_Fourth Edition_

# ECOLOGY OF FRESHWATERS

## A VIEW FOR THE TWENTY-FIRST CENTURY

_Brian Moss_

Emeritus Professor, University of Liverpool, UK

WILEY-BLACKWELL

A John Wiley & Sons, Ltd., Publication

Blackwell Publishing was acquired by John Wiley & Sons in February 2007. Blackwell's publishing program has been merged with Wiley's global Scientific, Technical and Medical business to form Wiley-Blackwell.

*Registered office:* John Wiley & Sons Ltd, The Atrium, Southern Gate, Chichester, West Sussex, PO19 8SQ, UK

*Editorial offices:* 9600 Garsington Road, Oxford, OX4 2DQ, UK
  The Atrium, Southern Gate, Chichester, West Sussex, PO19 8SQ, UK
  111 River Street, Hoboken, NJ 07030-5774, USA

For details of our global editorial offices, for customer services and for information about how to apply for permission to reuse the copyright material in this book please see our website at www.wiley.com/wiley-blackwell

*Library of Congress Cataloguing-in-Publication Data*
Moss, Brian.
  Ecology of freshwaters : a view for the twenty-first century / Brian Moss. — 4th ed.
    p. cm.
  Includes bibliographical references and index.
  ISBN 978-1-4443-3474-6 (hardcover : alk. paper) — ISBN 978-1-4051-1332-8 (pbk. : alk. paper)
1. Freshwater ecology.    I. Title.

  QH541.5.F7M67 2010
  577.6—dc22

                                                    2009050256

A catalogue record for this book is available from the British Library.

Set in 9/11pt Photina by Graphicraft Limited, Hong Kong
Printed and bound in Malaysia by Vivar Printing Sdn Bhd

1   2010

Books are to be returned on or before
the last date below.

ECC

LIBREX—

# Dedication

For my wife, Joyce, my daughter Angharad,
my friends and colleagues, and all who have not sacrificed
their honesty and principles for personal
aggrandisement, wealth and power

*O quam cito transit gloria mundi*
(How quickly the glory of the world passes away)
**Thomas à Kempis, 1418**

---

**Companion website**

A companion website for this book is available at:
www.wiley.com/go/moss/ecology
The website includes figures from the book for downloading.

# CONTENTS

Companion website for this book:
www.wiley.com/go/moss/ecology

# Chapter 1

# INTRODUCTION

## 1.1 WHY?

Textbooks usually sound a bit pompous. It's in their nature as the factual 'text': that which has to be known. Yet some, at least, come from the passions of their authors wanting to pass on their enthusiasms, reflected in the facts. But the relative importance of facts changes as understanding grows and the facts only increase in number as time passes. A huge number appear in articles, books and websites on almost everything, and although there is a lot of repetition, sometimes direct, sometimes just new examples of general principles, and sometimes recycling, by newer methods, of ideas that originated long ago, the amount is nonetheless daunting. Most of the scientific literature is written as if no one wants to communicate anything, anyway. The writing is pompous, self-serving, full of unnecessary jargon and distinctly off-putting. Quite a lot of it is deceptive in that something is written as if it is an entirely new revelation when this is far from the case. I have had to wade through a lot of it, often needing to read things several times for glimmers of understanding to emerge. Not surprisingly the population in general cannot be much bothered with scientific findings. The positive side is that when one teases out

the meaning, it is completely fascinating! This is the fourth edition of this textbook. The previous editions have grown bigger and bigger so I decided to write a shorter fourth completely from scratch, mostly because I wanted to break away from the near complete emphasis on Europe or North America that most freshwater textbooks have had. Faced with so much information, however, this proved trickier than I had thought.

My first difficulty was that water is part of everything environmental. You cannot overestimate its importance. Planet Earth is very unusual, in the immediate Universe at least, in having a surface skin dominated by water. Two-thirds of its surface is ocean. Moreover, the evaporation and condensation of water, driven by the Sun's energy, controls the climate and hence what grows where and how well. The river systems, with their lakes and floodplains, stitch the land surfaces and the coastal seas together (Fig. 1.1) with the threads of water and mineral cycles, yet constitute only a small percentage of the total water. Most of it is in the ocean, polar icecaps or underground in the interstices of soils and rocks. More than 90% of the content of all living things is water; even land animals are totally dependent on a continual supply of it. We ourselves can only maintain our settlements where there is a reliable supply of freshwater, and because surface freshwater is relatively scarce, its division among different people and interests causes major political problems, even wars. If you are to write a book on freshwater, you have, at least, to pretend to be a polymath.

*Ecology of Freshwaters: A View for the Twenty-first Century*, 4th edition. By Brian Moss. Published 2010 by Blackwell Publishing Ltd.

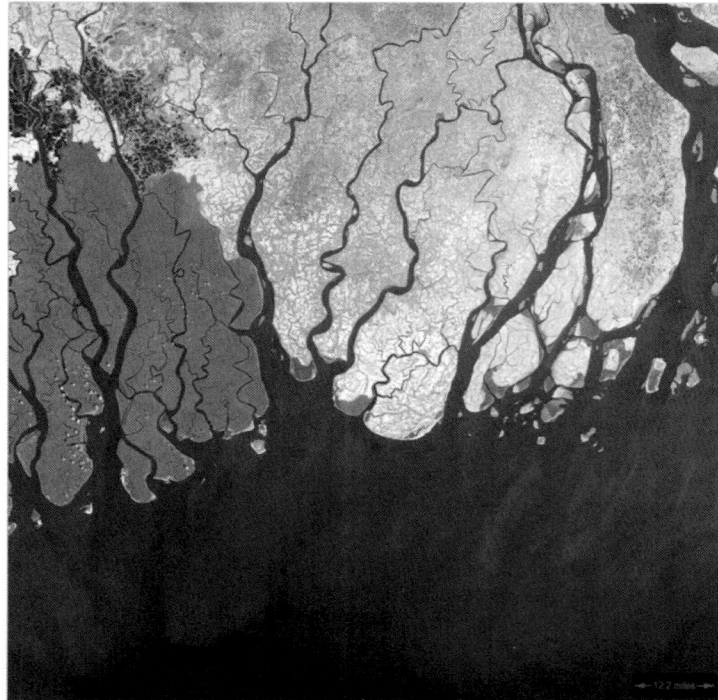

**Fig. 1.1** The Ganges Delta in Bangladesh seen from a satellite. The interconnectedness of the land, the river system and the ocean can be clearly seen from satellite photographs. (Copyright U.S. Nautical and Space Administration.)

One relief was that it was to be a book on freshwaters, so the ocean could be nearly ignored – but only nearly! A famous speech by a North American Indian chief, Seathl (Fig. 1.2), contains the sentence 'All things are connected'. The speech was about the natural linkages between land and, water, plants, animals and people, and there is some doubt that he actually said it. But to a professional ecologist, it rings completely true. All things really are connected. There are people who call themselves lake ecologists (limnologists), river ecologists (potamologists) and wetland, or mire, ecologists, let alone the larger camp of terrestrial ecologists, sub-divided into grassland ecologists, forest ecologists, desert ecologists or evolutionary ecologists, community and population ecologists, even theoretical ecologists, who thrive in warm offices rather than wet and windy hill-sides. Yet there is really only one tribe of ecologists and ultimately only one ecological system, the biosphere as a whole. One cannot write a book covering everything, however, so this one tries to single out the catchment (watershed or river basin) as the unit.

All the land surface is divided into one catchment (Fig. 1.3) or another, on which water falls then passes through streams and rivers, lakes and wetlands eventually to the sea or, in very arid regions, which cover nearly half the land surface, as vapour to the atmosphere. All of streams, rivers, lakes and wetlands are basically the same. They are depressions of the land through which freshwater passes, and there are many common features to them. There are also differences based on how quickly the water passes through and it is useful to look at them individually to discern what is happening. But fundamentally they march to the same drumbeat.

The connectedness appears in every aspect of ecology. Every action has consequences radiating in every direction. You cannot dam a small river in the highlands without having some effect on the river estuary perhaps hundreds of kilometres away. You cannot farm the land and expect a downstream lake to stay the same as it was before. You cannot change the climate and expect everything to go on as usual. The land and the freshwaters together have to be seen and discussed as a whole. Freshwater science is a microcosm of the whole of environmental science. There is something of everything in it.

**Fig. 1.2** Photograph of Chief Seattle (also Sealth, Seathle, Seathl or See-ahth) (*c.* 1786–1866), who was a leader of the Suquamish and Duwamish Native American tribes and after whom the city of Seattle is named. He made a speech in his native language, Salish, on the arrival of a newly appointed territorial governor, which has become important in environmental thinking. In it he is purported to have said: '*All things are connected. Whatever befalls the earth befalls the sons of the earth. Man does not weave the web of life; he is merely a strand of it. Whatever he does to the web, he does to himself'*. In truth he may have said something along these lines, based on notes taken at the time by Dr Joseph Smith, but these words, though nonetheless inspiring, were written by a scriptwriter, Ted Perry, in 1972 for a film called 'Home', produced by the Southern Baptist Radio and Television Commission.

There was a difficulty in drawing boundaries with time also. A very well-known ecologist, G. Evelyn Hutchinson (Fig. 1.4), used the metaphor of the environmental (or ecological) theatre and the evolutionary play. As the environment changes (and it does so continually), the players, who can be thought of as the genes, the individuals or the species, must change too if they are to stay on stage. And as each of these players changes, there are consequences for other players, who might be competitors, predators or prey, and who might also have to change. Some reference to evolution is needed, for that is what the process of change in organisms is about. Many of the ecological features of particular organisms reflect the conditions under which they first evolved. Cyanobacteria still retain the preferences for low oxygen waters that hark back to the anaerobic world, two or three billion years ago, in which they originated, but themselves began to modify by evolving oxygen-producing photosynthesis. The adults of many freshwater insects and the flowers of most aquatic plants are essentially aerial for it was from land-based ancestors that they entered the water. Time has many scales. Lakes and rivers have ecological histories, sometimes quite short for many were obliterated by the last glaciation and emerged anew only 10,000–15,000 years ago. Others may have persisted for some millions of years, but because climate changes naturally over that scale, they have been bigger or smaller, freely flowing or isolated from time to time. They also change from year to year and biological changes may be recognizable from minute to minute. The multimillion-year scales of evolution are not a major subject of this book but a study of ecological history is essential to understanding the processes of the present.

The third difficulty was in coping with ourselves. Most freshwater ecologists used to head for the hills in their research. They sought the least disturbed, ideally the pristine environments, where the results of the evolutionary play are still intact and where the design of the environmental theatre has not been wrecked by the incompetent architectural abilities of people. As a result we can draw for you pictures of intensely fascinating ecologies: the floodplain forests of the Amazon, with their seed-eating fish; the connections between wolves and bears in the functioning of river systems of the north-temperate zone; the division of the available food in the African Great lakes among fish so specialized that some scrape the scales or bite the eyes of others. We can take you to lakes and wetlands in seemingly endless landscapes of forest and savannah, steppe and even desert. We can be more escapist than the glossiest of travel brochures.

Yet what we also know is that these gems are just the meagre crumbs of what the world once was like, but no longer really is. People have been around for perhaps

**Fig. 1.3**  The north-west of England showing the land surface made up from abutting river catchments. The world's entire land surface is divided up in this way. Many catchments adjoin those of a larger river and eventually discharge to the seas and oceans, but this is not necessary. Many catchments are entirely land-bound and water leaves them, not at an estuary, but by evaporation to the atmosphere.

**Fig. 1.4** G. Evelyn Hutchinson (1903–1991), born in the UK and working mostly in the USA after a period in South Africa is well-known for his work in limnology and the writing of a major set of books on the subject. But he had a very wide vision of ecology and biogeochemistry and was widely familiar with oceanography, anthropology, paleontology, sociology and animal behaviour, whilst also being well versed in the arts and music. Such breadth is rare but often contributes the more interesting ideas and new trends to individual sciences.

one or two million years and evolved along with the natural ecosystems that give us great delight. The ways in which people meshed, as hunter–gatherers or even simple cultivators, with other animals and with plants, when people were neither numerous nor too ambitious, are parts of the fascination of natural systems. The reality for recent generations has been very different. The past 200 years have seen the progressive destruction of the detail of the freshwater, indeed of all environments (Fig. 1.5). There is no longer any completely pristine freshwater system in Europe and arguably, since we have contaminated the entire atmosphere with pesticides, emitted gases that fall as acid in the rain, and are now changing the climate, perhaps there are none anywhere (Fig. 1.6). Those who live in cities will see rivers embanked with concrete;

the ponds and lakes will often have signs warning of toxic blue-green algae; rivers in the lowlands will have been straightened and the woody debris that was so important for their ecology removed; lakes will have muddy deltas where the products of erosion wash in from cultivated land. The bears and wolves have long gone and even many of the fish that were once common, Atlantic salmon in Europe for example, are now rare. Previous ecological textbooks, including earlier editions of this one, pretended that the world was intact and tagged on human influences as secondary. That is truly no longer the case. The world is heavily damaged and more than half its natural ecosystems are seriously degraded. An honest textbook must reflect this.

So the final difficulty is one of motivation, for both of us, reader and author. Ecologists do not particularly want to write as historians of what once was, but no longer is. They do not want to appear as doomsayers, perpetually depressed and backward-looking. Nor do they want to instil the idea that things are going so steeply downhill that nothing can be done. To undermine optimism and morale is the greatest disservice and is self-fulfilling. Better to see things like this. We are studying perhaps the most interesting scene of the evolutionary play so far. People are immensely successful organisms, arch-competitors that have already out-competed many species and brought many already to extinction, and that milk is spilt.

Yet when one looks at the population fluctuations of an animal or plant, there are times when numbers (and thus impact) rise temporarily above the notional line of carrying capacity. For a very small part, a few decades, of our million-year history we have been above this line. It has had immense effects, but we live on a planet that has its own mechanisms of stabilizing its environment and may make its own adjustments, though these may be something of a shock to our eventual numbers. We can avoid that, however, for we know a lot about how these systems work. We already have the capacity to start readjusting and redesigning so that we maintain ecological systems that will not be the same as those in the past, but which will still be interesting, pleasant and functioning. It is there that freshwater, indeed all, ecological science starts to involve the human social sciences, for all things are also connected with human societies. In the final analysis, our present difficulties, frustrations and depressions can be a significant but reversible blip of human history not the start of an unending nightmare. There is a whole science of restoration ecology (Fig. 1.7):

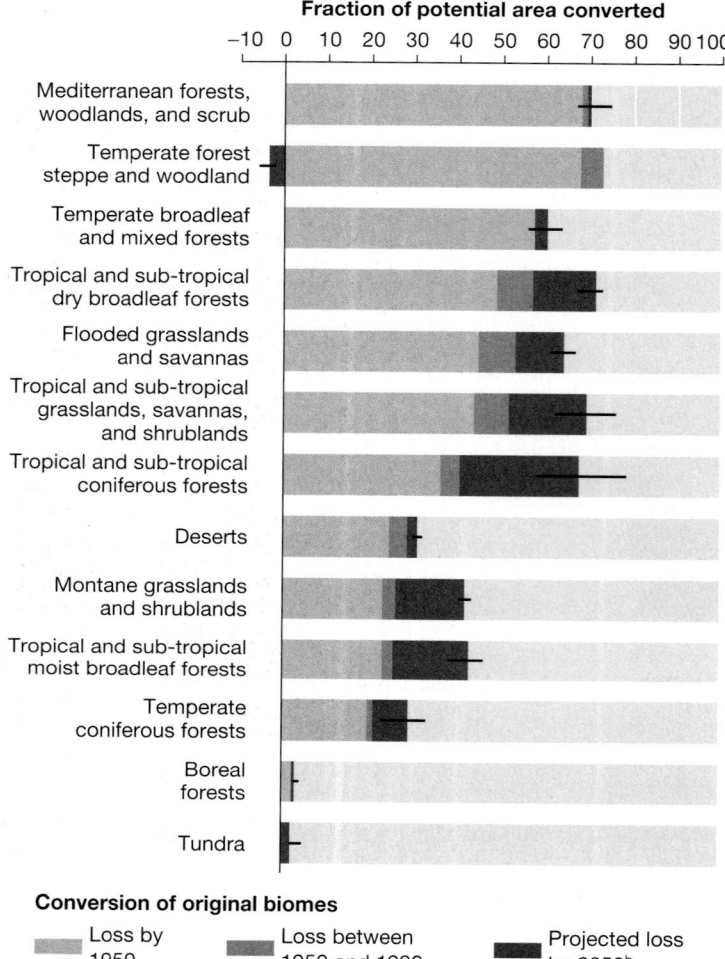

**Fraction of potential area converted**

−10  0  10  20  30  40  50  60  70  80  90 100%

- Mediterranean forests, woodlands, and scrub
- Temperate forest steppe and woodland
- Temperate broadleaf and mixed forests
- Tropical and sub-tropical dry broadleaf forests
- Flooded grasslands and savannas
- Tropical and sub-tropical grasslands, savannas, and shrublands
- Tropical and sub-tropical coniferous forests
- Deserts
- Montane grasslands and shrublands
- Tropical and sub-tropical moist broadleaf forests
- Temperate coniferous forests
- Boreal forests
- Tundra

**Conversion of original biomes**

Loss by 1950   Loss between 1950 and 1990   Projected loss by 2050[b]

**Fig. 1.5** Major damage and losses of major world biomes by 1950 and 1990, and projected on present trends for 2050. Where damage occurs to the biome in general, this is reflected in the freshwater systems contained within it to a considerable extent, for the waters draining the land are greatly affected by what happens on the land. Only the tundra and boreal forests have not suffered very extensive damage. Partly this may be because two groups of aquatic insects, the mosquitoes and the black flies, make them difficult to live in. (Source: Millennium Ecosystem Assessment.)

the putting together again of the bits that have been taken apart.

And against all these difficulties, there is one monumental bastion. Freshwater ecology is immensely interesting. I do not want to sound parochial about this. Anything is very interesting if you go deeply enough into it. But freshwaters are so much a part of our daily lives (go and turn the kitchen tap on) that they have a special place. One of my colleagues illustrated this by asking students to imagine somewhere where they would feel most relaxed. Almost invariably the scene involved water. A few years ago, I was informed by my

increasingly bureaucratic University administration that the course (newly called a module) I had taught for several decades in one form or another must have 'Aims and Objectives'. I replied that these were simple: to interest and enthuse. When they said that was against the rules and not adequate, but forgot to make a rule that I could not write in verse, I produced the following. It's the theme of this book.

> At this module's end, you'll know,
> That water comes from rain and snow,
> Dissolves most things then rests in basins,
> And seals the fates of arid nations.

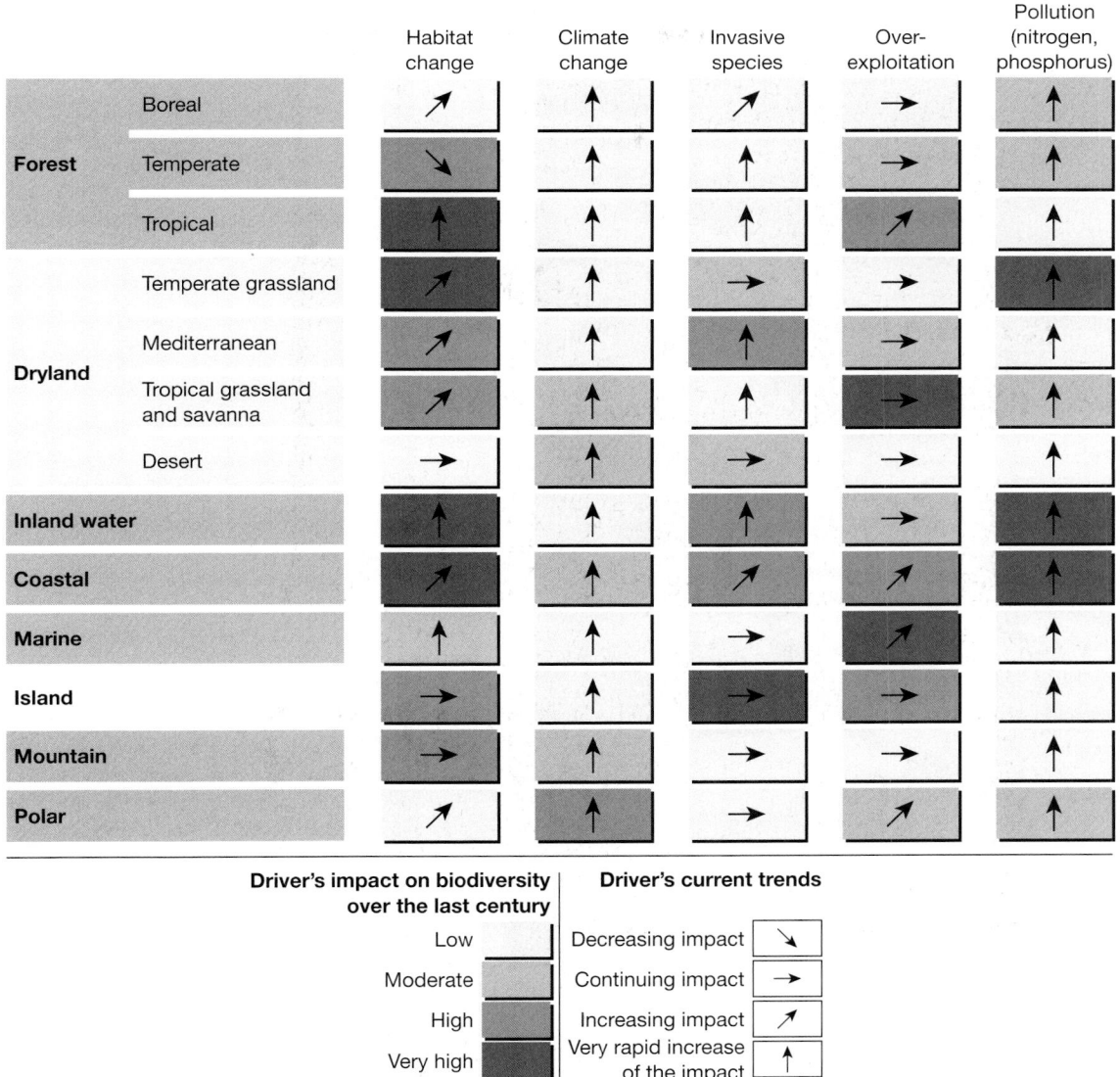

**Fig. 1.6** Trends in damage to major world habitats and their reasons. The intensity of shading indicates the degree of damage so far. The arrows indicate whether this damage is decreasing (pointing downwards), staying the same (horizontal), or increasing to a moderate (sloping upwards) or high (vertical) degree. Changes are grouped as habitat change (mostly complete destruction), climate change, invasive species, overexploitation (by fisheries, for example) and eutrophication (pollution by excessive nutrients). Inland waters have suffered perhaps the greatest damage so far and are under the greatest future threats. (Source: Millennium Ecosystem assessment.)

**Fig. 1.7** The River Brede in southern Denmark was previously greatly modified by straightening and deepening to more efficiently drain surrounding agricultural land. Recently parts have been restored to their former course and the floodplain re-established. Segments of the original straightened channel can be seen along with the restored meanders, side channels and floodplain.

Its stage is shifting, fleet and short;
Life, for its denizens, is fraught.
How well they've coped, you'll clearly see:
The bug, the bloom and the water flea.

Alas what is a wondrous world,
Is by humans often churled.
And so we'll teach of lakes polluted
And bubbling rivers dammed and muted

And by the end I hope you'll feel
You know the problems, keen and real,
But also see remediation
And share our endless fascination

## FURTHER READING

I have not peppered the text with numerous references, for the simple reason that there are now so many scientific papers, the text would be overwhelmed if I were comprehensive; and there would inevitably be a great deal of selectivity if I were not. Some worthy people left out might be mortally offended. Information gathering anyway has changed immensely in the past ten years. Use of key words in search systems such as the Web of Science or Google Scholar will turn up the background for any statement with little difficulty. People produce the information however, and they should be given proper credit. I have thus written sections on further reading for each Chapter to do this and guide readers to particularly relevant articles, especially books and reviews.

With relevance to this chapter, G.E. Hutchinson's classic '*Treatise on Limnology*' is published as four volumes, with enormous reference value. There are many texts on freshwater ecology, each with its own approach, and looking at several is always a good idea. Wetzel (2001), Kalff (2003) and Goldman & Horne (1994) have strongly North American biases. Lampert & Sommer (2007) has European emphasis whilst Boulton & Brock (1999) covers Australasia. Beadle (1981) and Davies & Day (1998) are books for Africa, and Talling & Lemoalle (1999), for the tropics. Bronmark & Hansen (2005) emphasizes more the biology of organisms, whilst Burgis & Morris (2007) is a very readable account of lakes, Hynes (1979) of rivers and Worthington & Worthington (1933) a delightful and eminently readable account of East African waterways and ecology as they once were. For English readers, Macan's books

(1963, 1970, 1973), biased towards the English Lake District, are classics and Mason (2002) is an introduction to the problems that all waters are now suffering. The global situation is amply documented in the Millennium Ecosystem Assessment (web site, www.millenniumassessment.org/en/index.aspx). Hutchinson (1965) introduces the analogy of the ecological theatre and the evolutionary play.

There is a tendency in education now to be superficial. You do the course, learn the textbook, answer the multiple-choice questions, pass the exam, throw away the notes, and move to the next thing. I think you lose a lot with that approach. I think you learn most from being and doing rather than as a passive spectator, which all that that approach makes you. You get into a subject by project and practical work, seeing what is going on in the field, investigating it. A book cannot give you this, but in Chapter 17, there are several problem exercises, which, if you can produce sensible solutions, will tell you if you have learnt something.

# Chapter 2

# WATER, A REMARKABLE UNREMARKABLE SUBSTANCE

## 2.1 INTRODUCTION

Water is unremarkable and at the same time, exceptionally odd. The very fact that it is unremarkable (it is the most familiar of substances in everyday life; we handle it almost hourly) is because it is so odd. It is the only substance on Earth that commonly exists in all three of its solid (ice), liquid, and gaseous (water vapour) forms. On a day in spring in the north, when snow is melting, you will be aware of all three together as the water runs out of the melting snow and the vapour from your breath condenses in the cold air. This property is crucial for two reasons.

First, life on Earth depends on there being a liquid available. Biochemical systems cannot function as gases because the dispersion and random movement of the molecules does not allow close control of chemical reactions, nor as solids because chemical reactions are too slow in solids whose molecular movements are restrained. Second, there are no other natural substances that normally occur in quantities as liquids at the Earth's surface. The nearest are hydrocarbons in oil deposits, but these are already derived from living organisms. Water was necessary for the living organisms that produced them. The very existence of life depends on the properties of water.

The remarkableness rests on the fact that, by rights of predictable chemistry, water should exist only as a gas at Earth temperatures. Water is the hydride of oxygen and should show a graded series of properties with the hydrides of the related elements, sulphur, selenium and tellurium, in the Periodic Table (Fig. 2.1). Hydrogen sulphide, hydrogen selenide and hydrogen telluride are all gases at Earth temperature and pressures. As the lightest of these compounds, hydrogen

|  | Melting point (°C) | Boiling point (°C) |
|---|---|---|
| $H_2O$ | Actual 0 Expected (−100) | Actual 100 Expected (−80) |
| $H_2S$ | −85.5 | −60.7 |
| $H_2Se$ | −60.4 | −41.5 |
| $H_2Te$ | −49.0 | −1.0 |

**Fig. 2.1** The hydrides of the oxygen series in the Periodic Table include water, hydrogen sulphide, hydrogen selenide and hydrogen telluride. Based on the usual progressive change in properties down the columns of the table, water should have much lower freezing and boiling points than it does.

*Ecology of Freshwaters: A View for the Twenty-first Century*, 4th edition. By Brian Moss. Published 2010 by Blackwell Publishing Ltd.

**Fig. 2.2** Ice, broken off from the melting front of a glacier, floats in the lake formed at the foot of the glacier. The melting ice is at 0°C and the water at a little higher temperature. The ice floats because the water molecules of its crystal structure are more distantly spaced than those in the liquid water.

oxide, $H_2O$, should also be a gas. Water thus evaporates and freezes at much higher temperatures than expected.

The consequences of these properties are important. The mean air temperature at the Earth's surface is around 13°C. Earth's surface extremes of temperature run to well below the freezing point of water (0°C) and to well above it in the molten lavas that emerge when volcanoes erupt. Even elsewhere, the heat of the summer sun can bring the soil temperature to 60 or 70°C, painful to bare feet and perilously close to water's boiling point of 100°C. Both during a year, and over longer periods such as glacial epochs, changes in temperature can readily shift water from its (to living organisms) usable liquid form, to ice or vapour. Small changes in climate can lock enormous amounts away in polar glaciers or render moist regions arid. Small fluctuations in weather can mean that water supplies dry up or run amok as floods. Freshwater organisms, in the course of their evolutionary history have had to cope with these uncertainties. Human societies, equally

dependent on liquid water, face them continuously. Water is abundant on Earth, but mostly in unusable form for land and freshwater organisms and people, as ice, in deep ground-waters or, particularly, as the saline ocean. The usable supply of freshwater is small and vulnerable.

There is more. Water is densest not at its freezing point, but at nearly 4° above it so that water bodies freeze from the surface (Fig. 2.2), insulating the water underneath from further cooling and generally always leaving liquid water for living organisms beneath the ice. Water also dissolves a huge range of other compounds, making it the near universal solvent that is needed for a biochemical medium; it has a high specific heat, changing temperature relatively slowly and buffering temperature extremes for organisms living in it; it has a high viscosity, making it a 'sticky' medium for organisms living in it and its surfaces have a skin, a surface tension. All of these properties have effects on living organisms and rest on the particular molecular structure of water.

## 2.2 THE MOLECULAR PROPERTIES OF WATER AND THEIR PHYSICAL CONSEQUENCES

These are the bare bones of the structure of water: two hydrogen atoms and one oxygen atom, the hydrogens are held at nearly 0.1 nm from the oxygen, jointly making an angle of 104° 27' with it; the six electrons of the outer orbit of the oxygen are shared with the one from each of the hydrogens to give the eight that complete the shell of oxygen and the two that do likewise for the hydrogen. If that were all there was to it, water would be an unremarkable covalent compound and a gas at Earth temperatures. There would be no life on Earth, no ocean, no ice caps, simply a very hot, completely dry, laval waste.

The initial clue to why things are different comes from the angle at which the hydrogens are held. Theory predicts it should be 90° but it is more. The tiny phenomenon that makes all the difference is that the shared electrons are slightly more attracted to the oxygen than the hydrogens. The difference is small, but it makes the hydrogens slightly positive in charge and the oxygen slightly negative. The two slightly positive hydrogens repel one another, widening the angel between them. Much more importantly, since opposites attract, the hydrogen of one water molecule attracts and forms a bond with the oxygen of another. The molecules become joined together in a superstructure (Fig. 2.3) and that is the key.

A solid contains molecules that are very close together, often, as in a crystal, in a fixed geometric pattern. A gas has its molecules bearing no relation to one another but moving randomly at relatively far distances. Liquids have their molecules much closer together than in a gas, but much further apart than in a solid, and without the bonding that occurs to hold many solids together. Water, when a liquid, has its molecules close but also held together by hydrogen bonding, which is what the attraction between hydrogen and oxygen of different molecules is called. To break that structure, to convert liquid water to vapour, requires a lot of energy. Such energy is not available at low temperatures and as much as 100°C is needed for the conversion. Without the hydrogen bonding, water would become a gas at around minus 80°C.

### 2.2.1 Ice and melting

Ice has a crystal structure based on tetrahedrons of water molecules (Fig. 2.3). This holds the molecules relatively far apart and gives a low density to the ice. Ice floats on liquid water. At its melting point, as more heat energy is applied to the ice, this structure is broken and starts to collapse inwards. The liquid water at the melting point is denser than the ice. The water molecules in the meltwater still retain some structure, held together by the hydrogen bonding, so the total amount of energy needed for melting (the latent heat

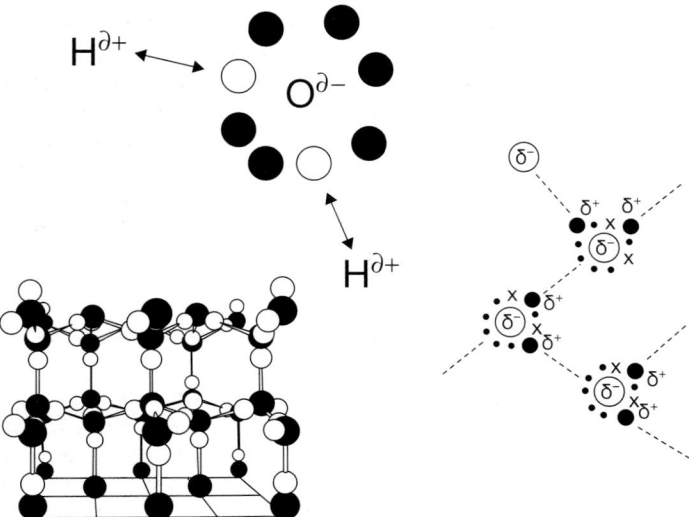

**Fig. 2.3** The slightly greater attraction of the shared electrons to the oxygen atom leads to the oxygen being slightly electronegative and the hydrogens electropositive in the water molecule. Neighbouring molecules are thus attracted (hydrogen to oxygen) and hydrogen bonds bind them together (lower right). In ice (lower left), the crystal structure is maintained by these attractions, but they persist to some extent also in liquid water.

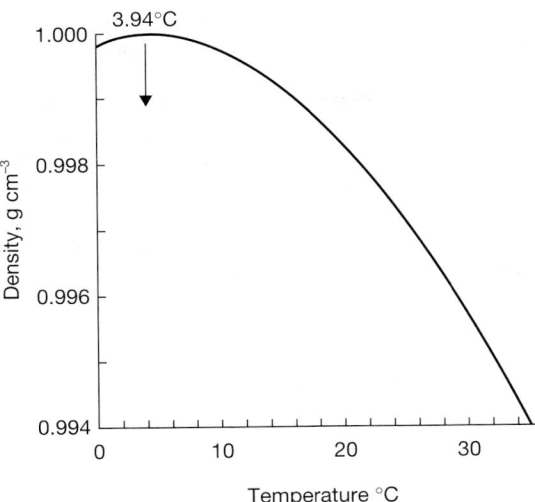

**Fig. 2.4** Pure liquid water is densest (1.000 g cm$^{-3}$) at 3.94°C. The density is slightly lower at the melting point (0.9998). Ice has a density of about 0.920, so floats on water at all higher temperatures, though of course it will melt rapidly, the higher the water temperature.

of fusion) is small. Water thus freezes and thaws rather easily. Beyond the freezing point, as the water warms, this structure is retained to a large extent but partly disrupts and freer water molecules start to collapse into the spaces of the structure. The density of the water thus increases a little. By about 4°C, more precisely 3.94°C for pure water under normal pressures, this process of collapse is balanced by the tendency of the molecules to vibrate more vigorously and move away from one another. At 4°C, therefore, the water is at its maximum density and as it warms more, it becomes less dense (Fig. 2.4). In reverse, when a water body cools through 4°C, the 4°C water sinks and colder water starts to float on it, resulting in lower density colder water, at the melting point, layering on the surface, where ice forms. Water bodies thus freeze from the top and because the ice provides some insulation to further heat loss to the atmosphere, it is unusual for them to freeze solid to the bottom.

### 2.2.2 Buffering and evaporation

Above 4°C, the water steadily gets less dense, so warmer water floats on cooler, but its temperature changes only slowly as heat is applied. This is because water has a high specific heat. It takes a lot of energy to break down the hydrogen bonds that hold water molecules together and because temperature is a measure of the degree to which molecules are vibrating or moving freely, temperature change is resisted. Liquid water thus buffers inputs (or losses) of heat because its structure resists the change. This keeps many freshwater habitats equable with narrow temperature ranges (sometimes only half as much as that of nearby aerial habitats) during the year.

If enough energy is applied, the water approaches its boiling point. This can occur naturally in volcanic areas where water is heated by underlying hot rocks. The heat required to evaporate water at the boiling point is substantial (over six times that needed to melt ice per unit mass) because the hydrogen-bonded structure has to be completely destroyed to convert liquid to vapour. Water is thus slow to evaporate, though with inputs of energy from the Sun and in dry atmospheric conditions where there is a large deficit of moisture in the atmosphere, it readily does so.

### 2.3 HOW MUCH WATER IS THERE AND WHERE IS IT?

Hydrogen and oxygen are among the commonest elements on Earth. Water is the most common compound in which they occur together. Water is not scarce. There is an enormous amount of it in the oceans, but it is wanting on the land surfaces, in the atmosphere and for the freshwater systems that are linked closely with them. Water is thus the most important limiting factor for plant growth and hence for ecosystem production on land. Freshwater in river and lake systems comprises only 0.02% of the total water on Earth. There is a little more, frozen into the polar ice caps and glaciers (2.1%) and in deep ground-water supplies (0.6%) where water rests in saturated pervious rocks, but the ocean holds 97.2% of the total.

### 2.3.1 Turnover and the hydrological cycle

On the other hand there is a fast turnover in the water cycle. The water cycle (Fig. 2.5) describes the gross movements of water molecules among the atmosphere, rivers, lakes, estuaries, and the ocean through rain and snow (precipitation), flow and evapotranspiration.

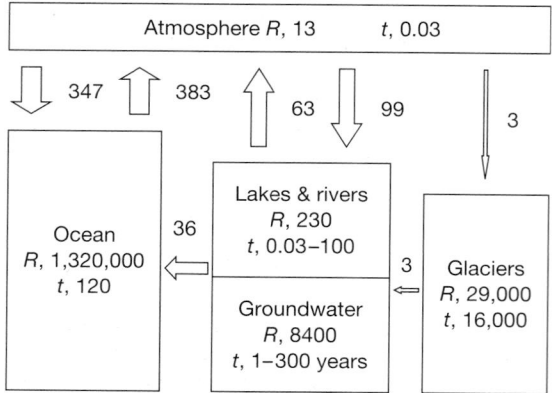

**Fig. 2.5** Most water is in the ocean, least in the atmosphere. The diagram shows the average amounts ($R$) in thousands of km$^3$ in the various components. Arrows show the annual flux, in thousands of km$^3$ yr$^{-1}$, through precipitation, evaporation, run off and melting. $t$ gives the residence time in years. This is the average length of time a molecule of water is likely to be retained in a particular component.

One particular water molecule may spend thousands of years in the ocean but its sister may spend only minutes or seconds in the sea after reaching it from a river before being evaporated back to the atmosphere. On average a water molecule will spend 11 days in the atmosphere before being condensed to rain or frozen as snow, and 2.3 years in the surface water (river/lake/estuary) system. It will spend 12,000 years in the glaciers and 300 years in the ground water. The rapid replacement of water in the surface freshwater system is one reason why restoration of polluted freshwaters is comparatively easy and the long average retention time in the oceans a good reason for avoiding contamination, for the problems can be with us for thousands of years.

## 2.3.2 Changes in geological time

The water balance, the distribution of water among the various components of surface freshwater, atmospheric vapour, ice, ground water and ocean, has varied over geological time, because the Earth's climate has changed a lot. All surface freshwaters are temporary features in this respect but there has been an ocean continuously for at least 4 billion years, although it has changed shape as continents have moved and with

them the pattern of ocean currents and the climate regimes.

There seem to have been three, at least, main states of the Earth's water balance in geological time. Sometimes almost all of it has been in the ocean, leaving the land surfaces mostly as desert and what remained of the freshwater basins salty through evaporation (see below), as in the Devonian (360–400 Ma; million years ago) and late Permian (250 Ma) Periods. The Carboniferous Period (290–360 Ma) was in contrast clearly a very wet one, judging from the evidence of the extensive swamps that were the origins of coal deposits and there is much evidence of fossil dried-out lake basins from the early Permian Period, which succeeded the Carboniferous. Sometimes, as in the early Tertiary (65 Ma), there has been maximal humidity on land. The wet Tertiary period led to a phase of drying in which large arms of the ocean were cut off and transformed into inland lakes.

The third general state of the Earth's water has seen much of the water locked into glaciers. The Pleistocene glaciation, from about 1.7 million years ago until 10,000 years ago effectively re-set the landscape of much of the temperate world but there have been several much older glaciations, including one at 600 Ma, which extended from the poles to within 10–15° of the Equator. The lands of the Earth have thus variously been very dry, very wet or frozen. The reasons are complex, but involve the movements of the Earth's plates, changing the patterns of the continents and oceans, and rhythms in the orbit of the Earth around the Sun, which takes it sometimes slightly nearer, sometimes slightly further away.

We have just emerged from a frozen period that may have begun when continental drift in the late Oligocene (25 Ma) moved Antarctica into its present, polar position creating a circum-polar current around the continent that isolated it from warmer waters moving southwards from the Equator and promoting accumulation of much ice on its mountainous land surface. Ice began to form around the North Pole in quantity somewhat later, only 2.5 to 3 million years ago but the consequences were that high-latitude freshwater systems froze solid whilst those at lower latitudes were wetter through reduced temperatures and lesser evaporation. When eventually the ice started to melt back, temporary lakes formed against the retreating ice front. These could be huge. The Laurentian ice-lake, the precursor of the St Laurence Great Lakes that now straddle the USA and Canada, was 300,000 km$^2$ in area; a similar large lake preceded the Baltic Sea and there was another in West Siberia which has left no remaining large water body. Expansion, then melting back of the polar and mountain glaciers has caused considerable change to the freshwater systems, including the creation of millions of new lake basins.

The pattern of freshwaters changes also because geological events such as volcanic activity, crustal movements and landslides alter the configuration of the landscape and thus the nature of valleys and basins. Like the effects of natural climate change, such happenings are continual. One lake in Iceland fell in water level by several metres in 2000 because a small earthquake opened up a large crack in the rocks at the edge, down which enormous amounts of water have drained, exposing a large area, now of black laval beach sands and gravel.

## 2.4 PATTERNS IN HYDROLOGY

The hydrology of a system is a description of the amounts of water passing through it and their seasonal distribution and variability among different years. This is usually expressed as a hydrograph, a graph of amount of water (the net run-off or discharge, equivalent to the difference between precipitation and evaporation in the catchment) passing down the river system. Hydrographs vary enormously from place to place and between years in the same place.

Polar and high mountain regions (Fig. 2.6) have some of the simplest patterns. Snow accumulates in the catchments in winter, melts in spring and summer to form a vigorous run-off into the basins, passes through the systems with relatively little evaporation and eventually reaches the sea. There are, however, in polar regions, some areas of intense dryness where accumulated snow will usually sublime straight to the atmosphere without an intervening step of liquid water. In some, warmer years, there may be melting and passage of liquid water into basins, but evaporation is intense from these also. The basins may have liquid water in them only in parts of some years. Salts, derived from rock weathering and washed in from the catchment with the water are not washed through but accumulate in salt pans. Systems in which there is a flow through of liquid water are called open or exorheic basins, those in which water leaves the basin only by evaporation are closed or endorheic basins.

In the course of geological time a basin may alternate between endorheic and exorheic dependent on climate change.

### 2.4.1 Temperate regions

Endorheic and exorheic systems are paired also in cold temperate climates, indeed in all climate regimes. In cold temperate regions (Fig. 2.6), wetter areas will have a pattern in which snow may accumulate on the catchment in winter and the freshwater basins will be flushed with torrents of meltwater in spring. If the region is slightly warmer, rain runs off more or less continuously in the winter and spring. Evaporation will account for some of the water but evaporation rates will be low in the lower temperatures of winter. The net run-off will thus be high and indeed most of the water entering the basins will come in winter and spring. It will not enter evenly, however.

There will be a spate following a period of rainfall or melt, followed by much lower flows in the streams in drier periods. During and just after rain, most of the water will have passed over the land surfaces or perhaps only through the superficial soil layers. In the dry periods, water that has passed into the deeper layers of soil or even underlying rock will supply the streams. This flow is called the base flow. In summer, net run-off is often zero or negative as evapotranspiration accounts for all of the summer rainfall and even some water stored in the soils. There may be brief periods of increased flow following summer storms, but most of the river flow will be maintained from the groundwater store. If there is no store to supply a base flow, the stream will dry up. This is often the case in smaller streams, which have a temporary character to them. In autumn, as temperatures fall, net run-off increases again and the streams rise to their winter levels for several months or for the time before the weather becomes so cold that the snow-beridden landscape freezes and run-off ceases until spring.

Rivers accommodate these seasonal changes in flow by adjusting the size of their beds. Even upland small rivers will have a riparian (bankside) zone that is covered in water during spring at least and sometimes all of winter, but is exposed in summer. Bigger rivers will accommodate the higher flows through the development of features such as meanders and a floodplain (Fig. 2.7). Meanders increase the length of the river and hence the capacity of the channel in summer;

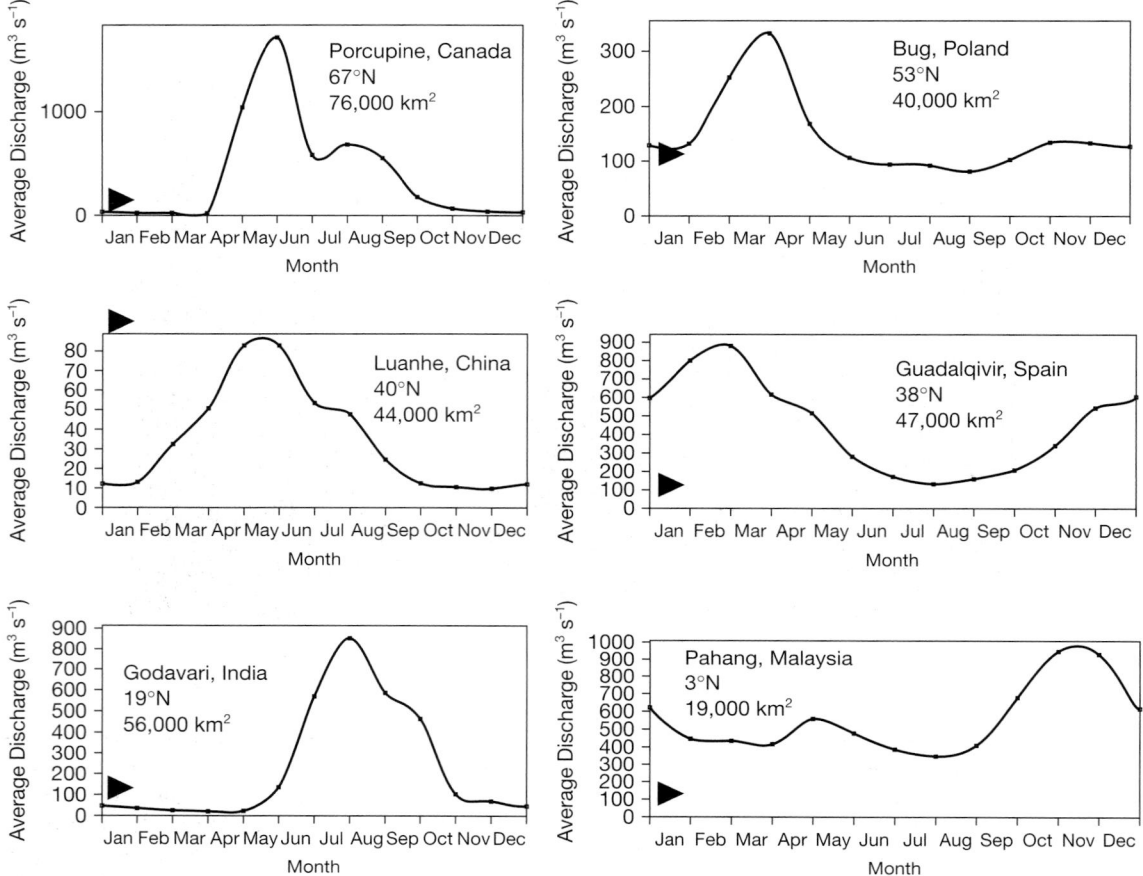

**Fig. 2.6** Annual hydrographs, averaged over several years for a tiny selection of the world's rivers. All are from the northern hemisphere, so that they are comparable seasonally and from catchments of a few tens of thousands of km$^2$ so that they reflect climate regimes rather than areas. The Porcupine is an arctic river, the Bug a north temperate one, the Luanhe and Guadalquivir from warm temperate regions of differing aridity. The first four reflect a summer–winter seasonality, with the effects of ice melt shown particularly in the Porcupine; the Godavari has a wet season and a dry season and the Pahang, only modest seasonal changes. The graphs are taken from www.sage.wisc.edu/riverdata/, which has comparable information on over 3000 rivers. Arrows are set at the same absolute discharges for comparison.

floodplains are the channel that the river needs to accommodate the winter flows. They are parts of the river bed, not dry land that is sometimes flooded. Lakes accommodate these changes in amounts of water entering them from their inflow rivers by changing their levels. This means that parts of their shorelines will be exposed in summer and in shallow basins these may be quite extensive in area. In deeper lakes, the area exposed may be small because the change in

inflow is relatively small in relation to the total volume of the basin.

### 2.4.2 Warm-temperate regions

The patterns of cold temperate regions become more exaggerated in the warm temperate region (Fig. 2.6). There will be little or no snow, so water runs off the land

**Fig. 2.7** The huge meanders of the River Amazon are flanked by a forested floodplain up to 30 km wide.

throughout the winter. The net run-off will be lower, the higher the temperature, because of increased evaporation with increased temperature. Run-off will cease earlier in summer with increased temperatures and resume later in autumn, so river and lake levels will be low for a longer period and the chances of complete drying out in summer will also increase. Shallow lakes will be more likely to dry up completely and the level changes in deep lakes will be more pronounced. On balance, more basins are likely to be endorheic as these conditions become more extreme, and although there is no shortage of endorheic areas in cold temperate regions (in Oregon and the steppes of central Asia for example), there are huge areas in which closed basins are the norm in the warm climates of Australia, the Mediterranean and Middle East, the south-western USA and Africa (Fig. 2.8).

### 2.4.3 Tropical cycles

Climate in the tropics (Fig. 2.6) gives patterns in which the same interplay of run-off and evaporation is at work but to extremes. The wet tropics, rain forest areas for

example, may have continual rain-fed river flow and there may be no periods where rivers are dependent entirely on base flow from ground water, even though there is usually some seasonality in the amount of rainfall. Water levels will change as rainfall changes, often irregularly through the year. In the dry tropics, there may be only short bursts of rainfall; streams may sometimes flow only for a few days at a time before drying up. Lakes may fill with water for a year or two then dry up and become salt pans for long periods, even decades. If they are large enough, they may change level considerably and also respond in area of water, and salinity. In dry periods they will be much smaller and much saltier.

To these general patterns in hydrology set by the climate regime, there will be local complications. A river system in the tropics may paradoxically rise in the dry season. This may be because it is receiving a water supply from the distant reaches of a very large catchment. Water reaches the lower parts of the Amazon floodplain, for example, from snow melt in the Andes, two or three months later. This is the time it takes to travel the distance from one side of South America to the other. All very large rivers will have

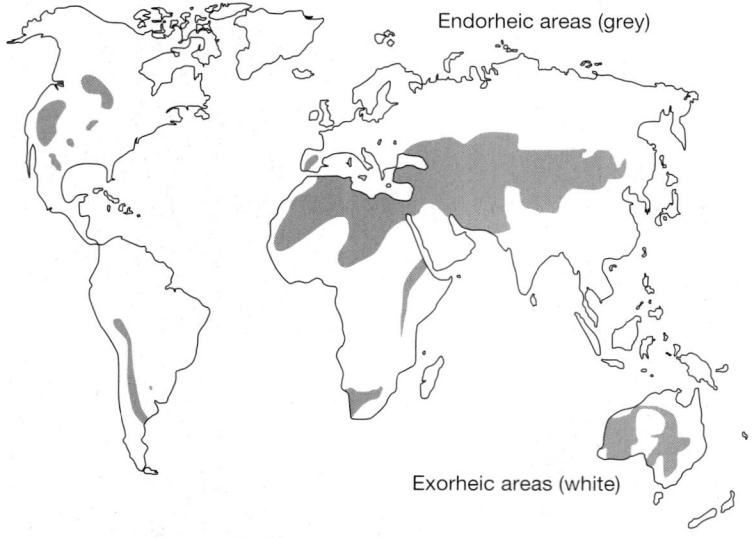

Endorheic areas (grey)

Exorheic areas (white)

**Fig. 2.8** Just over half the land surfaces are exorheic areas, in which at least some of the water falling on the catchments flows from atmosphere to ocean, with only part of it returned to the atmosphere by evaporation. The grey shading covers the remaining, still very substantial area, which is so arid that water entering the catchments as precipitation leaves only by evaporation, leaving behind salts that were dissolved in the water. Such areas are closed basins or endorheic. The ocean, of course receives liquid water but loses it only by evaporation. It is thus the world's largest endorheic lake and is also salty.

similar complications. A second complication is that because water is in such short supply, it is often tapped for irrigation schemes, or flows are regulated for generation of hydroelectricity or irrigation storage. These interventions have often been so considerable that natural patterns have been nearly obliterated. Living organisms, however, have evolved their life histories in response to the natural patterns and such alterations may be terminally disruptive to them.

## 2.5 BODIES OF WATER AND THEIR TEMPERATURES

Water tumbling down streams and through rivers is generally well mixed and acquires the temperature of its surrounding air after a short period. A polar stream will be frozen in winter and in summer will be cold, perhaps only a few degrees; a tropical one will be well over 20°C for all of the year. The molecular physics of the water molecule will be reflected in how rapidly the water changes temperature, but in little else. Where the water forms a distinctive body, where it is retained *en masse* for some time – a lake – it is a different matter. Lakes form in dozens of different ways (Fig. 2.9; Chapter 11) but their essence is that the water has a long stay, a residence time generally of weeks to years, compared with rivers and streams where it might only be minutes or days. This residence allows the water

mass to display some of the properties of the physical structure of its molecules.

### 2.5.1 Lakes and latitude

We will take a series of idealized lake basins at sea level from the Poles to the tropics, first a shallow series, then a deeper series. Shallow lakes (say 3 m or so mean depth) can easily be mixed by wind. They will thus be isothermal, the same temperature from top to bottom for much of the year. In summer, shallow lakes will track the changes in air temperature and in the warm temperate and tropical zones they will continue to mix in the winter or cooler season.

Towards the Poles and in the colder temperate regions (Fig. 2.10), however, they will cool more and may eventually cool to 4°C. At this point the dense 4°C water sinks to the bottom and further cooling, if the wind is not too strong, will result in colder water floating on it. Eventually, as the water reaches 0°C at the surface, ice, which is less dense than liquid water, begins to form, with a layering or stratification of warmer waters below it. This is called inverse stratification because the warmest (4°C) water is at the bottom. Under the ice, there is no significant mixing. In some polar and mountain lakes, the ice cover may be permanent, and in warm temperate and lowland tropical lakes, of course, it is absent. In between, the

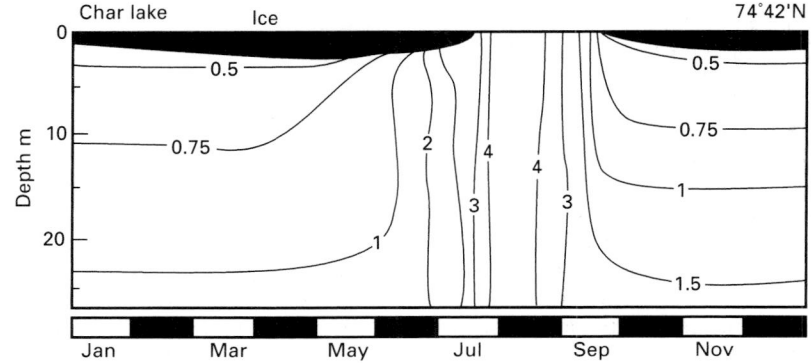

**Fig. 2.9** There are many ways in which lake basins have been formed. Most of the lakes in the north temperate region (upper left, the St Lawrence Great Lakes) were formed by ice scouring the land surface, damming river valleys with moraines, melting as huge blocks sunk in meltwater-borne sands and gravels and various other ways. Along plate margins, where earthquakes and volcanic activity are normal, lakes can be formed in dormant craters (upper right, a small crater lake in Uganda) or by separation of plates leaving wide rifts or by simple geological sinking of the land. Animals including beavers and (lower left) ungulates in South Africa can disturb soils that blow away in the dry season to leave a basin that fills with water. People are probably the sources, through damming, of most new lake basins at present. The example (lower right, Barton Broad, UK) is of a lake formed about 1000 years ago by people digging out peat deposits in a river floodplain for fuel. The parallel islands were the undug parts where the peat was piled for drying.

**Fig. 2.10** Stratification in a shallow Arctic lake. The pattern is cold monomictic. Numbers are °C. Shallow lakes of warmer regions where ice does not form in winter will be polymictic, mixing to the bottom year around, though on hot still days there may be a temporary stratification that breaks down overnight. (Based on Schindler et al. 1974.)

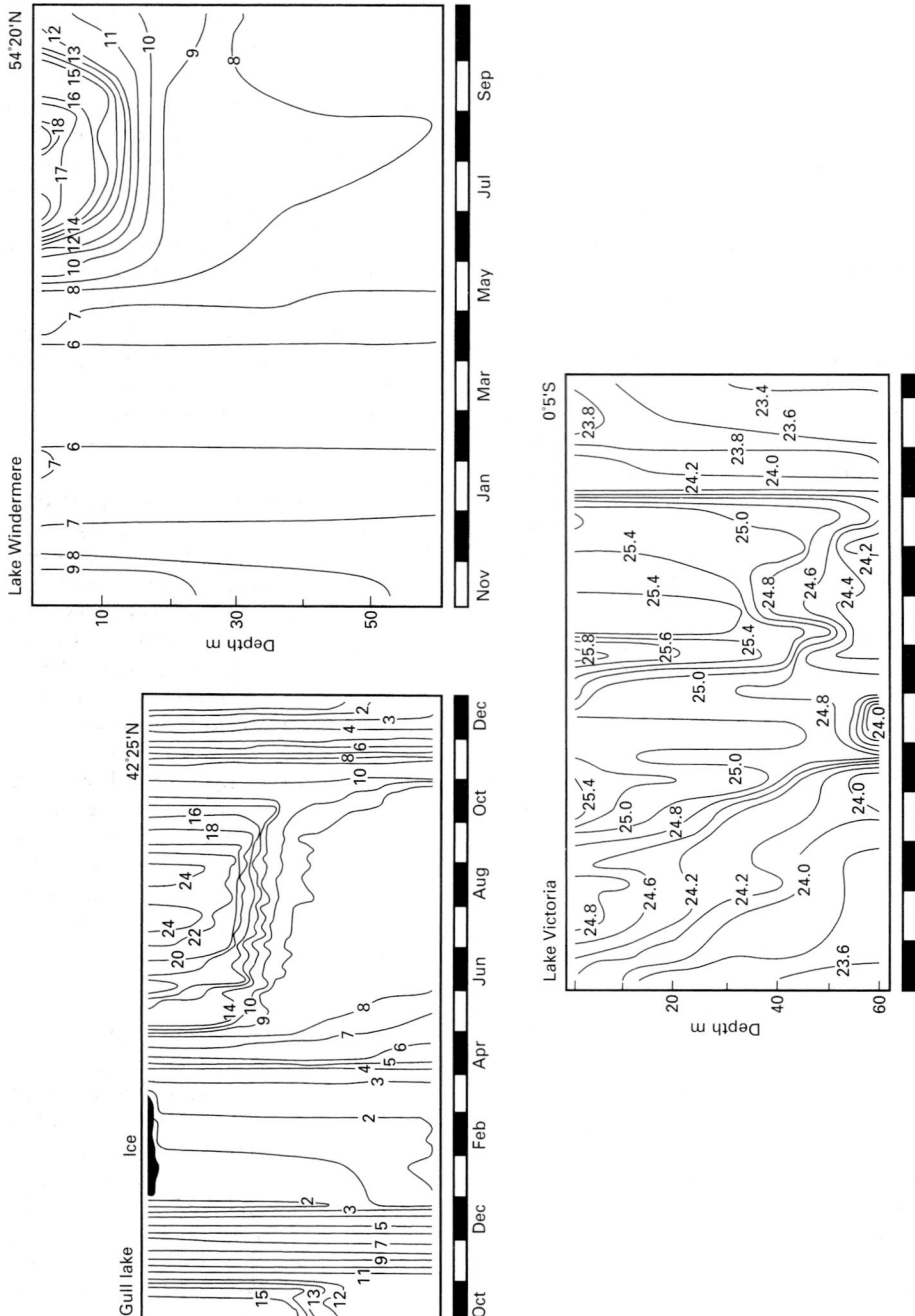

**Fig. 2.11** Stratification patterns vary with climate. Upper right is the pattern in a maritime, cold temperate lake, with no ice formation in winter and direct thermal stratification in summer. Similar patterns, at slightly-higher overall temperatures, are shown in warm temperate lakes. Numbers are °C. Upper right is the dimictic pattern of a temperate continental lake, with inverse stratification in winter, direct stratification in summer and two mixing periods, in spring and autumn. The lower diagram is for the tropical lake Victoria. There is no ice formation and the lake is directly stratified at high temperatures for most of the year. Slightly cooler periods, caused by increased windiness, cause some mixing in July and to a lesser extent in January. (Based on Jenkin (1942), Moss (1972) and Talling (1966).)

period of ice cover will generally increase with latitude from a few days to several months.

## 2.5.2 Deeper lakes

In a similar series of deeper lakes (Fig. 2.11), a similar pattern of inverse stratification will be found in winter at the colder end of the series but more complicated events occur in the summer, or warm season, or year around in the tropics. In deeper water, in the warmer periods, wind strength may be too feeble to mix the water to the bottom. As the surface waters absorb energy from the Sun (see Chapter 5 for details), they warm. The water absorbs this energy quickly and it thus does not penetrate very far into the water mass. What little wind there is may mix just the surface layers, perhaps a few metres, which then become uniform (isothermal) and float on the deeper, cooler, denser water. The upper layer is called the epilimnion, the lower the hypolimnion and the transitional layer in-between where the temperature falls rapidly is the metalimnion. The temperature gradient is called the thermocline, but this term and metalimnion are often used interchangeably. This pattern is called direct stratification.

In the polar regions, there will be no direct stratification in summer. The wind is too strong and the water remains isothermal throughout once the ice has melted and the inverse stratification under ice has been overturned. This pattern is called cold monomixis. The lake mixes (mixis) but once (mono) during the year and the stratified period is during the winter. If the lake is permanently frozen over, it is called cold amictic (unmixing). Further towards the Equator, in the cold temperate region, there will be winter inverse stratification under ice, then a period of mixing in spring, during which the water warms by a few degrees, before direct stratification begins in early summer. The epilimnion water may then reach 20°C, whilst the hypolimnion might be at less than 10°C.

In extreme cases, deep in the continents, spring may be very short and the ice melt succeeded by summer warming so rapidly that the mixing period occurs entirely at 4°C so that the hypolimnion remains at that temperature. In late summer, as the angle of the Sun decreases and solar energy is unable to prevent a cooling of the surface waters, the epilimnion will cool towards the temperature of the hypolimnion and with the help perhaps of an autumn gale, the water mass will mix to isothermality before cooling more towards winter freezing. This seasonal pattern is called dimixis; the lakes are dimictic, with two periods of mixing during the year.

Warm temperate regions have lakes that do not freeze but are well mixed in winter and then have intense direct stratification in summer, with quite warm hypolimnia. The pattern is warm monomixis. As the climate really warms in the tropics, a variety of patterns can be found (Fig. 2.11). Sometimes there is warm monomixis, with summer epilimnion temperatures close to 30°C and mixing during the cooler season only a degree or two below this at the temperature of the hypolimnion. The density of water changes more quickly per degree C the warmer it becomes above 4°C, so stratification differences of only a few degrees at high temperature are as stable as those involving 10°C or more in cooler lakes.

In the tropics there may also be near-permanent stratification (warm amixis), where intensely hot conditions close to the Equator create temperature gradients that are rarely mixed by wind. Such conditions are promoted by shelter in dense forest and sometimes by progressive accumulation of dissolved substances in the deep water which increase its density more than by just lower temperature alone, a phenomenon called meromixis. Very deep meromictic lakes may go through a warm monomictic cycle in their upper layers, whilst never mixing at all in their deepest layers, stabilized by accumulation of dissolved substances. Deep, chemically stabilized layers that do not mix are called monimolimnia (singular, monimolimnion). Other lakes that are exposed but do not freeze in winter may be permanently mixed (polymictic). They are usually quite shallow.

## 2.5.3 Effects of altitude and oceanicity

Mountains, and proximity to the sea, add another dimension to this. For a given latitude, the idealized sequence seen at sea level as one moves from the tropics to the poles, of warm amictic to warm monomictic to dimictic to cold monomictic to cold amictic, can theoretically be repeated with increasing altitude if lake basins exist. Thus the lakes at the tops of the highest tropical mountains may be permanently frozen, though global temperature increase in recent decades has converted some of them to polymictic. Likewise, closeness to the sea at a given latitude will lead to slightly warmer

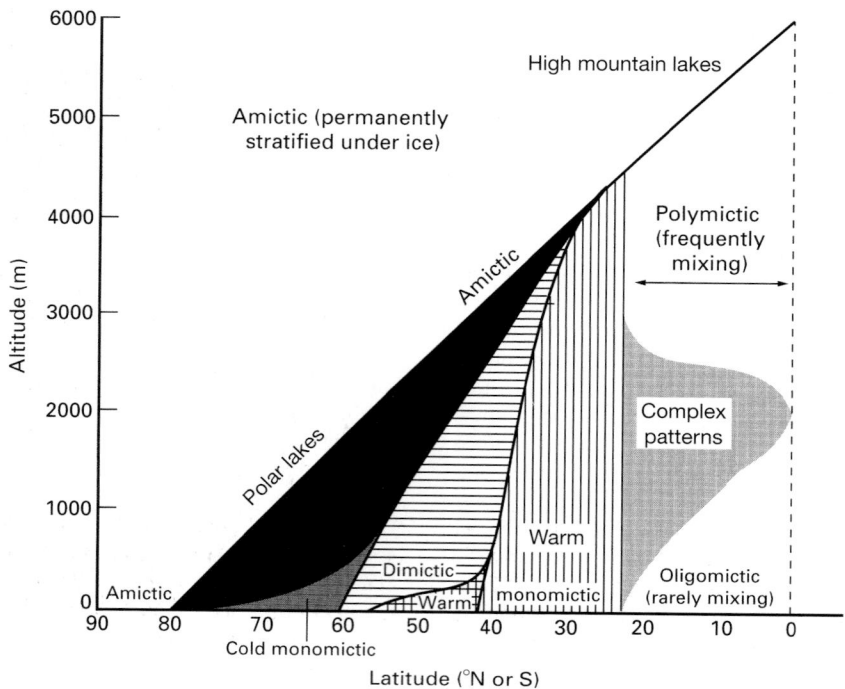

**Fig. 2.12** The main patterns of thermal stratification as it changes with altitude and latitude are summarized. At mid-altitudes in the tropics (i.e. below the high-altitude lakes at the tops of high tropical mountains and above the torrid lakes of the wet tropical lowlands, a variety of patterns of alternate mixing and stratification may occur, depending on local climate. (Based on Hutchinson & Loffler 1956.)

conditions than found at the same latitude deep within a continent. English lakes tend to be warm monomictic; lakes at similar latitudes in Canada or Russia will be dimictic. Figure 2.12 summarizes the generalities of lake stratification for lakes that are theoretically deep enough to stratify. Shallow lakes may be polymictic in any situation where they do not freeze. The pattern of stratification is very important in determining the nature of the ecosystem in a lake.

## 2.6 VISCOSITY OF WATER, FLUID DYNAMICS AND THE DIFFUSION OF GASES

There is a further set of properties linked with the molecular structure of water that is very important in the ecology of freshwater organisms. Water, being a liquid, is a fluid. It flows; the molecules, or domains of them linked together in bunches by their hydrogen bonds, are free enough to move relative to one another. But also, because of the retention of some crystalline structure owing to the hydrogen bonding among the molecules, they will stick to surfaces and to each other. Water thus has a viscosity, a stickiness and forms a relatively dense medium through which other molecules find difficulty in passage by simple diffusion. It can be imagined as a dense thicket of trees with the branches touching and interleaving, in which a creature only about as big as the spaces between the branches will not get much delayed if it tries to get through.

If we think of a fluid as a collection of adjacent blobs or tiny droplets, viscosity is a measure of the resistance of these blobs to change shape if a force is applied to them. Formally, viscosity is the rate of change of angle of distortion divided by the shear stress. Two sorts of local forces (as opposed to distant ones such as gravity) act on a blob of water. One is pressure, which acts normally (at right angles) to the surface and is created

Large object
*Re* high >10
Pressure ≫ drag

Medium sized object
*Re* <10. >0.1
Pressure and drag
both important

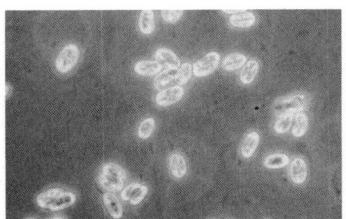

Small object
*Re* ≪ 0.1
Drag and viscosity
dominate

**Fig. 2.13** Objects moving through a fluid, or over which a fluid moves, experience two forces. Pressure acts at right angles and is proportional to size, density and speed. Drag (sheer stress) acts tangentially and is dependent on size of body and stickiness (viscosity) of the fluid. Reynolds number, *Re*, is: density × velocity × length divided by viscosity. Broadly it is the ratio of pressure forces to drag forces.

by the weight of water above or of an object moving towards the blob or the blob moving against a fixed object. The other is the force due to the stickiness, which acts tangentially as blobs move across a surface or relative to one another. This is the shear stress. It can be thought of as friction between the blobs or between a surface and a blob, and is the distorting force.

Some fluids, like gases, have very low viscosity; that of liquids is higher. Water is not so viscous as glycerol, treacle or tar, but its viscosity does present a problem to organisms. It is a variable problem dependent on the size, density and relative speed of movement of the organism. If a moving body is very large, a big fish or seal 2 m long, say, the resistance to its passage because of viscosity is quite low, and resistance to its passage from inertial or pressure forces will be much greater. If it is a 1-μm bacterium, however, the resistance owing to both inertial forces and viscosity will be enormous and the relationship between the bacterium and the fluid will be similar to that of a ship moving through thick tar. Inertial forces become irrelevant because viscosity is so great. We talk therefore of a viscous environment and define this by the ratio of the (density × speed × length) of the moving object, divided by the viscosity. This ratio, which is dimensionless, is called the Reynolds number (*Re*). For a large vertebrate, *Re* is high, much greater than 10 say; for an alga or bacterium it is very low, perhaps of the order of 0.001. Small organisms will thus move sluggishly and if they do not move will sink very slowly even if they are much denser than the water. Life at low Reynolds numbers is dominated by stickiness.

Life at intermediate Reynolds numbers (Fig. 2.13), such as experienced by larger organisms like the larger invertebrates or smaller fish, means coping with both viscous and inertial forces. Viscous forces are referred to as drag. Coping with drag means expending energy and thus evolution has selected shapes that minimize the drag. Over the surface of an organism in a fluid, there is a layer in which viscous forces are prominent. This is called the boundary layer. In it, the stickiness of the fluid to the organism minimizes mixing of the blobs and they may not move at all. Layers of water in the boundary layer beyond the immediate surface will stick to those closer to it but less than they would to the organism's surface. Those a little further away will have a little more freedom; they will be less affected by friction with the organism's surface and as the organism moves they will flow in a smooth or laminar (layered) way across each succeeding layer. Eventually friction with the organism's surface will be negligible and at that point the limit of the boundary layer has been reached and the fluid mixes and swirls in turbulent motion. Boundary layers tend to be thinner as relative motion increases because the shear stresses lever them away from the surface. They are generally only millimetres in thickness for invertebrates and fish.

Boundary layers are useful, however, as they lubricate the movement of the organism and help it to overcome the drag effects of the water mass. If we imagine a spherical organism moving through water, the water, as it impacts on the front of the sphere, comes to a temporary halt. Its pressure is thus high. As it then begins to slide along the surface of the organism through the laminar boundary layer, its pressure should decrease as it speeds up but it meets the viscous resistance of the boundary layer and pressure increases again. It pushes the boundary layer backwards and a point comes when the opposing pressures cause the boundary layer to separate from the surface into a little maelstrom of turbulence. This impedes the slide of the sphere through the water.

There are, however, shapes that allow the boundary layer to remain intact, called streamline or aerofoil shapes (Fig. 2.13). These are commonly seen in fish, and copied in submarines and aeroplanes. Streamlined bodies have a pointed nose and a maximum width about one-third of the length back, then taper to a point at the rear. As water moves back from the nose, the low angle of the shape allows the moving water to move along the boundary layer without levering it away. Pressure in it first increases to the shoulder (the widest part), but not sufficiently to destroy the boundary layer. Pressure then decreases towards the tail as the angle to the direction of movement declines and the water slides smoothly past the tail as a streamline. Energy is thus not dissipated in causing turbulent mixing of the boundary layer and the water outside it. The same principles apply whether the organism is moving through the water or the water, as in a stream, is moving past a sessile organism. A non-streamlined shape may result in the organism being torn away by the turbulence caused by the shear stress but a streamlined shape allows the water to move smoothly past the organism and to leave it in place.

### 2.6.1 Diffusion

The next chapter will deal with the great importance of things dissolved in the water for freshwater organisms. Some are needed for osmoregulation, others as nutrients for growth; yet others are excretory products. In all cases, the molecules need to get into or out of the organism. The analogy of the thicket of branches mentioned above again comes into play. It is difficult even for small molecules to find their way, sometimes nearly impossible for bigger ones. Molecules in the water will tend to move randomly and their speed of movement will depend on their size (the smaller the faster) and the temperature (the warmer the faster). If they are uniformly distributed to start with they will simply rearrange themselves by random movements in an infinite variety of uniform concentrations. If there are more in one place than the next, their movements will tend to even out this difference. There may be more dissolved nutrient in the outside water than inside a cell, for example and diffusion will tend to balance this by a net movement towards and into the cell. This tendency to even out the concentration ultimately resides in like molecules tending to repel one another and the tendency, that is the speed at which evenness is achieved, will be proportional to the steepness of the concentration gradient.

Diffusion is very slow, however, in a medium like water, especially with its thicket of hydrogen-bonded molecules, and in very still water cells may become very short of required nutrients. Movements of molecules are helped, however, by sometimes hitching rides. If a molecule reacts with water to form a compound, it may be carried by the water molecule or by parcels of water molecules moved around *en masse* by wind or gravity. Organisms have also evolved transport enzymes that aid movements of molecules into their cells, sometimes against concentration gradients. We often talk of problems created for organisms by their environment, but where evolution has found a way of overcoming these phenomena, there is no longer a problem.

### FURTHER READING

The present problems of freshwaters have spawned dozens of books on water. For the properties of water, Hutchinson (1957) is still a standard work, whilst Ball (1999), Caro (1993) and especially Pielou (1998) are very readable. Hydrology also has a vast library and Ward & Robinson (1990) is a standard work, with Gregory & Walling (1973) also well respected. Leopold (1994, 1997) is eminently readable having perhaps inherited his talents from his father, Aldo Leopold, a great conservationist and a lucid and attractive writer. Anything from this family is well worth reading. Do not spurn older books in the library. They are sometimes better written than modern works that are replete with jargon designed to impress rather than to inform. Ruttner (1953) is still, in my view, the clearest textbook on limnology ever written and certainly inspired me 40 years ago. Kling et al. (1987) give background to the topic of Exercise 1 in Chapter 17.

# Chapter 3

# WHY THE CHEMISTRY OF WATER IS SO IMPORTANT

## 3.1 INTRODUCTION

One of the best examples of the power of advertising persuasion, almost as absurd as selling ice to Inuit (though, with global climate change (Chapter 16), this may become less odd) is the massive sale of bottled water in Europe and North America, where the public supply is generally of superior quality and vastly less expensive. The labels on the bottles frequently carry a chemical analysis of the water, usually in terms of the pH and the concentrations of sodium, potassium, calcium, magnesium, sulphate, bicarbonate, chloride and sometimes nitrate. You can deduce the general origin of the water from this (though often the numbers do not balance in the way they should and may be bogus) but a water chemist will also note that they are a very crude and incomplete description of a solution that might contain tens of thousands of different compounds, not just eight or nine ions.

### 3.1.1 Polar and covalent compounds

Most things will dissolve, to a small extent at least, in water and this is a consequence of its molecular structure. Its slight polarization of electrons, the tendency for the oxygen to be slightly electronegative, the hydrogen electropositive, is enough to allow water to react with ions. Such reaction is a measure of true solution. It also allows it to dissolve slightly polar organic compounds, particularly those with hydroxyl and amino groups, such as sugars, alcohols, amino acids, amides and organic bases. But it does not truly dissolve completely covalent compounds that are not electrically charged. These (e.g., fats and oils, hydrocarbons, and gases such as oxygen and nitrogen) can only form a non-reacting mixture. Their uncharged molecules and the charged ones of water repel one another, and the mixture is a reluctant one, with few molecules of these substances able to be maintained in a simple physical equilibrium among the water molecules. A measure of true solution (reaction) is that more of the substance dissolves as temperature increases. Conversely, in physical mixtures, less of the substance is present as temperature increases. Warming and the consequent increased molecular motion tend to cause the substance to move out of the mixture (Fig. 3.1).

No one knows the exact composition of any natural river or lake water. We know the most common substances in them, but there is a huge array of others, probably many thousands of them; some chemists think there are millions, especially organic compounds, present in tiny concentrations. The process of creating this complex mixture begins with the condensation of water droplets that fall as rain from the atmosphere.

*Ecology of Freshwaters: A View for the Twenty-first Century*, 4th edition. By Brian Moss. Published 2010 by Blackwell Publishing Ltd.

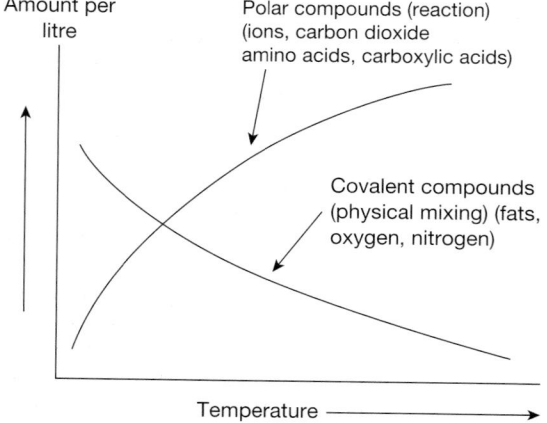

**Fig. 3.1** Ionic compounds have greater solubilities in water as temperature increases because solubility involves a chemical reaction with the water and in general chemical reactions proceed faster and to a greater extent as temperature increases. Covalent compounds and the polarized molecules of water tend to repel one another, however, and can form physical mixtures only by diffusion into one another. Increasing temperature tends to increase diffusion away from the mixture so lower amounts of covalent compounds can coexist in the mixture as temperature increases.

The droplets will dissolve ions from dust, flecks of sea spray swept up in storms from the ocean, and carbon dioxide. The water droplets will also form physical mixtures with dust particles and the covalent atmospheric gases such as oxygen, nitrogen and the noble gases. After water reaches the ground it will mix with and dissolve more substances from the weathering of rocks and soils, and the secretions and decomposition products of land organisms with which it comes into contact. It may gain, and then lose, some substances, as plants absorb them or microorganisms process them. When it enters streams and lakes, similar processes will further change it. Concentrations of substances will vary depending on how fast the water moves through soil and over rock, how active the organisms are with which it comes into contact, and the climate. Hot places lead to evaporation and concentration and to salty waters. It helps to consider some of the details in turn, building the composition of the water from the moment of its formation as a droplet in the atmosphere.

## 3.2 THE ATMOSPHERE

The atmosphere contains many gases, not just the familiar oxygen, nitrogen, carbon dioxide or even the rarer argon, neon, krypton and xenon. There is methane, methyl iodide, ammonia, dimethyl sulphide, nitrous oxide and a host of other very reactive gases produced by living organisms and thought to be important in regulating atmospheric composition because they react with oxygen. There are also atmospheric pollutant gases produced by industry, agriculture or waste disposal, such as persistent organic pollutants, often chlorinated aromatic compounds from industry and pesticide residues. Water droplets in the atmosphere will pick up all of these though the concentrations may be very low.

For the moment, we will look at the commoner gases. They fall into two groups: carbon dioxide on the one hand and oxygen, nitrogen and the inert gases on the other. The latter group does not truly dissolve, though we usually refer to 'dissolved' oxygen. These covalent gases form mixtures with the amount mixed in directly proportional to their partial pressure in the atmosphere and inversely to the temperature. The solubility of oxygen under atmospheric pressure is shown in Fig. 3.2. The consequence is that natural waters are quite low in oxygen concentrations, with at most about 14 mg $L^{-1}$ of water. This compares with concentrations in the atmosphere of about 270 mg $L^{-1}$ of air at standard temperature and pressure.

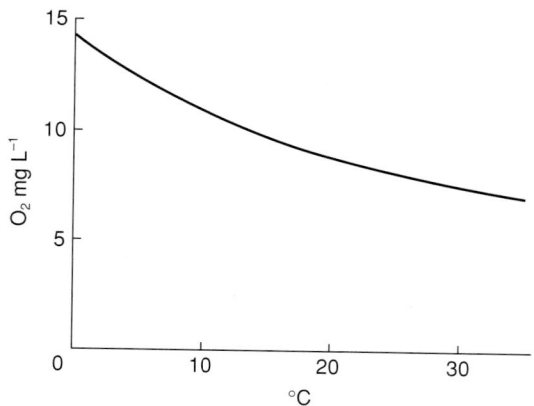

**Fig. 3.2** Oxygen is covalent and very little oxygen can be dissolved (in fact physically mixed) in water. This is an important issue for the respiration of freshwater organisms and indeed for many other aspects of water chemistry.

In sluggish rivers and especially in shallow, swampy, standing waters, uptake of this oxygen by bacteria may be more rapid than it can diffuse in from the atmosphere and natural waters may temporarily become severely deoxygenated relative to their equilibrium (saturation) concentrations. Evolution has produced many ways of coping with this (see Chapter 6). Gaseous nitrogen levels in water are higher, simply because nitrogen is more common in the atmosphere but still quite low as dinitrogen gas also is a covalent compound. Some prokaryotes are able to fix this nitrogen into amino groups hence providing, through their eventual decomposition, a truly dissolved nitrogen supply in the form of nitrate and ammonium. There is no indication that the levels of dinitrogen dissolved in water seriously limit the rate of fixation.

### 3.2.1 Carbon dioxide

Carbon dioxide is relatively scarce in atmospheric air (about 7 mg $L^{-1}$ of air or 380 parts per million by volume at present) but is relatively enriched in rain water because of its high solubility. Unlike oxygen and nitrogen, but like water, it is slightly polar and can react with the water. It diffuses into water droplets in the atmosphere and forms a weak acid, carbonic acid. This acid dissociates to form bicarbonate ions, according to the following equilibria:

$$CO_2 + H_2O \Leftrightarrow H_2CO_3 \Leftrightarrow HCO_3^- + H^+ \Leftrightarrow CO_3^{2-} + H^+$$

The reaction involves hydrogen ions and therefore determines an equilibrium pH (minus the logarithm of the hydrogen ion concentration, $-\log_{10}[H^+]$) of around 5.5 for natural rain water and a concentration of about $10^{-5}$ M or 0.44 mg $CO_2$ $L^{-1}$. Only a little of the carbon is in the form of bicarbonate ions and carbonate ions are effectively absent from rain water. Figure 3.3 shows how at different pH values, different proportions of the forms of inorganic carbon can exist. The slightly acid solution of atmospheric water droplets also often picks up small quantities of sea salt, especially within a few tens of kilometres of the coasts and this may increase the pH slightly, but the rain is still naturally acid when it reaches the ground. Man-made pollutants such as sulphur and nitrogen oxides may increase the acidity and reduce the pH to lower than 4. The effects of these are discussed in later chapters. For the moment we are considering the natural baseline.

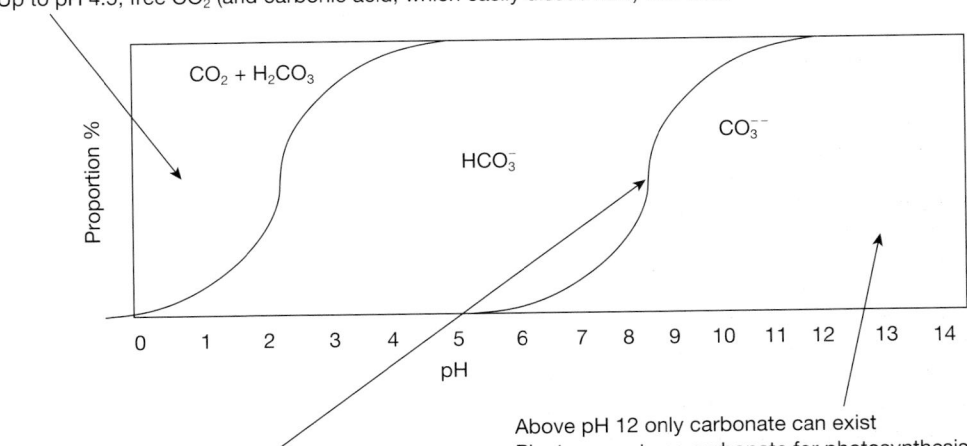

**Fig. 3.3** Carbon dioxide is polar and truly dissolves, but once in solution, its reactions with water and hydrogen ions lead to a set of chemical equilibria in which the form of the carbon (molecular $CO_2$, bicarbonic acid ($H_2CO_3$), bicarbonate ($HCO_3^-$) and carbonate ($CO_3^{--}$) ions) and their proportions are both influenced by pH and contrive to determine the pH. This is important because some plants and algae cannot use bicarbonate in photosynthesis and none can use carbonate.

## 3.3 MAJOR IONS

When the rain water (or snow meltwater, for over much of the world, snow is the main form in which water reaches the ground from the atmosphere) percolates into the soils, it starts to react with other inorganic substances. Rocks and soils are made up of large numbers of minerals. Some of these are primary, having been formed as crystals in the solidification of lava to form igneous rocks of volcanic origin. Others are the secondary products of past weathering and other geological processes that have created sedimentary and metamorphic rocks. Together they give a relatively rich source of ions for the water to dissolve and to add to the load it has already acquired from dust and sea spray in the atmosphere.

The extent to which mineral elements are dissolved depends on their attraction to water molecules. In turn this depends on their charge or valency (the number of electrons by which the outer orbit of the atom exceeds or falls short of the number in the outer orbit of the closest related inert gas) and on the size of the ion. The attraction increases with the charge (either positive or negative) but decreases with increasing size of the ion. This is because a greater surface area of the ion spreads the charge and therefore weakens the attraction. If $Z$ is the charge on, and $r$ the radius of the ion, the affinity for water can be measured as the ionic potential, $Z/r$.

### 3.3.1 Effects of ionic potential

The efficiency of water as a solvent, however, does not simply increase with increasing ionic potential of the solute. Elements with $Z/r < 3.0$ or $> 12.0$ are readily dissolved but those with $Z/r$ between these values tend to be precipitated. Elements with an ionic potential $< 3.0$ form cations derived from metals (Fig. 3.4) such as sodium, potassium and calcium. The charge is sufficient for attraction to the water molecules and to bind the ions with water (the results being called hydrated cations) in solution.

However, ionic radius is not a simple function of atomic weight and some heavier elements have quite small ionic radii despite a great weight and a high charge. In these, which have an ionic potential between 3.0 and 12.0, the charge is sufficient to attract the oxygen atom in water so closely that the binding between the oxygen and one of the hydrogens in the water molecule is weakened. A hydrogen ion is then ejected into solution and a metal hydroxide is formed. Such hydroxides have little surplus charge left for the attraction of water molecules, and they precipitate. Aluminium and silica are good examples. So are iron and manganese, though these transition metals have two valency states and can also behave like the first group.

In a third case, of elements with ionic potentials $> 12.0$, the charge attraction for the oxygen in water is very great. Both the hydrogens of a water molecule are ejected into solution as $H^+$ (where they bond with water molecules to form $H_3O^+$, hydrated hydrogen ions, and remain in solution) and an oxy-anion is formed. Such oxy-anions are called complex, for they involve two elements (one being oxygen), and the ionic potential of the complex ion (as opposed to those of its elemental components) is reduced to a value at which it attracts water molecules and remains in solution. Nitrate, carbonate and sulphate are good examples, with the position of phosphate (see Fig. 3.4) bringing it close to the borderline between the soluble oxy-anion and the insoluble middle group.

The charge properties of water thus interact with those of other elements to bring ions into solution to varying extents, and the inorganic composition of natural waters, where the highly soluble $H^+$, $Na^+$, $K^+$, $Mg^{++}$, $Ca^{++}$, $HCO_3^-$, $SO_4^{--}$ and $Cl^-$ are normally major components, reflects this. The final composition, however, also reflects the availability in the surface of the Earth's crust of elements for potential solution. To some extent this relative availability is an accident of astrophysics and the composition of the gas cloud from which the Earth originally formed. Because of this, almost none of the more soluble elements will approach saturation, except in conditions of very high evaporation. And in mixtures of ions the affinity of one to another may overcome the attraction of either to water and lead to precipitation. For example, both calcium and carbonate are highly soluble each in the absence of the other, but readily precipitate as $CaCO_3$ if mixed together. Elements with ionic potentials between 3 and 12 also tend to be scarce for they are much less soluble.

The major ion concentrations of rain and some natural freshwaters are shown in Table 3.1. They very much reflect the local geology and therefore the minerals available for reaction with the water. Igneous rocks tend to be dense and massive (lacking internal pores) and are only slowly weathered by the action of freezing and thawing and rain. They contain some

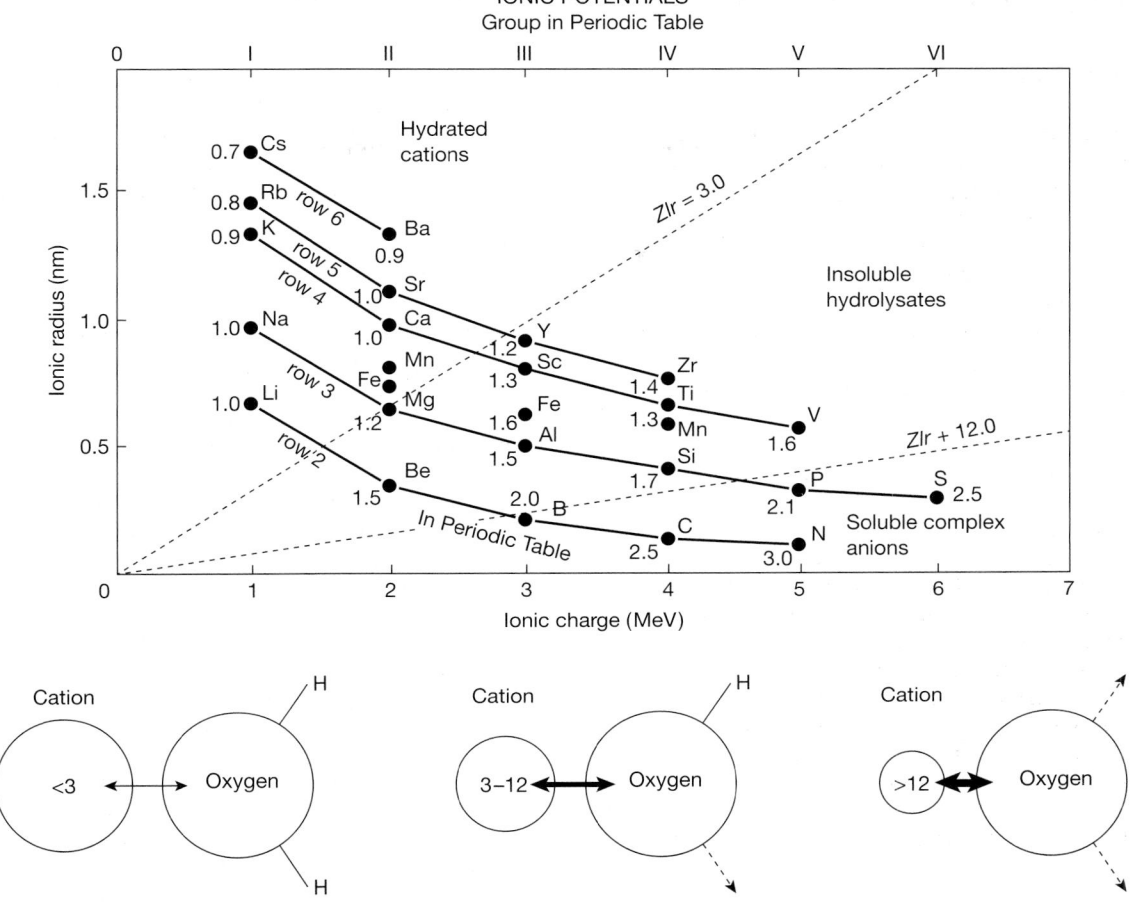

**Fig. 3.4** The solubility of major ions is determined by the charge or valency (Z) and the ionic radius (r). High, intermediate and low values of their ratio lead to very different solubilities and properties. In particular, those with ratios between 3 and 12 tend to precipitate out and are normally quite scarce in dissolved form. Some of these, particularly P and Fe, are required in quite high quantities by living organisms and their availability may limit production (see Chapter 4).

**Table 3.1** Major ion concentrations of some fresh waters.

|  | Rain (UK and USA) | World mean | Tropical water (Tasek Bera, Malaysia) | English Lake District | Norfolk Broads | Endorheic lake (Lake Nakuru, Kenya) |
|---|---|---|---|---|---|---|
| pH | 4.8–5.5 | 6.6–8.0 | 5.24–5.3 | 6.5–7.1 | 7–9 | 10.1–11.0 |
| Na (mg L$^{-1}$) | 0.12–3.1 | 10 | 1.04–1.24 | 3.3–5.0 | 37–46 | 4669–38,000 |
| K (mg L$^{-1}$) | 0.07–0.74 | 1 | 0.47–0.51 | 0.3–0.9 | 4.3–9.4 |  |
| Ca (mg L$^{-1}$) | 0.16–3.7 | 17 | 0.4–0.43 | 2.1–8.3 | 14.3–128 | Trace–3.7 |
| Mg (mg L$^{-1}$) | 0.04–0.3 | 10.3 | 0.28–0.29 | 0.5–3.5 | 5.9–11.0 |  |
| SO$_4$ (mg L$^{-1}$) |  | 2 | 3.05–3.41 | 4.5–9.9 |  |  |
| Cl (mg L$^{-1}$) | 0.55–5.1 | 5 | 0.02–1.97 | 5.9–10.1 | 48–77 |  |
| HCO$_3$ (mequiv L$^{-1}$) |  | 0.85 | 0.06–0.07 | 0.05–0.3 | 4–5.7 |  |
| Conductivity (µS cm$^{-1}$) | 50 | 140 | 13.9–14.4 | 42–70 | 560–720 | 10,000–162,500 |

quite soluble minerals but these are only slowly made available for solution. Sedimentary rocks are made up of the products of weathering of former rocks that have been eroded and redeposited. They are less massive, and already composed of distinctive particles, with some spaces, or very soluble natural cements between them, that can be relatively readily dissolved for the water to act upon the particles. Natural waters, despite the variation imposed by different geologies, are mostly dilute ionic solutions and this, like the shortage of oxygen poses problems for organisms whose internal functioning demands rather higher concentrations of many elements (see Chapter 4).

Table 3.1 gives some details of major ion composition of a range of waters, and illustrates the information that can be drawn from some simple chemical analyses. The labels on bottled water bottles offer a parallel opportunity. The values in Table 3.1 are typical values rather than absolute means and are mostly given in mg per litre, except for pH (units) conductivity ($\mu$S cm$^{-1}$) and bicarbonate, which is given in mequiv L$^{-1}$. This is because it is analytically impossible to give a precise value for bicarbonate because it enters into equilibrium reactions during analysis. What is done is to titrate it against hydrochloric acid but the measure gives the total of weak acid salts, usually dominated by bicarbonate but also always including some weak organic acids in natural waters. A crude approximation can be given for bicarbonate by multiplying the value in mequiv L$^{-1}$ by 61 to give mg L$^{-1}$.

Rainfall, as expected, shows only modest concentrations and a pH around 5.5 (though some rain is acidified by pollutants and has lower values). Its ratio of sodium to calcium is relatively high, reflecting the sea spray component in it. By comparison the world average freshwater has around ten times as much major ion, reflecting ions picked up from rock weathering and a lower sodium to calcium ratio in consequence. Water draining through tropical rain forest in Malaysia has comparable or lower values than those of rain. There is little to be picked up from weathering in the very ancient, long-leached soils and some of the rain's ions are taken up by the vegetation and stored in the soils. The English Lake District has a range of rocks, though none of them highly calcareous and is very wet so that water passes rapidly through the soils, picking up ions but not achieving the world average, whilst the waters of the Norfolk Broads in the dry east of England pass through calcareous glacial drift and even chalk bedrock to give very high calcium and bicarbonate levels and total concentrations much higher than all

the previously mentioned examples. Lake Nakuru, in Kenya, is startlingly different. It has very high concentrations of sodium and carbonate through evaporative concentration and negligible concentrations of calcium, which is precipitated out into white sediments exposed at the margins when the lake levels fall in the dry season.

## 3.4 GLOBAL PATTERNS IN MAJOR IONS: GLACIATION AND ENDORHEISM

The major ionic composition of waters varies locally with the geology (e.g., the contrast between the English Lake District and Norfolk Broads in Table 3.1) but there are also some bigger patterns. One is related to climate history, another to age, a third to vulcanism and a fourth to current climate. Much of the northern hemisphere was glaciated until quite recently. The warm temperate regions and the tropics, except on high mountains, were not covered by ice. Ice, as it formed towards the poles and then moved towards the Equator, was a powerful agent of rock weathering. Ice grinds, gouges and splits rock particles. As it melts back, the meltwater sorts, and deposits sands and gravels, silts and clays, and replaces and refreshes with new minerals the former underlying soils. As warmer conditions return, the newly flowing waters have rich pickings of new minerals and the waters are comparatively concentrated for some time.

Studying the composition of lakes that have been recently formed when glaciers have melted back can show this. Figure 3.5 shows the terrain around Glacier Bay in Alaska and the ages of lakes that have been exposed in the progressive retreat of the glaciers. The water chemistry can then be related to the age of the lake. Figure 3.6 shows how the ionic concentrations of the waters are at first high, but then decline as the catchments are progressively leached. The values of dissolved organic matter increase as the catchments build up vegetation and organic contents in their soils and nitrogen levels also increase to a plateau. Nitrogen (see Chapter 4) enters from the atmosphere through biological processes of nitrogen fixation and these processes take some to time to establish.

The concentrations in the sediments laid down in lakes forming after the glaciation tell the same story of initial high concentrations. These sediments can be sampled using borers that remove an intact core from the earliest sediments laid down to the most recent and the sediments can be dated (see Chapter 11) by a

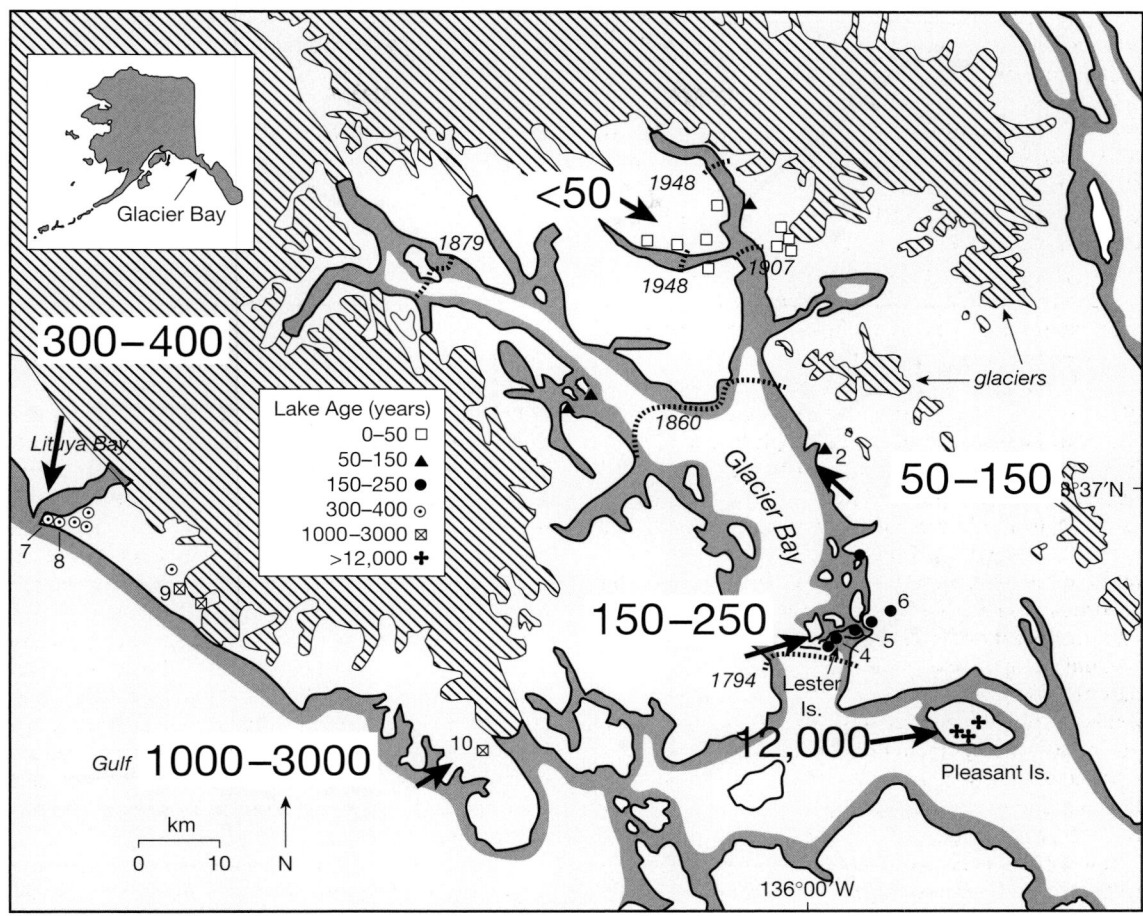

**Fig. 3.5** Glaciers have been retreating from Alaska Bay for several hundreds of years, slowly at first, now more rapidly with global warming. As the ice retreats it exposes new lake basins so that a sequence of lake ecosystems of known ages can be studied and changes in their water chemistry followed. (Based on Engstrom et al. 2000.)

variety of methods. The concentrations eventually fall as the soils are progressively leached out (Fig. 3.7) but the waters are still relatively high in ions (though absolutely dilute nonetheless) 10,000 years on compared with ancient geological regions that have not been disturbed by the ice (e.g., the tropical Malaysian water shown in Table 3.1).

### 3.4.1 The water chemistry of ancient landscapes

Very old soils and landscapes occur on ancient continental surfaces: parts of Australia, Africa, and South

America, away from the influence of any recent vulcanism. Where there has been no recent glaciation or volcanic activity generating newly weatherable minerals or new rocks at the surface, the soils will have been slowly leached for very long periods, often millions of years as opposed to the few thousand of glaciated landscapes. Most of the soluble elements will have been dissolved, leached out and transported to the sea long ago so that present-day rain water has little on which to draw from the soils. The rivers of the Amazon, Orinoco, Zaire and Zambezi are low in ions.

The soils they drain are ancient and exhausted, comprising mostly insoluble oxides of iron, which gives a redness, and silicon, which contributes white quartz

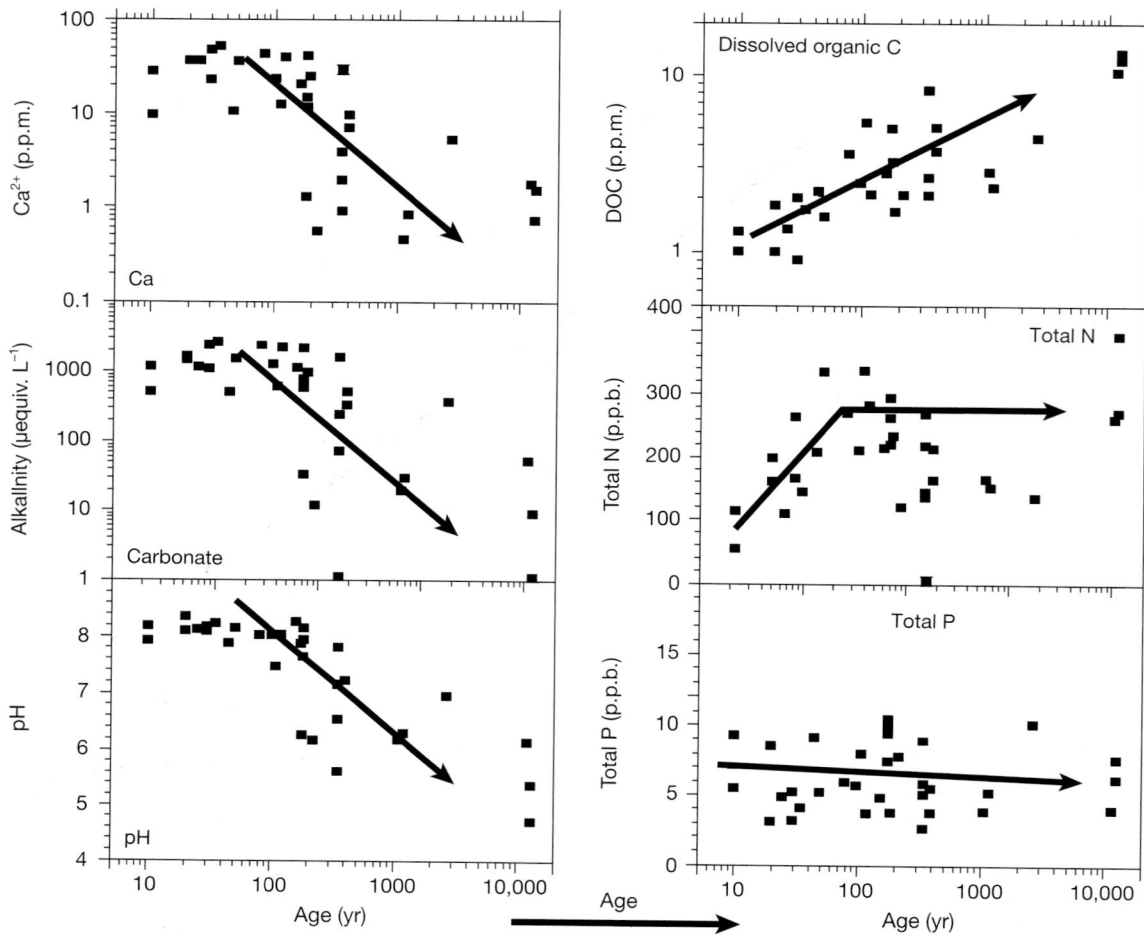

**Fig. 3.6** The newest lakes of Alaska Bay (Fig. 3.5) have waters with relatively high concentrations of the ions derived from rock weathering (Ca, $HCO_3$) and high pH. But as the local catchments become leached by rain, pH falls, and so do the concentrations of these ions. Phosphate is also a little higher at first but is relatively insoluble anyway (see Fig. 3.4) so declines only a little. In contrast, elements fixed from the atmosphere, such as nitrogen, tend to increase as the biological community becomes established and stores more and more carbon in the system. Overall, however, the lakes are richer in ions in their earlier stages than when they have aged. (Based on Engstrom et al. 2000.)

particles. What soluble ions are left are usually bound up and retained by the land vegetation, and although at the bottoms of the soil profiles unweathered bedrock is available, the profiles may be many metres deep, in contrast to the metre or two of the fresh soils of the glaciated regions. Weathering at depth is slow, for water may not easily percolate and extremes of temperature are rare. The products of weathering may not easily pass to the waters that flow from the surface

layers to the streams. Glaciation and time have thus created a general gradient of decreasing mineral content from the poles to the Equator.

### 3.4.2 Volcanic activity

But no natural pattern is entirely regular. This one is disrupted by another major geological process,

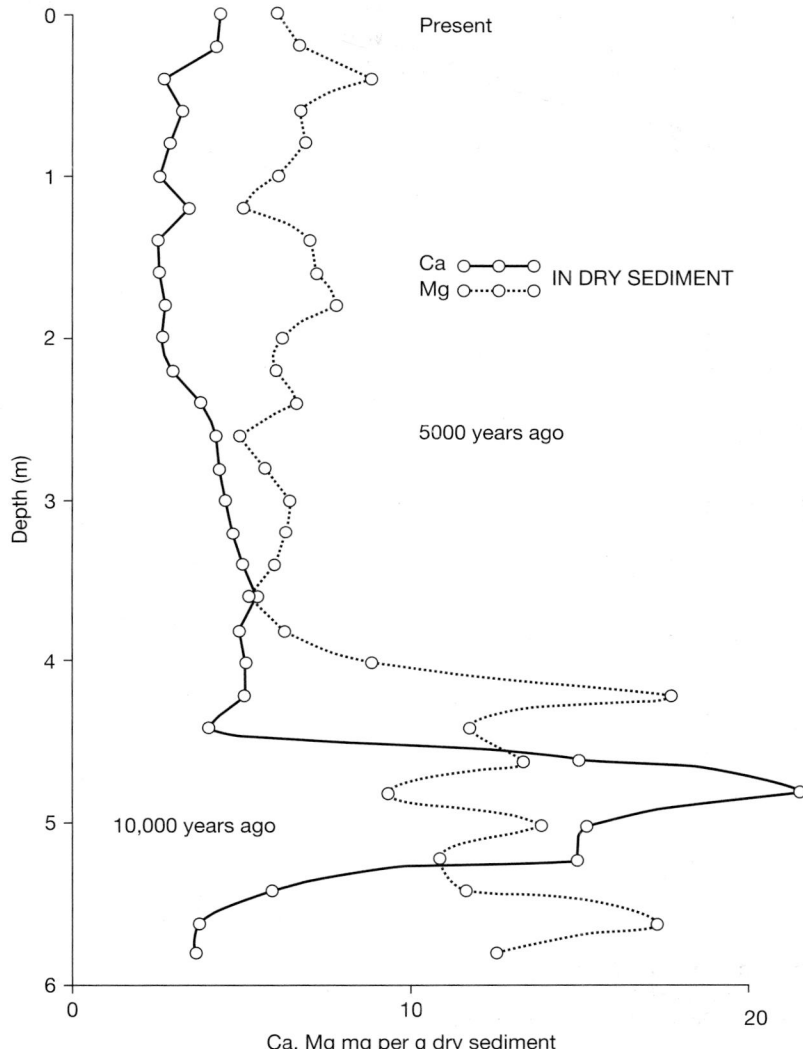

**Fig. 3.7** The same phenomenon as in Fig. 3.6 can be seen in sediment cores from lakes that were formed more than 10,000 years ago as the glaciers retreated from Europe. The earliest sediments are richer in calcium and magnesium (and other ions) than later sediments. Freshly exposed minerals provided the initial boost, but as the soils were leached, the supplies dwindled and the waters became progressively less concentrated. (Based on Mackereth 1965.)

that of plate separation and the vulcanism associated with it. Along the lines of the Earth's surface where plates are separating or disappearing into ocean trenches, new rock is formed as volcanic ashes are blown out and molten lavas ooze from the underlying mantle. Where water percolates into hot rock close to the surface, the solution reactions are speeded up and minerals may dissolve in greater quantity than in other areas. Hot springs and geysers produce waters of exotic composition (Fig. 3.8) and, as the water cools, secondary minerals, elemental sulphur

even, are deposited. These regions give us insights into the early Hadean and Archaean environment of the Earth, $3–4 \times 10^9$ years ago, when vulcanism was predominant. They are still widespread along the Pacific coasts in Japan, Indonesia and New Zealand, the mountain chains of western North America, the Andes and East Africa and the islands of Iceland and the Azores, along the mid-Atlantic ridge, sometimes giving in close proximity, highly saline volcanic waters and the waters derived from ancient tropical soils.

| Temperature (°C) | 67.5–95 |
|---|---|
| $Cl^-$ | 3–453 |
| $SO_4^{--}$ | 16–497 |
| $Na^+$ | 36–434 |
| $K^+$ | 10.2–42 |
| $Ca^{++}$ | Undetectable–8.8 |
| $Mg^{++}$ | Undetectable–2.4 |
| $SiO_2$ | 139–338 |
| pH | 2.3–9.3 |

**Fig. 3.8** Hot springs, where water is heated underground by volcanic lavas, have greatly differing chemical compositions than waters that have percolated through soils and rocks at more modest temperatures. Some are very acid, others highly alkaline; all tend to have high ionic concentrations. Values are in mg $L^{-1}$. Otherwise unusual elements, such as arsenic, may also be abundant. Locally, as in areas like Yellowstone National Park, such waters will dominate the freshwater ecology, but on a world-scale, the geology is more quiescent and water chemistry is determined by slow weathering of rocks rather than by high temperature cooking! (Based on Brock 1978.)

## 3.5 OPEN AND CLOSED BASINS

There is also a climate-based pattern, and one that arguably is the most important of all. It depends on the balance of precipitation and evaporation. There are wet regions where evaporation is low and there is considerable run-off of water to the rivers and the ocean. The waters pick up a modicum of ions but are generally dilute. And there are arid regions where rainfall is low relative to evaporation. Water runs off the land but never reaches the sea. It is quickly evaporated where it collects in low places in the landscape. Such places are salt pans or saline lakes. Water enters as streams but leaves only as vapour and the salts it contained are retained and become more and more concentrated until an equilibrium is reached where chemical precipitation takes some

out of solution to form minerals on the bottom and crusts at the edge.

These regions are not unusual on the continents. They occupy only a little less than half the land surfaces, where the normal lakes are saline (see Fig. 2.8). If you live in most of Europe or North America, you will be familiar with exorheic (externally drained) waters, where lakes have outflows as well as inflows and rivers normally reach the sea. You might think of salty inland waters, called endorheic or internally drained, as odd or unusual, but you should not. They are perfectly usual to much of humanity and they are present even in Europe, in Spain and Greece, and in North America, in the states and provinces that lie in the rain shadow of the Rocky Mountains. The saltiness of endorheic waters poses problems for living organisms, different but no less than the diluteness of exorheic waters.

## 3.6 THE BIG PICTURE

On a world scale, and including both the fresh and marine waters, the processes discussed above fall into a big picture. The rivers that do run to the sea in openly drained regions, with their modest concentrations of salts, are part of this picture. But the ocean has no outlet. It might be seen as the world's largest endorheic lake that has accumulated salts from the land surfaces and has a series of chemical equilibria that lead to precipitation of some salts and, for the past 500 million years or so, a relatively constant composition. The ionic composition of the world's natural waters can then be summarized in a single diagram that expresses these ideas (Fig. 3.9). If the total concentration of salts is plotted along the vertical axis, and the ratio of sodium concentration to the sum of calcium and sodium on the horizontal axis, the world's waters fall into an envelope like the wings of a bird.

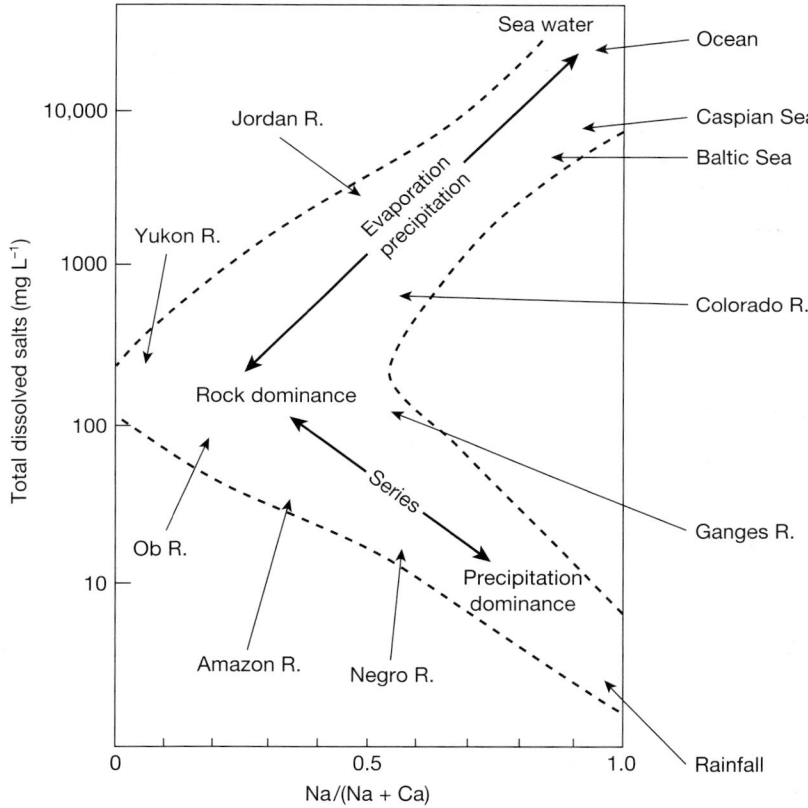

**Fig. 3.9** Plotting the total ionic content of waters against their ratio of sodium to sodium plus calcium gives an orderly pattern like a bird's wings. Sodium is a relatively soluble ion; calcium is more easily precipitated into sediments and eventually rocks. A low ratio is characteristic of waters derived from rock weathering, a high ratio, of waters from which calcium has already been precipitated. At the topmost wing tip are concentrated waters such as those of the ocean and inland seas, which are endorheic and from which calcium is precipitated as evaporation concentrates the solutions. Rain, on the lower wing tip, with much lower concentrations, has an ionic composition dominated by sea spray and hence a high Na/(Na + Ca) ratio. Between these extremes, dominated by precipitation (in the chemical sense) and at the junction of the wings, are exorheic waters where the rainfall composition is modified by rock weathering. Note that tropical waters tend to have a higher ratio than temperate ones. Hot climates lead to some concentration and precipitation, even in exorheic waters, on the one hand, and the ancient, long-weathered soils of many parts of the tropics (compared with the very new ice-regenerated soils of higher latitudes) have lost their calcium to leaching long ago, but have a continuous new supply of sodium from the oceans through the sea-spray effect on rainfall. (Based on Gibbs 1970.)

At the bottom right are rain waters. They have a low absolute concentration, for they pick up only a few salts in the atmosphere, mostly from sea-spray aerosol droplets. They also have a high percentage of sodium among their major ions because ocean water is an endorheic water. Sodium concentrations are relatively high in endorheic waters because of the high solubility of sodium's salts, whereas calcium, in contrast, precipitates out as carbonates. At the top right, therefore, are the concentrated waters of the oceans and of endorheic inland lakes: the Dead Sea, the Aral Sea, the Caspian Sea, along with countless smaller basins of the arid world. In the middle, where the wings join, are the hugely varied waters where different geologies contrive to give a range where calcium and sodium concentrations vary but where conditions are exorheic. Progress from the bottom right through the centre to the top right essentially reflects the changing water composition from rain through rivers to either inland saline lakes or the biggest lake of all, the ocean.

## FURTHER READING

The texts mentioned in both Chapters 1 and 2 all give good accounts of major ions, Hutchinson's Treatise again being authoritative. Andrews et al. (2004) is a very readable overall introduction to environmental chemistry. Because of the particular properties of water, freshwater ecology has developed along chemical lines perhaps much more than terrestrial ecology. A general working knowledge of water chemistry is thus very useful. Talling & Talling (1965) reviews African water chemistry and is very good in contrasting exorheic and endorheic waters. Brock (1978) is a book that recounts a long-term research programme on the hot springs of Yellowstone National Park in the USA. Yellowstone is a fascinating system located in a huge dormant volcanic crater and illustrates many aspects of ecological linkages and management. It was the world's first designated National Park. Brock (1967) is a short readable review of hot spring ecology.

# Chapter 4

# MORE WATER CHEMISTRY: THE KEY NUTRIENTS, TRACE ELEMENTS AND ORGANIC MATTER

## 4.1 INTRODUCTION

The major ions of Chapter 3 are called major because they are the most abundant. They influence the nature of the plant and animal communities in freshwaters. The amounts of free carbon dioxide and bicarbonate (Fig. 3.3), for example, determine which groups of algae and aquatic plants will grow, because some species are unable to use bicarbonate for photosynthesis and others can. The aquatic mosses and the higher plant genera *Isoetes*, *Littorella* and *Lobelia* and many of the green algae of the group called desmids, can only use molecular carbon dioxide. At high pH most of the carbon is bicarbonate (Fig. 3.3) and free carbon dioxide is scarce. Such plants and algae are thus confined to waters of low pH where carbon dioxide is abundant and bicarbonate is scarce and bicarbonate-users, which can also use molecular carbon dioxide, do not have a competitive advantage.

Among animals, major ion contents determine the richness of the snail and large crustacean fauna because much calcium is needed for shells and carapaces (Fig. 4.1). Some molluscs are confined to very calcareous waters; others are found in less calcium rich waters, but in general more species and greater biomass

are found in the richer waters. Calcium may thus be acting, for this particular group, as a growth-limiting factor. In practice, many substances help determine the occurrence of a particular group or species, and a wide range may also help determine growth or production. But some are more widely implicated than others in determining production. Phosphorus and nitrogen appear to be particularly important and these are the focus of this chapter.

## 4.2 CONCEPTS OF LIMITING SUBSTANCES

Why these two particular elements should be relatively scarce and so important can be looked at in two ways: the geological accidents of the initial composition of the Earth on the one hand; and a bias in our understanding dependent on the extent that human activities have altered the relative availabilities of nitrogen and phosphorus on the other. The compositions of planets must certainly be accidents of what was the composition of the dust and gas cloud that formed the solar system. Beyond that the compositions are products of the size of the gas clouds that condensed to molten masses to become each planet. The larger the cloud, the greater was the gravitational pull and the more of the lighter elements that could be held and prevented from dispersing to outer space. The availability of elements to surface waters on Earth is also a function of planetary

*Ecology of Freshwaters: A View for the Twenty-first Century*, 4th edition. By Brian Moss. Published 2010 by Blackwell Publishing Ltd.

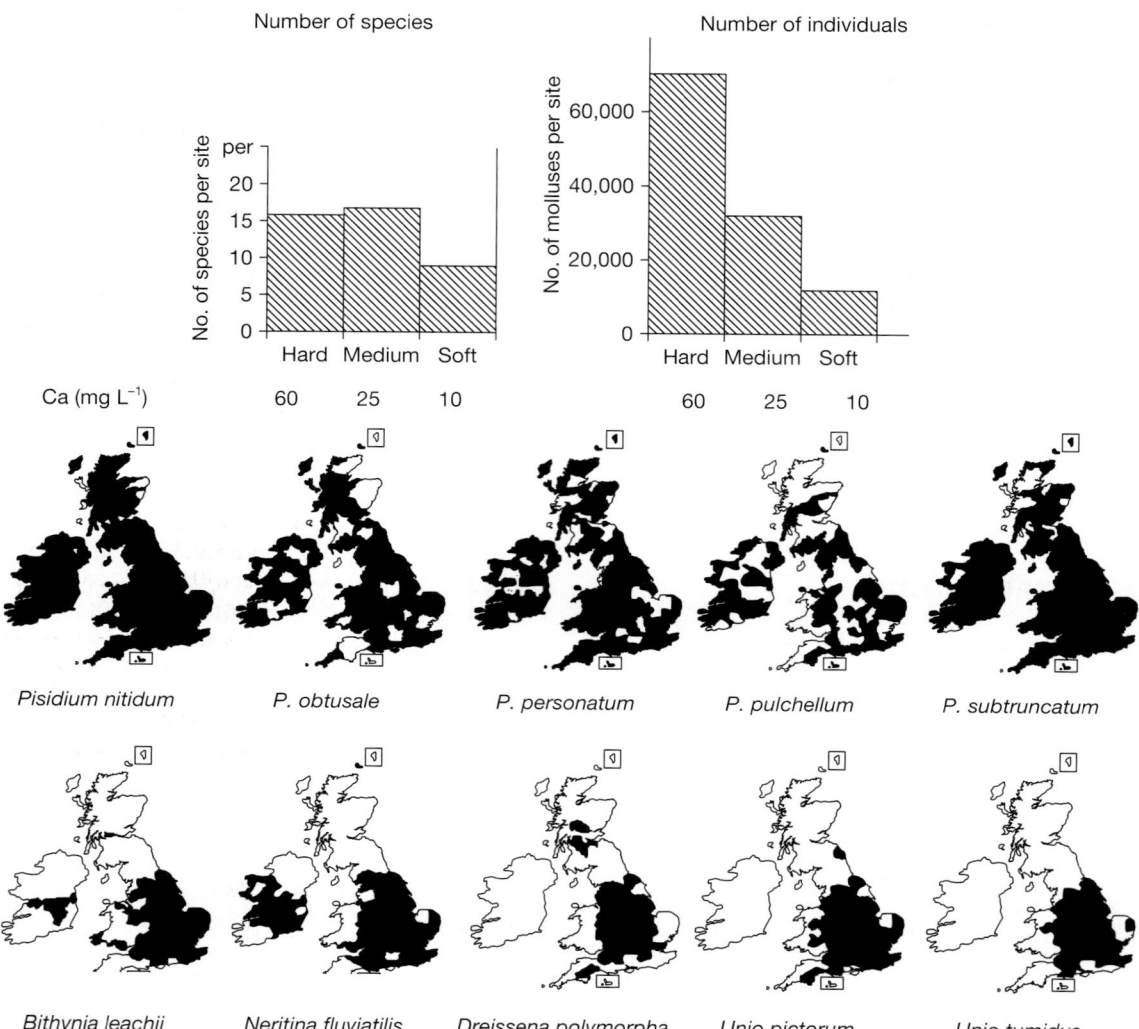

**Fig. 4.1** Molluscs require a lot of calcium for shell formation, and the number of species in the UK, as well as the total mollusc population increases with increasing calcium concentration in the water (upper panel from Dussart 1976). Some molluscs, as shown by the upper line of distribution maps do occur in calcium poor waters in the north and west of Britain but they tend to be small species and they grow better in higher calcium waters in the south and east, to which large species tend to be confined (lower panel of maps). (From Boycott 1936.)

size and cooling and the rate at which lighter elements could move upwards in the molten mass before five or more billion years ago, when a solid crust started to form. It is also a product of the rate at which new material from the underlying mantle is ejected as volcanic ash and lava through cracks in the crust along the lines of plate separation And beyond that, and of greatest importance for living organisms, it is a function of how living organisms themselves, in the course of four billion years or so of evolution have redistributed the elements in the surface crust among the atmosphere, ocean and continental blocks.

There is increasing evidence that the composition of the atmosphere and oceans is not random, but maintained within a fairly narrow range, equable to our particular biochemistry, by the activities of living organisms. James Lovelock pointed out that the composition of the atmosphere and oceans, and presumably also soils and freshwaters, departs greatly from the strictly chemical equilibrium that would be reached in the absence of life. There would, for example be little free oxygen and a great deal of carbon dioxide in the air and a much higher salt and nitrate content in the oceans. Through the balance of photosynthesis and respiration, the storage of carbon in soils and sediments, and the production of gases such as methane and dimethyl sulphide, all by living organisms, the oxygen concentration is kept up and the carbon dioxide content down towards their current values. Likewise, in the ocean, chemical precipitation and bacterial denitrification (see below) reduce both salt and the otherwise toxic nitrate concentrations to within tolerable ranges. Cells must have membranes that are necessarily thin to absorb substances, and thus unable indefinitely to resist the powerful osmotic forces of an external very concentrated brine.

Living systems appear thus to have mutually evolved with the chemical state of the planet in ways that manipulate their environment and optimise their use of it. Natural selection is a very powerful testing system and we might expect that situations where one or other element needed for life becomes seriously deficient would have been avoided. However, in experiments, this can apparently be clearly demonstrated. Figure 4.2 shows the results of one in which an hour-glass shaped lake in Canada was divided into two by a plastic curtain sealed into the bottom and edges and a variety of substances added to one side with the other left as a control. Addition of phosphate (Fig. 4.3) consistently gave much greater growth of planktonic algae in the water. It appears to have been limiting growth before it was artificially increased, and the term nutrient limitation has become common currency in freshwater ecology for substances that appear to restrict potential growth.

**Fig. 4.2** David Schindler fitted a plastic curtain across the narrow isthmus that divides this lake (Canadian Experimental Lakes Area, Lake 304) into two basins and used one basin as a control with which to compare experimental treatments in the other, distal one.

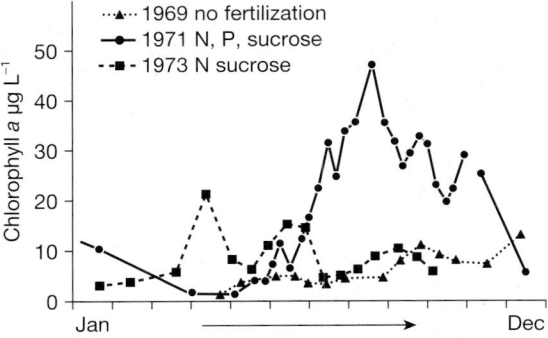

**Fig. 4.3** Effects on biomass of phytoplankton (measured as its chlorophyll $a$ content) of fertilizing Lake 304. In 1969 there was no fertilization; in 1971, totals of 0.4 g $PO_4$–P, 5.2 g $NH_4$–N and 5.5 g sucrose were added per $m^2$ in 20 weekly increments. In 1973, ammonia and sucrose were added in similar amounts but no phosphorus. Stimulation of growth was obtained only when phosphorus supplies were boosted. (From Schindler 1974.)

Such experiments in whole lakes are rare. The experiments are usually carried out on a smaller scale, in large containers suspended in a lake, or laboratory flasks, or with diffusion pots filled with agar containing the substance under study submerged in streams. Many experiments have shown a stimulation by phosphorus, with the conclusion that phosphorus was limiting. With graphic and convincing experiments like that shown in Fig. 4.3, the convention has grown that phosphorus supply limits growth in most freshwaters. Some experiments, however, show nitrogen to have the effect, and some a co-limitation by both phosphorus and nitrogen. Nitrogen has been believed to be more likely to be limiting in warm temperate and tropical lakes (Fig. 4.4), where phosphorus can

be regenerated from sediments when they are exposed to air at the edges in the dry season and where high temperatures promote bacterial conversions of nitrate to nitrogen gas, which is not available to many organisms. Nitrogen has also been believed to be the main limiting nutrient in the ocean and coastal seas.

When a survey was made, however, by James Elser and his colleagues, of thousands of such experiments now published, in freshwater and marine habitats, and, using fertilized plots of land or experiments in soil-filled pots, in terrestrial vegetation, the results did not support these widely held conventions. Rather they showed (Fig. 4.5), in all three habitat types, that the most common result was a co-stimulation by both nitrogen and phosphorus compounds and that single

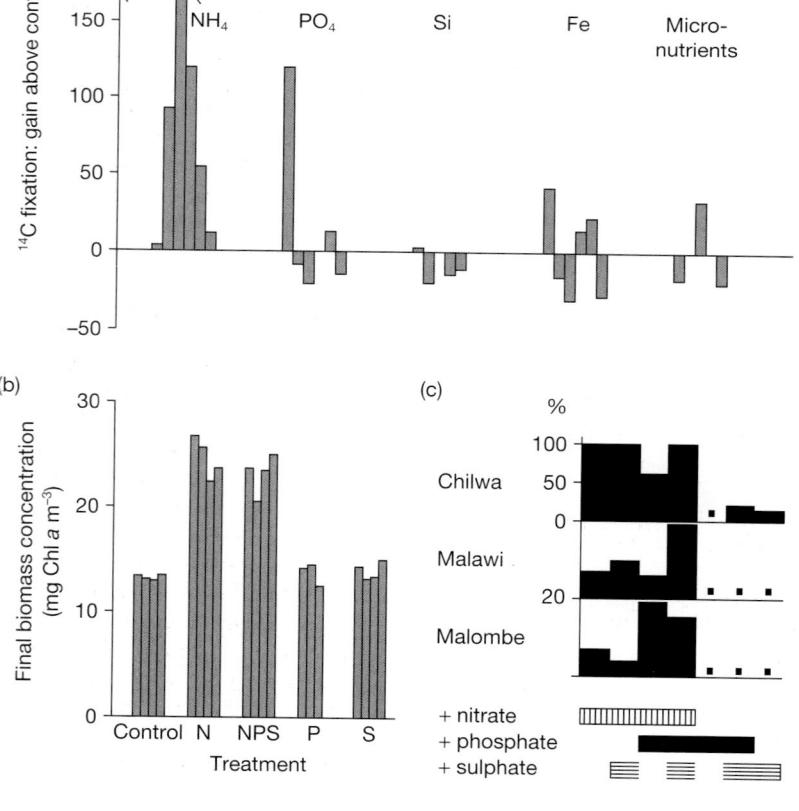

**Fig. 4.4** Tropical lakes often show apparent limitation by nitrogen, or nitrogen and phosphorus together. Examples here (Talling & Lemoalle 1999) are from: (a) Lake Titicaca, in which the response to the nutrient addition was measured by photosynthetic uptake of $^{14}$C after 5–6 days; (b) Lake Victoria, with the response as production of chlorophyll $a$ after two days; and (c) three lakes in Malawi, with responses measured as percentage of the maximum level of chlorophyll compared with controls.

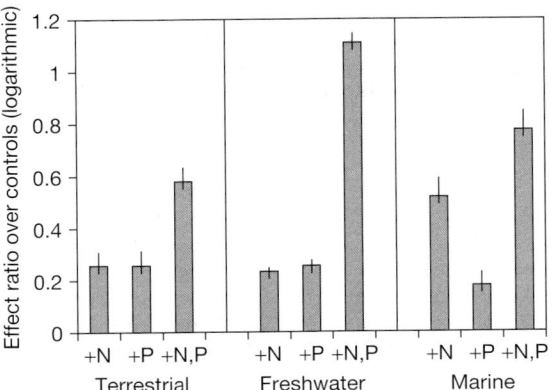

**Fig. 4.5** Summaries of 425 terrestrial, 1633 freshwater and 487 marine bioassay experiments in which the growth or biomass responses of plants or algae were measured when nitrogen or phosphorus or both were added. Results are shown as the logarithm of the response in the treatment to that in the control. N and P together gave the greatest response in all habitats. (From Elser et al. 2007.)

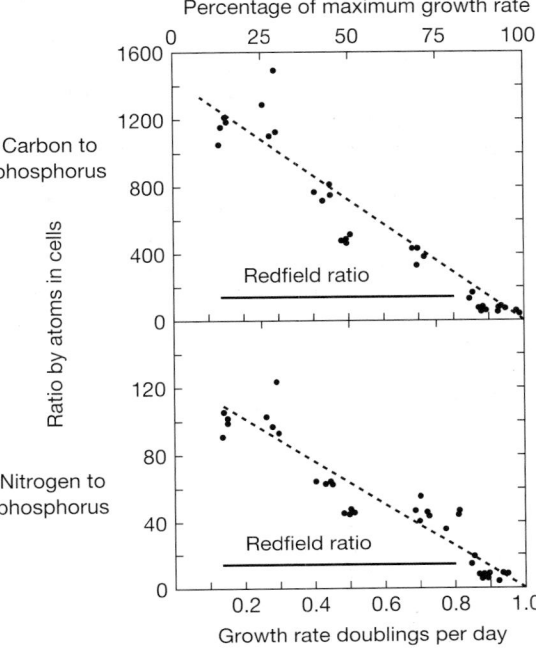

**Fig. 4.6** Goldman et al. (1979) showed that altering the ratios of carbon to phosphorus, and nitrogen to phosphorus, affected the growth rate of a marine alga, *Monochrysis lutheri*. Maximum rates were achieved when the ratios in the cells conformed to the Redfield ratios, which are frequently found in open ocean habitats, which are least affected by human activities.

stimulation by either nitrogen or phosphorus was generally about equally as common, with perhaps a greater bias towards nitrogen in marine systems.

These results are very significant, but they need further interpretation. The experiments are carried out in closed systems in which a dose of substance is given at the start rather than the continuous supply usually provided in natural systems by inflow from the catchment and natural regeneration through grazing on the plants or algae and excretion by the grazers. The system is usually simplified to just the plants or algae. Sometimes the experiments are carried out in only lightly modified habitats, in other cases in places where human influences have already been severe. There is thus the possibility that the results may sometimes be artefacts of the experimental arrangements, though this objection cannot be made to experiments on whole lakes, or large enclosures within them that achieve the same results. So it is likely that the experiments do mean something.

In 1979, a paper appeared (Goldman et al. 1979) in which open ocean phytoplankton algae were studied. It was shown that the composition of the algae for carbon, nitrogen and phosphorus was in a ratio around 106:16:1 (by atoms). In the laboratory, algae with this ratio, or close to it, grow maximally fast, because the elements are being supplied at optimal and

non-limiting rates (Fig. 4.6). The implication was that the oceanic algae were not nutrient limited. Biomass was not high because they were being grazed as they grew, but the growth rate was not impeded by a particular shortage of one element or another. This optimal ratio had been noted many years earlier by Alfred Redfield and is known as the Redfield ratio. The significance is that the open oceans are the habitats least affected by human activities that alter the rates of supply of nitrogen and phosphorus. On land, and in fresh and coastal waters, relative availabilities of nitrogen and phosphorus have been greatly altered by the use of mined phosphate deposits for fertilizers and food production, and the artificial production of ammonia by the industrial Haber process. There is now about as much combined nitrogen in circulation from the latter as from natural processes. The conclusion that we might thus draw is that in a world not affected by these recent alterations in the availability of nitrogen and phosphorus, living organisms would have experienced conditions that, through evolutionary processes, adjusted their systems to natural ratios that led to optimal growth. If there was limitation, it was co-limitation by all the necessary elements. The systems were so finely tuned that nutrient limitation by one element or another was unknown and that our perception of this phenomenon has been determined by the artificial ratios now created.

Elser et al. (2007) found a predominance of co-limitation of nitrogen and phosphorus, consistent with this view. Nitrogen and phosphorus are absolutely scarce in available form on the Earth's surface for reasons given below, so the idea of them restricting the biomass that can be supported is valid, but the concept of there being just one limiting nutrient, nitrogen or phosphorus in undisturbed situations, perhaps is not. But ours is a greatly altered world and such individual limitations are now common. Phosphorus becomes limiting where nitrogen supplies are artificially boosted and vice versa. Indeed they are part of the serious problem of eutrophication or nutrient pollution, which greatly exercises freshwater ecologists (Chapters 8 and 14). In a parallel way, our interference with the carbon budget of the Earth through our burning of fossil carbon deposits as fuels, is creating the problem of a rapidly changing climate (Chapter 16).

## 4.3 NUTRIENTS

Living organisms require about 20 elements: H, O, C, N, P, Na, K, Ca, Mg, S, Cl, Fe, Mn, Cu, Zn, B, Mb, Co, V, and Si for some. Because of the accidents of ancient cosmology and geology, few of these elements are absolutely or relatively scarce in relation to the biochemical needs of living organisms. The important ratio is that of supply to need. An element may be quite scarce but rather little of it may be needed so scarcity is not a problem. Many heavy metals required for living organisms as enzyme co-factors, such as cobalt, zinc and molybdenum, are in this category. Other elements are relatively more abundant on Earth but are required to greater extents, so are relatively scarcer from the organism's perspective. Phosphorus is like this. Yet others are absolutely abundant but very insoluble, such as iron under oxidizing conditions, and silica, needed for the cell walls of a few groups of organisms such as the diatoms. Table 4.1 illustrates these points. It sets the values of phosphorus to unity then shows the relative abundance of other elements in the Earth's crust. Then it shows the relative amounts needed by living organisms, again relative to phosphorus as unity. Finally it shows the ratio of supply to need. All the elements shown, which are those derived from the crust (the lithosphere) rather than the atmosphere, are relatively less scarce than phosphorus.

**Table 4.1** The relative supply to and relative needs of living organisms for elements derived from the lithosphere. The ratio of supply to need is shown in the final column. This ratio is greater for all elements than that for phosphorus, which is therefore the relatively scarcest of the elements needed by living organisms. (From Hutchinson 1973.)

| Element | Available in lithosphere relative to P | Needed by organisms relative to P | Ratio of supply to need |
|---------|----------------------------------------|-----------------------------------|-------------------------|
| Na | 32.5 | 0.52 | 63 |
| Mg | 22.2 | 1.39 | 16 |
| Si | 268 | 0.65 | 413 |
| P | 1 | 1 | 1 |
| K | 20 | 6.1 | 3.3 |
| Ca | 40 | 7.8 | 5.1 |
| Fe | 54 | 0.06 | 893 |
| Zn | 0.07 | 0.04 | 1.8 |
| Mo | 0.0014 | 0.0004 | 3.5 |

## 4.4 PHOSPHORUS

Supplies of phosphorus in pristine freshwaters are comparatively low because phosphorus is derived largely from rock weathering, which is slow and the element is relatively scarce. Clay particles in soils also tend to bind phosphorus quite tightly and although the enzymes associated with plant roots can loosen it easily enough, phosphorus is resistant to simple leaching by water. Its ionic charge to radius ratio also tends to reduce its solubility (Fig. 3.4).

Land vegetation has evolved mechanisms to scavenge available phosphate using fine roots, efficient enzymes and mycorrhizae store phosphorus in its own biomass, because it is scarce, and thus relatively little available phosphorus is allowed to exist in the soil water before it is rapidly reabsorbed. Some does escape, however, and phosphorus might be leached into freshwaters as a variety of different compounds. There are several phosphate ions ($PO_4^{3-}$, $HPO_4^{2-}$, $H_2PO_4^-$), phosphates attached to organic compounds and phosphate held in insoluble form in eroded soil particles, including colloids and in organic debris eroded from soil by moving water. When water is analysed it is difficult to separate all of these and they are usually determined in operational categories as: soluble inorganic phosphorus (which reacts cold to give a blue dye with ammonium molybdate, so is also called soluble reactive phosphorus or SRP); soluble organic phosphorus (which does not react until it is hydrolysed with hot acid); particulate phosphorus (PP) (held in suspension and again unreactive until hydrolysed); and the sum of all of these, total phosphorus (TP). Soluble inorganic phosphorus is an approximate measure of availability to living organisms (approximate because some organic phosphates are easily taken up). Because it is generally thought that bacterial activity can ultimately convert all forms to soluble reactive phosphates, total phosphorus is usually taken as a measure of the total amount potentially available in the water.

## 4.5 NITROGEN

A last group of elements needed by living organisms is abundant but easily converted, through biological activity, to relatively unavailable forms. It seems odd that one of these, nitrogen, should be a key element likely to limit production, because there are huge amounts of it in the atmosphere, indeed it is the most abundant gas in the air. The problem is, however, that it is present in a form that only a few organisms, the nitrogen fixers, can readily use and that the process of nitrogen fixation requires anaerobic or microaerophilic conditions that are comparatively uncommon in a world that has been well oxygenated for at least 500 million years. Nitrogen fixers are all prokaryotes, though some may occur in symbioses with some ferns or vascular plants, pre-eminently the legumes (Fabaceae) and alder (*Alnus*). Free-living nitrogen fixers also occur in soils and in water and have the common property of being able to create microaerophilic conditions close to the enzymes that convert nitrogen gas to amino groups within their cells.

They may do this by modifications to their own internal metabolism or by associating with other organisms that reduce oxygen levels. Some cyanobacteria (blue-green algae) fix nitrogen in special cells, called heterocysts (Fig. 4.7), where the part of the photosynthetic mechanism that emits oxygen is lacking. Others may fix in microaerophilic environments such as sediments without need of such special metabolic arrangements. Soil nitrogen-fixing bacteria associate in clumps in soil crumbs with oxygen-consuming aerobic bacteria to the outside of the clump and those associated with fixation in the middle. Bacterial nitrogen fixers in plants occur in special root nodules where the host cells consume oxygen or even produce small amounts of haemoglobin to mop up surplus oxygen.

Nitrogen fixed in these organisms becomes available to others when they are eaten or die. The amino groups in proteins are converted to ammonium ions by bacteria. Other species of bacteria convert ammonium to nitrite, using oxygen to oxidize the ammonium and release energy. Another group converts the nitrite to nitrate for similar reasons. Nitrate and ammonium (though not generally nitrite) are available for uptake by algae and plants and are converted back to amino groups in amino acids and proteins and ultimately recycled through the steps already described. Unlike phosphate, both are very soluble and readily transferred in water from catchment to river and lake.

Nitrate is, however, vulnerable to further bacterial activity. It is a powerful oxidizing agent and if free oxygen is scarce, denitrifying bacteria can use nitrate to oxidize organic matter, converting the nitrate to nitrogen gas and sometimes oxides of nitrogen, such as $N_2O$ in the process. This activity is inevitably greatest in low-oxygen habitats and particularly so in wetlands with organic soils, but it occurs even in open waters

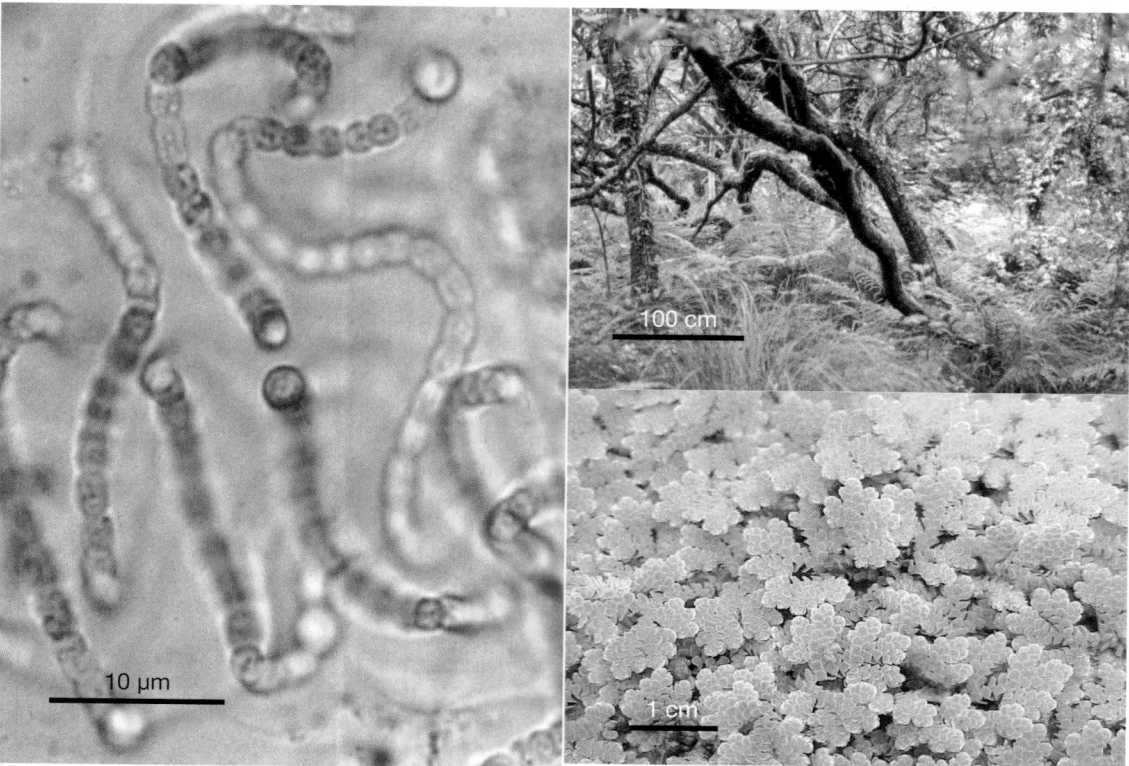

**Fig. 4.7** Nitrogen fixation, the conversion of dinitrogen ($N_2$) to amino groups ($-NH_2$) can be carried out only under microaerophilic (low oxygen) conditions by prokaryotes, sometimes free-living, sometimes associated with higher plants. Among the former, filamentous cyanobacteria can fix nitrogen in aerobic habitats if they have specialist cells called heterocysts in which low oxygen tensions can be maintained (left). The respiration of surrounding plant tissue creates similar conditions in the roots of legumes, alders (*Alnus* spp) (upper right) and the floating fern, *Azolla* (lower right).

because of the low ability of water to dissolve oxygen and the frequency therefore in which it may become deoxygenated. It is this process that balances the global nitrogen cycle, with levels of nitrogen fixation being ultimately balanced by those of denitrification.

## 4.6 PRISTINE CONCENTRATIONS

Table 3.1 showed concentrations of major ions in a variety of world freshwaters and the point was made that these are generally very dilute solutions except where evaporative concentration has made them much more salty. The same principle of very low concentrations applies to nitrogen and phosphorus compounds, but to an even greater degree. Figure 4.8 shows the concentrations of total phosphorus and total nitrogen in streams draining catchments in the USA where the terrestrial ecosystem remains intact and no farming or forestry has taken place.

There are two sets of data for total nitrogen (which, in analogy with total phosphorus, includes the nitrogen not only in available forms but in organic compounds and fine particles in the water, but not dissolved nitrogen gas). One includes the actual measurements; the other set is corrected for nitrogen that is attributable (through rainfall) to atmospheric pollution largely from nitrogen oxides produced in motor vehicle engines, but also from volatilization of ammonia from the dung and urine produced on intensive farms. The concentrations of TP and TN even before this correction are very low. They average about $15 \mu g L^{-1}$ of TP

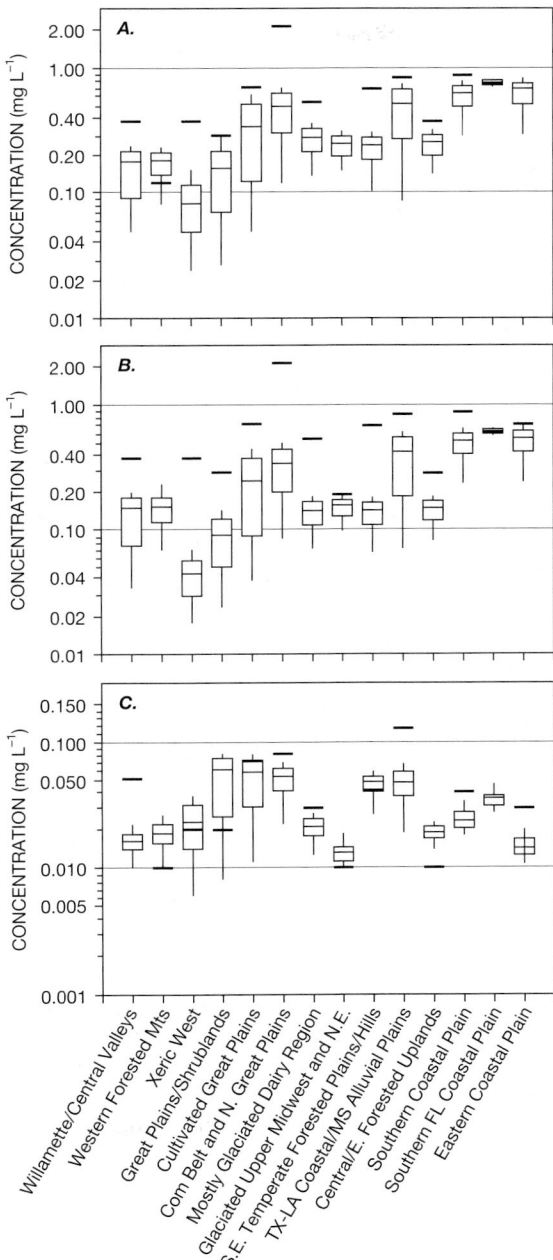

and $150\ \mu g\ L^{-1}$ of TN. The ratios of TN to TP in these near pristine catchments are also close to the Redfield ratio (16 to 1 by atoms, 7 to 1 by weight), as in little disturbed open ocean water. This contrasts greatly with values found in rivers in farmed and developed areas. There it is not uncommon to find ten to one hundred times such values (Fig. 4.9), reflecting human activities.

Human activities, except where they are devoted to reducing the problem created by farming and waste disposal in the first place, always increase the amounts of N and P reaching freshwaters. The classic experiment demonstrating this for nitrogen was carried out in the Hubbard Brook Experimental Forest in New Hampshire, USA. The valley of a side tributary of the main stream in this naturally forested catchment was clear felled, with the tree debris left in place, and the effects on water quality of the tributaries draining the catchment were followed for several years (Fig. 4.10). There was a substantial increase in concentrations of major ions and nitrate from the felled valley. Mechanisms that retained nutrients within the intact, forested system had been destroyed. The same thing happens wherever natural vegetation is cleared for any sort of development. Nutrients are lost and maintenance of production for agriculture or plantation forestry therefore will always need replacement of these nutrients by fertilizer. Since monocultures of crops and trees do not have the intricate conservation mechanisms of natural systems, the fertilization has to be continued year by year, some of the nutrients being taken away with the crop and the rest running off into the freshwater habitats and eventually to the ocean, causing many problems on the way.

## 4.7  TRACE ELEMENTS AND SILICON

Of the 20 or so elements required for life, including all the major ions and key nutrients, 11 in all including the C, H and O required for organic compounds, have been so far discussed in this chapter and Chapter 3. All but one (Si) of the remainder (Fe, Mn, Co, Cu, Zn, Mo, V,

**Fig. 4.8** Concentrations of total nitrogen (upper) and total phosphorus (lower) in streams draining undisturbed catchments in various geographical regions of the USA. Even undisturbed catchments receive quantities of nitrogen through air pollution so the middle panel shows values corrected for this contribution. Bars show the median values and the 10, 25, 75 and 90 percentile values. This means that 10% of all values lie below the 10-percentile line, 25% below the 25-percentile line, etc. Also shown as detached lines are the 25 percentile values of all catchments in the regions, i.e. including those disturbed to varying degrees by urbanization, forest plantation and agriculture. (From Smith et al. 2003.)

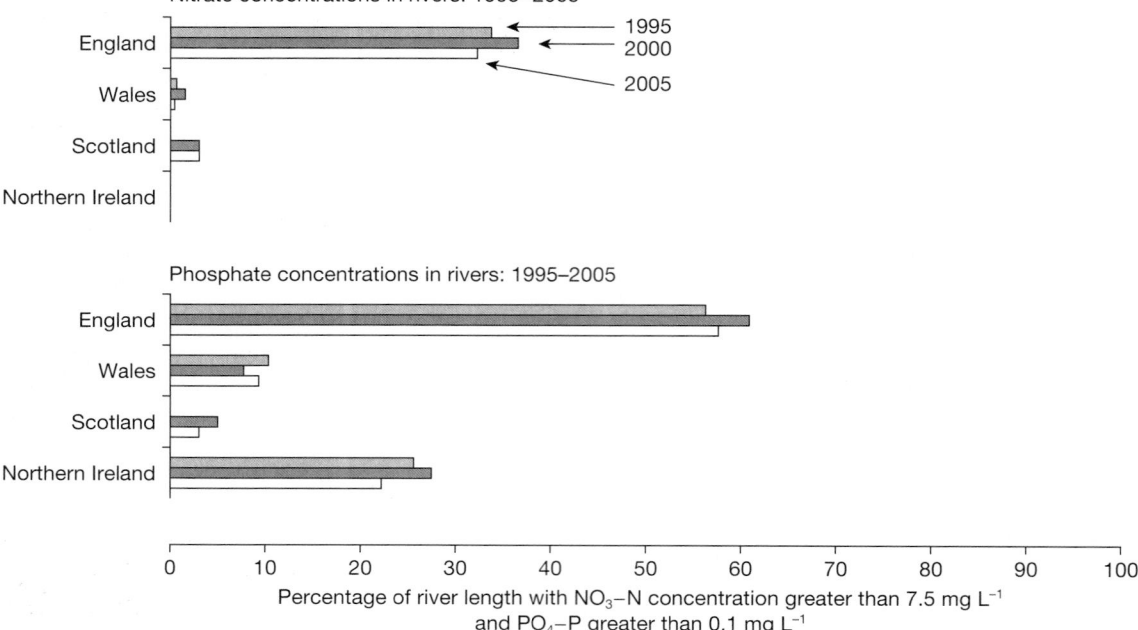

**Fig. 4.9** The nutrient concentrations in British rivers are particularly high though published government statistics are often expressed in ways that aim to minimize the severity of the situation. Here values are given first in terms of nitrate and phosphate, which underestimate the total values (TN, TP) conventionally used, and the data are expressed in terms of the percentage river length with concentrations exceeding a chosen arbitrary value. The values chosen here for nitrate are about 50–100 times the TN values and about ten times the TP values of pristine streams in the equivalent climatic areas shown in Fig. 4.8. There are huge nutrient concentrations in many English rivers from agriculture and waste water treatment works. The situation in Scottish and Welsh rivers appears better but the way that the statistics are expressed conceals the fact that concentrations are almost everywhere well above the pristine standards. The source of these data is the Deparment of Environment, Food and Rural Affairs, UK.

B, I, Si) are usually referred to as trace elements because most occur in very small concentrations, both in living organisms and usually in the environment. Iron is the exception; it is very abundant in rocks and soils. Silicon, the last element, is a special case. It is very abundant in rocks and soils but required by only a few groups of organisms: the diatoms and related algal and protozoon groups. However, it is relatively insoluble and its availability may determine the distribution and productivity of these groups.

The trace elements, despite their low external availability, appear for the most part to be available in excess of the needs of organisms and rarely limit growth. There are some exceptions. In the remoter parts of the ocean, iron appears to be limiting, partly because of the distance from its main source, the soils of the land, and there have been some reports of soil deficiencies,

and thence of deficiencies in water, in some areas of ancient rocks, for example Australia, where the soils have been subject to millions of years of leaching. In the recently glaciated regions, where fresh rock has been exposed to weathering, there are very few such reports. There are considerable problems in investigating the behaviour of trace elements, however, and thus there is not yet enough information to describe general patterns of their availability and behaviour.

The difficulties lie in their low concentrations in water and in the likelihood that the water will be contaminated, during sampling by the equipment used, which usually has been fashioned to some extent from metal, though the former age of brass and steel samplers, skilfully made in laboratory workshops and very heavy, has passed. Even laboratory dust can contaminate the samples so ultraclean conditions must

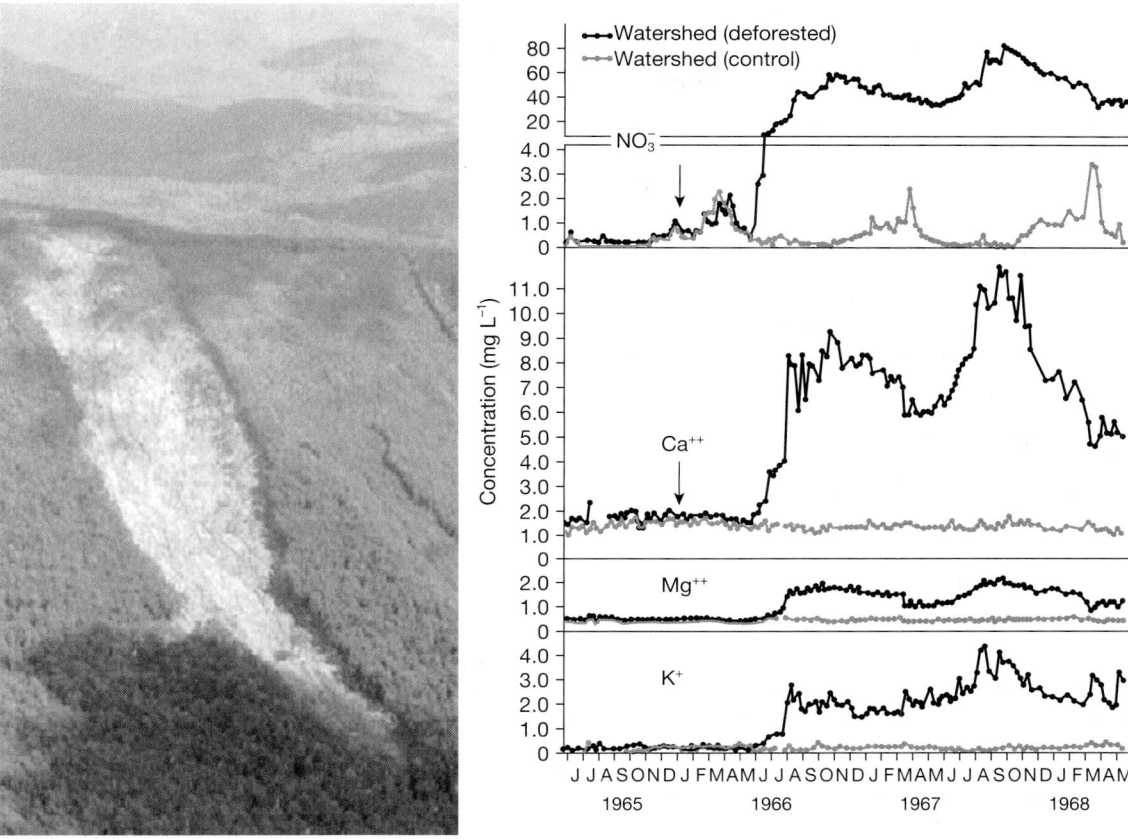

**Fig. 4.10** In the Hubbard Brook Experimental Forest, tributary catchments (watersheds) were clear-felled of their native forest, whilst others were left intact as controls. Deforested watersheds showed a major loss of major ions and nitrate that was measured for several years and would continue until the soils were completely leached out. Based on the work of G.E. Likens and H. Boorman.

be used. Mining operations, especially those producing lots of dust, also compromise understanding of natural patterns and the widespread use of minerals leads to much contamination. Vehicle tyres, for example, are rich in heavy metals and tyre wear on roads is reflected in metal concentrations draining from roads to nearby ditches and the freshwater system.

Silicon becomes available to organisms as silicate ions. It is present in many minerals in complex forms because silicon, like carbon, has four valencies, which give it the possibilities of forming a myriad of compounds. It is released from rocks by weathering processes, when silicate minerals are hydrolysed. Such weathering also releases major ions such as potassium and produces clay minerals, which have particles small enough to be easily moved by water. Silicate

availability thus follows two main patterns. First it is most available where weathering is greatest, in warm moist conditions. Secondly, as the rocks become weathered over very long periods and the original minerals become scarce, silicate becomes scarcer. In the ancient soils of the tropics, for example, most of the material is of insoluble iron oxides and quartz. These are highly resistant to further weathering. The weatherable minerals were decomposed long ago and the supply of silicate, like that of the major cations, becomes very small.

We might thus expect silicate supplies to be low in the polar regions, because of slow weathering, greater in the temperate zone, where fresh minerals have been exposed by glaciation, and greatest in the warm temperate zone and tropics where there has been some geological disturbance, for example from vulcanism in the recent past. Supplies should be lowest in the most ancient landscapes of the tropics. The same generalization might be made also for the trace elements.

## 4.8 ORGANIC SUBSTANCES

Most of the chemical substances present in natural waters are organic carbon compounds. They are derivative substances from living activity, rather than primary substances, like the inorganic ions that promote such activity, but are nonetheless very important in supporting further activity. There may be many thousands of them in any natural water sample and in terms of absolute amounts there may be vastly more 'dead' organic matter than there is living. Although very sophisticated techniques of mass spectrometry and gas chromatography exist to measure the amounts of these compounds, they depend on reference standards and thus on initial identification of the substances. Most of them have not been identified, however, and the organic content of waters is still usually described in general terms. The origin of many of these substances is probably in the catchment soils where terrestrially produced organic matter decomposes to simpler organic substances, and in the wetland habitats that surround lakes and rivers. These sources produce a range of products, some of which (amino acids, small carboxylic acids, small carbohydrates, alcohols) are readily metabolized by bacteria, others of which are more refractory and sometimes washed into the streams as colloids.

These refractory substances are often long-chain carboxylic acids and phenolic compounds, yellow or brown in colour, and acid in nature. They were first called *gelbstoff* (yellow matter) by German limnologists. A first separation of them can be achieved by treatment with alkali, then acid, which precipitates one group, the fulvic acids, but not a second group, the humic acids. A third group, the humins, is not soluble in alkali. The fulvic acids are smaller, relatively more oxygenated molecules, possibly oxides of the humic acids. Both may be derivatives of the humins, which originate from wood and leaf decomposition. Collectively they can be estimated by the absorption of light of wavelength about 440 nm (blue light which is strongly absorbed by yellow material) in the water sample.

The abbreviation DOM (dissolved organic matter), or if amounts are expressed as carbon, rather than mass, DOC, is usually used to describe the totality of dissolved

and colloidal organic compounds. Dissolved organic matter is that material which will pass through a 0.45 μm filter. About 80% of DOM is accounted for by humic compounds, of which perhaps 30–40% are aromatic (benzene ring) compounds. Some of these are so refractory that they may be hundreds to thousands of years old. Others of them, the smaller molecules, are more reactive and may combine, as chelators, with trace metals, which indeed may be a mechanism for keeping these relatively insoluble elements in solution. We might expect up to 8 or 10 mg $L^{-1}$ of DOM in most waters, much more in those derived from peaty landscapes (Fig. 4.11). The waters of many streams of Finland and Russia and northern Canada, draining a soggy landscape of conifer forest, muskeg and bog are as brown as brewed coffee or tea and may have of the order of hundreds of milligrams per litre of brown substances.

### 4.8.1 Patterns in DOM availability

There are likely to be patterns in DOM availability dependent on latitude and geology. Extremely cold climates, such as those of the Polar circles tend to be rocky and barren of vegetation or covered by tundra. There is low terrestrial production, so little source of catchment DOM. Cold, but wet climates further from the poles tend to accumulate peat at the surfaces of their soils. Peat is partly decomposed plant material, deoxygenated and waterlogged. Bacterial activity will be able only partly to decompose the dead plants so the DOM that runs off may be copious and also potentially less refractory. It might thus be expected to be more reactive and take a greater part in the metabolism of organisms in the receiving freshwaters. The tundra and boreal forest landscapes will thus tend to have browner waters and DOM may be a very important component in their ecology.

In warmer, temperate regions, covered by deciduous forest, there will also be substantial amounts of DOM. Bacterial decomposition will have been greater in the forest soils so the DOM may be less reactive when it reaches the waters. Where the climate is warm but plant growth seasonal, we might expect less DOM because of greater decomposition in the terrestrial soils. There will be many nuances to these broad patterns, however. Very acid soils in the warm temperate zone, for example the sandy soils of Cape Province in South Africa, where heathy vegetation, called *fynbos*, is characteristic, tend to release very brown

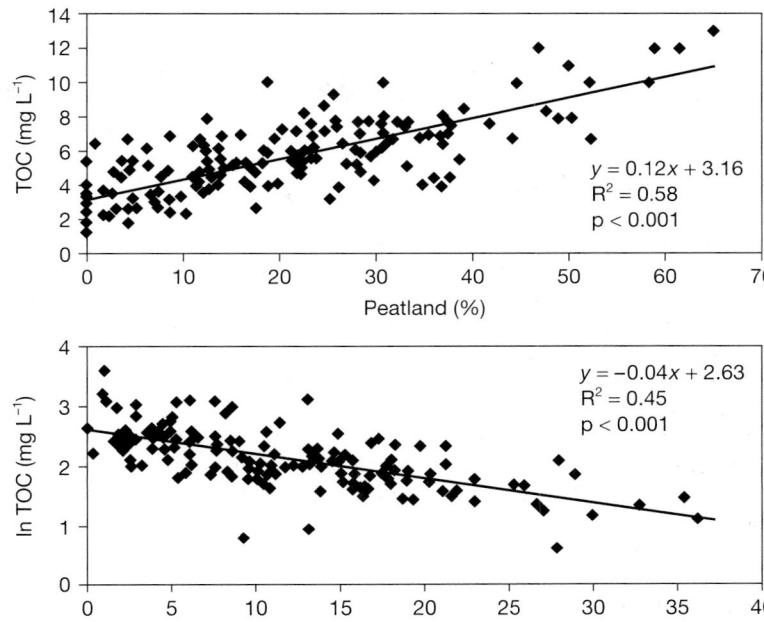

**Fig. 4.11** The amounts of total dissolved organic matter (TOC), measured as carbon, increase steadily as more and more of the catchment is covered in peatlands (upper panel). To convert concentrations approximately to organic matter, multiply by 2.5. Conversely, the greater the percentage of open water lakes in the catchment, i.e. the less land vegetation, the lower are the values. The data are from northern (upper) and southern (lower) Finland (Kortelainen et al. 2004).

waters. The acidity inhibits bacterial decomposition in the soil.

The tropics present a greater complication. Arid areas will have rather little DOM derived from the catchment. Most organic matter will oxidize in the hot season before it can reach the waters. But wet tropical areas, with year around forest growth and decomposition and abundant rainfall will tend to release large quantities from their catchments. Although decomposition on the forest floor is rapid, the turnover of organic matter is high and intermediate products of decomposition will be vulnerable to leaching. Indeed the Rio Negro, draining part of the Amazon rain forest basin is so called (Black River) because of its abundance of DOM. In general we expect more DOM in warmer, wetter regions with abundant terrestrial vegetation, less in colder, dryer areas, barren of vegetation.

The nature of the water body will also affect the DOM concentration. Although even the remoter regions of a catchment will contribute some, rather refractory, DOM (it has had far to travel with many opportunities for breakdown on the way), much of the DOM may come from within the immediate riparian zone or flood-plain of a river or lake basin and be derived from the emergent wetland plants. This material, being more immediate, is more likely to be reactive and to contain a larger proportion of small organic molecules that might easily be used by microorganisms in the water. There are two pathways for production in the open waters of lakes and rivers. The first is dependent on *in situ*, autochthonous, production by algae and plants and direct consumption by herbivores (the grazing pathway). The other is dependent on the DOM derived from the catchment and the plants of the surrounding wetlands and riparian zones, which is first metabolized into bacteria before being consumed by Protozoa and small metazoans (the 'microbial loop' or detritus pathway). The higher levels in this pathway might also be the same herbivores that directly consume the autochthonous production, giving a linkage between the pathways. There is some controversy about the relative importance of these pathways and between the relative importance of DOM derived from the littoral (thus within the lake) and that derived from the terrestrial catchment (genuinely allochthonous) (see Chapter 11) but it is clear that freshwater systems receive a great deal of fixed energy from their catchments as well as most of their nutrients.

## 4.9 SUBSTANCE BUDGETS

Later chapters will go into detail about how substances, required by living organisms, are transformed within the systems of rivers, wetlands and lakes, but there is some value in taking an overall distant view, ignoring the details in favour of the larger trends. There are great cycles of every element when geological time and rock formation are considered. The Earth is finite and much of the material in it is locked away so deeply that it has no role in the biosphere. Small amounts emerge in volcanic eruptions and lesser activity and equally small amounts disappear back into the interior as plates meet and one or other is forced downwards. But the major cycles involve the atmosphere, the oceans and freshwaters (hydrosphere) and the rocks and soils (lithosphere).

Within this system, where the biosphere holds sway, there are cycles for elements such as the major cations

and phosphorus in which substances are weathered from rocks, pass down rivers to the ocean, are swallowed by the sea and eventually precipitated as sediments. The sediments become compressed by their own weight and eventually, during geological upheavals, may be raised up to become land, and the weathering processes begin again. For some elements, such as nitrogen, sulphur and carbon, the cycle also includes the atmosphere. Figures 4.12 and 4.13 show these global cycles for phosphorus and nitrogen, which are representative of the two types, with some indication of the quantities involved.

To understand the processes at an intermediate level, in a section of the freshwater system, a river or a whole lake, for example, simple general models can be drawn up to act as a basis for considering details at a later stage. The aim of the models is to explain the concentration measured in the water as a consequence of processes happening to the system. The simpler model

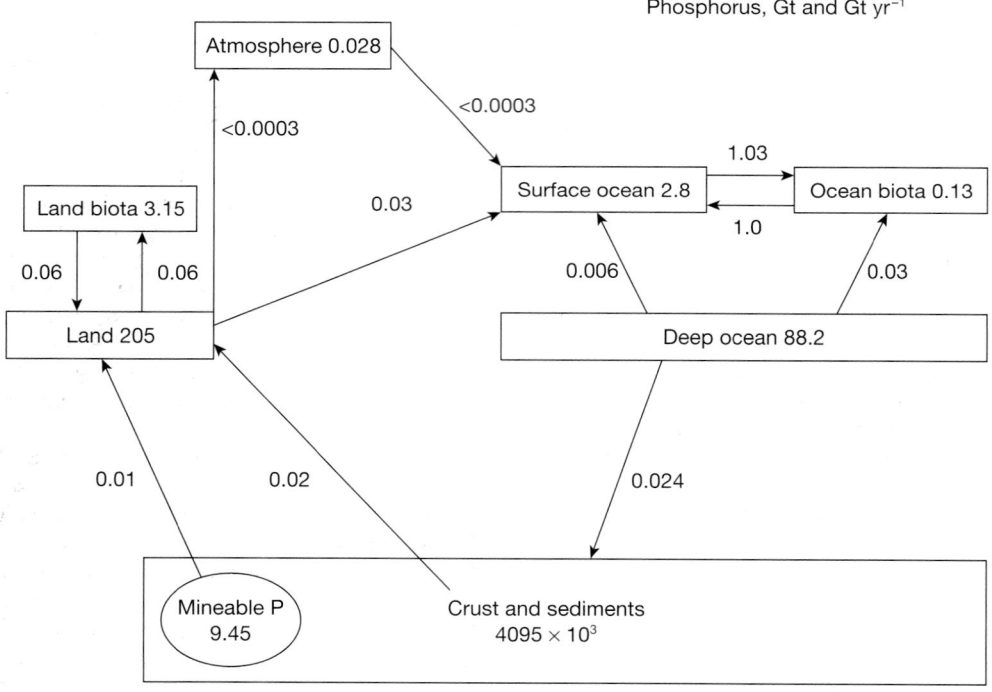

**Fig. 4.12** Major features of the Earth's phosphorus cycle. The bulk of the P is in the crust and sediments; the atmosphere has very little role to play. Amounts held in the reservoirs (boxes) are in gigatonnes (1 Gt = $10^{15}$ g) and the fluxes (arrows) in Gt yr$^{-1}$. Values are taken from various sources and are likely to be in error by up to 50%. This is simply because of the difficulties of estimating anything on the global scale, because of the enormous variation from place to place. Freshwater values are included with those of the land. Values will not exactly balance therefore, but are probably of the right order of magnitude.

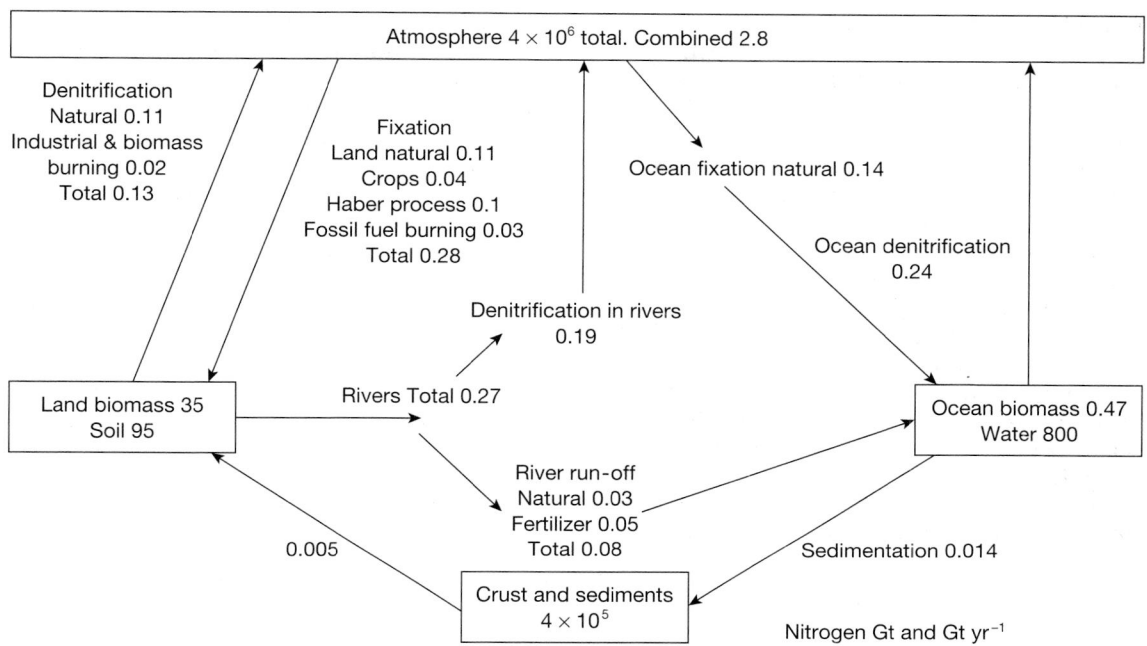

**Fig. 4.13** Major global transfers of nitrogen. Values are largely taken from Gruber & Galloway (2008) but as for Fig. 4.12 are approximations. The huge reservoir of the atmosphere is obvious as is the role of human-initiated sources.

is the lithospheric one. First there are inputs to the system, called loads. They will include rock weathering and delivery of the substance by percolation of water underground, material brought in by animals (birds or hippopotami feeding on land and excreting in the water, for example), and amounts derived from human activity, such as waste water or fertilizer run-off. These are collectively called $L_c$ (load from the catchment). We distinguish between point sources, such as a discrete pipe outfall from an industry or wastewater treatment works, or a stock unit, and diffuse sources, which are those that are not so closely locatable but come in from many small sources, such as individual fields or patches of vegetation. There is also a small load from rain falling directly on the water body, $L_r$. For different bodies of water, the relative amounts from different sources will vary. The forms in which the substance enters will vary also, both in terms of chemical species dissolved and whether they are in dissolved or particulate form. The concept of total amount of substance is thus a useful simplification.

Once delivered to the body of water, several things can happen: the amounts will be diluted, some will be

taken up by organisms and recycled through food webs and excretion, some will be lost to the sediments and some will simply pass through to the outflow and be part of the loading to the next river or eventually the sea. We will ignore the multiple recycling by organisms, as that is effectively neutral at this level. It does not affect the total concentration, merely the forms in which the substance is held. Dilution will depend on the volume of water. The bigger the system the greater the dilution and likewise the greater the flow of water into it, the greater the dilution. This is true of the point sources. Diffuse sources should be uninfluenced by the volume of inflow, except where the processes in the catchment change as the rainfall changes. Heavy rain may wash out more of a substance than light rain for example, but these details are ignored in the general model. Finally, some substance may be lost permanently to the sediments, but may rest there only temporarily, and be regenerated back to the water by chemical mechanisms or by the action of organisms.

The concentration of a lithospherically derived substance $[m_l]$ is then directly proportional to the total loading, $L_c + L_r = L_t$ but inversely proportional to the dilution, measured as the mean depth of the system ($z$) and the flushing rate, $r$ (the number of times the water mass is replaced by the inflow per year). It is also inversely related to the fraction of the load that disappears permanently into the sediment ($s$). If the sediment is a net source (more comes out than goes in, a situation that could pertain for a temporary period), $s$ is negative. The units of $[m]$ are typically in g m$^{-3}$, the units of $L$ are g m$^{-2}$ yr$^{-1}$, of $z$ are m and of $s$ and $r$ are yr$^{-1}$. Thus:

$$[m_l] = L_t/z(r + s)$$

In the case of the concentration of atmospheric-derived elements, $[m_a]$, the fixation from the atmosphere is a component of the total load, but it may be useful to distinguish $L_a$ from $L_c$, $L_a$ being the contribution from atmospheric gas. Loss of gas through biological processes like denitrification is accounted for by a term in the denominator, $g$, with the units yr$^{-1}$, so:

$$[m_a] = (L_t + L_r + L_a)/z(r + s + g)$$

The usefulness of these equations is in working out what will happen to the concentration if, for example, rainfall and hence flushing rate changes, or if a new source of loading is added or one is removed (especially relevant where human activities are concerned). Processes such as denitrification, which are influenced by changing temperatures, can also be factored in. The model is a tool; it is not a way of calculating concentrations highly precisely. It assumes that the water body is instantly completely mixed, for example, whereas, especially with lakes, this is not the case especially in summer. Rivers mix more thoroughly, however. The model can be used to think about effects of seasonal changes, in inflow, for example. It also highlights the role of the sediments, which is considered in the next section, for there are generalities about sediments that can be usefully applied to all water bodies.

## 4.10 SEDIMENT–WATER RELATIONSHIPS

All water bodies lay down sediments. It is a simple fact of gravity that particles, either from weathered rock, eroded soil, washed-in organic debris or material produced in the water body, be it lake or river, will come to rest somewhere. Fast-moving streams will deposit only gravels and sands but lakes, especially shallow ones, and wetlands, dominated by plants will produce a great

deal of their own particulate material to add to that washed in. In the equations above, there is a more or less inverse relationship between $s$ and $r$. The greater the flushing rate, the less the likelihood of important effects of sediment, but the longer the water is retained, the more likely. The reciprocal of flushing rate is residence time, the average time that a molecule of water will spend in the water body (Chapter 2).

Sediments can be very reactive and their activity increases with decreasing particle size. Gravels and coarse sands are more or less inert and will have little effect on the water in contact with them. But finer sands incorporate some smaller particles, including organic matter, and sediments with smaller particles do this to an increasing degree. In general the finer and more organic the sediment, the greater will its influence be on the chemistry of the interstitial (between the particles) and the overlying water. There is a huge variety in the composition of sediments, but some common features in their activity.

By their nature, sediments are relatively solid and unmixing. They will have acquired bacteria as they formed, for bacteria are ubiquitous and attach to any particle. The bacteria will begin to decompose the organic matter and the immediate products of decomposition will include carbon dioxide, phosphate and ammonium ions and then nitrite and nitrate as the ammonium is further oxidized. This aerobic decomposition will continue in very coarse sediments and at the surface in finer ones, but in the latter, only millimetres or at most a centimetre or so below the surface, the bacteria will use up the limited supply of oxygen in the limited volume of water in the interstitial spaces faster than it can be resupplied by diffusion. The interior of sediments, other than very coarse ones, rapidly becomes anaerobic. Bacterial activity does not entirely stop, for there are plenty of anaerobic bacteria capable of using alternative oxidizing agents so long as stocks last. Nitrate is the first to be drawn on as denitrifying bacteria use its oxidizing potential to oxidize organic matter and convert nitrate to elementary nitrogen. Oxidized iron (Fe III) and manganese (Mn III) can then be converted to reduced forms (Fe II, Mn II) with the removed electrons used in oxidation. Then sulphate can be reduced to sulphide by genera such as *Desulphovibrio*, and finally hydrogen ions can be used to convert organic matter to methane with generation of energy.

The interior interstitial water of sediments may thus be poor in combined nitrogen but rich in phosphate and reduced iron and manganese and sulphide. If sulphide concentrations are high enough, a black precipitate of ferrous sulphide will form, which gives sediments their dark colour. Where sulphate has been very abundant, in saline waters, for example, the sediments may be intensely black. At the sediment surface, in the presence of oxygen, nitrogen compounds generated from decomposition will be abundant, but phosphate is precipitated with oxidized iron and manganese, and held tightly in the surface layers, which have a lighter brown colour compared with the deeper layers, and are known as the oxidized microzone. Nitrogen compounds may diffuse out of the surface layers, but relatively little phosphate escapes.

Matters change when the sediment is highly organic with labile compounds or when the water above becomes depleted of oxygen. This can happen in stratified conditions (Chapter 2) when water under ice or in the hypolimnion in summer is isolated from the atmosphere for a long period. In the first case (highly organic sediments) diffusion into the sediment may be too slow to keep even the surface layers oxidized and in the second there is simply no oxygen to diffuse in. The processes previously going on deeper in the sediment now go on also at the surface. No nitrogen compounds now escape, but reduced iron and phosphate and copious amounts of methane do. Thus sediments, depending on circumstances, can act as sinks (storages) or sources to the water body for phosphorus (though of course the phosphorus must have entered the sediment from the water body in the first place, so temporary store may be a better term than source). They can be regenerators of inorganic nitrogen compounds or places where nitrogen is lost to the atmosphere and they can be converters of oxidized carbon to reduced carbon in methane, which, being a greenhouse gas, has implications for climate regulation.

Enough has now been said to illustrate that a good freshwater ecologist must have a reasonable understanding of water chemistry if sense is to be made of the behaviour of freshwater systems and their organisms. But there is one further physical component, electromagnetic radiation, particularly light, that needs to be dealt with first.

## FURTHER READING

The effects of carbon speciation on photosynthesis are examined in an interesting experimental way in Sand

Jensen et al. (1992), whilst the effects of calcium on mollusc distribution are covered in Boycott (1936), a classic paper of its time, Dussart (1976) and Heino & Muotka (2006). Schindler (1977, 1978) comprehensively reviewed evidence that phosphorus is now a strongly limiting factor to freshwater production worldwide. Examples of nitrogen limitation on production or diversity include Moss (1969), Talling & Lemoalle (1999), James et al. (2003, 2005), Barker et al. (2008b) & Hameed et al. (1999). The meta-analysis of thousands of bioassay experiments, which is the source of Fig. 4.5, is described in Elser et al. (2007). The concept that living systems determine and regulate the chemistry of the biosphere is covered by its originator, James Lovelock in Lovelock (1965, 1979, 1988, 2003 and 2006), Lovelock & Margulis (1974) and Margulis & Lovelock (1974), whilst issues of limiting nutrients in general and challenges to the idea of single limiting nutrients in pristine contexts are taken up in Goldman et al. (1979), Moss (1990), Bergstrom & Jansson (2006) and Lewis & Wurtsbaugh (2008). Hecky et al. (1993) discuss variations in the Redfield ratio and Vitousek et al. (1997) review human effects including those of increased nitrogen in the biosphere.

Issues of major cycles in key elements are taken up for carbon by Alin & Johnson (2007) and Cole et al. (2007) and Gorham (1961) reviews the origins of many elements. Classic work on the retention of ions by natural systems and their loss when vegetation is damaged is described in Likens et al. (1970, 1977), whilst Smith et al. (2003) give data for pristine concentrations in the streams of undisturbed catchments. Wetzel (2001) puts particular emphasis on the ecology of dissolved organic matter.

Equation 4.1 is derived from Vollenweider et al. (1975) and issues of nutrient budgeting using a technique called export coefficient modelling are discussed by Johnes (1996) and Johnes et al. (1996). Lean (1973) and Kilham & Kilham (1990) are stimulating papers on the very rapid cycling of phosphorus in the water and the contrasts in phosphorus supply between temperate and tropical systems respectively.

Although often now ignored in the reference sections of papers concerning wetlands and chemical transformations in waterlogged soils, Mortimer (1941–1942) was the originator of understanding these processes and deserves the credit for little really new has been added since. Fenchel & Finlay (1995) discuss the fascinating world of life with a shortage of oxygen.

# Chapter 5

# LIGHT THROWN UPON THE WATERS

## 5.1 LIGHT

In the mythical biblical account of the creation, light had a very prominent part, for on the first day, light was separated from darkness, and light was thrown upon the waters. It retains this prominence in modern understanding. All underwater habitats are shaded and some are very dark indeed. This is simply because water and the substances that naturally become dissolved in it absorb very easily the electromagnetic radiation – ultraviolet, visible and infrared, among others – from the Sun. Photosynthetically active radiation (PAR, that which can be fixed into chemical energy by plants and algae) covers broadly the same range of wavelengths as visible radiation. Ultraviolet radiation is important in that it acts as a mutagen and may be damaging and infrared radiation is crucial in its effects on warming of water. But the absorption of PAR alone means that, just as with the availability of nutrients, freshwater ecology is strongly influenced by the physics and chemistry of the environment.

Electromagnetic radiation has been measured in a variety of units (calories, watts, joules, lux, lumens) but most usual now is a measure of the number of photons or particles of light, the Einstein. At the top of the atmosphere, beyond the effects of the gases held in it, the amount of radiation received from the Sun depends on the state of the Sun and the angle at which the radiation is received. Because the Earth is tilted on its axis of spin relative to a line connecting the centres of the Earth and Sun, the northern hemisphere is slightly closer to the Sun for half (the northern summer) of the year, as the Earth rotates around the Sun, and the southern hemisphere for the other half, in the southern summer. The Equator is always at the same distance during this annual cycle and the differences between the summer and winter increase from none at the Equator to very considerable differences at the poles. The daily rotation of the Earth as it spins on its axis gives the difference between day and night and the relative periods of day and night change with season and distance from the Equator, where they are equal.

It is hotter at the Equator than at the Poles because of the effect of the curvature of the Earth. At the Equator, the area presented to what we can think of as a sunbeam, is small because the angle of the plane of the Earth's surface to that of the path of radiation is close to 90°. Away from the Equator, on a spherical planet, the angle widens so the energy of the sunbeam is spread over a wider area. In summer, with the tilt of the hemisphere towards the Sun, the projected area of the beam is smaller, and the energy more intense than at the corresponding latitude on the other side of the Equator, where the hemisphere is tilted away from the Sun (Fig. 5.1). This also decreases the light period (the

*Ecology of Freshwaters: A View for the Twenty-first Century*, 4th edition. By Brian Moss. Published 2010 by Blackwell Publishing Ltd.

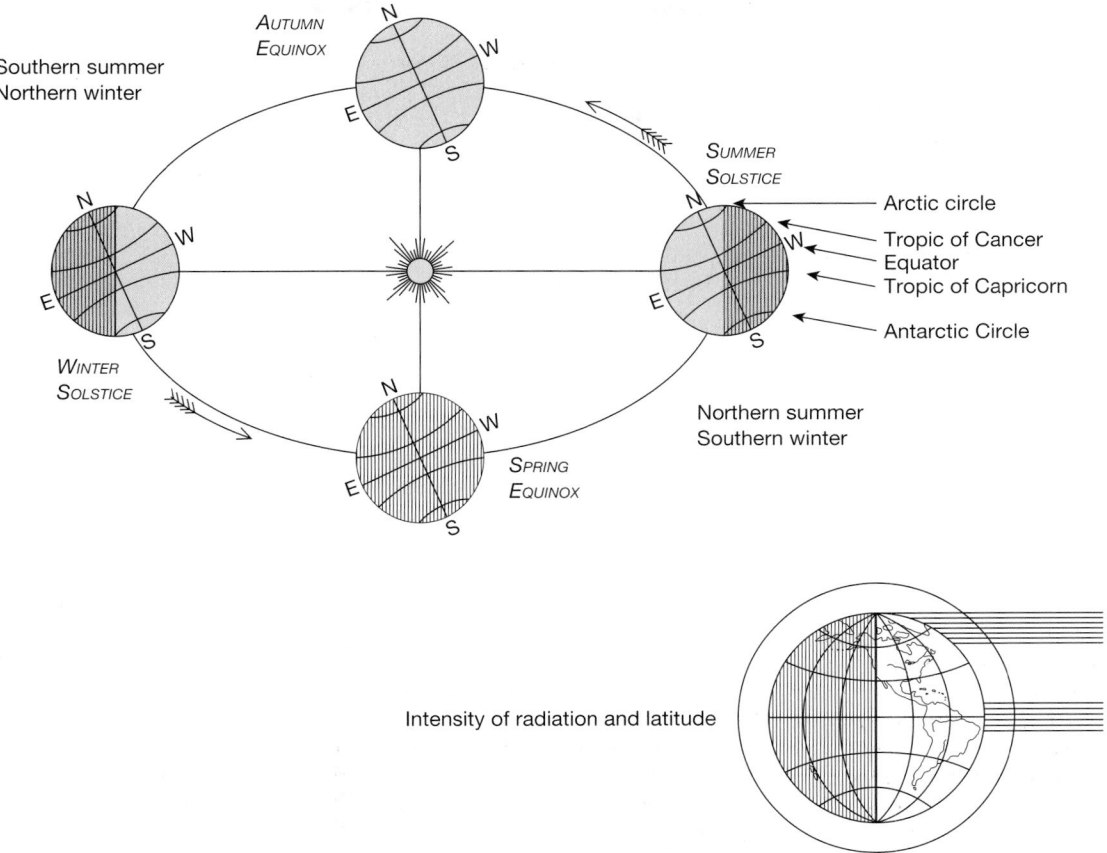

**Fig. 5.1** The availability of light at a given place depends first on latitude, north or south of the Equator. The constant tilt of the Earth's axis creates conditions for alternating winters and summers in the northern and southern hemispheres. And the angle that the surface of Earth makes with the line joining the centres of Earth and Sun determines the intensity of radiation received per unit area.

photoperiod) in winter and increases it in summer. At the Poles in mid-winter, the Earth's surface is close to parallel that of the path of radiation but the Pole is tilted away from the Sun and shaded by the Earth, so there is permanent night. In mid-summer at the poles the same parallel path with a tilt towards the Sun gives near permanent day. These simple relationships of day length, and intensity of radiation received, create the potential climate and photosynthesis conditions at the Earth's surface, but the actual amount of energy received is modified by the absorption of radiation by the atmosphere and then the absorptive properties of water itself.

### 5.1.1 Effects of the atmosphere

The atmosphere is a complex mixture of gases, all of which absorb some wavelengths of radiation. The spread of wavelengths of relevance to freshwaters (there are radio waves and gamma radiation also) runs from about 300 nm to 1500 nm. The visible (photosynthetically active) part is from about 400 to 700 nm and the total amount of energy (called the solar constant) received at the top of the atmosphere is around 6 micromoles photons (microeinsteins) $m^{-2}$ $s^{-1}$ (or in older units 1352 watts $m^{-2}$). On a cloudless day about a third of the total energy is taken out by absorption

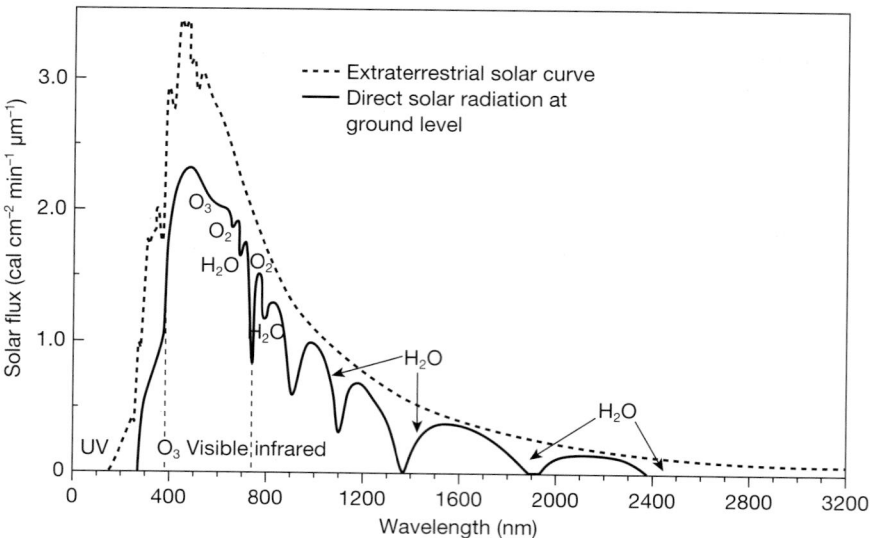

**Fig. 5.2** Radiation received at the top of the atmosphere is absorbed by the gases in the atmosphere, as indicated, so that what is received at the ground or water surface is less rich in long (infrared) and short (ultraviolet) radiation. A confusing variety of units is used when considering energy relations. To convert the calories per cm$^2$ and min$^{-1}$ to Watts m$^{-2}$ sec$^{-1}$, multiply by 39.7.

by the gases of the atmosphere, but selectively by wavelength. Ozone in the upper atmosphere removes much UV radiation; water vapour and carbon dioxide remove infrared radiation. This absorption warms the atmosphere and the energy is converted to slightly longer wavelengths and eventually re-radiated to space (Figs 5.2 and 5.3). What reaches the ground and water surfaces is thus reduced in ultra violet and infrared radiation and relatively enriched in visible radiation, because atmospheric gases take relatively less of this out. At the top of the atmosphere about 45% is in the visible range and at the ground about 50%. Figure 5.2 shows how the spectrum of the radiation changes as the atmosphere selectively absorbs particular wavebands and Fig. 5.3 summarizes the energy exchanges between the atmosphere and the ground.

The amount of visible radiation reaching the ground (maximally about 2 microeinsteins m$^{-2}$ s$^{-1}$) broadly follows the amounts reaching the top of the atmosphere but there will be deviations caused, for example, by different cloudiness in different places. In turn these will reflect local climate conditions, which are not only driven by the amount of radiation received from the Sun locally, but its influence elsewhere in driving major ocean currents that redistribute the energy by

warming or cooling the air masses above them. The heat and light availability in a given place is thus a complex matter dependent on factors that have feed back effects on one another. However, the picture is broadly that in Fig. 5.4.

## 5.2 FROM ABOVE TO UNDER THE WATER

At a water surface, some of this energy is then reflected back into the atmosphere. More will be reflected, the lower the angle of the Sun to the water surface. Least is reflected therefore towards the Equator (about 2%). About 5% is reflected at 30° latitude but then much more as latitudes increase. The reflectance loss is called the albedo. The nature of the water surface will also be important; the calmer the conditions the more is reflected, but rough water can more or less prevent much reflection. At this stage about 50–90% of the visible radiation will be left just under the water surface and this amount is what is potentially available for photosynthesis.

The radiation energy can then be absorbed by the water, the substances dissolved in it and by particles (plankton, detritus, inorganic particles washed in from

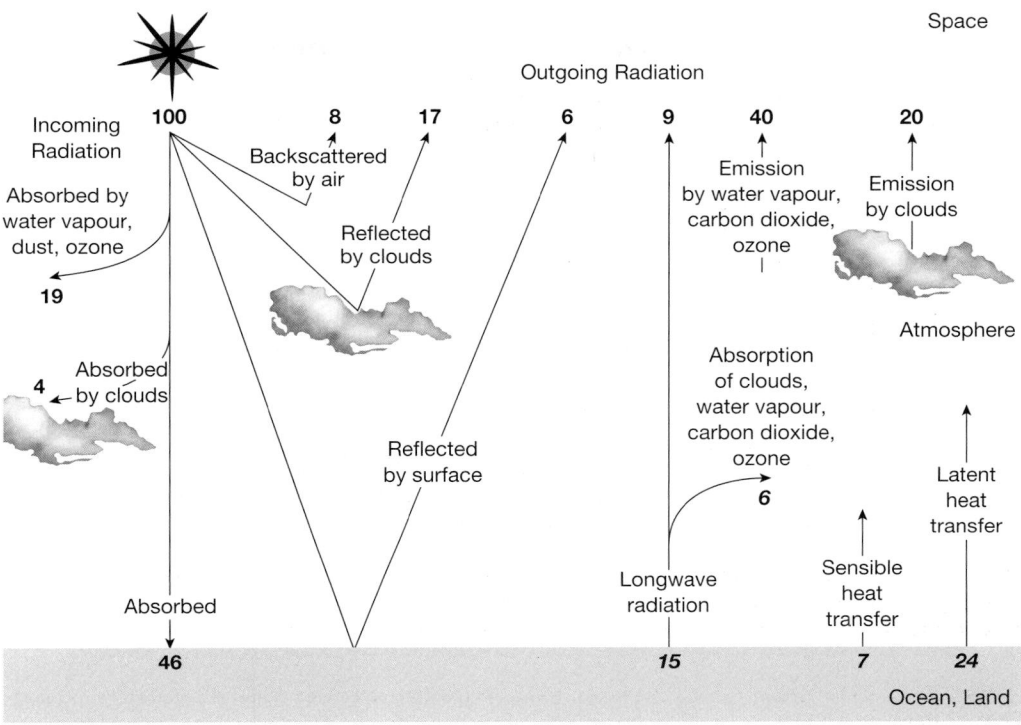

**Fig. 5.3** The Earth is almost in energy balance, which means that as much radiation as is received, is eventually re-radiated out to space. At present, Earth is warming as a result of changes in atmospheric composition, but this change falls within the uncertainties of measuring the various fluxes of energy shown here. Of 100 units at the top of the atmosphere, about 46 are absorbed at the ground. Re-radiation of this is at a longer wavelength than it is received. Finding the balances in this diagram will help you understand the processes.

**Fig. 5.4** The amount of energy received at the ground or water surface that is usable in photosynthesis is primarily a function of latitude but also varies with local cloudiness, and atmospheric dust. Here the average amount received in July is shown. The least amount (in Antarctica) is shown as the darkest shading (at the southern pole, July has almost permanent night), the greatest as without shading. Cloudiness causes differences over land and ocean. The range is $0-350$ W m$^{-2}$ with a mean of 158. The maximum is just north of the Equator as July is midsummer for the northern hemisphere. This band shifts south of the Equator in January. Data from NASA.

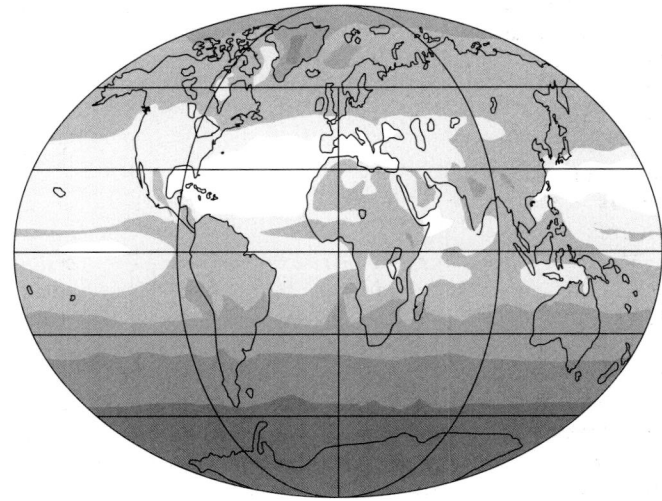

**Fig. 5.5** A Secchi disc and a photometer used variously to measure light penetration into water. The photometer is an old model. Newer ones use a much smaller photocell, but in older models, coloured filters can be placed over it to measure the penetration of different wavebands.

soil) suspended in it, or scattered by the suspended particles. Radiation therefore passes downwards (downwelling) and partly back upwards by back scattering from the particles and molecules. It may be measured by a photometer covered with filters to isolate particular wavebands (Fig. 5.5) or by a much more expensive spectroradiometer that will measure the amounts of energy at particular wavelengths as the detection cell is lowered through the water column. The rate at which the light is attenuated (the sum of absorption and scattering) depends on what is dissolved in the water, especially coloured substances, such as the brown humic DOM compounds, what is suspended, and the wavelength. Short wavelength light is more penetrative than long wavelengths in pure water (Fig. 5.6). Blue (around 440 nm) is absorbed about 30 times less rapidly than red (650 nm) in pure water.

For a given wavelength the rate of attenuation is described by a simple logarithmic equation:

$$I = I_0 e^{-kz}$$

where, for a vertical distance in the water of $z$ metres, $I_0$ units of radiation are reduced to $I$ units at a rate of $k$ m$^{-1}$, and e is the base of natural logarithms. This means that for each metre a set fraction $k$, is absorbed. If $I_0$ is 100, and $k$ is 0.1, there will be 90 units left after 1 m, 81 after 2 m, 72.9 after 3 m and so on. Variable k is called the absorption, extinction or, strictly, attenuation coefficient. It may be calculated by expanding the logarithmic equation so that:

$$k = 1/z \, [\log_e I_0 - \log_e I]$$

If the values of $\log_e I$ are plotted on the horizontal axis of a graph and those of the corresponding $z$ values on the vertical axis and the best straight line drawn by eye or calculated, the ratio of $\delta I$ to $\delta z$, the gradient, gives a value for $k$ (Fig. 5.7). For pure water, $k$ will increase with wavelength but will average about 0.02. It will be finite because even pure water absorbs light. For a relatively clear water, not much stained by humic compounds, $k$ values might be in the range, for different

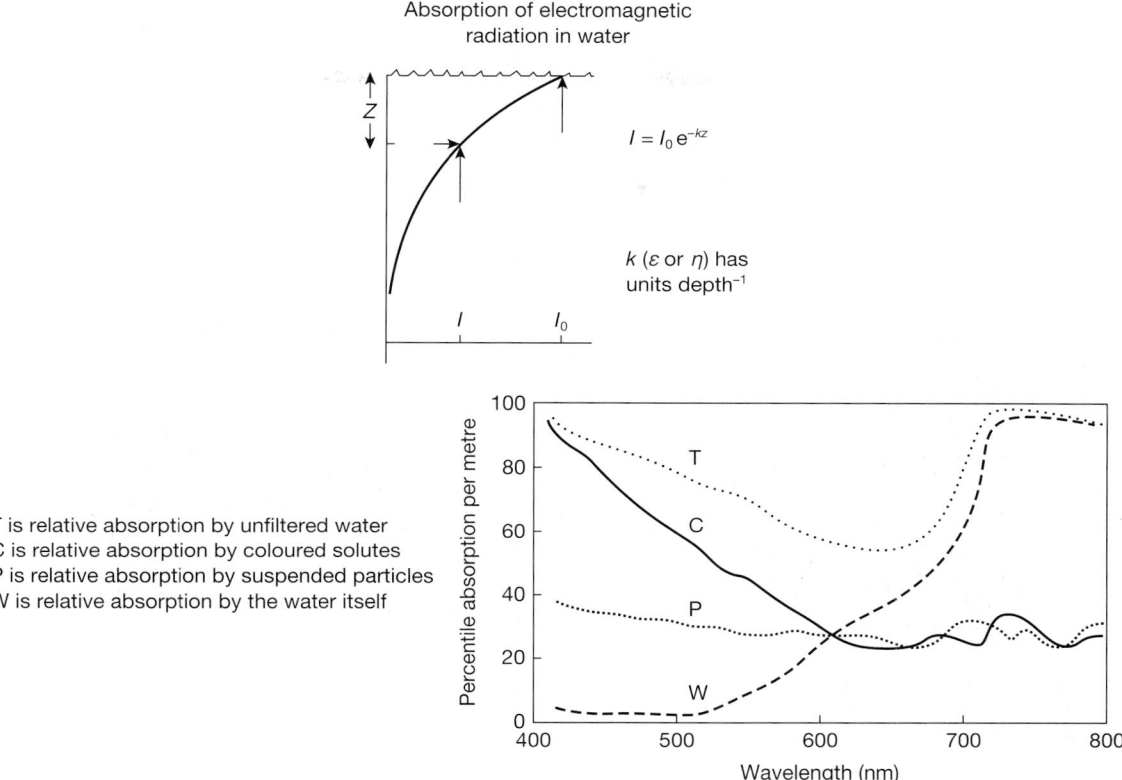

**Fig. 5.6** Light absorption in mixed water is logarithmic and follows a logarithmic equation. The percentage absorption per m at different wavelengths for a particular column of water is shown in the lower diagram. Percentage absorption is another way of expressing the extinction coefficient. W is absorption of the water itself and this increases with wavelength. Particulate matter (P) and even more so the yellow coloured dissolved substances (C) absorb most strongly the shorter wavelengths. The combined effect (T) of all three components is to give maximum absorbance at both very short and very long wavelengths leaving yellowy-green light, 590–690 nm, to be most penetrative and to give freshwaters their most common colour. Waters with little dissolved organic (C) matter or particulate matter (P) look bluer.

wavelengths, of 0.05–0.2. Heavily humic waters could have values of up to 2 and waters carrying heavy burdens of eroded soil or clay or phytoplankton, values up to 20 or so (Table 5.1).

It is usually inconvenient to have to measure the penetration of every individual wavelength so usually light meters are calibrated to measure 'white light'. It isn't white of course. In very clear waters it will become bluer with depth as the less penetrative longer wavelengths are more rapidly absorbed, and in humic stained waters, which absorb blue very rapidly, it will become yellow with depth. In all cases the mean absorption coefficient will become slightly smaller with depth as the more penetrative wavelengths are relatively enriched.

A common approximation, which has the advantage of being more easily envisaged than absorption coefficient, is to calculate the depth at which 1% of the visible radiation present at the surface is left. In very clear waters this might be of the order of several tens of metres, in humic stained waters, perhaps 2–3 m and in heavy suspensions of particles it could be as little as 25 cm. The 1% level is also a convenient approximation for the depth at which growth of algae is possible through photosynthesis, called the depth of the euphotic zone, $z_{eu}$. It is also called the

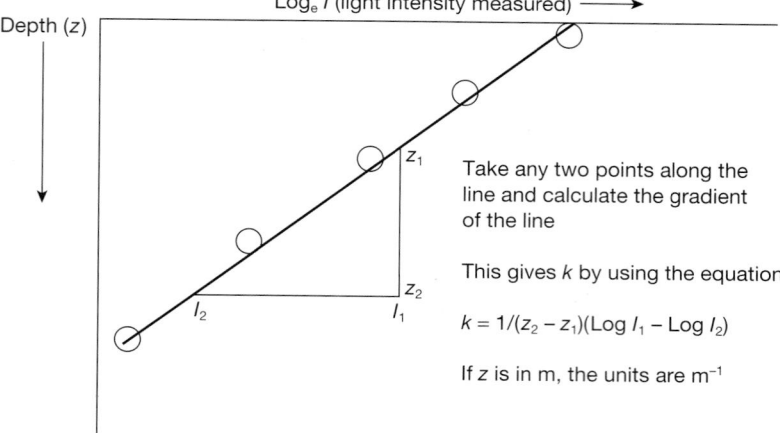

Calculation of absorption (extinction) coefficient

Depth (z)

$\text{Log}_e\,I$ (light intensity measured) ⟶

$z_1$

Take any two points along the
line and calculate the gradient
of the line

This gives $k$ by using the equation

$z_2$

$I_2$    $I_1$

$$k = 1/(z_2 - z_1)(\text{Log}\,I_1 - \text{Log}\,I_2)$$

If $z$ is in m, the units are m$^{-1}$

**Fig. 5.7** The extinction coefficient
can be calculated by plotting log of
light intensity against depth, which
gives a straight line, whose slope is
the extinction coefficient.

**Table 5.1**  Extinction coefficients and estimates of the compensation (euphotic) depth, $z_{eu}$ for natural waters and pure water.

|  | Extinction coefficient (m$^{-1}$) | Compensation depth (m) |
|---|---|---|
| Floodplain rivers | 10–15 | 0.2–0.4 |
| Lakes, coastal seas | 0.1–10 | 0.4–40 |
| Mid-ocean | 0.02 | 200 |
| Pure water | 0.005 | 920 |

compensation depth (Table 5.1) for at this depth photosynthesis carried out by the algae, the gross photosynthesis, just balances or compensates, the respiratory needs of the algae, so no new growth is possible.

Much of the water column in a very deep lake or in a turbid river may lie below this depth and thus be unable to support such growth. The euphotic zone may also be crudely estimated by a very simple instrument, the Secchi disc (Fig. 5.4). Secchi discs measure transparency and comprise a metal plate about 20 cm diameter, divided into quadrants alternately painted black and white. An observer lowers the disc into the water column until it just disappears and measures this depth. The disc is then pulled up and the depth at which it reappears is recorded. The mean of these two depths is called the Secchi depth and is very approximately about 0.4–0.5 the euphotic depth.

## 5.3 FROM PHYSICS AND CHEMISTRY TO BIOLOGY

The properties of water at a molecular level and *en masse* provide the stage for the action carried through by the organisms that live in it. It is not a one-way process, for, as in such matters as the secretion of organic compounds or the absorption of light by suspended plankton, the biota also continually reconstructs the stage. In the next chapter these biotic players are introduced and in subsequent ones the continuing ecological play is examined.

## FURTHER READING

Most limnology textbooks will give good accounts of light and light penetration, but the standard specialist work is Kirk (1994).

# Chapter 6

# EVOLUTION AND DIVERSITY OF FRESHWATER ORGANISMS

## 6.1 INTRODUCTION

Biodiversity is a recent term that has replaced the former, and simpler, 'diversity' of living organisms. New terms are often coined when some much older concept suddenly becomes fashionable though they do not necessarily imply any greater understanding of the topic. In this case the interest comes from the decline in diversity owing to widespread destruction of the Earth's habitats, something long known to professional ecologists. The remarkable thing is that, even with the current losses, there is a huge variety of living organisms, and if those that have formerly lived, but are now extinct, are considered, the range of living organisms is stupendous. The numbers raise questions, not only for freshwaters, but generally. Why are there so many? Is there some redundancy in that there might be ten different species all scraping algal films from stones in a single stream? Can some be dispensed with? Is there an upper limit to the number than can exist in a given space at a given time? How is the variety best expressed (e.g., as individual genes, genotypes, populations that are discrete breeding groups, or as higher groupings such as genera, families or phyla? Why is there rather greater diversity, however you measure it,

*Ecology of Freshwaters: A View for the Twenty-first Century,* 4th edition. By Brian Moss. Published 2010 by Blackwell Publishing Ltd.

in some places or latitudes than in others? And what generalizations can be made about the particular organisms that have colonized freshwaters?

New techniques, in which individuals can be characterized by base sequences in their DNA, have elaborated a previously well-known fact. All individuals are genetically unique. Among some, identical twins, asexually producing unicells and parthenogenic invertebrates, for example, the differences might be confined to somatic mutations, but in most others they are derived from the processes of sexual recombination and are much greater. In prokaryotes, enormous variation at the genetic level has been found, for bacteria appear to be able to transfer and share genes willy-nilly in the closeness of their microscopic domains. In their versatility in carrying out chemical transformations crucial for biogeochemical cycling, they are clearly more diverse than all of the visible plants, animals and fungi put together. On the other hand, in creating structures to support these processes: from soil crumbs to whole ecosystems, the larger organisms rule and any attempts to claim greater importance for one domain or the other are nonsensical. The biosphere thrives on its overall diversity.

Because of the enormous power of natural selection in eliminating the less effective in the competition for resources, there must be some fundamental significance to the high degree of diversity, and reduction of it must imperil the long-term continuity of the systems of which it is part. Increasing evidence suggests that reduced diversity impairs the functioning of the ecosystem in a given habitat, whether it be the recovery of grasslands from drought, or the damage caused by deer grazing to forests which have lost their top predators such as wolves (Chapter 7). It might sometimes appear that there is great redundancy at any one time, but when mechanisms for the survival of ecosystems in the face of many natural gological and climatic changes and fluctuations are considered, this seems increasingly unlikely.

## 6.2 THE ECOLOGICAL THEATRE AND THE EVOLUTIONARY PLAY

In G. E. Hutchinson's attractive metaphor (Chapter 1) the ecological theatre is the planet; or rather the solar system, for the Sun is central to the play. The theatre has had a changing stage for the whole of its 4.5–5 billion years of history and was at first inimical to living organisms. Until around 4 billion years ago, in a period now called the Hadean, it was too hot for liquid water to condense. It was also rank with the toxic gases spewed from the volcanoes that were formed in the thin solidifying crust that was slowly covering the interior of liquid magma. The atmosphere was sulphurous, and reducing in nature. There was no free oxygen. Oxygen reacts too readily with other elements to exist alone without the continual help of living organisms.

Slowly the crust became thicker, insulating the still hot but cooling interior. It remained restless with new material emerging from great cracks, solidifying as plates and being moved across the now plastic underlying mantle by convection currents, to disappear down trenches and be re-liquefied. In the deeper, still liquid, interior, heavier elements such as iron and nickel sank, lighter ones such as silicon and aluminium floated upwards and their minerals formed the continental platforms borne on plates of denser lava.

### 6.2.1 The seas form

By about 3.85 billion years ago, the planet had cooled sufficiently for the seas to have formed, because fossils, or at least fossil biochemicals, attributable to bacteria, appear in sedimentary rocks soon after, and structural fossils not long after that. Both fossils and sedimentary rocks require liquid water for their formation. It was still a very warm planet and the atmosphere remained anaerobic and maintained by volcanic emissions. The continents were different in shape and position from their present counterparts and the seas must have been fresh, not salt, at first. The salinity of the present oceans has had to be acquired by leaching from the minerals of the continents and the sea floor, though the freshwater phase was not long, perhaps 100 million years. It was a crucial phase for the early evolution of life, however.

The first fossils herald the beginning of the Archaean period. They were probably of anaerobic, heterotrophic or chemosynthetic bacteria, gaining their energy from oxidation of organic compounds or inorganic reactions respectively. The organic matter would have had to come initially from inorganic reactions. Passage of sparks simulating lightning, for example, through a gas mixture resembling that which emerges from volcanic vents, produces a range of amino acids and other organic compounds, though the famous initial experiments of Miller and Urey on this topic probably used an atmosphere that was atypically rich in component elements.

A range of relatively simple prokaryotes emerged quite rapidly, including photosynthetic forms that used hydrogen donors such as hydrogen and hydrogen sulphide to reduce carbon dioxide, but it is unknown whether the present representatives of these (Fig. 6.1) are closely similar or rather different from their ancestors. Bacteria leave few fossils. It is likely, however, that they have changed little. The morphologically basic anaerobic forms that have persisted in anaerobic refuges, though the Earth's surface is now well oxidized, could hardly be more elaborate than their ancestors. All the bacterial groups have representatives in fresh and salt water and their early history is a mystery. For up to two billion years, however, it is certain that the planet was anaerobic and populated only by anaerobic prokaryotes.

The ecological stage was still changing, however. There seems to have followed a long period of nearly two billion years in which the surfaces of the oceans slowly became oxidixed whilst the deeper waters remained anaerobic until, about 600 million years ago, almost the entire planet became aerobic. The surface oxidation was undoubtedly created by development of oxygen-releasing photosynthesis by the Cyanobacteria and related groups, about two to three billion years ago, using water as a hydrogen donor for photosynthesis (Fig. 6.2).

### 6.2.2 Eukaryotic cells

Eukaryotic cells become abundant in the fossil record much later, just over 1 billion years ago, when the

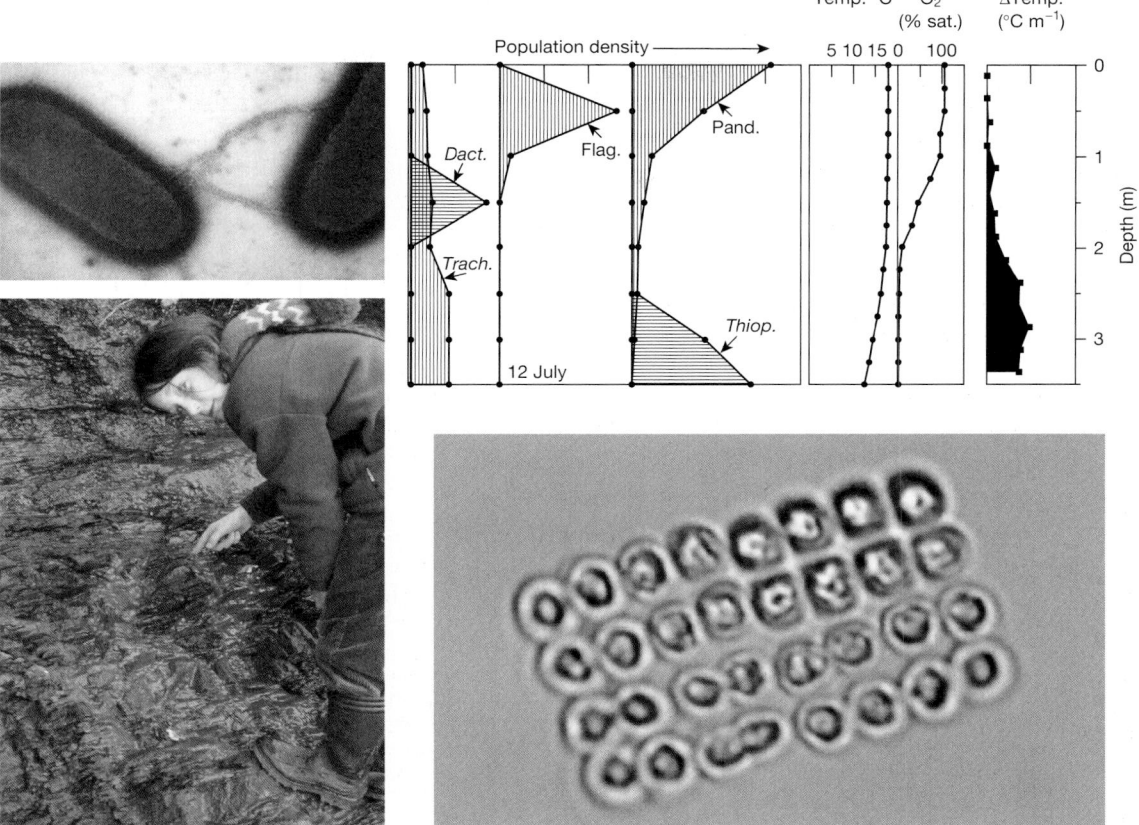

**Fig. 6.1** Rapid evolution in bacteria is favoured by mechanisms of free exchange of genes by various mechanisms including bridges called pili (upper left), but extreme conditions favour retention of specialist traits. Anaerobic bacteria, probably very similar to those that evolved on the early Earth, when free oxygen was very scarce, persist locally where free oxygen is lacking. Chemosynthetic iron bacteria, oxidizing $Fe^{++}$ to $Fe^{+++}$ make rusty deposits where water emerges as springs (left). In a small, shallow pond that stratifies in summer (upper right) because of shelter from the wind by woodland, a colonial purple sulphur bacterium, *Thiopedia* sp. (lower right, about 30 μm × 15 μm, photograph by R. Wagner), that uses hydrogen sulphide as a hydrogen donor in photosynthesis, grows densely in the deoxygenated bottom waters. Aerobic algae layer themselves in the light gradient above it. (Pand, *Pandorina morum*; Flag, a unicellular green flagellate; Trach, *Trachelomonas volvocina*, a euglenoid alga that requires iron and manganese to construct the theca external to its cell; and Dact, *Dactylococcopsis raphidioides*, a cyanobacterium with gas vesicles that suspends itself at an intermediate depth.) Cyanobacteria, having evolved in zero to low oxygen concentrations, frequently favour microaerophilic environments even now. (From Moss 1969.)

surface of the oceans had been becoming increasingly aerobic for perhaps a billion years. Evolution of the eukaryotic cell as a symbiosis of prokaryotes has been associated with rise of oxygen concentrations to potentially toxic levels. However, one group of apparent eukaryotes, the stramenopiles seem to have been present at least since the early part of the Proterozoic (around 2 billion years ago) and from evidence of molecules supposedly associated with them, perhaps from the anaerobic period of the Archaean, over 2.5 billion years ago. It may be that the start of the eukaryotic symbiosis reflects advantages that were not created by the changing oxygenation but that high oxygen levels began to select strongly for this particular arrangement, which allows protection of oxygen sensitive enzymes deep within the cell envelope. It may

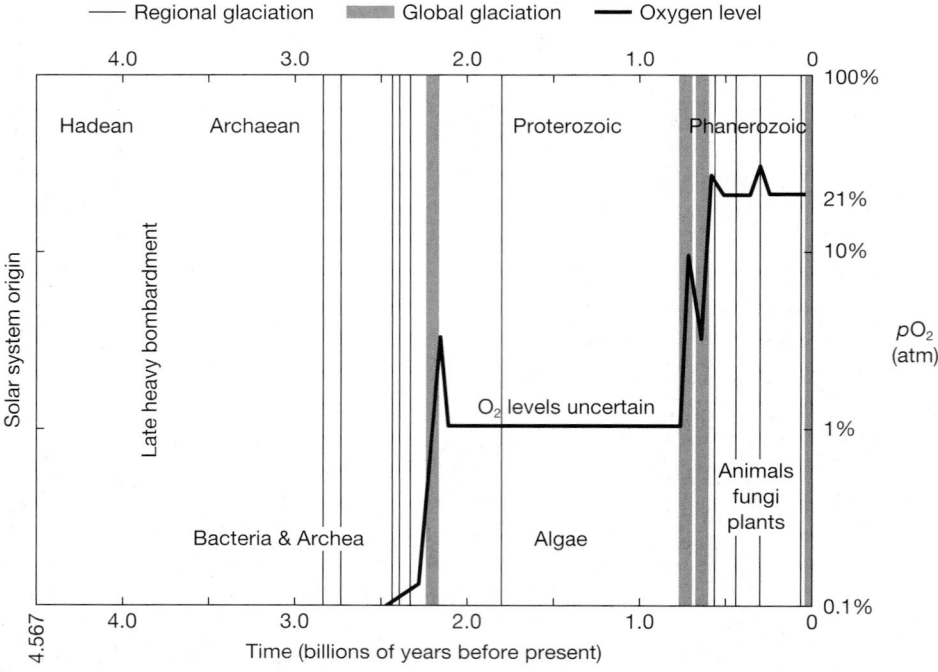

**Fig. 6.2** Free oxygen was virtually lacking in the biosphere until around 2.5 billion years ago when photosynthesis using water as a hydrogen donor evolved in the Cyanobacteria. It stayed at around 1% of the composition of the atmosphere for a further 2 billion years, as reducing substances continually mopped it up, but rose to its present 21% after multicellular plants had developed and the Earth's surface had been nearly exhausted of reducing substances.

also be that the large multicellular eukaryotes were unable to meet the needs of diffusion into their bodies without the existence of large external oxygen concentrations.

Throughout these momentous changes in the oceans and atmosphere, there were land masses and if there were land masses there were also streams and lake basins. And in those basins must have been communities of freshwater microorganisms. It seems unlikely however, that there were many freshwater multicellular organisms at the time, the Cambrian Period, when there seems to have been a major increase in such creatures in the oceans. The evidence is, however, tangential. The chances of long-term preservation of fossils in freshwaters are minimal, for freshwaters are readily disturbed and destroyed by drought on the land masses. The evidence seems to suggest that, other than by prokaryotes, freshwaters have been secondarily colonized from the oceans and from the land.

## 6.3 THE FRESHWATER BIOTA

Freshwaters by no means lack variety (Fig. 6.3) but in contrast to the ocean and land, freshwaters have fewer species. There are no existing phyla or classes, and few orders that are confined to freshwaters. There are, however, different ways of looking at this apparently simple set of statistics. The absolute extent of freshwater habitats is tiny compared with the ocean. The density of biodiversity in terms of number of species per unit volume is nonetheless huge in freshwaters, compared with the ocean. Ten thousand of a total of forty thousand fish species occur in freshwaters, the rest in the sea, but this works out at one marine fish species per $10^5$ km$^3$ of water but one fish species per 15 km$^3$ of freshwater. It is wiser to abandon the creation of league tables of what is greater or lesser, a peculiar pathology of how human societies are regarded at present, and simply focus on the meaning of biodiversity in freshwaters and elsewhere.

**Fig. 6.3** Freshwaters have a lesser range of diversity than land and the oceans, but it is not meagre. Some very common groups living in, or strongly associated with water, include (left to right and top to bottom): Cyanobacteria, desmids (green algae), charophytes (also green algae), higher plants, oligochaetes, crustaceans, molluscs, insects, crocodilians, snakes, frogs, newts, birds, mammals such as the water vole, and hippopotamus, and people.

No one knows exactly how many species there are and indeed definitions of what constitutes a species differ. However, it seems clear that there are many more conventional morphospecies (those recognizable by distinctive structural characteristics) than yet described, especially of invertebrates, and insects in particular. Estimates vary but range from the presently described 1.75 million species up to informed guesses of ten or twenty times as many. The situation is particularly difficult for prokaryotes, where the convention, that a species is a group of interbreeding individuals, breaks down with rather free exchange of genetic material among broadly similar-looking simple cells. Higher taxonomic groups are better known and it is now very rare for a new phylum to be described. Phyla, and in plants Divisions, thus constitute a more reliable basis for comparisons among the habitats of land, ocean and freshwaters. Even then there is some argument about what constitutes a phylum, especially among prokaryotes and among the smaller, often-unicellular eukaryotes, now called the Protoctista that used to be called the algae, Protozoa and 'primitive' fungi.

### 6.3.1 How many phyla and where?

Taking one (of several) widely used schemes (Margulis & Schwartz 1998), there are 93 phyla or divisions of

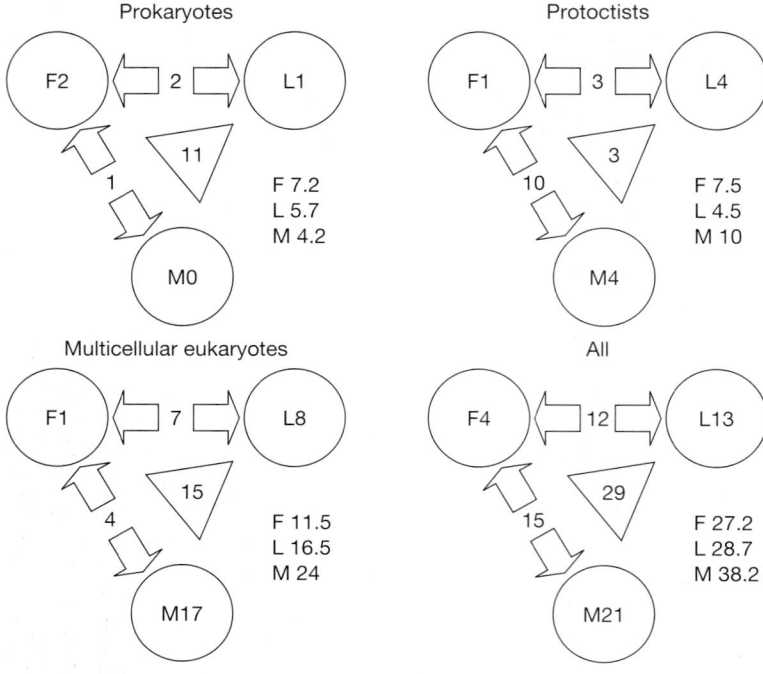

Prokaryotes

F2 ← 2 → L1

11

1

M0

F 7.2
L 5.7
M 4.2

Protoctists

F1 ← 3 → L4

3

10

M4

F 7.5
L 4.5
M 10

Multicellular eukaryotes

F1 ← 7 → L8

15

4

M17

F 11.5
L 16.5
M 24

All

F4 ← 12 → L13

29

15

M21

F 27.2
L 28.7
M 38.2

**Fig. 6.4** Distribution of Phyla (animals) and Divisions (the equivalent of Phyla in prokaryotes, plants and fungi) among freshwater (F), land (L) and marine (M) habitats. The numbers in the circles show groups confined to that habitat, those between arrows those shared between pairs of habitats. Numbers in triangles are those found in all three habitats. An overall measure of relative diversity is given as the sum, for each habitat, of those exclusive to it plus half of those shared with a second habitat plus one third of those occurring in all three. Data are shown and calculations made for the Prokaryote groups, the Protoctists (largely unicellular eukaryote groups) and the multicellular eukaryotes. Apart from prokaryotes, where freshwaters are the most diverse, the ocean is most diverse, but diversities on land and in freshwaters are not greatly different at this level.

prokaryotes and eukaryotes. Figure 6.4 shows how these are divided among the marine, land and freshwater realms in terms of groups that are confined to one or the other and those that are shared. Among prokaryotes, most are shared among all three but rather more are confined to freshwaters than to the sea, and since land prokaryotes must exist in essentially a small freshwater habitat, needing a film of free water to function, either freely or as a parasite, there is a tendency for greater richness in fresh water than marine water. This may reflect the probable freshwater habitat of origin of prokaryotes. Among the Protoctista, the focus shifts to marine waters and the marine–freshwater interface, whilst among multicellular eukaryotes, the plants and animals, but not the fungi, it remains with the sea but diversity in land habitats becomes more prominent. The picture is one of origin of prokaryotes in freshwaters, followed by a secondary colonization of saltwater and land. Protoctists, and then multicellular eukaryotes, evolved largely in a marine environment, then colonized the land mostly via freshwaters. There are no phyla that occur on land and in the ocean without also being present in freshwaters.

### 6.3.2 Plants

The ocean is clearly now the richest place for animal phyla, the land for plants. Freshwaters are poorer in phyla. Among plants and fungi, no Divisions are solely confined to freshwaters, but the horned liverworts (Anthocerophyta), whisk ferns (Psilophyta), Ginkgophyta, Gnetophyta, Cycadophyta and Coniferophyta are all now confined ostensibly to land. Parts of the life histories of the Anthocerophyta and Psilophyta do require free water habitats for fertilization of their eggs by free-swimming spermatozoids, however, so these are, in a sense, freshwater organisms. The other groups have evolved pollen which accomplishes fertilization without the need for a water film. The flowering plants (Spermatophyta), now the most abundant group, contain a small proportion of freshwater species and even fewer marine species. The higher plants seem to have arisen in water, either marine or fresh, probably the latter, from the Chlorophyta, or green algae. They then successfully colonized the land, where they have undergone their main development, then secondarily recolonized freshwaters and the sea with forms that have retained many of their land characteristics, such

**Fig. 6.5** Insects and aquatic plants epitomize groups that have secondarily colonized freshwaters from the land and still show many terrestrial characteristics. Among plants, the charophytes (*Chara vulgaris*) (top left) are large algae that probably have a direct aquatic origin and lack any terrestrial features. Their gametes, spermatozoids and oogonia, require free water for fertilization and are produced underwater. They lack cuticles. At the other extreme, emergent plants such as reeds, sedges, trees and papyrus (*Cyperus papyrus*) (bottom right), retain many land features, including production of flowers above the water surface, pollination by wind and insect vectors, thick, water retaining cuticles and stomata in their epidermis for water and gas regulation. Some plants have both submerged leaves and floating leaves, such as frogbit (*Hydrocharis morsus-ranae*) (lower left) but even completely submerged vascular plant such as the pondweeds (*Potamogeton* spp) (top right) still produce flowers above the water surface, are pollinated by land agents, have at least a thin cuticle and even retain some vestigial, though functionless stomata.

as land-based pollination agents and even vestigial stomata, the devices on the leaves that evolved to regulate gas and water exchange with the air (Fig. 6.5).

### 6.3.3 Animals

Among the animals, there is a long list of phyla that are confined to the ocean. A very short list, indeed one only, the Onycophora, or velvet worms, a group of cave- and soil-inhabiting, thin, cuticled worms that require very moist habitats, is confined to the land. There is a list,

about as long as that of phyla confined to the sea, of groups that occur both in freshwaters and the sea (Table 6.1).

An examination of the multicellular freshwater biota shows a number of characteristics. None of the groups is confined to freshwaters. They are shared among the land, the ocean or both. This represents a two-pronged colonization by marine organisms that have successfully coped with freshwater conditions, and land animals that have secondarily moved back to water. The sponges, jellyfish, flatworms, nematodes, nematomorphs, rotifers, nemertines, gastrotrichs, some of the

**Table 6.1** Animal phyla confined to the sea or freshwaters and shared between the sea and freshwaters.

| Confined to the sea | Confined to freshwaters | Present in the sea and freshwaters |
| --- | --- | --- |
| Placozoa (a single species of tiny animals with very little tissue differentiation) | Tardigrada (water bears) | Porifera (sponges) |
| Ctenophora (comb jellies) | | Cnidarians (jellyfish, medusas) |
| Gnathostomulids (jaw worms) | | Platyhelminthes (flatworms) |
| Rhombozoa (parasitic worms of molluscs) | | Nematoda (Nematodes) |
| Orthonectida (also parasitic worms) | | Nematomorpha (nematomorph worms) |
| Priapulida (also worms but free-living) | | Rotifera (rotifers) |
| Loricifera | | Acanthocephala (thorny – headed worms) |
| Kinorhyncha | | Nemertina (ribbon worms) |
| Entoprocta (sessile colonial animals) | | Gastrotricha (gastrotrichs) |
| Echiura (spoon worms) | | Chelicerata (horseshoe crabs, spiders, sea spiders, ticks and mites) |
| Sipuncula (peanut worms) | | Mandibulata (insects, centipedes, millipedes, symphyla, pauropods) |
| Pogonophora (beard worms) | | Annelida (oligochates, polychaetes and leeches) |
| Brachiopoda (lampshells) | | Crustacea (crabs, crayfish, prawns, copepods, brine shrimps, water fleas, woodlice, krill) |
| Phoronida (filter-feeding worms) | | Mollusca (snails, bivalves, mussels, sea slugs, nudibranchs, chitons, octopi, squid) |
| Chaetognatha (arrow worms) | | Bryozoa (ectoprocts) |
| Echinodermata (starfish, sea urchins, sea cucumbers) | | Tardigrada (water bears) |
| Urochordata (sea squirts) | | Craniata (vertebrates: fish, amphibians, reptiles, birds, mammals) |
| Hemichordata (acorn worms) | | |
| Cephalochordata (lancelets, amphioxids) | | |

crustaceans and cheliceratans, the annelids, molluscs, bryozoans, and tardigrades and some of the vertebrates (the fish) are so closely similar in features and life histories to their marine relatives that they seem to represent simple direct movement of their ancestors from the sea through the estuaries and thence to the freshwaters.

Others probably made the same transition and thence the transition to land organisms, but left no intermediate freshwater descendents. From a stronghold on the land they then secondarily colonized freshwaters and include some of the Chelicerates (spiders, mites), the insects, the reptiles, birds and mammals. This is a parallel story to that of the flowering plants. The amphibians and those plant groups such as the mosses and liverworts, which have both land and freshwater phases in their life histories are probably also in this latter group, but equally could represent

organisms metaphorically on their way from sea to land via freshwaters as much as those reverting to freshwater from the land (Fig. 6.6).

## 6.4 LIVING IN FRESHWATERS

Living in water poses some disadvantages as discussed in Chapters 2–5. These include the problems of slow diffusion, high viscosity and the relative shortage of certain nutrients. Living in freshwaters poses additional problems, which underlie the patterns of diversity among the phyla discussed above. A freshwater organism faces a medium that is much more dilute in salts than its cell sap or body fluids, and a habitat which is inherently unstable. Few freshwater bodies have any permanence in geological terms or even in terms of much shorter timescales.

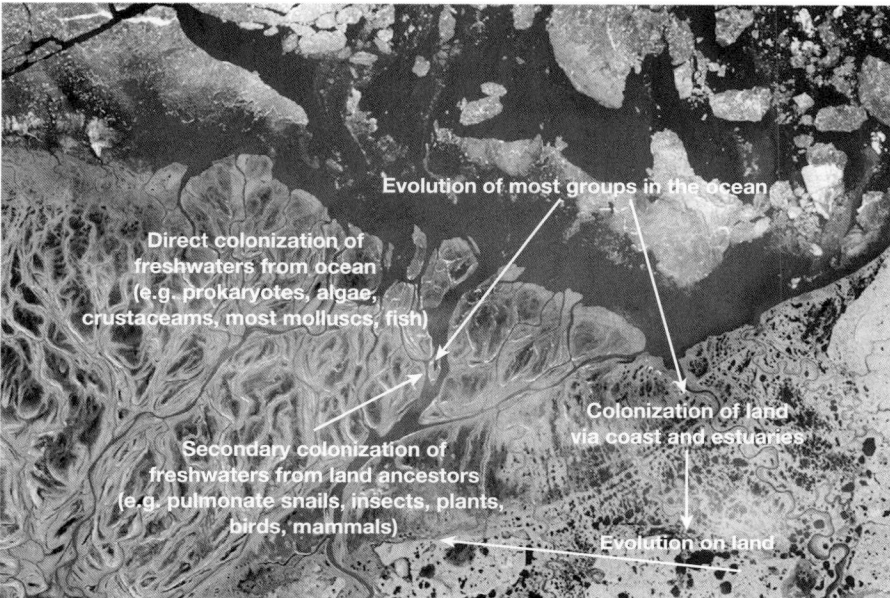

**Fig. 6.6** Pathways of evolution of some major groups of freshwater organisms.

## 6.4.1 Osmoregulation

The ocean, on the other hand, is a chemically monotonous, highly stable environment with a continuous history of many millions of years. It has 3.3–3.7% of salts, more than 80% of which are sodium chloride, has been chemically relatively unchanged since the Earth acquired its current well-oxygenated atmosphere, up to a billion years ago and varies from place to place by only a few per cent. Freshwaters have 0.01–1% of salts, a hundredfold range, or much more if some highly saline endorheic basins are included. Sodium chloride constitutes around 5% and potassium is very scarce. Seasonal fluctuations in salt content may be up to ±80%. Sea water has pH values of 7.8–8.3, a thirtyfold range in hydrogen ion concentration, freshwaters, less than 4.4 to more than 11, a range of at least four million-fold. Freshwater organisms thus have to cope with great extremes, both in colonizing new habitats and in survival once they have reached them.

Low salt concentrations in the external water mean that water is continually absorbed by osmosis through the body membranes of freshwater organisms, and cells are liable to burst if not somehow protected. In plants, the resistance of the rigid cell walls copes with this but in animals, where flexibility is needed for movement, the only solution is to get rid of the water as fast as it enters. This takes energy and is done by special organs or glands: protonephridial systems, contractile vacuoles, nephridia, blood gills and glands. In contrast, marine organisms take up little water by such osmotic processes and use little energy in maintaining their water balances. Getting rid of water in freshwater animals also means that salts, inevitably dissolved in this water, are continually lost and the animal must therefore absorb them, against a concentration gradient from the medium to maintain its internal salt content (Fig. 6.7). This it does by various glands and in its food, but this also requires energy, and a consequently greater supply of oxygen to release it through aerobic respiration. Where animals can be matched between the ocean and freshwaters (lobsters and crayfish, for example) the marine version is usually larger, perhaps reflecting a greater availability of energy for growth with the need for less for osmoregulation.

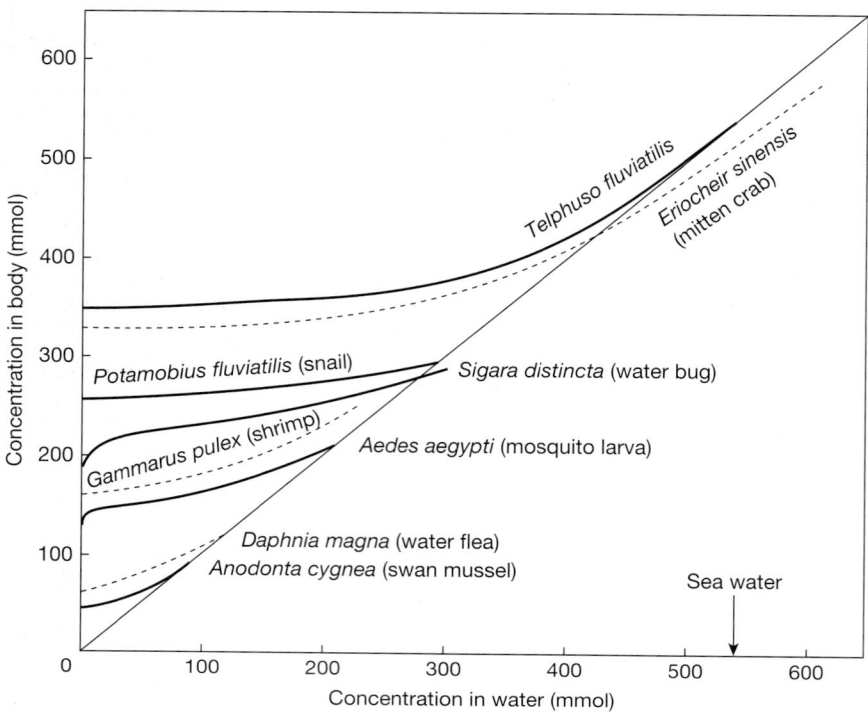

**Fig. 6.7** Osmoregulation in brackish and freshwater organisms. Freshwater organisms have to be able to regulate the concentration of their body fluids in a medium that often has much lower concentrations. Thus all of the organisms shown here have relatively steady internal concentrations as external concentrations are experimentally changed. There are limiting concentrations where such regulation fails, in these cases between 17 and 63% of sea water. The more tolerant freshwater crabs, *Telphusa* and *Eriocheir*, are probably recently evolved from marine ancestors and can tolerate seawater by osmoconforming. At the higher levels, they adjust their body concentrations to that of the external medium, but at lower concentrations, like the other species shown, they osmoregulate.

### 6.4.2 Reproduction

This energy shortage may also underlie a lower reproductive investment in freshwater animals. Many fewer eggs are produced than in marine equivalents and they are often carried by the adult until they are developed into self-sufficient young rather than released willy-nilly into the water. Chances of local survival are thus increased but chances of effective dispersal are decreased. The freshwater *Hydra*, for example, carries 1–2 eggs, the equivalent marine *Cordylophora* twice as many. Marine oysters produce a hundred million eggs, freshwater mussels, like the swan mussel of similar size, only up to 2 million. Special larval stages are also rarer in freshwaters. This may reflect the need for rapid turnover in life histories in a habitat that may be disturbed unexpectedly by drying or freezing or replacement by washout.

### 6.4.3 Resting stages and aestivation

This theme of uncertainty is taken up also in the production of anabiotic devices: stages of the life history resistant to difficult conditions, such as resistant, dormant eggs or cysts, which are rare in the ocean (Table 6.2). Dry mud from ponds, if wetted, will hatch out a myriad array of animals; dried marine mud will not. Such devices were early evolved in the colonization of freshwaters and are especially common among

**Table 6.2** Occurrence of anabiotic (resting stage) devices and free-swimming larval stages in marine and freshwater invertebrates. (Based on Pennak 1985.)

| | Resting stages | | Free-swimming larvae | |
|---|---|---|---|---|
| | Marine | Fresh water | Marine | Fresh water |
| Protozoa | Rare | Very common | | |
| Porifera | Gemmule-like structures rare | Gemmules, reduction bodies | Coeloblastulae, stereogastrulae | Flagellated embryo in a few species |
| Coelenterata | None | Thecated embryos | Medusae, panulae, actinulae | A very few medusae |
| Turbellaria | None | Cocoons, fragmentation cysts, 'winter' eggs | Müller's larvae, Göttes larvae | None |
| Gastrotricha | None | Opsiblastic eggs | None | None |
| Rotifera | None | Resting eggs, winter eggs, anabiotic adult stages | None | None |
| Nematoda | None | Resting eggs, desiccated individuals | None | None |
| Tardigrada | No representatives | Various stages: tun, cyst stage, anabiotic stage, cryptobiotic stage | No representatives | None |
| Nemertea | None | Cysts | Pilidium | None |
| Ectoprocta | None | Statoblasts (six types), hibernacula | Cystid, cyphonautes | 'Ciliated' larva |
| Entoprocta | None | Hibernacula | Ciliated larva | None |
| Oligochaeta | None | Cysts | None | None |
| Copepoda | None | Resting eggs, diapause cocoon stage | Nauplius and copepodid stages | Nauplius and copepodid stages |
| Ostracoda | None | Resting eggs, advanced instars able to withstand cold and drying in diapause | Atypical nauplius | Atypical nauplius |
| Isopoda | None | None | None | None |
| Amphipoda | None | None | None | None |
| Decapoda | None | None | Nauplius, protozoae, zoea, mysis, phyllosoma | None |
| Mysidacea | None | None | None | None |
| Pelycypoda | None | None | Trochophore, veliger | Only glochidia, a secondary device for parasitism |
| Gastropoda | None | None | None | None |

smaller organisms, such as the Eubranchiopoda. Many freshwater insects, derived largely from land ancestors, have diapausal stages, resistant to cold, freezing, drying or anaerobiosis. Freshwater organisms are often more tolerant of freezing than, say, intertidal marine organisms, and aestivation, a resting stage of the whole adult animal is most common in freshwaters.

The African lungfish (Fig. 6.8), for example, will burrow into the mud of drying swamps and secrete a water resistant cocoon within which it survives the dry season, emerging as the new rains raise the water table. Similarly some snails will seal their shells with a mucoid epiphragm in dry periods. Production of resting stages means the possibility of effective colonization

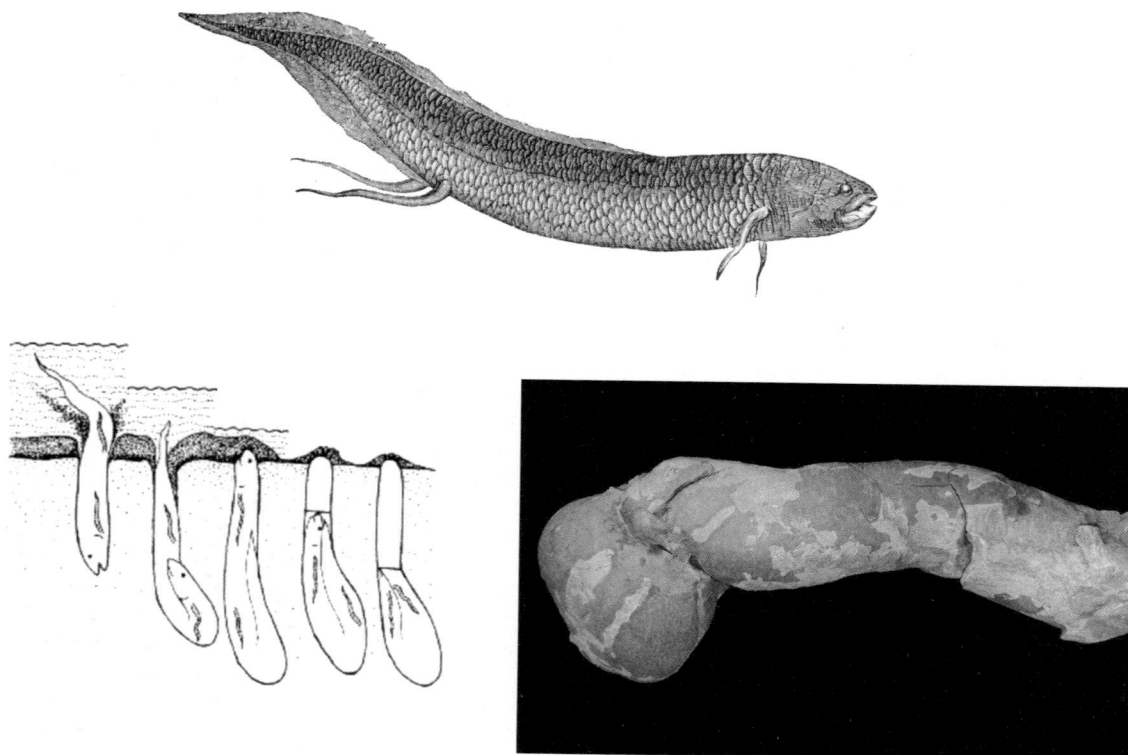

**Fig. 6.8** There are several species of lungfish in Africa and South America. *Protopterus aethiopicus* (top) survives the dry season by burrowing into wet mud (bottom left) and forming a mud cocoon around itself in which it survives in a dormant condition until the swamps are again flooded.

of new basins when these stages are inadvertently picked up on mud or plant fragments by itinerant birds and insects or the wind, or rolled away in floods and this too may be seen as a device to cope with a relatively temporary habitat. Permanent springs with a reliable ground-water source often have species, such as planarians, isopods and leeches, lacking anabiotic stages.

These difficulties lend a spartanness to the appearance of freshwater organisms. Crustaceans, annelids and molluscs in freshwaters lack the structural embellishments notable in their marine relatives. The bright colours, bioluminescence and elaborate shapes of the latter, devices to cope with predation or to demonstrate superior fitness in the competition for mates are generally lacking. The freshwater cadres are the tough inhabitants of a demanding place, with little to spare for the extravagances of soft marine living!

### 6.4.4 Getting enough oxygen

If regulation of their salt and water content is a particular problem for freshwater organisms, they share, with marine organisms, the problem of obtaining sufficient oxygen for aerobic respiration. The problem is less acute in the oceans, however. The seas are large in volume, low in primary productivity. Decomposition processes can cope with the available supply and only in very confined, landlocked basins, with long water replacement times, such as the Black Sea and narrow fjords, is there a problem and then only in the deep bottom water in summer.

The proximity of land to freshwaters, however, and the load of organic matter washed in, coupled with a generally higher productivity through greater, land-derived supplies of nutrients, means increased problems of balancing oxygen supply and demand for freshwater animals. Often the supply of organic matter greatly exceeds the ability of oxygen to diffuse in from the atmosphere to maintain reasonably high concentrations in the face of intense bacterial decomposition. Indeed in some shallow, swampy habitats, natural deoxygenation is so great that extreme adaptations have developed among animals and plants to cope with it.

All eukaryotic organisms living in water, however, face some problem with their oxygen supply. For plants such as reeds or papyrus that emerge into the atmosphere, there may still be a problem, for their roots are contained in an often anaerobic sediment and to function oxygen must diffuse, or even be pumped down to them (see Chapter 9). For fully submerged species, the problem of the slow diffusion of gases in water (Chapter 2) is serious. It can be obviated by maximizing the surface area of the body in relation to its volume, or by moving rapidly through the water so that 'new' water is continually brought into contact with the surface, as long as the surface is permeable to gases. Surface area for absorption can be increased by the use of thin sheets of tissue called gills or the development of fine and filmy thin leaves in the case of submerged plants. The bigger the organism, the more this must be done, for the surface to volume ratio, in the simplest case of a sphere, $4\pi r^2 : 4/3\pi r^3$ increases only by the square of the radius as the volume increases by the cube. To an extent, flattening the body compensates for this, but flattening cannot proceed indefinitely as organs have to be accommodated. Beyond about a millimetre path length for diffusion, specialized structures are needed, and the solution, in animals, is often to have evolved gills (Fig. 6.9). Rotifers, water fleas and flatworms are small enough to manage without, but many invertebrates, particularly insects have considerable gill surfaces borne on the abdomen or elsewhere.

### 6.4.5 Insects

Freshwater insects, like freshwater vascular plants, appear all to be secondary colonists from land ancestors and show a range of adjustments. Many have aerial, air-breathing adults but aquatic larvae or nymphs. Where the adults are aquatic they may still retain air-breathing mechanisms by holding a bubble of air against their undersides in the case of some bugs, or under their wing covers in the case of diving beetles. They absorb oxygen from the bubble, which is replenished during visits the water surface, but underwater, for a time, oxygen diffuses into the bubble from the water to maintain the air/water equilibrium concentrations, which are relatively high in oxygen (21%). However, as oxygen is absorbed, the concentration of nitrogen rises and nitrogen diffuses out to the water. Theoretically a dynamic equilibrium should be established with the nitrogen diffusing back in, but the speed of these processes is generally too low to avoid progressive reduction in size of the bubble, its eventual collapse and a need for its replacement at the water surface.

By holding the bubble supported by its surface tension on a mat of hairs, the plastron, bubble collapse can be delayed, but surface replenishment is never totally avoidable. This antecedent of the aqualung is matched in some water spiders by an analogue of the diving bell. The spiders spin a bell of silk, fixed to water plants and pointing downwards. They bring down bubbles from the surface to fill the bell and may be able to survive on this supply, and its replenishment by diffusion, for days. Having to return to the water surface to replenish the oxygen supply of course involves an increased risk of predation from larger animals. On the other hand most of these air-breathers are predators themselves, requiring a large oxygen supply for the fast motion involved in pursuing prey. The smaller bodied, and the gill-breathers are able to remain indefinitely in refuges provided by plants and other structures underwater.

### 6.4.6 Big animals, air breathers and swamps

The biggest freshwater animals, such as hippopotami and the few species of freshwater seal, are amphibious and air breathers; the biggest totally submerged freshwater species are the larger fish and the price they must pay is in the energy of pumping water past the gills or in vigorous movement to force a water current over the gills. Predatory fish have the greatest oxygen demand and tend to have more streamlined bodies enabling faster movement. Herbivorous and detritivorous fish have evolved such characteristics to a lesser extent, but still need large gill areas. Gills, being necessarily permeable to gases, are also permeable to small ions and water and thus compound the problems of water and salt regulation.

In swamps, with their enormous productivity of emergent plants (see Chapter 9) and shallow waters, not only the sediments but often the overlying waters

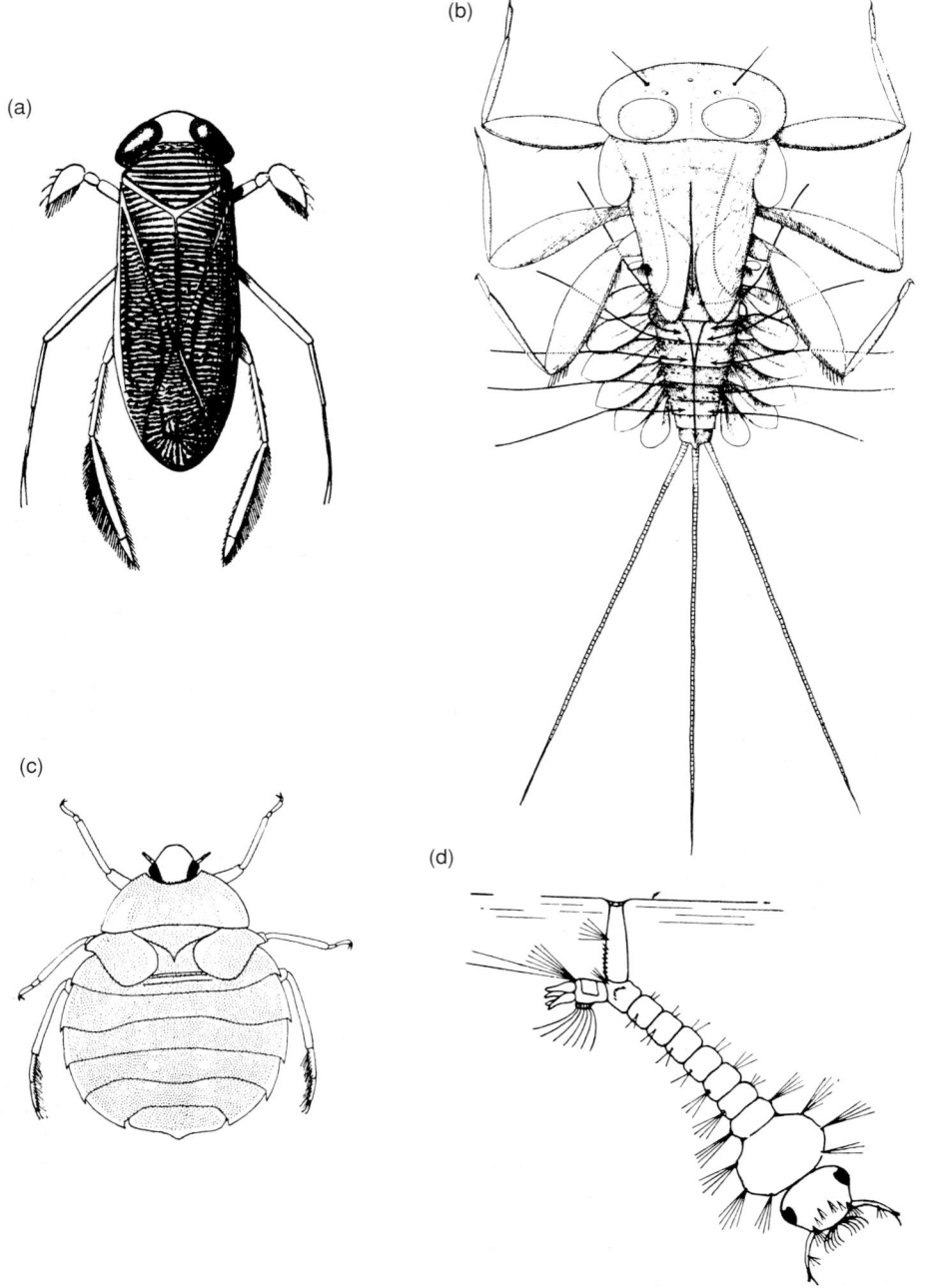

**Fig 6.9** Supply of sufficient oxygen is crucial to freshwater animals. Many beetles and bugs (*Sigara*, top left) visit the water surface frequently to capture a bubble of air, which sticks to their undersides and supplies them for a time. Eventually the bubble collapses and must be replaced. Others, such as the larva of the mosquito genus, *Culex* (bottom right) attach to the surface tension film and breath atmospheric air through a large spiracle. Many simply absorb oxygen from the water over their whole bodies, or, as in the nymph of the mayfly, *Ecdyonurus* (top right) have, on their abdomens, flat, paired gills, which provide large areas for absorption. The beetle, *Aphelocheirus* (bottom left) has a plastron, or velvety mat of hairs on its underside, which supports a bubble of air for a long period. Oxygen dissolves from the water into the bubble and this obviates frequent visits to the surface. (Based on Fryer 1991 and Hynes 1979.)

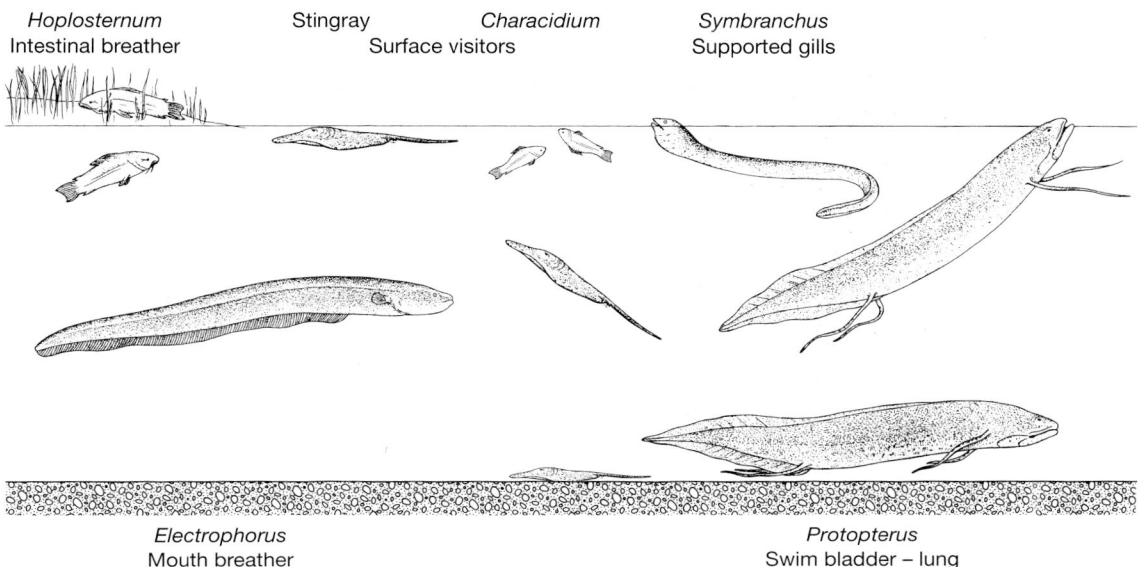

*Hoplosternum*
Intestinal breather

*Stingray*          *Characidium*
       Surface visitors

*Symbranchus*
Supported gills

*Electrophorus*
Mouth breather

*Protopterus*
Swim bladder – lung

**Fig. 6.10** Fish living in swamps are frequently dependent on breathing atmospheric air. Gills are ill-equipped for this as they collapse if not supported by water so additional devices are needed. These include increasing the blood supply to other absorptive surfaces that do not collapse, such as the intestine, swim bladder or mouth, or by changing behaviour so that the fish live mostly in the surface, better-oxygenated waters, or even on the swamp vegetation mat for extended periods.

are anaerobic. Their invertebrates tend to be rich in haemoglobin, which presumably gives them some oxygen storage, and an equilibrium concentration in the body that is higher than in body fluids lacking this pigment. Even then they may have to expose themselves at the surfaces of swampy peat mats to obtain sufficient oxygen, as in the tropical oligochaete, *Alma*. Many swamp fish have evolved air-breathing mechanisms or adopted behaviour that keeps them close to the better-aerated surface layer of water (Fig. 6.10).

Gills have become supported in some fish on bony or cartilage struts, which prevent their collapse when the fish opens its mouth into the air, or the mouth has become highly vascularized. In the extreme examples of the African and South American lungfish, the swim bladder, originally an organ for adjusting buoyancy, has become rich in blood vessels and developed into a lung, into which air is regularly breathed during visits to the water surface. Newly hatched fish using these devices would be particularly vulnerable to predation. In some cases, the parents lay eggs in bubble rafts, produced by mouth secretions, which float at the surface. These keep the young in the surface waters

whilst providing some protection until the larvae need to become free-swimming when their yolk sacs are exhausted.

## 6.5 DISPERSAL AMONG FRESHWATERS

All organisms need to be able to disperse for many reasons. Their immediate habitat may change; they may be threatened with extinction by local predation or competition; their own activities may have altered their local surroundings unfavourably. Freshwater organisms are no different but it is possible that the vulnerability of their habitat to external change may have placed a greater imperative on methods of dispersion, although it is difficult to establish this, there being no absolute scale to measure dispersability, nor a consistent one of measure of difference among populations. Easily dispersed organisms, in theory, will show greater genetic uniformity among populations in different places, whilst those that spread less easily might be expected to have evolved considerable genetic differences in their isolated fastnesses.

### 6.5.1  Small things are the same everywhere?

Very small organisms disperse easily, in dust particles, droplets, bodily in moving water or attached to other organisms. They exemplify the problem of measuring dispersability. One school of thought maintains that for microorganisms and possibly even for animals less than about a millimetre in size, everything is everywhere and the environment selects. In other words, microorganisms and small animals are so easily dispersed as to be ubiquitous and grow wherever local conditions allow. The evidence for this rests on recognizing similar species worldwide from their morphological characteristics. With bacteria this is a trivial criterion because many look very similar even when they perform very different functions, but for the eukaryotic microorganisms like the protozoa and algae (the Protoctista), it is true that collections from many parts of the world show many similar genera.

The existence of a species depends on a balance between its rate of colonization and rate of extinction in a given place and even if extinction rates for microorganisms are large, they are matched by huge colonization rates through the atmosphere. It is calculated that about $10^{18}$ viable bacteria are transported between the continents annually. Population sizes of small organisms are also very large (a small pond may have $10^{18}$ bacteria, $10^{16}$ protoctists and $10^{11}$ small animals) and so the chances of extinction are very small, barring utter catastrophe. One $cm^2$ of pond sediment might have 1000 ciliates of 20 species. Treating this sediment by warming, drying, rewetting or the addition of food can reveal another 110 spp amounting to 50% of all species in the pond and 8% of all named ciliates.

### 6.5.2  Or are they?

Looking the same, however, is not being the same and this view of everything small potentially being everywhere has been widely challenged by very careful taxonomists who find significant distinctions among ostensibly similar organisms in different places. Sometimes apparently very similar appearance belies quite different genetics. Genetically very different populations occurring close to one another are interpreted as meaning that dispersal is slow and that as a result, isolated populations have become adjusted, through drift and selection to the detailed mosaic of local conditions. Molecular methods that are now able to distinguish very small differences in local populations sometimes show a great deal of variation between populations and sometimes much similarity. Where differences are shown, the problems are that, in many microbes, mutation and sharing of genes are very common and that differentiation will occur rapidly even where immigration is continuous. Difficulties also lie in deciding what degree of genetic difference constitutes real biological and ecological difference. It has long been known that all individuals have their genetic distinctions from others and that variation within a species, defined as a breeding group or a group exchanging genes, is normal, indeed essential. As the technology of recognizing difference becomes ever more sophisticated, the problem becomes more intractable.

For larger organisms, there is no doubt that a great deal of differentiation occurs and no argument that there is an immense biogeographic complexity. The mayflies of northern Europe, or even of a small part of Sweden, for example, are clearly different from those of Papua New Guinea or southern Spain. Some generalist species may occasionally be shared, but species are usually clearly different. Here the problem of discerning patterns rests not in knowing the significance of small differences, as it does in microorganisms, but in having comprehensive data on which to work, such is the inadequacy with which the Earth's biodiversity has yet been described.

### 6.5.3 Vulnerability and dispersal in freshwaters

An answer to the question of whether freshwater organisms are remarkably different from those of the land or sea in their dispersive abilities, because of the vulnerability of their habitat, is still elusive. Sometimes species do appear to be widely distributed, for example many species of submerged aquatic plants, such as the hornwort, *Ceratophyllum demersum*, whilst even in flying insects, genetic differences appear to be sometimes quite large in closely occurring populations (Fig. 6.11). The incidence of anabiotic stages, which may act in passive dispersal in many freshwater invertebrate groups, compared with their marine counterparts, may suggest a particular talent for dispersal but such stages are no less scarce in terrestrial organisms. We may simply be noting that the ocean is

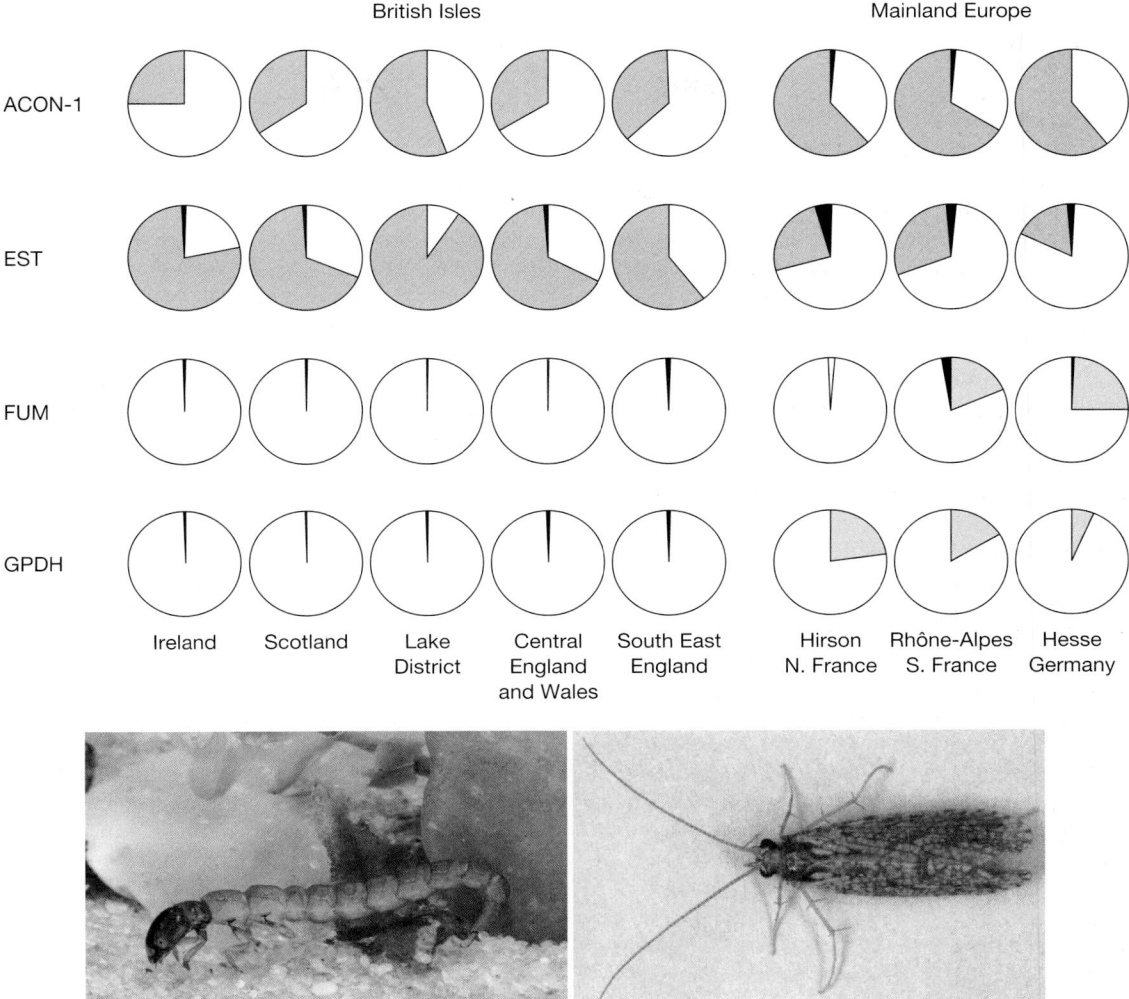

**Fig. 6.11** Genetic studies using sequencing of particular genes can throw light on how easily species become dispersed. The caddis fly *Plectrocnemia conspersa* has filter-feeding aquatic larvae that hatch into aerial adults. Four genes (extreme left column) were studied in eight populations in the UK and on the European mainland. Gene frequencies (shown in pie diagrams with different alleles indicated by different shading) were relatively uniform over the UK, suggesting relatively easy spread over short distances, but differed from those of the mainland, where they were also relatively uniform. This suggests that distribution over longer distances is not difficult so long as major barriers like the sea do not get in the way. (From Wilcock et al. 2001; pictures by Biopix.)

a particularly stable habitat rather than that freshwaters are particularly vulnerable. One emerging piece of evidence may be convincing, however. The increase in intercontinental movement by ships, air, trade goods and people in the last century has led to an unprecedented introduction of new species to freshwaters, many of which have established and often become problems by outcompeting the native plants and animals. This suggests that dispersability may, in the absence of this artificial help, be a problem for freshwater organisms though few could be expected to negotiate a huge barrier of salt water. That several groups of fish, the eels and salmonids for example, do so readily at different stages in their life histories defies this, however.

## 6.6 PATTERNS IN FRESHWATER DIVERSITY

Natural selection has been very effective in providing solutions to the problems of osmoregulation, oxygen supply, and dispersal. The diversity of species in freshwaters, considering the small size of the usable freshwater resource (Chapter 2) and the vulnerability of freshwaters to the disturbances of a dynamic geology and climate, is considerable. It is not uniform, however. There are patterns that reflect the nature of the particular freshwater habitat and its recent geological history. For example, there will be more species the bigger the lake or river system (Fig. 6.12). Size, however, does not simply mean greater structural complexity or variety of potential niches; it may mean also greater stability, in the sense of persistence of the water body in the face of geological and climate changes. The patterns are not simple and freshwater diversity can best be understood by considering the combined influences of geological and climatic history, climate, size, and nature and permanence of the water body at a particular spot. We tend to know rather more about fish faunas than other groups, because fish are large and often of economic significance. Fish are thus frequently used below to illustrate what are likely to be general patterns.

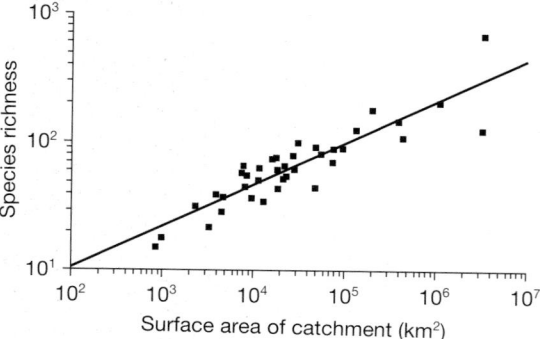

**Fig. 6.12** Species richness tends to increase with size of water body in lakes and size of river system, measured as discharge or catchment area. Greater size offers more niches. These data relate catchment size to fish species richness in 39 West African river systems. (From Hugueny 1989.)

There is undoubtedly a gradient with latitude (Fig. 6.13). Polar waters are relatively scarce in species. Their short growing seasons and frozen catchments support only low production, and occasional complete freezing of lakes has often prevented the persistence of large animals like fish. Travelling towards the Equator, the number of species generally increases. Long growing seasons, abundance of food and high turnover of generations have meant extensive speciation, provided the water body is long-lived enough. The issue of permanence is perhaps more important than the temperature. Lake Baikal (Fig. 6.14) in southern Russia is cold but huge and has a very diverse community, including freshwater seals. It persisted as a body of water during the glacial epochs that obliterated the more northerly lakes, driving their organisms southwards to refuges in the warm temperate zone from which, even after 10,000 years they are still moving back.

### 6.6.1 Fish faunas

The UK, for example has only 42 native species of freshwater fish, including those that spend only some of their life history in freshwaters. The former communities of the interglacial periods were reduced to very simple ones in very cold lakes at the edge of the ice sheet at the height of the glaciation with only a few species of whitefish (Coregonidae). As the ice melted back, fish capable of living in the sea and freshwaters moved into the newly flowing meltwater rivers, and other fish migrated through river systems that were continuous with the European mainland so long as sea levels were low and the present North Sea was a land basin connecting the UK with what is now mainland Europe. This migration was stopped, however, when sea levels rose as meltwater accumulated and the UK was isolated as an island about 7000 years ago (Fig. 6.15). At equivalent latitudes on the continents, the migration was not so arrested and the freshwater systems have far more species.

In the tropics, the glaciations led to wetter conditions than at present. In Kenya, for instance, the rift valley bore the extensive Lake Gamble, extending its span from the volcanoes of Menengai in the north to Longenot in the south, which has now dried down to the much smaller basins of Naivasha, Nakuru and Elementeita. These lakes have themselves dried out quite frequently in the past few thousand years and are poor in species, though they may provide spectacular

**Fig. 6.13** Latitude also affects species richness. Lower latitudes have not been disturbed by recent glaciation and have longer growing seasons allowing more predictable food supplies and supporting specialization of ecological niche. These data are from 120 rivers and lakes in the northern hemisphere in North and South America. There are over 100 times as many fish species in the tropics, compared with the polar region.

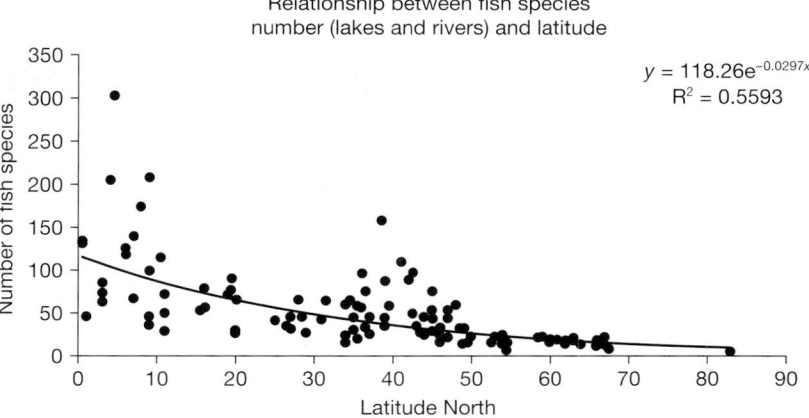

Relationship between fish species number (lakes and rivers) and latitude

$y = 118.26e^{-0.0297x}$
$R^2 = 0.5593$

**Fig. 6.14** Lake Baikal (left) in Russia is the world's deepest lake and is very ancient. It has evolved a great many species that are confined to it (endemics), including a seal (top right) and many gammarid crustaceans and sponges (bottom right). (Photographs by NASA, Greenpeace and UW.)

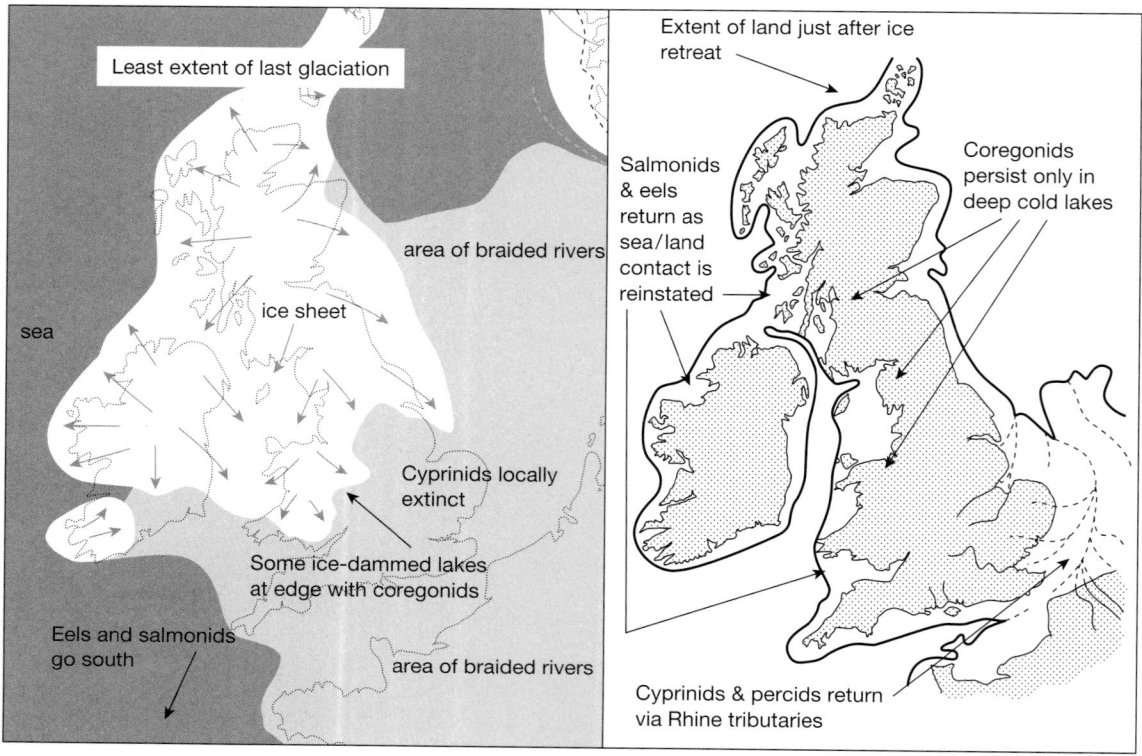

**Fig. 6.15** The last glaciation made most British fish extinct. Salmonids and eels were able to migrate southwards and some coregonid species persisted in ice-dammed lakes in southern England. As the ice retreated and whilst sea levels were low, cyprinid and percid fish, pike and others were able, for about 2000 years, to move into Britain and Ireland via the continental river systems. Salmonids moved back from the ocean, as did eels. In the warming climate, coregonids and Arctic charr became confined to colder, deeper lakes in the north. Recolonization ended with the rising of sea level and the cutting off of Britain as islands, 7000 years ago, by which time only a limited community (44 species) had been able to establish.

numbers of those such as lesser flamingo and cyano-bacteria that persist in them. Even the huge, but comparatively shallow Lake Victoria is believed to have dried out, or at least been reduced to a series of smaller lakes, about 14,500 years ago. The deeper East African lakes, such as Tanganyika, Malawi and Albert, how-ever (Fig. 6.16), have probably had existences, albeit with fluctuating water levels, for several million years and this may underlie their considerable diversity.

Determining the exact extent of this fish diversity is not easy, however. There is no rigid standard by which taxonomists delineate species, especially when, as often in the past, they have had to work with pre-served specimens that have lost their colours and can-not manifest any behaviour. Structural characteristics

have thus been the main criteria. Lakes Victoria and Malawi are thought now to have about 700 species each, mostly of one particular, prominent group of fish, the cichlids, but Lake Tanganyika, which is bigger and possibly more ancient than Lake Malawi, apparently has only 250. The inherent genetic diversity, as mea-sured by molecular methods, is greater however in Lake Tanganyika than in Lake Victoria and the dis-tinction may be an artefact. Lake Victoria has suffered many greater assaults from human activity in recent years and this has led to intense study of its fish, whilst the fauna of Lake Tanganyika has been less studied is still known mostly from early work.

A stable habitat in a tropical regime offers pre-dictable, abundant food and selection tends to produce

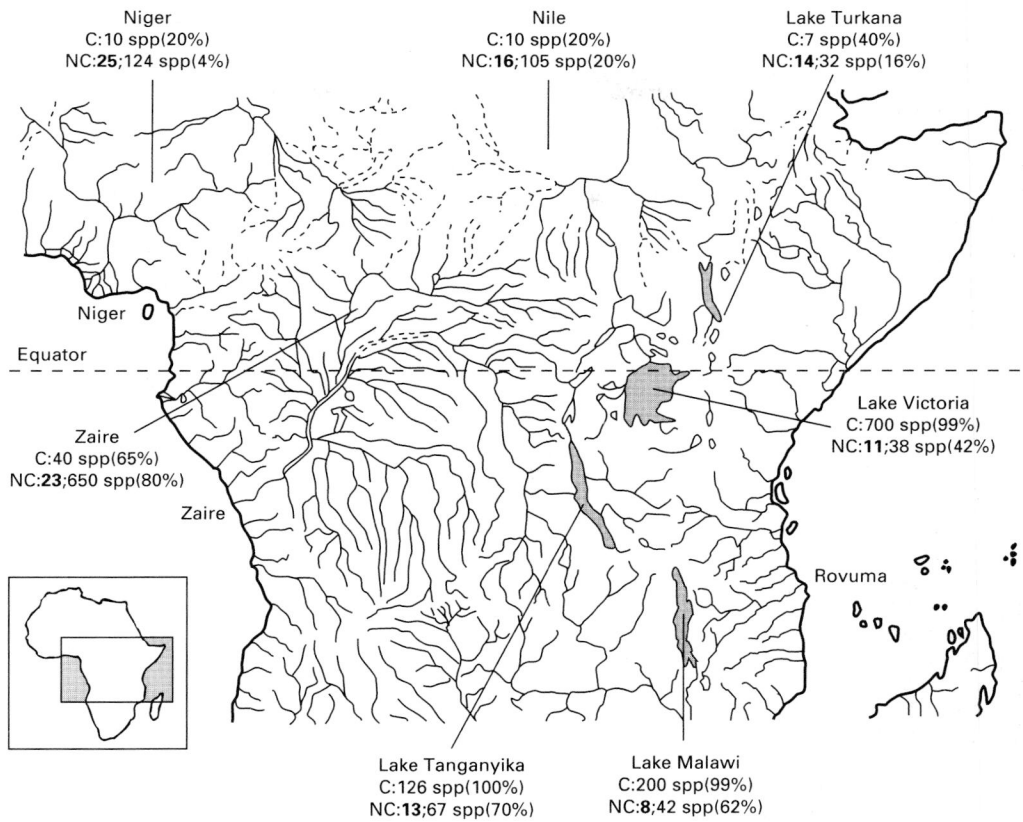

Niger
C:10 spp(20%)
NC:**25**;124 spp(4%)

Nile
C:10 spp(20%)
NC:**16**;105 spp(20%)

Lake Turkana
C:7 spp(40%)
NC:**14**;32 spp(16%)

Niger **0**

Equator

Lake Victoria
C:700 spp(99%)
NC:**11**;38 spp(42%)

Zaire
C:40 spp(65%)
NC:**23**;650 spp(80%)

Zaire

Rovuma

Lake Tanganyika
C:126 spp(100%)
NC:**13**;67 spp(70%)

Lake Malawi
C:200 spp(99%)
NC:**8**;42 spp(62%)

**Fig. 6.16** Africa was not glaciated, except for some extension of the higher mountain glaciers. Its fish faunas have thus been able to develop over very long periods and show great species richness and a high degree of endemism. Numbers show total number of cichlid (C) and non-cichlid (NC) species and the percentage, in parentheses, that are endemic.

many species each specializing to a large extent, in, for example its diet, location or breeding conditions. The fish fauna of Lake Malawi, for example (Fig. 6.17) has species that specialize in feeding on algae attached to the different parts of rocks (top, side) or on loosely or firmly attached algae. There are fish that feed on the eggs of others, or on their fins and scales. Invertebrate feeders specialize on soft worms, which they seek with their fleshy lips in the sediment, or on crustaceans which they delicately pick with teeth like forceps or on molluscs which they crush with specialized teeth or plates in the mouth. That climate alone is not a guarantee of diversity, however, is shown by the endorheic Lake Chilwa just to the south of Lake Malawi, where frequent drying out has left a native fish fauna of only about 12 species, only three of them

abundant (Fig. 6.18), and all of them very generalist in their feeding and breeding needs, as befits an unstable, unpredictable environment where flexibility is a better stratagem than specialization.

Lake Victoria is something of an anomaly. Lying astride the Equator, it has a rich fish fauna (or at least had until it was severely depleted by human activities) but apparently dried out comparatively recently. When it dried, many previous species may have found refuges in small residual bodies of water in its main basin or at its edges and in river estuaries, but there appears to be an additional, to an extent accidental, factor at work. Many of the Lake Victoria species are small spiny fish of the Family Cichlidae, particularly of one group, the haplochromines. As in the other large East African lakes, these fish have produced species flocks in which

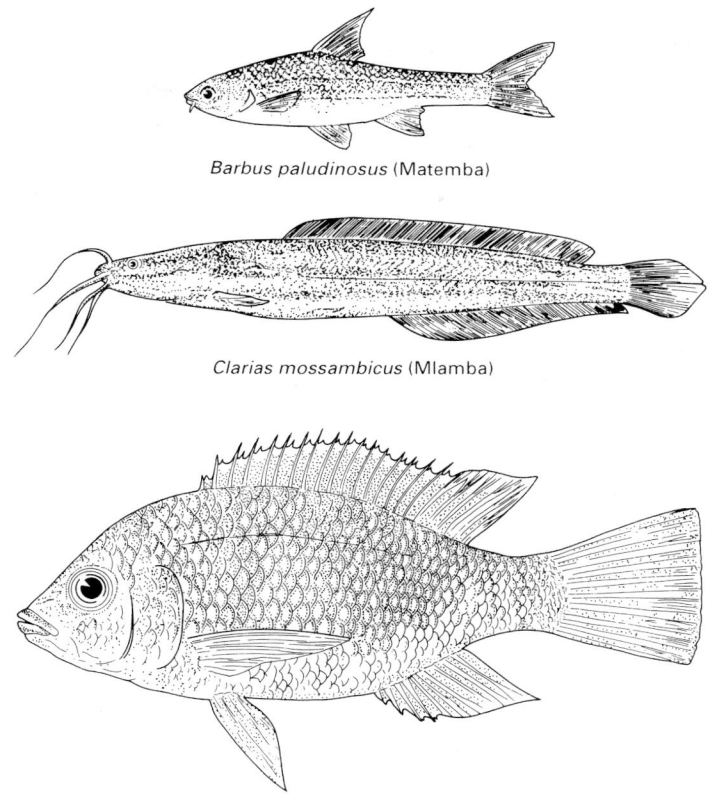

*Barbus paludinosus* (Matemba)

*Clarias mossambicus* (Mlamba)

*Tilapia shirana chilwae* (Makumba)

Stomach contents (% of total items)

|  | Higher plants | Green algae | Blue-green algae | Diatoms | Crustacea | Snails | Insects | Rotifers | Fish |
|---|---|---|---|---|---|---|---|---|---|
| *Barbus* | 14 | 22 | 1 | 1 | 56 | 0 | 3 | 1 | 1 |
| *Clarias* | 12 | 4 | 1 | 1 | 47 | 1 | 15 | 0 | 20 |
| *Tilapia* | 28 | 23 | 13 | 10 | 14 | 0 | 0 | 7 | 5 |

**Fig. 6.18** The three main species of fish in Lake Chilwa, Malawi, and the average stomach contents of samples of several hundred fish of each species. Lake Chilwa undergoes irregular phases of drying out; its fish species have very broad diets and unspecialized habitat requirements which allow them to cope with this variability. Each fish species, however, takes more of one particular item than the other two fish.

**Fig. 6.17** (*opposite*) Specialization that has occurred in diet for a number of closely related small species of the genus *Haplochromis* in Lake Malawi. In some cases whole heads, in others details of the pharyngeal bones (the triangular diagrams), upper part of the mouth (arch-shaped diagrams), or individual teeth are shown. Most descriptions are self-evident, but the mimic resembles a harmless (to other fish) plant eater, though in fact it scrapes scales from the bodies of other fish species, whilst the employers of subterfuge are fish-eaters (piscivores) that lie on the bottom, resembling rotting carcases. Curious small fish come to inspect them and are soon eaten as the 'carcase' comes to life. Pickers delicately pick small animals from rock surfaces, whilst diggers use their sensitive lips to feel for animals whilst probing in sand or sediment. The eye biter is reported to remove eyes from larger fish, but also eats whole small ones. (From Fryer and Iles 1972.)

many closely related species live sympatrically, that is in the same geographical space, without interbreeding, though if forced to breed in the laboratory, they may often produce fertile hybrids. These species are endemic, occurring nowhere else. With the variety of habitats available and time to produce increasing specialization, the existence of several hundred, perhaps as many as 700 related species as in Lake Malawi is remarkable but understandable. For it to have occurred in a lake that dried out only about 15,000 years ago, like Victoria, needs some quirk of circumstances.

## 6.7 THE FISH OF LAKE VICTORIA

Lake Victoria had very clear water, and the ancestral fish to the some hundreds of haplochromines now present in the lake appears to have had a gene complex that could produce greatly different colours in males. Molecular studies suggest that the Lake Victoria species flock has about ten times less variability in its mitochondrial DNA than the Lake Malawi flock and that it comes from a single ancestral species of the genus *Thorachromis*, which it shares with the flock in the nearby Lake Edward, derived from riverine fish of this genus of the Congo or Nile.

The gene complex can produce blue males, males with red/yellow backs or red/yellow bellies. These colours appear to have been used as markers for mate selection by the females, who preferentially reproduce with particularly bright males, whether red/yellow or blue. The females vary in colour too (plain, orange blotched, black and white) but are more subdued and the selection mostly appears to be by females for males rather than the other way round. This seems to have led to sympatric speciation and differentiation of closely similar species, but differently coloured species, at first capable of interbreeding but progressively unable to do so. Based on this separation, specialization in feeding was able to follow and with rocky areas separated by stretches of sand and mud, this sympatric species differentiation has been repeated separately in many different areas.

The system appears to have depended on the clear water for perception of different colour values among the females. Closely related species have males at opposite ends of the colour spectrum (one blue, one red/yellow) and under monochromatic light in experimental conditions, the females cannot distinguish the males of their own species from those of the closely related one. The clearer the water, the more variability there is

in the males of a given species (thus giving greater possibilities for further speciation) and consequently the more species in a genus. In deep water, where differential absorption of light leads to restriction of wavebands (see Chapter 5), there are fewer species, for colour perception is restricted. Currently the water is cloudier over many areas of Lake Victoria for reasons of eutrophication (see Chapter 15), and variation in colour in populations in turbid water is also much lower so that speciation may be slower in cloudy water where subtle colour distinctions are not easily perceived. The prolific species flocks of the African lakes all occur in the clear lakes (Secchi disc transparency 3–22 m) but not in those that are more turbid (Secchi disc transparency 0.2–1.3 m).

## 6.8 LOW DIVERSITY FRESHWATER HABITATS

In contrast to these examples of very high diversity, there are equally illuminating ones of very low diversity. Hot springs and caves are two of these. Hot springs (Fig. 3.8) arise where water, having percolated underground in volcanic areas is forced back to the surface through superheating by very hot rocks. Springs may emerge as mixtures of warm to boiling water and steam, bubbling through vents or mud pots with an exotic mixture of gases thought to resemble those of the early atmosphere of Earth. The regions of such springs often have a strong sulphurous smell. The water as it emerges may be chemically very unusual with high concentrations of heavy metals and arsenic, derived from the chemical reactions taking place between superheated water under pressure and igneous minerals in the Earth's crust.

The hottest springs have few species, all of them prokaryotes. Boiling water does not preclude growth of some heterotrophic bacteria, but cooling to around 70°C is necessary for the first photosynthetic organisms, cyanobacteria and some anoxyphotobacteria to persist and then flourish in slightly cooler water. The first colonizers tend to be morphologically simple unicells but filaments develop at lower temperatures. It is not until below 48°C, however, that the first eukaryotes appear (Fig. 6.19) in the form of filamentous green algae and small fly larvae. Even then the diversity is low and it takes another 10–15° of cooling to produce a diversity comparable with averagely cool freshwaters. Extreme conditions, irrespective of

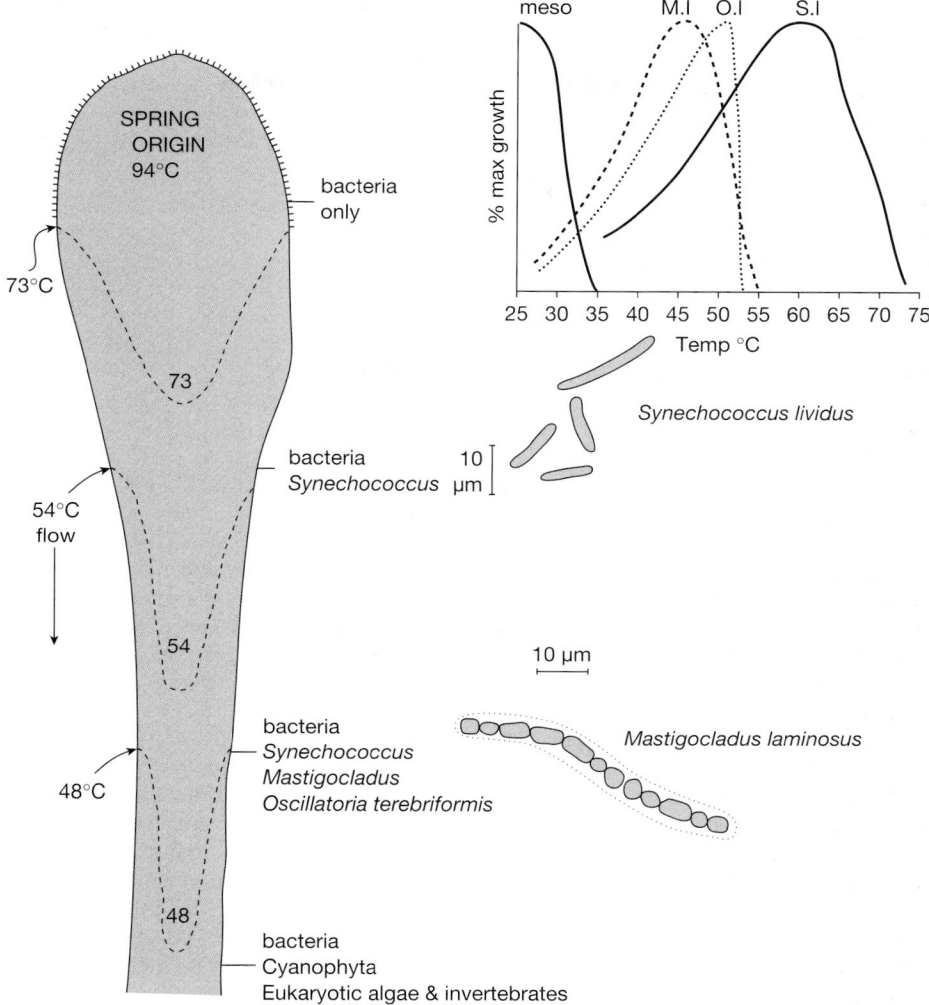

**Fig. 6.19** Some features of the ecology of hot alkaline springs in Yellowstone National Park, USA. A map of a spring shows how bacteria, coccoid cyanobacteria, filamentous cyanobacteria then eukaryotes successively colonize as the water cools from boiling point. Thermal tolerances for growth rate are shown in the graphs (meso, mesothermal eukaryotic community, M.l, *Mastigocladus laminosus*, Ot, *Oscillatoria terebriformis*, Sl, *Synechococcus lividus*.

location or age of the habitat can thus be associated with low diversity.

### 6.8.1 Caves

Caves are extreme in different ways and again have a very restricted, but very specialist biota. Caves form particularly in limestone regions where slightly acid rain water percolates and dissolves cracks and eventually large caverns deep underground. Sometimes they contain subterranean lakes and complex stream systems. The cave environment may be very steady and predictable but the lack of energy and the difficulties of operating in complete darkness seem to have restricted the diversity. This is not true, however, of the greatest

**Table 6.3** Characteristics of some cave habitats in the south-east of the USA (based on Poulson & White 1969)

| | pH | Ca (mg L$^{-1}$) | Temp (°C) | Number of species | Diversity (relative log units) | Biomass (kg ha$^{-1}$) | Substrate organic matter (%) |
|---|---|---|---|---|---|---|---|
| Entrance (terrestrial) | | | −10–30 | 100–300 | 1.5 | 1000 | 5–20 |
| Twilight zone (terrestrial) | | | 0–20 | 50 | 0.5 | 0.3 | 2–10 |
| Cave stream bank (terrestrial) | | | 7–15 | 5–11 | 1.1 | 0.02 | 0.5–5 |
| Cave stream, (aquatic) | 7.3 | 50 | 10 | 0–3 | 0.5 | 0.1 | 0.5–1 |
| Cave stream, (underground course of surface stream) | 7.5 | 37 | 11.8 | 8–20 | 0.4 | 0.05 | 2–6 |
| Drip pools | 7.9 | 64 | 15.8 | 0–2 | 0.2 | 0.001 | 0.1–0.5 |

and darkest ocean depths, so an element of disturbance and time must underlie the relative poverty of cave communities (Table 6.3). There is a twilight zone near the entrance, with trogloxenes such as bats and pack rats, a middle zone of variable temperature and complete darkness, also populated by bats and sometimes birds that roost in the darkness, then the deeper zone of complete darkness and steady temperature, containing the truly troglobitic fauna. It is not an entirely steady environment, however, for there may be strong air currents generated by temperature changes outside the system and variable flows of water from trickles to torrents after heavy rain outside. Energy for the freshwater cave community is provided by chemosynthetic bacteria and inwashed organic matter.

Cave animals tend to be small and readily distributed because of the wide interconnections of many cave systems, but limited in diversity. They move in stream waters and through runnels and cracks. Typically they may include a few species of amphipods and isopods, a salamander, a crayfish and a fish. The local geology to some extent determines the diversity. In the Appalachian mountains of the USA, the caves are under solid cap rock and prone to collapse and become isolated. There is an overall relatively higher species diversity, related species do not occur together and there are many rare species of limited distribution. In the interior plateaux of Kentucky and Tennessee, where the caves are less isolated, there is lower species density, frequent sympatry and wide distribution.

Cave animals tend to have lost some sense organs, particularly eyes, but have become highly developed in others, particularly chemical sensors. There are no predators, only detritus feeders and temperature and oxygen concentrations are very steady for the deep troglobites. Among one relatively well studied group of fish, the amblyopsids, there are no escape responses, a reduced regulation of metabolic rate when oxygen is experimentally reduced and no inherent light–dark rhythms. Crayfish, however, show annual rhythms reset by a subtle drop in temperature when spring rains bring in more food.

There is very high efficiency in food use in troglobyte fish, but slow swimming and low efficiency in finding food compared with surface species (Fig. 6.20). Food is very scarce. They are active throughout the 24 hours of a day, allowing them to search as much water as possible. They produce only a few large eggs and have large fry, traits seen among animals in other steady environments. But caves have generally low diversity – a function of food shortage and monotony and a short geological history.

## 6.9 A SUMMARY OF THE FRESHWATER BIOTA AND ITS PROBLEMS

Freshwater habitats thus illustrate that biodiversity and its distribution are not simple phenomena. What occurs is a reflection of past geological history on the one hand, accident and circumstance on the other. Size of habitat matters, partly through the greater complexities of a larger stage, partly because a large habitat is more likely to have survived the vicissitudes of changing climate. The high diversity of large tropical lakes is thus partly a function of latitude and long growing

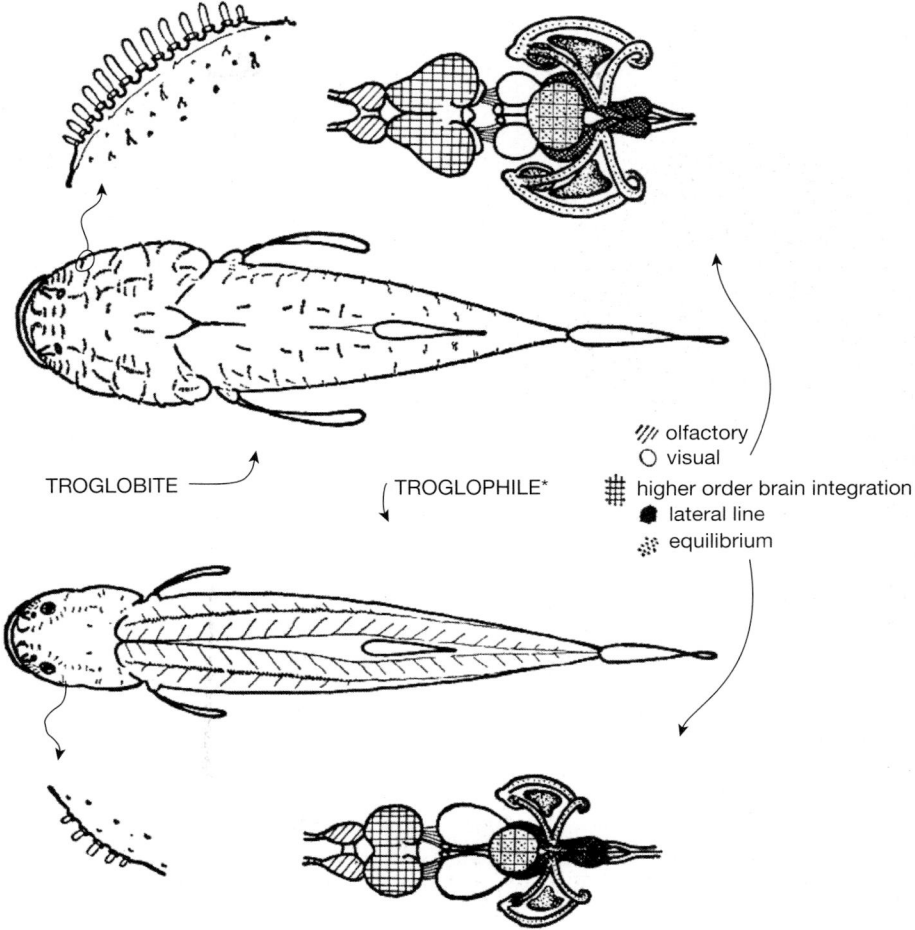

**Fig. 6.20** Contrasts in brain development between a deep cave fish, *Amblyopsis spelaea* (a troglobite), and a fish from the twilight zone at the cave mouth, the troglophile, *Chlorogaster agassizi*. The troglobite has many more touch sensors on the side of the head, greater brain development for integrated activity but much less for visual activity. It has much smaller eyes. (From Poulson & White 1969.)

season and to some extent a function of distance from the centres of polar glaciation. Extremes can reduce diversity, even in habitats of great fundamental antiquity because of high immediate disturbance. Hot springs must be the least secure of places. In the end, freshwaters undoubtedly do have fewer species than the Ocean, but they are not devoid and the diversity in relation to the size of the freshwater resource is large. A general summary is shown in Fig. 6.21. To survive on the freshwater stage means considerable flexibility, an ability to adjust the make up to the changing scene,

a good bladder or its equivalent and a willingness to live from a packed suitcase and move on when the theatre goes temporarily bust.

## FURTHER READING

Understanding freshwaters demands some knowledge of most environmental and biological sciences. Press et al. (2003) is an excellent text on geological processes and the evolution of the environment on Earth, whilst

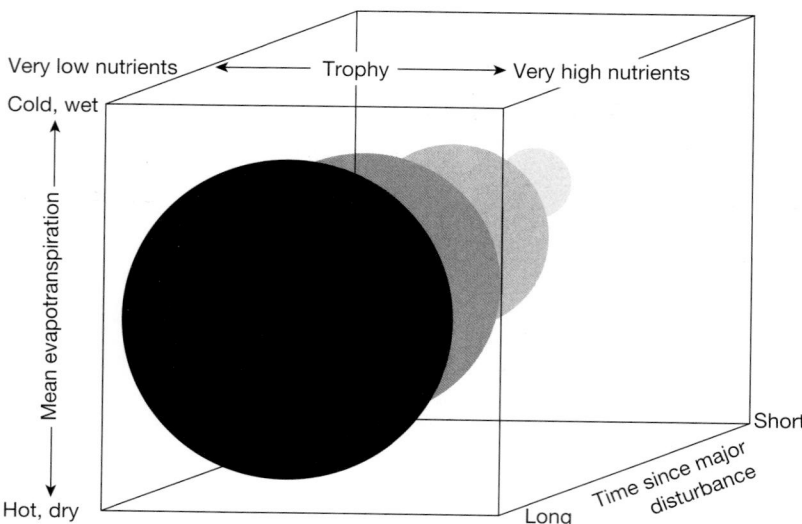

**Fig. 6.21** In freshwaters, diversity is greatest (heavy shading) where conditions are neither extremely cold, indeed frozen, nor so hot and dry that drought is frequent. It is low (light shading) where nutrients are exceptionally scarce and where they are extremely abundant for reasons of simple scarcity on the one hand and takeover by highly competitive species on the other. And it is greatest the longer the location has not suffered major disturbance through glaciation or other climatological or geological extremes. (From Moss et al. 2009.)

Margulis & Sagan (1987) deal more comprehensively with changes in the microorganisms. Two good books on biodiversity are Gaston & Spicer (2004) and Leveque & Mounolou (2003), whilst Fortey (2008) gives an attractive and interesting account of why taxonomy is important and how it is done. Beebee & Rowe (2007) introduce new molecular methods, yet to make much impact in freshwater science, but undoubtedly destined to become more important. Margulis & Schwartz (1998) give a very useful catalogue of phyla, whilst Hooper et al. (2005) review the links between biodiversity and ecosystem functioning. Fenchel et al. (1997) and Fenchel & Findlay (2004) present the idea that among microorganisms, things are less diverse than you might think.

Balian et al. (2008) introduces a series of papers that will tell you exactly (more or less!) how many species of animals have been recorded from freshwaters (125,530, of which 75,874 are insects), whilst Chambers et al. (2008) do the same for vascular plants (2614). No one has dared to try it yet for prokaryotes and protistans. Moss et al. (2009) review the likely effects of climate change on freshwater biodiversity. Schmidt-Nielsen (1997) is an admirably clear writer on all aspects of animal physiology including osmoregulation and respiration in aquatic habitats and Goldschmidt (1997) and Salzburger & Meyer (2004) review the rapidly changing field of evolutionary and speciation mechanisms in the fish of the African Great Lakes from less formal and formal points of view.

# Chapter 7

# HEADWATER STREAMS AND RIVERS

## 7.1 INTRODUCTION

It all starts as drips and trickles. Rain falls; moisture condenses from mists onto leaves and runs down trunks and stems; snow and ice melt. The water percolates into soils and saturates them. Eventually some emerges lower down the slopes as springs. Much of it runs off hard rocks, the squiggles of flow running together until something we might call a trickle forms. It might last only until a few hours after the rain stops. Its course may change the next time it flows for it may be born of the changing irregularities of clumps of grass as much as the greater solidities of the ground. Into these trickles will be washed debris and soil, worms and insects, leaves and twigs and at this stage there may be little that can be called a distinctive freshwater system. But eventually, the rivulets from bigger and bigger headwater areas merge, and there is some sort of permanence to the channel, though not necessarily to the flow of water in it. A stream system is born.

Its nature will depend on where it is located and just as examples were drawn from the polar, the cold temperate, the warm temperate and the tropical regions of the Earth in previous chapters, so this pattern and its subdivisions of endorheic and exorheic systems

*Ecology of Freshwaters: A View for the Twenty-first Century*, 4th edition. By Brian Moss. Published 2010 by Blackwell Publishing Ltd.

will be held to in those that describe the functioning of stream and other freshwater systems. There is an additional dimension too of time. But first I will attempt to reconstruct what these systems were like before the major human influences of the past century or so; then I will show what has changed. Eventually, at the end of the book, I will sketch likely futures.

## 7.2 GENERAL MODELS OF STREAM ECOSYSTEMS

To understand how streams work, there are first some basic principles for all ecological systems, then some general models for streams, then the details of how streams work in a particular place, either a climate regime or a specific location. Understanding at all these levels is needed now that ecosystems have been seriously damaged and need repair, but at the level of individual places the degree of detail is colossal. No wonder we attempt to generalize, as I shall have to do, to cope with the amount of information. Nonetheless, for many ecologists and everyone else it is the particular place, not the general model that generates the love and concern needed to make sure that it is conserved.

The basic principles are those of all ecosystem ecology, broadly laid down by Arthur Tansley and Robert Lindemann early in the 20th century and elaborated by Howard and Eugene Odum in its middle. An ecosystem (Fig. 7.1) is a recognizable combination of a

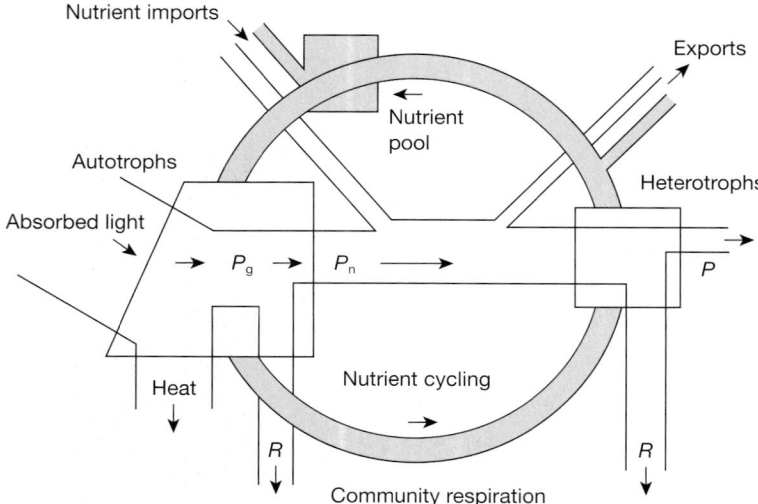

**Fig. 7.1** Basic structure and function of an ecosystem. Energy flows in from the Sun and is used in gross primary production ($P_g$) or lost as heat. Of the gross production, some is used for autotroph respiration, the rest is passed on to heterotrophs (direct grazers or decomposers, then predators). All heterotrophs are shown in one box with their production, $P$ and respiration, $R$. Nutrients may enter the system from elsewhere and may be exported from the system. Many are recycled within the system.

physical place and structure, a set of organisms (and their products such as organic detritus) that lives in this place and has been fitted through natural selection to survive, for the present, in it, and a set of processes by which these organisms manipulate energy and materials and interact with the place and each other. The processes involve the absorption of solar energy by photosynthesizers and the exploitation of this energy by food webs that include herbivores, detritivores and microbial consumers, and usually at least one level of predator. Operation of the food webs results in recycling of the 20 or so elements needed by living organisms (Chapter 4) and there may be some import of these from adjacent systems and some exports as material is blown or washed out. Energy may also be imported as organic matter from adjacent systems and similarly may be exported. Tansley talked of a nearly self-contained system, but, having worked only in the compartmented agricultural landscapes of the UK, probably had a view of containment that was tighter than our present concept.

The ultimate key features of all ecosystems are an efficiency of nutrient use (parsimony of nutrients in their available forms) because certain elements are scarce (Chapter 4), a characteristic structure, contributed by physical (bedrocks and rock debris, water flow and chemistry) and biological (intact food webs, detritus and debris, soil, water chemistry) features and a connectivity (in physical space and through imports and exports of organisms and materials) with adjacent

systems. Ultimately there is only one system that is self-contained, meaning that there are no material imports or exports, and that is the entire biosphere. And even that imports solar energy, so the self-containment, barring the alleged invasions of living particles from outer space, mostly by science fiction writers, is really the solar system.

A very general model of the upper parts of stream and river ecosystems (Fig. 7.2) includes the land area from which the water is derived (the river basin, catchment or watershed) with a recognizable ecotone, the riparian zone or bankside straddling the stream channel and the land. The stream has a physical structure and characteristics, which give it its basic identity. These will include a channel that the water is cutting and which will change direction (plan form) in response to gravity, irregularities in the bedrock and material such as sand, gravel, stones and boulders that the water has moved when the flow has been high and which are now temporarily at rest. The same will apply to the stream banks. They may seem fixed when seen in dry weather, but in reality they are very much changing.

Part of the physical structure is also the nature of the water flow, its amount, timing, turbulence and speed and these characteristics will be very variable from place to place. They will also be affected by a further characteristic of the physical structure provided by organic debris that will have washed in from the immediate riparian zone or, after large floods, from more distantly. This might mean wads of leaf litter,

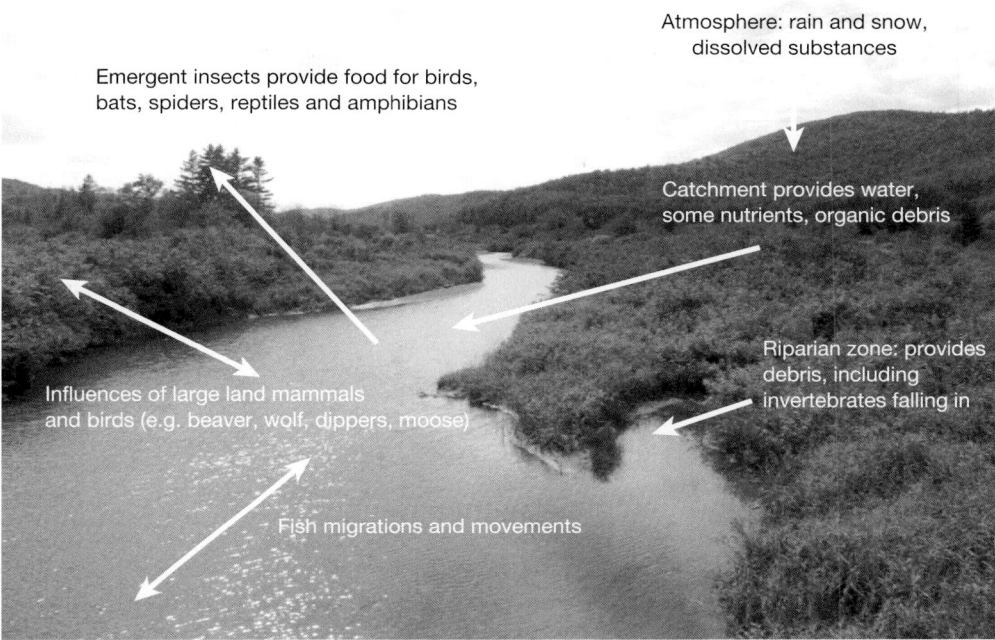

Atmosphere: rain and snow, dissolved substances

Emergent insects provide food for birds, bats, spiders, reptiles and amphibians

Catchment provides water, some nutrients, organic debris

Riparian zone: provides debris, including invertebrates falling in

Influences of large land mammals and birds (e.g. beaver, wolf, dippers, moose)

Fish migrations and movements

**Fig. 7.2**  Some features and processes within a headwater stream system.

branches and even huge tree trunks. In ecosystems such as forests the living plants will provide a great deal of the characteristic structure. This is sometimes true of freshwater systems, such as swamps or shallow lakes with beds of aquatic plants, but it is least true of the headwater stream system, where rocks and the washed-in terrestrial debris provide the structure. The growing plants in the stream have a minor structural role but will include films of microscopic algae on the rocks, and perhaps some mosses and liverworts and macroscopic red algae. In tropical systems some specialized flowering plants, the podostemonads, grow like blobs of chewing gum over the surfaces, poking up their flowering stems a little way into the current. Photosynthesizers are scarce for two reasons. First overhanging forest or woodland shades the site. Even in desert streams there is usually overhanging vegetation. And secondly, the nutrient retention mechanisms of the catchment vegetation will mean that inorganic nutrients, to support the growth of algae and plants in the stream, are always scarce.

The films of organisms on the rocks will not only include photosynthetic algae but also Protozoa and

bacteria that process dissolved organic matter entering from the catchment soils. Connections of this kind are particularly important in streams and we distinguish allochthonous production (energy sources produced outside the immediate system) from autochthonous production (produced by photosynthesis within it). Leaf litter is a particularly important allochthonous source in many streams. Feeding on the primary production, be it allochthonous or autochthonous, will be several guilds of leaf-shredding, film-scraping, deposit-feeding and filter-feeding invertebrates and living on these will be both invertebrate and vertebrate predators.

Connectivity is manifest. Many of the invertebrates will be aquatic only as juveniles and will have adult stages that require a suitable riparian or more distant terrestrial habitat. In terms of maintenance of the system characteristics, some of the most important fish are migratory, even taking in the ocean as part of their life span, and mammals such as otters, bears, and wolves are increasingly implicated in the functioning of pristine streams. All of these have strong terrestrial connections. A predominant former view of the scientific community was that the physical habitat mostly determined the nature and operation of the biological community (bottom up control). That view is probably truer of headwater streams where the force of moving water is so prominent, than of other systems, but even for such streams it is now realized that top-down effects, where organisms operating through the food webs create important parts of the structure and functioning, are substantial.

## 7.3  A BASIC LESSON IN STREAM FLOW

On average about 100 cm of rain and snow fall on the Earth's surface every year and after evaporation and transpiration on land about 20 cm is left to run off into the streams, though there is huge variation from place to place. The amount that enters the streams thus depends not only on the local precipitation as rain or snow but also on what determines local evapo-transpiration, for example the temperature regime and vegetation. Local soils and geology are also involved. They affect the balance between run-off (the flood flow) from the ground surface and storage in the soil or deeper layers of ground water and later percolation to the stream (the base flow). The balance between run-off and percolation is affected by the amount, duration and intensity of each rainstorm, the geographic distribution of the rain within a catchment, the insolation, tempera-ture and humidity, the wind, the nature of the tran-spiring vegetation, the layering and compaction of the soil, its existing water content and structure (whether it has root and worm holes and what size the particles of soil are and whether there is a thick or thin litter layer at the surface), the aspect and altitude of the slope down which the stream is flowing, the permeability of the underlying rock and even the shape of the catchment. As in the value of houses, location is the key thing and the thickness of the many hydrology textbooks reflects a desire to quantify a very complex and very chaotic situation. The emphasis on hydrological measurement is because freshwater is scarce and an important neces-sity for drinking water supply and agriculture.

Many details of hydrology are simply part of the background 'noise' of variation to which stream organisms have adapted. There are nonetheless certain characteristics of moving water of particular import-ance to them. These involve the amount and nature of the flow and the way that water creates structures within the channel that form the basic habitats for organisms. A further dimension is that much of the flow in the channel may be under the stream bed rather than above its surface, except where the channel is based on solid bedrock. Most channels are not such simple impermeable troughs, like a rain water gutter on a house, but gutters filled with rock debris and sediment such that there is a visible flow above the sur-face of the debris but also a flow through the debris. This is known as the hyporheic flow and it may exist even if there is no visible flow at the surface and may provide habitat for many small animals such as small crustaceans, oligochaetes, Protozoa and nematodes down as far as a metre below the apparent stream bed.

## 7.4  FLOW AND DISCHARGE

Water flow is never stable except during a prolonged dry period. During such a period, the flow, if any, will be the base flow maintained by what runs out of the soils and the ground water, and this will often decrease as a dry period is prolonged. In rainy periods, the flow will change by the hour. The discharge, which is the volume flowing down the channel per unit time, can be measured as the product of flow rate (current velocity) and cross-sectional area of the channel. Flow rate varies with depth within the channel and proximity to the bottom and edges where friction delays the flow, so a mean flow has to be determined using a flow meter from measurements at several locations across the profile of the stream. At any point, the mean flow is found at around 60% of the depth below the surface. Sometimes streams are continuously gauged, in which case a weir, with a V-shaped overflow, is installed and a float used to record on a chart the depth of water behind the weir. Depth can be related to discharge by empirically determined graphs and a continuous record can be obtained. This is important because occasional 'spot' measurements can be very misleading. Flow changes very rapidly during and after rainstorms and as snow melts in the catchment in spring.

The change in flow over time is described by a hydro-graph (Fig. 7.3). In a rainstorm, discharge at first increases rapidly, often to many times the base flow. It then steadily falls back to the base flow unless there is another bout of rainfall. During the storm, the extra water comes as surface run-off or as interflow, which is water that has entered the soil at a level above that of the ground-water table and flows through the soil a little before it enters the stream. The significance of this is that it picks up more ions and organic compounds

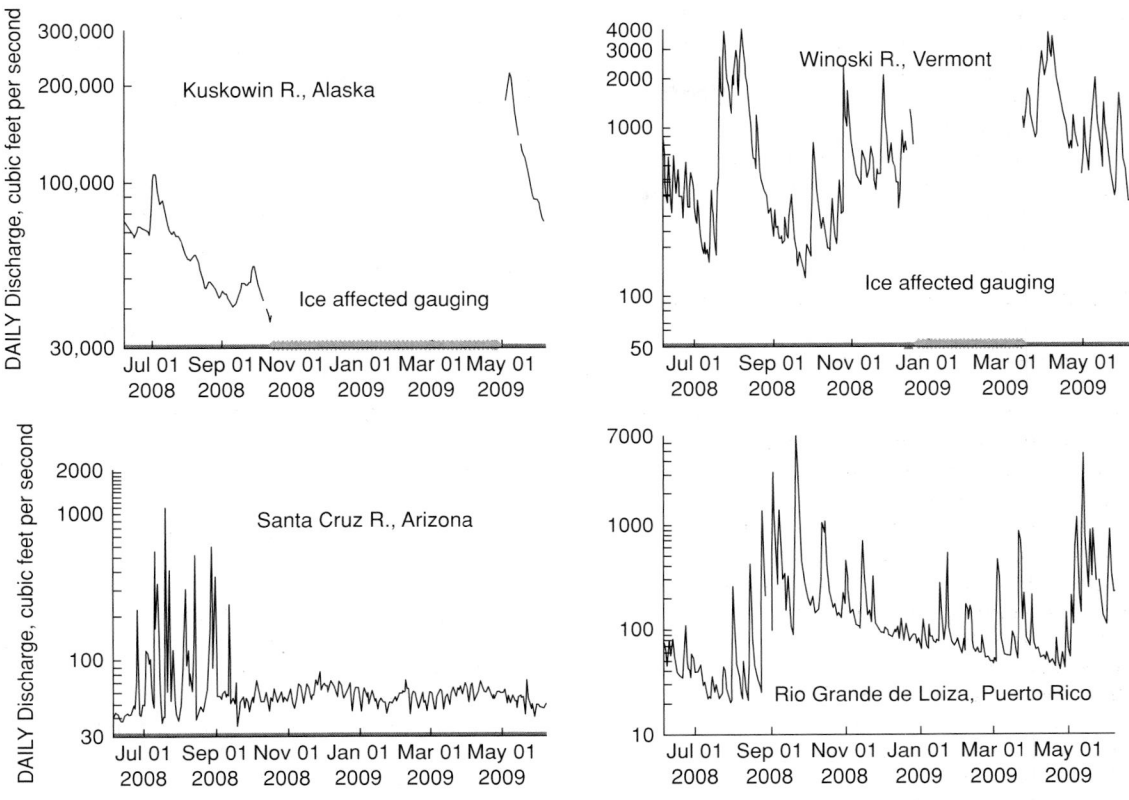

**Fig. 7.3** Typical hydrographs over a year (July 2008 to June 2009) based on daily measurements of stream discharge for polar (upper left), cold temperate (upper right), warm temperate (lower left) and tropical (lower right) rivers in the USA. The effects of rainstorms are seen as short-term peaks, followed by a rapid reduction back to the base flow. Discharge is shown in cubic feet per second. To convert to $m^3\,s^{-1}$, multiply by 0.0283. (Data from the United States Geological Survey.)

from the soil than can the surface run-off. Chemistry as well as discharge varies continuously in small streams. The pattern of successive storm hydrographs is also of interest. A series of sharp peaks indicates a flashy stream where there will be little opportunity for storage in the soil and ground water and hence a reduced base flow and a possibility of drying up in dry periods. A broader hydrograph keeps levels high for longer and more water will infiltrate the soil and base flows will be enhanced.

## 7.5 LAMINAR AND TURBULENT FLOW

The nature of the flow will also change with time. At base flows it is most likely to have a large laminar (smooth) component, but as discharge increases it will become more turbulent. This is important because organisms are likely to be torn away from the substratum more easily during turbulent flow when shear stress, a measure of tearing forces, increases. In laminar flow, layers of water slide gently past one another with movement being small close to the bottom or the surfaces of smooth rock. The shear stress in laminar flow is given by the viscosity multiplied by the rate of change in velocity from one layer to the next. The lowest velocity is next to the bed, the greatest just below the surface. Such flows are rare and require even channels as well as low discharges.

Turbulent flow sets in above a critical velocity and is promoted by 'rough' beds with projecting boulders and is characterized by chaotic movements, swirls and eddies. The threshold for turbulent flow to set in is indicated by the Reynolds number (*Re*) (Chapter 2), which is given by the density of the water multiplied by the velocity and the hydraulic radius of the channel (cross-sectional area divided by the wetted perimeter and approximating to the mean depth) divided by the viscosity. Turbulence sets in in bigger, faster streams. You can demonstrate this with a domestic tap. Turn it on lightly and smooth laminar flow will ensue. Open it up more and the flow soon becomes turbulent.

Turbulent flows have much greater shear stress and come in two kinds: streaming, and at the higher velocities, such as in rapids, shooting. There is again a formula for this, called the Froude number, *F*. If velocity times depth divided by the square root of the acceleration due to gravity is <1, the stream is relatively tranquil with streaming turbulence. But if *F* > 1 it will be shooting and very erosive.

The shearing force in turbulent flow (*T*) is given by (viscosity + eddy viscosity) multiplied by the change in velocity with depth. Eddy viscosity is a measure of the intensity of mixing. The greater the mixing, the greater is the value of *Re*. In turbulent flow, the maximum mixing is close to the bed and the maximum velocity about 0.05 to 0.25 down the depth profile, depending on channel shape, roughness and sinuosity (bendiness). On a bend the position of maximum velocity moves towards the outer bank, where erosion is then greatest. All in all, the more and faster the flow, the greater the shear stress, the more raging the river. Mathematics is really only a statement of common sense.

## 7.6 PARTICLES CARRIED

What the water carries in suspended materials, and may eventually deposit, also matters to living organisms, for deposits are colonizable habitats, and suspended material reduces turbulence by increasing the viscosity but also absorbs light otherwise usable for photosynthesis. Some particles are rolled along the bed in the laminar flow layers but most of the load is carried in turbulent water. A critical velocity is first needed to erode a particle from the bed and this can be relatively high because small, often clay, particles (0.001–0.1 mm) tend to stick together, then falls for the easily eroded sands before steadily rising for bigger particles such as gravels, pebbles and boulders. The largest particle size a stream can move is called its competence and this will vary with the state of the flow. If this falls below the

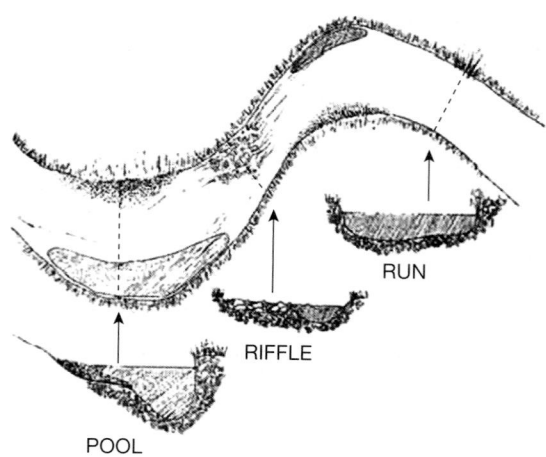

**Fig. 7.4** Riffles, pools and runs occur in a quasi-orderly way in headwater rivers, providing very different habitats. Riffles are shallow with very turbulent water and are formed where stones and cobbles, moving downstream, tend to bunch on the insides of bends. Pools form where erosion deepens the water to the outsides of bends, and runs are fast moving water in smoother straighter stretches.

critical velocity, the particle will be deposited, only to be moved on again as flow increases and the velocity rises. Thus a stream will have temporary beds of sand and gravel and strewn boulders, the legacies of the previous high flow, which may persist for long periods.

The channel will rarely be straight and will develop many physical features (Fig. 7.4). Irregularities in the local topography will deflect it, but it will also tend to meander as a way of increasing its capacity (its volume) to cope with its higher flows. It will tend to erode the outsides of bends, giving vertical banks and deepened pools, and deposit material on the shallower inner sides leaving a gently shelving shoreline. It will also develop a sequence of shallower riffles where gravel and sand accumulate in piles that steadily move down river as material at the tail end shallows the water and increases the flow rate, so moving the material on, and material temporarily accumulates at the upper end as the flow is blocked by the pile. Flow will be slower through the deeper pools, faster over the riffles. In drier periods the channel may break up into braids as islands of deposited material, sometimes stabilized by vegetation, split the flow. Again in small streams and modest rivers, these will be temporary.

## 7.7 THE RESPONSE OF STREAM ORGANISMS TO SHEAR STRESS

It is shear stress that really matters to the organisms of streams. They can stay in place in torrential water so long as they can find places with minimal shear stress. Large animals such as big fish will cope well with the problems of flow and turbulence by their streamlining. For small ones the problem is to avoid the worst excesses by clinging onto rocks, living in the laminar boundary layers, or being able, often helped by streamlined form, to scuttle quickly to areas of reduced turbulence. What matters is not the overall flow but the conditions on the surface or under rocks or in the interstitial water of gravels and sands where the animal actually lives. A raging torrent, provided it has a reasonably irregular bottom, will thus have plenty of animals, small adherent algae and biofilms on its rock surfaces.

Among these organisms, there are the resisters and the avoiders (Fig. 7.5). The avoiders may use size and movement to remain in a reach, and include large

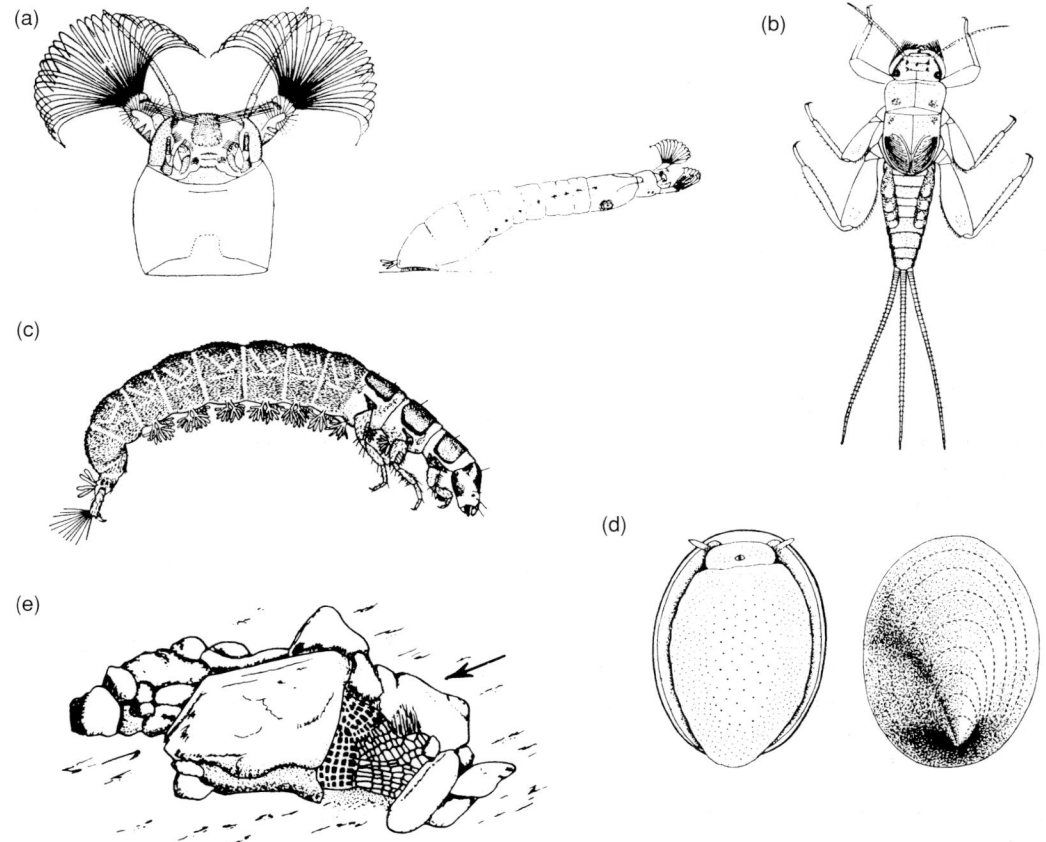

**Fig. 7.5** Different strategies for resisting shear stress in freshwater invertebrates include: the use of silk pads in which to hook onto surfaces (*Simulium*, a); a flattened body for staying within laminar boundary layers (*Trichorythus*, b); protection behind piles of small stones (*Hydropsyche*, c, e); and suckers (*Ancylus fluviatilis*, d). These animals also represent various feeding guilds, including scrapers of rock and other surfaces, such as the freshwater limpet, *Ancylus*. Others are collectors of fine particles from the water flow: the blackfly larva, *Simulium*, which collects particles on its head fans, the African mayfly nymph, *Trichorythus*, which filters with brushes on its mouth parts, and the caddis fly larva, *Hydropsyche*, which spins a net across the entrance to a chamber of small stones which it has constructed (e). (Based on Hynes 1979 and Fryer 1991.)

crabs and shrimps in warmer waters, crayfish in cooler ones and may be several centimetres long with fast scuttling movement. Smaller crustaceans such as the amphipod *Gammarus* also move rapidly, whilst even smaller animals such as oligochaetes and fly larvae may burrow in deposits of the hyporheic zone. Some are flattened and live under rocks or in the thin boundary layer of laminar flow that coats stones and bed rock and are simply thinner than the boundary layer. All of the microrganisms are like this.

The categories are not entirely separate for some of the avoiders, such as the nymphs of mayflies, may also be streamlined resisters, often with one, two or three tails that realign the animal head on to the current if it is displaced sideways. It is like keeping the bow of a rowing boat into the waves, for if it goes side-on it may capsize. Other resisters acquire ballast in the form of cases of sand grains or gravel that they glue together and glue also onto the rocks, or, like leeches, have suckers that likewise attach them.

The arch-resister is perhaps the larva of the blackfly, *Simulium* spp (Fig. 7.5). It spins a pad of silk that it glues to the rocks and to which it attaches by small hooks at the base of its abdomen; if it does get displaced it also has a 'climbing rope' of silk that extends to the pad on the rock from its head and with which it can haul itself back into place. If, as often happens to stream animals, all fails and it is swept into the flow, a phenomenon called accidental drift, it can also move, with a looping movement of its abdomen, from wherever it eventually lands to a suitable place on which to spin its pad and resume filtering the water for fine particulate food with fans on its head.

Like many stream insects it hatches out to an aerial adult responsible for reproduction and egg laying to produce the next generation of larvae. Its food source is then the blood of mammals, which it gets by causing a painful bite in the skin. In the tropics it also carries the nematode worm that causes river blindness (onchocerciasis). The contrast between adult and larva once caused me to reflect on the lessons it might hold for Heads of University Departments and to write a poem to open a small conference of people who research these animals, mostly because of their role as disease vectors.

> The blackfly is a nasty beast,
> which bites you where you 'xpect it least.
> In shorts, by bubbling streams and rills,
> Upon your tender bum it mills.

> A pity that it's reprehensible,
> when its young is quite so sensible,
> providing morals plain to see,
> for any watchful HOD.

> The larva's head fans catch each mote,
> like hints of gossip you should note.
> And ultimately should enquire
> if they're just smoke or really fire.

> It hangs quite tightly on with wads
> of silk in which its hooks it prods.
> Thus surviving currents fleeting
> Not unlike each term's staff meeting

> And when it has to, loops its girth
> to more congenial bits of Earth,
> where its head fans won't be hit
> by flying lumps of words unfit.

> However, there's a bad prognosis
> if you achieve metamorphosis,
> and then at times of grating stress
> you get yourself into a mess.

> No matter what your senior state,
> the canvas straitjacket's your fate,
> if, feeling in the darkest dumps,
> you start to bite your colleagues' rumps!

## 7.8 COMMUNITY COMPOSITION IN STREAMS

Erosive streams and rivers are very disturbed systems. High flood flows will render chaos to any structure that has been built up. They will move sand and gravels, even large boulders and tree trunks. Between high flows, a degree of biological structure will be established and there will be a semblance of a stable community. But, in its details it will be an artefact of the moment. There has been much discussion of what determines biological communities and many attempts to identify recognizable repeatable lists of species for particular places. Sometimes, as in the plant communities of terrestrial habitats such as forests, this can be done, but even then there is always an individuality to particular sites. In streams, communities are predictable to some extent but the individuality is extreme because of the frequent disturbance. All is not totally random, however. The community will be made up of organisms adapted to stream conditions so it will still show some order, if only at the family rather than species level.

First there are four distinctive groups generally present for which there is reasonable information: the algae on stones (the epilithon), the plants, the macroinvertebrates and the fish. This is not to say that other groups are absent or unimportant. The bacteria and fungi, the microinvertebrates, such as Protozoa, nematodes and small Crustacea, and the amphibians and reptiles may be very significant, but we know less about how they fit in.

Which members of these groups are actually present will depend first on which have reached the site. Especially in cold regions, distributions are still being established through migration, as the last ice of the previous glaciation continues to retreat, and we do not know how rapidly most species can migrate. There seems to be enormous variation in the dispersal abilities of different species, whether they move by air or by water. Genetic studies using DNA markers in one species, the caddis fly, *Plectrocnemia conspersa* (see Chapter 6), showed a great similarity in populations with radii of about 20 km and increasing variation beyond that. This suggests easy dispersal over 20 km or so, a distance probably adequate to cope with all but the most extreme disturbances to an individual stream, but other studies show much more variation among close-by populations, indicating much lower dispersive ability.

Barriers such as waterfalls may prevent larger animals, including crabs and shrimps and fish from moving further upstream. And among those reaching a particular site, some will be unable to reproduce in the particular conditions prevailing. Some macroinvertebrate groups for example require high oxygen concentrations found in turbulent flows; others only survive in organic deposits laid down in quieter streams. Some that can survive the conditions may be made locally extinct by an extreme flood or a drought and may take time to recolonize, if they ever do. Then, within the group of persistent species, available structure and its food resources and the effects of predation will determine the balance of numbers of each. Vertebrate predation in particular can markedly alter the community of macroinvertebrates through size-selective predation (preferentially taking the bigger or smaller). Basically the predator will take the largest prey animal that it can ingest as this represents the most efficient investment of energy in catching the prey. Large invertebrates will be rapidly removed and smaller ones may then flourish in the absence of competition from the larger. Invertebrate predators tend

to operate in the opposite way, being unable to handle prey that is nearly as large or larger than themselves and so concentrating on small animals that they can manoeuvre into their mouths.

### 7.8.1 Algal and plant communities

Where there is sufficient light, a film of algae will grow over the stones in a stream as part of a 'biofilm' that also includes bacteria, fungi, Protozoa and dead organic matter (Fig. 7.6). The latter often comes from the pads of mucilage that algae produce to attach themselves to the stones. The bacteria and fungi will colonize this material and also will take up organic matter from the water and the protozoa will feed on all of these microorganisms. Growth will be least in winter but a biofilm may persist year around giving a slimy feel to the stones. Smaller stones and gravel will not be colonized for they are so frequently moved by the current that the film will be worn away as fast as it can form. Diatoms (Bacillariophyceae) tend to predominate in spring. They need silicate for their cell walls and they may be strongly adpressed to the rocks and stones on mucilage pads (e.g. *Cocconeis*), or held by a pad at one end of a long cell (*Cymbella*), or held on simple or branched stalks (*Gomphonema*). Green algae (Chlorophyta) and filamentous Cyanobacteria are also common, particularly in summer, when the invertebrate grazers have browsed off the diatoms, which are easily digestible, despite the silicate walls, for the walls are highly perforated. Larger filamentous algae may grow in quieter waters and sometimes, long skeins of filamentous diatoms may be found. In general these are abundant only when the stream has been polluted by nutrients, however, though in pristine streams, moderately large red algae (Rhodophyta) such as *Lemanea* may form bluish-grey tufts and the flattened thalli of *Hildenbrandia* may coat the rocks with a maroon colour.

Bryophytes (mosses and liverworts) are the most common plants in pristine erosive streams, together with the podostemonads in the tropics. The latter are highly specialized flowering plants with flattened photosynthetic stems and tiny leaves or none at all. Although mosses are widespread and their communities quite diverse, they have received little attention. Large flowering plants generally do not survive abundantly in erosive streams, simply because the deposits that they need for rooting are inevitably scarce. There may, however, be clumps of water buttercups

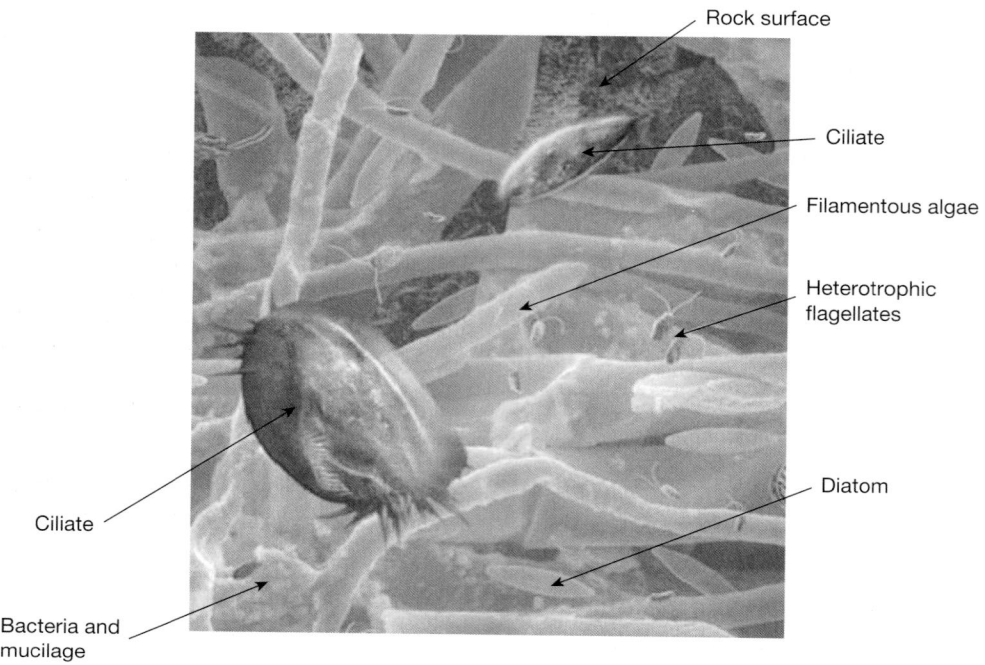

Rock surface

Ciliate

Filamentous algae

Heterotrophic
flagellates

Diatom

Ciliate

Bacteria and
mucilage

**Fig. 7.6** Biofilms are complex communities on a microscopic scale and normally coat all surfaces in freshwaters, including rocks in streams. (From a colour poster designed by Andrew Dopheide and Gillian Lewis, University of Auckland.)

(*Ranunculus*) and other genera. Where the stream begins its transition to a meandering floodplain system and widens, more deposits will persist and dense beds of water crowfoot, water cress and other plants will be found, themselves promoting the accumulation of silt and providing a highly structured complex habitat for invertebrates. These communities are discussed in Chapter 9.

### 7.8.2 Macroinvertebrates

Macroinvertebrates have been the darlings of stream ecologists for decades and are the best known of the stream biota. A number of groups consistently occur in lists of species from almost any erosive stream. Prime will be the stoneflies (Plecoptera), mayflies (Ephemeroptera) and caddis flies (Trichoptera). These three groups include species that scrape the biofilms from stones, shred leaf detritus, filter fine particles from the water or are predators. Limpets and gastropods also scrape stones, and are abundant in the more calcium-rich

waters. A major insect group whose various members will feed on biofilms on stones is the Diptera (two-winged flies), whose larvae are adept at processing organic matter and which includes the very diverse chironomids and, a filter feeder, the blackfly larvae. Other insects include alder flies (Sialidae) and damsel and dragon flies (Odonata) whose larvae or nymphs are predators. Crustacea (shrimps, crabs, crayfish and isopods) may be abundant, shredding leaf detritus and feeding on deposits. Oligochaetes will usually be found where organic detritus accumulates on the bottom. The surface film may bear, in quiet pools at low flows, a variety of bugs (Hemiptera), including the water skaters, and many beetle species will be present, usually as predators either as larvae or adults. Leeches are common, feeding on invertebrates, or sometimes parasitic through blood-sucking on fish and other vertebrates, whilst predatory water mites (Hydracarina) and predatory flatworms (triclads) will frequently be found in tangles of detritus.

Research papers will frequently include lists of families or species. Often, perhaps almost always, these will be incomplete as some animals are difficult to identify and may require hatching out to adults to determine their name finally. About 1000 invertebrates have so far been recorded from one small stream, the Breitenbach stream in Germany. Sampling of streams is usually done by agitating the bottom by foot or hand and catching the disturbed animals in a net held downstream. Because of the extreme patchiness in such a shifting habitat, many samples will have to be taken and sorting them takes time so that they have to be preserved in alcohol. This precludes any hatching out of adults. Some groups are quite difficult and need specialists who are becoming increasingly scarce as commercially driven fashions in the training of biologists favour cell- and gene-based subjects at the expense of whole organisms and ecosystems.

For example, water mites are typically lumped together collectively as Hydracarina but if a specialist is available to look at the sample a great richness may be revealed. Table 7.1 shows a list from Ford Wood Beck in the English Lake District where this was the case. In other instances the fauna may be very poorly known and sampled under expedition conditions where only a single sample was possible, rather than monthly or more frequent sampling that will reveal seasonal occurrences of particular animals. Table 7.2 shows a list from New Guinea streams where only insect families were found. Almost certainly other groups would have been detected by more samples. What is often noticeable though, is that broadly the same groups of invertebrates figure in many lists. Compare the lists from Ford Wood Beck (Table 7.1) and a stream in Tanzania (Table 7.3) for example. There are differences: there are no crabs in the UK, but many other groups are present in common, though of course the particular species will differ almost completely.

Thus there is a widespread pool of families and groups that might be expected in streams wherever

**Table 7.1** Macroinvertebrate community of Ford Wood Beck, English Lake District. (From Macan 1963.)

| Phylum | Order | Number of species | Most abundant species | Total number per $m^2$ |
|---|---|---|---|---|
| Platyhelminthes (flatworms) | Tricladida (flatworms) | 1 | *Polycelis felina* | 48 |
| Mollusca (snails) | Pulmonata (snails) | 1 | *Ancylus fluviatilis* | 42 |
| Crustacea (crustaceans) | Amphipoda (freshwater shrimps) | 1 | *Gammarus pulex* | 1432 |
| Arachnida (water mites) | Hydrachnella (water mites) | 23 | | Numerous |
| Insecta | Ephemeroptera | 9 | *Baetis rhodani* | 1811 |
| | Plecoptera (stoneflies) | 14 | *Nemoura cambrica* | 441 |
| | Hemiptera (bugs) | 1 | *Velia caprae* | Few |
| | Coleoptera (beetles) | 4 | | 17 |
| | Neuroptera (lacewing flies) | | *Sialis fuliginosa* | Few |
| | Trichoptera | 18 | *Agapetus fuscipes* | 304 |
| | Diptera-Tipulidae (craneflies) | 3 | | |
| | Diptera-Muscidae (two-winged flies) | 1 | | |
| | Diptera-Simuliidae (blackflies) | 4 | *Simulium* spp | 40 |
| | Diptera-Chironomidae (gnats) | 6 | *Orthocladius semivirens* | Many |
| Total | | 86 | | >>4135 |

**Table 7.2** Macroinvertebrate communities in streams in Papua New Guinea. Values are means from six streams in the New Guinea highlands and data were obtained under expedition conditions and are likely to be underestimates of the total diversity. (From Dudgeon 1994.)

| Phylum | Common name | Order (number of families) | Number m$^{-2}$ |
|---|---|---|---|
| Insecta | Mayflies | Ephemeroptera (4) | 10,564 |
| | Bugs | Hemiptera (1) | 158 |
| | Two-winged flies | Diptera (6) | 6195 |
| | Beetles | Coleoptera (3) | 2140 |
| | Caddis flies | Trichoptera (3) | 2594 |
| | Dragonflies and damselflies | Odonata (2) | 364 |
| Totals | | Mean number of species 20.4 | 19,848 |

they are sampled, but the balance of groups and species will vary greatly. The physical habitat, the balance of quiet water where silt and sand can accumulate, and fast erosive water, will determine the relative proportions of deposit feeders such as oligochaetes and many chironomids and groups that scrape biofilms from stones, like many of the nymphs of mayflies and caddis flies. Higher ionic content of the water will allow more crustaceans and snails to persist (Chapter 3) and in an open grassy or tundra landscape, with less overhanging vegetation, there will be more algae, a higher autotrophic productivity and more grazers than in a forested stream. A lake upstream of the sampling site will provide much fine particulate matter because its plankton is washed downstream and this will favour filter feeders such as *Simulium* and caseless caddis larvae. Table 7.4 gives data from three Icelandic streams that illustrate these points. Vestari Jökulsà drains a bare rocky landscape close to a glacier, has few species, mostly grazing a sparse biofilm on the rocks. Svartà drains a large area of tundra from which detritus washes into the river and has a richer fauna, also with more varied grazer species but also with some deposit feeders, two species of fish and a duck; and Laxà lies below a large lake. It is the richest in both species and production, as measured by its average catch of Atlantic salmon.

Fish and invertebrate predators may also structure the community by selective feeding. Streams in Ohio had a predatory fish, bass, *Micropterus salmoides* and an algal grazing fish, a minnow, *Campostoma anomalum*, on which the bass fed. In pools within the streams, high bass numbers were generally accompanied by low minnow numbers and vice versa. A pool was fished out

and a fish-proof fence constructed along the centre line. Minnows were added and the crop of filamentous algae declined significantly over the next few weeks. In a pool with minnows, three bass were added and this changed the behaviour of the minnows, which moved from the deeper parts of the pool to the shallows and were gradually eaten. As a result algal crops increased greatly (Fig. 7.7).

More complex experiments in Swedish streams have involved both leeches (*Erpobdella octoculata*) and trout (*Salmo trutta*). Enclosures were established with netting over a cobbled bottom; a control (no predators), and treatments with leech addition (26.7 m$^{-2}$), trout addition 0.9 m$^{-2}$) and addition of both predators were used. Trout avidly ate pond shrimps (*Gammarus*) and as these dominated the invertebrate community, total invertebrates were reduced in treatments with trout. Leeches did not touch *Gammarus*, but, as also did trout, reduced numbers of *Asellus*, a crustacean, and mayflies. Trout selected large prey, leeches small and since most prey were algal grazers, the amount of algal biofilm increased.

Behaviour can also be influenced by the presence of predators. Drift is a common phenomenon in streams, by which organisms are swept up in the current and washed downstream, during which time they are more vulnerable to predators. Drift may be accidental or a deliberate activity, however, and used for dispersal. It often takes place at night when fish, which generally need to see their prey, are more hampered. In experiments in artificial streams in New Zealand, a mayfly, *Deleatidium* continued to drift at night in the presence or absence of a day-feeding fish, brown trout, or a

**Table 7.3** Composition of animal communities in two subhabitats of an upland East African stream near Amani, Tanzania. Values are numbers m$^{-2}$, with SD (n = 9 or 10) in parentheses. Feeding guilds are P, predators, Sc, scrapers, Sh, shredders, D, deposit feeders, and C, filter collectors. Note that the standard deviations are large in relation to the means. This is typical for stream communities, where the animals are very heterogeneously (patchily) distributed. (From Abdallah et al. 2004.)

| Group | Common name | Family | Guild | Riffles | Pools |
|---|---|---|---|---|---|
| Platyhelminthes | Flatworms | Planariae | P | — | — |
| Annelida | Oligochaetes | Lumbriculidae | D | — | — |
| | | Tubificidae | D | — | 2 (6) |
| Gastropoda | Snails | Planorbidae | Sc | — | — |
| Crustacea | Crabs | Brachyura | Sh/P | 6.4 (2.4) | 1.6 (5.0) |
| Acarina | Water mites | Hydracarina | P | 114 (107) | 5.7 (4.9) |
| Arachnidae | Spiders | Arachnida | P | — | — |
| Anisoptera | Damselflies | Cordulidae | P | — | 3.8 (12) |
| | | Gomphidae | P | 3.2 (0.8) | 3.8 (8.0) |
| Zygoptera | Dragonflies | Chlorolestidae | P | — | 2.0 (2.00) |
| | | Lestidae | P | — | — |
| | | Platycnemidae | P | — | — |
| | | Calypterygidae | P | — | — |
| Hemiptera | Bugs | Corixidae | P | 150 (146) | 506 (636) |
| | | Veliidae | P | — | 2.0 (6.0) |
| | | Hydrometridae | P | — | 10.8 (14.6) |
| | | Gerridae | P | — | — |
| Diptera | Two-winged flies | Ceratopogonidae | D | 1.6 (6.0) | 3.8 (12.0) |
| | | Chironomidae | D | 78 (78) | 47 (30) |
| | | Dolichopodidae | P | 1.6 (6.0) | — |
| | | Simuliidae | C | — | — |
| | | Anthericidae | P | 9.6 (17.2) | — |
| | | Tipulidae | Sh | — | — |
| | | Tabanidae | P | — | — |
| Trichoptera | Caddis flies | Ecnomidae | C/P | — | 3.8 (3.8) |
| | | Hydropsychidae | C/P | 43 (86) | 3.8 (3.8) |
| | | Polycentropidae | P | 1.6 (6.0) | — |
| | | Leptoceridae | ? | — | — |
| | | Sericosomatidae | Sc | — | — |
| Ephemeroptera | Mayflies | Baetidae | Sc | 14 (35) | 25 (34) |
| | | Caenidae | D | 1.6 (6.0) | 39 (173) |
| | | Heptageniidae | Sc | — | 15 (48) |
| | | Trichohythridae | D/C | 1.6 (6.0) | 7.6 (18.4) |
| | | Oligonuridae | C | — | 3.8 (12) |
| | | Leptophlebiidae | Sc | 75 (120) | — |
| | | Ephemeridae | D | — | — |
| Coleoptera | Beetles | Gyrinidae | P | — | 1.9 (2.1) |
| | | Elmidae | Sc | 11.2 (18.4) | — |
| | | Dytiscidae | P | — | — |
| | | Hydrophilidae | Sc/P | — | — |
| | | Noteridae | Sc | 12.8 (36) | — |
| Amphibia | Frogs | Ranidae | Sc | 3.2 (12) | 24 (39) |
| Osteichthes | Fish | Siluridae | P | 1.6 (6.0) | |
| Total | | | | 534 (404) | 712 (676) |

**Table 7.4** Animal communities (number of species in each group) of three Icelandic rivers draining, respectively, a bare glacial area, an area of tundra and below a large lake. Indications of total community size and of fish production are also given. Production increases through the sequence. (From Gislason et al. 1998.)

| | Vestari Jökulsà (bare glacial) | Svartà (tundra) | Laxà (below lake) |
|---|---|---|---|
| Coelenterata | | | 1 |
| Bryozoa | | | 1 |
| Nematoda | | 1 | 1 |
| Hirudinea | | | 2 |
| Oligochaeta | | 1 | 1 |
| Gastropoda | | | 1 |
| Bivalvia | | | 1 |
| Hydracarina | | 1 | 1 |
| Trichoptera | 1 | 1 | 2 |
| Plecoptera | | 1 | |
| Chironomidae | 14 | 9 | 24 |
| Simuliidae | 1 | 1 | 1 |
| Limoniidae | | | 1 |
| Empididae | | | 1 |
| Muscidae | | | 1 |
| Copepoda | | 1 | 1 |
| Fish | 2 | 3 | 3 |
| Ducks | | 2 | 14 |
| Invertebrates per m$^2$ | 5300 | 17,500 | 207,000 |
| Salmon catch (1974–94) per km for similar rivers | 0.8 | 1.15 | 1.57 |

mainly night feeding fish, *Galaxias vulgaris*. However, the number on the stone surfaces was lower by day in the presence of trout and lower by night in the presence of *Galaxias*, which disturbs the cobbles in its feeding and causes more drift. In nearby rivers, abundance of the fish was associated with higher biomasses of algae on the stones.

## 7.9 STREAMS IN COLD CLIMATES: THE POLAR AND ALPINE ZONES

The simplest stream systems are the coldest and the driest. Let us start with the coldest. In polar and alpine regions, glaciers accumulate snow in winter and to some extent melt in summer, releasing water to a complex and fluctuating set of channels (Fig. 7.8). In winter there may be no flow and everything will be frozen solid, but the pressure of the ice can cause some melting at the bottom of the glacier and in times of warming

climate, as at present, melting may be substantial even in winter as the glacier recedes.

More water will pour out in spring, carrying with it suspended clays and other particles ground from the underlying rock as the glacier moves over it. Glacial meltwater is grey and milky in appearance and very cold, at first 0°C. Melting will be least in the morning and will increase during the day as the Sun warms the ice. It will vary from day to day with the weather and the contributions of melted surface snow and melting ice at the base will fluctuate also. There will be differences in conductivity in these sources and also in deeper ground water that will also flow out from the deposits at the foot of the glacier, washed out in previous years. Discharge and chemistry of the outflow streams will thus vary greatly.

The water will pass into a complex of channels, for sands and gravels will also wash out when flows are high and be deposited in an irregular terrain over and around bare rock. Immediately there will be little

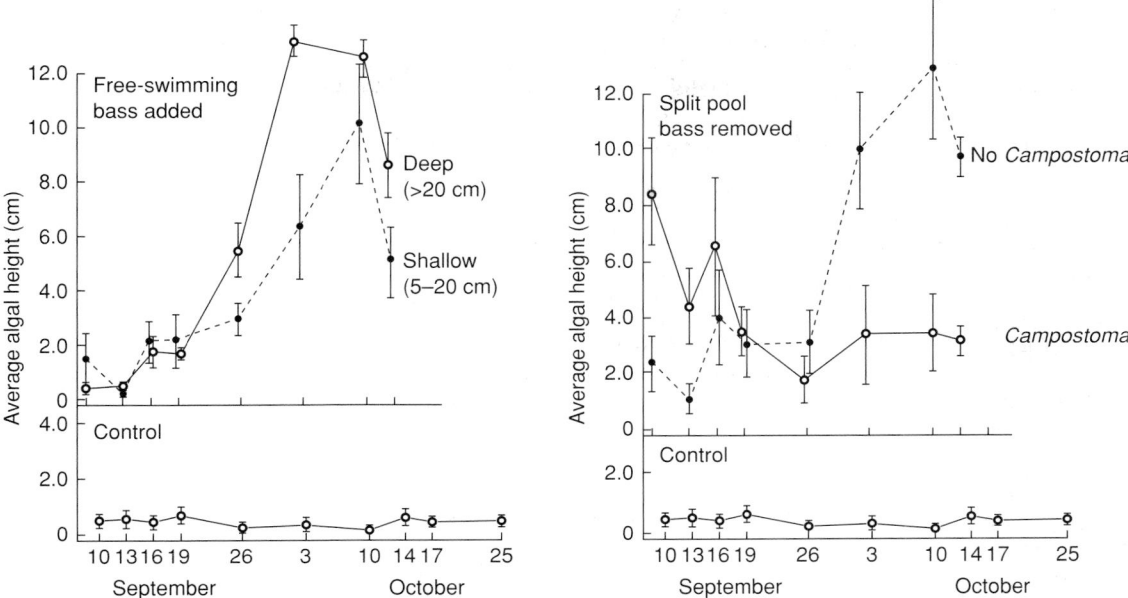

**Fig. 7.7** When predatory fish, bass, *Micropterus salmoides*, were added to sections of a stream previously only with herbivorous minnows (*Campostoma anomalum*) in the fish community, there was a dramatic increase in algal growth (measured as height of the community) on the rocks in both shallow and deeper water, compared with controls (left). When bass were not present, removal of minnows also led to large algal growths, whilst presence of the minnow was associated with little growth. Food chain effects can have as great an effect on primary producer biomass as physico-chemical conditions. (From Power et al. 1985.)

**Fig. 7.8** Streams emerging from a glacier are milky with suspended clay, highly variable in flow dependent on the rate of melting, and bare of organic structure. They rapidly become colonized, however.

vegetation but pioneer saxifrages and grasses, mosses and lichens will establish around the stream, whilst at greater distances the land may remain barren and either frozen or dry. Eventually the vegetation will coalesce into a tundra of grasses, sedges and lichens, mostly perennial and of low productivity because of the low temperatures and short growing season. Trees do not develop until the midsummer temperature reaches 10°C and between this point and the permanent snow and ice line there are several sorts of stream.

A stream fed by glacier melt is termed kryal. Lower down its course, where vegetation has developed and most of the water comes from summer snow meltwater that passes through the vegetated soils of the landscape, it is called rhithral. If you like classifying things, there are also cold streams called krenal deriving their water from springs fed by the ground water. These are more constant in flow and composition and support a more complex community than the rhithral and especial the kryal streams.

### 7.9.1 Invertebrates of kryal streams

There are animals in kryal streams even close to the foot of the glacier. Mostly they are insects with flying adult stages and particularly they are dipteran (two-winged) flies. In general the diversity of the invertebrates increases as the temperature of the water increases. It increases also as the habitat becomes more stable and less disrupted by changes in the deposits as the channels become larger, and less subject to the daily and hourly vicissitudes of melting. Eventually the channels are constrained by the roots and rhizomes of the tundra vegetation. In the coldest water, up to about 2°C, midge fly larvae of the family Diamesinae dominate to the near exclusion of others. As temperatures rise to 4°C they are joined by oligochaete worms and flies of the Tipulidae (whose adults are the crane flies or daddy-long-legs) and then by increasing numbers of dipterans, plecopterans (stoneflies), trichopterans (caddis flies) and ephemeropterans (mayflies) as the temperature warms to the 10°C that characterizes the first forests and a change in the nature of the streams (Fig. 7.9).

### 7.9.2 Primary producers

The kryal and rhithral streams of this scheme are very open. They may have dwarf willow thickets around their courses and they may receive organic matter

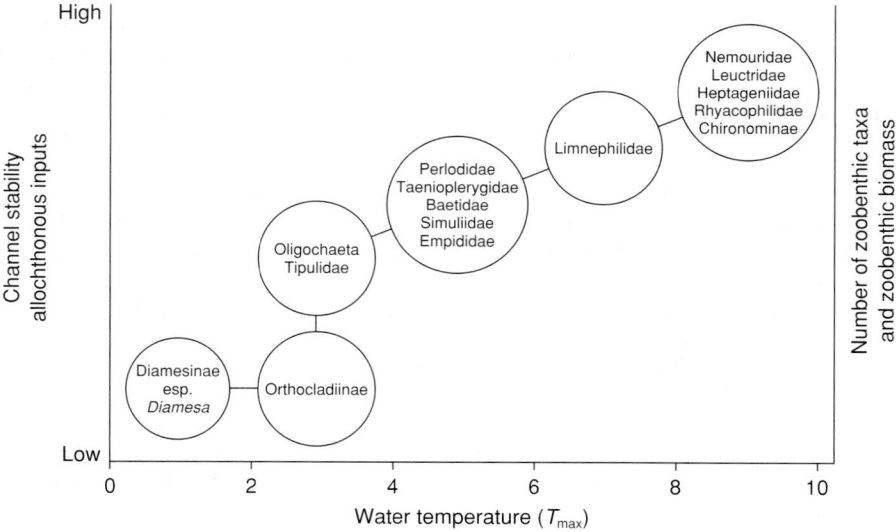

**Fig. 7.9** As the water warms in a European mountain glacier stream, there is a succession of invertebrates, with deposit feeders at first, then scrapers as algal growths begin to develop. Number of taxa and biomass also steadily increase. (From Milner et al. 2001.)

from these and blown in as pollen, but they flow rapidly and there is little chance of substantial amounts of allochthonous organic matter accumulating for long enough for it to be eaten. The main food source is from algae in the biofilms and small plants such as mosses that cover the rocks. These need a supply of nutrients and this will be very low in such streams.

Concentrations of available phosphorus are often close to the limits of detection and some of the algae produce tapering hairs that have been shown to contain phosphatase enzymes capable of lysing otherwise unavailable phosphates. Such streams will also be naturally very low in nitrogen, though atmospheric pollution has raised nitrogen levels in rain everywhere, including the polar regions. Natural nitrogen supplies require development of nitrogen-fixing organisms and soils where oxygen is low through build up of organic matter and bacteria to decompose it. Glacial streams tend to be well oxygenated and suitable soils for nitrogen fixation do not develop in the krenal areas. Some cyanobacteria, such as *Tolypothrix* and *Stigonema*, which have the specialist cells or heterocysts required for nitrogen fixation in aerobic habitats, do develop in the streams, however. The weathering of finely powdered rock under the glacier may, on the other hand produce more adequate amounts of needed cations. An additional problem for the autochthonous producers is the milkiness of the water and the low light penetration. Extinction coefficients will be very high. The algae will grow best in spring when the flow is modest as temperatures are still low and the meltwater is too sluggish to carry a high suspended load.

Zoologists have long dominated stream ecology and algae tend to have been ignored and lumped together as the biofilm. However, algae occur in greater diversity than the animals and have their own suite of adaptations to the habitat. Krenal and rithral cold streams will have a complex, but shifting vegetation (Fig. 7.10) with many species of diatoms and some filamentous cyanobacteria that form the mucilaginous biofilms. There may be tufted or protruding algae extending out a centimetre or so, such as the cyanobacterium *Tolypothrix*, or red algae like *Lemanea* and the green alga *Prasiola* and particularly the mucilaginous holey colonies of the chrysophyte *Hydrurus foetidus* that seems especially characteristic of the coldest waters.

There is a patterning across the streams with a splash zone to the outside with the reddish-orange *Trentepohlia*, a green alga, and the thickly sheathed cyanobacterium *Gloeocapsa*, both of which may be able, in alpine zones, to tolerate habitats exposed to high ultraviolet radiation by the shielding accessory orange pigments and a group of compounds called the mycosporine-like amino acids. The algae growing on the rocks are collectively called the epilithon (Gk *lithos*, rock) but there is a trend now to refer to all algae that are not planktonic as periphyton. The term really means 'around plants' and has been widely misused by a generation of scientists no longer properly schooled in the classics. Though myself not one of them, I fear that in this book I will nonetheless have to go with the flow.

### 7.9.3 Food webs in cold streams

Determining what animals eat is not straightforward. Examination of the guts is useful but tedious to do and what remains undigested gives no clue to what has already vanished. In recent years, a technique has developed using the naturally occurring stable isotope carbon-13. Aquatic plants and algae tend to discriminate against this isotope in taking up carbon dioxide or bicarbonate. Land plants discriminate against it less. Possibly this is because the difference in mass between $^{13}C$ and $^{12}C$ makes a lot more difference to diffusion rates in water than it does in air. From the ratio of $^{13}C$ to $^{12}C$, usually expressed as the difference from that in a reference standard, in an animal's body, the degree of use of allochthonous and autochthonous sources can be discerned. Studies on krenal streams have shown a clear use of autochthonous material with allochthonous material still a small component in rhithral streams. The significance of this is in the contrast with cold temperate forested streams (see below).

Even as they warm, the streams of these very cold climates remain low in diversity. They are extreme systems with low temperatures and greatly fluctuating conditions. But if the diversity is examined by latitude (Fig. 7.11), there is a distinct decrease towards the higher latitudes. This seems to be due to the greater isolation of the systems further north and of Antarctica. Much of the Arctic is on islands and Antarctica is very much isolated by huge oceans. The alpine mountain glaciers of lower latitudes, however, are on land continuous with the rest of the continent and there have been more possibilities for colonization.

Studies on nutrient relationships are scarce and the links between the tundra and the streams are little understood. There are some tantalizing hints, however. In northern regions, especially on islands, seabirds may

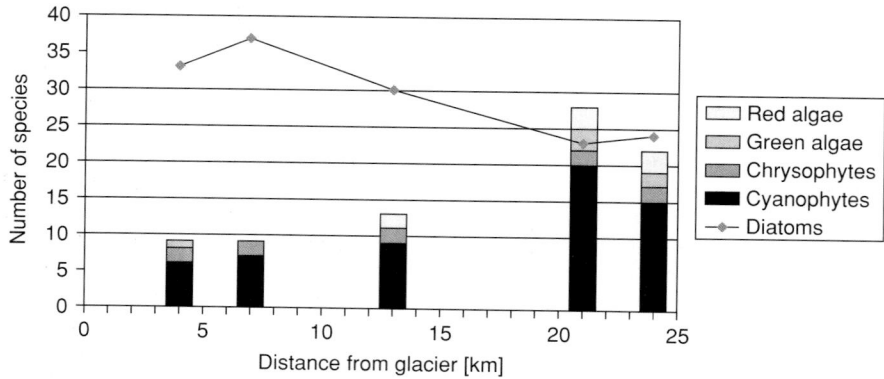

| Growth form | Maximum thickness | Critical velocity | Sketch | Taxon |
|---|---|---|---|---|
| Coating | 2 mm | 2 m s$^{-1}$ | | *Phormidium autumnale* |
| Tuft | 1 cm | 0.8 m s$^{-1}$ | | *Tolypothrix* |
| Tubular tissue | 10 cm | 4.5 m s$^{-1}$ | | *Lemanea* |
| Lacunate mucilage | 20 cm | 1.5 m s$^{-1}$ | | *Hydrurus foetidus* |
| Tubular tissue | 10 cm | >2 m s$^{-1}$ | | *Prasiola* |

**Fig. 7.10** Communities of algae change steadily in glacial streams. Numbers of diatom species are generally high and cyanobacteria (cyanophytes) are generally present, with red algae developing with greater distance from the glacier. Current flow, expressed as shear stress, also selects for particular growth forms. The tubular thalli of the red alga, *Lemanea*, are particularly resistant and will persist up to current speeds of 4.5 m s$^{-1}$. (From Rott et al. 2006.)

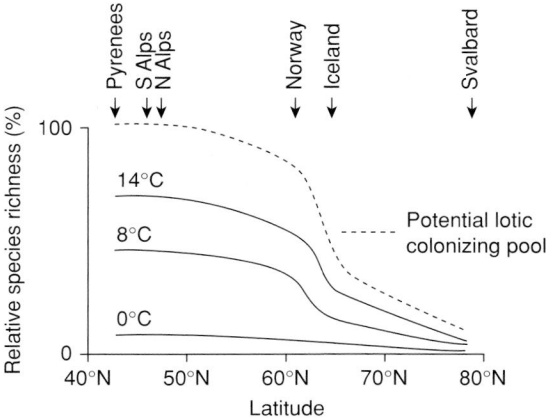

**Fig. 7.11** Diversity of krenal streams with latitude. The dotted line represents a theoretical maximum based on the total number of available species and its greater value than any of the existing curves suggests that existing habitats may still be undersaturated, possibly as a result of there not having been yet enough time for full colonization. The extreme conditions close to the Pole are tolerable by very few species. 'Lotic' is scientific jargon for moving water. (From Milner et al. 2001.)

be major sources of nutrients, bringing them from the sea to the land in their guano. Where foxes have been introduced to the Aleutian Islands, sea bird numbers have declined through predation and soils are less fertile (Fig. 7.12). This must impact upon the streams too as the snow melt penetrates the soils to supply the streams. But it is in the next general climatic zone, the cold temperate that links between land and water through large animals and through the nature of the vegetation become very prominent.

### 7.9.4 Fish and birds in polar streams

Fish do not occur in the very isolated Antarctic glacial streams but do penetrate into Arctic ones, though there may be only one or two species. Two streams in Alaska illustrate their potential effects. They are close together in the Arctic National Wildlife Refuge at 67°1′N and are tributaries of the Ivishak River. One is a rithral stream, called the mountain stream in this study and the other, a krenal stream is called the spring stream. Both have riparian vegetation of willow bushes in a setting of tundra. The physical environments were

different (Fig. 7.13). The spring stream was steadier in temperature and warmer; 1–8.7°C with a mean of 5.8 compared with a range of −0.4°C to 9.5°C with a mean of 1.6°C in the mountain stream. During the summer when the streams were gauged, the flow was higher and flashier in the mountain stream. Rocks on the bed were marked with paint and their positions recorded. A measure of stability of the bed was obtained by recording how many moved between samplings. It was more than twice as many in the mountain stream (57–66%) than the spring stream (4–20%). In the streams were some fish, Dolly Varden char (*Salvelinus malma*) and a pair of dippers, insectivorous birds, and their two chicks also fed in the spring stream.

The essence of the study rested in a comparison of the food webs under these contrasted conditions and these were determined by analysis of gut contents. There is much interest in the structure of food webs in modern ecology, particularly with respect to how connected they are (i.e., of all possible links between organisms (at its greatest, $(n \times (n - 1)/2)$, where $n$ is the number of species), how many links are actually realized, and the extent to which many organisms previously thought of as strict plant-eaters, detritus eaters, scavengers or carnivores are actually omnivores with, respectively, greater emphasis on plants, dead plant material, animal carcasses or live animal prey. There are controversies about the stability of food webs (their ability to continue to function even if a disturbance removes some species) and the number of links. In the past it has been thought that the simpler the web, the more resilient it would be, as fewer organisms with bigger ecological niches would be more capable of filling in gaps left by those removed. Currently, reliance on mathematical modelling seems to suggest that the more complex the web the more stable and an analogy is drawn with the rivets on a ship or aircraft body. There are many more rivets put in than actually needed, to hold the body together in an emergency.

In these Arctic streams the webs were relatively simple and there were more species in the spring web (though algae were, as often, lumped together in functional categories whilst animals were characterized to genus and further where possible). The macroinvertebrates are those caught in a Surber sampler, which is a square frame held on the bottom and from within which stones are individually rubbed by hand so that any animals are displaced into a net (about 0.25 mm mesh) held just downstream. Smaller animals are thus not considered. Among the macroinvertebrates

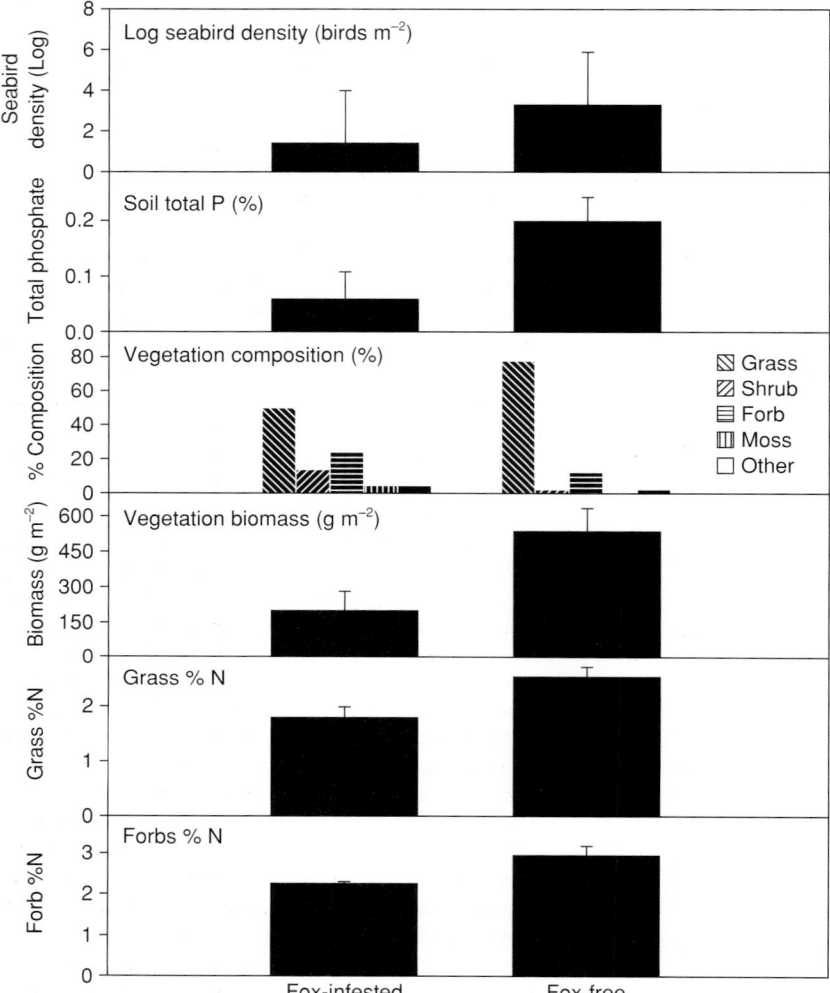

**Fig. 7.12** Nutrients are generally scarce in pristine systems but supplies can vary dependent on factors other than the nature of the soils and vegetation. Introduction of arctic foxes (*Alopex lagopus*) to boost the fur trade onto some of the Aleutian Islands resulted in increased predation on seabirds, a reduction in phosphorus and nitrogen transferred through bird guano from the sea to the land, a reduction in vegetation biomass and a change in community composition from grassland to tundra. Streams would thus receive fewer nutrients from their catchments than in the absence of foxes. (Based on Croll et al. 2005.)

there were 25 species in the spring, 20 in the mountain stream and much more biomass (4617 mg m$^{-2}$ cf. 635). This probably reflects the greater stability of the spring stream and its greater bryophyte coverage. All the animals were, with the exception of small biomasses of water mites, oligochaete worms and flatworms, insects of the Diptera, Ephemeroptera and Plecoptera and the primary consumers fed most frequently on diatoms in the biofilms (Fig. 7.14).

A measure of linkage in the food web suggested that it was similar in both streams but the average number of links in the component food chains was 3.04 in the spring stream, and 1.83 in the mountain stream. This was mainly due to the presence of the dippers, but when their effect was statistically removed, chain length remained higher in the spring stream. There was also much more biomass, by about 25 times, of invertebrate predators, such as large stonefly nymphs in the spring stream, though the ratio of invertebrate predators to invertebrate prey was much lower in the spring stream. This was attributed to greater availability of refuges in the structure provided by the mosses, whilst the differences in biomass were attributed to the greater stability of the environment of the spring stream. The dippers

(a)

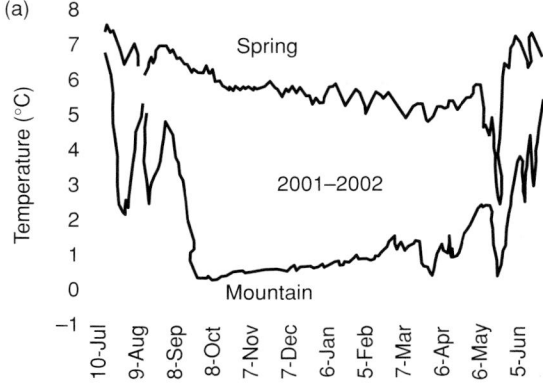

(b)

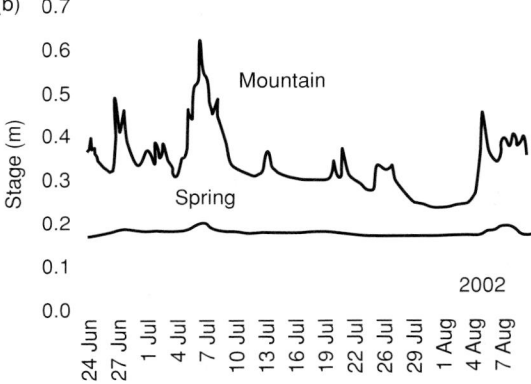

**Fig. 7.13** Comparison between the physical environments of two Alaska streams, one a mountain stream, and the other emanating from a spring.). Stage is a measure of discharge. It is the height of water above a fixed V-shaped notch in a weir set across the stream. (From Parker & Huryn 2006.)

ate small fish and this in particular lengthened the food chains of the spring stream though there were greater lengths even so in the spring stream.

This study was descriptive and there was only one stream of each type. Strictly speaking descriptive studies tell nothing of the mechanisms by which ecosystems work (there has to be an experimental manipulation compared with a control to do that) and statistically, there should be replication of each sort of stream. Otherwise it could be argued that either the spring stream or the mountain stream or both was not typical of its type. On the other hand, the interpretations do make sense in the light of other observations

and conclusions drawn from an intellectual context can sometimes be very valuable. The difficult conditions of working in very cold regions often preclude ideal approaches.

## 7.10 STREAM SYSTEMS IN THE COLD TEMPERATE ZONE

Most freshwater scientists are cold-temperate in location if not by nature and this has been true for at least a century. Ideas and concepts tend thus to be biased towards the systems of this zone. Thus in the 1980s, a very useful model of how stream systems operate, proposed by North American scientists working in the deciduous forests of New England, the River Continuum Concept (Fig. 7.15), caused some controversy when people tried to apply it inappropriately to non-forested regions or systems that had once had forest but no longer had through conversion of the landscape to agriculture. For my present purposes of contrasting streams in broad climatic zones, it does well for the forested landscapes of the cold temperate regions. Much of the forest of the boreal zone still stands. It has a predominance of conifers in cold temperate climates that leave much of the ground wet and for streams and wetlands to be prominent. It is the warmer, more equatorward parts of the cold temperate zone with former drier deciduous-dominated forests that have been most altered. They have been extensively settled by agricultural people whilst the preservation of the boreal forest may owe not a little to the swarms of blackfly and mosquitoes that make life difficult in the boreal summer.

The pristine small streams and rivers of the cold temperate zone are overhung with vegetation. Trees in the riparian zone shade out the bottom and make photosynthesis *in situ* difficult. The nutrient flow from the forest to the stream is also low because forest systems have evolved mechanisms to scavenge scarce nitrogen and phosphorus from the soil before it can be lost to the forest system. Yet these streams may have large populations of invertebrates and fish. The reasons lie in the connections between the forest, the stream and ultimately the ocean. Indeed the contrast between substantial amounts of past research on the minutiae of invertebrate populations within the stream, important though it has been for much understanding, and the broader picture needed for the conservation and management of these systems, could not be greater.

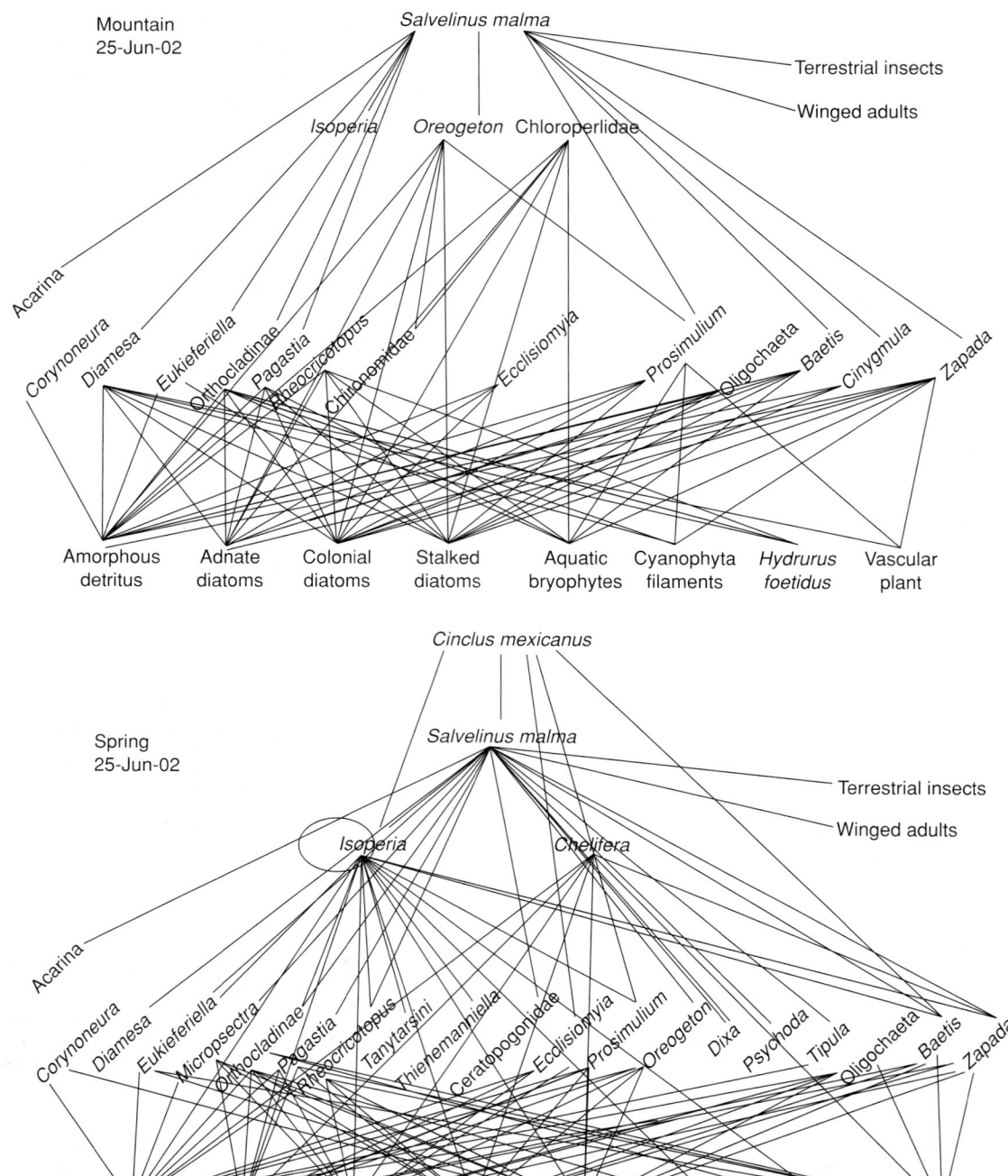

**Fig. 7.14** Food webs in two Alaskan streams, one a mountain stream and the other emanating from a spring, in June. Circle indicates cannibalism. (From Parker & Huryn 2006.)

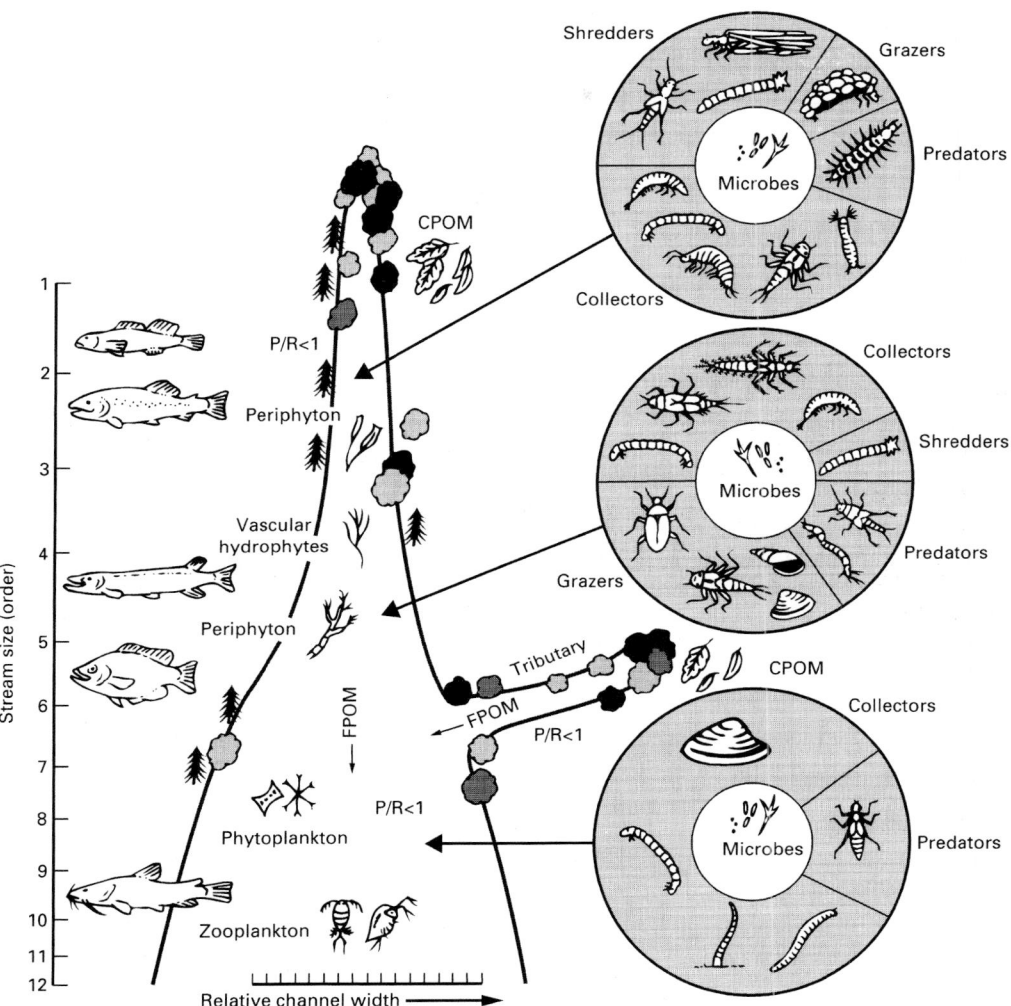

**Fig. 7.15** The river continuum concept of Vannote et al. (1980). Changes in the community are given in relation to the order of stream. In river systems, the smallest streams with no tributaries are called first order streams. Second order streams are formed by the joining of first order streams, third order by the joining of at most second order streams and so on. The sequence of typical fish and the major primary producers are shown to the left of the diagram. P stands for autochthonous primary production, R for community respiration. CPOM and FPOM are coarse and fine particulate organic matter respectively. Circles to the right show typical bottom invertebrate communities.

## 7.10.1 Allochthonous sources of energy

Energy in the form of leaves, bracts, pollen, twigs, branches and trunks falling, blown and washed into the stream supports the cold temperate system. Many studies have shown that the smaller and softer components of this material, largely leaves, provide most of the energy for the food web whilst the larger components, trunks and branches, create obstructions and temporary dams that aid the retention of the leaves in the channels long enough for them to enter the food web. For sizeable stretches of such a river it may be difficult to see much of the water, so great is the amount of timber debris. But trees do not shed leaves rich in nutrients. As a leaf senesces, much of the nutrient is translocated back into the stems and branches for reuse by new leaves. Shed leaves are mostly of cellulose and lignin, with dosings of phenolic compounds such as tannins that the tree produces to discourage insect grazers.

A poor food is thus provided to a medium that also lacks much nutrient. However, there is a group of fungi, the hyphomycetes, which has spores that are tossed around in the turbulence but are shaped like hooks or anchors, so that they easily latch into softening waterlogged leaves. These fungi, like the mycorrhizal fungi that scavenge nutrients for trees from forest soils, are efficient at accumulating nutrients from the tiny concentrations in stream water. They have enzymes capable of digesting lignin and cellulose and they steadily, over a period of weeks, convert the original leaf into a lump of partly digested carbohydrate enriched with the protein of the fungal mycelium. This is called conditioning; it is carried out by several fungi working together; and it proceeds most efficiently for leaves that are initially softer, such as alder, willow, larch, oak and lime, compared with the harder leaves of beech, pine and spruce.

### 7.10.2 Shredders, filter-collectors and deposit feeders

The conditioned leaves attract a guild of invertebrates, called the shredders, which tear the leaf apart to reach the mycelium, breaking it into small pieces as they do so and leaving a skeleton of the more resistant veins. Such animals include shrimps (*Gammarus*), other crustaceans such as *Asellus*, the water hog-louse and the larvae of tipulid and other flies. The fine particles of uneaten leaf, together with the faeces of the shredders and the organic matter washed in from the soils of the catchment in rainstorms, become suspended in the current and are colonized or recolonized by bacteria and fungi, which continue the process of conditioning.

As they pass downstream, fine particles are intercepted by filter feeders, such as *Simulium* and also a group of caddis flies that spins nets across gaps between stones. The concentrated fine material becomes the food of these, which in turn produce more fine particles of faeces to add to the flow. Some fine material settles in quieter places in the stream and there deposit feeders, oligochaetes, some mayfly nymphs such as *Ephemera danica* and chironomid larvae (Diptera) burrow into it,

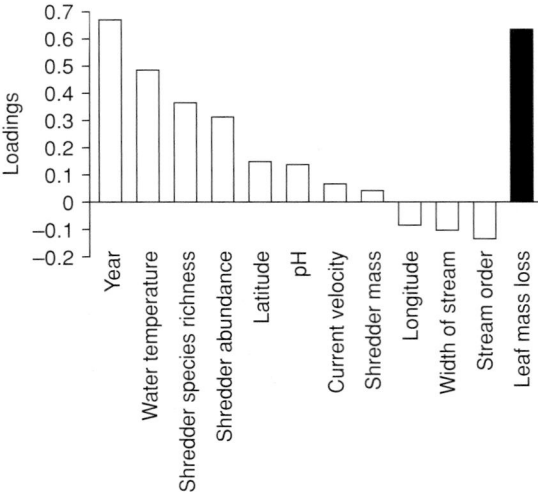

**Fig. 7.16** Effects of shredder diversity on leaf breakdown. Data were taken from studies on 23 Swedish streams. The rate of leaf breakdown, measured as loss in dry weight was most strongly related to year, temperature, shredder species richness and shredder abundance. Species richness was more important than either shredder abundance or shredder biomass. Values on the vertical axis (loadings) are correlation coefficients. The greater the value, the more important the effect, either positive or negative. (From Jonsson et al. 2001.)

swallowing organic matter, digesting the protein-rich microbial cells and defaecating undigested remains for further colonization and conditioning.

In this way the coarse leaf material is eventually converted to animal tissue and carbon dioxide and there is some evidence that the material is more efficiently processed the greater the diversity of the members of particular feeding guilds (Fig. 7.16). They may tackle different parts of the leaves, different fungal materials, or each operate most efficiently in some of the fluctuating physical conditions of streams than others. The issue of biodiversity is much discussed especially at a time when organisms are being made extinct at a high rate by human activities and demands are often made of ecologists to 'prove' that all the biodiversity is necessary with the implication that some, if not quite a lot of it, is redundant and can be lost without detriment. It can be shown that ecological processes do operate better with the characteristic diversity of the habitat than with reduced diversity but it would be impossible practically to have to do this in every place for every guild and every process. An alternative approach is the argument that since natural selection is so ruthless in eliminating poor competitors, survival is always difficult. Thus if diversity persists it must a priori have functional meaning.

### 7.10.3 Stream orders

Hydrologists conveniently classify streams into orders such that streams with no tributaries are called order 1. Order 1 streams merge to form second order streams, which when they join become third order streams. A big river system like the Mississippi or Amazon might have ten or eleven orders. The number of streams and rivers of a given order in such a system steadily decreases as order increases, as does the combined length of each order. In general, as order increases the streams pass from being erosive to depositional, the slope of the terrain decreases, the accumulated catchment area increases and so the discharge increases. The mean current speed increases but the range of velocities in the channels gets broader so that a big river will have some water not moving at all in its floodplain and fast moving water in the middle of the channel.

This is to get ahead of this account to some extent but it underlies the idea that as one moves up from order 1 to about 4 in a forested system, the number of shredder species increases, but then declines (Fig. 7.17). This is because the river will be widening, and shading by overhanging trees will affect only the edges of a channel that will be becoming overall better illuminated. Algal biofilms, mosses and some vascular plants will start to colonize the river bed, and this will be helped as the physical stability of the system increases with a greater catchment area to even out the flows. The proportion of filter feeders may increase relative to the shredders, but in particular invertebrate scrapers will become more abundant, exploiting this new source. Such scrapers were, of course, the main components of the open polar and mountain streams (see above).

### 7.10.4 The River Continuum Concept

The system has thus moved from a situation where gross photosynthesis ($P_g$) in the channel has been much lower than the respiration of the animal and microbial community plus that of photosynthetic organisms (community respiration ($R_{com}$)) so that $P_g \ll R_{com}$ and fungi and shredders are processing allochthonous leaf material, to one where both allochthonous and

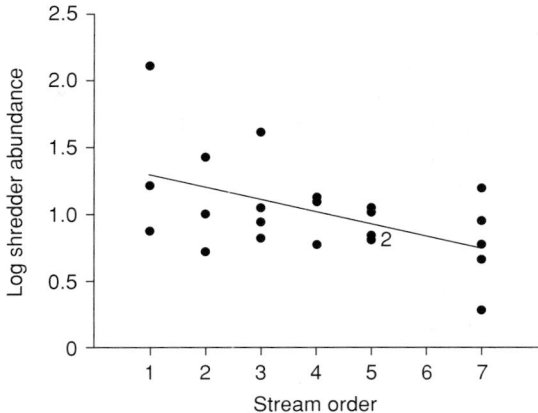

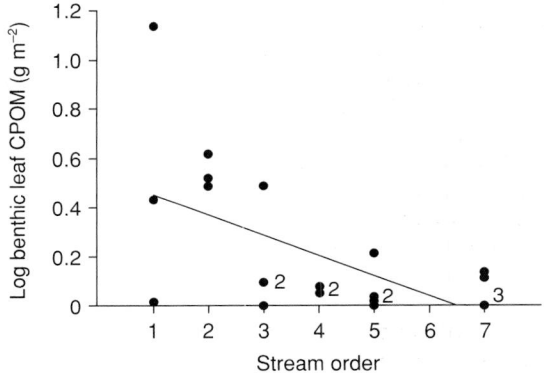

**Fig. 7.17** In line with the River Continuum concept, shredder abundance, and the availability of coarse particulate organic matter (CPOM), decreased with stream order in a set of Swedish rivers. (From Jonsson et al. 2001.)

autochthonous material are both contributing substantially ($P_g = R_{com}$) and perhaps eventually for a time, before the river becomes big and muddy, where $P_g > R_{com}$. This is the essence of the River Continuum Concept (Fig. 7.15). It is important to realize that these changes in $P_g$ relative to $R_{com}$ apply just to the stream channel, which is not an entity in itself but part of the larger catchment system that is really the valid ecological unit. The stream community is consuming leaf material in much the same way as the soil animals of the forest floor, and for the system as a whole (trees + forest floor + stream), $P_g$ will overall equal $R_{com}$, or if some organic material is being stored in the soils or passed downstream to the floodplains and sea, $P_g$ will be greater than $R_{com}$. The ratio depends on where one draws the boundary of the system.

### 7.10.5 Invertebrates fall in too

As well as leaves that fall or blow in from the forest in the lower order streams, an immediately richer food source of insects and other terrestrial invertebrates will also fall from the trees into the water. Fish, in particular, benefit from these. The habits adopted by stream invertebrates to cope with shear stress will often position them such that the larger fish cannot reach them, under stones or in quiet refuges of twig debris. Smaller, benthic (bottom living) fish may be able to winkle them out, but larger ones are dependent on what is suspended in the water. Some of it will be the drift of the stream animals but a lot of it will fall in from the canopy. Over 100 animals can fall in per m$^2$ of stream per day, including ants, wasps, spiders, snails, flies, grasshoppers and collembolans and the total available may be greater than that of the animals produced in the stream. Moreover the fish often select the terrestrial animals for they are frequently bigger, unable to move to refuges in the water and quite buoyant. They are also easily visible against the light if they are trapped in the surface tension film of water. The mass falling in, based on several studies, can be up to 450 mg m$^{-2}$ day$^{-1}$ and in summer this food source may be so important to the fish that if it is experimentally blocked by sheeting, the fish will move to other reaches of the stream where it remains available.

### 7.10.6 . . . and emerge

This link with the forest is not entirely one way. The insects that live in streams and emerge as adults will swarm and mate in the air over the stream and the riparian zone. Dominated by dipteran flies, particularly chironomid midges, they may provide almost all of the food for birds, bats, spiders and lizards that inhabit the riparian zone and close-by forest. Again the numbers may be large with hundreds of thousands of animals emerging from every metre squared per year, with a dry mass of 500 to 23,000 mg m$^{-2}$ yr$^{-1}$. In one study, such emerging insects made up a quarter of the food of the ten bird species occupying a 200-m wide swathe to either side of a Japanese river. Wrens in another riparian zone took these insects as 98% of their diet and stable isotope studies have indicated up to 100% of the diets of spiders in an Arizona creek came from emerging insects. Many of the birds dependent on these sources of food are migratory and their population dynamics will be influenced by the emergence rates. Ecosystems far afield, to which the birds migrate, will thus be influenced.

### 7.10.7 Indirectly, wolves are stream animals

There is another dimension to this linkage between stream and forest. The riparian zones of streams provide attractive browsing for large herbivores such as elk, moose and other deer. For moose, at least some aquatic plants are essential to meet the sodium requirements in its diet. In Yellowstone National Park in Wyoming, elk are very abundant, so much so that in the winter, when they have to move down from the high mountain pastures as the snow sets in, they have to be fed hay. In summer the pastures, including the open woodlands are overgrazed and the willow thickets that normally characterize the riparian zones of the streams have been lost.

This is not a normal situation and arises because the natural predator of elk, the timber wolf, was shot out from the area in the 1920s, and because subsequent control of the elk by shooting was discontinued in the 1950s as inappropriate in a National Park. Since then the elk herd has multiplied. In 1996 wolves were reintroduced into areas of Yellowstone. They have thrived and have begun to control the numbers and behaviour of the elk. The constricted nature of the stream bottoms is a risky habitat, where the wolves may corner the elk and the elk have learned to stay away from them. The result has been that the willow thickets have grown again (Fig. 7.18), bringing with them an increased number of beavers and an increased diversity of birds. It has not yet been recorded how the invertebrate communities of the streams have changed but with such a major structural change there must have been significant effects.

### 7.10.8 Scarcity of nutrients

The growing picture is thus of streams so intricately linked with their terrestrial catchments that it is unthinkable now to separate them as distinct ecosystems. And there are more, and more extensive, links to do with nutrient supply. The general rule (Chapter 4) is that pristine ecosystems are parsimonious with a limited available nutrient supply (Chapter 4). The northern forests are no exceptions. Something, however, must supply to the hyphomycete fungi the nutrients

1996, without wolves

2002, with wolves

**Fig. 7.18** Animals that are conventionally considered terrestrial can have significant effects on streams. This is the same view of Blacktail Creek in Yellowstone National Park in 1996 and 2002. In 1996 elk heavily grazed the stream bottom. After reintroduction of the native wolf, elk behaviour was changed and willows (*Salix* spp) grew much better, increasing local bird diversity and beaver populations and markedly changing the nature of the river channel. (From Ripple & Beschta 2004b)

needed to prime their conditioning of the leaves and to the bryophytes and biofilms for their growth. The concentrations available from the forest, however, are very low and it appears that functioning of the system depends also on an extra supply . . . from the ocean, provided by migratory salmonid fish.

### 7.10.9 Salmon

An important group of fish in the cold temperate rivers of the northern hemisphere is the salmonids. The Atlantic salmon is joined by the sea trout off Europe and eastern North America whilst the sockeye, coho,

chinook, chum, pink, steelhead, and coastal cutthroat are salmonids of the Pacific basin. Many salmonids have a dual life. They are spawned in the gravel beds of headwater streams or associated lakes, following a mating in which the female digs a depression, the redd, in the gravel with her tail, and lays eggs, which the male fertilizes. She then covers the eggs with gravel to hide them from predators but also to ensure a free flow of oxygenated water over them through the wide interstices between the stones. This happens in the winter, and in the following spring the eggs hatch to alevins dependent at first on their yolk sac but then on small organisms in the biofilms on rocks in the stream bed.

As they grow they become dependent on macro-invertebrates on the stream bottom, where they remain for about a year, and are called parr before beginning to change physiologically into smolts that will move down river to the sea and out into the fastnesses of the ocean. There, for at least a year, they will feed as carnivores on other fish and large invertebrates before moving back to the river system where they were born. Their navigation across sometimes several thousand miles of ocean is still something of a mystery but they sense the water from where they were born even when its is mixed with sea water along the coast. Every water is subtly different and the salmonids are better instinctive chemists than we are deliberate ones.

They do not feed once they enter the river and to reach the spawning grounds in the headwater rivers, they may have a journey still of some hundreds of kilo-metres, with waterfalls, rapids and debris to negotiate.

Some do not survive the journey. The carcasses of the Pacific salmonids are scavenged by both black and brown bears, who will welcome a protein-rich meal. In some river systems salmon provides the bulk of the bear's diet for several months of the spawning runs. The bears will also intercept the salmon as they congregate to await favourable flows to jump up waterfalls. The bears wander through the forest in search of berries, defae-cating and urinating and adding nutrients ultimately from the ocean to the soil. This we know from the ratio of nitrogen-15 to nitrogen-14, which is characteristic-ally different in the oceans and ocean animals than in terrestrially grown ones. Eventually the nutrients may be absorbed by plants in the riparian and somewhat wider zones. Close to the river up to 25% of the nitrogen in the trees may come from the ocean (Fig. 7.19).

Eventually the surviving salmon, in an already exhausted state, reach the spawning areas, where they

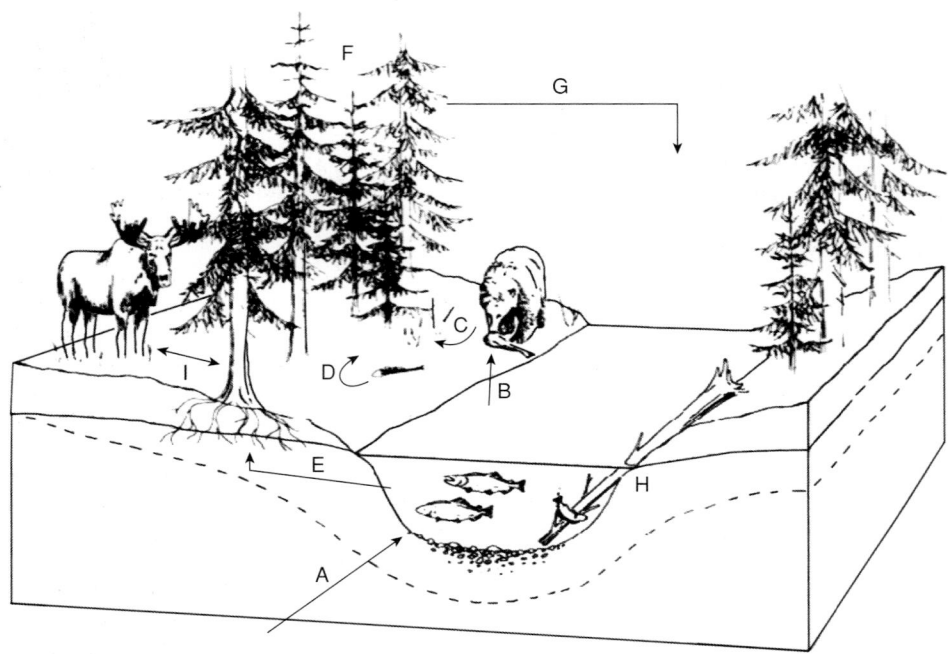

**Fig. 7.19** The relationships among Pacific salmon, bears, rivers and forest are complex. Spawning salmon bring nitrogen derived from the ocean (A); bears eat significant amounts of salmon (B) and excrete onto the forest floor (C). Discarded and uneaten carcasses are colonized by bacteria and invertebrates (D). Released nitrogen percolates into the forest soils directly and through the hyporheic water table (E) and is taken up by tree roots, promoting higher growth rates in the riparian trees (F). The trees provide (G) shade, bank stabilization, allochthonous organic matter and woody debris, all contributing to favourable fish habitat with the woody debris also retaining fish carcasses (H) whose released nutrients are used by fungi conditioning the debris for consumption by shredders, which eventually provide food for the salmon parr. (From Helfield & Naiman 2006.)

mate, losing much of their biomass and energy in the process. Most then die and their carcasses litter the spawning grounds, despite the swift flow of the water. This is because tree debris hinders their being washed down river. As they decompose in the late winter and spring, their contained phosphorus and nitrogen add to the nutrient pool of the headwaters, and to the production of fungi and biofilms, invertebrates and ultimately the salmon parr. When this link was broken by overzealous forestry that allowed no tree debris to enter the streams, the salmon recruitment was much reduced.

## 7.11 WARM TEMPERATE STREAMS

Climate changes steadily, of course, with latitude and altitude, with distance from the ocean and in the lee of mountain ranges. There is an infinity of climate regimes on Earth, but there is nonetheless some merit in thinking about them in broad groups, a recurrent theme in this book. The warm temperate regimes take over from the cold temperate as frozen winters give way to ones where the temperature rarely, if ever, plunges to freezing, where most of the annual precipitation falls in winter as rain and where the cool moist summers of the cold temperate region are replaced by hot, dry ones, where streams may cease to flow and be reduced to isolated pools or dry down completely (Fig. 7.20). The lands around the Mediterranean and those of parts of California, Chile, South Africa and Australia typify such a climate. And the nature of the animals living in such streams (Table 7.5) is much fitted to a place that might be expected to dry out.

In pristine catchments, the vegetation is of open woodland or parkland, sometimes shrublands (maquis, chaparral or fynbos) with resinous, evergreen trees producing small hard, woody leaves (sclerophylls) that tolerate drought with their thickness and which are shed from the trees more or less continuously. In California, redwoods (*Sequoia*), Douglas fir (*Abies*), tanoak (*Lithocarpus*) and madrone (*Arbutus*) may predominate with manzanita (*Arctostaphylos*) and scrub oak (*Quercus*). In New Zealand and Chile, the southern beeches (*Nothofagus*) are common and in Spain, sage (*Salvia*), juniper (*Juniperinus*) and myrtle (*Myrica*). There will be riparian woodland but it may not be extensive or dense. The pronounced autumn leaf-fall of the cold temperate region is absent and there is much less timber debris in the streams to hold whatever

**Fig. 7.20** Warm temperate streams frequently dry out in summer, and the biological community must take refuge in resting stages or in waters elsewhere.

leaves blow in. Moreover the small hard leaves are less likely to catch on snags, but cascade down with the current in winter or lie in a thin layer on the bottom of the pools or the dry bed in summer. They may form substrates for biofilms but are unlikely to be tackleable by shredders until abrasion in the flow has already reduced them to fragments.

In winter a fauna of scrapers and filter feeders may be found, for the open channels will support photosynthetic biofilms on the rocks, and to the sides of the summer channel some emergent vegetation of grasses and rushes (*Juncus*, *Phragmites*, *Arundo*, *Scirpus*) as well as some riparian bushes such as oleander (*Nerium*) and *Limonium* will bear a periphyton as the stems are inundated in the winter. The often bare soils of the catchment will erode easily in the winter rains, bringing fine organic matter into the flow and the sediments accumulated among the grasses and bushes will move in the often violent floods that follow the winter rainstorms. The community in the stream in winter will be more like that of the polar and alpine regions in its lack

**Table 7.5** Strategies for surviving drying out of a stream. (Based on Boulton & Brock 1999.)

| Strategy | Examples |
| --- | --- |
| Flying adults capable of evacuation and recolonization | Dragonflies and damselflies, beetles, bugs, mayflies, caddis flies, stoneflies, two-winged flies |
| Drying-resistant eggs or juveniles | Flatworms, oligochaetes, snails, two-winged flies, some beetles, mayflies, stoneflies and caddis flies |
| Survival in deep, still damp burrows | Crayfish, crabs, smaller crustacea, oligochaetes, water mites, nematodes, some midges |
| Survival in saturated hyporheic sediments | Nematodes, oligochaetes, mites, some mayfly nymphs, beetle and midge larvae |
| Survival under moist leaf litter or damp vegetation | Nematodes, oligochaetes, amphipods, snails, beetles, midge larvae and caddis fly nymphs |

of shredders and unlike that of the closer cold temperate streams that take the river continuum concept as their blueprint.

The taxonomic composition of the communities will vary a great deal between summer and winter, reflecting the very different conditions. The reasons why communities are as they are have been discussed above. Traditionally communities have been analysed in terms of their taxonomy but an alternative is to look at biological features, or traits. These might include such characteristics as shown in Table 7.6. When this was done for two streams, the intermittent Hunting Creek and the perennial Sulphur Creek, in California, the taxonomic compositions in the wet and dry season, and between streams, varied greatly, but trait composition varied less, revealing features appropriate perhaps to the totality of the Mediterranean stream environment. The dry season communities of the perennial stream tended to show much desiccation resistance, with terrestrial eggs, moderate to strong body 'armour', and small size, whilst the wet season animals tended to eat coarse organic matter, but had no armour and short-lived adults. In the intermittent stream, animals in the dry season had tendencies to short lives, aquatic adults, with adult diapause (a resting stage in the life history) and ovoviparity (the bearing of live young) whilst in the wet season they also showed short life and diapause, and bore single eggs and a tendency to burrow in sediment. Some of these traits are clearly well fitted to a fluctuating environment (diapause, burrowing, short life). Others, like body armouring remain to be explained, but may be related to the more violent flow conditions.

Many Mediterranean streams will dry in the summer, stranding their communities in pools, as the connections first between the channel and riparian vegetation, then among the shallow riffles, are lost. There is a richness in the names of such temporary streams: caap, laagate, wadi, wash, donga, nullah, fiumara; and in the terms used to describe their hydrology: intermittent (generally wet but sometimes dry), ephemeral (unpredictably wet and for only short periods), episodic (dry most of the time but when wet remain wet for long periods), seasonal (regularly alternating wet and dry every year), all summing up a regime where potential evaporation in summer may be more than 1000 mm and rainfall is zero.

Where the stream breaks up into deepish pools that persist, there may be a rich endemic fauna, for small fish may be able to persist where larger, predatory ones must move or die. Oxygen levels in the pools may be low at the high temperatures of summer and it is the more robust beetles and bugs, with their thick chitins and ability often to breathe air, or fly away for much of their life history, and odonates and atyid shrimps that persist. The more delicate mayflies, caddis flies and stoneflies with adult stages that last only a few days, fare less well. If the stream dries completely, all is not lost. In winter there will be recolonization from adult insects that fly in, or from reactivation of diapausal stages of those that simply cocoon themselves into the mud.

The upper levels of the food webs of warm streams have been little studied but the diversity of reptiles and amphibians is likely to be much greater than in cold temperate streams and, especially polar ones, for

**Table 7.6** Some characteristics of invertebrates usable for analysis of trait characteristics in streams. (Based on Bêche et al. 2006.)

| Trait | Possible variants |
| --- | --- |
| Maximum size (mm) | <2.5, 2.5–5, 5–10, 10–20, 20–40, 40–80 |
| Body armour | None (soft-bodied), moderate (sclerotized), case or shell |
| Body shape | Flattened, cylindrical, spherical |
| Life span | <1 year, >1 year |
| Voltinism (generations produced per year) | <1, 1, >1 |
| Aquatic stage | Egg, larva or pupa, adult |
| Adult longevity (days) | <1, 1–10, 10–30, 30–365, >365 |
| Resistance | Desiccation resistant, diapause, none |
| Diapause stage | Egg, larva or pupa, adult, none |
| Dispersal | Active or passive, by air or water |
| Reproduction | Sexual, parthenogenic, other asexual |
| Egg type | Free or attached eggs, single or clutched, laid in plants, laid on land or ovoviviparous (developing in adult) |
| Respiration | Through skin, gills, plastron, aerial and with or without respiratory pigments |
| Movement | Flight, surface film swimmer, underwater swimmer, crawler, burrower, living permanently in sediment |
| Food | Fine particulate organic matter, coarse particulate organic matter, attached algae, plants, dead animals, microinvertebrates, macroinvertebrates, vertebrates |
| Feeding mode | Absorber, deposit feeder, shredder, scraper, filter-collector, piercer (of plants or animals), predator, parasite |

these animals are poikilotherms. They are also mostly predators and may exert strong top-down controls on the food webs. Possibly amphibians are more important than the fish, for their life history is well fitted to temporary streams, with tadpoles exploiting algal biofilms in the wet stage and adults the terrestrial insects of the dry season. In Australia, the platypus (*Ornithorhynchus anatinus*), is the equivalent of water rats and otters in the cold zone, feeding on crayfish (yabbies in Australia), shrimps and fish. Frogs, toads and water snakes are prominent in the diet of otters in Spanish streams at the southernmost limits of the otter's range.

## 7.12 DESERT STREAMS

There are many similarities between desert streams (Fig. 7.21) and Mediterranean climate streams. The differences are those of degree. Mediterranean streams will generally flow for at least part of every year. Desert streams may not flow for several years, but when they

do the system is similar. Traits to withstand drought are important, but the violence of flash floods, when they occur, may be such that resting animals are carried away with eroded sediment before they can hatch. Repopulation is by insects that fly in and lay eggs for the most part. In Sycamore creek, in the Sonoran Desert in Arizona, USA, 98% of the community of a pre-existing small flowing stream was washed out in a late summer flood, but the stream was repopulated within three weeks. Major invertebrate groups included the familiar mayflies, stoneflies, caddis flies, beetles, bugs, dipterans, odonates, oligochaetes and triclads, but with an overwhelming dominance of insects. Large algal populations of diatoms and cyanobacteria had developed within two weeks. Deposit feeders (85%) dominated the biomass, then predators (10%) and scrapers (5%). Shredders and filter feeders were very scarce. This stream is also notable because direct measurements of photosynthesis and respiration have been made. Experiments in plexiglass chambers set in the stream bed allowed relationships among photosynthesis, respiration, temperature, light and algal biomass

**Fig. 7.21** Desert streams have riparian zones just like all other streams but the vegetation tends to be lower growing and scrubby. (Photograph by D.R. Patterson.)

(measured as ash-free dry weight or chlorophyll *a*) to be established through changes in dissolved oxygen concentration under light and dark conditions (see Chapter 9). Unlike headwater streams in cool temperate climates, this was an autotrophic system with $P_{gr}:R_{com}$ ratio about 1.46. Table 7.7 shows energy budgets for this stream (though expressed in units of organic matter) and for a heterotrophic stream in the cold temperate zone.

## 7.13 TROPICAL STREAMS

The 'tropics' is a simple term that hides a very great complexity of habitat. There are high tropical mountains with glaciers; there are extremely wet areas and deserts, savannahs and grasslands. It is thus impossible

to designate a 'typical' tropical stream system and the greater diversity of tropical biotas, coupled with a much lesser density of scientists to study them, and thus much less information, compounds the problem. In the past there has been a tendency to apply the general models for temperate regions to tropical systems and this has led to much controversy. There is a substantial literature, for example about whether the river continuum concept (Fig. 7.15) applies in the tropics, with some papers alleging that it does and others finding few shredders and therefore asserting that it does not. In scientific circles there is kudos to be had by proposing general models that the proposer hopes will be adopted widely, but although Newton's Laws and Einstein's principles certainly do have this universality, such simple laws are unlikely to be able to describe the structure and behaviour of complex systems. There are general principles but local details will continually obviate them.

Probably the most useful approach to tropical streams, indeed to all systems, is to view them as individuals in a continuum created by the mutual variation of a few major features that determine how they function. For streams in general these will include water supply and its seasonality and predictability, including frequency of drying up, local vegetation, possibilities of provision of allochthonous matter and the biogeographical history that has led to the current local biota.

Some tropical streams rise in headwaters that are heavily forested and receive rain in every month of the year, though often more in some months than in others. Often the water chemistry is not far different from rain because rock weathering over many thousands of years has deepened the soils so much that fresh, weatherable rock is now very far below the surface whilst rain has leached out the surface layers over very long periods. Other streams in scrub or savannah may be much more like Mediterranean streams with a riparian zone of open woodland or grassland, and a propensity at some times of year to dry down to a series of isolated pools, with flash floods at others. Desert streams in the tropics may only flow once in decades.

In the forested streams of the tropics (Fig. 7.22), litter fall differs from temperate regions in that there is a continuous supply, sometimes augmented by greater amounts after heavy storms with high winds, hurricanes for example in the West Indies, and monsoon downpours in southern Asia. There have been some suggestions that there is less woody debris in tropical

**Table 7.7** Energy budgets for a desert stream (Sycamore Creek, Arizona) and a forested north-temperate stream (Bear Brook, New Hampshire). Values in parentheses are percentages of inputs and of outputs. From Jones et al. (1997) and Fisher & Likens (1973)

| | Sycamore Creek (g m$^{-2}$ day$^{-1}$) | Bear Brook (kcal m$^{-2}$ yr$^{-1}$) |
|---|---|---|
| Inputs | | |
| *In situ* photosynthesis | 5.43 (90) | 10 (0.3) |
| Allochthonous organic matter | 0.61 (10) | |
| Allochthonous organic matter (coarse) | | 2669 (82.4) |
| Allochthonous organic matter (fine) | | 562 (17.3) |
| Autoch : Alloch ratio | 9 | 0.003 |
| Outputs | | |
| Exported organic matter (coarse) | | 0 (0) |
| Exported organic matter (fine) | 0.91 (15.1) | 1201 (37.1) |
| Microbial respiration | 3.02 (50) | 2031 (62.7) |
| Macroinvertebrate respiration | 0.71 (11.8) | 9 (0.3) |
| Storage in stream | 1.4 (23.1) | 0 (0) |
| *P : R* ratio | 1.5 | 0.005 |

**Fig. 7.22** Students sampling a tropical montane stream in the Usumbara Mountains of Tanzania. There is a densely forested catchment and riparian zone and an abundance of woody debris.

forest streams and therefore less potential for leaves to be held long enough to contribute to the local food web, but there seems no reason to expect this in general and in Ugandan forests I found it often impossible to locate the smaller streams except where paths had been cut across them because of the dense vegetation and debris overlying them.

It has also been suggested that the chemistry of the tropical leaves may make them less palatable than temperate leaves. Trees produce many alkaloids and other toxic substances that deter insect grazers and which remain in the leaves when they die and fall from the tree. On the other hand, such substances are also produced by trees in cooler climates and appear to be no deterrent. Experiments do show greater and lesser rates of breakdown in different species but these are more usually related to woodiness of the leaf than subtler chemistry.

Inspection of the lists of macroinvertebrates in tropical streams reveals, at least superficially, a fauna familiar to the biologists of temperate countries: dipterans, ephemeropterans, plecopterans, trichopterans, odonates, snails, oligochaetes and all other familiar groups are present. Many of the families are the same, though in particular regions some will be absent and different ones present, but the species are always very different. Sometimes, in the past the feeding mode of tropical species has been presumed based on what the family does in temperate regions but this may be very misleading. In one study, of streams in the foothills of the Bolivian Andes, in which gut contents were examined, only about half the tropical families fed similarly to their temperate counterparts and fine detritus was a major component of the guts (Fig. 7.23). Microbial activity is likely to be rapid in warm waters and there might be a greater availability of such fine organic matter. The authors suggested that in line with existing views elsewhere, tropical stream invertebrates were often generalist feeders, essentially omnivores.

**Fig. 7.23** (*right*) Few animals feed strictly at only one trophic level. Most are omnivores with stronger tendencies towards one source of food but able to exploit one or more others. This appears especially so in the tropics where there is generally an abundance of food year around. The diameter of the circles for these groups in a Bolivian stream indicates their relative preferences. Only one is not an omnivore. (From Tomanova et al. 2006.)

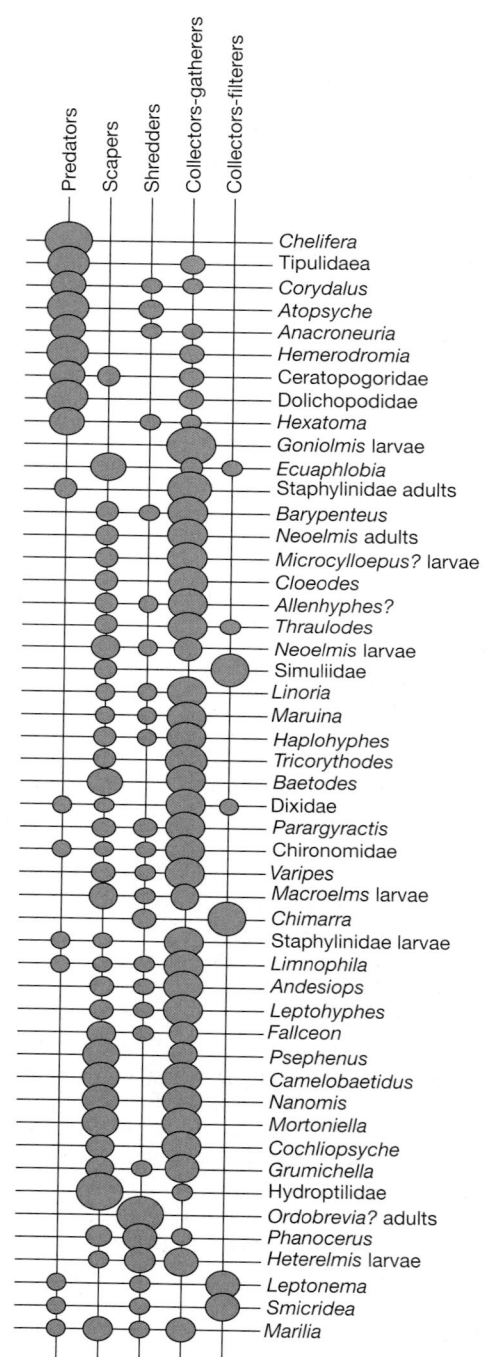

Large Crustacea are perhaps more common in tropical streams than in temperate ones. The latter have crayfish and occasionally crabs, but large atyid shrimps and crabs are very widespread in tropical streams. Different species have different feeding preferences but many are clearly omnivorous. Some of the shrimps can filter fine material from the flow by holding limbs like fans into the current whilst also using the same limbs like paint brushes to sweep fine detritus from rock surfaces into their mouths. Others clearly shred leaf material. In Puerto Rican streams, leaves placed in 1 cm × 1 cm mesh bags and therefore accessible to shrimps such as *Xiphocaris elongata* were eaten at rates of around 4% per day, whilst leaves in finer (1 mm × 1 mm mesh) bags disappeared at around 2% per day. Even that is a high rate of loss compared with temperate regions. Other studies (Fig. 7.24) in the same streams, in which shrimps were excluded from areas of the bottom using electric fencing have shown that in the absence of shrimps fine organic matter accumulates and algae grow more prolifically. Certain other invertebrates, such as chironomids also became more abundant.

The contribution of allochthonous leaves in tropical forested streams seems not to be denied. Some controversy rests on whether they feed into the food webs as fine detritus following microbial activity alone or whether invertebrates shred them. Where shredders appear absent from fauna lists this may be because of insufficient knowledge of the feeding behaviour or it may be that the sampling methods used did not fully reveal the larger crustaceans, especially crabs. These often hide in debris dams or rock crevices by day and emerge at night. The traditional methods of disturbing bottom substrate by foot or hand into a net held downstream may thus miss such animals.

In streams in the rain forest of the Usambara Mountains in Tanzania, the invertebrate fauna, sampled by such methods, appears sparse and dominated by insects, many of which are predators. The streams are almost bare of leaves though twigs and tree trunks abound in them. I placed leaves of a common forest tree, *Ficus mucedo* in very tight woven bags, in coarse (1 mm) bags and simply tied together in bundles without any bags and placed them in one stream. I was very surprised to find most of the exposed bundles had disappeared, only the stalks being left, after only one day. After a week all these leaves had disappeared whilst those in the bags were intact (Fig. 7.25). The reason was that crabs had eaten them. The crabs were omnivores, eating leaves, animals and mosses and grew to large size; 10 cm across the carapace was not uncommon. They consumed the leaves at a rate of around 30% per day, which is nearly ten times higher than other measures of crustacean shredding, and leaves falling into the stream also disappeared at this rate. I caught leaves on a sheet and compared the rate of fall with the mass of leaves in the stream to calculate the rate of loss.

What was puzzling was how the crabs gained enough calcium for their carapaces from water that was very low in ions (around 50 µS cm$^{-1}$). One possibility is that the crabs move into the forest during rainy periods and eat molluscs. There is one species that specializes in living in the otherwise very acid water that accumulates in holes in trees, which it neutralizes by importing mollusc shells, giving a calcium-rich solution.

This latter raises the issues of how tropical headwater streams are linked with the surrounding forest. We have some information on energy budgets, but little on the sorts of interactions that involve wolves and bears in temperate streams, though the richer fauna of the tropics would suggest even more such links, which are well known for large tropical floodplain rivers (Chapter 9). Whole system energy studies show some interesting features, however. For example, the metabolism of a Puerto Rican stream has been studied using measurements of the oxygen concentration in the water throughout the day and night (see Chapter 9 for details). For the Puerto Rican stream, $P_g$ was, 70 g $O_2$ m$^{-2}$ yr$^{-1}$ in the canopied headwaters, shaded by trees, and 453–634 in the lower, less shaded reaches. $R$ was higher than $P$ in both sections, with around 770 in the headwaters and 1550–1660 in the lower reaches. $P$ was less than $R$ throughout and the reasons for this appear to be because allochthonous material was being used in the upper reaches. In the lower reaches, $P$ was limited because the abundance of shrimp and fish grazers kept the periphyton populations very low and the potential for photosynthesis was not realized.

Other studies on Puerto Rican streams showed a general tendency for shredders to be abundant in the canopied headwaters and scrapers to increase downstream but for filter-collectors to be more abundant upstream. Again this was probably due to a local phenomenon in that predators on these animals, such as fish and shrimps, were abundant downstream and removed them, but because of waterfalls and other barriers the predators could not penetrate upstream. Use of stable isotope methods in a Atlantic coastal forest

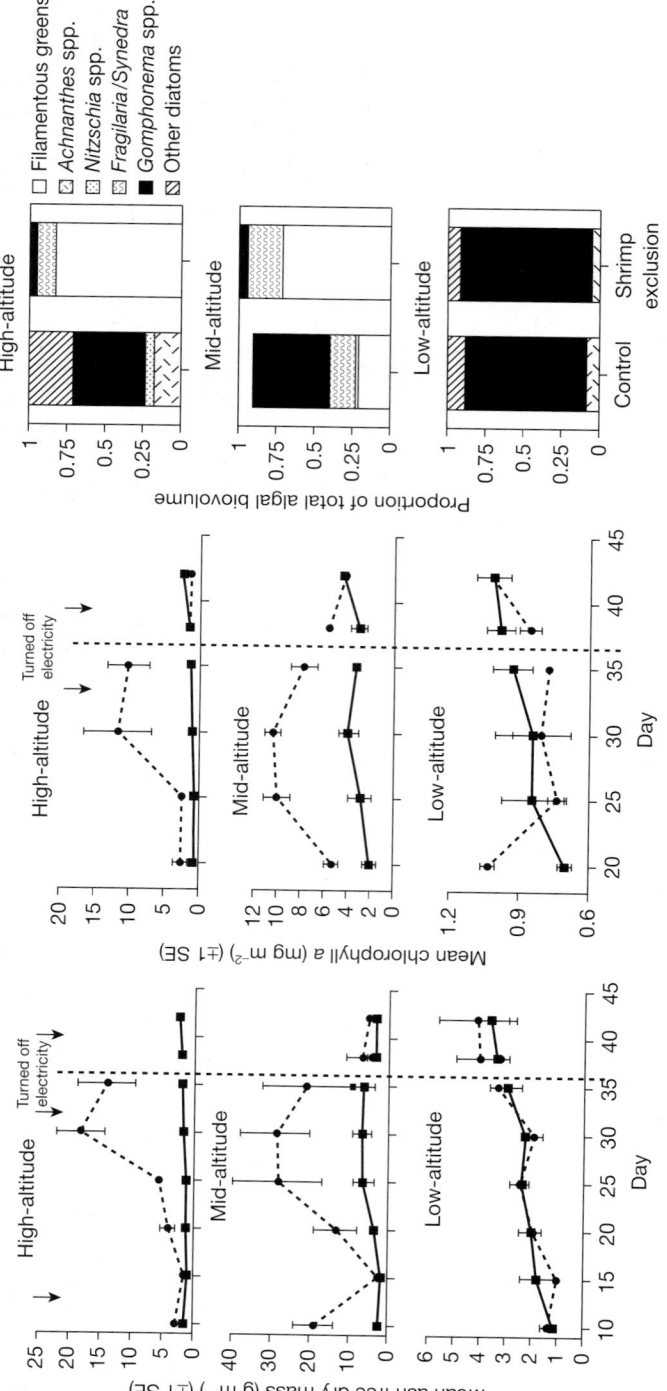

**Fig. 7.24** Large shrimps are common in montane streams in the tropics, where fish are often scarce or absent because of barriers such as waterfalls. Large shrimps (*Atya* sp and *Xiphocaris elongata*) were removed by electrofishing from sections of the Rio Espiritu Santo at altitudes of 10, 90 and 300 m above sea level and thereafter excluded by electrified barriers (dotted lines), compared with controls (solid lines). At the mid- and high altitudes this resulted in accumulation of organic matter and greater growths of algae (right). There was no such effect at the low altitude probably because the role of the shrimps was taken over by high densities of snails. Exclusion of shrimps also led to changes in the composition of the algal community left. (From March et al. 2002.)

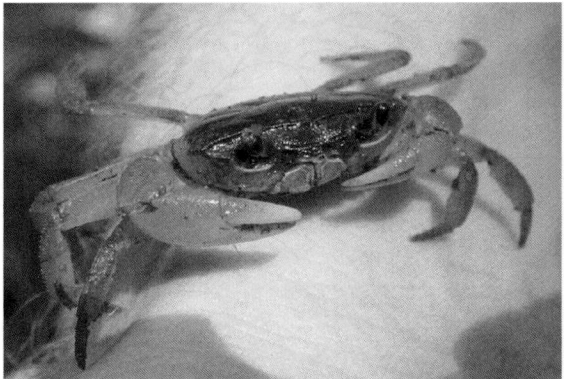

**Fig. 7.25** Crabs are important shredders in many tropical streams and often dominate the biomass. In a stream in Tanzania, crabs removed almost all of bundles of leaves in a few days, whereas smaller invertebrates and microorganisms with access to leaves in coarse and fine mesh bags had no effect in the same period. (From Moss 2005.)

stream in Brazil also showed considerable feeding on allochthonous material in the forested headwaters but nonetheless put more emphasis, for the most abundant baetid mayflies and the shrimp *Macrobrachium*, on material produced by algae within the stream. The sites sampled were largely quite open ones, however, with good light penetration.

Generalities about tropical streams, beyond the principle that available food resources will engender appropriate animal communities, are thus hard to find. As information accumulates, more may emerge but it is equally likely that the sheer complexity of the tropics will obviate this and perhaps also possible that the generalizations made for temperate regions will also be confounded by more detail as new aspects of their biology are explored. But now, like the water in the river, we move on and will consider the systems of rivers as they have ceased to be pristine and have become damaged by human activities.

## FURTHER READING

There is no shortage of literature on stream and river ecology. Two journals, *Freshwater Biology* and *Journal of the American Benthological Society* are particularly rich and there have been several specialist text books in recent years, including Allan & Castillo (2009), Giller & Malmqvist (1998) and Naiman et al. (2009). Hauer & Lamberti (2006) give much detail on research methods in streams, and Williams (2006) concentrates on temporary streams. Calow and Petts (1992) is still a useful reference.

Recent reviews on a variety of stream topics are: Decamps et al. (2004) (riparian zones), Malmqvist (2002), Clarke et al. (2008) (invertebrates). Cardinale et al. (2006) (biodiversity), Moore (2006) (ecosystem engineer species), Baxter et al. (2005) (linkages between the stream and the land, a very important review). Bilton et al. (2001), Bohonak & Jenkins (2003) (dispersal),

Northcote & Lobon-Cervia (2008) (experimental studies on trout). A former literature dominated by studies relating invertebrate communities to physicochemical features is being enriched by experimental studies on biological interactions, including Dahl (1998a,b), Konishi et al. (2001), Parker et al. (2007a) and McIntosh & Townsend (1996) and the quite wonderful results of the experiment of reintroducing wolves on stream systems are documented in Ripple & Beschta (2004a,b) and Beschta & Ripple (2008). A wide variety of references is now available on streams in different geographic locations including, Gislason et al. (1998) for the Arctic, Helfield & Naiman (2006), Naiman et al. (2002) for cold temperate (and many references in the text books quoted above for these regions), and Bêche et al. (2006), Boulton (2003), Cheshire et al. (2005), Dobson et al. (2002), Greathouse & Pringle (2006), Lake (2003), Ortiz-Zayas et al. (2005), Pringle et al. (1993), Gray (1981), Wright & Covich (2005) and Yule (1996) for tropical and warm temperate. And if you find the sheer amount of stream literature overwhelming (I did!), the best antidote is to get hold of a net and an identification book and go and look in your nearest stream and see for yourself.

*Chapter 8*

# USES, MISUSES AND RESTORATION OF HEADWATER STREAMS AND RIVERS

## 8.1 TRADITIONAL USE OF HEADWATER RIVER SYSTEMS

Salmon have yearly migrated up the valleys of the Rocky Mountains in Canada, and the ranges of Alaska, following a period of fattening in the Pacific Ocean. There are seven Pacific species and four of them, the sockeye (*Oncorhyncus nerka*), pink (*Oncorhyncus gorbuscha*), coho (*Oncorhyncus kisutch*) and Chinook (*Oncorhyncus tshawytscha*) migrate up the Fraser River in British Columbia and into its tributaries to spawn, moving seasonally in cohorts, formerly of millions of fish. For many hundreds of years, and to some extent still, despite suppression of indigenous groups by the colonial authorities during the 18th to early 20th centuries, they have been the basis of food and wealth for many north-western American peoples (Fig. 8.1). Customs varied from tribe to tribe, but in general family groups within the tribes 'owned' the rights to particular stretches of river or fishing locations within the river. Salmon, as well as items such a sea otter pelts for dwellers close to the coast, particular quarried stones for tool making, metals, deer hides and meat were harvested in what was a hunter–gatherer but not nomadic society. Villages were set close to the rivers

and comprised different sized houses, from very large to very small huts.

Excavation of one such village, at Keatley Creek in British Columbia, about 240 km north-east of Vancouver, revealed five large huts, a smaller number of medium-sized ones and many small ones housing a calculated total population of 1500 people. The smallest huts, of only 40 m², and supporting three families, revealed a lifestyle that was spartan. Clothing was of beaten bark and bony food residues were of the watery, least calorific, pink salmon. Fuel was scarce and charcoal remains few. Several families, living in much greater opulence, occupied the largest huts. Apparently they traded salmon oil, berries, dog meat, jade, slaves and other luxury goods. There were remains of leather clothing, seashell necklaces, and artwork with jade. Food comprised deer and the rich, oily species of salmon, the sockeye and chinook. There was evidence of many cooking and warming fires.

Knowledge from archaeological sites, and of the historic period, gathered by anthropologists such as Franz Boas, reveals that a hierarchical society prevailed. A few families were very wealthy and owned the rights to fish with 2-m wide long-handled nets from platforms built on particular overhanging rocks where there was minimal danger of being swept into the current, and where the sockeye and chinook salmon were forced close to the edge. They also owned deer fences in the hills where animals could be cornered for slaughter, and

*Ecology of Freshwaters: A View for the Twenty-first Century.*
4th edition. By Brian Moss. Published 2010 by Blackwell Publishing Ltd.

**Fig. 8.1** The Keatley Creek village (lower left, house hollows) depended on a system based on salmon (upper right) fisheries that persisted (upper left) until the 20th century, when the potlatch system of ceremonial gatherings, held for the giving of gifts (lower right) became undermined by external trade goods and fell into disrepute. (Photographs, University of British Columbia, British Columbia Archives.)

quarries for particular rocks used for tools, ornament and trade. Other families had rights to lesser fishing sites, on the banks, where only the smaller pink and the coho salmon were in reach but the occupants of the smallest huts did not even have these but were slaves working for the middle and upper classes and living on their cast-offs.

The richer people had responsibilities that ensured a sustainable harvest and an insurance against famine. From time to time, when there was a local surplus they would prepare a large feast, the potlatch, and assemble surplus produce such as deer meat, salmon oil and blankets of mountain goat wool to be given to guests from other villages in the region, where perhaps resources were currently scarcer. Often these occasions

were associated with weddings or the accession of a new chief. The larger the potlatch, the greater the status the donors enjoyed within the regional tribe, but there was a snag. The gift had to be returned by the recipients some time later, with a small amount of interest, and then further reciprocated.

If it were not, status was lost. This ensured that potlatches were infrequent and that overharvesting of salmon and other natural produce was avoided, because overfishing would result in a fall in harvest and an inability to return the gifts. The system worked well so long as the gifts were pegged to the quantity of local resources. It was nearly destroyed by the introduction of trade goods by Europeans, which devalued the local produce in barter for metal and cloth goods. The system had many features of a sustainable society that could endure and indeed did, for at least 1500 years. It encompassed features that seem inherent in human societies such as property rights, title holding, public accountability and rules of exchange. It was also a social insurance against variation in harvest and incorporated environmental ethics into a religious system. Animals were believed to be reincarnated as gods and failure to share wealth was believed to result in punishments by the animals, such as a failure in the salmon runs.

The Fraser River close to the Keatley Creek village is 30 m wide, cascading in rapids through a canyon, and the run of Chinook salmon in spring was estimated at 8 million fish before commercial fishing began lower down the river. Some fish could be 30 kg in weight. Sockeye salmon were caught in July, dried in air and eaten or traded. Discarded fish heads were boiled down for their oil. The Keatley creek village was abandoned, however, in AD 850, along with two other local villages and for a time this was unexplained. What had happened became clear when examination of deposits in terraces, slightly above the river lower downstream, showed a sequence of fine sediments sandwiched between the coarser gravels of fast flowing water. The sequence could be dated from charcoal, using $^{14}$C dating in a cooking and storage pit that had been covered by the deposits. For a time, probably several years or decades, the river had been blocked and converted into a lake, with the dam, probably a natural rockslide disturbed by a small earthquake, preventing the salmon from running upstream. A modern equivalent in 1913 also stopped salmon runs. The inhabitants of Keatley Creek would have had to move, and become dependent on alliances with neighbouring villages to support them until they could return to their own fishing sites.

This example demonstrates how human societies can use, in a sensible and sustainable way the natural resources at their disposal, and also the consequences of their dependence on them. It is a local dependence that modern societies have discarded through agriculture, trade and export, but at the expense of near exhaustion of many natural resources and creation of wastes that jeopardize future comfort and security. We have merely increased the stakes in a gamble that we may lose no less than the Keatley creek villagers lost when a landslide stopped the salmon runs. That will be the story of modern use of upstream rivers and indeed of all our freshwater resources.

## 8.2 DEFORESTATION

Headwater rivers are often in upland regions where soils are thin and settled peoples fish, hunt, or raise stock rather than grow crops, though this is possible if slopes are terraced. Impacts on the streams are less than in the floodplains of the lowlands, where human populations are higher, but they are still considerable. Fishing is now unusual because former upstream fisheries have been undermined by removal of migratory fish lower down or obstruction of their movements by dams. The secondary consequences of settlement and pasturage may greatly alter the catchments.

Pasturage means the deliberate removal of forest, which, except in very dry or very high areas, is the usual natural cover for hilly regions the world over. Even when it was not deliberate, deforestation happened because stock browse on tree seedlings and regeneration of the forest is then not possible. Native grazers, such as deer, antelope, wild sheep, wild goats and cattle, forest buffalo or bison, are kept in check by predators such as wolves, tiger, leopard and lynx and so herbivore numbers are prevented from reaching damaging levels. In a natural forest, the clutter created by fallen timber provides both the structure needed for fully functioning streams but also creates places protected from grazers where tree seedlings can grow. Large grazers will not risk breaking a leg to reach seedlings nested in interlocked branches and fallen trunks on the forest floor.

Human settlement will also mean clearance of forest for fuel and if the forest, even if it is unsettled, is used for a timber harvest, dead wood may no longer be left in place or allowed to accumulate. The river, as well as the forest, will be denied the debris that is crucial to its full functioning. This may also have distant as well as local consequences. Peoples of the tundra-bordered Arctic coastline depend on forest debris that has cascaded down the rivers, and eventually washed up on the beaches, for fuel and building, and material for tools and hunting weapons. Human settlement will also mean hunting out of predators, for they may attack domestic stock, and an increase in deer and smaller seed-eating animals such as squirrels and rodents, thus reducing the ability of the forest to regenerate, through the unchecked damage they cause. Beaver, with their habits of creating temporary dams, will be hunted out or will be unable to find suitable riparian timber with which to build. One way or another the forest is doomed and the rivers will change accordingly.

**Fig. 8.2** Upland streams in the UK may appear to be in good condition, but often are severely damaged. This river, in the Trough of Bowland, is acidified, its riparian forest has been removed and prevented from regrowth by overgrazing by sheep, and bank erosion has widened it so that the water is shallow in summer and usually too warm for successful breeding of the characteristic native brown trout.

The local consequences are immediate. Pasturage and, on lesser slopes, eventual cultivation, begin to increase soil erosion, especially if the soils are soft and peaty, and the leaching of nutrients that start to change the stream environment. Soils become less able to retain water as their organic content is oxidized away and not regenerated by tree litter. Debris dams across the river are washed out and not replaced. Rainstorms lead to high floods and in dry periods the basal flow may be greatly reduced. In the lesser flows the fine deposits of soil will block and blanket the gravels required for the survival of salmon eggs, and tree debris will no longer retain the carcasses of the spawned fish.

The invertebrate community will change from one of shredders and collectors to one of algal scrapers, supported by nutrients washed in from the land in the more open environment. In patches of sediment, aquatic plants may colonize. At the edges, overgrazing by sheep and trampling of the edges by cattle will lead to erosion and the stream will widen, but since water

flows in summer will be reduced, it will become shallower and will therefore warm more in the summer sunshine. Indeed it may warm sufficiently to stop cold-water fish such as brown trout (*Salmo trutta*) from spawning. Paradoxically the open terrain (Fig. 8.2) may be valued by people, as in the open fells of the hillier parts of England, the casual observer being unaware that these are ecologically very damaged systems.

## 8.3 ACIDIFICATION

In the 1970s, an awareness grew that waters in the uplands of Europe and eastern North America had become more acid than they would naturally be. Values well below the natural pH of rain (around 5.5, Chapter 3) were found and were being associated with losses of fish from streams. Acidification, it turned out from studies of sediment cores from lakes (see Chapter 11), had begun in the mid-19th century in Europe and had been recognized at the time, but the

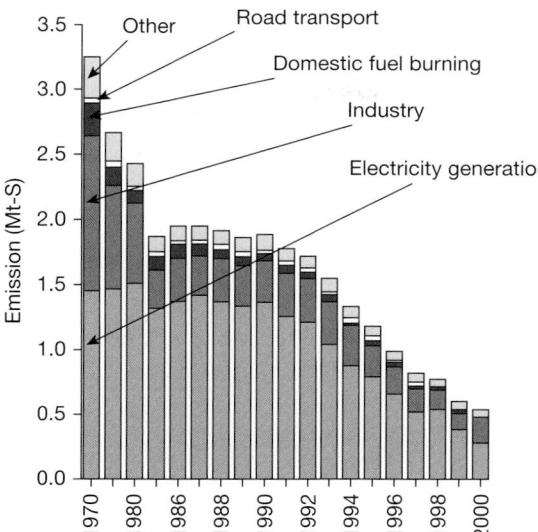

**Fig. 8.3** Trends in sulphur emissions in the UK. Emissions were, and are dominated by electricity generation and industrial fuel burning, but total emissions have been greatly reduced since 1970 by neutralization of the sulphur gases at the source by reaction with calcium carbonate. (Based on NEGTAP 2001.)

problem had intensified with the industrial expansion of the late 20th century. The problem was traced to the production of sulphur oxides (largely $SO_2$, but with others involved, so that the term $SO_x$ is usually used) from the burning of coal and oil in power stations and other industrial plants. Domestic coal burning had also been responsible, but had been much reduced in the UK after the 1950s following dense smogs that had led to severe bronchitis among city dwellers. Sulphur also enters the atmosphere from natural volcanic emissions and release of dimethyl sulphides on the decay of marine phytoplankton, but industrial emissions doubled the total release by the 1970s (Fig. 8.3).

In the atmosphere, $SO_x$ was oxidized to sulphuric acid and on reaching the ground, sulphuric acid reacted with soil minerals, removing bases such as calcium, mobilizing metals, particularly aluminium, and leaving a surplus of hydrogen ions to run off into streams and lower the pH. The direct effects of reduced pH included interference with the enzymes that fish embryos use to break through the enclosing egg membranes, so that they failed to hatch, and production of mucus around the gills of adult fish so that gas exchange was hampered and they asphyxiated. Some invertebrate groups were also directly affected, including crustaceans, which failed to form the calcareous components of their exoskeletons, and insects. Moreover the aluminium dissolved from the soil minerals had several further effects. It accumulated in invertebrates and then further in small stream birds such as dippers (*Cinclus cinclus*) and interfered with eggshell formation, so that recruitment of young was reduced and populations fell. Similar effects have been shown for other water birds that feed on invertebrates (Fig. 8.4). Aluminium also precipitated phosphorus compounds from waters so that natural productivity was reduced.

Acidification had its initial direct effects on the terrestrial vegetation, killing trees in an already much deforested landscape. It also had long-term effects. Emissions of $SO_x$ have been reduced by scrubbing the gases released with wet calcium carbonate at the power stations and the sulphate content in the atmosphere has fallen, but several decades of acidification have reduced the acid-neutralising capacity (ANC) of catchment soils by leaching out previous stocks of bases. In a soil developed in a particular place, there is usually a net loss of bases as new base formation from the weathering of minerals is not quite matched by losses by leaching (Chapter 3). Acidification accelerated this, resulting in a severe base depletion that has not yet been replenished by rock weathering and may not be in the foreseeable future. Stream waters have thus increased in pH, but remain acid despite the reduction in sulphur emissions. Responses in stream communities have been slow (Fig. 8.5). Often local treatment of symptoms by dripping in suspensions of lime has had to be used to restore fish communities.

This may have to continue for even longer, however, for as sulphur oxides have been reduced (Fig. 8.3), they have been replaced in the atmosphere as acidifying agents by the nitrogen gases produced by vehicle engines and burning of vegetation (nitrous oxide and nitric oxide), and emission of ammonia from animal wastes (Fig. 8.6). Nitrogen emissions have increased three- to tenfold over natural levels and industrial nitrogen fixation is now as great as natural fixation. The nitric acid that now reaches the ground not only acidifies but also contributes to the problem of nutrient pollution, called eutrophication. New technology in the developed world (e.g., catalytic converters in vehicle engines) will undoubtedly progressively reduce these emissions but there will be a lag in response not least

**Fig. 8.4** Acidification of streams in Pennsylvania due to acid precipitation and mining pollution led to reduced wing size and mass (upper right) of the Louisiana water thrush, which feeds on invertebrates in streams, and to delayed egg laying (lower right). Open symbols are unacidified sites (pH 7.1–7.3); closed symbols are acidified sites (pH 4.5–5.4). Acidification also led to reduced food availability, lower population density and reduced fledgling survival. (From Mulvihill et al. 2008.)

because of the loss of ANC from the soils. In the developing world, especially in Asia, the problem of acidification is now increasing and all the problems that became apparent in eastern North America and industrial Europe in the 1970s are now emerging in China, India and elsewhere.

The risk of acidification problems can be assessed from data on local geology and soils (cation exchange capacity and base saturation) and local rainfall, and expressed first as the critical load of sulphate, nitrate or hydrogen ions, below which it is judged that no serious effects will be experienced. Serious effects are damage to the local vegetation causing increased vulnerability of forest trees to frost, drought or pests, or, in the case

of nitrogen loading, reduced diversity and increased grazing damage from insects seeking more nutritious tissues. Inevitably, terrestrial problems are accompanied by problems in the streams. Critical loads can be as low as 12–30 milliequivalents of $H^+$ $m^{-2}$ $yr^{-1}$ in igneous rock areas or >300 in areas of basic sedimentary rock. In general, sensitivities are highest in cold, dry areas with soils with low base saturation, lesser in warm wet areas with high base saturation (Fig. 8.7). Table 8.1 compares rainwater composition in an acidified region of Europe and a yet unacidified dusty area of north-east India. The dust provides substantial buffering capacity. Risks of problems are indicated by the ratio of actual load to critical load and it would

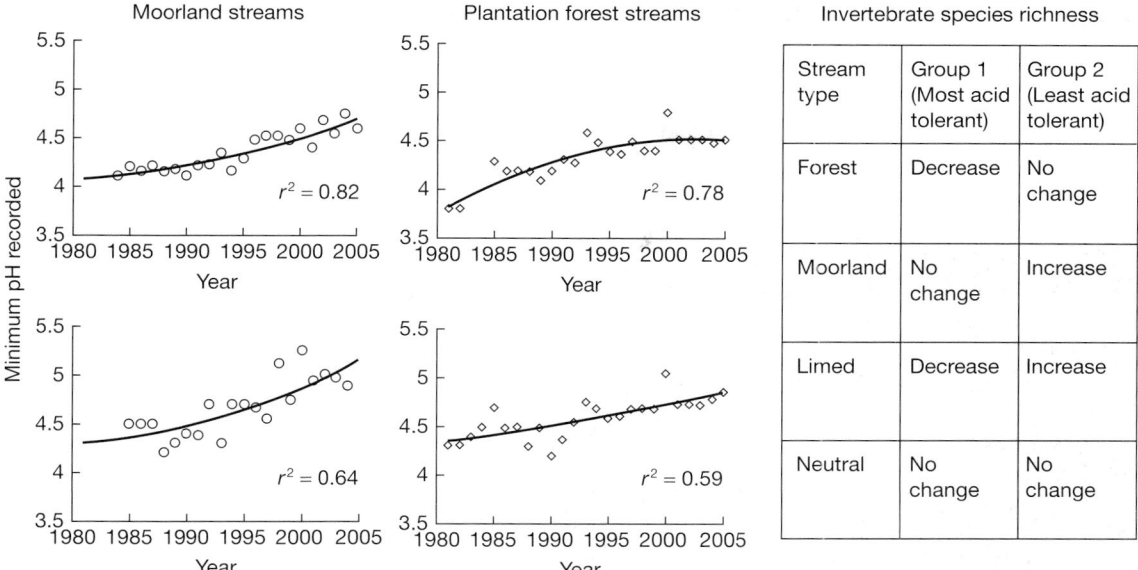

**Fig. 8.5** Upland streams in the UK, including those in central Wales (left) have all improved chemically since sulphur scrubbing at power stations reduced sulphur emissions to the atmosphere. Ecological responses have not followed to the same extent (right) though there has been some decrease in the number of very acid tolerant invertebrate species and an increase in the least acid tolerant. Intermediate groups have shown little change. Liming, a procedure frequently used in the past to neutralize the acid had relatively little effect. The reason may be that severe acid episodes still occur when heavy rain washes through still large pockets of acidified soil. (From Ormerod & Durance 2009.)

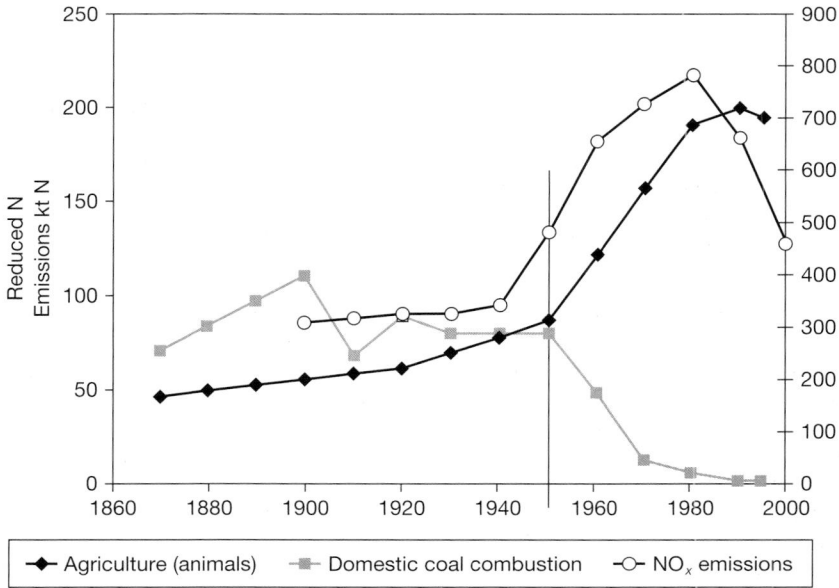

**Fig. 8.6** Changes in nitrogen emissions in the UK. Agriculture and coal burning produce a lot of the very volatile ammonia. As coal burning has been reduced, there has been an increase in agricultural sources. $NO_x$ is produced from vehicle engines, whose usage has expanded greatly since 1950, indicated by vertical line.

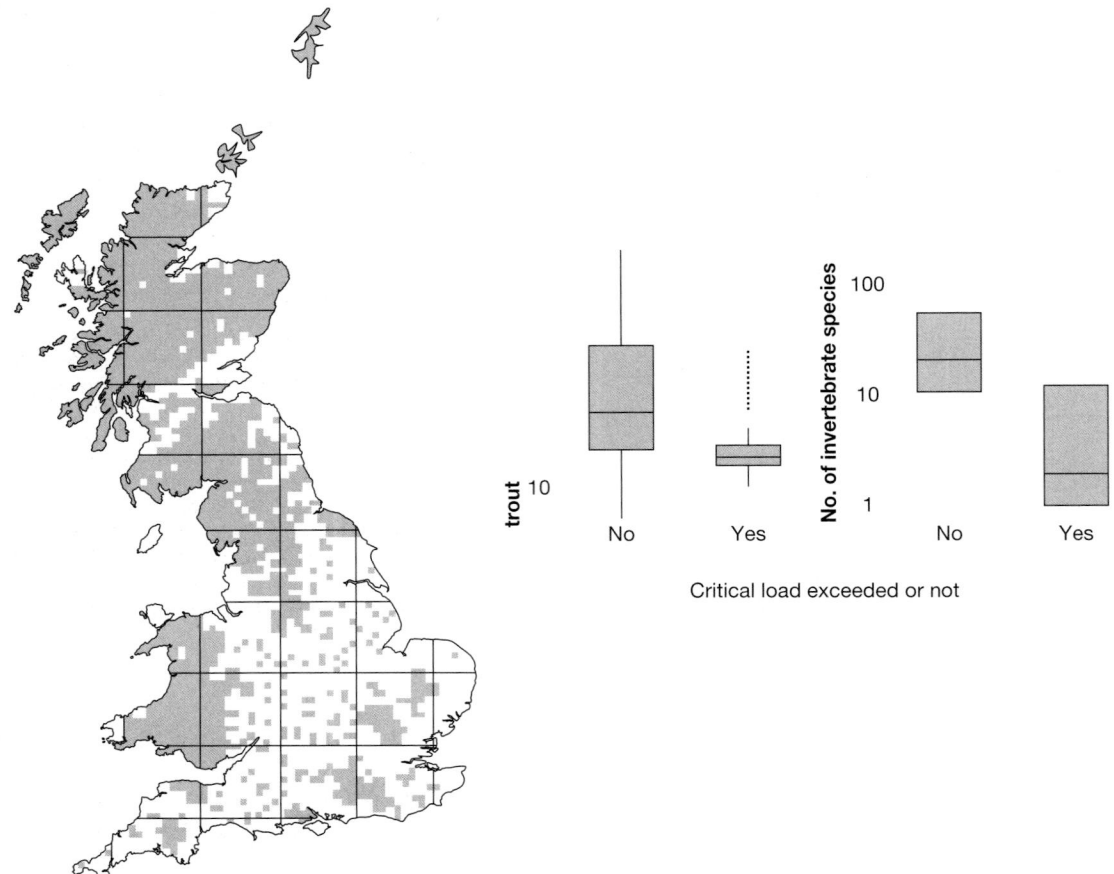

**Fig. 8.7** Critical loads for hydrogen ions are those that ecosystems can tolerate without showing long-term deterioration. They vary from place to place depending on rainfall, dustiness and ability of the rocks and soils to neutralize the acids. Useful measures are maps showing by how much hydrogen ion the critical load is exceeded. In the UK it is exceeded on base poor rocks in the north and west and on sandy glacial drift in southern England (dark shading in left panel). Exceedance of the critical load is shown by reduced trout density and a decline in the number of invertebrate species present. (Based on NEGTAP 2001.)

appear that although risks may decrease a little in Europe and North America, they still affect up to 17% of the land area and are increasing substantially in Asia, Africa and South America (Fig. 8.8). Nitrogen problems will spread the risk away from industrial areas.

## 8.4 EUTROPHICATION

Destruction of forest inevitably breaks mechanisms that conserved nutrients in the natural system and replaces them with agricultural systems that leak nutrients. Stock excreta are washed overland in rainstorms and the hooves of relatively densely crowded animals increase soil erosion, which transfers both silt and particulate nutrients to streams. Ploughing, tillage and fertilization for crops do likewise. The amounts of nutrients that are lost vary with the intensity of the farming but concentrations of phosphorus and nitrogen in stream waters will rise tenfold or more compared with intact systems (see Chapter 4). The losses would stop as stocks in the soil are used up were it not for the fact that new nutrients are continually imported into the catchment from elsewhere as stock

**Table 8.1** Typical composition of precipitation in an acidified region (central Europe) and a dusty region (north-east India). In μequiv per litre. (From Rodhe et al. 2002.)

|  | **Acidified** | **Dusty** |
|---|---|---|
| Anions |  |  |
| Sulphate | 70 | 20 |
| Nitrate | 30 | 10 |
| Chloride | 15 | 15 |
| Bicarbonate | 0 | 15 |
| Sum | 115 | 60 |
| Cations |  |  |
| Ammonium | 30 | 20 |
| Sodium | 15 | 13 |
| Calcium | 12 | 20 |
| Magnesium | 5 | 5 |
| Potassium | 3 | 2 |
| Hydrogen | 50 (pH 4.3) | Negligible (pH 6.2) |
| Sum | 115 | 60 |

feed and artificial fertilizer. In the mediaeval period in Europe, and in contemporary tropical systems, when these imports were, or are, not available, there is evidence that farms became less fertile as nutrient stocks are washed out and not replaced rapidly enough by soil nitrogen fixation and rock weathering.

Eutrophication, as this transfer of nutrients is known, is a serious problem when the stream water reaches a large river or lake, but it also has effects in streams. It will increase production a little, by increasing the rate of leaf litter processing, if leaves still remain as a potential food source in a denuded landscape; it will increase periphyton growth and eroded soil may accumulate on the bed. Periphyton, once released from

**Fig. 8.8** (*below*) Acid precipitation has been most studied in Europe and North America, but as the large nations of the tropical world industrialise, it is becoming a global problem. Based on the local geology and the ability of the soils to neutralise acidity as well as the balance of rainfall and dustiness, the darker areas in this map are those where the risk of acidity problems in freshwaters is greatest. (Based on Rodhe et al. 2002.)

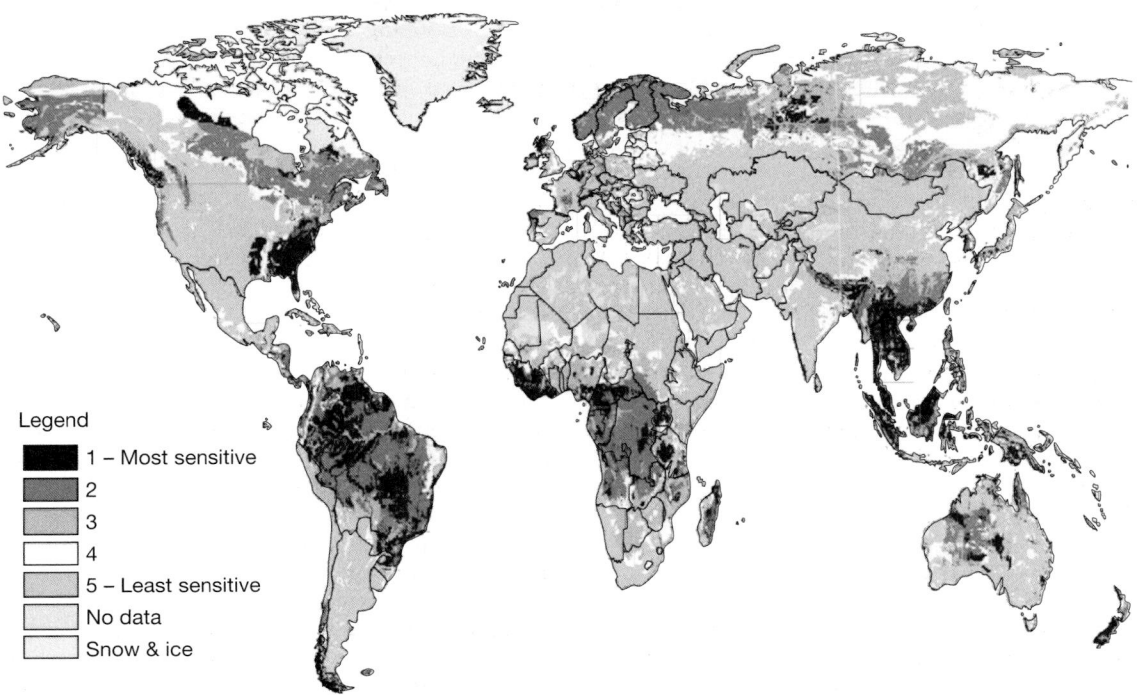

Legend
- ■ 1 – Most sensitive
- ■ 2
- ■ 3
- □ 4
- ■ 5 – Least sensitive
- ■ No data
- □ Snow & ice

limitation by lack of light as bankside trees are felled, will respond to increased nutrients in many areas and rocks previously coated with a thin biofilm of diatoms may acquire coarse strands of filamentous diatoms in spring and wadges of green algae, often the blanket weeds, *Cladophora* spp, later in the year. The invertebrate community will change to one dominated by scrapers, as the woody debris that held back leaf material that supported shredders, will no longer be so abundant. There may be more fine organic material exported from tilled land and this may encourage more filter collectors, as well as deposit feeders. Sometimes this may result in nuisance swarms of insects such as blackflies in early summer.

## 8.5 COMMERCIAL AFFORESTATION

Where trees have been maintained in an otherwise developed catchment, they will often not be native species. Forestry is an industry and uses species or varieties that are fast growing, often exotic, conifers rather than broad-leaved hardwoods that grow slowly and may live for centuries. Plantation trees are softwoods, felled after 40 or 50 years. Debris is not allowed to build up on the forest floor for fear of fires and woody debris is not allowed to fall into streams. Modern forestry uses every product of the tree, shredding even small branches to make chipboard and bark to sell for mulch and garden paths. The needles of conifers are woody and full of resins that impede microbial breakdown. They too build up on the bottoms of streams and clog the beds. Indeed it was failure of salmon recruitment owing to forestry practices in parts of Russia and Canada that started to reveal the important role of salmon carcasses and their nutrients in maintaining recruitment of the species. Plantations are often fertilized also and the coniferous trees may exacerbate acidification problems by their uptake of bases that are then removed with the timber. In the tropics similar problems occur with *Eucalyptus* trees being grown for fuel or palms for the oil in their seeds. Forestry does no more for the quality of stream ecosystems than other forms of crop agriculture.

## 8.6 SETTLEMENT

With agriculture comes also the expansion of small settlements to villages and villages to towns. People produce biological wastes no less than stock. Initially sewage disposal comprised a dung heap from which organic matter, nutrients and bacteria and viruses washed into rivulets in rain and then into streams. Those living close to a stream would use it directly. They also derived their drinking water from it or from wells in the local ground water that also became contaminated. The consequences were a high incidence of gastrointestinal diseases and from time to time truly dreadful outbreaks of typhoid and cholera, from which, in the crowded slums of the industrially developing world, as now in the burgeoning cities of the tropics, many died.

The next step is disposal in a pit behind the house but this too eventually becomes impossible for lack of space to put the pits, nuisance smells and the risks of enteric diseases. Isolated houses may still have the modern equivalent of the pit, the septic tank, in which sewage rots down and a sludge is pumped out from time to time and taken elsewhere for disposal, whilst a nutrient-rich effluent percolates to the deep soil layers. But the effluent from a septic tank is not innocuous and a high density of septic tanks is not possible in a village or town. Nitrogen compounds in septic tank effluents may be denitrified in the soil and phosphorus may be retained in the soils for a time but eventually the soils become saturated and nutrients reach the ground water and eventually the nearest stream. The more mechanized arrangements of the sewage treatment works, or with its modern name, the wastewater treatment works, however, are more immediate.

The effects of raw sewage discharge and also the organic matter thrown into rivers by industries such as tanning and food processing have been recognized for a long time (Fig. 8.9). The load of organic matter is too great for the supply of oxygen needed by decomposer bacteria and oxygen levels fall, often to zero. Anaerobic bacteria proliferate and the grey threads of a filamentous bacterium, *Sphaerotilus natans* start to appear like dirty cotton wool on the stream bed. As the oxygen recovers a little, Protozoa, and other bacteria become abundant and decomposition is completed. By this stage most of the macroinvertebrate fauna and the fish have been eliminated, but the more tolerant invertebrates, oligochaetes and chironomids begin to recolonize, followed by moderately tolerant Crustacea such as *Asellus*, and leeches. The nutrients released from decomposition support wads of blanket weed. Eventually, perhaps several kilometres below the source of pollution, nutrients have become diluted, algal growth

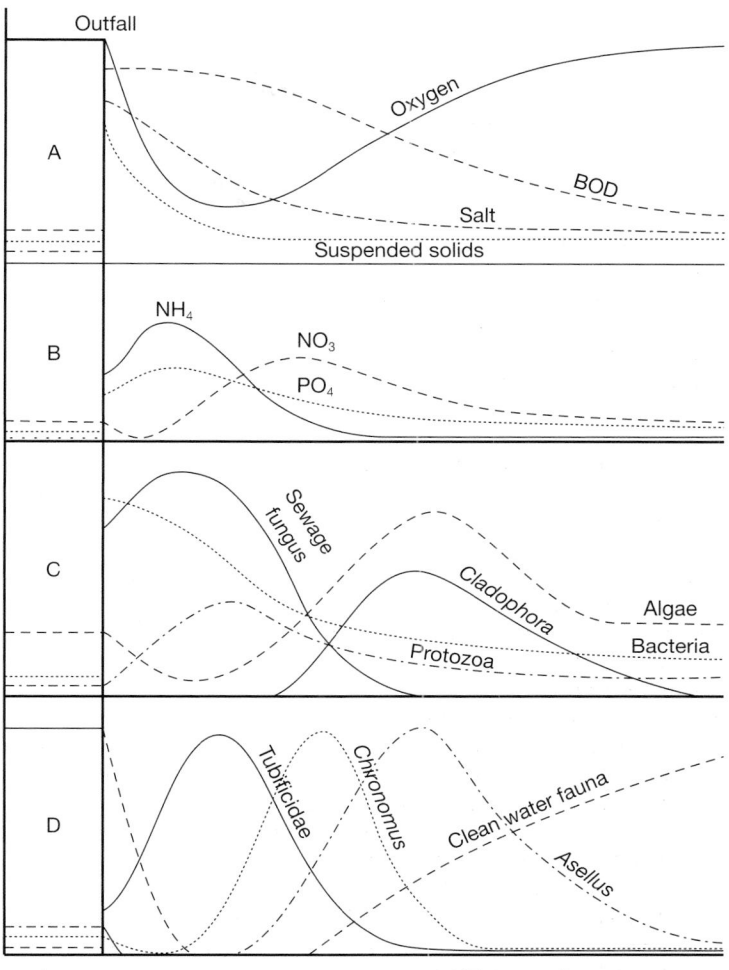

**Fig. 8.9** This diagram has become a classic since H.B.N. Hynes first used it to summarize the effects of a gross discharge of organic matter to a river. Pollution and recovery go through a sequence of linked stages involving the chemical environment and biological response. BOD, Biological oxygen demand. (Based on Hynes 1966.)

is reduced and the former diverse invertebrate fauna and the fish return. That is, provided there has not been a new source of pollutant to set back the process. Commonly settlements collect along river courses and this has usually been the case.

Settlements also add pollutants beyond gross organic matter. Towns attract industries and industries have produced in the past a diverse collection of wastes: heavy metals, acids, alkalis, deoxygenating chemicals such as hypochlorite, phenols, gasworks liquors and a myriad of products and waste substances from an array of industries from food processing to smelting, pesticides and plastics. Sometimes heat from the cooling of

power stations and even radioactive isotopes have added to the problems, though these are more usual in the lowland reaches closer to the coast. Many of these substances are now regulated in the western world and treated at wastewater treatment works (hence the new name) but new ones emerge continually. By-products of new processes may have unexpected effects. Some industrial detergents act like endocrine substances to disrupt gender and reproductive behaviours in fish and invertebrates, and hormonal contraceptives are excreted from the body and pass almost unchanged through the treatment works to retain similar effects in animals other than humans. Cycled back in drinking

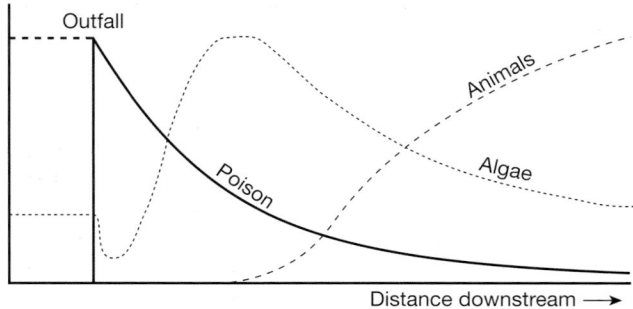

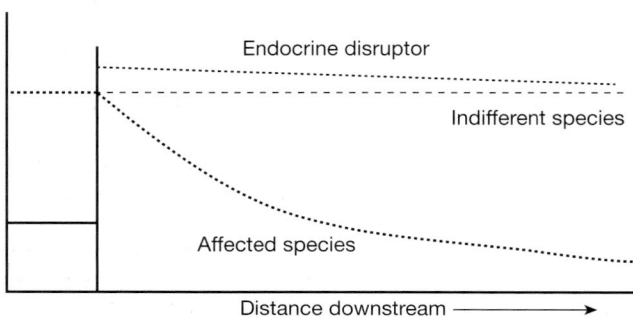

**Fig. 8.10** Hynes (1966) devised a similar diagram to summarize the effects of a lethal toxin (upper). Such pollution is less common (except for accidents) now in Europe because of increased stringency of industrial legislation, but severe incidents still occur and, as with gross organic pollution (Fig. 8.9), the developing world is developing its environmental problems in parallel. The lower diagram illustrates an increasingly common scenario, everywhere now, of a sublethal, trace organic substance having selective effects on reproduction of some organisms, leading to a community change and loss of biodiversity.

water they may also have effects on human sperm counts.

If waters are naturally complex chemical mixtures (Chapters 3 and 4), that complexity is amplified by what is added through human activities. The earlier chemical pollutants tended to be outright lethal to river communities (Fig. 8.10). Animals were killed and communities recovered once the pollutant had been sufficiently diluted by the river flow. The new micro-organic pollutants are more insidious. They have sublethal effects that have ramifications for the community as a whole through alteration of behaviours and food webs and which are much less easily detectable and remediable than a simple fish kill. Moreover, pollutants rarely come singly and estimating the effects even of a single pollutant in a complex system is difficult; predicting that of a cocktail of pollutants is virtually impossible. As with gross organic matter, the developing world is following in the footsteps of the developed world when it comes to heavy metal pollution from industry and mining. Mercury is still used in separating small particles of gold and other precious metals from river sediments in South America and organochlorine pesticides banned in the western world are still sold (by western companies) in the tropics.

## 8.7 ENGINEERING IMPACTS

Once settlement has begun, its ramifications reach out like tentacles. Settlements need water supplies and as they become bigger, water pumped from the stream is insufficient, especially in dry areas or periods. It also becomes more likely to be contaminated with disease organisms as human activity increases. Recognition of this in the late 19th century led to the damming of rivers in the uplands for water storage and the establishment of treatment works for the provision of safe and drinkable water. Settlements also need electricity and food. Damming has been used to create a head of water to drive hydroelectric turbines and to store water for irrigation of drier downstream areas. Many dams were made in the 20th century particularly in the 1960s and 1970s. There are now around 45,000 large dams (>15 m or with a dam volume of 3 million cubic metres) worldwide and an unaccounted number, probably over a million, of smaller ones.

But damming has its negative side and many big dams have created as many problems as they have solved. Again a syndrome of circumstances sets in. The dam stops migratory fish from reaching upstream spawning grounds and the very fact of storage alters the size and seasonal pattern of river flow. In turn this alters the nature of the river community. The most problematic aspect, however, is that, especially with irrigation dams, rather little of the flow is released below the dam. What is referred to as 'environmental flow' may be only a few per cent of the natural flow and the river system below the dam is effectively destroyed. Floodplains (see next chapter) are left dry, rivers no longer reach the sea, salt water penetrates far inland, fisheries are destroyed and irrigated land in dry areas becomes salinized and eventually useless. Seventy per cent of the world's freshwater is now used in commercial crop irrigation. The issues of creating dams and reservoirs are discussed in Chapter 15.

Even if the river is not dammed it may be engineered. Settlements are often unwisely developed close to river channels that meander across valleys on timescales of decades to centuries. Human perception, based on experiences of only years, is that the channels are fixed and so buildings are constructed very close to them. Eventually these buildings become threatened as the channel moves and human communities seek to tame them with concrete or rock revetments. The channel is deepened and straightened and again loses most of its ecological structure and natural character. It becomes a drain and the flood storage associated with a natural river system is lost to the detriment of increased damage downstream after heavy rain. In turn this means more engineering. Once the natural geomorphology of the river starts to be altered, the process is unstoppable and in decades the river has become a mere conduit. Even in the remoter areas of Scandinavia, headwater rivers have been deepened and woody debris and even large rocks removed to facilitate floating of cut timber down to the sawmills. Almost all of the river systems of Europe, below the altitude at which settlement is possible have been severely altered. There are no pristine entire river systems at all.

## 8.8 ALTERATIONS OF THE FISH COMMUNITY BY MAN

The river channel may also be directly used for commercial activities. Fishing for food has been a long-term use of erosive rivers, probably to no detriment so long as it was on a small scale. Modern angling for recreation and commercial fish culture, however, are different matters.

The American brook trout (*Salvelinus fontinalis*) and the rainbow trout (*Onchorynchus mykiss*) were introduced to Britain in the late 19th century. Initially they were confined to hatcheries, for breeding was not successful in the wild. Hatchery fish have been used to stock recreational fisheries where the voraciousness of the rainbow trout, and the ability of both to tolerate greater extremes of temperature, dissolved oxygen and, for brook trout, pH, than the native brown trout, make them especially favoured by fishery managers. Some populations have now bred in the wild and it is not clear whether stable coexistence of these more resilient fish with brown trout and salmon is possible.

There has also been a great increase in farming of rainbow trout for the food trade. From about 40 farms in the UK in 1970, producing less than 1000 tonnes per year, the industry grew to nearly 360 farms producing nearly 16,000 tonnes by now. Fish farms take water from the rivers and return an effluent that may have a greater biological oxygen demand (from fish faeces). It may also contain antibiotics, and disinfectants, used to protect eggs against disease. Fish escape from the farms, and may introduce diseases, always liable to be rife under hatchery conditions, to the wild stocks of other species. Viral haemorrhagic septicaemia (VHS) and infectious pancreatic necrosis (IPN) are examples.

The hatcheries favour genetically tailored strains, selected for high growth rates, and disease resistance under hatchery conditions. Such fish may also be treated with steroids to produce only females, which grow fast, and to delay breeding so that spawning does not weaken fish, grown fat for angling, before they have been caught. Such fish may interbreed with native stocks. The progeny might survive in most years, but a severe year might result in widespread kills under conditions that naturally selected wild fish would survive.

The tendency to stock rivers with exotic fish for anglers has also been widespread in the USA where game-fishing commands large sums of money, and where natural communities may have suffered considerably. Training of fishery managers in the past has emphasized the production of large fish for anglers, though a more sympathetic attitude to conservation of the smaller native species may now prevail. An article by E. P. Pister (1985), a fisheries manager in the California Department of Fisheries and Game, describing his training and subsequent maturation to conserve small endemic fish of the desert springs and streams, rather than to remove them in favour of stocking exotic species for anglers, is enlightening reading. One of the introductions he formerly managed in the Owens River valley of California to the near extinction of four native fishes, was the European brown trout.

Commercial activities may also bring in other exotics, deliberately or accidentally. Perhaps most notorious have been introductions of crayfish and mussels. The American signal crayfish, introduced to mainland Europe in the 19th century and later to farms on English rivers as a fast growing, more resilient species than the European crayfish species, brought with it a fungal parasite, *Aphanomyces astaci*, to which it is resistant but which has reduced the English species to near extinction. The zebra mussel, *Dreissena polymorpha* (Fig. 8.11), native to the Black Sea region, has displaced many native molluscs in North America and is expected to spread through most of the continent, as it has through most of Europe. It particularly favours

hard substrates and does not grow so well on soft sediments unless it can gain a toehold on an isolated rock or piece of debris, when it may build up a colony that is then self-supported. Extensive colonies will clear the water of suspended matter, but also entirely obliterate the native fauna.

There have now been many thousands of species introductions among different continents, many of them incidental through use of freshwater as ballast in ships travelling empty of cargo and discharging the ballast in another freshwater port when they take on a new cargo. Riparian plants, sometimes introduced by nurseries for garden use, may also be problems. In the USA, the European purple loosestrife, *Lythrum salicaria*, has ousted many native species and forms dense monospecific swards along river banks and in wetlands, whilst in the UK, the giant hogweed, *Heracleum mantegazzianum* (notorious for skin rashes caused by

**Fig. 8.11** The zebra mussel (*Dreissena polymorpha*) (right) is just one of a series of exotic species, including crustaceans, molluscs, fish and plants that are now more easily introduced than previously from other continents and which are tending to increase in numbers and to out compete the native biota. Zebra mussels, which are about 2–3 cm long, filter water very rapidly, removing planktonic food that would sustain other animals and once having gained attachment on a hard surface will form colonies with huge numbers. Attempts at control (left) are generally too late and ineffective, despite the vigour with which they are pursued.

its sap on human skin exposed to bright sunlight), the Japanese knotweed (*Fallopia japonica*) and the Himalayan balsam, *Impatiens glandulifera*, have had similar effects. In all cases the spread of the plant has been exacerbated by removal of riparian forest and more open conditions and nutrient-polluted water.

Compared with lowland rivers (Chapters 9 and 10), upland erosive streams and rivers have been changed by human activities to a lesser extent, but the change has still been major and fundamental. Only the remoter rivers retain their pristine structural characteristics, their mutual links with the surrounding forests and the sheer richness of their ecological relationships. And even these are affected to some extent by atmospheric pollution and acidification. Where human settlement has occurred, the changes are as serious as they have been in the lowlands and there is a long history of attempts to mitigate them, at first usually in the interests of human health.

## 8.9 SEWAGE, TOXIC POLLUTION AND THEIR TREATMENT

Pollution by sewage of rivers in the industrial regions was the start of this concern. Fast flowing rivers

had been harnessed in the 18th and 19th centuries in Europe and New England to provide power for machinery: cotton gins, metal hammers and looms. The towns, later cities that grew in these places, such as Manchester and Sheffield, Birmingham and Stoke in the UK, were the first to suffer enteric disease epidemics. Between 1901 and 1915, a Royal Commission on Sewage Disposal in the UK produced nine reports and determined that sewage should be treated to remove organic matter and pathogens. It set limits for the quality of effluent released from sewage treatment works, based on its content of suspended solids and its biological oxygen demand (BOD). Biological oxygen demand is measured by enclosing the effluent, suitably diluted if necessary, in a bottle and determining the rate at which oxygen is consumed under standard conditions of temperature in the dark. The Commission's findings have been the basis for sewage treatment worldwide.

Their effect was to require more stringent treatment of sewage (Fig. 8.12), which had previously simply been spread on fields (sewage farms) if it had been treated at all. Processes developed in which the sewage is macerated and the gross solids settled as sludge. The sludge was spread on fields at first but then treated by bacterial digestion in sealed tanks in which anaerobic

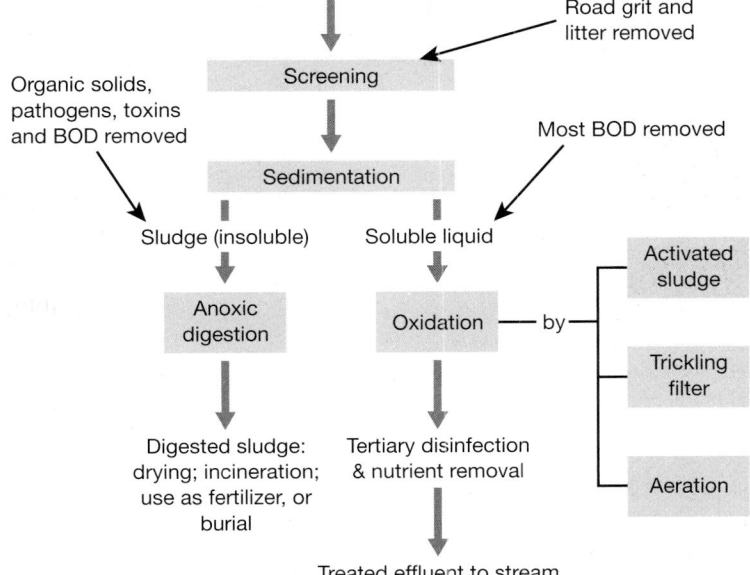

**Fig. 8.12** Waste water treatment comes in three stages of primary (removal of solids, grit and litter), secondary (oxidization of organic matter in sediment by anaerobic digestion, and from water by microbial processing) and tertiary (nutrient removal and in the USA, disinfection with chlorine or ultraviolet light). It is now possible to produce a very high quality effluent for discharge to streams, but there are still problems with trace organics, accidents and poor management of the works.

bacteria generate heat. The heat kills most pathogens and the sludge is converted to a more or less pleasant solid, not unlike garden compost, that can be used on the land. Methane is also produced and can be used to generate power to run the pumps needed at the works. The supernatant water is treated either by trickling it through deep beds of stones over which a film of bacteria and protozoa develop (trickling filters) and break down the dissolved organic matter, or by agitating it in tanks, with paddles or bubbled air, when flocs of the same microorganisms do the same job.

After treatment the water is held in tanks to sediment remaining particles (bits of microbial floc for example) before being released to the river with a much lower deoxygenating capacity than the former raw sewage and with most of its pathogenic microorganisms killed. Mostly these are eaten by Protozoa in the films or flocs. A few remain but are rapidly diluted in the river and mopped up by the river community. Many sophistications to these processes were developed during the 20th century so that effluents can be produced that could, if necessary, be turned into potable drinking water with only a little extra disinfection treatment. On the other hand, the efficiency of a works depended to a large extent on the commitment of the local authority running the works and its managers. Well into the middle of the century some works were producing substandard effluents, and during heavy rainstorms, the works capacity was exceeded and raw sewage was discharged to the rivers. Frequently this and sundry accidents led to pollution incidents and fish kills.

Commonly industries were also discharging chemical effluents direct to rivers, many of them very toxic. This was legislated against, though there are still many illegal pipes dating back to their installation over a 100 years ago and many of them uncharted. The legislation required such effluents to be recovered at the works or discharged via the sewage treatment works, which became known as wastewater treatment works as a result. Bacteria are very versatile, and on trickling filters exposed to such substances, a specialist bacterial film will often develop capable of destroying or rendering less toxic many industrial effluents. The legislation then set limits to the precise concentrations or amounts of specific substances that could be discharged to the rivers and costs were appropriately levied on the originating industries. In the 1970s, it was realized that the system, although much superior to that 50 years or more earlier, was still fairly ramshackle in the UK (and also most other European countries) and new moves were made to improve it.

In the UK, responsibility was taken in 1974 from local authorities (town councils and the like) and given to much bigger Water Authorities, responsible for all of waste treatment, water supply and river quality. The Authorities were few and big and organized in areas that matched single river catchments or groups of adjacent rivers and catchments. This was conceptually a sensible move and the larger organizations were given abilities to raise funds to improve the many treatment works that were in poor states of repair and function. It did lead to a problem, however, that the same organization was often a river polluter, through accidents and malfunctioning of treatment works and simultaneously the body that had to prosecute itself for the pollution. Prosecutions were rare! In 1988, the functions of providing domestic water and treating waste were sold to private companies and the regulatory role retained by a government agency, the National Rivers Authority, renamed the Environment Agency when it took on further responsibilities for air pollution and solid waste disposal in 1996.

The history of legislation in other countries has been different in detail but broadly the same in principle. Many of the developing countries still have poorly developed sewage treatment systems, even those such as China, India and Brazil with thriving economies. Meanwhile in Europe, Australasia and North America there have been two further significant developments. The problem of eutrophication, nutrient pollution, was recognized through its manifest symptoms in lakes in the 1940s and is discussed in later chapters. The nutrients are mostly discharged first into rivers, however, and the problem has to be seen in a catchment–river context.

Wastewater effluents, even when treated to the highest standards for organic and pathogen content remain, as a result of the mineralization of organic matter by the treatment bacteria, rich solutions of nitrogen and phosphorus compounds. Pristine waters draining from untouched catchments will have total phosphorus (TP) concentrations of the order of ten or a few tens of micrograms per litre and total nitrogen concentrations about ten times higher, say around $0.15$ mg N $L^{-1}$ per litre (Chapter 4). Conventionally treated effluents will have up to 20 mg $L^{-1}$ of TP and up to 100 mg $L^{-1}$ of N, thus a thousand times more P and several hundred times more N.

In settled catchments, these sources of nutrients frequently dominate the nutrient budgets of rivers and lakes and from the 1970s onwards, North American and Scandinavian countries, Germany and Switzerland, began to remove P and to a lesser extent N from their effluents by various techniques. These included precipitation (stripping) by calcium, iron and aluminium compounds and manipulations of the activated sludge tanks by which vigorous oxidation promoted bacterial uptake of phosphorus. From the 1960s to the 1980s quite a large proportion of the phosphorus in sewage came from laundry detergents and there were pressures (both legal and voluntary) on the detergent industry to reduce its use of phosphorus. Sodium tripolyphosphate is an excellent builder in detergents. Builders chemically combine with calcium and magnesium ions in the water and prevent the formation of scums that these ions would otherwise form with the surfactant (a soap equivalent) whose job it is to emulsify and remove the fatty body deposits that are the major problems of dirty laundry.

Change in detergent composition, even when phosphate is replaced by other builders such as sodium zeolite, somewhat reduces the costs of chemical precipitation of phosphorus, though not proportionately, but still leaves an effluent much richer in phosphate, from human excretion, than is desirable to combat eutrophication. Legislative phosphorus bans on detergents have thus become less popular with governments wishing to support their industries, though they are still discussed as an interim measure in developing countries. More effective has been legislation to control the N and P discharged at the wastewater treatment works, as this is more likely to give a solution to the eutrophication problem. The European Union passed its Urban Waste Water Treatment Directive in 1991 and this sets severe limits on the contents of effluents. Generally total phosphorus concentrations must be lower than 2 mg $L^{-1}$ and total nitrogen <15 mg $L^{-1}$. Conditions are more stringent (1 mg P, 10 mg N) for very large works.

But there are loopholes because most legislation represents a compromise worked out during its drafting between lobbies that may be financially disadvantaged and the representatives of the community in general. The aspects of the Directive concerned with nutrients only apply to the larger works (serving at least 2000 person-equivalents), for example, and only to works discharging to waters that are 'susceptible to eutrophication'. All waters are of course susceptible, but member states legislatures are not always as well informed as the readers of this book will be, and some, notably the UK and Ireland have resorted to tortuous arguments to avoid having to go to the expense of properly treating their effluents. Mostly rivers used for water supply have been so designated. Other countries, such as The Netherlands, Germany, France and Scandinavia, have designated all or most of their land surfaces as susceptible.

Overall, however, the quality of waste effluents in Europe and North America is continually improving. It has also helped that the chemical industry is keen to recover phosphate from the sewage works for reuse. It has problems of contamination of mined rock phosphate, which it has hitherto used, with heavy metals such as cadmium. Effluent treatment represents a first step in combating eutrophication. There remain large quantities of N and P draining diffusely from both arable agriculture and stock husbandry, however. And there is a wide variety of substances other than nutrients that are associated with diffuse agricultural and industrial pollution.

## 8.10 DIFFUSE POLLUTION

The solutions to these problems are less tractable. Hitherto most emphasis has been placed on phosphorus control because extremely convincing work in the 1970s showed that for many lakes, phosphorus was limiting to algal growth rather than nitrogen. Moreover phosphorus, because of its chemical properties (Chapter 4), is easily precipitated from wastewater effluents and where population densities are high (Fig. 8.12), the bulk of it came from wastewater treatment works. More recent work (Chapter 4) suggests that lowland lakes, shallow lakes and lakes in warmer regions may be more likely to be nitrogen limited and that nitrogen increases have key effects in reducing biodiversity. In the future nitrogen controls will be increasingly required. But nitrogen comes more from agricultural land than from sewage (Fig. 8.13).

Removing nitrogen at wastewater treatment works is more expensive than removing phosphorus as its compounds (nitrate, nitrite and ammonium) are very soluble, though good oxidation converts most to nitrate that can be absorbed on resins. These same solubilities, however, make it difficult to control the diffuse sources of nitrogen from the land. Nitrate enters the rivers from thousands of small trickles, springs and subsurface

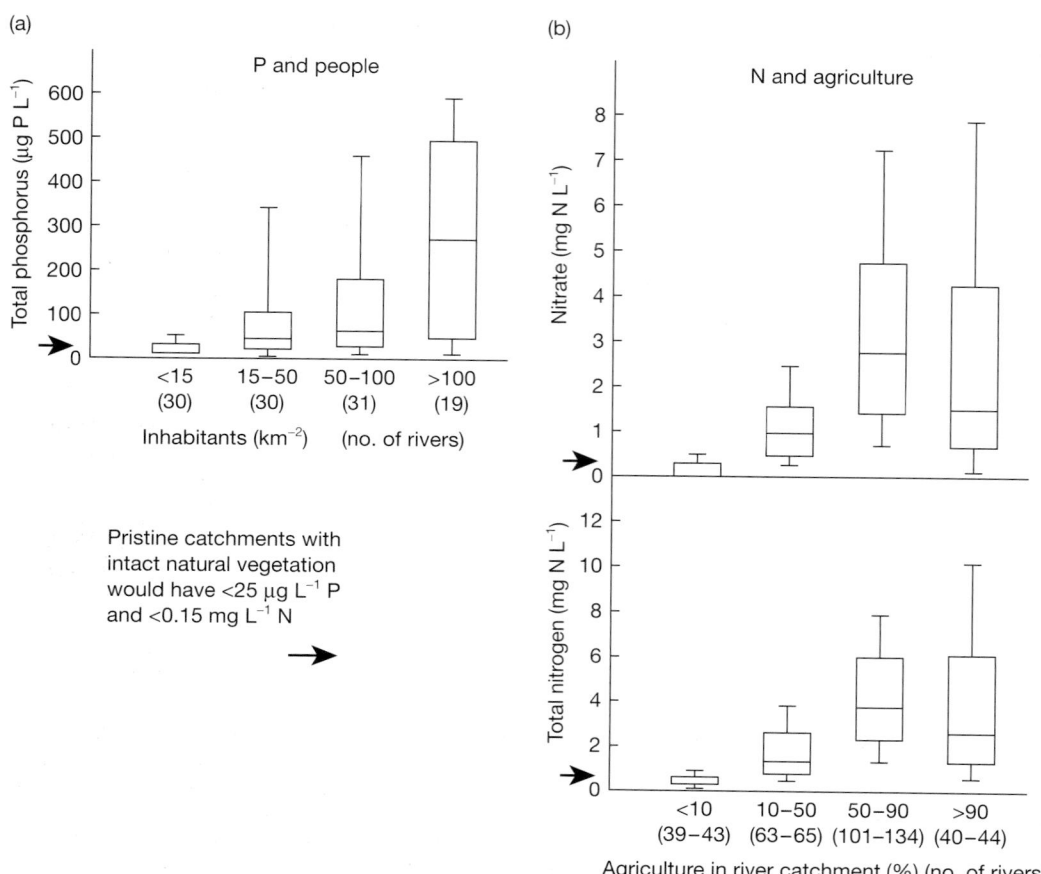

**Fig. 8.13** Total phosphorus concentrations in rivers are closely linked with the human population density (and waste water production) in the catchment, whilst the total nitrogen concentrations are more closely predicted by the percentage of the catchment devoted to agriculture. This does not imply, however, that agriculture cannot be a major phosphorus contributor, nor waste water a significant source of nitrogen.

sources, likewise the phosphate that is increasingly escaping soils as they have become saturated with decades of fertilization (Fig. 8.14). One solution is lower fertilizer use and more recycling within the farm but this is hard to control. A second is to remove large enough areas of land from agriculture to allow semi-natural vegetation, especially wetland, to remove nitrate by denitrification and phosphate by absorption. Reduction of contamination from persistent organic pollutants, such as pesticides, is even more difficult.

The needs for greater agricultural production as populations rose rapidly in the 20th century stimulated the development of potent pesticides. Typically these

were organohalogen, particularly organochlorine, compounds with substitution of hydrogen on linked benzene rings by varying numbers of halogen atoms. They were highly toxic, very stable to decomposition, volatile, of low solubility in water and high solubility in fat and included DDT and hexachlorobenzene. Demands of industry led to production of similar compounds such as polychlorinated biphenyls (PCBs) for use as insulators in electrical equipment, and destruction of these compounds by burning produced equally toxic by-products called dioxins and furans. New refrigerants and propellant gases for spray cans included the chlorofluorocarbons (CFC). These were not toxic but

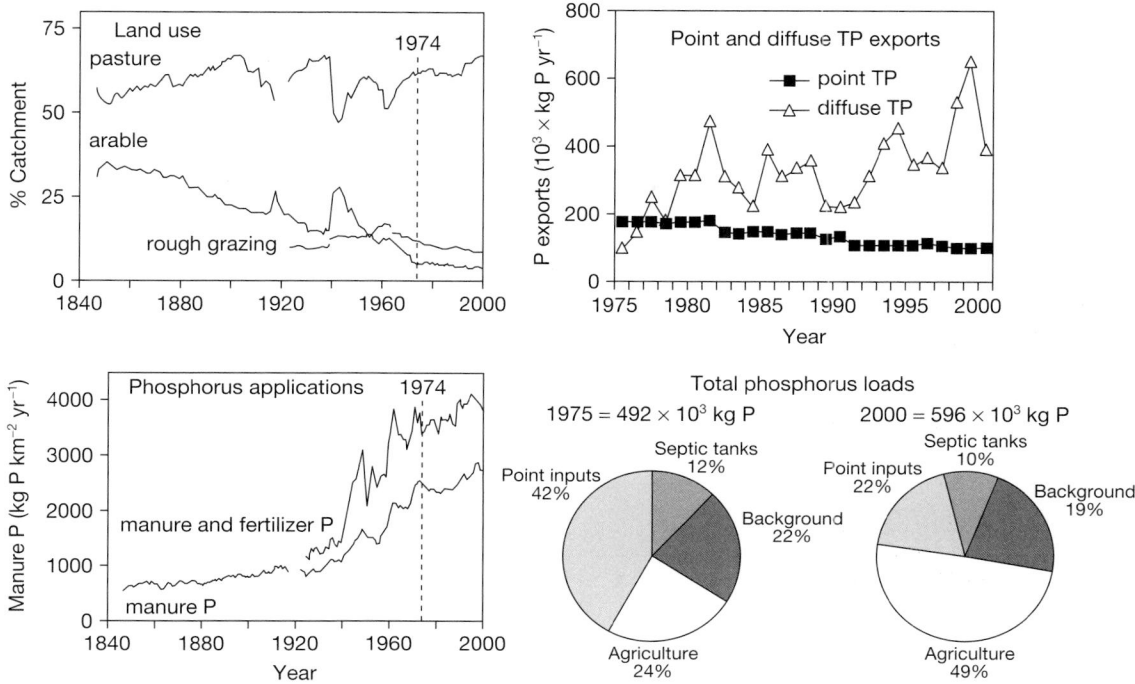

**Fig. 8.14** Although it was acknowledged for many years that agricultural soils were relatively minor sources of phosphorus for rivers, the situation is changing. Intensive agriculture, increased fertilization and saturation of the absorption sites in soils all conspire to increase the amount of phosphorus derived from soils. In northern Ireland, in the rivers draining to Lough Neagh, arable cultivation has declined relative to pasturage but total P loads have steadily increased (left), despite, in 1974, the fitting of nutrient removal processes for the human waste water. There has been a steady increase (upper right) in diffuse loads, the total load has increased, and agriculture now provides a greater proportion of it. (Based on Foy & Lennox 2006).

proved problematic as they reacted with ozone high in the stratosphere, removing an essential shield to dangerous radiation in the atmosphere. The other compounds proved to be inert as well as toxic and they persisted for lengthy periods in the environment and also became more concentrated in the tissues with successive steps in the food chain.

One result was an increase in toxicity of fish, particularly fatty ones and in some areas near the factories of production or sites of major accidental spills, fishing remains banned or restricted. In birds, these compounds caused metabolic changes resulting in thin eggshells and reduced success in hatching. The more dangerous compounds (Fig. 8.15) have now been banned, but most still persist in the food webs and are likely to do so for many decades. Substitutes have been found but there will always be some risk; pesticides are

designed to kill. New compounds, the polybrominated diphenyl ethers, for example, which are flame retardants, are also now proving to have toxic effects. The number of new substances entering the markets each year numbers several hundred and it is impossible to screen them all for what might be subtle yet significant effects in ecosystems. Industry prefers to develop and use them and wait to see if effects appear. A more precautionary approach of thorough testing first would be desirable.

Yet more varied are the substances thought to act as endocrine disruptors, including insecticides DDT, endosulfan, dieldrin, methoxychlor, kepone, dicofol, toxaphene and chlordane; herbicides such as alachlor, atrazine and nitrofen, the fungicides, benomyl, mancozeb and tributyl tin and nematocides such as aldicarb and dibromochloropropane. Plasticizers

| POP | Use | Structure |
|---|---|---|
| Aldrin | Crop insecticide (corn, cotton) | |
| Chlordane | Crop insecticide (vegetables, citrus, cotton, potatoes) | |
| DDT (dichloro-diphenyl-trichloroethane) | Crop insecticide (cotton), protection against malaria, typhus | |
| Dieldrin | Crop insecticide (cotton, corn), domestic pests | |
| Endrin | Crop insecticide (cotton, grains) | |
| Heptachlor | Insecticide (termites and soil insects) | |
| Hexachlorobenzene | Fungicide for seed treatment | |
| Mirex | Insecticide (termites, fire ants), fire retardent | |
| Toxaphene | Insecticide (livestock, crops) | |
| PCBs (polychlorinated biphenyls) | Industrial chemical (paint and plastic additive) | |
| Dioxins | Unintentionally produced during combustion, manufacturing (paper and metal recycling) Smoke | |
| Furans | Unintentionally produced during combustion. Found in commercial PCB mixtures | |

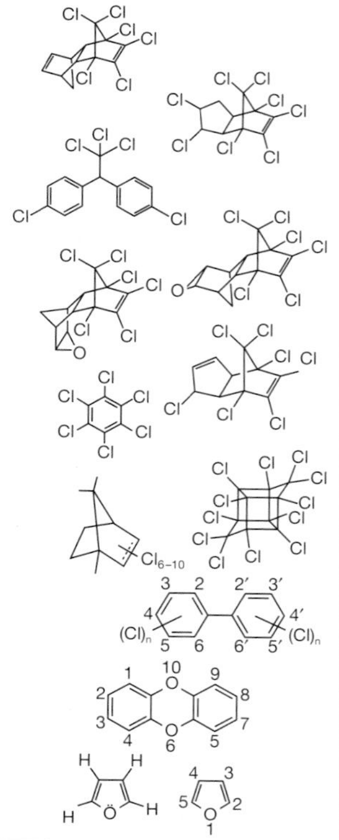

**Fig. 8.15** Twelve substances or groups of them have been considered so dangerous to living organisms, that despite the effectiveness of some of them as pesticides, their use for most purposes and in some cases manufacture, has been banned by international agreement. These are the 'dirty dozen' of the Stockholm Convention of 2001. The convention: (1) immediately banned the pesticides aldrin, endrin, dieldrin, chlordane, heptachlor, hexaclorobenzene, mirex, and toxaphene; (2) prohibited polychlorinated biphenyl (PCB) production and mandated a phase out of use; (3) promoted action to minimize release of by-product persistent organic pollutants (POPs); (4) established a goal to eliminate dichloro-diphenyl-trichloroethane (DDT), with exceptions for health crises; (5) provided mechanisms to assist developing nations to eliminate POPs; and (6) aimed to identify and act against other POPs.

such as bisphenol A and phthalates, contraceptive hormones, industrial detergents such as nonyl- and octylphenol, PCBs and dioxins and even some heavy metals (Pb, Cd, Hg) are also active. There are traces of all these substances in many rivers because their often-volatile properties promote evaporation in warmer regions and condensation in cooler ones or higher altitudes after passage through the atmosphere. Mostly the concentrations are now not lethal to most organisms but sublethal effects may be more important when whole ecosystems are disrupted.

Finally, mercury is a problem for headwater river systems. Mercury is used in many industrial processes, but its compounds are very toxic. The element itself is also highly volatile and like the persistent organic pollutants, tends to condense in colder climates from the atmosphere, so that boreal and Arctic streams are very vulnerable. Moreover mercury ions can be methylated by bacteria when they become easily taken up by animals, causing malformation and various metabolic problems. Methylated mercury also accumulates in fatty fish. Use of mercury is now strongly discouraged but elements are indestructible and it will be a long time before mercury released from industrial processes has found its way into sinks such as sediments where it is effectively removed from circulation.

## 8.11 RIVER MONITORING

Since 2000 an entirely new dimension has been introduced to river management in Europe. The European Water Framework Directive is a potentially radical piece of legislation that brings the concept of ecological quality to water management and it is useful to review the development of water monitoring approaches to appreciate its significance. Throughout the 20th century methods were developed for estimating water quality in rivers. They originated with the problems of gross organic pollution in the 19th century and began with the monitoring of dissolved oxygen concentration, ammonia concentration and BOD. These were natural things to measure (Fig. 8.9) for organic pollution reduces oxygen concentration, increases BOD and increases ammonia concentrations (which can be toxic to fish). Analyses for pH and heavy metals were added later and waters have been classified on scales of bad to excellent based on arbitrarily determined standards for these few determinands. These statutory standards, against which prosecutions for river pollution were made, had the advantage that the analyses were precise and the courts could easily understand whether they had been exceeded or not.

Sometimes illegal discharges are made at night and washed downstream by the next day when pollution inspectors might take samples following a fish kill some distance downstream. It is then difficult to associate the discharger with the incident. Bottom invertebrate communities, however, show effects for days to weeks after an incident and can be used to locate the origin of a polluting discharge. Many schemes developed in Europe and North America associating changes in macroinvertebrate communities with polluted conditions, and the nature of the community was characterized in some sort of numerical index.

For example, the National Water Council in the UK devised the biotic score. Using expert advice, scores from 1 to 10 were assigned to particular invertebrate families, reflecting their intolerance of gross organic pollution (Table 8.2). Oligochaetes, for example were assigned 1. They are extremely tolerant. Many families of mayflies were assigned 10, as they are extremely intolerant. By identifying the invertebrates in a sample, listing the families and then adding the scores for each family found, a composite index can be obtained (the biotic score), which might be less than 10 for an industrially polluted river in a city or as much as 200 for an organically unpolluted mountain river in the remoter uplands. In general the classifications given by the

water chemistry (oxygen concentration, etc.) and the biotic score are parallel but deviations do occur where the water chemistry is good but the invertebrates retain the effects of a past polluting discharge.

There are some problems with this approach. Any biological measure is likely to have a greater variance than a chemical measurement and variance means uncertainty, a difficult concept where prosecution of alleged offenders is concerned. Secondly, the biotic score for a pristine site will vary dependent on the nature of the site. A depositional river with lots of sediment-collecting families (which are tolerant of organic matter for they feed in deoxygenated sediments) will have naturally lower scores than a rocky river with lots of scraper families. Scores thus have no absolute meaning for a particular site. The same score might mean severe pollution or none at all. And thirdly, the scores measure only susceptibility to gross organic pollution. They do not reliably measure any other of the many ways in which a river system might be altered.

The first problem is an inherent one, returned to below, the second was confronted by use of reference-based systems. In these an estimate is made of what the score would be for a particular site were it undamaged and the actual score is compared with this. The greater the damage to a site, the more its score will deviate. The British RIVPACS (River Invertebrate Prediction and Classification System) works in this way. A set of several hundred of the highest quality rivers in the UK was sampled for invertebrates using a standard kick-sampling method, and a range of physical and chemical determinands measured for each site. These included such things as slope, distance from the source, pH, chloride content, and nature of the bottom substratum.

A computer program then linked the lists of invertebrate species or families to the physico-chemical conditions, so that for a newly sampled site, the program would predict the families that ought to be found (and hence predict the biotic score) for these particular conditions. The actual score measured could then be compared and expressed as a percentage of the expected score (Table 8.3). This system is intellectually attractive in measuring the quality relative to a standard rather than to an arbitrarily derived value. But it still has the disadvantage that it is based largely on the effects of organic pollution, examines only one characteristic, the invertebrate community, of the ecosystem, and measures change relative only to the best remaining qualities of rivers, which, in a country with a high population density that has been agriculturally dominated for several thousand years, are far from a pristine state.

**Table 8.2** National Water Council biological scores system. Scores are summed for each family present to give the Biotic Score.

| Score | Families |
|---|---|
| 10 | (Mayflies) Siphlonuridae, Heptageniidae, Leptophlebiidae, Ephemerellidae, Potamanthidae, Ephemeridae<br>(Stoneflies) Taeniopterygidae, Leuctridae, Capniidae, Perlodidae, Perlidae, Chloroperlidae<br>(Beetles) Aphelocheiridae<br>(Caddis-flies) Phryganeidae, Molannidae, Beraeidae, Odontoceridae, Leptoceridae, Goeridae, Lepidostomatidae, Brachycentridae, Sericostomatidae |
| 8 | (Crayfish) Astacidae<br>(Dragonflies) Lestidae, Agriidae, Gomphidae, Cordulegasteridae, Aeshnidae, Corduliidae, Libellulidae<br>(Net-spinning caddis-flies) Psychomyiidae, Philopotamidae |
| 7 | (Mayflies) Caenidae<br>(Stoneflies) Nemouridae<br>(Net-spinning caddis-flies) Rhyacophilidae, Polycentropodidae, Limnephilidae |
| 6 | (Snails) Neritidae, Viviparidae, Ancylidae<br>(Caddis-flies) Hydroptilidae<br>(Bivalve molluscs) Unionidae<br>(Crustacea) Corophiidae, Gammaridae<br>(Dragonflies) Platycnemididae, Coenagriidae |
| 5 | (Water bugs) Mesovelidae, Hydrometridae, Gerridae, Nepidae, Naucoridae, Notonectidae, Pleidae, Corixidae<br>(Beetles) Haliplidae, Hygrobiidae, Dytiscidae, Gyrinidae, Hydrophilidae, Clambidae, Helodidae, Dryopidae, Elminthidae, Crysomelidae, Curculionidae<br>(Caddis-flies) Hydropsychidae<br>(Dipteran flies) Tipulidae, Simuliidae<br>(Triclads) Planariidae, Dendrocoelidae |
| 4 | (Mayflies) Baetidae<br>(Alderfly) Sialidae<br>(Fish leeches) Piscicolidae |
| 3 | (Snails, bivalves) Valvatidae, Hydrobiidae, Lymnaeidae, Physidae, Planorbidae, Sphaeriidae<br>(Leeches) Glossiphoniidae, Hirudidae, Erpobdellidae<br>(Crustacea [Water hog louse]) Asellidae |
| 2 | (Diptera [midge larvae]) Chironomidae |
| 1 | (Bloodworms) Oligochaeta (whole class) |

## 8.12 THE WATER FRAMEWORK DIRECTIVE

The Water Framework Directive attempts to remedy these restrictions whilst giving a more comprehensive framework for water management than has been possible hitherto. It is based on the idea that management should be on a catchment basis (though uses the term 'river basin' instead of catchment). Remarkably this has not been the case in the past, the freshwater system being seen as separate somehow from the surrounding land when it came to regulation and management. The Directive also covers all the streams and rivers, lakes and reservoirs, estuaries and coastal waters of Europe

**Table 8.3** Biotic scores and River Invertebrate Prediction and Classification System (RIVPACS) predictions for a site (Lower Severalls) on the River Parrett in Somerset. ASPT is average score per taxon. (From Wright 1995.)

(a) Environmental data

| Variable | Data | Variable | Data |
|---|---|---|---|
| Water width | 3.6 m | Altitude | 35 m |
| Mean depth | 35 cm | Distance from source | 7.2 km |
| Substratum composition: | | Slope | 5.2 m km$^{-1}$ |
| boulders and cobbles | 33% | Mean air temperature | 10.5°C |
| pebbles and gravel | 36% | Air temperature range | 11.8°C |
| sand | 22% | Latitude | 50°53′N |
| silt and clay | 9% | Longitude | 2°46′W |
| mean size on a logarithmic (phi) scale | −2.57 | Alkalinity | 4.7 meq L$^{-1}$ |

(b) Families found (asterisked) and families predicted with their percentage probability of occurrence, by RIVPACS for this site

| | | |
|---|---|---|
| Oligochaeta (100)* | Chironomidae (100)* | Elmidae (100)* |
| Baetidae (100)* | Sphaeridae (99.9)* | Gammaridae (99.7) |
| Glossiphoniidae (96.5)* | Simuliidae (95.4) | Limnephilidae (94.2)* |
| Hydrobiidae (90.7)* | Hydropsychidae (89.6) | Tipulidae (89.3)* |
| Erpobdellidae (89.1)* | Ephemerellidae (88.4)* | Asellidae (86.7)* |
| Dytiscidae (84.2)* | Hydroptilidae (83.7) | Ancylidae (79.3)* |
| Lymnaeidae (78.6)* | Haliplidae (75.6)* | Caenidae (71.2) |
| Planorbidae (69.1)* | Planariidae (68.7)* | Rhyacophilidae (67.2) |
| Polycentropodidae (66.6) | Leptoceridae (65) | Sialidae (64)* |
| Sericostomatidae (54.4) | Leuctridae (54.4) | Ephemeridae (54.4) |
| Goeridae (52.5) | Leptophlebiidae (51.6) | Physidae (44.1)* |
| Hydrophilidae (38)* | Dendrocoelidae (33.9)* | Notonectidae (6)* |

(c) Scores

| | Biotic | Number of taxa | ASPT |
|---|---|---|---|
| Observed (O) | 98 | 23 | 4.26 |
| Expected (E) | 178 | 32 | 5.6 |
| O/E | 0.55 | 0.72 | 0.76 |

so it takes in the surface water system, except for the open oceans, in its entirety. It requires that water be no longer treated as a free good and requires an economic analysis so that users pay for what they use. This too is innovatory for some major users, such as irrigators, pay only trivial sums, though dominate use, whilst smaller users, such as domestic consumers, pay at vastly higher rates. It requires that certain very hazardous substances, some pesticides and industrial products for example, be removed to levels below the detectability of the most sophisticated current technology. Hitherto, small concentrations have been tolerated. But most significantly it requires the restoration of all aquatic habitats to good ecological quality, by 2015. This proviso should have enormous implications.

Member States of the European Union first have to create a typology of different sorts of rivers, lakes and estuarine and coastal waters. This is a simple pigeon-holing of different kinds based on unchanging, largely geographical characteristics such as latitude, depth, area, catchment size, and local geology. The important thing is that the characteristics should be those not influenced by human activity. Then, for each of the types, the pristine state has to be described and the Directive lists many factors that must be included, from the plants and algae, invertebrates and fish communities to the geomorphological structure, hydrology and water chemistry, which includes not just oxygen and pH but nutrients, salinity and polluting substances. Hitherto, in most countries, river water quality has been routinely measured on a mere handful of chemical characters. The Directive requires a suite of perhaps 100 or more structural, hydrological, chemical and biological characters. The pristine state is called 'high ecological quality' and is specified as having 'no or very minor human influence'. It may be determined by finding examples, by using palaeoecological records or by using expert judgement. As the provision of 'very minor human influence' means that virtually no such sites exist in Europe and as palaeoecological information is always incomplete (Chapter 11), expert judgement is likely to be the most important mechanism.

Ecological quality must then be defined on a scale running from high through good, moderate, poor and bad for each of the types of aquatic system, again in terms of the same long list of features, so that the current quality of any given site can be determined. The Directive gives little help as to how these grades shall be defined except that it says that 'good' is slightly different from high. By any definition of 'slight' this should impose very high standards and this is important because of the provision that all sites will be restored to at least good status by 2015. The Directive is radical in that to achieve good status it should not be possible to do this without management of the entire catchment and consideration of all the many human activities, from sewage disposal and agriculture to highways and housing that can have ecological effects on waters. It requires truly joined-up policy and planning. There are loopholes by which Governments can avoid having to restore sites, drinking water reservoirs on rivers, for example, if it is not in the public interest or if it would be too expensive, but each case has to be justified. But in the long run, the provisions of the Directive should vastly improve freshwater sites.

## 8.13 IMPLEMENTATION OF THE DIRECTIVE

Progress in implementation so far has been slow, largely because of traditional attitudes among the regulatory agencies. Water management has, for a century, been seen as an occupation for engineers and chemists. Despite the importance of fisheries, biologists have been tangential in decision-making. The Directive puts ecology into the centre. Water quality has previously been monitored largely by chemical approaches, which have used just a few determinands and seen quality as a rather simple feature. Ecological quality is a very different thing. A pristine site will have the three fundamental ecological characteristics: parsimony of nutrient availability; characteristic structure (both physical, which might include an abundance of tree debris, and biological, which will include complete food webs, not least the bears and wolves and other top predators of the riparian zone); and connectivity with other systems, which embraces hydrological continuity and integrity (no dams or weirs, no river engineering, no removal of water for irrigation). A pristine system will also have built-in resilience, the ability to adjust to natural changes in the physical environment; there will not be a single characteristic species list or set of physico-chemical conditions; there will be an envelope of possible conditions determined by hundreds of thousands of different features.

This point has hitherto been ignored and the government agencies responsible for enforcement of the Directive have yet to determine what they mean by good ecological quality. What they have done so far is to create scales for a few, mostly chemical determinands, without reference to how these will be influenced by other factors. They are assuming that ecosystems are simple collections of variables that are put together like boxes on a shelf and that a given site will have a single set of characteristics for a given ecological quality. The cart is being put before the horse. The only logical way of approaching the requirements of the Directive is first to determine scenarios for high and good quality then work backwards to determine how to measure the key features of ecological quality using the determinands specified in the Directive. The current approach appears to contain a hope that the meaning of good quality will emerge pragmatically from the application of systems of measuring individual components. This is far from a sophisticated understanding of how ecosystems work. It is a chemist's approach to an ecological phenomenon and might achieve rather little, for ecological improvement cannot come if there is a lack of ecological understanding. On the other hand, some steps in the right direction will be taken, even if there are inevitable reverses.

## 8.14 WIDER CONSIDERATIONS: ECOSYSTEM SERVICES

The ultimate intention of the Water Framework Directive is restoration of ecological quality. Some modification of rivers will always be necessary, however, so long as the human population on Earth remains high. Probably the developing countries will go through the trajectory of the developed in terms of river damage. Indeed the grossly polluted rivers of the Far East are currently in much the same state as those of industrial Europe in the early 20th century. Europe, with the Water Framework Directive and other legislation, is dealing with these problems and has already countered much of the gross organic pollution. The irony is that it has continued to use the methods and monitoring appropriate largely to organic pollution whilst a host of other problems has developed. Ideally, however, the developing world may be able to short circuit the process and avoid some of these problems. The experience of history argues against this, however, so that the restorative techniques now being developed for erosive rivers will have to be used worldwide.

We live, one hopes, at the nadir of environmental quality. There has been so much damage to natural ecosystems that there are now fears that this will compromise human survival, at least in a civilized and comfortable way (see Chapter 16). The problem is not just one of aesthetics: ugly canalized river systems, a predominance of grey and depressing concrete in urban areas and a countryside of large fields lacking the detailed interest of former times. It is one of loss of essential goods and services provided by natural systems. The Millennium Ecosystem Commission in 2004 recognized four groups of such services: Provisioning, Regulating, Cultural and Supporting. Natural predators control the depredations of pests on crops and natural systems provide extensive grazing and products such as timber and, for many people, food (provisioning services). The very composition of the atmosphere is regulated by the balance of photosynthesis and respiration, the storage of carbon in peat in the vastnesses of the Arctic tundra, boreal forest and elsewhere, and the production of reactive gases by soil bacteria and marine phytoplankton (Chapters 3 and 4). Water is stored and purified by wetland systems; other wetlands protect coasts against erosion and storms. All these are regulating services. Ecosystems provide cultural services through recreation, not least angling (Fig. 8.16) and bird watching, but may also have deep spiritual significance, especially for traditional peoples, those in the western economic world having become increasingly alienated from these (cultural services). Supporting services are essentially functions such as photosynthesis, maintenance of biodiversity and nutrient cycling that underpin the other three and are subsumed into them.

Increasingly, economic studies that take these services into account are demonstrating major importance (Table 8.4). Natural ecosystems appear to be far more valuable to society as a whole, as opposed to their individual owner, in their undisturbed state than when they are exploited (Fig. 8.17). The current serious climate change (see Chapter 16) is just the most recent of a battery of damage. Fisheries have been almost uniformly overexploited, oil reserves are being used up much faster than new ones are being discovered and a human population that will continue to rise until it is about 50% greater than at present will make increasing demands. Paul Ehrlich produced an equation that proposes that the product of population size × resource use and waste production × power of technology = environmental damage. All three components continue to rise.

## 8.15 RESTORATION, REHABILITATION AND RECONCILIATION ECOLOGY

There will thus have to be increasing emphasis on repairing much of the existing damage let alone curbing future damage. The interconnectedness of natural systems implies that this cannot be just the preservation and conservation of limited areas, such as nature reserves and national parks, which is our present approach. It will have to pervade the entire surface of the planet so that natural goods and services continue to be provided. It is impossible to manage without them. Colossal amounts of energy would be required to replace, say, the natural regulation of the atmospheric composition by some human-run air-conditioning plant. The natural one is very complex and is continually

**Fig. 8.16** The opening of the salmon fishing season on the River Tay in Scotland in 1961 illustrates how ecosystems can provide provisioning (the fishery is important in the local economy) and spiritual services. A bottle of whisky is broken over the bow of a boat whilst a piper plays a traditional air. (Photograph, The Times archives.)

**Table 8.4** Valuation of ecosystem services per hectare for terrestrial habitats (mean of all systems), wetlands, including both freshwater and coastal systems, and lakes and rivers. Question mark means that valuations had not been possible when the work was done. Dollar valuations are at 1995 rates. (From Costanza et al. 1997.)

| Service | Example | Terrestrial (US $ per ha) | Wetland (US $ per ha) | Lake/river (US $ per ha) |
|---|---|---|---|---|
| Gas and climate regulation | Carbon dioxide and methane balance | 141 | 133 | ? |
| Hazard protection | Storm protection, flood control | 2 | 4539 | ? |
| Water regulation | Storage, pollutant dilution, quality improvement | 5 | 3815 | 7552 |
| Erosion control | Soil conservation, silt control | 108 | ? | ? |
| Nutrient cycling and waste treatment | Nitrogen fixation, denitrification | 448 | 4177 | 665 |
| Biological control | Provision of predators, grazers | 23 | ? | ? |
| Refugia | Nurseries, habitat for migrant species, over wintering grounds | ? | 304 | ? |
| Resources | Timber, food, fuel, fodder | 181 | 362 | 41 |
| Culture and recreation | Tourism, recreation, aesthetics, spiritual, scientific, mental health | 68 | 1456 | 230 |

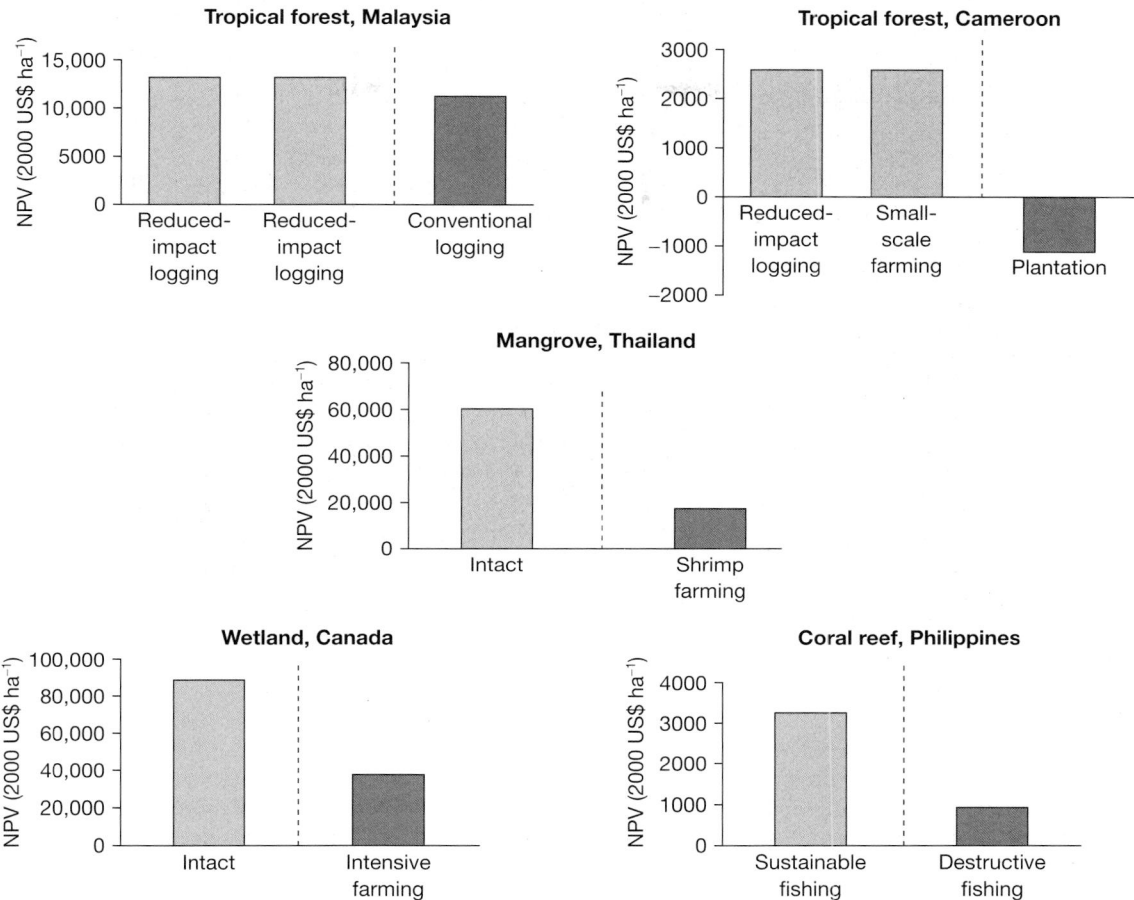

**Fig. 8.17** Valuation of ecosystem services suggests that intact ecosystems are more valuable in the long term to the community as a whole than when developed for the short or longer-term gain of individual landowners. NPV, net present value. (Based on Balmford et al. 2002.)

tested through the operation of natural selection on all its components. Replacement is inconceivable. If the systems fail, we cannot survive.

There will thus eventually be increasing emphasis on restoration ecology, the reconstruction of natural systems. There is already much interest in this as reflected in the terms of the Water Framework Directive, discussed above. The term is a misnomer, however, because restoration really means returning to the exact former ecosystems and this is impossible. First they existed with very low human populations with barely damaging technologies; second, some components have already been made extinct; and third, we do not know exactly

how they were put together for lack of detailed information. A more accurate term for what we can do, is rehabilitation ecology, the re-creation of a semi-natural system that resembles the natural ones but is inevitably not the same and is more limited in scope.

Rehabilitation ecology is what we do when we manage a nature reserve to encourage growth of particular plant and animal communities, or cover a domestic landfill or minerals waste tip with some sort of vegetation so that it can be used as a park or sports pitch or a reasonably pleasant, if not very diverse 'natural' area. It is what we do when we ameliorate the water quality in an individual lake or improve, usually temporarily, the habitat in a stream that has become silted, by tipping in rocks and gravel or fencing the edge from erosion by cattle. It is all very worthy but has failed to stem the tide of environmental destruction. What we now have to do will be much more extensive. We have to restore functions to large tracts of land and water, indeed to almost all of it, where this has been lost and we have to do it on the assumption that there will always be a large human population that has to be fed and needs a reasonable standard of comfort. These latter two provisos, however, cannot embrace the current excesses of the developed world, nor can they assume that most of the world's population will be required to live in abject poverty so that a minority can live in luxury.

What we are now contemplating is reconciliation ecology. Reconciliation ecology means re-creating ecological systems that provide essential functions yet allow for human needs. Reconciliation ecology requires a much greater effort than has ever previously been contemplated in rehabilitation ecology. There are few guidelines, for there are still many gaps in our detailed knowledge but essentially reconciled systems must mimic natural ecosystems as closely as possible, for these are our only guides. The guidelines derive from the fundamental features of natural systems: parsimony of nutrients, characteristic structure, and connectivity, for only if these are in place can the systems retain the resilience that protects their function from disturbance

## 8.16 RECONCILIATION ECOLOGY OF RIVER SYSTEMS

What does this mean for headwater river systems? Currently there are many limited techniques for river 'restoration'. Streams can be broken out of culverts where they have been channelled underground so that the land above them could be used for farming or development. They can be re-meandered where they have been straightened; gravel can be dumped to form new riffles in streams silted by soil erosion; small dams and weirs that are no longer needed can be removed; native fish can be restocked and aliens destroyed; small side channels can be dug for fish habitat; banks can be fenced to minimize stock erosion. Sometimes floodplains have been re-created (see Chapter 10) over limited lengths. But almost all schemes in the erosive sections of rivers have been very small and of limited

value. Plans for the rivers of the future will have to be more ambitious.

Reducing the losses of nutrients from landscapes that will have to remain settled and agricultural is difficult. Both phosphorus and nitrogen can be easily removed at wastewater treatment works from sewage, and most other pollutants can be taken out if enough funds are invested. Some are relatively intractable, such as endocrine disruptors, but given sufficient risk or legal pressure these are not insoluble problems. The greatest problem is from agriculture, for the sources are diffuse: indeed every field drain, every gateway where rain water cascades out onto a lane or road, taking soil particles with it, and every manure pile that is exposed to the weather. There are ways of reducing these losses, but they are yet inadequate.

Gateways can be sited to drain into fields rather than out of them, manure can be rapidly spread back on the land and ploughed in, a return of mixed (arable plus stock together) farming can minimize use of additional fertilizer, though not entirely dispense with it. Fields can be ploughed along the contours rather than across them, which minimizes erosion, and wide strips of grassland can be left among those ploughed, to retard erosion. Slow release fertilzsers can be used and our arrangements for food production and supply to shops can be made far less wasteful, meaning that less land needs to be in cultivation. Buffer zones of semi-natural vegetation can be used to absorb phosphate and denitrify nitrogen, the former only for a time, however. Soils become saturated with phosphorus in the end. Buffer zones, unfortunately, need to be very large to be effective. A token few metres by the side of a stream are likely to help little. Nitrate levels currently running into streams are of the order of ten to one hundred times higher than in pristine conditions. If concentrations have to be reduced to say one tenth of current levels, this means that 90% of the land has to be taken out of farming if current methods of intensive agriculture are used. If farming is made environmentally efficient, as opposed to efficient in the limited economic sense that is currently used, more land can be farmed whilst river nutrient levels are lowered. This is the essence of reconciliation ecology. Profits will be lower for agriculture and the food industry but this is merely repaying a debt of environmental costs that has hitherto been ignored by a very primitive economic system.

Re-creating structure is only slightly easier. Reconciliated forests can be managed to provide useful timber whilst also serving their environmental roles, but again financial profit can only be modest. A first step must be the re-establishment of undisturbed riparian forest zones and the ability of the rivers to re-acquire tree debris in natural quantities from native, not exotic species. This will be opposed by those concerned with downstream flooding (debris holds back water), but this will no longer be seen as a problem, for what will be flooded will be the buffer and riparian zones where flooding is a benefit, rather than agricultural land.

Some concessions will be needed for streamsides already built over, but there will have to be a ban on further building and a ban on rebuilding when existing buildings become derelict. Re-establishment of downstream floodplains (see Chapter 10) will mean less need for engineering of the upper river sections so much channelization can be removed. A river will re-establish a natural line (called the plan form), in equilibrium with the amount of water flowing from the catchment, and the load of rock and sand particles it carries, if left long enough, so that expensive re-engineering can be avoided except where existing buildings need to be protected. Buffer zones and sensitive farming will reduce the amounts of silt that clog the beds currently, so that natural gravel beds and rockier areas will be uncovered without the expensive artificial dumping of gravel that steadily moves down river and out to sea.

Some dams and reservoirs will always be necessary, but the societal changes demanded by the current crisis will lead to water saving measures and less irrigation of the land. They may, in contrast lead also to more hydroelectric power generation, but it should be possible to move many obstructions to the passage of migratory fish and to provide workable fish passes around those that have to remain. Many fish can negotiate barriers of 1–1.5 m, and salmon species can often jump up to 3 m. Most dams are far higher, but fish ladders can break the ascent into manageable steps. These might comprise a series of stepped pools on a gentle incline beginning some distance below the dam or climbing, as a spiral, within the dam itself. One problem is to encourage the fish to enter, because the flow down the ladders is often much less than that coming through the dam sluices. Series of diverting baffles may help. Some dams have powered lifts in which the fish are transported from bottom to top. Scottish law has demanded provision of fish passes on all dams since 1860, but even as late as 1933, the Grand Coulee Dam on the Columbia river in the USA was built without a fish pass, and blocked 1600 km of river spawning sites to migrating salmon. If no provision has been made when the dam was constructed, fish can be netted at the foot of the dam and carried by road around it at the peak of the spawning season. Hatcheries may have to replace previous natural spawning areas, perhaps now covered by lake sediment.

Passage downstream through dams may also be difficult. The blades may kill fish moving into turbine intakes, and those taking the fall of perhaps tens of metres over the dam wall will be smashed on the rocks below. Turbine operation can be arranged to minimize damage, but death rates may reach 10–20% even so. A series of dams on a river may thus kill almost all the migrating smolts. The fish may not even reach the dam outlet because the reservoir lacks the strong currents that guide them down-river. Again they can be netted and moved by road, but this is expensive and increasingly recourse is made to a completely artificial system of stocking of the river with adults of non-migrating salmonid fish reared in hatcheries.

The fishes' problems will not be over even when they are in the river below the dam. Though a minimum flow to be released from the dam is usually stipulated by law, the contrasts between low and high flows may be very great and change rapidly, especially with hydroelectric dams. The Kennebec River in Maine experiences flows of about $8.5\ m^3\ s^{-1}$ at night when little power is being generated, but up to $170\ m^3\ s^{-1}$ by day when the turbines are working fully. Twenty-five per cent of the river bed may be uncovered at night, stranding small fish, whilst the sudden high flows may damage them by abrasion against rocks. Far greater environmental flows in much more natural diurnal patterns will be demanded by reconciliation approaches.

Connectance laterally between the river and its catchment through the riparian zones and up and downstream can thus be achieved. Other aspects of structure, based in the links between large mammals such as bears and wolves, will be highly controversial and generally opposed, especially in a UK that has become progressively alienated from its natural environment through its dominant urban culture. But the difficulties are perceived rather than real for the remoter northern and western rivers of the UK. Scotland already has a problem of over browsing of its remaining forest by deer and a sheep farming agriculture that is profitable only through subsidies. More tourist revenues as well as greater ecological quality and function could be generated by reintroduction of the wolf to large areas of the highlands. Such introduction is not inconceivable elsewhere. There are plenty of communities in Europe, Russia and Canada that coexist comfortably with wolf and brown bear populations. We cannot survive on a philosophy generated by Little Red Riding Hood.

Solution to the problem of acidification now rests largely with time to allow base regeneration by rock weathering and new soil formation, admittedly a slow process, and continuation of measures to reduce $SO_x$ emissions at power stations and factories. Inevitable reduction of fossil fuel burning (Chapter 16) at power stations will help and the imminent shortage and high pricing of petrol will reduce the emissions of $NO_x$ through reduced car use. It is possible that further new technologies will emerge to convert $NO_x$ to nitrogen gas in the vehicle engines also.

All this may seem currently unachievable. It means major changes in lifestyles of the western world, the demise of the current highly organized and manipulative systems of food production, supermarket chains, convenience foods and intensive farming systems; it means a more spartan existence using less energy, wasting less in the way of food and materials and recycling almost everything. It means less dependence on the labour and goods and agricultural produce of distant countries. It does not mean necessarily a less happy and fulfilled existence; it may lead to great improvement in these. But it will happen. Ours is not a planet that can be pushed beyond its finite resources and, for all our knowledge and power, we cannot change our fundamental dependence on these resources. We have to learn how to use them better, and moving in the way that natural systems operate is not only a good model, it is the only possible model.

## FURTHER READING

Good general reviews on the problems of headwater rivers are Malmqvist & Rundle (2002), Dudgeon (2000) and Dudgeon et al. (2006). Iwata et al. (2003) concerns deforestation effects in the tropics and is the basis of Exercise 9. Heathwaite et al. (1996) review nutrients in rivers and Newman (1997) is an interesting study of the balance of nutrients in farming. The importance of river-transported driftwood in the Arctic is related in Alix (2005). The Keatley Creek study and the fish-based system of coastal peoples in North America have a large literature. Reader (1988) and Pringle (1996) are readable introductions. More details are in Hayden (1997), Hayden & Cannon (1982), Hayden & Rider (1991), Trosper (2003), Ryder & Church (1986), Speller et al. (2005) and Prentiss et al. (2007). Acidification has a huge literature. NEGTAP (2001) is a well-written and comprehensive review from a UK point of view, but with wider value. A selection, with emphasis on general issues and recovery includes Stoddard et al. 1999, Weatherley (1988), Rodhe et al. (1995), Sullivan (2000), Bouwman et al. (2002), Driscoll et al. (2001), Ormerod & Durance (2009), Kowalik et al. (2007), Kuylenstierna et al. (2001) and Sommaruga-Wograth et al. (1997). Specific effects of acidification on dippers include Buckton et al. (1998) and Ormerod et al. (1991). Buckton & Ormerod (2002) looks at specialist river birds in general. Exotic species also have a large literature, and can be approached through Caraco et al. (2006), Lodge et al. (2000), Strayer (1991, 2009) and Strayer et al. (2006). A technique of assessing the general structural complexity and damage in rivers is River Habitat Survey, which is discussed in Raven et al. (1997) and Brewin et al. (1998). Dams and reservoirs will be considered in detail later, but a comprehensive review of the wider issues is World Commission on Dams (2000).

Chapter 9

# MIDDLE STAGE AND DEPOSITIONAL FLOODPLAIN RIVERS

## 9.1 INTRODUCTION

All streams wiggle. They meander or wander from side to side as their channel attempts to accommodate the higher flows of the spring or wet season by expanding its length and volume. And sometimes the flows will be too great for the excavated channel so that they spill over onto land to either side, creating a floodplain. In erosive rivers, however, this is a temporary feature from which the water soon recedes, leaving plants bent in the direction of the flow as the main channel swirls and bubbles on.

But as the river gets larger, it somewhere switches from being an erosive, headwater river to a depositional river, leaving behind more silts, sands and gravels, than it erodes. Some persist in the main channel, smoothing it, for although current speed increases on average downstream, the range of velocities within the greatly increased profile is greater and there are quite low speeds at the edges and at the bottom. The higher flows spread over the floodplain, leaving sediment as the waters recede. The current slows more and more as the water spreads sideways, so that larger particles fall out close to the main channel, or in it, often behind obstructions such as large tree logs, and the smaller

silts and clays more distantly. Deposition within the main channel leads to its splitting into braids with islands of gravel between them; deposition at the edge creates raised banks or levees, which may be several metres high. Water spills over them at high flows, spreading to fill the floodplain, but cannot get back to the main channels as water levels recede so that extensive tracts of swampy ground, lagoons and lakes are formed.

The main channel and its braids are not fixed in place. They will meander under the pressure of the highest discharges to accommodate the water, and the meanders will slowly move over many years. The flow will erode them on the outside of the bends where the speed is greatest, but deposit material on the inside where it is lower. Sometimes the deposition will cut off meanders as oxbow lakes, batons or billabongs. A new meander will then start to form because the discharge still needs to be accommodated. The depositional flood-plain system thus develops a wonderful complexity (Fig. 9.1). There are different degrees of water cover, permanent in the main channel, under water for weeks or months in the middle, often dry for years on end at the very extremes of the floodplain. There is a variation in topography, with semi-permanent basins full of water in the oxbow lakes, which eventually fill in with sediment and vegetation, areas of varying wetness on the main plain, and usually dry islands on the levees and between the braids. In turn, what is ultimately a pattern of different degrees of wetness supports an

*Ecology of Freshwaters: A View for the Twenty-first Century*, 4th edition. By Brian Moss. Published 2010 by Blackwell Publishing Ltd.

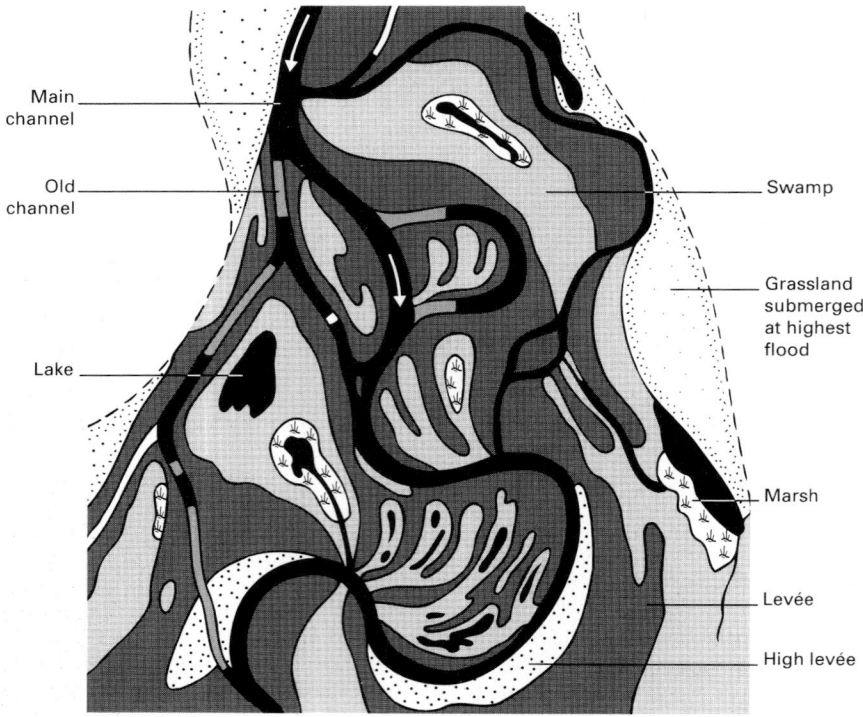

**Fig. 9.1** Floodplains support high biodiversity not only because they are wet but because they have many different physical features, created by the movements of the river channels, the laying down and redistribution of sediments, the ponding of water and the frequent fluctuations in these.

equally interesting and complex mixture of biological communities from dry to wet forests and grasslands, permanent and temporary swamps, and open water.

Floodplains are among the most productive ecosystems on Earth and, because of the variety of habitats they provide, areas of high biodiversity. They are also widely used by many traditional peoples who harvest timber, grass for thatching, and food, or use the rich wet grasslands for grazing and the fertile damp soils at the edge for cultivation. All this depends on the natural water flow and its predictable seasonal pattern of rise and fall of the flood, sometimes called the flood pulse.

Where humans are concerned it also depends on an understanding that the floodplain is part of the river bed that is sometimes dry rather than dry land that is sometimes flooded. Traditional users always build their permanent villages where the risk of flooding is zero or extremely low, or use temporary camps. Where flows are interfered with, floodplain systems can be destroyed

and frequently have been. Where the wisdom of the ancients has not been heeded in siting villages and farms, there has been loss of life and property through a wrong perception of the nature of the floodplain. The tragedy of floodplains is that their nature and values have not been appreciated and so they have been drained, engineered and destroyed (Fig. 9.2) on the one hand, and because the urgent needs for living space of a poor and increasing human population has forced it into living where habitation is dangerous, on the other. Eventually the natural flood may reassert itself.

## 9.2 CHANGE FROM AN EROSIVE RIVER TO A DEPOSITIONAL ONE

The distinction between headwater, erosive river and depositional river develops gradually (Fig. 9.3). The river bed may at first develop pockets of finer sediment,

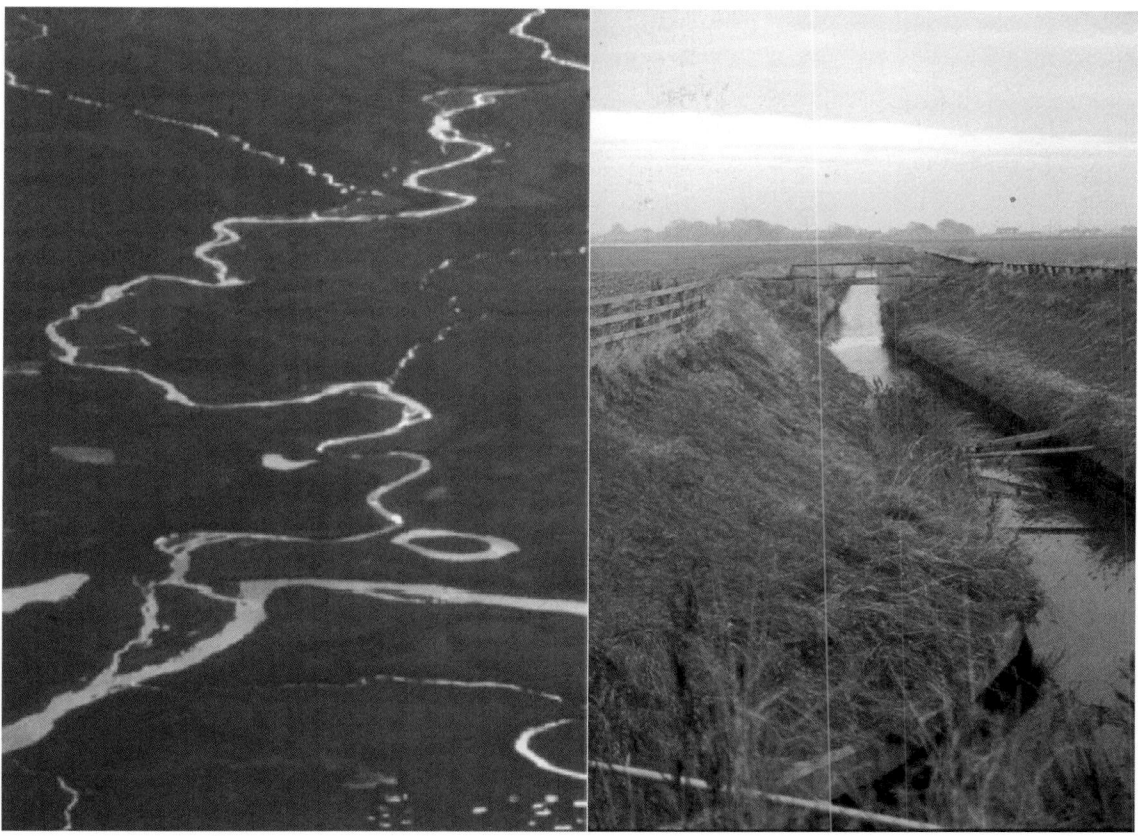

**Fig. 9.2** Natural floodplains (left) contain all the complexity shown in Fig. 9.1. Those that have been engineered in the interest of drainage (right) are uniform, drear and boring with straight, deepened and embanked channels, and a former floodplain that has been dried out, flattened and its habitats destroyed.

which support submerged plants. The widening channel in the middle stages, even if overhung at the edges by trees, will become well lit over an increasing fraction of the bed, which will also allow more plants to grow in water still quite shallow.

Then, in the lower reaches, four gradual changes may take place. Depth will increase, and the water may then bear enough silt from erosion of the catchment to prevent much light penetration to the bottom, so the submerged plants may disappear. Secondly, at the edges, rooted or floating plants, which cope with the turbid water by emerging into the air above it, may start to form permanent swamps. In the bed, the animal community, still dependent on fine organic debris, will largely be deposit-feeding.

Thirdly, as the river becomes larger, water is retained in parts of the channel for longer periods, and there may be time for a suspended community, the plankton, to develop before it can be washed down river to the sea. This community may at first be of animals, the zooplankton, feeding on suspended fine organic debris but in the lower stages of a large river, photosynthetic plankton (phytoplankton) may grow, swirled with the silt and gaining enough light as the eddies sweep it to the surface. Submerged plants may also recolonize the edges. At this stage the lowland river will be almost lake-like. Meanwhile, on the floodplain, the shifting sediments moved by successive annual floods of varying size create the complex floodplain habitat described above. This chapter begins with the colonization of

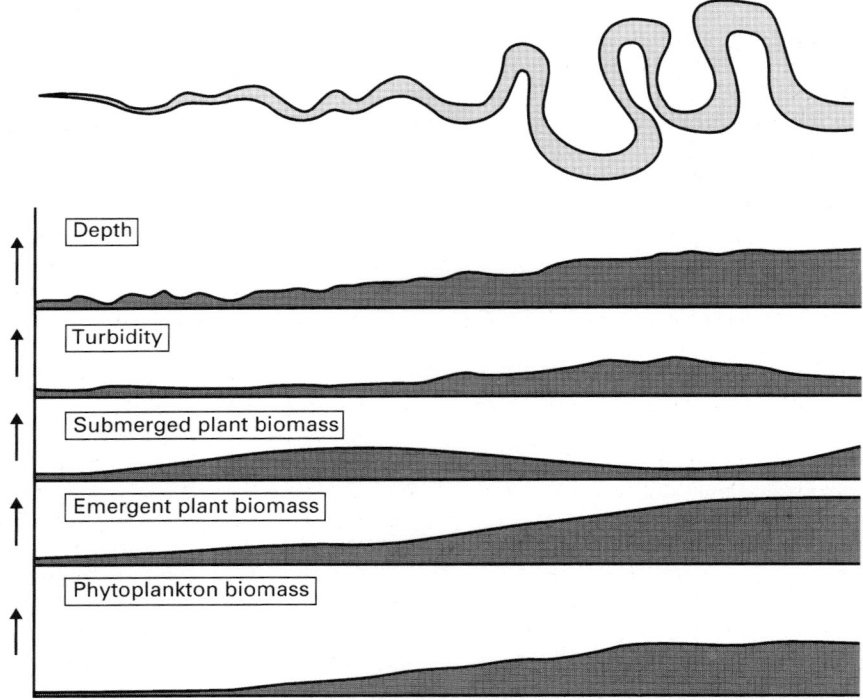

**Fig. 9.3** The transition from headwater stream to floodplain river is a gradual continuous process with trends in the turbidity and producer communities as shown.

middle stage rivers by submerged plants, then looks at the development of swamps and floodplain ecosystems.

## 9.3 SUBMERGED PLANTS

Submerged higher plants (Fig. 6.5) show many common features. Often they have reduced root systems, little woody tissue and large internal air spaces (lacunae). Cuticles are spare, covering thin and sometimes dissected leaves and there is an emphasis on vegetative spread by stolons, rhizomes or contracted shoots called turions or winter-buds. Reliance on vegetative reproduction is often ascribed to difficulties of pollination under water, yet some species have evolved thread-like pollen, which is transported by water currents.

Further features reflect the disadvantages of deoxygenation of roots in sediment, low diffusion rates of gases in water, and the shaded underwater environment. Reduced root systems are often related to the relatively high concentration of mineral nutrients in the interstitial waters of many sediments (Chapter 4).

Experiments with isotopes of nitrogen and phosphorus have shown ample uptake from the sediment by even small root systems and translocation to the shoots. This needs energy, but root respiration may be difficult in sediments that are deoxygenated by bacterial activity. The production of lacunae and air-tubes through which oxygen may be moved to the roots is one solution to the problem (see later).

The lack of woody supportive and water-conducting tissues is understandable in a dense, viscous environment, and the air spaces give buoyancy. The thinness and dissectedness of submerged plant leaves is not so straightforwardly explained. Turbulent water tends to pull plants from their anchorage, and to batter them against adjacent rocks. Small species, might avoid this problem by growing tight mats of leaves close to the bottom, but risk being covered by shifting sand during spates. Taller plants can avoid burial but risk mechanical damage. Flexible, narrow leaves would seem to be well fitted to cope with turbulence, but are no less common in still lakewaters than they are in swift streams.

Perhaps the main reason for selection of such leaves lies in the problems of photosynthesis. Diffusion of $CO_2$ into the leaves is slow, and light is scarce. Submerged leaves show features like those of the 'shade' leaves deep in the canopy of woodland trees. Their thinness increases the ratio of outer photosynthetic tissue to inner tissue where internal shading reduces photosynthesis, but where respiration still continues. Chloroplasts are often present in the surface cell layer, the epidermis, of shade and submerged leaves, but not in those of plants of well-lit places. This places photosynthetic tissue where it can best benefit from restricted light, and where the pathway for diffusion of $CO_2$ from the water is smallest.

The problem of obtaining $CO_2$ is acute in waters of low pH where inorganic carbon concentration is low with no reserve of bicarbonate ions (Chapter 3). A group of submerged plants, called 'isoetid' forms (Fig. 9.4), has features favouring use of $CO_2$ dissolved in the pore waters of the sediments, where decomposition of organic matter increases the concentration very greatly. Their root systems are well developed (for increased absorption); their leaf surfaces have thicker cuticles (which minimizes loss by diffusion back to the water); and they tend to be small and to live in clear, soft waters where the bicarbonate content is not only low, but so also is that of other nutrients, such as phosphorus and nitrogen compounds, so that competition for light with overlying phytoplankton and more vigorous plants is minimized. They may also use crassulacean acid metabolism to store carbon dioxide temporarily as carboxylic acids at night when they can absorb it but not use it in photosynthesis.

Some of the problems faced and overcome by plants in colonizing waters are shown by an elegant comparative study of plants in Danish streams (Sand Jensen et al. 1992). Seventy-five species were essentially terrestrial but could grow submerged, 45 were amphibious and 41 were obligately submerged. Among the amphibious forms, heterophyllous species produce some leaves resembling land plants and others of typically submerged form. Others (homophyllous) produce only one sort of (all purpose) leaf. Sand Jensen et al. measured the photosynthetic rates as oxygen production of representatives of each of the four groups under standard submerged conditions.

Photosynthetic rates increased along the sequence terrestrial to amphibious heterophyllous to amphibious

**Fig. 9.4** Isoetids, for example *Littorella uniflora* (left) and *Isoetes* sp (centre), typically grow on sandy sediments or gravels, are small (left) and can absorb carbon dioxide from their roots in the low-bicarbonate waters where they have some advantage over the ranker, bigger bicarbonate users, such as the mares tail, *Hippuris vulgaris* (right).

**Table 9.1** Comparative photosynthetic physiology of Danish stream plants. Plants were grown in natural stream water. Median values of the experimental results are shown. (From Sand Jensen et al. 1992.)

| Group | Photosynthesis (mg $O_2$ $g^{-1}$ DW $h^{-1}$) | | Final | | Chlorophyll (mg $g^{-1}$ DW) |
|---|---|---|---|---|---|
| | Ambient $CO_2$ | Enhanced $CO_2$ | pH (units) | $CO_2$ (mM) | |
| Terrestrial | 2 | 8.4 | 8.95 | 6.2 | 8.0 |
| Amphibious (Homophyllous) | 4.3 | 13 | 8.95 | 6.0 | 7.5 |
| Amphibious (Heterophyllous) | 10.8 | 27 | 9.05 | 4.8 | 7.1 |
| Obligate submerged | 14 | 34.7 | 10.48 | 0.04 | 6.1 |

homophyllous to submerged, but the differences could be muted (Table 9.1) by enhancing the $CO_2$ content of the stream water. Only the obligate submerged group were able to use bicarbonate (indicated by a marked rise in pH). The chlorophyll $a$ concentrations in the plants also decreased along the series, suggesting a greater efficiency of photosynthesis underwater by the obligate submerged forms. The experiments suggest that obtaining sufficient carbon has been a key problem for aquatic plants to overcome. The 'terrestrial' plants which survive underwater in streams can do so only because stream water is oversaturated with $CO_2$ from ground water which passes into streams with high concentrations derived from soil respiration.

## 9.4 GROWTH OF SUBMERGED PLANTS

As well as a carbon dioxide supply and other mineral nutrients, plants need adequate light as well as particular features of the environment that may favour a given species. Values of light intensity at which net photosynthesis (and hence growth) is just possible (gross photosynthesis > respiration) vary with plant species but have been determined in two English rivers to be between 10 and 40 J $m^{-2}$ $s^{-1}$. Maximum summer irradiance was about 320 J $m^{-2}$ $s^{-1}$ at the water surface, so a fraction of at least 3–13% of the available light was required.

By substitution of values of 320 for $I_0$, 10 or 40 for $I$, and typical values of 1 or 2 for $k$, the extinction coefficient (Chapter 5), some idea can be obtained about the maximum depth at which net growth will still be

possible in rivers. The calculated depths range from 1 to 3.5 m, with three of the four values below 2.1 m. Many middle-stage rivers have depths much less than 3 m and although the calculations must be made separately for each case, this example suggests that there will often be enough light for plant growth to be possible on their beds. It also suggests that, in deeper rivers, the underwater light availability will be critical and that much reduction in incident light, for example by tree shading, could prevent growth even in shallow water. The low rate of $CO_2$ diffusion into the bulky tissues of aquatic plants, as well as the relatively low concentrations of $CO_2$, found at high pH, could possibly lead to limitation of photosynthesis by carbon shortage.

This does happen, but sometimes light is in even shorter supply or it is mitigated because the plants can use the often more abundant $HCO_3^-$ directly as a carbon source. This is difficult to demonstrate unequivocally. Experiments are set up in sealed containers, with no gas phase, where equal amounts of total inorganic carbon at pH 5 or pH 9 are supplied to replicate plants. At pH 5 essentially all the carbon is present as $CO_2$ or as $H_2CO_3$, whereas at pH 9 the chemical equilibria markedly favour $HCO_3^-$ (Chapter 3). If photosynthesis (measured as [14]C uptake, or sometimes oxygen production, see below) is significantly greater at the higher pH than at the lower one, then direct bicarbonate use is believed to have occurred. This has been demonstrated in species characteristically occurring in hard, bicarbonate-rich waters, for example *Ceratophyllum demersum*, *Myriophyllum spicatum*, *Elodea canadensis*, *Potamogeton crispus*, *Lemna trisulca* and *Chara* spp while aquatic mosses and plants of more acid, soft waters, particularly the 'isoetids' such as *Lobelia dortmanna* and *Isoetes lacustris*, seem to be confined to use of free $CO_2$.

Because of their bulkiness, and hence long diffusion pathways, aquatic plants may nonetheless be at severe disadvantage compared with algae when $CO_2$ is scarce. In still water, use of tiny electrodes to measure the pH within millimetres of the leaf surface has shown that pH can be raised by carbon uptake by one or two units close to the leaf surface (Fig. 9.5) and this means that measurements of pH taken even centimetres away from the plants will give a misleading picture of the difficulties they are facing. The rate of supply of either $CO_2$ or $HCO_3$ to the leaf surfaces will be influenced by flow rate, and replacement of water at the leaf surface, however, and photosynthesis should increase with current speed up to some value where factors other than the rate of supply of carbon become important. Increasing net photosynthesis of aquatic plants has been shown with flow rate at velocities up to 0.5 cm s$^{-1}$ but this is a very low flow for rivers, and although the flow within a plant bed will be much reduced, the flow outside the bed would need to fall well below 1.0 cm s$^{-1}$ to have much effect. This might happen in dry periods, but the self-shading within a plant bed makes it more likely that light would become limiting long before carbon supply.

Productivity might be limited by nutrient supply. However, high contents of nitrogen and phosphorus are generally found in aquatic plant tissues. In glasshouse-grown plants growth of a variety of species increased with contents up to about 0.13% (as dry weight) of phosphorus and to 1.3% of nitrogen. Greater tissue concentrations gave no increase in growth rate. Wild-growing plants showed tissue concentrations greater than these critical values in most cases, except for plants rooted in sands.

Many river species, however, will be rooted in fine gravel or sand and nutrient availability will be lower than in silts and finer sediments. Work on algae in upland streams suggests a shortage of phosphorus (but the algae do not have the benefit of nutrient supplies in the sediment), and much higher phosphorus

**Fig. 9.5** (*right*) Absorption of carbon dioxide and bicarbonate by the plant itself and associated periphyton can create steep gradients of pH close to the plant surface. Results are shown from an experiment (Jones et al. 2000) in which plants were given low, medium and high levels of nutrients to stimulate differing degrees of periphyton growth. Bars show the thickness of the periphyton. The curves show change in pH over a few millimetres distance from the plant surface.

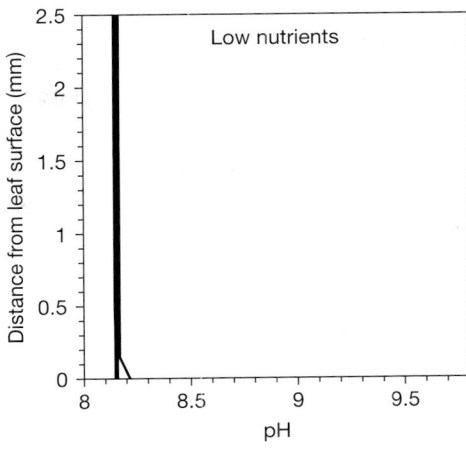

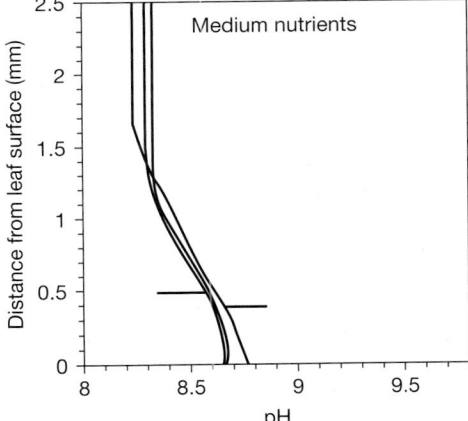

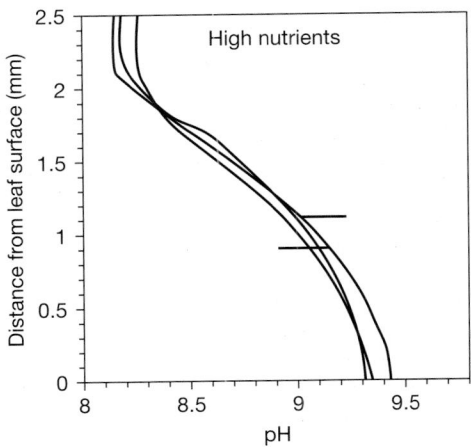

threshold concentrations for maximum photosynthesis of submerged plants than quoted above may be found in some plants. The apparent increase in weed and algal biomass in lowland rivers in recent years, where most rivers have been fertilized by agricultural run-off or sewage effluent also suggests a previous natural nutrient limitation. However, agricultural development has generally also meant removal of dense riparian woodland, so light availability has increased simultaneously. A recent review (Sand Jensen et al. 2007) suggests that light availability is the predominant limiting factor.

## 9.5 METHODS OF MEASURING THE PRIMARY PRODUCTIVITY OF SUBMERGED PLANTS

It is useful to know the rate of production of aquatic plants but the method chosen will depend on why

the measurement is needed. The overall production of mixed plant beds, and their associated algae may be wanted, or specific information may be sought, plant-by-plant, with or without the complications of the algal epiphytes that grow on them. A comparative view of the results of production estimates is shown in Table 9.2. Methods can involve the enclosure of plants in experimental containers (with consequent partial control of conditions) or can cope with the plants in their natural, but varying environment.

### 9.5.1 Whole community methods

The earliest 'whole-community' method was simple and involved the cropping, drying and weighing of the plant biomass at the time of its peak growth. Losses (grazing and mechanical damage) during the growing season were assumed to be small and the difference between biomasses at the start (negligible) and the end

**Table 9.2** Annual productivity of various aquatic plant communities. Values are given in kg organic matter (ash-free dry wt) m$^{-2}$ year$^{-1}$.

| Communities | Average | Range | Maximum |
|---|---|---|---|
| Freshwater phytoplankton | | Negligible–3.0 | |
| Submerged plants: | | | |
|   temperate | 0.65 | | 1.3 |
|   tropical | | | 1.7 |
| Floating plants: | | | |
|   duckweed | 0.15 | | 1.5 |
|   water hyacinth | | 4.0–6.0 | |
|   papyrus | | 6.0–9.0 | 15.0 |
| Reedswamps: | | | |
| *Typha* (reedmace, cattail) | 2.7 | | 3.7 |
| *Carex* (sedge) | | 0.34–1.7 | 1.7 |
| *Phragmites* | 2.1 | | 3.0 |
| Tree swamps: | | | |
|   alder/ash | | 0.57–0.64 | |
|   spruce bog | 0.5 | | |
|   cypress | | 0.7–4.0 | |
|   hardwood | 1.6 | | |
| Comparisons | | | |
|   tropical rain forest | 2.3 | | |
|   boreal forest | 0.9 | | |
|   savanna | 0.8 | | |
|   temperate grassland | 0.6 | | |
|   open ocean phytoplankton | 0.14 | | |

represented the net growth or net photosynthesis. A practical problem was (and remains for any method) that, if the natural variability of the habitat was to be allowed for, large numbers of bulky samples had to be taken. More important were the problems that underground parts (rhizomes, roots) were usually ignored and that losses of biomass during the season were often considerable. For six available estimates for submerged plants, a mean value of 0.65 has been obtained for the ratio of below-ground to above-ground biomass. A similar survey of losses of biomass during the growth season gave values for the turnover rate for a mean of 12 values of 1.9. Turnover rate is the ratio of total annual production (derived from methods discussed below) to maximum biomass and would be unity if there were no losses during the season. Values significantly greater than 1.0 suggest major losses. Values less than 1 are just as problematic for they imply overwintering of considerable biomass, usually as roots and rhizomes.

A better method of determining overall community production is the upstream–downstream oxygen change method of H.T. Odum, developed in the 1950s (Fig. 9.6) and already mentioned in Chapter 7.

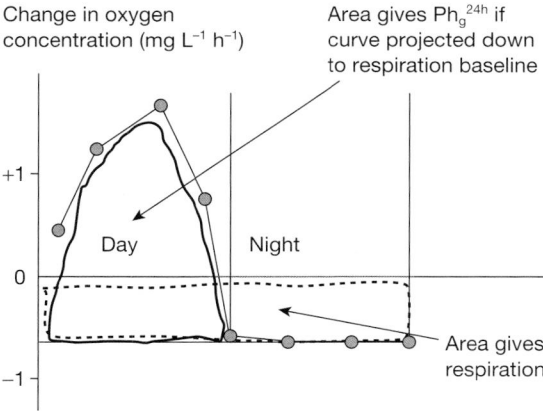

Fig. 9.6 In H.T. Odum's upstream–downstream method for determining productivity, oxygen concentrations are measured at positions in a river about 100 m apart. The change in oxygen concentration (vertical axis) after correction for exchange with the atmosphere is plotted against time. The daytime part of the curve is projected downwards to a line projected from the night-time respiration rate. The area roughly indicated by the solid line then gives the gross photosynthesis, $Ph_g$, whilst the dashed that of line gives the community respiration.

A uniform stretch of river perhaps 100 m long is chosen and over 24 hours the concentrations of oxygen are frequently (desirably continuously) measured at its upstream and downstream limits. From the difference between the two oxygen curves so obtained, after rephasing to allow for the time it took for water to travel the length of the stretch, the net change in oxygen concentration over 24 hours is calculated. It is taken to equal the gross photosynthesis minus the sum of (a) respiration, (b) the net effects of diffusion between water and atmosphere, and (c) accrual, the addition of oxygen in seepage water along the banks. Accrual, which cannot easily be measured, is usually assumed to be negligible. Diffusion is estimated from the oxygen saturation levels and temperatures during the period or determined directly from addition of an inert gas such as propane and measurement of its rate of loss. Respiration is calculated from the oxygen changes during the night extrapolated to the whole period.

### 9.5.2 Enclosure methods

The advantage of the above method is that it studies an unenclosed community; the disadvantages are that exchange of gases with the atmosphere can result in the need for large corrections, giving large possible errors and that a great deal of water may move in the hyporheic zone, the 20 or 30 cm of gravels and sands below the bed surface, whose oxygen concentrations are not measured but where considerable respiration may be going on. It also does not separate the contributions of different components of the system: the plants, the epiphytic algae growing on the plants, the algae on sediments and rocks, and the respiration of the microbial and animal communities. Enclosure methods allow some such separation but the problem is then that the components may not behave in the enclosures as they would in the open environment.

The first enclosure method relied on oxygen changes and was developed for phytoplankton by two Norwegians, T. Gaarder and H.H. Gran in 1927 but can be used for plants also. Samples of the plant material are placed in clear containers (usually bottles) and in containers made opaque with paint or black tape, and incubated in the natural habitat for several hours. Oxygen is released in the clear container (light bottle, LB) by photosynthesis, but is simultaneously respired by the plants and any associated heterotrophs. The change in oxygen concentration in the light bottle is thus:

$$\Delta O_2^{LB} = [O_2^{LB}] - [O_2^I]$$

where $[O_2^I]$ is the initial oxygen concentration and $[O_2^{LB}]$ the oxygen concentration measured in the light bottle after an exposure of $t$ hours.

In the dark bottle, respiration will have reduced the oxygen concentration, with a change:

$$\Delta O_2^{DB} = [O_2^I] - [O_2^{DB}]$$

where $O_2^{DB}$ is the oxygen concentration after $t$ hours. Respiration rates in the dark and in the light bottles are taken as similar, though this may not always be so. The gross oxygen production per hour and per unit dry weight of plant is calculated as the sum of the increase in oxygen concentration in the light bottle plus the decrease in the dark bottle, divided by the weight of plant used ($w$) and the time of incubation ($t$).

Gross photosynthesis =
$$([O_2^{LB}] - [O_2^I] + [O_2^I] - [O_2^{DB}]) (tw)^{-1}$$

The initial oxygen concentration thus need not be known. However, if the amount of plant material is large compared with that of heterotrophs present, the change in the light bottle approximates to net plant production and that in the dark bottle to plant respiration, and a measure of $[O_2^I]$ will allow these to be separately calculated.

Enclosure in bottles is abnormal for plants of flowing waters and photosynthetic rates could be altered (use of stirrers in the chambers can partly compensate for this); there are also difficulties in extrapolating the results of short experiments to entire season production. The amount of photosynthetically useful radiation is continuously monitored and the ratio of whole-day radiation to that during the experiment is used to scale-up the values. This assumes that photosynthesis is governed entirely by light and this may not be true.

A second enclosure method measures the uptake rate of carbon as its radioactive isotope, [14]C, supplied as NaH[14]CO₃ and was developed by a Dane, E. Steeman Nielsen in 1952. The method is sensitive and incubation periods can be much shorter than in the oxygen method. The plants are thus more likely to show rates close to their unconfined natural ones. The bicarbonate added rapidly equilibrates with the $CO_2$–bicarbonate

system in the water and the addition is usually very small. Carbon-14 is taken up more slowly, because it is heavier, than the more abundant [12]C and corrections may be made for this. After a time, the plant is removed, and exposed to fumes of concentrated hydrochloric acid to remove any adherent inorganic [14]C. Epiphytes can be removed and the amounts of [14]C incorporated into the epiphytes and plant separately measured by standard techniques using digestion and scintillation counters. Calculation of primary production assumes that the ratio of [14]C uptake to total C uptake is in the same ratio as the supply of [14]C to the total amount of inorganic carbon present:

total carbon uptake =
(total inorganic carbon ([14]C taken up))/[14]C supplied)

The total inorganic carbon present can be determined by routine analytical methods. The advantages of this method are offset by the problem that what is actually measured (gross or net production) is not known accurately. If the [14]C taken up stayed in the cells and was not respired, gross production would be measured; if it was taken up in the ratio [14]C : [12]C = $x$, and respired in the same ratio, then net production would be measured. In practice, it is probably taken up in ratio $x$ but respired in some different ratio, $y$. It is assumed that respiration does occur but the difference between $x$ and $y$ will determine how close to the true net rate of production the estimate is.

### 9.5.3 Other methods

Paradoxically, approaches that use little equipment, but more ingenuity, may give the most reliable estimates of production for aquatic plants. They depend on a knowledge of plant structure and a willingness to carry out tedious but simple measurements. Thus they have to be applied on a species-by-species basis with adaptation of the method to the biology of the particular species concerned. *Ranunculus penicillatus* var *calcareus* is common in lowland chalk rivers in southern England and grows stems up to 4 m bearing finely segmented leaves every 20 cm or so. Determining the biomass is not difficult with a sampler that cuts the weed from a known area, and the underground biomass is relatively small. Leaves continually break off or are cut by caddis-fly larvae such as *Limnephilus* to provide material for their cases. Stems are broken by water voles and moorhens to line their burrows and nests respectively. Hugh Dawson estimated production from the total losses of leaves and stems from an area plus the biomass left intact. He measured leaf loss by counting the number of nodes that had lost their leaves along stems sampled at frequent intervals and found it to be about 8.5% of the maximum biomass obtained. Whole-stem loss was determined by marking a sample of stems with coloured plastic rings. From the rate of loss of marked stems, an estimate of 77% of the maximum biomass was found for the stem loss.

By placing nets downstream of the areas under study, Dawson found remarkably little 'export' of plant material. The detached stems caught on other stems and often re-rooted, so that the total net loss was small (about 30 g dry wt m$^{-2}$ compared with a total annual production of 300–400 g m$^{-2}$. Most of the produced material, even at the end of summer, was retained and decomposed where it was produced, suggesting that downstream export was unimportant.

## 9.6 SUBMERGED PLANTS AND THE RIVER ECOSYSTEM

The middle stages of rivers, between the upper erosive stream whose food web is dominated by a supply of organic matter from the surrounding land and the vast and swampy floodplains of the lower, depositional rivers, are likely to have submerged plants and some emergent plants as the ultimate determinants of their ecosystems. Submerged plants provide microhabitats, spawning and egg-laying sites for invertebrates and fish, cover from predators for prey and lurking sites for predators. They also supply labile organic matter and entangle organic matter such as leaf litter washed from upstream. The beds may also affect water chemistry, particularly by the removal of nitrate ions. Nitrate removal may be through growth, in which case it is only temporary, as the nitrogen will be released on decomposition of the plants, or it may be by bacterial denitrification (Chapter 4). The plant beds, in encouraging the accumulation of deoxygenated mud and in providing organic matter, may promote denitrification.

In the Arctic, plant growth may be mostly of filamentous and thalloid algae, particularly the red algae and large globular colonies of genera such as *Nostoc* and some of the green algae. The growing season is short and few annual submerged plants can make much growth. Emergent perennials do better, overwintering as rhizomes, and willow thickets may be prominent, providing an early bite for caribou and moose. Further south, a range of vascular plants is able to grow as well as algae, and submerged species become more prominent. It is difficult to be sure exactly how much growth would characterize pristine open rivers in the cold temperate and warm temperate zones because atmospheric nitrogen distribution from human activities has boosted the nutrient levels almost everywhere and development of the banks has allowed greater access of light.

Probably the natural growth would be sparse, with attached algae and mosses on the rocks having prominence. The dense weed beds, for example those of *Ranunculus penicillatus* referred to above, of such rivers in the developed parts of Europe are almost certainly reflections of the huge amounts of nutrients and eroded sediment that pour into them from farmed land. Frequently the 'weeds' are cut to prevent back up of the flow and summer flooding (see below). Warm temperate rivers may often dry up which will limit the growth of plants, at least submerged ones, in them and there may be continued dependence on organic matter washed in from the land, albeit that the leaves of Mediterranean type bushes and trees tend to be hard and resistant to decay as a result of their adaptations to dry conditions.

Tropical rivers in forested regions sport the podostemonads (Fig. 9.7), a group of about 250 highly adapted plant species (Podostemaceae) whose stems mould themselves like green chewing gum over the rocks, putting out flowering branches from time to time. Other groups are also present, but rather little is otherwise known about the ecology of such communities in tropical waters.

## 9.7 FURTHER DOWNSTREAM – SWAMPS AND FLOODPLAINS

As the river widens and begins to deposit more silt at the edges of the main summer or dry season channels, where its flow is reduced, and on its winter or wet season floodplain, emergent aquatic plants, with the bulk of their photosynthetic biomass above water, form swamps, marshes, wet grasslands and forests. Swamps normally have water standing above the peaty soil surface and are dominated by trees, floating mats or tall herb species, often sedges (Cyperaceae), rushes

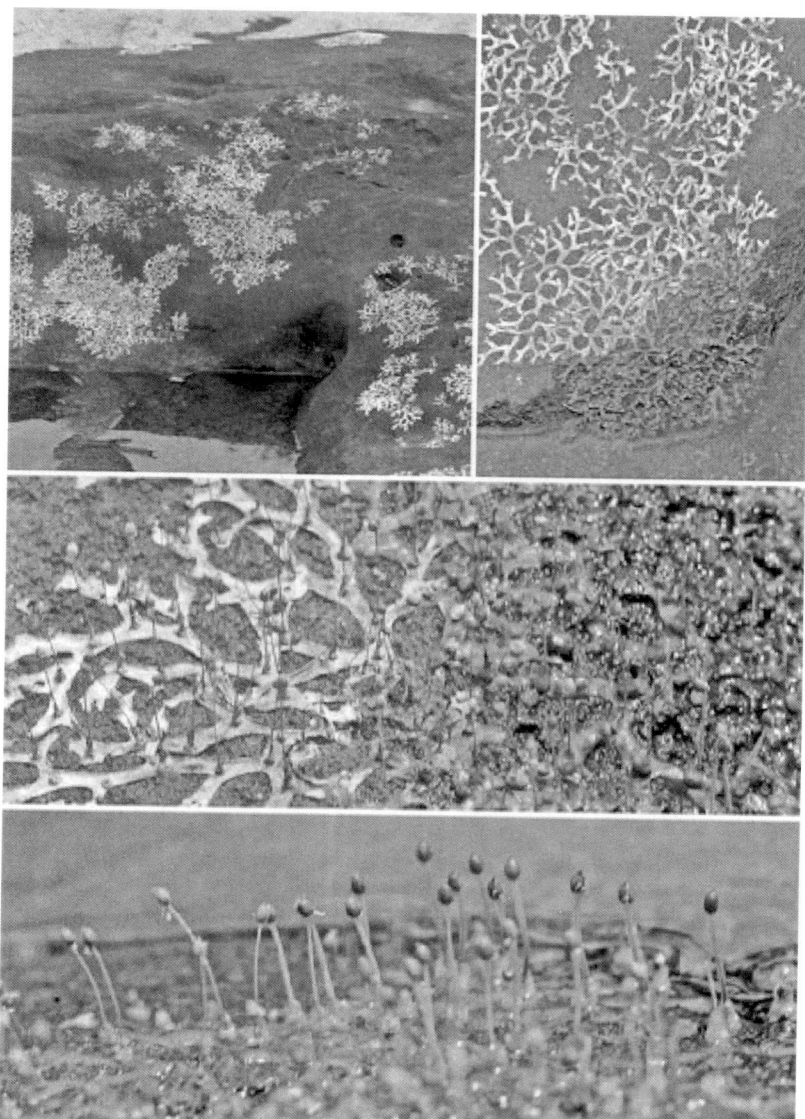

**Fig. 9.7** *Polypleurum ubonense* is a podostemonad found in Thailand. It grows close to rocks in fast flowing streams, and produces flowering heads that emerge from the boundary layer close to the rock, so that seeds can be easily dispersed.

(Juncaceae) or grasses (Poaceae) in the northern hemisphere and restiads (Restionaceae) in the southern.

The warmer the climate, the more likely it is that trees will predominate but much depends on depth of water and the length and amplitude of the flooding. Cold climates will support only sedges and grasses, temperate climates and predictable moderate flooding will promote a transition from grasses and sedges to trees; the greater seasonal variability and more dramatic flood rise of parts of the tropics promotes floating communities including water hyacinths in South America and papyrus in central Africa, but also dense swamp forests even where the rise and fall of the water is tens of metres. Swamp grows closest to the main channel of a river. Marshes, on the other hand, form the more distant short grasslands on more mineral

**Fig. 9.8** Some typical plants of emergent swamps. Reed, *Phragmites* (upper left) has several species and is common on most continents. *Cyperus papyrus* is confined to central and east Africa but is predominant in swamps over a large area, whilst *Victoria regia* (bottom left) is a well-known Amazonian water lily with leaves 1–1.5 m diameter. Water hyacinth (*Eichhornia crassipes*) has become notorious as an exotic species in Africa and Asia, but is not a problem in floodplains of its native South America.

soils flooded perhaps for only part of the year and wet grasslands are somewhat drier, grading imperceptibly with the marshes as the marshes do with the swamps. The swamps and marshes in undisturbed river valleys may occupy a huge valley floor, the basis of a rich ecosystem often involving indigenous peoples totally dependent on it. The swamps and marshes act as huge filters for silt, change the chemical composition of water passing through them and are highly productive ecosystems.

### 9.7.1 Productivity of swamps and floodplain marshes

Swamps and marshes are among the most productive of the world's ecosystems (Table 9.2). They are dominated over large tracts by single, large, vigorous species (Fig. 9.8). In north-temperate regions, reed, *Phragmites australis*, reedmaces or cattails, *Typha* spp, bullrushes, *Scirpus* spp and other monocotyledons often predominate, with tree-swamps of alder (*Alnus*) and willow (*Salix*). In warm temperate climates, members of the Restiaceae (South Africa, New Zealand), the saw-sedge (*Cladium jamaicensis*) or swamp trees – the swamp cypresses, *Taxodium* and tupelo, *Nyssa* (southern USA and Caribbean) – are found. In the tropics, the *igapo* is a more diverse swamp forest in parts of the valleys of the black-water Amazon tributaries, whilst papyrus (*Cyperus papyrus*) characterizes many central African swamps, and many floating species dominate those of subtropical South America. A full list would be much more extensive and the floodplain marsh grasslands may be very diverse because of the varied terrain with

**Table 9.3** Energy budget for a freshwater swamp. Values are in kcal m$^{-2}$ yr$^{-1}$. (From Howard-Williams 1977.)

| Primary producers | Net primary production | Herbivores | Net production | Algal feeders | Net production |
|---|---|---|---|---|---|
| *Phragmites communis* (australis) | 15,000 | Plant-eating insects | 40–60 | Chironomidae | 10 |
| *Utricularia vulgaris* | 150 | Muskrats | <10 | Snails | 30 |
| Planktonic algae | 500 | | | *Asellus aquaticus* | 10 |
| Periphyton | 1000 | | | | |
| Total | 16,650 | | <70 | | 50 |

islands and lagoons as well as the range of emergent communities. Submerged plants will be present in channels in the swamp, though the emergent and floating vegetation will provide most of the biomass.

The high productivity stems from the favourable environment. Only in extreme drought is water short; a continuous supply of river-borne silt brings abundant nutrients; carbon dioxide is readily available from the atmosphere to the emergent parts, and through the water to the submerged; and light probably becomes limiting during the growing season only when the stands become dense enough for self-shading to occur.

We usually measure the productivity of swamps by methods which depend on the harvesting of biomass, partly because of a belief that little of the production is directly grazed, most entering the food webs as detritus following the productive period. The few estimates made of turnover of the biomass, however, suggest that losses during the growth season may be quite high. The Allen curve approach, developed for measurement of fish production (see Chapter 15), follows the mass and fate of individual shoots as they grow throughout the season. A graph of number of shoots per unit area, versus size of shoot for successive occasions, encloses an area underneath it that gives the total production. This value can be divided by the peak biomass to give the turnover. Cohorts of emerging shoots of a grass, *Glyceria maxima* in the UK, showed an annual ratio of above-ground production to maximum above-ground biomass of >1.5. Values of this ratio for other temperate emergent plants (*Phragmites*, *Typha*, *Scirpus*) are close to 1 but for papyrus in African swamps were 1.8–3.6, suggesting that the biomass is replaced up to nearly four times each year.

Equivalents of the light and dark bottle method using large transparent and opaque enclosures covering patches of vegetation can also be used to measure emergent plant production but are technically difficult because of the need to measure changes in atmospheric carbon dioxide during the incubation, which requires a portable infrared gas analyser. There are also methods used by terrestrial ecologists in which the changes in carbon dioxide concentration are measured as parcels of air move across the vegetation in a steady breeze. However, the instrumentation is complex as air movements have to be measured as well as carbon dioxide concentrations and swamps are not easy to move through for installation and use of delicate equipment. Many estimates of swamp production thus depend on biomass changes and are probably underestimates because the underground component is often not measured.

### 9.7.2 Swamp soils and the fate of the high primary production

Several things can happen to the abundant organic matter produced by swamp plants and in general we are uncertain precisely how it is apportioned in many places. It can be directly grazed; it can be washed downstream for processing elsewhere or, in the dry seasons of the tropics and subtropics, consumed by fire; it can be fed upon by detritivores as it dies, becomes colonized by microorganisms and falls to the sediment; and it can be preserved in the waterlogged, anaerobic sediments as peat. Processing through the grazer food webs in the oxygen-rich environment of the emergent shoots appears minor. Budgets (see, e.g., Table 9.3) suggest that only a small fraction of green tissue is eaten by insects, such as grasshoppers and leaf miners, and that although birds such as geese may eat both green tissue and seeds, and rodents such as muskrat and coypu will excavate rhizomes, the impact of these activities is small.

Perhaps this is because the plant biomass is bulky, because of the air spaces in it (see below) and has a high water content, hence a low energy content per unit volume. The same limitations may apply less to the detritivores as the biomass collapses into the water and becomes compressed into the sediment. It may be, however, that most of the material is burned, washed down river to the sea or stored as peat. The soils of floodplains in cool climates may comprise several metres of peat, representing many years of accumulation where microbial decomposition is limited by temperature as well as oxygen; the soils of tropical floodplains are often much less organic and much of the produced organic matter may be recycled within the year (though there are notable exceptions in the rain forest peat swamps of South-East Asia (Chapter 12)). Generally drier conditions, higher temperatures, more grazing species and the frequency of fire will facilitate this.

### 9.7.3 Oxygen supply and soil chemistry in swamps

Swamps are naturally highly deoxygenated places and the smell of sulphurous compounds on the breeze can be evocative. Oxygen diffuses slowly into water and sediment and, because of the huge production and microbial and animal respiration, swamp sediments, and in warm periods, the overlying water, are near anaerobic. Deoxygenation limits the rate of decomposition and favours rapid peat build in colder areas that remain wet throughout the year.

Waterlogged soils pose problems for plants because their reducing nature changes the chemistry of the interstitial and even the overlying water (see Chapter 4 for details). The degree of reduction is measured as the redox potential. A calomel ($Hg_2Cl_2$)-platinum electrode is immersed in water or wet soil whilst connected into a circuit that includes a standard hydrogen electrode. Free electrons move to the calomel-Pt electrode to an extent reflecting the number available and are measured on a galvanometer as a relatively negative potential, in millivolts. A large number of free electrons

available for donation indicates a reducing environment. In an oxidizing medium, electrons move away from the calomel-Pt electrode giving a relatively positive electrode potential difference. Well-oxygenated waters may have redox potentials greater than +500 mv; in deoxygenated ones redox potential will eventually fall to negative values.

As heterotrophs decompose organic matter in sediments, and the oxygen concentration falls, so progressively does the redox potential, to values of about +200 mv when anoxic conditions are reached. Decomposition will have produced inorganic ions such as phosphate and ammonium to add to the ions already present in the interstitial water. Bacterial respiration, becoming anaerobic, may produce organic acids (butyric and acetic). The carbon dioxide content will have risen and the pH will consequently have fallen (Chapter 4).

As oxygen is depleted, oxidized ions may be used by microorganisms to process organic matter. Some protozoa and many bacteria (e.g. *Achromatium*, *Bacillus*, *Pseudomonas*) reduce nitrate to $N_2O$ or $N_2$ through denitrification. Deoxygenation also favours nitrogen fixation by free-living bacteria (*Clostridium pasteurianum*) and bacteria in nodules on the roots of swamp trees such as alder (*Alnus*). Eventual decomposition of these organisms gives a supply of ammonium ions to the soil.

Denitrification is generally complete as the redox potential falls to +100 mv, when anaerobic bacteria, unable to oxidize carbon compounds further, may release ethylene, and bacteria, or perhaps inorganic chemical processes, begin the reduction of $Mn^{3+}$ ions to the more soluble (and toxic) $Mn^{2+}$. At slightly lower redox potentials, *Clostridium* and other bacteria reduce the orange-red ferric ion ($Fe^{3+}$) to green-grey, also more soluble, ferrous ($Fe^{2+}$) ions. If water is moving through the soil these soluble ions may be washed out (gleying) leaving a pale green or grey appearance.

Just below a redox potential of 0 mv, bacteria produce methane (*Methanobacterium*, *Methanomonas*), hydrogen (*Clostridium* spp) or phosphine ($PH_3$) (marsh gases) which may ignite on release as 'wills o' the wisp'. *Desulphovibrio delsulphuricans* and *Desulphomaculatum* oxidize $H_2$ or organic matter by reducing sulphate in the interstitial water to sulphide. In turn the sulphide may precipitate $Fe^{2+}$ to form black, iron-sulphide in the most intensely reducing soils. These processes produce soils with potentially toxic ions ($Fe^{2+}$, $Mn^{2+}$, $HS^-$) and organic acids, and ammonium rather than nitrate as a nitrogen source for roots.

The chemical changes that occur on waterlogging are reversed if the flooding is seasonal and alternates with drying. Carbon dioxide concentration may then decrease, pH may rise and oxygen may diffuse into greater depths. The reduced iron may be oxidized to $Fe^{3+}$ to release energy by iron bacteria of the genera *Gallionella* and *Sphaerotilus*, giving deposits of rust-coloured ochre. Oxidation of sulphides to sulphate by sulphur bacteria (e.g. *Beggiatoa*) may produce insoluble gypsum if calcium is abundant, or sulphuric acid if it is scarce, as in many peats. This reduces the pH to 2 or 3 and forms acid-sulphate soils. Ammonium ions may be oxidized by nitrifying bacteria (*Nitrosomonas*) to nitrite and then (*Nitrobacter*) to nitrate. On reflooding the nitrate will be denitrified so a swamp with a seasonally fluctuating water level may ultimately remove much combined nitrogen from the water. Indeed, if the concept is still valid (see Chapter 4), plant growth in floodplain systems appears to be nitrogen limited.

This interlinked set of inorganic chemical and bacterially mediated reactions thus produces a swamp soil, and an overlying water, which look to be problematic for the higher organisms which colonize them, in more ways than oxygen lack. But evolution has developed solutions and swamps are as vigorously populated as any other system.

### 9.7.4 Emergent plants and flooded soils

Swamp plants can survive waterlogging because they tolerate deoxygenation of their roots or avoid it by supplying air from the atmosphere to the roots via the emergent leaves and stems. Flooding kills many non-swamp plant species because their roots are unable to respire aerobically, and the toxic products of anaerobic metabolism (acetaldehyde or ethanol) reach lethal concentrations. It is not that swamp plants prefer deoxygenated conditions, however. They often grow better in drained soils than in waterlogged ones in cultivated conditions when they are freed of competition with other plants.

A remarkable community of nearly 1000 species of trees, many of them endemic, grows in the 300,000 km² floodplains of the River Amazon. They are flooded to depths of 10 m or more for many months; the water becomes hypoxic with less than $1\ mgO_2\ L^{-1}$ and as much hydrogen sulphide, the temperature is up to 29°C; and especially where the water comes from the Andes, bearing sometimes grams of suspended matter per litre, light penetration is very shallow. These trees remain green underwater, though chlorophyll concentration may fall, and may grow a little at the beginning and ending of flooding when more light is available, but in general they simply tolerate conditions that would quickly kill trees in other habitats. They have usually xeromorphic (dry-adapted) leaf features, such as thick waxy cuticles, which may prevent waterlogging and they make their main growth in the non-flooded season, when drought may become a problem. Indeed adult and seedling mortality rates appear to be higher in the dry than in the flooded season. The key to survival during the anaerobiosis of flooding seems to be previous accumulation of large amounts of carbohydrates that can be respired when photosynthesis is not possible.

Among other swamp plants, avoiders of difficult conditions may produce shallow roots (pine, *Pinus* and rushes, *Juncus*) or may continually replace damaged roots (some grasses). Wet soils not actually inundated but exposed to the air, will be least anaerobic towards the surface. In swamp forests, the trees may produce aerial roots, which protrude above the soil surface and absorb oxygen through pores (lenticels) in the bark. Tolerators limit the formation of toxic anaerobic products within the roots, excrete them to the water or form non-toxic ones instead of ethanol. They may also be able to detoxify ions such as $Fe^{2+}$ and $Mn^{2+}$, which diffuse into the roots from the soil.

Most swamp plants have systems of internal air spaces and it is often assumed that these act as channels for the diffusion of oxygen to the roots and rhizomes. Sometimes they do, though diffusion alone may be too slow to give a ready supply. In water lilies, there is mass flow of air from the emergent leaves to the rhizome. If polyethylene bags containing air are sealed over the young leaves by day, the bags collapse as air is withdrawn from them. Internal pressure, slightly greater than atmospheric, is created in the air spaces of the leaf by absorption of heat. The inner parts of the leaf are in contact with the atmosphere through stomata on the upper surfaces, but the rate of diffusion of air through these is insufficient to prevent build up of pressure in the young leaves. The pressure in the young leaves forces air down through the petioles and into the rhizome from which air is exhaled via the older leaves. As the leaves age, the stomata enlarge and diffusion through them is much faster. In rice, there is a mass flow of air through the continuous bubbles that coat the outside surfaces of the submerged parts of the leaves and stems.

Not all emergent plants, however, have such bubbles or unoccluded air spaces. Sometimes plates of cells interrupt the internal passages. Diffusion through these is slow and mass flow is prevented. Nonetheless even closed lacunae provide internal surfaces, in contact with air, on which toxic reduced ions (e.g. $Mn^{2+}$, $Fe^{2+}$, $HS^-$), diffusing into the root can be oxidized. Diffusion of oxygen from some roots may have this effect at the outer surface in contact with the soil where iron compounds may be precipitated. If you dig into waterlogged soil, the effects of these can sometimes be seen as rusty red pipes around the roots in an otherwise blue-grey or black soil.

Some marsh plants, for example *Filipendula ulmaria* and *Phalalaris arundinacea*, do not have any air spaces. In these, metabolic mechanisms may sometimes better explain flood tolerance. Finely divided adventitious roots (those arising along a buried or submerged stem) may be produced providing a large surface area through which ethanol and acetaldehyde can diffuse out. This happens in several flood-tolerant trees, especially where there is moving water to remove the excreted compound, and can be seen in willows on river banks whose root bundles dangle into the water. Secondly, the rate of anaerobic metabolism can be controlled to minimize ethanol production. Lastly, the end products of anaerobic metabolism can be diverted to less toxic compounds – pyruvic acid and glycolic acid (willow), malic acid, shikimic acid (iris and water-lilies) or amino acids. Eventually these compounds must be oxidized if root function is to continue and this is done either by translocating them to better aerated parts of the plant or waiting until oxygen movement to the roots has increased.

There is a great deal of interest in how swamp plants survive because flooding is a frequent hazard for food crops, many of which are grown on floodplains that have been drained (see Chapter 10) but are still vulnerable to flooding. Many varieties of rice are tolerant and even prefer inundated conditions. There is a complex of genes that aids survival, sometimes by promoting rapid elongation of stems to above the water surface by production of ethylene within the plants, sometimes by producing adventitious roots that are surrounded by better-oxygenated water than that of the flooded soil. Once above the water surface there is the possibility that oxygen can be conveyed down to the roots. With changing climate and greater risks of flooding, natural swamp plants may provide genes for breeding or further lessons in survival. The flood tolerators of the Amazon may be especially valuable.

## 9.8 SWAMP AND MARSH ANIMALS

Floodplains often have spectacularly large populations of fish, birds and mammals because of the great diversity of habitat and the high productivity. Invertebrates are equally remarkable and abundant but less spectacular. As for the plants, coping with natural deoxygenation determines the fauna. Groups of air-breathers (Chapter 6), beetles, some Diptera, and pulmonate (lung-breathing) snails, are predominant, together with specialized members of some otherwise water-breathing groups. An African oligochaete worm, *Alma*, for example, has developed a deeply grooved tail, which is richly supplied with blood vessels. The tail is extended to the surface of a waterlogged, deoxygenated floating mat of vegetation and the groove flattened out in contact with the air. Some snails, for example *Biomphalaria sudanica*, have both gills and lungs.

Among the fish, air-breathing is crucial for those that stay in the swamp all year. At low-water they are confined to the deeper channels and pools where the stagnation of the water, and the large numbers of animals in a small volume, make deoxygenation more severe than in the flood season. It may also make, for the observer, a spectacular collection of fish, turtles, water snakes and alligators in, for example, the sloughs (pools) of the dry season Florida Everglades, a large American floodplain system (Fig. 9.9). Modifications for air-breathing in swamp fish have already been introduced (Fig. 6.10).

Air-breathing fish can remain permanently within the swamp, which, despite its hypoxia, is a permanent and predictable habitat, compared with the temporary aquatic conditions of the outer floodplain grasslands or forests. This favours an economy in reproduction, with relatively few, but large eggs produced, each with a high chance of survival and often guarded by the parents, sometimes in floating nests of vegetation or mucus froth. Where the swamp dries out seasonally, some annual species may survive as eggs buried in damp mud (e.g. some Cyprinodont fishes) or (some lungfish, Fig. 6.8), as adults cocooned in a muddy chamber lined with body slime. The fish breathe through a tube emerging at the mud surface.

**Fig. 9.9** The sloughs of the Florida Everglades (Chapter 10) are deeper places in the floodplain, often maintained free of vegetation by the movements of alligators, and providing dry-season refuges for many other animals.

### 9.8.1 Whitefish and blackfish

In the Mekong river floodplain, the swamp-tolerant fish are referred to as 'blackfish', because by coincidence they are dark in colour, with small or few scales and come from a group of families that include the siluroids and anabantids (catfish), channids (ophiocephalids), osteoglossids, bichir and lungfish. Usually they are permanent swamp dwellers with adaptations for air-breathing. In contrast are the silvery, scaled 'whitefish' of other families, with very different characteristics. The terms 'blackfish' and 'whitefish' conveniently describe similar functional groups in many especially tropical, floodplains.

The whitefish tend to be migratory. They move upstream from the dwindling channel of the river in the dry season and breed in the headwaters, or an upstream floodplain in high flood, where they move to the fringes where oxygenation is greatest. Later they feed on the still inundated floodplain then retreat to the main river as the flood goes down. The whitefish produce many small eggs, which are scattered, and

each of which stands only a small chance of survival. This strategy is appropriate where the conditions for breeding (well-oxygenated water and often some form of structural support for the eggs) may be short-lived and where rapid reproduction is needed in an environment likely to change rapidly and unpredictably. Flood height may vary a lot from year to year (Fig. 9.10).

The contrast between the tolerators of the permanent swamp, like the blackfish, and the migratory whitefish who take advantage of it seasonally, is reflected to some extent also in the mammals and birds, though not of course in contrasts in the way they obtain oxygen. All are normal air-breathers with lungs. Among the former, the sitatunga (Fig. 9.11), a central African antelope, is a more or less permanent swamp dweller with feet splayed to allow it to walk over soft, often floating, beds of vegetation, whereas another antelope, the red lechwe (Fig. 9.11), migrates onto the floodplain grasslands as the water retreats and fresh growth begins. Something of the same pattern can also be seen in the indigenous human societies associated with floodplain wetlands (see below).

**Fig. 9.10** Flood heights (stages) can vary a great deal from year to year. These data (Ilg et al. 2008) are from the River Elbe in Germany, which had an unusually high late summer flood in 2002.

**Fig. 9.11** Sitatunga and Nile lechwe are both associated with African floodplains, but the lechwe migrates onto the floodplain as the flood recedes and away from it as the waters rise. Sitatunga, however, with their large splayed feet are permanent dwellers of the floating swamp mats and other swamp vegetation. (Photographs by Zambia Safari Company and Wildlife Direct.)

## 9.9 LATITUDINAL DIFFERENCES IN FLOODPLAINS

Water always behaves like water. Always it causes deoxygenation of the soils and sediments it covers; and almost everywhere there is some pattern of differential rainfall that causes a rise and fall in water level in big rivers. Flood and ebb are obviously grand contrasts in the state of a place. Differences among floodplains with latitude are thus very much variations on the theme of flood and ebb with the fascinating variation depending on the period and depth of flooding and the extremity of drying out. Behind complete differences in the composition by species of the communities, the common features of biology can always be seen. Moreover, floodplains have probably been occupied by human groups for very long periods, sometimes using their resources for hunting and fishing, sometimes for herding and forms of agriculture that take advantage of the seasonal availability of moist soils at the fringes of the floodplain. Some thousands of years ago, former civilizations in the Middle and Far East developed irrigation systems to maintain the moistness of soils at the edge of the plains in the dry season. Most of these traditional societies and systems have been undermined by the voracity of western technology and the sheer expansion in human populations and the next chapter will have to be devoted to the damage that has now been done to floodplain systems almost everywhere. But in giving some account of geographical differences here, I have also illustrated the subtleties of usage by traditional peoples.

### 9.9.1 Polar floodplains

Little moves in the extreme northern winter. Everything is frozen; snow hangs heavily on the dwarf trees that poke only a couple of metres above the ground towards the tree line, then blankets the tundra. There may be some river flow below the thick ice, but it is small because the catchments are frozen and only deep ground and volcanic spring water may be above zero. Permafrost prevails only a short distance into the ground. When spring comes, it comes earliest to the south and many Arctic rivers flow northwards, often for hundreds or thousands of kilometres in North America and Eurasia. They are big rivers covered with millions of tonnes of ice in winter. About 10% of the world's river discharge to the ocean comes through

about ten rivers discharging to the Arctic Sea, among them the Yenisey, Ob, Lena, Yukon and Mackenzie.

They are still big far to the south where they are surrounded by boreal forest whose debris naturally accumulates in them. When the thaw starts in the south, it is colossal in volume and it starts to push debris and yet fully unmelted but broken up ice blocks ahead of it. Inevitably as the volume of these grows and a narrow place in the valley is encountered a dam of ice and debris forms, ponding back water behind it into a temporary lake, filling the floodplain often for kilometres back. Flows dwindle below the ice-dam for a time but eventually it must burst giving a dramatic surge of water and accumulated sediment and debris downstream and northwards until the next such blockage is encountered. During the temporary stoppages water will spread out to raise the levels of the millions of ponds and lakes that characterize the tundra floodplains, their basins formed by a variety of mechanisms, involving soil movement in alternating freezing and thawed conditions, or simply scooping out of the rock when the polar glaciers pushed southwards only a few thousand years ago.

The Mackenzie River in Canada has a floodplain and huge delta that has been little altered by man. The delta spreads over about 10,000 km$^2$ and is studded with about 25,000 mostly very shallow lakes in a terrain of tundra and a few dwarf trees. The lakes are not uniform, for some are at the same level as the channels of the river, others are perched a little way above it, and others perhaps a metre or two higher, for reasons of underlying irregularities in the rock or in the behaviour of the frozen underlying glacial deposits as they swell and melt just above the permafrost. The region is relatively arid with only 200 mm of rain and so the main water supply is the river flood. The summer, when the flood has passed, though cool, is a period of intense evaporation. Lakes at river level have chemical compositions dominated by river water with a relative abundance of calcium and bicarbonate ions. They are also turbid. Lakes at just above river level are flooded every year but isolated once the flood has passed. In these some plants may develop as the turbid matter settles out with some precipitation of calcium carbonate as marl, so that the calcium to magnesium ratio falls a little and magnesium becomes more prominent. And in the highest lakes, which are not flooded every year, precipitation of marl in the clear waters, which are heavily grown with submerged plants, and evaporative concentration leave magnesium and sulphate as the more abundant ions.

**Fig. 9.12** The River Alti on the Finland–Norway border and Sami reindeer herders. (Photographs by J. Brittain and Reindeer Blog.)

Smaller floodplain rivers are located around the Arctic Sea in Europe (Fig. 9.12). The Altaelva and Tana (Tenjoki), with catchments in Norway and shared between Norway and Finland, respectively are among those least changed by intense human activity. Both are surrounded by catchments with birch forest and lichen tundra, with small populations (<0.5 km$^{-2}$) of Sami herders and fishermen and much larger populations of reindeer. The rivers are open, with swamps of low willow thickets, and large sand bars close to the sea, and represent perhaps the least extreme conditions of deoxygenation, for the waters are swift and low temperature allows greater oxygen dissolution. Large numbers of the piscivorous (fish-eating) goosander (*Mergus merganser*) collect on the sand banks of the Tana in late summer as they moult their feathers. Fish in the rivers are derived from two groups in a pattern reflecting that recounted for the UK in Chapter 6. One group has migrated back from the sea as the polar glaciers have retreated and includes Atlantic salmon, brown trout, Arctic charr, eel, three-spined stickleback and flounder (respectively, *Salmo salar*, *S. trutta*, *Salvelinus alpinus*, *Anguilla anguila*, *Gasterosteus aculeatus* and *Liopsetta glacialis*) whilst the other, including whitefish, pike, minnow, burbot, perch and nine-spined stickleback (*Coregonus* spp, *Esox lucius*, *Phoxinus phoxinus*, *Lota lota*, *Perca fluviatilis* and *Pungitius pungitius*) has moved up from refuges in the south. Fishing is a major activity, with traditional birch fences still being built across the rivers to trap the fish, though more modern netting is also now used and tourist sport fishing has been developed as a source of income. Agriculture is negligible (the growth season is too short) but wild cloudberries (*Rubus chamaemorus*) are collected from the tundra, whilst pearl mussels (*Margaritifera margaritifera*), though now depleted in numbers, are still sought.

### 9.9.2 Cold temperate floodplains

It is not easy to find examples of intact floodplains in the cold temperate region. There has been too much development for intensive agriculture, so that catchments have been changed and the river channels engineered to prevent water movement from the main channel to the floodplain, so that it can be cultivated. Some fragments remain, however, and the Biebzra River, at around latitude 53°N in north-east Poland is one (Fig. 9.13), where about 164 km of meandering

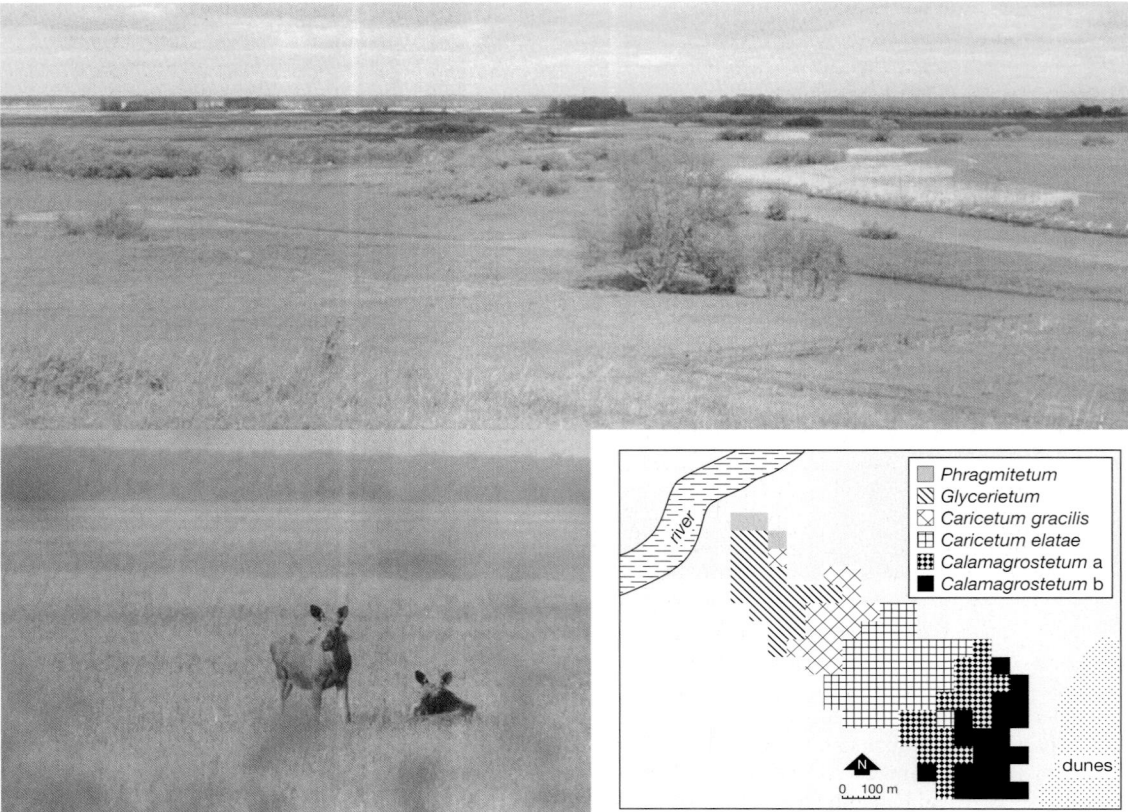

**Fig. 9.13** The Biebrza marshes are one of the few remaining intact floodplain systems in Europe south of the Arctic Circle. They support a complete native fauna including moose (elk) and their predators. The vegetation is complex but a zonation with water depth away from the river can easily be seen. (From Wassen et al. 2002.)

river, 10–35 m wide in summer, still supports a floodplain corridor a kilometre or more wide and 116,000 ha in area. Many of its tributaries have been altered and it is threatened by construction through it of a major trans-European motorway that would alter the hydrology and upset movements of animals, but it yet remains as a rich system probably typical of what Europe once boasted but has now destroyed.

The system is structured around its vegetation. Swamps of a tall grass, *Glyceria maxima*, and the reed *Phragmites australis* border the main channel flanked by communities of *Carex acuta* and *C. elata*, then of another grass *Calamagrostis*. But this is to oversimplify the vegetation, with its over 50 distinctive communities, in old river channels, on levees and in backwater ponds. It is very rich with 18 species of orchids and

about 80% of the Polish flora. As the edge of the floodplain is approached, more woody vegetation appears, of alder and willow, and fens and wet grasslands sometimes still maintained by cutting by local farming communities for hay. In eastern Europe there still remain small farms, only a few hectares in size, with a couple of cows, a pig, a vegetable field, a hay meadow and rights to cut hay on the floodplain. This process removes nutrients and promotes a greater plant diversity of small species in conditions where the competitive tall grasses and sedges cannot take over. It also prevents all of the outer floodplain from becoming forest as part of its natural succession and thus helps retain a diversity of habitats. The soils are sometimes sandy from river floods; the edges of the floodplain are old sandy moraines that have eroded over several thousand years. Elsewhere they are completely organic peats laid down by the swampy vegetation. Sometimes the peats are fairly base-rich and fed by flood water or base-rich ground water and support a minerotrophic mire or fen vegetation, rich in species. Sometimes, especially at the edges of the floodplain, they are fed by rain water, low in bases and pH, which wells up through the sands to produce bogs rich in *Sphagnum* and other bryophytes and bog forest with alder. In general with distance from the river, the soils get drier and less nutrient-rich, the water table fluctuates less, and the biomass of the vegetation is lower. Thus there is the characteristic pattern of floodplains, ultimately conditioned by the annual pulse of the flood in late winter and spring, and its fall in summer.

The Biebrza floodplain is rich in birds, mammals and fish and this also reflects the complexity of conditions and vegetation. There are over 235 species of birds, with cranes, bitterns, storks, ruff, dunlin, black grouse, little gull, several species of eagles, harriers, whooper swans, widgeon and other ducks. Some 500 elk (moose), and groups of roe deer, muskrat, beaver and wild boar graze the area, together with 17 species of shrews, mice and voles, collectively the prey of raptorial birds, and wolves, polecats, foxes and pine martens. In a short visit, my greatest thrill beyond the sheer wonder of the whole system, was to find the print of a wolf in a sandy patch at the edge of the fringing forest. There are 36 fish species, including unusual lampreys, burbot and bleak, now rare elsewhere. The invertebrate fauna has been barely explored and may never be fully documented if changes in farming and the building of the road, the Via Baltica, begin to remove this last remnant of floodplain systems that once occupied every lowland river in the centre of the continent.

### 9.9.3 Warm temperate floodplains

A classic warm-temperate floodplain is a system that has been nearly destroyed by political considerations in the Middle East, but which may yet be reinstated. It is that of the Euphrates and Tigris rivers in Iraq with their indigenous marsh arabs, or Madan. Travellers such as Wilfred Thesiger and Gavin Maxwell paint a picture of the Madan (Fig. 9.14), permanently dwelling in tall reed swamps. These spanned the 15,000 km$^2$ around the confluence of the Tigris and Euphrates near the Arabian Gulf. *Phragmites australis* grows to 4 m in height and dominates the swamp; it is flanked by

seasonal swamps of *Typha angustata* and a sedge *Scirpus brachyceras*. The Madan are descended, in part, from the Sumerians who founded the great Mesopotamian civilization at the edge of the marshes 6000 years ago. In the early cities of the area, such as Babylon, the river waters were also harnessed for irrigation outside the floodplain by systems of considerable ingenuity.

A Sumerian legend, however, has it that Marduk the Great God, built a platform of reeds on the surface of the waters and created the world. Perhaps this was how the ancient marsh arabs built their houses as it still was until very recently. On the platform simple houses of reed bundles were built and also elaborate *mudhifs*, or guest houses, up to 20 m long and 6 m wide. The bases of their construction were pillared arches of reed 2 m in girth and tightly bound. Inside these structures an elaborate social life was possible in comfortable carpeted surroundings.

Outside the buildings, the platform housed the three to eight water buffalo that were the mainstays of a marsh family. These placid animals were taken to graze, where the water was shallow enough for them to touch bottom, on sedge or water plants (*Polygonum senegalense, Jussiaea diffusa, Potamogeton lucens, Cyperus rotundus*) and on return at nightfall were fed the young shoots of sedge or reed cut during the day. Buffalo provided milk, meat and dung for fuel, whilst birds were shot for meat, or, in the case of pelicans for the soft pouch skin which, once cured, formed excellent drum and tambourine skins.

Fish, particularly *Barbus sharpeyi*, were speared with forks from lines of boats set across channels, or poisoned with flour and dung bait laced with extracts of the toxic plants, *Digitalis* or *Datura*. Gill nets were laid, and the fish sold to the cities. Boats were usually of wood, brought in from the coast but, as elsewhere, simple canoes were built from *Typha* bundles bound together. On the swamp edges, rice was cultivated and provided a staple diet; the ricefields also attracted wild boar. A metre or more at the shoulder and aggressive, the boar accounted for many injuries to Madan who surprised them whilst punting through the channels or cutting reed.

The Madan were originally largely self-contained; visitors commented on their hospitality and the complexity of clan and tribal relationships. They suffered also from poor health – high infant mortality, yaws, schistosomiasis, dysentery, and tuberculosis. Increasingly, health care was made available and there had been trade in woven reed mats and fish with areas outside the marsh. The pattern was set for maintenance

**Fig. 9.14** It is yet unclear how much of the traditional lifestyle of the marsh arabs has survived drainage of the Euphrates–Tigris marshes. These photographs by Nick Wheeler were taken in the early 1970s (Young & Wheeler 1977), showing water buffalo herding and a meeting house, or *mudhif*.

of a traditional culture benefiting in a sympathetic way from other influences. The current situation of most Madan is probably far different from this description, however. For reasons purportedly of agricultural development, a former Iraqi Government dug canals, which have drained the marshes. Denied the traditional marsh resources and influenced by the brutalization inevitably following the Gulf War in the area, the Madan seem likely to be forced to join the mainstream of westernized ways. Commentators who have observed this share the regret that Thesiger and Maxwell would have articulated no less sadly.

### 9.9.4 Tropical floodplains

Australia is one of the least populated of the world's regions, and across its northern tropical parts of Western

Australia, the Northern Territories and Queensland, from Broome to Cape York, about 80 major river basins, covering 1.5 million km$^2$ including the Magela, Mary and Arafura, have yet survived development for agriculture and modification of the rivers. It is very hot and the extreme wet–dry climate brings heavy rains over just a few months, largely from November to February, with an intense dry season from March to September. Potential evaporation is more than twice the annual rainfall and rivers that flow vigorously in the monsoon season, dry up completely. The seasonal pattern is predictable and, as elsewhere, but especially so here, drives the ecology of the floodplains. The aboriginal peoples of the area recognize a subtle calendar of weather that is confirmed by the meteorological readings (Fig. 9.15). What is more variable, because of the violence of the wet season flows, is the pattern of vegetation on the plains. Sediments shift greatly, water

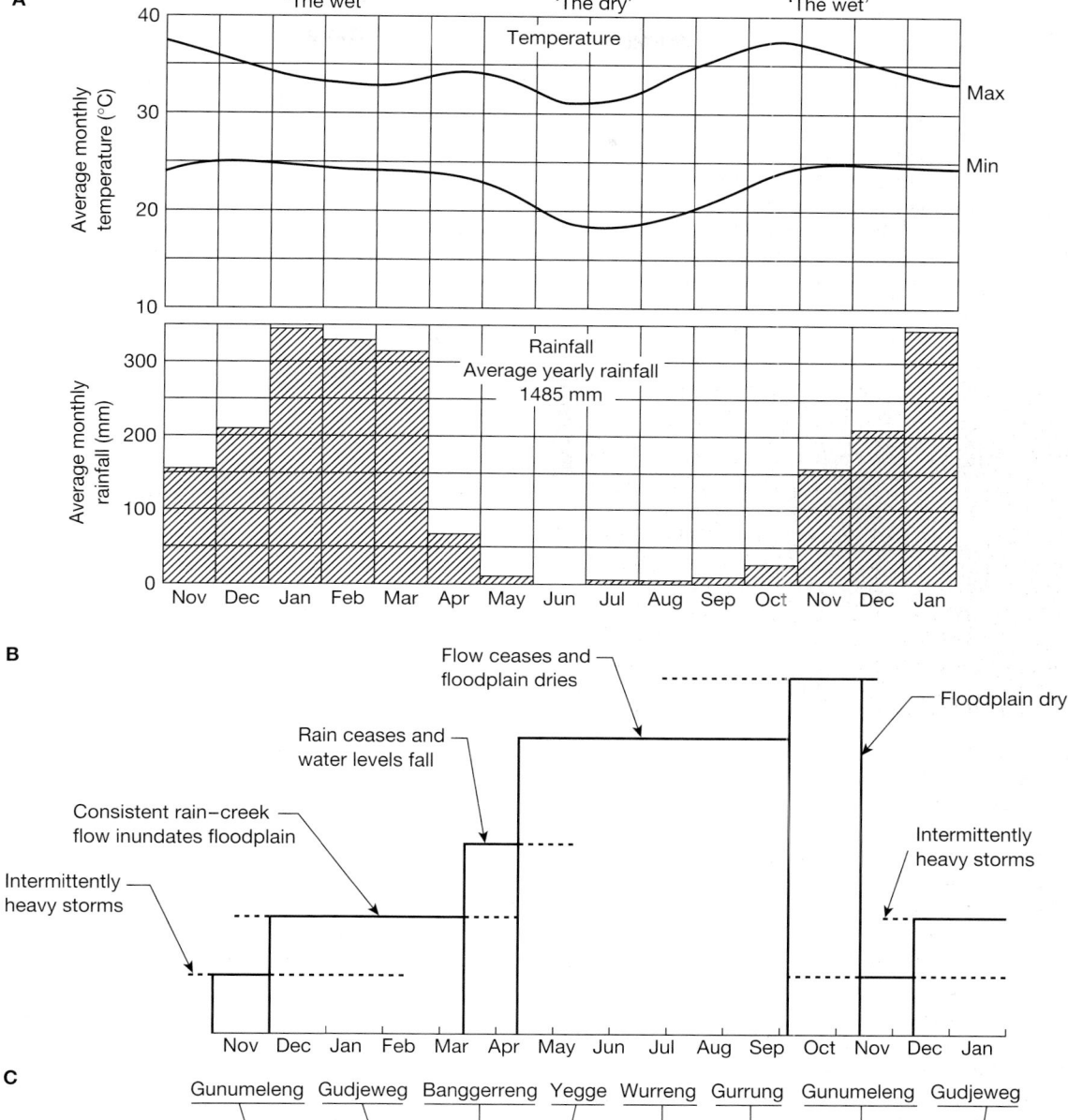

**Fig. 9.15** General features of weather in northern Australia relevant to the floodplain systems. The traditional aboriginal terminology for the seasons and hydrological events is also shown. (Based on Finlayson 2005.)

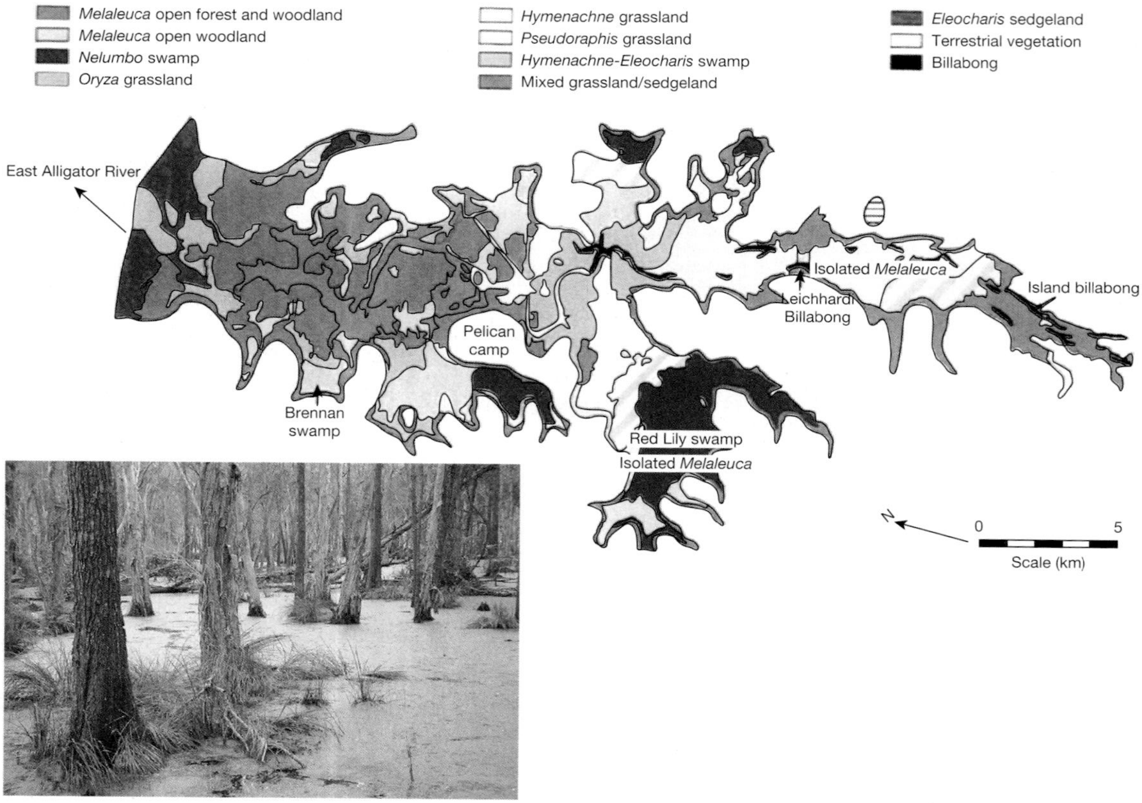

Legend:
- *Melaleuca* open forest and woodland
- *Melaleuca* open woodland
- *Nelumbo* swamp
- *Oryza* grassland
- *Hymenachne* grassland
- *Pseudoraphis* grassland
- *Hymenachne-Eleocharis* swamp
- Mixed grassland/sedgeland
- *Eleocharis* sedgeland
- Terrestrial vegetation
- Billabong

East Alligator River

Pelican camp

Brennan swamp

Isolated *Melaleuca*
Leichhardt Billabong
Island billabong

Red Lily swamp
Isolated *Melaleuca*

Scale (km)
0          5

**Fig. 9.16** Map of the vegetation in part of the floodplain of the Magela River, northern Australia and (inset) a section of flooded *Melaleuca* woodland. The pattern of the vegetation is not regular as it is in wetter regions (Figs 9.13 and 9.17) owing to the less predictable pattern of rainfall and flooding. (Based on Finlayson 2005.)

holes and billabongs (oxbow lakes, but the term is now used for any depression that holds water in the dry season) may fill in or be created elsewhere. Fire is normal in the dry season. Salt water may move up the river channels from the mangrove lined estuaries for 100 km but eventually peters out. The ordered patterning of vegetation, parallel to the main river channel, from permanent swamps to the wet then drier grasslands of the floodplains in regions where water flows for all of the year is rare, and a vegetation map may look almost random (Fig. 9.16).

In the dry season, the most prominent feature is the open woodland of paperbark *Melaleuca* trees (*M. viridiflora*, *M. cajaputi* and *M. leucadendra*) with other tree species such as *Baringtonia* and *Pandanus*. The leaves are small and thick, for they must survive a climate close to desert. The ground is brown, sandy and dry, sometimes with whitish salt deposits, except where the oases of deeper water holes support greener patches with trees, sedges and grasses around, and lilies and submerged plants within them. Here congregate the crocodiles, snakes, turtles and fish, including the barramudi (*Lates calcarifer*) as well as invertebrates that will repopulate the river and roam over the rest of the floodplain when the rains come in November and create water sometimes several metres deep. When this happens the floodplain greens up with a variety of communities: sedgelands of *Eleocharis* with a grass related to rice, *Oryza meridionalis*, wet grasslands of *Phragmites vallatoria*, *Hymenachne acutigluma*, *Pseudoraphis*, *Leersia* and *Echinochloa*, patches of water lilies and lotus, *Nelumbo*, *Nymphaea* and *Nymphoides*. Fish and reptiles move out to spawn and feed; large flocks of birds, including sometimes millions of magpie geese

(*Anseranus semipalmata*) appear and graze on *Eleocharis* and its rich underground tubers, and the seeds of *Oryza*.

The fish, like many in tropical communities with low-oxygen warm waters, include many omnivores and few strict piscivores and the aquatic food web appears strongly dependent on algal production, either the epiphytes on the aquatic plants or the filamentous skeins of *Spirogyra* and *Vaucheria* that thrive in the wet season, to be grazed down by shrimps, turtles and fish, which in turn are taken by the two top predator crocodilians (*Crocodylus porosus* and *C. johnsoni*). Dependence on the algae is reflected in the carbon isotope signatures of the animals. Their relative enrichment in $^{13}$C does not reflect the sedge, grass and tree signatures, but those of the algae and the relative enrichment in $^{15}$N suggests omnivorous feeding. Nitrogen-15 becomes enriched by three to four times at each step of the aquatic food chains and may be used to trace the links. In these floodplains the enrichment is often much less, suggesting feeding from at least two trophic levels.

As the waters recede, great migrations of animals follow, the birds to wetter regions elsewhere, the reptiles, shrimps and fish to permanent water holes, and many invertebrates form cysts, eggs and other resting stages. The plants die back to underground rhizomes or tubers, or survive as seeds, often with corky or aerenchymatous tissues or in air-filled pods that can float as the vicissitudes of the next wet season change the patterns of water. The dry peeling bark of the trees, so quintessentially Australian, epitomizes the intense drought. It is a rich system, both in its diversity and in the intactness of the ecological processes, but there are threats even in this remote area. Feral water buffaloes (*Bubalus bubalus*) escaped from farms, and breeding freely, have caused overgrazing, and feral domestic pigs (*Sus scrofa*) and introduced cane toads (*Bufo marinus*) have changed the communities. Where the buffalo have been culled, *Eleocharis* has grown more vigorously but some vegetation described by early travellers, dominated by *Phragmites*, has not re-established but has been replaced by *Hymenachne*. It is not known whether this would have happened anyway or if a former system can ever be restored once it is disturbed.

### 9.9.5  The Sudd

The Nile is a permanent river, unlike many in the Australian tropics. It has harboured large numbers of

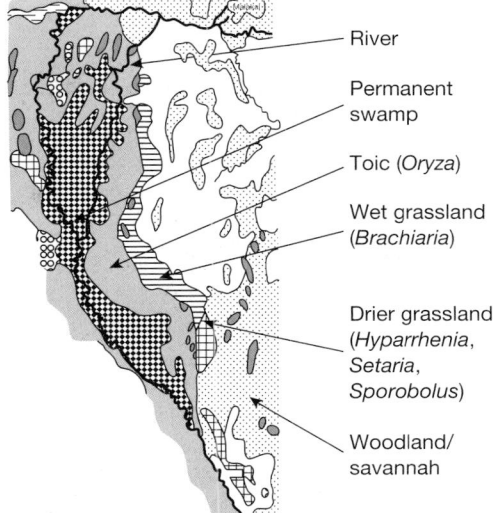

**Fig. 9.17**  Vegetation map of the Sudd. (From Van Noordwijk 1984.)

people in consequence. In the southern Sudan, where its floodplain is wide, it provides a living place for migratory cattle herders. The Nuer are a nilotic people living in the valleys of the White Nile (Bahr el Jebel), Bahr el Ghazal and River Sobat around their confluences in the Sudd swamp in the Southern Sudan (Fig. 9.17). Like the Dinka who occupy the eastern part of this region, to the Nuer's western, they have a mixed economy and a social system that rests heavily on the flood cycle (Fig. 9.18).

Heavy rain falls, between April and September, onto the flat plain, floored by clay, lacking trees and crossed by large rivers. Close to the rivers (Fig. 9.17) is a permanent swamp of papyrus, reed, *Phragmites mauritianus* and floating or part-floating beds of water hyacinth (*Eichhornia crassipes*) and hippo grass (*Vossia cuspidata*). To the edge of the permanent swamp are regularly flooded swamps with *Typha australis* and grasslands called toic. The toic has grasses such as *Echinocloa pyramidalis*, *E. stagnina* and wild rice, *Oryza barthis*, and is annually fertilized by silt-laden river water.

Further distant from the rivers the toic is replaced by grasslands, which flood (to depths of up to a metre and largely with rain water) in the wet season and are less fertile. The upland, which is not flooded, is reached often some tens of kilometres from the rivers. The area is rich in both large aquatic animals and many bird species that move onto the grasslands as the water

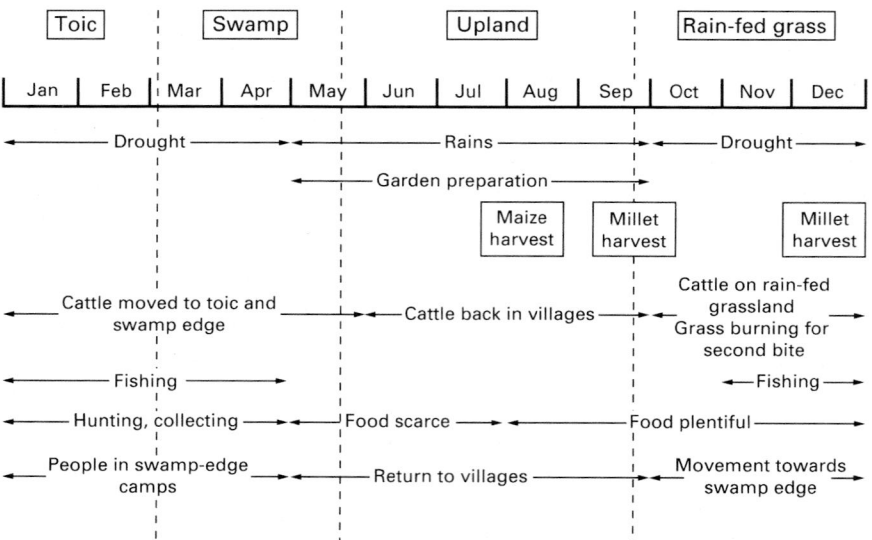

**Fig. 9.18** The Nuer year. (Based on Evans-Pritchard 1940.)

recedes. These include most of the world population of the Nile lechwe and several hundred thousand tiang, another antelope, a subspecies of the tsessabe (*Damaliscus korrigonus*).

The Nuer have permanent villages at the edge of the upland, close to the plain. They keep cattle and movement further into the upland is discouraged by the risk of nagana (cattle trypanosomiasis), a protozoan blood disease carried by the tsetse fly *Glossina morsitans*, characteristic of shady woodland. The floodplain is clearly unsuitable for permanent villages, but the Nuer must stay close to it for it provides grazing for the cattle. The swamps at its centre are a source of fish when milk yields are low in the dry season.

When the rains begin, in May, the village gardens are sown with millet (*Sorghum*), some maize, beans, gourds and tobacco, which will be harvested in July and August (Fig. 9.18). This work is done mostly by older people, the younger being still in temporary camps near the swamp where, at the end of the dry season, there is still some grazing and where the lagoons and diminished stream channels are a concentrated source of fish. Everyone returns to the village by June and the wet season provides an ample food supply based on milk and its soured products, and meat from sheep and goats. Blood is drawn from the necks of the cattle, coagulated and roasted.

Meanwhile fishing is difficult for the fish are dispersed in the flooded grasslands, which are difficult to cross. The lack of trees means that boats are scarce. When the millet is harvested, there are wedding, initiation and other ceremonies and the social organization is at its most complex. A second sowing of millet in August is harvestable by December, when the rains have stopped and when, particularly if the rains have been poor, food may be scarce.

The cattle are taken by the younger people onto the floodplain after August whilst the older remain to harvest the millet. The graze produced on the rain-flooded grassland is of low quality for cattle and soon has dried. Some areas may be burned to bring new shoots, but the main grazing is in the toic. Camps are made on mounds at the swamp edge, to which the older people also move after the millet harvest. These camps simply comprise wind-screens of swamp grass, and the social life is family-based and geared to the business of survival. Milk yields fall as the toic grasses shrivel and the millet store dwindles.

To the rescue comes fishing, the third focus of Nuer economy, together with collection of wild dates (*Balanites aegyptica*), wild rice seeds and water lily rhizomes (*Nymphaea lotus*) to eat. The swamp fish include catfish (*Bagrus, Clarias*) and lungfish (*Protopterus*), which are speared behind temporary grass dams as they attempt to move back to the river. A line of withies, thin branches of ambatch (*Aeschynomene*), may be pushed into the mud in front of the dam. The quivering of these as the fish move against them signals the target for the spearsman. Lungfish aestivating in the mud may be sounded out by tapping the surface with a pole or by recognizing sounds the buried fish make when a finger is scraped over a gourd. They can then be dug for. There is some hunting, largely for products such as skins of waterbuck for bedding or of hippo to make shields. Cattle stealing, especially by the Nuer from the Dinka, is not unknown.

When the rains return, the older people move back to the villages to prepare the gardens and the cycle is completed (Fig. 9.18). Each of its three parts is essential; diseases such as rinderpest prevent any great expansion of the cattle population; the climate precludes total dependence on grain, the crops of which often fail; and the dispersion of the fish in the wet season means that fishing cannot be the sole source of food. After 1961, a rise in the discharge of the Nile, linked with a 1–2 m rise in the levels of Lake Victoria at the head of the river, led to an extension of the permanent swamp and a marked reduction in the grassland. The Nuer turned more to fishing though they regard themselves primarily as cattle keepers. In recent years the floods have fallen again.

In all of these accounts of floodplain systems, and in the many more examples that I could give, a human dimension has been universally present. But these are examples where it is generally sympathetic to maintenance of the floodplain system. That of the Tigris–Euphrates, however, was almost completely destroyed in the 1990s. Most floodplain systems have been equally spurned, as will be shown in Chapter 10.

## FURTHER READING

Aquatic plants, both submerged and emergent have been favourite subjects for research for many years because of the physiological problems that they must face. General accounts are Cook et al. (1974) and Sculthorpe (1967). Swaine et al. (2006) is a rare paper that refers to podostemonads. Nutrient uptake is reviewed by Denny (1980), Barko & Smart (1980), Lockaby & Conner (1999) and Casey & Downing (1976), carbon dioxide availability by Raven (1970), Boston & Adams (1983, 1986) and Maberly & Spence (1983). Wium-Andersen (1971) and Wium-Andersen & Andersen (1972) began a great interest in isoetid

metabolism and the uptake of carbon dioxide by roots. Parolin (2009) describes the remarkable abilities of Amazonian trees to survive flooding and Sand-Jensen et al. (2007) argue that light availability is the key feature of aquatic plant survival. Deoxygenation *per se* and in the context of flooding tolerance by non-aquatic plants is covered by Crawford (1989), Dacey (1980) and Lynn & Waldren (2003) and latterly by Jackson & Colmer (2005) Jackson & Ram (2003) and Jackson et al. (2009). The development of plankton in floodplain rivers is discussed by Reynolds (1996).

Measurement of productivity of aquatic plants may be approached through Odum (1956), Seeley (1969), Steeman-Nielsen (1952), Dawson (1976), Matthews & Westlake (1969) and Kvet et al. (2008). It is a topic that was much studied in the middle 20th century and will now resurge as interest increases in global production and carbon storage as climate changes. Measurements and other aspects of production can be found in Imhof (1973), Howard-Williams (1977), Thompson et al. (1979), Westlake (1967, 1972) and Engelhardt & Richie (2001). Aspects of animal respiration physiology have been covered in Chapter 6 and Hoback & Stanley (2001) give a review of tolerance of hypoxia in insects. Jones (1964) shows what can be done with simple equipment under unsophisticated conditions.

For polar floodplains, the Mackenzie Delta and its water chemistry is discussed in Lesack et al. (1998) whilst Brittain et al. (2009) describe European polar floodplains. Issues of ice dams are discussed in Beltaos (2008) and Prowse & Beltaos (2002). The Biebrza floodplain is discussed in Wassen et al. (1990, 2002), Wassen & Olde Venterink (2006) and Winter et al. (2009). Tockner et al. (2003) summarize work on a second rare example of a relatively undisturbed European floodplain, that of the Tagliamento in Italy. Warm temperate floodplains in the USA and South Africa are described in Benke et al. (2000) and Jacobs et al. (2007). Thesiger (1964) is an account of living among the Madan in Iraq by a man who would have had no truck with current health and safety considerations and soft living, and is supplemented by Maxwell (1957) and Young & Wheeler (1977). Por (1995) covers the Pantanal in southern Brazil. My information on Australian tropical floodplains came from Finlayson (2005) and Douglas et al. (2005). Brito et al. (2006) covers similar aspects in a Brazilian example. The classic work on the Nuer remains Evans-Pritchard (1940).

# Chapter 10

# FLOODPLAIN ECOSYSTEMS AND HUMAN AFFAIRS

## 10.1 INTRODUCTION

The origins of settled agriculture are vague, for a transition from a hunter–gatherer existence to settled villages, fields and domesticated herds, was not an abrupt event but evolved gradually as populations increased, particular plants and animals were found to be controllable, and domestic and animal wastes were found to be stimulating fertilizers for crops. Sometimes, however, there are hints of the processes concerned and of the social and economic pressures that started to develop. Floodplain sites, with their abundance of water and natural high production are strongly associated with early agriculture and the eventual development of large cities. It is a syndrome that has led to severe damage, or the rise of civilization, dependent on how you wish to look at it.

At Kuahuqiao, near the coast of southern China, is a swampland site that was a river delta around 8000 years ago, became flooded by the sea, then re-exposed with changing sea level. Sediments at the site change from those of a forested swamp with alder around 7700 years BP (before present) to those of a more open vegetation with *Typha*, a wild rice, *Oryza rufipogon*, and other varieties of rice that show evidence of change towards

*Ecology of Freshwaters: A View for the Twenty-first Century*, 4th edition. By Brian Moss. Published 2010 by Blackwell Publishing Ltd.

modern cultivated varieties. Remains of houses set on wooden piles, of pigs and the parasites they share with people, of pots into the wet original clay of which stray rice grains have been accidentally pressed, of dogs, and a dugout canoe, have been found (Fig. 10.1). In soil cores preserved under a layer of marine clay, pollen grains, fungal spores and the ova of a nematode parasite, *Tricuris*, together with a sudden rise in charcoal, tell of the use of fire to clear the swamp woodland, and the establishment of pig and rice farming in the Neolithic Period. Remains of bunds suggest that the annual flood water was ponded back in the rice fields to extend the growing season, and oyster shells testify to a mixed economy that collected marine food as well as grew rice. It ended when the sea flooded the site in 7550 years BP after about 150 years, but it is probably just one of many examples worldwide of the start of exploitation of floodplains.

As human populations grew, with the ability to produce food in reliable quantities, so too did a more hierarchical system of organization, both needed to guarantee the production and distribution of the food on the one hand, and perhaps as a consequence of the availability of tradable goods on the other. In Mexico, there was a large shallow lake with several basins, collectively representing the swampy conjoined floodplain systems of several rivers that flowed vigorously for a few months, flooding the land to depths of up to 3 m, but then drying to trickles leaving a patchy landscape of ponds, islands and swamps of *Scirpus* and

**Fig. 10.1** The Kuahuqiao archaeological site in southern China. Zong et al. (2007) have shown how rice cultivation began here on floodplain soils that were later flooded by the sea.

*Typha.* For some centuries, as the Aztec culture began to develop from about 1500 BC onwards, its edges had been reclaimed by local groups of people for agriculture in the winter dry season. But as the Aztec cities grew in the region, their demands for food increased greatly and they were forced to annex supplies from more and more distant land. The Xochimilco and Chalco regions of the Lake of Mexico were seen as potential sources and the local people were suppressed by military force during the 14th century AD during the rise of imperial rule in the Aztec culture. The local system of creating chinampas was expanded into a vast agricultural system for maize and vegetable growing.

Chinampas are small fields, about 6–9 m by 3 m, raised above the swamp by digging channels around the field, and building up the soil level with the mud from the channels to a metre of so above the flood water level. Similar systems have been described in many countries. The work in Mexico could be accomplished for only about two months of the year, in the dry season, but the fields remained accessible by boat even during the flood. They are stabilized by trees, planted at the edges, and annually renewed by heaving sediment and water plants (tule (*Scirpus lacustris*), water hyacinth (*Eichhornia crassipes*), and tepalacate (*Hydrocotyle ranunculoides*)) onto them, giving a damp, naturally fertile soil that does not require artificial fertilization. Leguminous plants were interspersed with the maize with the benefit of their nitrogen fixing nodules and the tree shelter created a microclimate that could be several degrees warmer in winter than exposed land elsewhere. At over 2000 m above sea level, frosts are common. Under the Aztec emperor Itzcoatl (AD 1426–1440) and his successor, Motechuzoma Ilhjicamina (AD 1440–1467), the local population, required also to pay taxes and tribute in the form of woven cloth, was forced over about 20 years to reclaim about 120 km² of floodplain swamp, with about 65 km² of chinampas, numbering about 2.5 million fields. It took about 25 million person-days of labour, just for the construction. The Aztecs eventually declined under the pressures of Spanish colonization, but some of the chinampas remain, now used for flower farming (Fig. 10.2).

Both of these approaches to floodplain management, if not to social desirability in the latter case, are small-scale or sensitive to maintenance of the natural flood

**Fig. 10.2** Chinampas were raised beds dug in swamps for food growing in Mexico. A few still remain at Xochimilco, though now used for flower growing. Trees were used to stabilize the edges of the beds.

pulse. They were the forerunners, however, of a much more brutal approach. Perhaps it was convenient, because floodplain soils are very fertile, but the peculiar idea was embraced that the floodplain was dry land that was unfortunately sometimes flooded, rather than that it was part of the river bed that was covered with water for only part of the year, and with its outer reaches sometimes dry for several years. We talk of the 10-year flood or the 100-year flood as those which occupy the outer reaches only once in ten or a hundred years. The consequence of regarding the floodplain as dry land is that it then seemed logical to protect it from flooding at all. This was done by enclosing the main channel with embankments and deepening and straightening the river so as to allow the previously meandering shallow channel to cope with all the water and allow it to move rapidly to the sea.

Agricultural and even building land was gained and sometimes some protection from diseases born by floodplain insect vectors, but on balance and in the long term more may have been lost than gained. It is expensive to install and maintain flood control works and usually they are designed to cope with a 10- or 20-, sometimes 50-year flood. Floods of lesser frequency but greater magnitude will then overtop the defences and cause much damage to property. Hurricane Katrina that rained enormous amounts of water on the southern USA in 2005 and breached flood barriers in New Orleans is a case in point, but every year, some-where, there are serious floods of drained floodplains. The reaction is to put in bigger defences, particularly in cities. But as defences are raised upstream, the risks become greater downstream. One service provided by intact floodplains is to accommodate large amounts of

**Fig. 10.3** Former floodplains (2000 years ago) in England and Wales. A very large area was occupied, but now very little of it remains undrained. (From Newbould 1998.)

water which can then ebb away slowly to the sea. But once flood control has begun it becomes intensified and ultimately irreversible to any significant extent. In Chapter 8, the concept of ecosystem services was introduced. Floodplains provide a greater value of services than any other habitat, but this realization has come too late to save most of them in the developed world and those of the developing world are increasingly threatened. Figure 10.3 shows the former extent

of natural floodplains in England and Wales. There were once over 20,000 km². Table 10.1 shows how little is now left.

## 10.2 FLOODPLAIN SERVICES

There is increasing interest in economic valuation of ecosystem services so that they can be entered into conventional economic assessments such as the balance of costs and benefits of major projects, like dam building or conversion of land to agriculture or housing. Floodplains provide many very valuable services (Table 10.2) though they are not often widely appreciated. In general floodplains are regarded as undesirable habitats, best drained. The UK Government has excluded them as aquatic habitats in its planning for the implementation of the Water Framework Directive, preferring to regard them as dry land. This was clearly a political, face-saving rather than an informed decision. Since most UK floodplains have been drained, it would be impossible otherwise not to regard almost every lowland river in the UK as of bad quality, the lowest possible category.

Floodplain swamps are large sponges, with often-great surface area. A small increase in water level results in the temporary storage of water, which would otherwise rush downstream after a heavy storm to damage human settlements. The effect is to spread out the flood peak over time, reduce its height, and minimize erosion of the downstream banks. It is estimated that for the Charles River catchment in Massachusetts, the loss of the 2000 ha of wetland (a small proportion of the total catchment) would result in average annual flood damage downstream of $17M (1985 value). In the spreading out of the water, some is also lost by

**Table 10.1** Floodplain habitat in England and Wales. Values in parentheses are percentages of the original area. (Based on Newbould 1998.)

| Historic extent (ha) | Currently supporting breeding wading birds (ha) | Protected by legislation as Sites of Special Scientific Interest (ha) |
|---|---|---|
| 2,000,000 (100%) | 105,000 (5.3%)<br>Floodplain 69,000 (3.5%)<br>Part drained (grazing marsh and washland) 12,000 (0.6%) | 46,600 (2.3%)<br>Floodplain 16,000 (0.8%)<br>Part drained 30,600 (1.5%) |

**Table 10.2** Ecosystem services provided by four major freshwater systems. Darkest shading indicates major service, lightest relatively small, and intermediate shade an important service. Collectively these services have greater value to society than modification of the system for private short-term gain. Floodplains are particularly important in fish, peat and timber provision, in water regulation and improvement of quality, and in protection from flooding hazards.

| Service | Example | Headwater rivers | Lakes and reservoirs | Floodplain swamps (non-forested) | Floodplain swamps (forested) |
|---|---|---|---|---|---|
| **Provisioning** | | | | | |
| Food | Fish, wild game, fruit, grains | | | | |
| Freshwater | Water storage for drinking and irrigation | | | | |
| Fibre and fuel | Timber, fuelwood, peat, fodder, gravel | | | | |
| Biochemical and industrial products | Specific substances as medicines, industrial raw materials | | | | |
| Genetic materials | Genes for breeding of domestic crops and stock, ornamental species for gardens | | | | |
| **Regulating** | | | | | |
| Climate | Atmospheric gas composition, local weather | | | | |
| Hydrology | Groundwater recharge and discharge. Storage of water | | | | |
| Pollution | Removal of pollutants, sediment and nutrients | | | | |
| Erosion | Protection from bank erosion | | | | |
| Natural hazards | Mitigation of floods, storm protection | | | | |
| **Cultural** | | | | | |
| Spiritual and inspirational | Personal feelings, well-being. Religious significance. | | | | |
| Recreation | Boating, swimming, tourism, sports | | | | |
| Aesthetic | Appreciation of natural features. Contribution to mental health | | | | |
| Education | Formal and informal learning and training | | | | |

evapotranspiration, and this may also help alleviate downstream damage, though it also means a loss of water that might have been used for irrigation or domestic or industrial water.

There is some controversy over the amounts lost. Evapotranspiration from the swamp vegetation may actually be less per unit area than from an open-water surface by as much as 40%. The vegetation reduces its own loss by the closing of stomata in hot, windy conditions, whilst also shading and cooling the water surface. A wetland may thus save water. However, it will only save it if it would otherwise be spread out in a sheet as a lake behind a dam, for example. More water will be lost in total if the water spreads out in a swamp than if the water was allowed to move downstream in a direct channel.

Sediments and nutrients are retained in swamps, the former by the effects of reduced current, the latter if the swamp is laying down peat, which inevitably retains some mineral nutrients. Nitrogen will also be removed from the water by denitrification. These properties may improve the quality of the downstream water. Sediment might otherwise block irrigation channels or the main channel if used for navigation, or might need to be expensively filtered out if the water is used for industry or domestic supply. Excessive nitrogen and phosphorus can cause problems for lakes (Chapters 4 and 14) and increasing nitrate concentrations perhaps for human health, though the evidence is equivocal.

Civil engineers have seen mineral retention in swamps as a treatment for domestic and industrial effluents that is much cheaper than building and operating works for chemical treatment. Small 'artificial' wetlands of reed, *Phragmites*, are being established at many sewage treatment works and for farms and tourist attractions where there are large numbers of captive animals. Large natural swamps are also being viewed as potential treatment works. What are the limitations of such treatment?

The capacity of a swamp to cope with sediment and chemicals is not infinite; only for denitrification does adding a substance not cause changes in the swamp because the ultimate destination of the nitrogen is the atmosphere and not the swamp itself. Adding sediment to a natural wetland will cause successional changes. The swamp surface will rise relative to that of the water until a drier system is produced which floods for only part of the year and eventually not at all. Such successional changes, which eventually would preclude the use of the ecosystem as a nutrient retainer, may be slow, however, and retention in the short term may be very successful. In a natural floodplain, new areas of swamp would be established or the sediment eventually eroded and washed downstream.

Harvesting the vegetation and thus removing some of the accumulated nutrients might prevent succession in artificial wetlands. There is a fallacy, however, in this. Cutting of the above-ground plants at the height of their growth, when they contain most nutrients, will eventually kill them, whilst removal when they are senescing will result in little harvest of nutrients, which will, by then, have been translocated to the rhizome. In any case the major sink for the nutrients (other than the atmosphere for nitrogen) is the sediment. The plants create the optimal environment for sedimentation but

do not, when the vegetation is fully established, have any net uptake from year to year.

Swamp soils will retain metals, including toxic ones from industrial processes, and burial in the sediments may seem attractive. However, plant roots may absorb such elements and mobilize them into food webs, or the build up of such substances may ultimately kill the swamp plants or interfere with important bacteria in the sediments. Experiments with such disposal should be encouraged, but only with specially established artificial wetlands, not with natural ones where the properties of flood control, denitrification and natural sediment retention are too valuable to be jeopardized.

Recent surveys of such constructed wetland systems have tempered earlier enthusiasms and increased our understanding of how they might best be used. Many systems use common reed (*Phragmites australis*) but sometimes other species (*Typha, Phalaris*), and most effectively remove sediment and biological oxygen demand (a measure of the labile organic content of the water) and a varying proportion of the dissolved nitrogen compounds. They are much less reliable at removing phosphorus, and may become sources to the outflow water after a year or so.

Some reedbeds have been used for the treatment of raw sewage and have functioned poorly; the best results have been obtained where sewage effluent has been run into them for final 'polishing', where areas have been large in relation to the population served, where the growth season of the plants is long, and where a variety of plant types has been used in a mosaic of habitats through which the water flows. Original estimates of a requirement of about 1 $m^2$ of reedbed per person have been found to be too low and 2–5 $m^2$ may be more appropriate. This means that space requirements are high with a town of 100,000 people needing up to 50 ha to produce an effluent that has had most of its added N removed. Constructed reedbeds may be best used for hamlets, small villages or farms to treat the effluent from septic tanks or other pretreatment processes that have already removed much of the organic matter.

Constructed wetlands offer some advantages to wildlife conservation and they use no energy, pumps or mechanical devices (until they need to be dug out and regenerated). There can be no objection to further investigation to improve their performance in aspects for which they are well fitted. Natural floodplain swamplands, however, have aesthetic and wildlife values which are important and much greater than those of any constructed wetland. In the USA, 20% of threatened or endangered plants and animals are associated with wetlands. Floodplains figure prominently in lists of national parks and wildlife reserves. The cheap disposal of domestic or industrial waste cannot be justified at the expense of long-term damage to a habitat that is anyway being increasingly lost through drainage.

### 10.2.1 Floodplain fisheries

For many people inland fisheries are their major source of protein and, among fresh waters, floodplains provide some of the most productive and diverse fisheries, especially in the tropics. Part of the Amazon floodplain is a wonderful example, not only for the diversity of the fishery but the remarkableness of the floodplain swamp forest system. In the Amazon basin the rains are seasonal and water levels change greatly between the wetter season (December to June), when much water comes down river from the Andes, and the drier (July to November). Differences between high and low water may be 16–20 m (see Chapter 9). This means that the forests are flooded, sometimes to the treetops, and the lagoons and lakes alongside the rivers may vary in depth from 16 m to less than 1 m.

The fish fauna is diverse and productive with strong tendencies for the fish to migrate. One of its particular characteristics is dependence on the food supplied by the forests at high water. Among the characins, which, with the catfish, constitute 80% of the list of at least 1 300 species, are many species feeding on seeds, fruits, flowers, insects and monkey dung falling from the forest canopy. Fish returning to the main channels as the water recedes are fat from this source. Fruit and seed eating appears to benefit the trees also, because often only the fleshy fruit is eaten and the seed is not digested but is defaecated to germinate elsewhere.

The epiphytic microorganisms (periphyton) that grow on the trees and on tree debris during the flood, are another important food, especially for some large catfish species. Around Porto Velho, on the Rio Madeira, 87% of the commercial catch comes from nine genera of which a third of the species depend directly on forest seeds, and a quarter on forest detritus and periphyton; the rest are predators on the seed- and detritus-eaters. Reptiles (the black caiman (*Melanosuchus niger*), anaconda (*Eunectes murinus*) and turtles), and mammals (the boto or river dolphin (*Inia*

*geoffrensis*), manatee (*Trichechus inunguis*), capybara (*Hydrochoerus hydrochaeris*) and tapir (*Tapirus terrestris*) are also integral members of the system. Where hunting has reduced the numbers of predators, it has sometimes been noticed that fish production has fallen.

These animals may mobilize nutrients from the sediments and soils to the water when they feed on plants (manatee, capybara, tapir) or on larger fish (dolphins, turtles, caimans, anacondas). They move, at high water, into the swamps or flooded forest, where most of the fish spawn, producing young that require small planktonic organisms as their first food. The pulse of nutrients excreted by the pursuing predators may support planktonic production at the appropriate time. The system is summarized in Fig. 10.4.

A diverse fish fauna leads to a varied fishery and methods vary from the simple and cunning, but dependent on a deep knowledge of the habits of the fish, to the use of modern monofilament gill nets, backed by refrigerator ships. The former support subsistence, the latter commercial fisheries. The methods can be grouped into those exploiting fish in the main channel, the swamps and the flooded forest.

In the main channel, use of the gill nets depends on knowledge of seasonal migrations. Some characin genera, *Brycon* and *Mylossoma*, live in clearwater tributaries during the low-water season, but as the flood rises, move downstream into the more turbid main stem Rio Madeira to exploit the detritus and periphyton on the riparian trees in the main river valley. They move in a 10–14 day period when the water is a few metres below the peak flood. The fishermen watch for dolphin activity, which indicates a characin shoal, in the tributary. They then manoeuvre upstream of the shoal and place the 100–200 m gill net in a horseshoe pattern before beating the water with paddles to scare the fish, causing them to reverse direction and move into the net, which is then drawn tight with a rope threaded through the bottom of it. In May to July the same method is used for other species as they return from feeding in the tributary forests to move upstream in the main river.

In the swamps and the flooded forests, the methods depend on individual skills. The swamps harbour cichlid fish that move along the edges of the floating mats of vegetation. At night they can be paralysed with a light and stabbed with a 1.5-m, pronged spear. One voracious cichlid predator, *Cichla ocellaris*, is lured by movement through the water of a tassel of strips of red cloth or birds' feathers in which are embedded

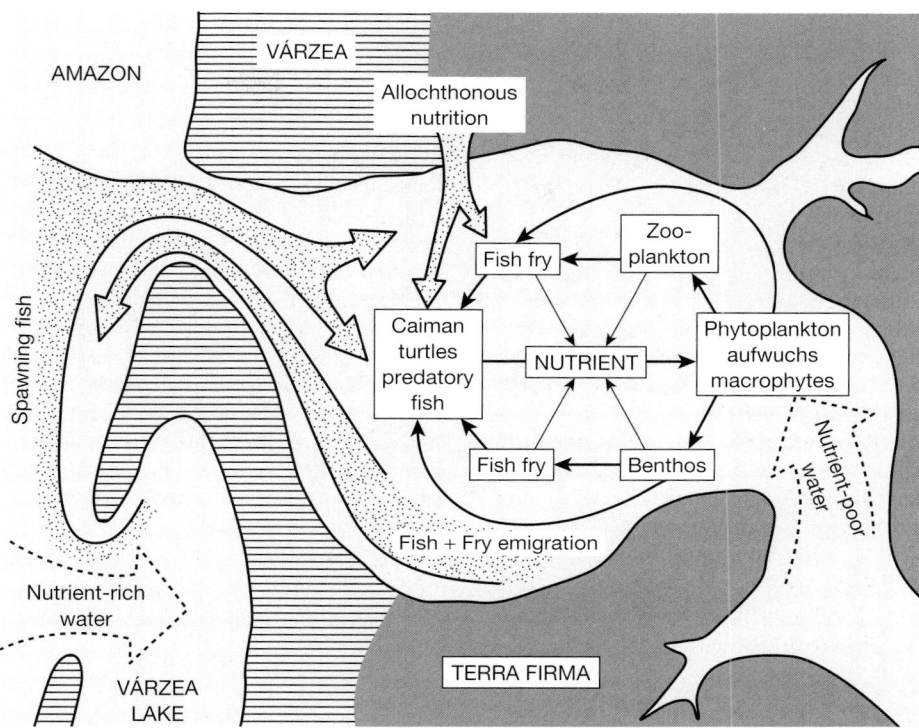

**Fig. 10.4** In the Amazon floodplains, the movement of animals into the floodplain at high water, and the excretion of large fish and predators, support a system for production of food for young fish. Adult fish feed largely on seeds, fruits, insects and mammal faeces falling in from the forested canopy. *Varzea* is floating grass-dominated swamp. *Terra firma* is forest naturally dry in the dry season and unflooded in the wet. (Based on Fitkau 1970.)

hooks. It mistakes the lure for its prey. The huge picarucu (*Arapaima*), which must return to the surface to breathe every few minutes, is harpooned when it does so.

In the flooded forest (a refuge against large-scale fisheries where nets would be tangled) individuals can be caught from knowledge of their diet. Seeds and fruit are released from the trees sporadically and are scarce. They represent large but infrequent meals and are usually snapped up as they fall (their characteristic shapes and sizes making specific 'plops' thought to be recognized by the fish). These noises, particularly those of the jauri, a palm tree (*Astrocaryum jauri*), can be simulated with metal ball bearings or nuts cast on lines. The fish are harpooned as they dart in to feed. Seeds can be used as bait also in simple rod and line fishing, with palm fruits or those of rubber trees (*Hevea*) or a cucurbit (*Cuffa*) the most successful baits.

## 10.3 FLOODPLAIN SWAMPS AND HUMAN DISEASES

There is a downside to floodplains too. To many people they may represent a threat: from disease, or the fear of being drowned in the flood. Such fears are reflected in the association of swamps with malevolent trolls, water witches and the like in traditional children's literature. Swamps have acquired a poor image, and nations have encouraged the drainage of them with alacrity, for some of the most devastating human disease organisms have also fitted their life histories to these productive systems. Hundreds of millions of people are exposed to malaria, schistosomiasis and filariasis, tens of millions to yellow fever, encephalitis, trypanosomiasis and lung and liver flukes. The vectors of dispersal are often wetland animals. Such vectors occur elsewhere, at lake margins and in irrigation ditches for example, but the

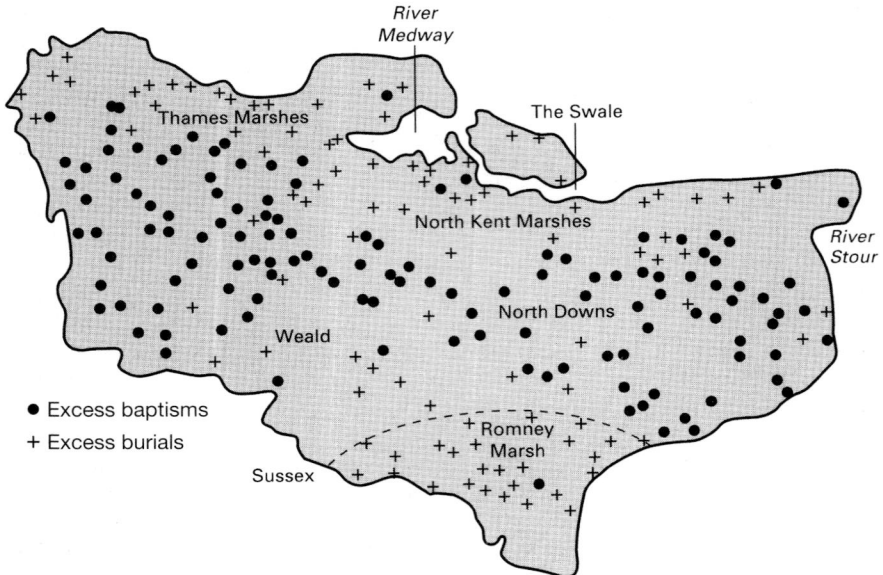

**Fig. 10.5** Excesses of baptisms (●) or burials (+) in Kent 1661–1681. Malaria (ague) resulted in an excess of deaths in the floodplain areas of the North Kent and Romney Marshes. (Based on Dobson 1980.)

extensiveness of floodplain swamps and the large associated human populations make such areas particular foci. Destruction of these areas is thus often advocated on health grounds.

Malaria is perhaps the most familiar. It was not confined to the tropics until relatively recently, for 'paludism' or 'marsh miasma' was a risk of the European fenlands until the 19th century. As late as 1827 people were fearful to enter the fens around The Wash in England because of the disease. In the 18th century, parishes in Kent associated with marshlands such as the Romney Marsh had much higher infant mortality than those of the uplands (Fig. 10.5) and clerics deigned to occupy these Parishes for fear of their health. Similar incidences of the disease occurred in the coastal marshes around the Thames and the Essex coast.

Malaria is a protozoan parasite of red blood cells, and is carried by about 60 of the 400 or so species of the mosquito genus *Anopheles*. The female needs several blood meals to complete development of her eggs and in feeding she may transfer cells of the malaria parasite *Plasmodium* between human hosts. There are at least four important *Plasmodium* species; some (*P. falciparum*) are more dangerous than others (*P. vivax*), but all are

fatal if not treated. *Anopheles* lay their eggs as floating rafts on almost any still water surface. Water among aquatic plants is ideal, as long as it is not completely deoxygenated, for there may be some cover from egg predators.

Control of malaria has long been sought because over 2 billion people are exposed to the disease; about 250 million suffer from it at any one time, with 1.3 million deaths each year. In 1956 the World Health Organization began a major campaign of spraying settlements with the inexpensive insecticide DDT (Chapter 8) to kill adult mosquitoes. This was very successful, but plans for spraying have often fallen into disarray for social or financial reasons or because war has intervened. Resistance to DDT has developed in some *Anopheles* species. Drugs are available, but resistance of the parasite to many of these has developed and costs often preclude their widespread use. A third line of control might be immunization against the parasite or genetic engineering of the host or parasite so as to decrease its transfer or virulence. Much research now concentrates on this.

If successful, the fourth-line destruction of the swampland habitat by drainage, a method used in the 19th century in Europe, might be avoided. Indeed drainage and replacement of the swamp with irrigated agriculture and a plethora of canals may sometimes provide better breeding habitat for the mosquitoes than the original wetland. In the UK, the marsh fever was probably *Plasmodium vivax*, carried by *Anopheles atroparvus*, which breeds in slightly saline water. From before the 16th until the early 20th centuries it was a debilitating disease of the poor who tended cattle on the rich marshland pastures.

The mosquito overwinters in dark, warm places such as those provided in the hovels of the marshmen, who developed resistance to the disease, helped by opium, alcohol, and more effectively, quinine from the Peruvian cinchona bark which they bought from the local apothecaries. Incidence of the disease declined from the 17th century onwards and this has been attributed to drainage. However, the mosquito breeds in small stagnant pools, and prevalence of the disease was greater in warm, dry years when such pools were not readily flushed out. The mosquito is still common and supported an outbreak of malaria in North Kent during the 1914–1918 War, based on reintroduction of the parasite by troops returning from Greece and India. It is more likely that decline of indigenous malaria was due to generally improving health and housing conditions and increased herds of farm stock which form alternative blood sources for the mosquitoes. Climate change may bring new threats as the mosquitoes of warmer countries become able to breed in the cold-temperate zones and if the current intensity of travel for holidays in the tropics continues to bring in infected human carriers of the disease.

Mosquitoes carry other diseases. *Aedes* and *Culex* transfer arbor, and other viruses, amongst which yellow fever and Japanese B encephalitis are well known and the former preventable by immunization. Others, such as Marburg virus, are presently incurable, though fortunately rare. More widespread (about 300 million current cases) is filariasis, often called elephantiasis after a characteristic symptom of swollen limbs. Several mosquito genera (*Mansonia*, *Culex* and *Aedes*) carry the microfilariae, the larval dispersal stages, of the nematode worms *Wuchereria bancrofti* and *Brugia malayi*. The microfilariae are released into the human bloodstream from large (often several cm) adult worms that grow in the lymph tracts, causing blockage and swelling of the tissues, and eventually death. The microfilariae are produced rhythmically in large numbers each day and are present in the bloodstream at the time when the local mosquitoes are most active.

*Mansonia*, an important vector of *Brugia*, has larvae, which, like those of other mosquitoes, breathe air, but not by spiracles held in the surface tension film at the water surface. *Mansonia* larvae have a saw-edged siphon bearing a spiracle and cut their way into the roots of floating aquatic plants, such as the water cabbage, *Pistia stratiotes*. They use the air supply contained in the lacunae of the plant. In this way they may be less exposed to predation than they would be at the water surface.

No less important as disease vectors in floodplains, are snails. Many carry stages of flatworms (flukes, Trematoda), which cause debilitating and often fatal disease. Most widespread are *Schistosoma* species, which cause bilharzia or schistosomiasis. The adult flukes occur in male–female pairs in the veins around the intestine or bladder of the human host. An individual may carry only a few pairs or very many, each producing up to several hundred eggs per day. The eggs have spines, the position and number varying with species, and pierce through the gut or bladder wall eventually to be voided with the faeces or urine. If, as often, this is in freshwater, the eggs will hatch to miracidia, which infect snails of particular genera. Later cercariae are released from the snails to reinfect humans when bathing or wading. Schistosomiasis can be controlled by provision of organized sanitation, though finance and custom may prevent this. As with many European public lavatories, the great outdoors may personally be far preferable to an overused pit. Also, the main source of schistosome eggs, the 10–24 year age-group and more particularly the 10–14 year olds, is the one most likely to make free in the open air.

Schistosomiasis is a debilitating disease, affecting whole villages and undermining much will for an active life. It can be treated with drugs, metrifonate, oxamniquine and proziquantel being safe, effective but relatively expensive. Control of the disease in the past has concentrated on killing the snails using copper compounds, which proved relatively ineffective, or the synthetic Bayluscide.

Such approaches do not work well on large swamps, though they are locally effective, for example in village ponds. Draining or filling-in of swamps has been recommended to remove the snails' habitat but this may ultimately increase the incidence of the disease. The irrigation schemes established in the Nile valley at Gezira following the damming of the floodplain by the Sennar Dam in 1924 led to an increase from 1% and 5% to 21% and 80% in the incidence of *Schistosoma* haematobium and *S. mansoni*, respectively in the local populations. Most of the 74 countries and 600 million people exposed to the disease will receive only local relief in the foreseeable future.

Schistosomiasis is only one, though the most widespread, of floodplain fluke diseases. Others include Busk's fluke (*Fasciolopsis buski*), affecting 15 million people, lung flukes (*Paragonimus*) and liver flukes affecting 5 and 30 million people respectively. All have snail vectors and also a second swampland host. For example, Busk's fluke, a large animal, 7–8 cm long, present as adults in human blood vessels, is carried in China and Thailand by the snail genera *Segmentina* and *Hippeutis*. The snails release not cercariae, but metacercariae, which attach to water chestnut plants where they change to cercariae. Water chestnuts (*Trapa natans*) are floating rosette-plants with a flower which, although initially above water, droops as the fruit forms and dips underwater. The metacercariae attach to the fruits, which are often collected and eaten uncooked by children, who become infected. Reservoirs of infection in the Far East are domestic pigs in which the adult flukes also live. The pigs may be penned over ditches so that their excreta fertilize the water, in which fish are cultured for food. The fluke eggs passing in the faeces then have a very good chance of reaching the snail host.

Liver flukes include *Clonorchis sinensis*, the Chinese liver fluke whose vectors are snails of the genus *Bithynia* and a fish, the Chinese grass carp (*Ctenopharyngodon idella*) under whose scales the cercariae develop. In Taiwan, *Opisthorchis felinus* similarly uses the common carp, *Cyprinus carpio*. In the Far East, fish is frequently eaten raw and the parasite is transferred. In Europe the sheep liver fluke, *Fasciola hepatica* may also infect humans, though not seriously, through their eating raw watercress, its intermediary host between snail and mammal. Finally, in West Africa and Asia, the usually fatal lung flukes are transferred to humans by the eating of raw freshwater crabs, on whose gills the metacercariae encyst.

## 10.4  CASE STUDIES

Scientists like to find general principles that can be applied everywhere and that is always very useful. But the richness of the environmental sciences comes from the details of locations and such details often illuminate some of the generalities but confound others. For me the excitement of ecology has always rested in the differences among places as much as the common features. Some case studies thus add flesh to the bones of generality about the use of and damage to floodplains.

### 10.4.1  The Florida Everglades

The Everglades (Fig. 10.6) is a complex of tree and sedge swamps based on a shallow river almost as wide, up to 100 km, as its 180-km length. It flows slowly from the lowlands around Lake Okeechobee to the sea at the south-western tip of Florida, USA The flow is only a few hundred metres per day and the river is at most 30 cm deep over much of the area. The main freshwater community is of emergent aquatic plants, dominated by the sawgrass, *Cladium jamaicense*, which grows several metres tall, so that the description 'River of Grass' (though in fact it is a sedge) is embodied in the title of a well-known book on the area by Marjorie Stoneman Douglas. Sawgrass is well named. It has silica reinforced teeth on the leaf edge that can cut through bread, especially the usually rather spongy American version.

Southern Florida is floored by a porous limestone (Miami oolite) and is very flat. Running along the east coast is a ridge of rock some 6 m above mean sea level, and the west coast also bears a slightly wider but still narrow and subdued 'upland'. In the basin between the two lie the Everglades, with the land dipping only 7 m from near Lake Okeechobee to the sea. Most of the 200 cm or so of rain falls in June and July, sometimes associated with hurricanes, which also occur in September. The winter is dry and the natural water supply to the Everglades is then at its least.

South of Lake Okeechobee was an area of several thousand hectares of peat, up to 4 m deep, laid down over several thousand years in swamps associated with the lake. This acted as a sponge, taking up water in wet periods and releasing it steadily all the year round. The flow penetrated the Everglades along three main water courses or sloughs, running south or south-westwards. When the water reached the sea, the sawgrass community was replaced by a tangled intertidal mangrove forest up to 30 m high (Fig. 10.7). The steady flow of fresh water confined the mangrove to the coast by stopping inland penetration of salt water.

Dotted among the sawgrass on islands of oolite standing a few centimetres above the general basin level are woods of slash pine (*Pinus caribaea*) and palmetto

**Fig. 10.6** The Florida Everglades is a large floodplain area with many different types of habitat reflecting local conditions, including sawgrass marsh (top left) and pine palmetto forest (top right), with a rich fauna appropriate to each, including the piscivorous anhingha (bottom left) and a subspecies of puma (bottom right), respectively. (Photographs by R. Hays Cummins and Greater Miami Convention and Visitor Bureau.)

(*Serenoa serrulata*) (Fig. 10.7) and sometimes clumps of hardwood trees. Small groves of other trees, swamp and pond cypresses (*Taxodium* spp), occupy depressions in the oolite where peat has accumulated. The sawgrass does not succeed to drier forest because fires, begun by lightning at the start of the rainy season, have occasionally burnt the surface vegetation and litter, though left undamaged the deeper peat and rhizomes of the sawgrass. The pine woodland is also fire-resistant and is replaced by hardwood only after a long period when fires have not intervened.

This complex of plant communities supports a rich fauna, of which the birds, some 250 species of them, are best known, for the area is at the junction of several migration flyways. Ducks, ibis, spoonbills, herons, pelicans, coots, plovers, gulls, terns, storks and cranes are abundant. Other vertebrates are no less exciting. The alligator is most famous, but the American crocodile lives in the mangrove swamps, and snakes and turtles are common. There are 57 species of reptile and 17 of amphibia. Some 25 mammal species – opossums, raccoons, wildcat, otter, white-tailed deer, mountain lion, black bear, and, offshore, the manatee and dolphin – have been recorded, and half of these depend significantly on the freshwater communities. The fish (240 species) and invertebrate faunas are even richer.

Not surprisingly, the first threat, now much reduced, to the Everglades, came from poaching of the rich fauna. In the 1890s, millions of feathers of egrets and

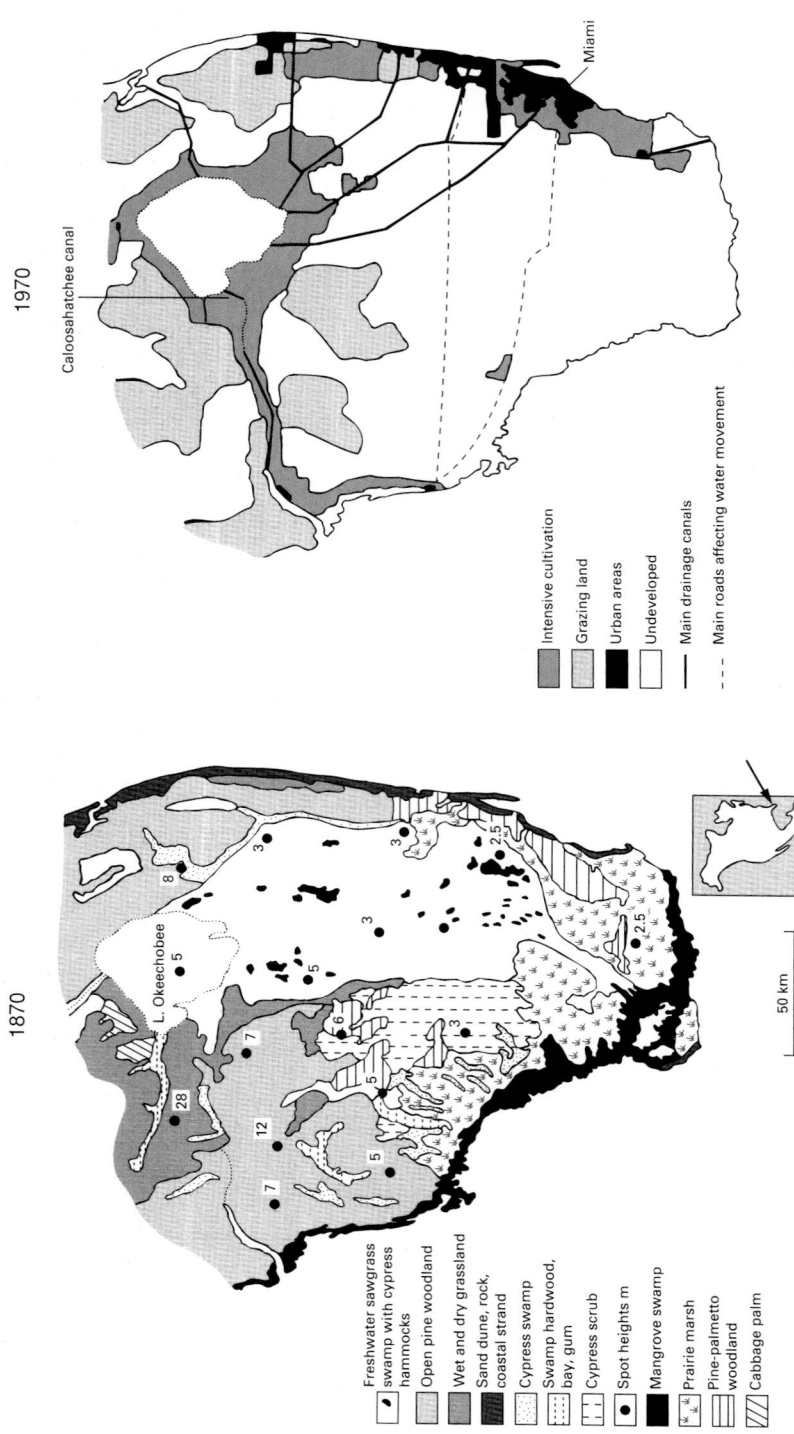

**Fig. 10.7**  Drainage of the Everglades has markedly altered the extent and pattern of the natural vegetation. (Based on Caulfield 1971.)

other birds formed the raw materials of a thriving millinery trade, and by 1930, 100,000 alligator hides were being processed into leather each year in Florida tanneries. The alligator population was reduced to only 1% of its original level by the 1960s, but it has now recovered owing to stringent protection and adds extra zest to golfing on courses in the southern USA where ponds are provided as hazards. The real danger for the Everglades' ecosystem, and also for the whole of southern Florida, now comes from interference with the natural drainage patterns.

Around 1882, it was realized that the peatlands around Lake Okeechobee would be extremely fertile, if they could be drained of the standing water that covered them for eight months of the year. A canal was dredged between the Caloosahatchee River and Lake Okeechobee (Fig. 10.7). Sugar cane and winter vegetables thrived on the drained areas. In 1925 and 1928, hurricanes were severe enough to cause flooding of water from Lake Okeechobee into adjacent drained areas, which had, by then, been settled. These areas had naturally accommodated floods but in 1928 between 1500 and 2500 settlers were drowned. Embankments were made around the lake and more drainage canals were dug so that future flood water could be drained rapidly to the sea. The canals (Fig. 10.7) emerge at the coast among the built-up areas of the eastern oolite ridge and divert the flow from its former southward progress through the Everglades. There are now some 2400 km of canals and 250 powerful pumps. Half the former freshwater area has been lost and remaining flows are only a tenth of their natural volume. Pressure for drainage has been stimulated not only by farming interests but also by the warm Florida climate. For decades the area has been promoted as a retirement and holiday haven and the demand for building land, otherwise confined to the coastal ridges, has been aggressive. The resident population of South Florida has increased from three to eighteen millions in the past 50 years.

The canal system incorporates large, shallow reservoirs called water conservation areas. These can be used for temporary storage of water released from Lake Okeechobee and are needed to delay the flow to the sea sufficiently for the ground-water aquifer, from which the coastal cities derive their freshwater supply, to be recharged. They had to be built because the natural peat sponge south of Lake Okeechobee, which bore exactly these functions, has been much reduced. Drainage results in rapid oxidation of the peat, which, once 4 m deep, now disappears at the rate of 2 cm per year.

A main road, the Tamiami Trail, skirts the southernmost of the reservoirs, and water may be released through culverts under it to the remaining southern portion of the Everglades. The supply is now insufficient and the natural seasonal rhythm of flow is not always maintained. Water is released to the Everglades largely when it is convenient for the drainage system. Between 1962 and 1965 none was released at all so that in 1968 it was necessary to pass legislation to guarantee at least a minimal supply for the Everglades National Park, a 5000-km$^2$ remnant of the original 10,000 km$^2$. In 1970, plans were blocked just in time to prevent a large part of the adjoining Big Cypress swamp from being developed as an airport.

In the pristine Everglades, animals congregated in the deeper parts of the sloughs in the dry season and breeding cycles were related to this. The concentration of invertebrates at the edge of the receding water provided the wood ibis, a wading bird, with a rich food supply during the fledgling season. Food and fledging are now often out of phase. Nests built on the swamp floor in the dry season may be destroyed by unseasonal inputs of water. The wood stork, which depends on a predictable supply of fish and Crustacea for its fledglings, has been reduced in numbers by 70% since the 1930s.

The overall lack of water is probably most crucial, however. The Everglades have always been subject to surface fires; indeed the diversity of their vegetation depends on fire to prevent succession in the sawgrass swamps. But the extreme drought now caused by diversion of the water supply, particularly in years of low rainfall, has led to especially destructive fires biting deep into the peat. Uncontrollable fires also threaten adjacent urban areas, as well as causing smoke pollution for long periods. In the dry season, fewer pools persist as refuges for fish and reptiles. This has led to heavier than normal predation and mass fish deaths due to deoxygenation.

The lack of water is affecting the cities also. The ground-water aquifer is not being recharged rapidly enough to prevent sea water moving into the oolite and contaminating the drinking water wells. New wells have had to be drilled further inland. A fishery worth 20 million dollars per year for estuarine shrimps, which move into the freshwater Everglades for part of their life history, is at risk.

The estuary of Florida Bay adds a final twist. Enclosed partly by the islands of the Florida Keys, the Bay formerly supported vast meadows of sea grasses, a community of completely submerged angiosperms. To the ocean side of the Keys is North America's only major coral reef. In the late 1980s the sea grasses began to disappear and more than 200,00 ha have now gone. Phytoplankton populations in the water have increased and there is greater turbidity. More recently there has been widespread death of coral species on the reef. The latter may be due to disease, but this is unlikely to be the entire cause. More likely is that declining water quality in the Bay is responsible. The reduced flows from the Everglades have led to increased salinity in the Bay. Increased intensification of agriculture and rapid movement of water through the canals to the sea, along the coast and perhaps into the Bay may also have increased the nutrient load, particularly nitrogen. Silt loads may also have increased through this route and together these factors are almost certainly linked with the changes in the seagrass meadows and coral reef.

Ironically, the problems in the Bay have emphasized the need to increase the flows through the Everglades and in 1996/97, work began on a major project to pump more water southwards through the system. Constructed wetlands will be used in an attempt to limit movements of nutrients from the sugar cane fields south of Lake Okeechobee. Some experts believe that the increased flow will decrease the salinity of the Bay and restore the seagrass meadows; others argue that unless the nutrient and silt contents of this water are also markedly improved, pumping of more low-quality water to the sea will simply worsen the problem. It may be a classic, but not unfamiliar case, of a positive feedback in the creation of problems once the functioning of a natural system is disturbed.

### 10.4.2 The Pongola river

At the end of what at least used to be one of the bumpier roads of South Africa lies Ndumu National Park, a section of unoccupied floodplain of the Pongola, a small river, but one of the best examples of how floodplain rivers can both serve their communities and be severely damaged by outside ambition. The Pongola cuts through a gap in the Lebombo Mountains of Kwazulu Natal then meanders some 70 km across a floodplain set like a green ribbon across the grey-brown dry expanse of the Makhathini Flats, an ancient sand dune system, until it joins the Usuthu River at Ndumu. Ndumu is a land (Fig. 10.8) of small, shallow lakes, or pans, filled at

the flood, bordered by sedges and grasses and drying down in the winter. There are groves of yellow-green barked fever trees (*Acacia xanthoploea*) and grasslands of *Cynodon dactylon*, on which crocodiles bask by day and hippopotami graze at night. Forests of fig trees (*Ficus sycomorus*) grow on the raised levees deposited by the floods. Birds abound, for the area is at the junction of the warm temperate and tropical parts of South Africa and like all transition regions and boundaries has a mixture of representatives from both sides. You can see the African fish eagle, pelicans, storks and flamingo among some 350 others. Herds of antelope, particularly nyala, and the two African species of rhinoceros are present.

But paralleling the road through the valley is a different aspect of the floodplain. It is the home of some 70,000 Tembe-Tonga people, whose traditional way of life depends, yet again, on the predictable rise and fall of the river flood. As the water rises in summer (Fig. 10.9), it brings in detritus from the catchment and spills over from the main channel to flood the grasslands and the 90 or so pans that flank its passage from Lebombo to Ndumu. With the flow move the fish from the winter channel to feed and spawn in the flooded grasslands and pans. Their gonads have already expanded and ripened in response to the changing day length at the start of summer. The Tembe-Tonga build fences of brushwood and grass across the side channels to trap the fish so that they may be taken out and dried as a future food store. Many fish nonetheless reach the pans and feed on the decaying floodplain grass detritus and invertebrates that benefit from it.

The plain is under water for some time but the Tembe-Tonga villages, like those of the Nuer (Chapter 9) are above the flood level at the edge. Activity expands as the waters recede in autumn. River detritus has settled from the water in the pans and in the clearer water, plants, particularly *Potamogeton crispus* and *Najas pectinata*, start to expand. Lilies, the floating *Trapa natans*, and large beds of reed (*Phragmites australis* and *P. mauritianus*) grow, renewing the food supply for invertebrates and fish, which eventually begin a movement back to the main channel. Many are isolated in the pans, however, and communal fishing using a line of baskets scooped through the water concentrates them for removal. In the emerging damp soils, grass growth produces rich swards and attracts in migratory birds such as the white-faced duck, and the cattle and goat herds of the Tembe-Tonga, who also clear some areas close to the river and grow beans, other vegetables

**Fig. 10.8** The Pongola floodplain in Kwazulu-Natal (upper left, in flood) includes a series of shallow lakes (pans) that support wildlife (upper right) and a community of fishermen–herders and cultivators (bottom left). It has been disrupted by the building of the Pongolapoort Dam, whose reservoir (lower right) is now used to regulate the flow.

and maize in soils that have been fertilized from the river silt.

In many ways the system has parallels with that of the Nuer in the Sudan (Chapter 9), and the comparison extends to threats to the system from river engineering. The waters of the Nile Sudd have long been eyed as a future water source for the northern Sudan and Egypt and there have been many proposals to by-pass the swamps with a 360-km canal, 60 m wide and 6 m deep to minimize losses by evaporation. It would disrupt the lifestyle of the Dinka, Shilluk and Nuer peoples but it was argued that their traditional way of life would be improved by the provision of organized cattle ranches, veterinary services, irrigated agriculture and generally improved social services that the wealth to be provided by the canal would provide. There was considerable concern in the southern Sudan, whose local authorities were not included in the planning consortia behind the project.

Excavation began in 1978 with the world's largest mechanical excavator (Fig. 10.10) and had covered 267 km by November 1983, when work was suspended by civil war in the Sudan. Planned crossing points for the canal have not been built and the structure now forms a barrier to the movements of cattle and wildlife. There has been little sign of provision of alternative social organization for the Nilotic peoples. If and when the canal is completed, it seems, from independent studies, that the proposed replacement lifestyle, even if provided to the extent promised, will be an inappropriate alternative for the conditions and that the Nilotic peoples will be disadvantaged to a large extent. The work has not been resumed and the dredger lies rusting and irreparable. The chances are, however, that the project will be renewed in the future with a new machine though changing climate and other circumstances may get in the way. The Pongola, however, did and still does face an uncertain future.

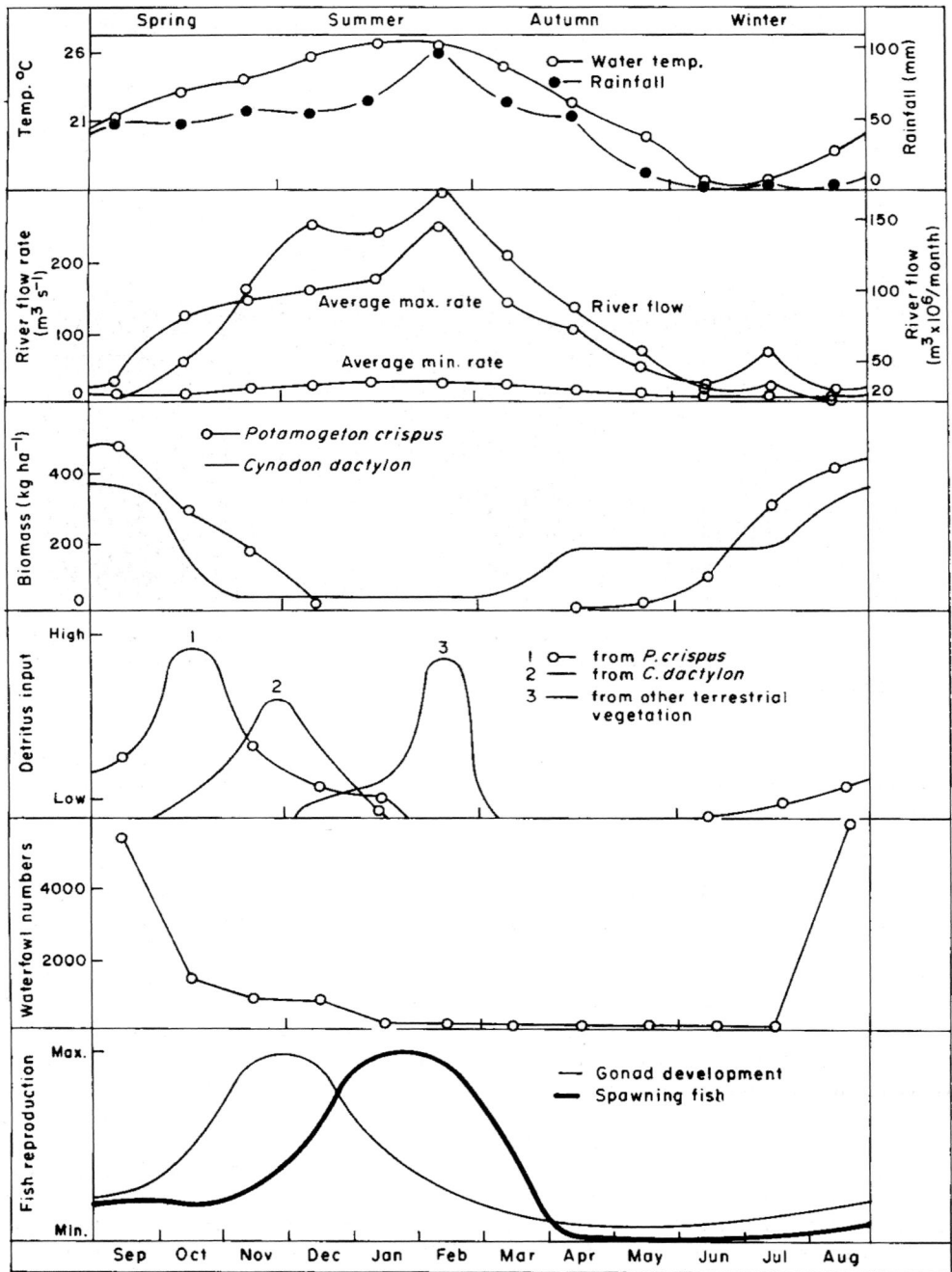

**Fig. 10.9** Seasonal events in the traditionally functioning Pongola floodplain. (Based on Heeg & Breen 1982.)

**Fig. 10.10** A very large dredger was used to excavate the Jonglei canal, which would by-pass the floodplain of the Nile in the Sudd region. The canal has not been completed and the dredger lies corroding. The floodplain system has yet survived. (Photograph by UNESCO.)

If you provide enough water, you can grow commercial crops almost anywhere. In the 1960s, agricultural trials showed that the Makhathini flats, if irrigated, could support a sugar cane industry. The world has a great appetite for sugar but the main aim of the project was to implant a block of white farmers to act as a political buffer close to what was regarded as a sensitive area close to the border with Mozambique. The Pongola was dammed in the gorge through the Lebombo Mountains by the Pongolapoort dam, to store the flood water for year-around irrigation of cane fields, but things did not go to plan. The irrigation scheme was never completed, the proposed 4000 sugar farms did not materialize and the weather was too dry to fill the dam immediately so that the flood pulse was obliterated for several years. There was even a fault in the dam wall that meant the reservoir could never be completely filled. Between 1973 and 1987, the dam was operated with no regard for the needs of the floodplain community. Sometimes the Tembe-Tonga scrabbled even for a little drinking water in holes dug in the river bed. Typhoid outbreaks ensued and there was extreme scarcity of food.

The promised economic benefits of sugar cultivation might have been welcomed by the younger generation, for the floodplain culture could support only a finite population and people were already having to move away to find work, but now there were neither traditional nor new economies. Eventually the dam proved a temporary boon when the waters of what would have been a devastating flood brought by cyclone Demoina in 1984 were absorbed by it, but it is now seen as a symbol of a previous oppressive political regime and 15 local Water Committees of all groups of users were established after 1988 to manage appropriate releases of water to support the traditional floodplain economy. The releases need to be big enough and at the right time for the biological rhythms of the system.

But nothing is stable for long in the present century. Genetically modified Bollgard cotton, the first GM crop to be grown in Africa, was brought in by the Monsanto Chemical Company in 1997 and adopted initially by about 3000 farmers in the valley, though this has now fallen to about 700. It survives well in the relatively harsh climate and has a guaranteed market. It is engineered through the insertion of genes from the bacterium, *Bacillus thuringensis* to be resistant to insect pests and is promoted as requiring less pesticide than normal cotton There are, however, pressures to repay loans for seed and equipment that in turn demand maximizing cotton production and there is evidence that pesticide use is much greater than anticipated, for it is less resistant to new pests such as aphids than to the bollworm against which it was engineered. The cotton farmers, a well-organized group, backed by strong commercial lobbies, want water released much earlier than the traditional floodplain users and have been successful in achieving this; the Water Committees are in disarray and the future is uncertain.

## 10.5  RIVER AND FLOODPLAIN MANAGEMENT AND REHABILITATION

Existing floodplain systems are clearly under considerable threat; many of the former two million square kilometres of them have already been destroyed (more than 95% of the former area in Europe) (Fig. 10.11); of these, most are used for agriculture (though their value for this is only about a tenth of their value as natural systems). Others have been built on; flooding of property, when it nonetheless happens, is so damaging emotionally and financially that it becomes a major political issue (the British Environment Agency spends about half of its one billion pound annual budget on flood defences and their maintenance; insurance companies in the USA pay over a million dollars each week for flood damage). Intact floodplains, left undeveloped, are the best defence against downstream flooding and provide many services, from building products (timber and reed) to grazing and agriculture based on the flood pulse. The Egyptian pharaohs based taxation levels on the height of the Nile flood and currently intact floodplains are valued per hectare more highly than any other habitat. Changing patterns of climate (Chapter 16) will lead to heavier and more concentrated rainfall and greater floods. In Europe, the Water Framework Directive requires that damaged habitats be restored to good ecological quality, though there are loopholes that allow already highly modified habitats to be ignored; wetland legislation in North America is also highly protective. Floodplains are rich in biodiversity and at the heart of many National Parks and major nature reserves.

There is a cornucopia of issues here for which some compromise has to be found. Floodplains should no longer be regarded as dry land that can be developed in any way (though that is often disregarded in the interests of immediate profit by property developers and governments unwilling to restrict private enterprise with socially desirable legislation). Where they have been developed, there is an argument for reinstating them, and this is easiest when they are simply used for agriculture, essentially impossible where they have been built upon significantly. And where possible there is strong justification for reinstatement of some of their features to return some of the services they formerly offered. Overall there is a hierarchy of approach from more sympathetic management to full restoration, spanning mitigation (minimizing damage where engineering of rivers has to occur in the interests of protection of property), enhancement (any improvement of environmental function) and rehabilitation (substantial renovation but falling short of restoring the intact system).

### 10.5.1  Plant bed management in rivers

Extensive plant beds retard the flow and increase the depth of small rivers in spring and summer and this may flood riverside land now used for crops. Summer flooding leads to deoxygenation of soil and deaths of the crop roots. In the past, in Great Britain, such flooding was acceptable and even controlled by systems of channels and sluices. The flooded 'water meadows' were used for grazing of a flood-tolerant native flora, annually fertilized by the river silt. Many of these ancient habitats, very rich in plant species, have now been destroyed by ploughing, following engineering operations to deepen and straighten the river channel. The fields have been seeded with flood-intolerant crop grasses or cereals and flooding is unacceptable to the farmers.

The frequency of summer flooding may have increased because of these changed farming operations. The removal of catchment woodland and drainage of riverside land may have increased the summer flows through reduced water storage and evapotranspiration. Secondly, the increased run-off of agricultural nitrogen to the rivers has increased the growth of a filamentous alga, *Cladophora glomerata* (blanket weed) and other 'weedy' plants. Thirdly, cultivation to the river edge and fears of brushwood falling into the channel and accentuating the flood risk, have meant removal of overhanging trees and bushes. Loss of this

(a)

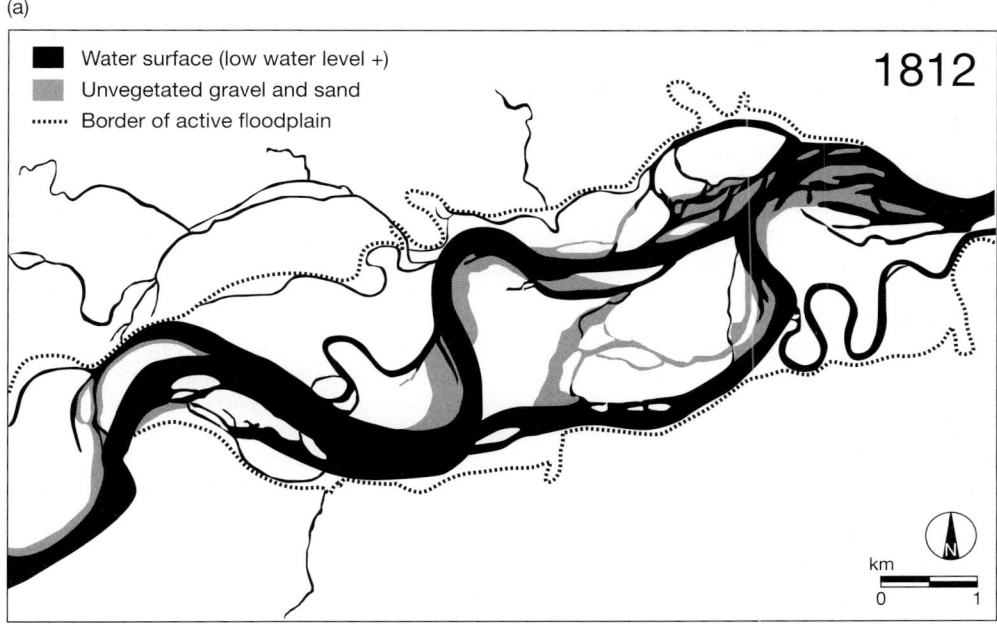

(b)

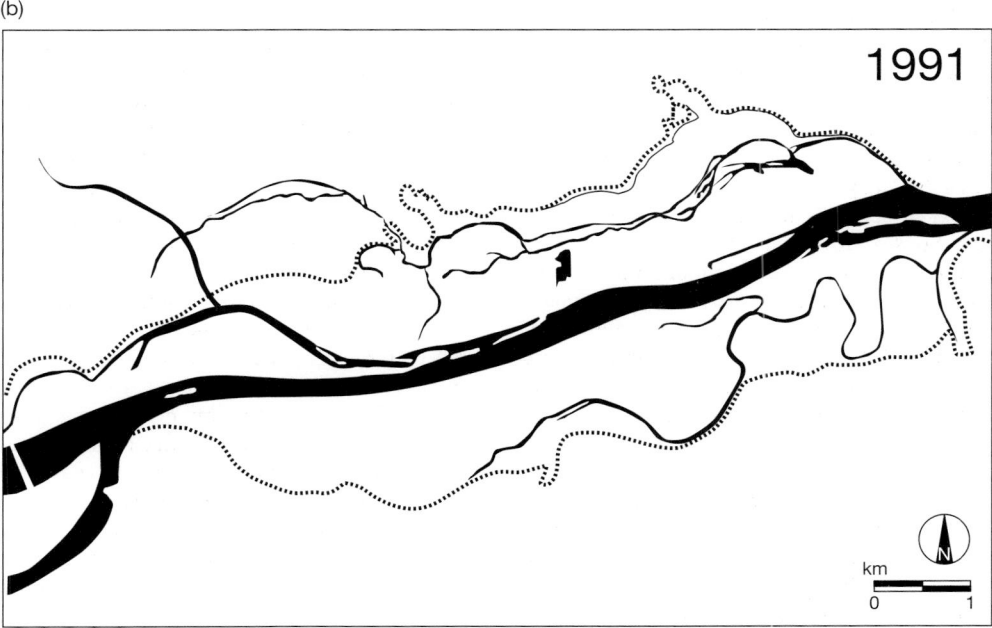

**Fig. 10.11** The Danube is just one of many European rivers whose floodplains have been destroyed in the interests of agriculture and development, with the river channel deepened and straightened. (Based on Hohensinner et al. 2004.)

shade lifts any previous light-limitation on the rooted plants and encourages their greater growth.

The plant beds are consequently cut in about a third of the main rivers, and about 32,300 km of ditches and dykes in Britain, usually by machine. Cutting is done two or three times a year and can be regulated to preserve some of the plants for fisheries and aesthetic purposes. The cut material must be removed to prevent its decomposition in the water, causing deoxygenation. Cutting, however, may increase the growth and biomass of the plants. Many are perennials with a yearly rhythm of growth in spring and early summer, flowering in mid-, and senescence in late-summer. Cutting just before flowering removes the suppressive effect on growth of the flowering hormones and encourages extension of side shoots. It also relieves the plant of the effects of its own self-shading, which also encourages further growth. Beds of *Ranunculus* in Dorset rivers were halved in biomass when cutting ceased. The biomass is closely related to the effectiveness of the beds in causing flooding. In Denmark, hand, rather than machine cutting has allowed much more improvement because some species, such as bur-reed (*Sparganium*) that are bulky and easily block the channel, can be selectively removed, whilst others such as the water crowfoots (*Ranunculus* spp) are left and a much more complex structure maintained for fish and invertebrate habitat.

Cutting is labour-intensive and thus costly. There has consequently been an increase in the use of cheap herbicides in recent years, especially in slower-flowing waters. Five compounds (2,4-D amine, dichlobenil, diquat, glyphosate and maleic hydrazide) are officially cleared for aquatic use in the UK though rather more compounds may actually be used. One in particular, diquat alginate, is favoured for treating submerged vegetation. The safety scheme, in approving a compound, attends largely to the risks to stock and people and has little regard to the ultimate effects on natural communities. Indeed it cannot, because data on such long-term effects are not available. Herbicides, unfortunately, are largely unselective and kill most aquatic plants. In turn this destroys the habitat for invertebrates and may cause deoxygenation as the plants rot. Herbicides may also be directly toxic to some animals. Repeated application can permanently destroy the habitat; recovery, however, is often complete from light applications, and the disturbance caused by the creation of habitat 'space' during the effective period may allow additional species to colonize. Unfortunately

this includes alien species that proliferate and displace the native flora. *Hydrocotyle ranunculoides* (Fig. 10.12), a bulky immigrant from the Americas, is currently spreading through the UK river system.

A wiser approach to plant management in rivers than herbicide use has been proposed by Hugh Dawson and his collaborators, who suggest the replanting of bankside trees to reduce the water plant biomass by shading. Trees on a northerly bank may cut down the incident light by about 20% in southern England and reduce the plant biomass by half. Trees and bushes planted on southerly banks will decrease light and biomass even more but may reduce the organic matter available to the animal community very significantly and this is of concern particularly to anglers, who like unnaturally large populations of large fish to catch. The leaving of gaps in the plantings of say 20 m in 100 m allows some compromise. The replacement of trees has advantages for riverine birds and otters, which make their nests and holts or dens among the roots of large trees, and as an attractive landscape feature. Furthermore, the costs of tree planting per unit length of river are about the same as the costs of a single year's cutting or herbicide treatment and additional maintenance over 10–20 years only doubles the initial cost.

### 10.5.2 Mitigation and enhancement

Most temperate rivers have been greatly altered and are confined in deepened and often embanked channels sometimes perched above the surrounding former floodplain. The surrounding soils, especially if peaty, will have oxidized and shrunk on drainage, sometimes by a metre or two. Even with embankment, there will still be some risk of flooding of the now agricultural or urban land of the plain, so the channel will be managed, though preferably not in the brutal ways of the past.

Previously its capacity to carry water was increased through dredging and deepening; it may have been straightened (canalization) to minimize siltation on bends, and its cross-section, particularly in urban reaches, may have been formed, sometimes with concrete, into a trapezoidal shape, which least impedes flow. Bank vegetation, overhanging trees, debris and aquatic plants were cut because these also impede the flow and increase the risk of flooding. All such measures decrease the variety of habitat for the channel

**Fig. 10.12** *Hydrocotyle ranunculoides*, a plant about 40 cm across is one of the latest introduced species to grow vigorously in European and Australian rivers. In its natural range in parts of North America it is, paradoxically, endangered.

ecosystems whilst the floodplain swamps were reduced to communities capable of growing in the ditches connected with powerful pumps to drain the land. The ideal ditch for a drainage engineer, however, was bone-dry in summer, especially where cereal crops were grown. Drainage was less intense where flood-banks were low and flooding risk higher and ditches in these systems can retain water and a rich flora. However, urban, industrial and agricultural pollution has often reduced water quality even in these so that many, clogged with grass, covered in duckweed and rich in ammonia from cattle wastes, lack much value.

The extent of river alteration is now very extensive. In the USA over 26,500 km of rivers are so managed, whilst in Britain a quarter (8500 km) of all main river lengths in the lowlands has been severely altered (canalized, dredged, piled), and virtually the remainder is managed in a lesser way (removal of aquatic plants, and bankside trees and shrubs). Management is equally extensive in mainland Europe. A canalized river (Fig. 9.2) is not pretty. Recent opinion, alarmed at the consequences of intensive agriculture, has forced more mitigation and some enhancement. The drainage

engineer's ideal of a straight, smooth trapezoidal channel may be softened by the provision of lengths of near-natural channel, by the keeping of bends as relief channels, and by limited planting of trees at the edge of a shallower berm adjacent to the main dredged channel (Fig. 10.13). These changes are welcome but usually only cosmetic. When it becomes necessary to provide submerged lengths of pipe to provide enough shelter for fish, then it seems clear that our approach has been unbalanced.

Other things can be done to mitigate and enhance (the difference between them is simply whether the work is done in anticipation or retrospectively) and those discussed for headwater streams in Chapter 8 apply equally to the middle and lower sections.

More ambitious enhancement is to set the flood-banks farther away from the river channel, when they have to be repaired or rebuilt. This creates a mini-floodplain or washland of greater or lesser value dependent on its width. The Ouse washlands in Cambridgeshire in the UK are an attractive area for water birds and constitute the land between the River Ouse and a straight artificial channel paralleling it, called the

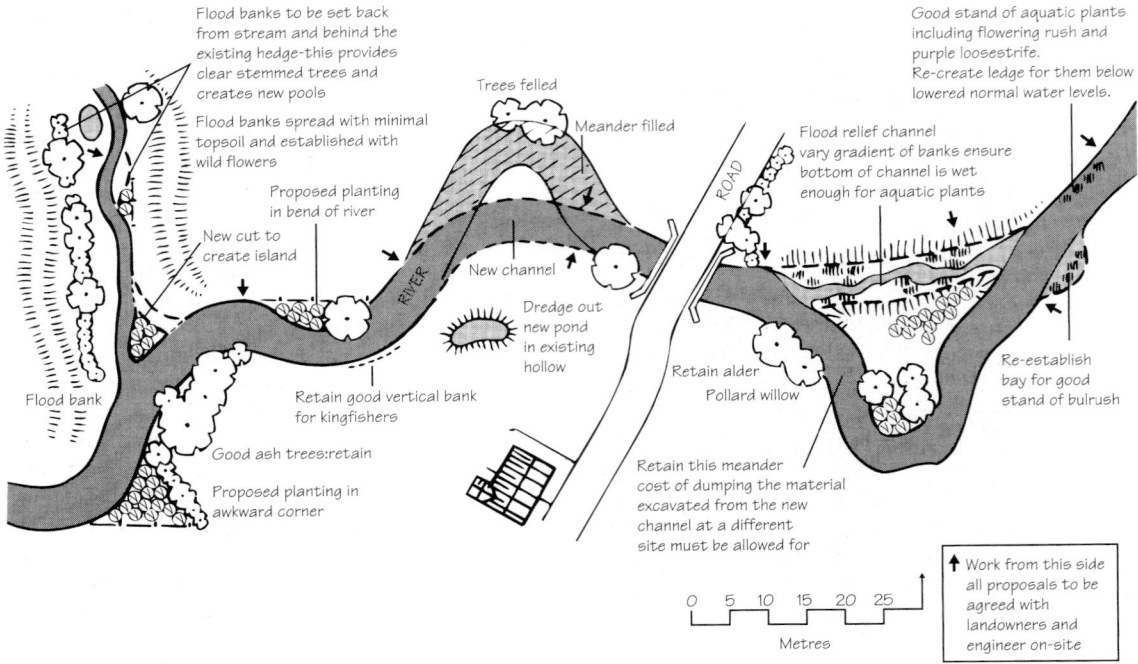

Flood banks to be set back
from stream and behind the
existing hedge-this provides
clear stemmed trees and
creates new pools

Flood banks spread with minimal
topsoil and established with
wild flowers

Proposed planting
in bend of river

New cut to
create island

Flood bank

Retain good vertical bank
for kingfishers

Good ash trees:retain

Proposed planting in
awkward corner

Trees felled

Meander filled

New channel

Dredge out
new pond
in existing
hollow

RIVER

ROAD

Good stand of aquatic plants
including flowering rush and
purple loosestrife.
Re-create ledge for them below
lowered normal water levels.

Flood relief channel
vary gradient of banks ensure
bottom of channel is wet
enough for aquatic plants

Retain alder
Pollard willow

Re-establish
bay for good
stand of bulrush

Retain this meander
cost of dumping the material
excavated from the new
channel at a different
site must be allowed for

0  5  10  15  20  25

Metres

Work from this side
all proposals to be
agreed with
landowners and
engineer on-site

**Fig. 10.13** Proposals for the engineering of drainage schemes have become more sympathetic, though still highly damaging to rivers. In this example of a proposed design, with some enhancement of river function, one meander has been straightened but another kept by provision of a flood relief channel. It represents the designer's ideal. The proposals may not prove acceptable to the landowners and engineer working on the site. (From Newbould et al. 1983.)

flood relief channel. High embankments are set to the outsides of the river and relief channel and floods can wash over the land, several hundred metres wide, between them.

On the former floodplain, enhancement measures have often been taken by conservation organizations to improve habitat for birds and this has been encouraged in Europe by legislation that has led to subsidy schemes to pay farmers to reduce the drainage intensity, raise water levels, reduce stocking densities and put on much less fertilizer. Former floodplains, especially where they have wasted and sunk are often still quite wet and unsuitable for cropping and the high profits of arable agriculture, though the extensive area of wheat, sugar beet and vegetable fields of the deeply drained fens around The Wash in eastern England is an exception that provides high profits but the dreariest landscape in the country.

In already damp former floodplains, the water table can be raised, using sluices in the drainage channel system, to the surface of the land or above in winter to force soil invertebrates to the surface as prey for wading birds. Lower water tables are kept in summer, though sufficient to maintain ponds on the floodplain to encourage ducks and other waterfowl to remain and breed, whilst allowing soil invertebrates to multiply in reasonably aerobic soil conditions. Cattle and sheep grazing (such areas are known as grazing marshes (Fig. 10.14) is allowed at levels that do minimal damage to nests on the ground and encourage a structured tussocky sward in some areas and a closer sward (higher stocking levels) in others, for geese. The names of schemes to promote such activity are ephemeral and change frequently, but the High Level Countryside Stewardship Scheme in the UK is the current title, replacing the former Environmentally Sensitive Areas Schemes that sought to maintain traditional landscapes through subsidy of traditional farming practices. Assessments of the optimal implementation and effects of such schemes are fertile topics for research but alas,

**Fig. 10.14** Where floodplains have not been too deeply drained, grazing marshes provide ditches and wet grasslands that may preserve some of the former biodiversity. It is essential to minimize fertilization of the grass and to maintain the water table close to the surface to keep water in the ditches throughout the summer.

the general conclusions have been that they have maintained the *status quo* and prevented further damage, but not led to any great enhancement except where the land was in the ownership of conservation organizations such as the Royal Society for the Protection of Birds or the National Trust rather than of private farmers and landowners. Farmers generally prefer to farm crops and stock not birds and reeds.

### 10.5.3 Rehabilitation

Enhancement and mitigation are useful, but largely cosmetic, or very small-scale even when they are effective. They can make things look better without giving any major benefit. Limited targets are the products of small minds. Rehabilitation also often falls into the same trap, if the schemes are too small, but can be seen as the first step in restoration. Only the whole

catchment and entire river system can be truly restored and that will never be possible. Human influence is now too extensive. But high degrees of rehabilitation over long stretches may approach restoration and are desirable goals. The key to successful rehabilitation is recognition that a river is not just a series of separate lengths, each of which can be treated alone, but a connected system in which the upstream lengths and the catchment all combine to determine its overall nature. Such a system takes a long time to adjust to changing conditions. Sediment loads and deposition, channel plan-form (meanders and bends), depth and width, riffles and deeper pools and floodplain habitats are not random features but respond to the overall as well as the local conditions. Many rehabilitation attempts have been disappointing for lack of proper geomorphological understanding, for unless all the former conditions of a river length are restored, including appropriate land use, it is rarely possible to reinstate the particular, pre-engineering features. A new design, a compromise that adds function, aesthetics, and diversity, yet reflects the new constraints, is needed for a successful project.

Denmark has taken the lead in ambitious river rehabilitation and there are now many examples (though still covering only a small percentage length of the damaged rivers and floodplains) where straightened channels have been re-meandered and the previously deepened channel bottom raised so that water again spills out after heavy rain onto the floodplain. Such restoration requires that land previously used entirely for agriculture be given back to the river system. Financial compensation is not normally paid for this; the landowner can still farm, but in a different way, gains in having a pleasanter environment, a potential trout fishery and public approbation in a society in which environmental responsibility is valued. In North America there have also been ambitious schemes, such as that to restore the Kissimmee River that flows into Lake Okeechobee and is ultimately part of the Everglades system, but the larger the human population density, the lesser have been the ambitions for river restoration.

River engineering schemes for flood control require continual maintenance, for they confine the power of the water and the water will tend to erode them away in time. An engineered river, given enough time will break back into a natural system that copes with the amount of water by re-establishing a meandering channel and a floodplain. But in doing so it might severely damage property and structures such as railway and road bridges and it might take some decades, even a century or two, to do this. Careful planning is thus needed to create a successful rehabilitation in a much shorter period. Old maps often show the former plan of the river (rivers often were used as historic boundaries between parishes or counties) but that plan depended on the nature of the catchment, the supply of gravels and silts and the run-off, all of which will have changed and will be impossible to change back to their former state.

A new design (Fig. 10.15) has to be created with much prior study by a team that includes hydrologists, geomorphologists, civil engineers and ecologists. In existing schemes often the physical characteristics (meanders, depths, gradient, overspill) intended have been successfully restored but the ecological quality has remained unchanged or low. Partly this might be simply a matter of time for readjustment and recolonization, partly it might be because the quality of the water has not been improved (the catchment remains much as it was) and partly it might be owing to lack of attention to the finer detail of the physical plan. The grain of habitat detail needed is often much finer than that conceived, though this is likely to be the least important of the three reasons. Typical rehabilitation

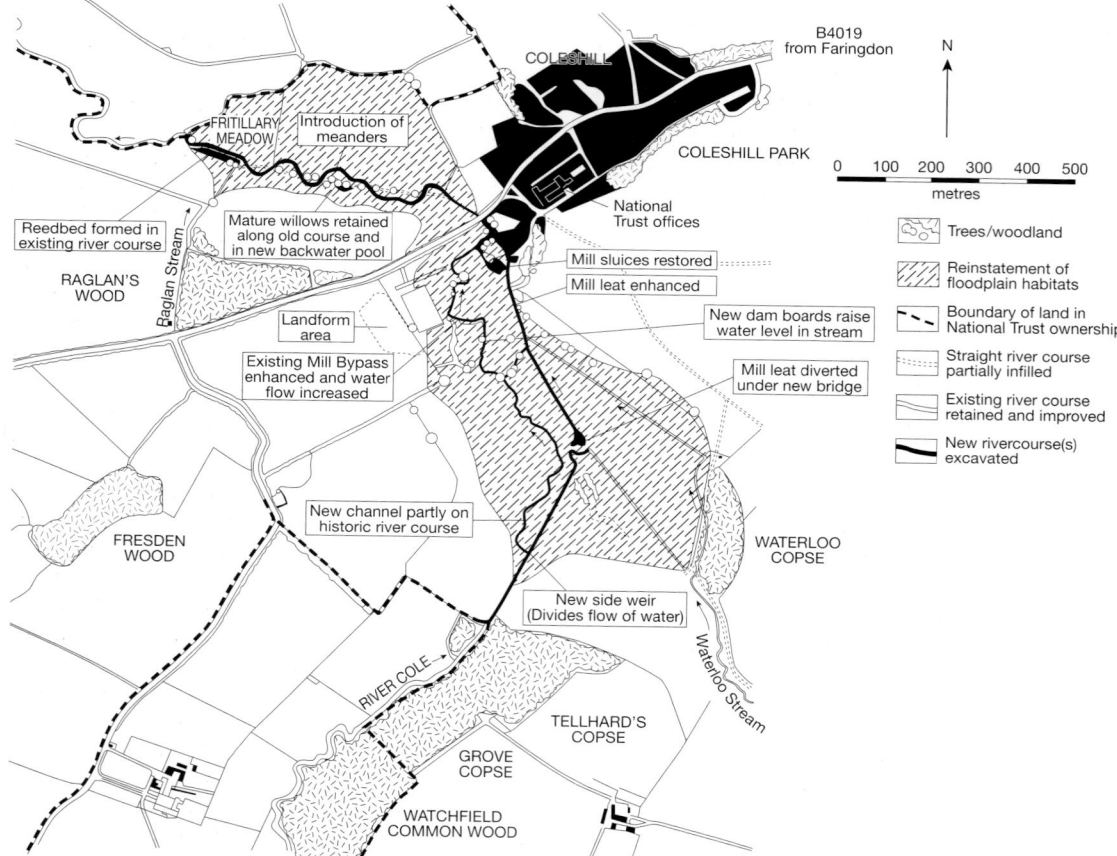

**Fig. 10.15** Design for rehabilitation of part of the engineered River Cole, a tributary of the River Thames in the UK. Covering 2.5 km of river, this has been one of the larger projects in the UK and reflooded part of the floodplain, re-meandered some of the river and reinstated some features of interest. It helped that the main landowner, the National Trust, was highly sympathetic. The project achieved all of its design goals, but increases in biodiversity have so far lagged behind. (Based on Holmes 1998.)

plans will include areas of bare gravel and shingle for the nesting of plovers, sandpipers and oyster catchers, bank cliffs for the nest holes of bees and wasps, kingfishers, swallows and martins, gentle batters (slopes on meander bends) for plants and their associated invertebrates. They will incorporate riffles and pools, edging swamp and flooded grasslands, overhanging trees and exposed roots for otter holts, crayfish holes and pike cover, oxbows and backwaters for fish spawning.

There has been much criticism that rehabilitation schemes have been too small (typically only a few hundred metres or a kilometre or two), too disregarding of the need for the catchment to be rehabilitated also, and underfunded so that there has been little follow-up monitoring to assess their success, or lack of it in improving ecological quality. Many have produced no real ecological benefit at all. That should not mean that no more should be undertaken; it simply means that much more ambition is needed. In the UK, where there have been many trivial river enhancements but few of any size, the remeandering stretch of the River Cole, a tributary of the Thames was rightly regarded as a landmark project (Fig. 10.15). Even a small light is of value in total darkness. But the standard should be set by schemes like that of the River Skerne in Denmark (Fig. 10.16).

## 10.6 INTERBASIN TRANSFERS AND WATER NEEDS

In the warm temperate and tropical zones, the problems for rivers and floodplains are not usually embankment and drainage, but diversion of the water for large-scale crop irrigation. Over two-thirds of the available freshwater in the world is diverted to irrigation. Local supplies are quickly used up and transfer from more distant sources is demanded, putting pressure everywhere on domestic supplies for essential uses and maintenance of a functioning river system, again in the interests of commercial profit.

This is a particular problem of arid areas – Australia, South Africa, central Asia – but is not confined to them. In 1984, the total of such transfers in Canada was 14 km$^3$ per year and there is a proposal to divert 50 to 60 km$^3$ from rivers flowing into the Arctic seas of Russia to the former Russian republics. Such transfers take little account of when and how much water is moved and the seasonal needs of organisms. Exotic fish, plants and invertebrates may incidentally be moved

with the water; reduced flows in the donor river may lead to a reduction in water quality, or the recipient river may be worsened and water-borne diseases may be spread. There will inevitably be pressures to transfer water to a greater extent as world populations expand, particularly in urban areas, but the process needs more care than in the past. In the meantime, there are controversies about how much water can be taken from a local river system for human domestic and commercial use. So much is now taken from some rivers, including major ones such as the Colorado in the USA that they no longer reach the sea and typically, the engineers and users of irrigation schemes allow only a few per cent of the summer flow to remain.

### 10.6.1 Assessment of the water needs

Following a major change in governance in the Republic of South Africa, a new water law was developed in 1998 that epitomizes some of the problems. Formerly the only resource supplied by rivers in the country was seen as the water itself and this water was allocated on a rights-based system that gave rights only to a very few people, largely major landowners for irrigation, and organized water companies for urban supply. The domestic needs for drinking and sanitation of the rural, and many of the poorer urban populations were disregarded.

The new Water Act established a right to adequate domestic supply for all and did it through a concept of maintaining the river system, not just the contained water, as the resource, with a system for allocation on the basis of need rather than preservation of historic rights. It introduced the concept of the 'ecological reserve' which was the amount of water needed to maintain indefinitely the river system with due regard to the variability of rainfall in a dry climate and the need to maintain the mechanisms within the system that allow its survival even in unusually dry years. If the system remained intact, the availability of water for domestic needs would be guaranteed. It was a sophisticated concept that requires a great deal of sympathetic education and negotiation for it to be accepted and not surprisingly it has revealed misconceptions (Table 10.3) that will be familiar worldwide. For the scientific community, it means developing methods to determine exactly what the reserve should be, for only amounts in excess of this reserve can be allocated to uses such as irrigation.

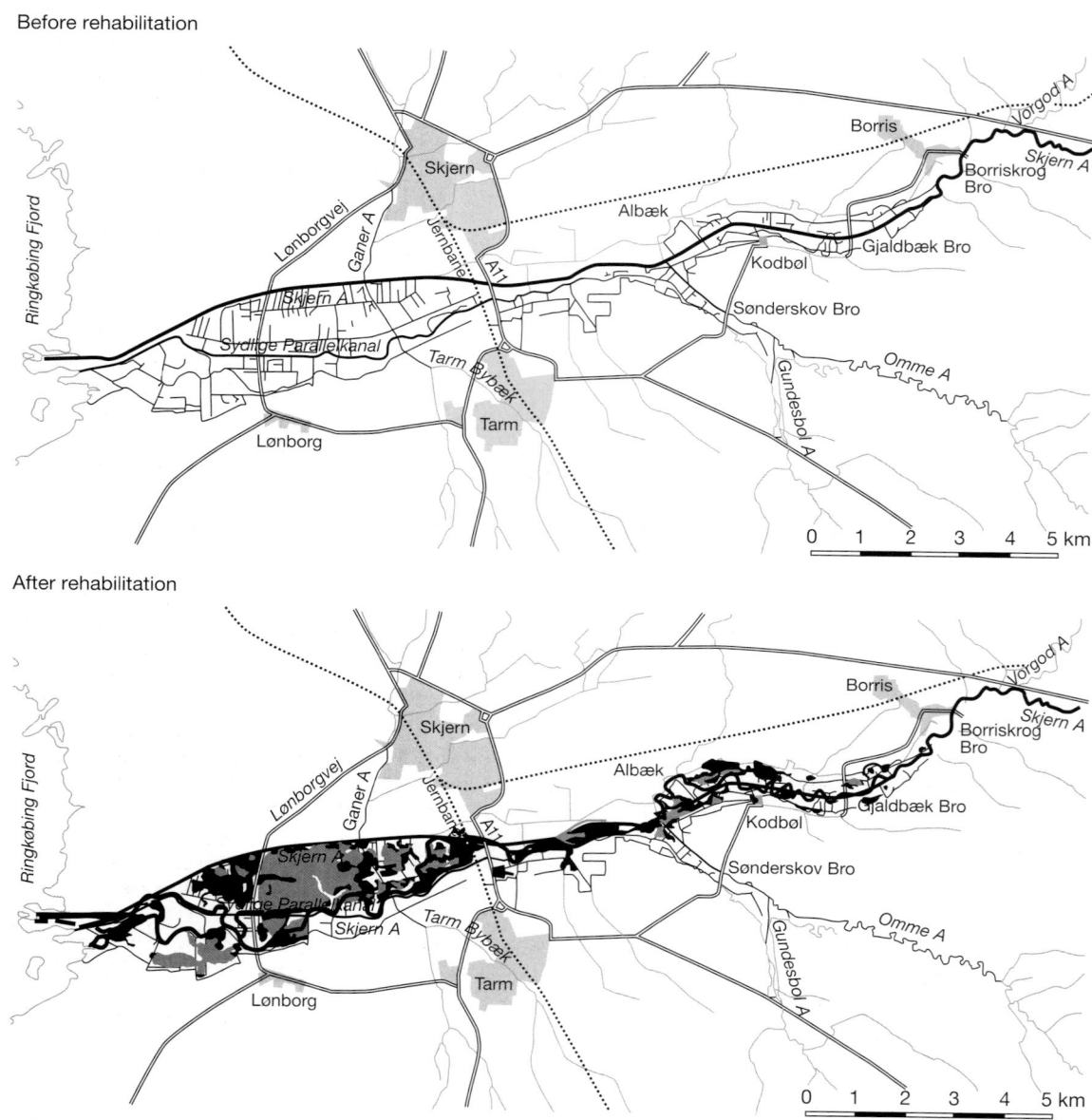

**Fig. 10.16**  The lower reaches of the River Skjern in Denmark were drained in the 1960s resulting in loss of the floodplain and problems of wasting of the soils and turbidity of the coastal waters. A major scheme of rehabilitation was completed in 2002, with re-establishment of large areas of open water (black) and reedswamp (dark shading), re-meandering of the river and major increases in wildlife populations. The scheme covered 22 km of the valley. (Based on Andersen 2005.)

**Table 10.3** Examples of statements, concerning the concept of the Ecological Reserve under the 1998 South African Water Act, made by the general public during a series of meetings on water management. (From van Wyk et al. 2000.)

| Statement | Assumptions implied or reinforced |
| --- | --- |
| The Reserve is water for 'bugs' | The ultimate purpose of the Reserve is to protect aquatic species. |
| We can only use the water that is left over after we have allocated some for the ecology. | People must compete with ecological systems for water; people's needs are secondary to the requirements of natural systems. |
| More water for the Reserve means less water in your stomach. | People must compete with ecological systems for water; higher levels of protection for the resource means less allocation to (and associated benefits for) people. |
| How can you tell people they can't have water because the fish need it? | People must compete with ecological systems for water; basic human need denied in favour of ecosystems. |
| Ecologists keep telling us about how the river ecosystem is the resource, and not just the water it provides. But what is a river except water? | Water is the only acknowledged component of the ecosystem; water provision is the only benefit to be had from river systems. |
| The Reserve is just there to give consultants jobs | The Reserve concept and processes to maintain it are by-products of self-serving participation by ecologists, engineers and consultants. By definition then, the purpose of the Reserve is not to serve the needs of society. |
| All we really need is sustainability. Why don't we just maintain all rivers at the lowest protection level then we can get maximal use out of them while still ensuring a sustainable resource? | The lowest levels of protection for the ecosystem translate to the provision of maximum benefits to people, i.e. protection and use are disjunctive and mutually exclusive. |
| If 10% of the money already spent on Reserve determinations had been spent on supplying water to rural areas, we'd have done more good. | Reserve determinations are perceived to be technical processes that waste resources in light of more urgent basic human needs; meeting short-term goals is more important than securing long-term sustainability. |
| How did ecologists in South Africa manage to negotiate so much power for protecting nature in the new water policy? | Nature and people are perceived to be separate entities with no interdependent needs. Resource protection seen to be for protection's sake and with no intention to accommodate human needs. |
| We need to rethink the Reserve. The Reserve is there to maintain the resource, which provides goods and services to people. | People depend on the resource. Resource protection enables and supports the use of resource-based benefits by people. |

Some previous work had been done on this. Rivers feeding the Kruger National Park in South Africa (Fig. 10.17) rise in lands under development for agriculture and forestry, and flow, in their lower courses, into a wild savannah with a spectacular assemblage of game. As well as being among the best managed of the world's wildlife areas, the Park is also a major tourist attraction and, as such, a large source of income for the country. Some of the rivers are already damaged.

The Letaba, Olifants and Crocodile Rivers are polluted and colonized by alien weeds; the Letaba and Luvuhu once flowed all year but now dry up in summer; the Crocodile is regulated to give a constant flow and no longer preserves its natural seasonal cycle. These problems have been largely caused by increasing agricultural abstraction and clearance of land, leading to decreased run-off and fast responses to flood and drought.

**Fig. 10.17** The Kruger National Park, South Africa depends on rivers flowing in from the developed catchment to the east of the Park. There is severe competition for the water from agriculture and forestry interests. (Photograph by P. Bolstad.)

The approach works on a series of building blocks to estimate needs in turn for consumptive (water supply for humans and for animal drinking, natural evaporation) and then non-consumptive uses. These include self-purification following a natural (say a drowned buffalo) or human pollution impact, sediment transport, prevention of reed encroachment, sufficient water depths for maintenance of pools for hippopotami and crocodiles and for fish movements over riffle areas, flooding of the floodplain and maintenance of its vegetation, and maintenance of appropriate temperature and water quality (especially salinity). Collectively these were called the environmental needs (now the ecological reserve).

An estimate of the environmental needs of the already developed Luvuhu River is given in Table 10.4, where a value of 61.1 million m$^3$ per year is given. This is about a quarter of the mean annual run-off. However, flows are frequently well below the long-term average. The value quoted is also higher than the total flow found under natural conditions during a degree of drought likely to recur once every 50 years and about the same as that found once every 20 years. A value given as a proportion of the mean flow is thus misleading. More significantly, the minimal required flow is greater than the total flow currently found in

most years under present conditions of development of the catchment. Further development is thus not advisable and indeed, current projects should be curtailed if the functions of the river in the Park are to be maintained. Thus we come again to the ultimate problem of whether the aspirations of the now huge numbers of our species can ever be accommodated, a subject to be examined in a final chapter, though no easy solution is available.

## FURTHER READING

A good review of the present state of floodplains is Tockner & Stanford, 2002. Perceptions of swamps, and children's changes in perception is illustrated in Anderson & Moss (1993), use of floodplains for rice growing in the Neolithic Period by Zong et al. (2007) and for chinampas by Arco & Abrams (2006) and Armillas (1971). An attempt to recreate them in Mexico is discussed by Chapin (1988). Backgrounds for the various case studies mentioned include: Darby (1983), Godwin (1978) and Moss (2002 – UK floodplains in the Fens and Broads; Caulfield (1971), Douglas (1947) and Davis & Ogden (1994) – Everglades; Howell et al. (1988) – the Sudd; Fitkau (1970, 1973), Goulding (1980,

**Table 10.4** Water needs of the Luvuhu River in the Kruger National Park in relation to natural mean annual run-off. Values are given in millions of m$^3$ per year (O'Keefe & Davies 1991).

| Use | Need | Subtotal |
|---|---|---|
| Consumptive use | | |
|   Animal drinking | 0.2 | |
|   Human use | 0 | |
|   River evaporation | 4.7 | |
|   Riparian evapotranspiration | 25.0 | 29.9 |
| Non-consumptive use | | |
|   Maintenance of fish habitat | 31.2 | |
|   Additional need for sediment flushing (1 in 10 yr flood) | 15.0 | 46.2 |
| Grand total | | 76.1 |
| Mean annual run-off | | 328 |
| Percentage needed by Park in average year | | 24% |
| Present human use in upstream activities (forestry, irrigation) | | 21% |
| Recent minimum flow | | 28 |
| Needs for Kruger Park under minimum flow | | >100% |

1981), Goulding et al. (1996), Junk et al. (2000) – Amazon floodplain forest; Heeg & Breen (1982), Rogers & Breen (1980, 1990a,b), Rogers (1980), Thirtle et al. (2003) – Pongola; and Richardson & Hussein (2006) and Dellapenna (2007) – Iraq marshes. Aspects of functioning and use of floodplains include Barko et al. (1977), Dugan (1994), Gersberg et al. (1983) and Smid (1975). Rouqouette et al. (2004) cover valuation. Geomorphological aspects and river engineering have a large literature, for example, Brookes (1995) and Sear (1994), and so have fisheries, e.g. Lowe-McConnell (1975, 1987), Welcomme (1979). Dawson (1978) and Dawson & Haslam (1983) discuss river management for plants. Philosophical aspects of restoration and appraisals of its success include Madsen (1995), Iversen et al. (1993), Ormerod (1999, 2004), J.L. Pretty et al. (2003), Roni & Beechie (2008) and Giller (2005). Enhancement aspects include Purseglove (1988) – a particularly attractive read, Lester & Boulton (2008), Newbould (1998), Holmes (1998) and de Waal et al. (1998). Interbasin transfers are reviewed in Davies et al. (1992) and the ecological reserve in O'Keefe & Davies (1991) and van Wyke et al. (2000).

# Chapter 11

# LAKES AND OTHER STANDING WATERS

## 11.1 INTRODUCTION

My practical introduction to lakes was at Abbot's Pool in Somerset. It had none of the grandeur of the great inland seas of the Caspian or Lake Baikal, or even the panoramas of Windermere or Loch Lomond. It was a small and shallow pond, created by damming a very small stream valley in the 19th century and enhanced by the addition of an island for the amenity of a Bristol tobacco importer and the relief of local labour during the depression of the 1930s. It was surrounded by a plantation of exotic larch and other trees along a small track off a road lined with apple orchards. It was so modest, yet it had all the features of a much larger lake, and, more importantly to me at the time, the excitement of being in a boat (a tiny one made of plasticised canvas with no seats) and dangling probes in the water that revealed some of these features.

In summer, as I lowered a thermistor (which measures temperature), I discovered that there was unexpectedly a stratification. It was not the classic division of epilimnion and hypolimnion (Chapter 2), more a slight rate of fall in temperature in the top metre and a half then a slightly greater one down to the bottom at 3.5 m. But that was enough to create a gradient of

*Ecology of Freshwaters: A View for the Twenty-first Century*, 4th edition. By Brian Moss. Published 2010 by Blackwell Publishing Ltd.

oxygen concentrations and water chemistry and in turn a layering of different sorts of algae and photosynthetic bacteria (Fig. 6.1) that I could sample with a device made from a glass tube and spring-loaded bottle caps. This had been constructed during wartime austerity by a Mr Jenkin, for his daughter Penelope Jenkin, one of the English pioneers of lake studies, who had daringly sampled the East African Great Lakes from a rowing boat in the 1920s. There was a satisfying sense of historical continuity for me.

There was a structure to the water mass of Abbot's pool that had a permanence of more than a few seconds. That is the essence of a typical lake, as opposed to a typical river or stream. There are, of course, transitional habitats, like the 'dead zones' of a river, where water is retained long enough for plankton to develop, which also develop a semi-permanence, and riverine lakes, where the structure might be changing from day to day if not second to second. One of the great misconceptions of the development of limnology, indeed of ecology in general, was that habitats exist in discrete types rather than as a collection, or continuum, that links each, essentially unique place, through gradual transitions with all the rest. But that is to jump too far too quickly. We need to look at the basic features of lakes first. And prime among these is that they occupy a basin, a hole in the landscape. Secondly, as indicated above, they have some sort of structure of the water mass; thirdly to understand processes in them, they cannot be separated from their catchment area. The fourth characteristic is that the immense amount of information about them can be ordered somewhat by seeing each lake as a product of the age and origin of the basin, the geology and land use of its catchment and the local climate; and the fifth is that they are not permanent but have histories of development and change that may be studied using the techniques of palaeolimnology.

## 11.2 THE ORIGINS OF LAKE BASINS

There are many ways that a hole in the ground, in which water can collect, can be formed. Abbots Pool was made artificially and so have a huge number of small water bodies, especially for fish culture in the Far East, for stock watering and many other human activities everywhere. In Europe there are decoy ponds (for trapping ducks), dew ponds and droving ponds (for watering cattle in the fields or on the move), dye ponds, flax retting ponds, forge ponds, hammer ponds (for supplying industrial steam hammers in the 19th century, ice ponds (before refrigerators), marl pits (where chalky soil had been dug out for sweetening acid land), mill ponds (to store the water to drive the machinery of grinding grain), moats (for defence of fortified houses), stew ponds (in which fish were kept for the winter when other meat was scarce), swimming ponds, traction engine ponds (steam engines needed lots of water and it had to be replenished frequently), peat cuttings (sometimes quite large in The Netherlands and eastern England) and watercress beds.

The world has an enormous number of artificial fish ponds, drinking water holes and reservoirs, hydroelectric and irrigation dams and rice fields. All of them are lakes of a sort and small, very shallow bodies dominate the area and number of the world's lakes. They do not dominate the volume of freshwater; that is the prerogative of a few deep basins, such as Lake Baikal, the Caspian Sea, the East African and North American Great Lakes, but depth is perhaps of less value than length of the edge and area when it comes to variety of habitat and value to people.

Despite the huge number of man-made water bodies, however, there is a way of forming lakes that has given perhaps even more and that is by ice action. Look at photographs, taken from satellites, of the arctic and boreal (evergreen forest) regions of Alaska, Canada and northern Russia and of the South Island of New Zealand or the tip of South America in Patagonia, and you will see that the landscape is pitted with millions of lakes. In the Arctic, they sometimes have a very regular appearance, like the dimples in a waffle and are formed as ice melts in summer and refreezes in autumn causing soil to be moved into heaps that form the edges of the ponds.

Throughout the polar and cold temperate regions there are many basins where the slow movement of glaciers, thousands of metres thick, rolling great boulders under them, ground out holes in the rock surfaces that eventually filled with water when the glaciers melted back. Because they were slow-moving rivers of ice, the glaciers often flowed down pre-existing river valleys, and when they started to melt back at a rate more or less matched by their advance forwards, they left great piles of debris, called moraines to later dam these valleys, forming long thin lakes like the finger lakes of New York State or the lakes of the Cumbrian Lake District and the Scottish Highlands in the UK.

When the glaciers melted back in earnest, colossal amounts of water washed out huge amounts of sand, gravel and ground rock flour to be deposited in wide plains at their feet. Chunks of ice up to several kilometers across broke from the glacier and were buried by the sands and gravels. Insulated there, they took many years to melt, but when they did, yet another glacially formed basin resulted, called a pothole or kettle hole lake. The plains of mid-western America, Europe and Argentina are studded with them.

All of these sorts of lakes are associated with the higher latitudes, because the last major polar glaciation, ending about 10,000 years ago did not penetrate much further south than about 45° north or south. But there are ice-formed lakes in the mountains everywhere in the world, even close to the Equator. Where a mountain glacier starts to form, the ice breaks rock from the mountain and gouges out a basin before spilling downhill. This basin, when the ice melts, gives a high-mountain tarn or corrie lake. There are classic examples on Mounts Kenya and Kilimanjaro in Africa, the Alps, Southern Alps, Rockies and Andes.

A third major way in which lake basins are formed follows the great fault lines that separate the plates of the Earth's surface. Along the western side of North and South America and the eastern coasts and islands of the Pacific Ocean, through East Africa and the Mediterranean region of Europe and the islands of the ridge that divides the Atlantic ocean into two, there are volcanoes and earthquakes, for these are areas where

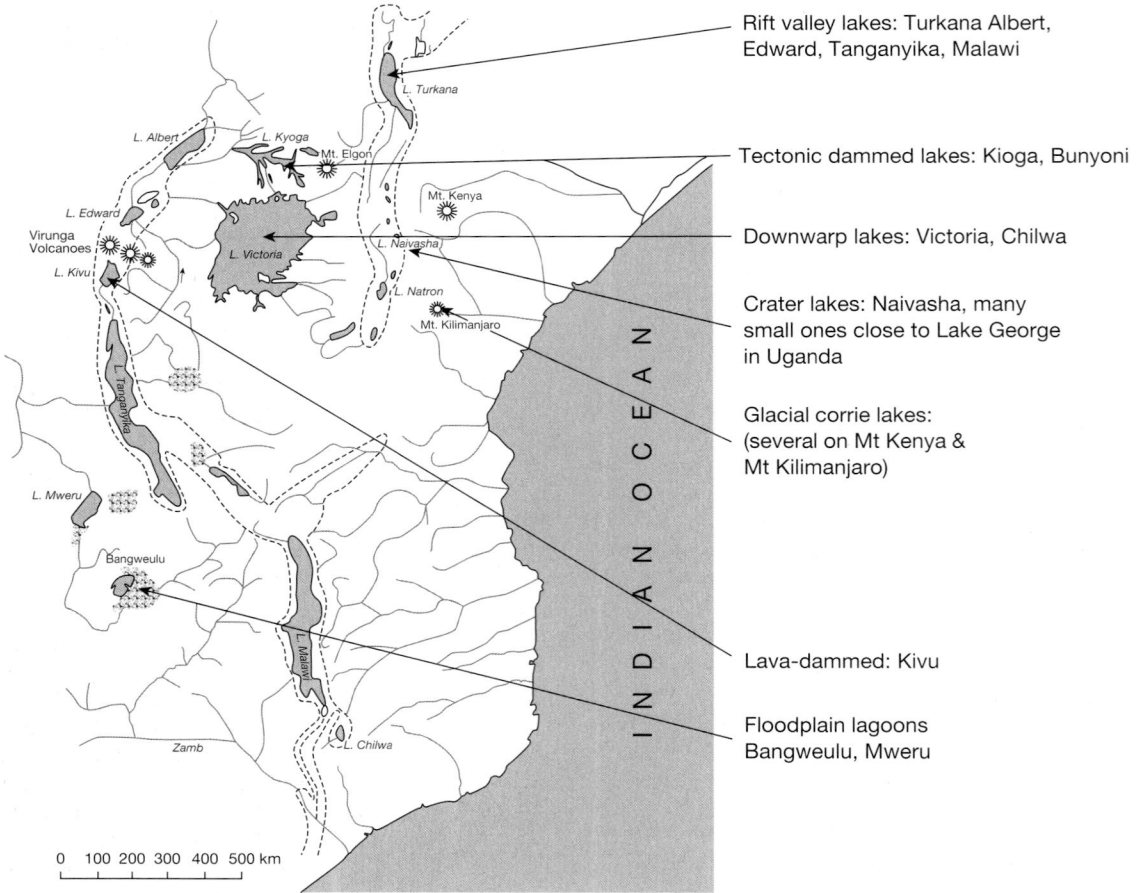

**Fig. 11.1** East Africa contains many lakes of many different origins.

earth movements are occurring. New rock is being extruded through the cracks or old rock is disappearing into them.

Earthquakes and lava flows can cause landslides that dam rivers and make lakes; volcanic craters, between eruptions that may only happen every few hundred years, can fill with water. The general disturbance in the land surfaces through separation of plates can make huge troughs, or rift valleys or simply cause the land over large areas to sink and in these basins water can collect. Africa epitomizes all this (Fig. 11.1). It is an ancient continent where the land surface until the Miocene period had been slowly worn down to a flatness and where the lakes occupied shallow basins

covering huge areas at the heads of the great river systems of the Congo, Nile and Zambezi.

But the earth movements began again, resulting in the forked rift valley that moves northwards to become the Red Sea and connects with the earthquake zones of the Middle East and Italy. In the African rift are the very big, elongate and deep lakes of Turkana, Albert, Edward, Tanganyika and Malawi in basins formed by plate separation that began, but has temporarily stopped. Between the rifts, general disturbance of the land surface by the huge forces operating below created Lake Victoria by subsidence, and its connected Lake Kioga. Kioga has an outline resembling that of a man-made reservoir, a hand with many fingers, caused by damming a river system, but in its case it was the rise of the rift wall, as a result of earth movements that made the dam. Lake Kivu was formed when the lava flows of the Virunga volcanoes blocked the path of the Ruzizi River. East and Central Africa is a land that was wetter 100,000 years ago and more, during the warmer periods that separated the advances of the polar glaciers, and there is evidence of this in ancient lake shores, now far from the existing water's edge. These shores bore the origins of mankind.

People, ice and earth movements thus have all been formers of lakes, but the list is not yet complete. There is the action of earth surface processes, water especially, and of animals other than man. River floodplains create lakes through the trapping of backwaters and the cutting off of meanders with the formation of oxbow lakes. Such lakes are formed in every big river system, though floodplain drainage has obliterated them in much of the developed world (Chapter 10).

Lakes form also from the action of water where there is chalk or limestone. Rain water dissolves the rock underground as it percolates (Chapter 3). Caverns and voids form that collapse leaving the karst (limestone country) lakes of Kentucky and the Balkans, central France and northern England. The ocean can form lakes too when it builds longshore bars of shingle and sand that may block river mouths and cause ponding of the freshwater behind them. The main lakes of Uruguay were formed in this way and there are examples all along the eastern coast of South America.

Finally, beavers when they may make dens safe from predators, incidentally create dams of felled timber that hold riverine lakes; alligators excavate holes in the soft chalks of Florida that retain water in the dry season for a collection of fish and reptiles that find refuge there (Chapter 10). And in a neat collaboration of animals and wind, shallow pools are formed in central African savannahs. Some species of termites, perhaps the world's most abundant animals, build mounds of soil that they ventilate with an air conditioning system driven by the beating of their wings. The evaporation of water cools the mound but the water is replaced by soil water wicked up from below and bearing salts. The soil in and around the mound thus becomes very saline. Antelopes, buffalo and zebra are attracted by the salt, which they lick, breaking the mound and disturbing the surrounding soil with their hooves as they do so. In the dry season, the wind blows the fine soil away and in the wet season, the large animals roll in the mud to remove skin parasites. They carry more of the soil away

stuck to their bodies. Eventually a depression deep enough to fill with water at least in the wet season is created. Another lake is formed.

## 11.3 LAKE STRUCTURE

The way a lake is formed gives it a basic structure, or morphometry. Lakes scraped out by ice tend to be shallow and shelving and have a very irregular shape, determined by the patterns of relatively harder or softer rocks in the area. Lakes created by ice deepening valleys and damming them with moraines, tend to be precipitously deep, long and thin. Deep and shallow are relative terms, but in these cases we might be thinking of maximum depths of a few tens to many tens of metres respectively. Pothole lakes formed by the melting of ice blocks tend to be shallow, more regular in shape but steep sided.

Then the catchment area contributes to the structure, by its size in relation to the lake volume and its nature. A large catchment area to lake volume ratio gives a more rapid flow through of water compared with a small catchment to lake ratio. The retention time will be shorter in the former case, longer in the latter, or put the other way, the turnover rate of the water mass in the lake will be greater or lesser respectively. The longer the water is retained the more its chemical nature will be changed by biological processes in the lake. Thus more nutrients will be taken up or denitrified and more calcium will be precipitated as marl, the longer the water is retained. In preparing drinking water, an inexpensive first step is to retain water in a reservoir as long as possible for silt to settle and nitrate to disappear. Retention time will also affect the physical structure of the water mass. Long-lived water masses will tend to stratify under ice in winter or directly in summer (Chapter 2); if the water is only retained for a day or two this might not be possible, but does sometimes happen. The simple ratio of volume of water flowing in to lake volume, which gives the turnover, is only an average value. The main flow through may retain the characteristics of a river or stream within the lake, leaving the water mass less disturbed away from this relatively small area. Stratification is a major determinant of the nature of the suspended plankton community (Chapter 6, Chapter 13).

A combination of morphometry and hydrology, the water flow and retention features, as well as the nature of the water flowing in contributes a lot in determining

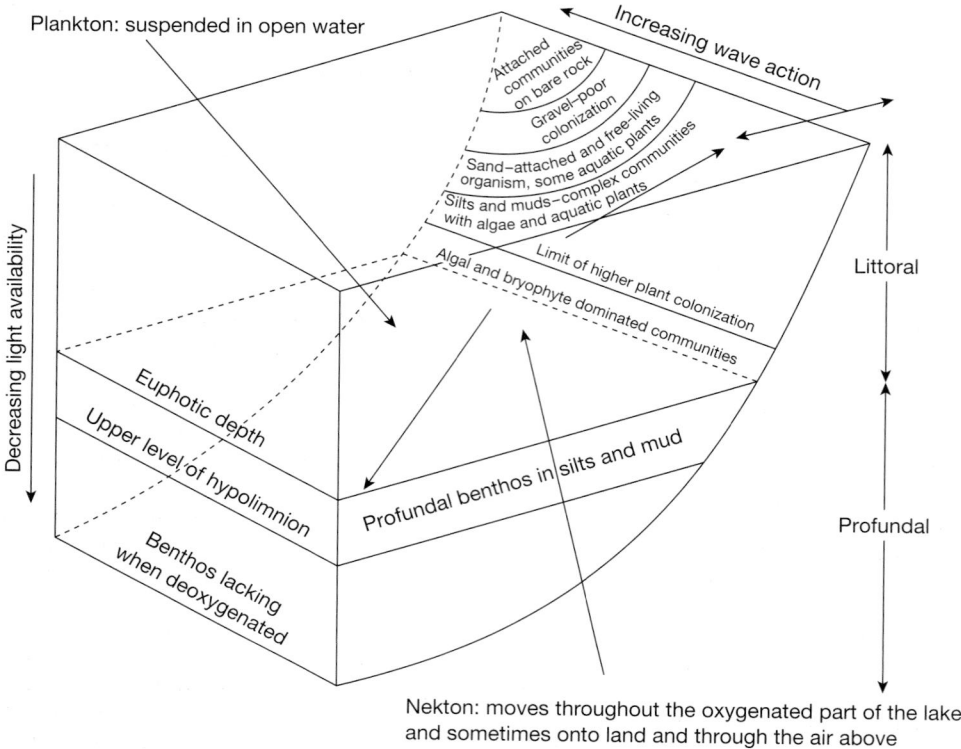

Plankton: suspended in open water

Increasing wave action

Attached communities on bare rock

Gravel–poor colonization

Sand–attached and free-living organism, some aquatic plants

Sand–attached and free-living organism, some aquatic communities

Silts and muds–complex communities with algae and aquatic plants

Limit of higher plant colonization

Algal and bryophyte dominated communities

Littoral

Decreasing light availability

Euphotic depth

Upper level of hypolimnion

Profundal benthos in silts and mud

Profundal

Benthos lacking when deoxygenated

Nekton: moves throughout the oxygenated part of the lake and sometimes onto land and through the air above

**Fig. 11.2** A general scheme for the communities within lakes and their terminology.

the biological structure of the lake. This can be seen first in the balance of the four main communities (Fig. 11.2): the plankton, the nekton, the littoral and the profundal. The plankton, which includes viruses, heterotrophic bacteria, photosynthetic algae and bacteria, small animals from Protozoa to crustaceans and rotifers, is suspended in the water, though a very few species float and some swim, though weakly. The longer the water is retained, the better the chance of it developing and the greater the stratification of the water mass, the more niches are available and the greater its diversity.

The littoral benthos is a more complex community that develops on the bottom wherever enough light can penetrate to allow net photosynthesis (total (gross) photosynthesis is greater than the respiration needs (Chapters 5 and 9)) of some combination of algae, photosynthetic bacteria and plants. These are associated with bottom-living animals and heterotrophic bacteria. A littoral community can develop irrespective of the

nature of the bottom (or substratum, or substrate). It can form on rocks, where the organisms share some characteristics with those of erosive streams, or where sands and gravels are left by the particular combination of water currents and wave erosion. It might then be quite sparse for moving gravel is destructively abrasive. Where the water movements are quiet, silts and clays are deposited, and rooted plants tend to predominate, sometimes zoned so that the shallowest water (say down to a metre) has emergent plants mixed with submerged, floating-leaved and floating species. Somewhat deeper water, say to 2 m, has all of these bar the emergents, and deeper water loses the floating and floating-leaved plants because wind disturbance at the surface breaks up the mats or their leaf petioles. Submerged species go down to such depths as enough light is available (Chapters 5 and 9), when the profundal benthic community takes over. The littoral zone also includes some plankton in the overlying water and this may be a different community from that of the middle of the lake, where the water overlies the pro-fundal zone. The term 'pelagic' describes this area.

In the littoral, large plants are always associated with algal and heterotrophic communities and there can be many combinations of features. Wave-washed rocky edges, for example, coated with attached algae, but with no large plants, may have well-illuminated sediments bearing submerged plants offshore in deeper waters. The sheltered bays of warm lakes may have dense communities of floating plants over depths of water that could not support photosynthesis at the bottom. Whether these should be regarded as littoral communities (they are edge-associated) or pelagic (open water) communities more akin to the plankton (they depend on the water for their nutrients, whereas bottom-associated plants may take nutrients from the sediments) is a moot point. Floating plants are often less affected by the minutiae of water currents because they are big and rafted into massive structures by interconnecting stolons, but some species, such as the duckweeds, are tiny and tossed about as much as a microscopic alga. Trying to classify things too minutely is generally a waste of time!

What is important is that many different littoral communities can exist in a single lake. Those of bays, sheltered from the prevailing wind to various degrees, will differ from those of rocky headlands exposed to the full force of the waves. They will also change from time to time as water levels go up and down, leaving the upper shores dry and sterile in drought years, and flooding what was damp grassland and edge forest in the wetter ones, establishing algae, animals and bacteria among the flooded debris, just as in a flood-plain. The littoral communities will also be determined by the nature of the catchment. Harder rocks will weather mostly to sands and gravels and the river deltas and shores will lack the fine material that is needed for many plants; weatherable catchments will not only produce much fine material but also different qualities of organic debris, perhaps more nutrient rich than the raw brown peaty material of acid, igneous catchments, and bearing very different communities of plants.

In recent years the term wetland has been coined for habitats, both fresh and saline that are wet and dominated by large plants. Floodplain swamps are examples. There are also similar swamps in standing water habitats, not only edging lakes with open water or covering shallower lakes, but also in habitats where the water table is, on average during the year, at the soil surface. Such bogs, fens, carrs and marshes have traditionally been regarded as terrestrial habitats and claimed by terrestrial ecologists, but really they are variations on the theme of lakes (Fig. 11.3) and are treated in Chapter 12 as particular sorts of littoral zones. This is unconventional but really very logical. The natures of the plants of such habitats and the chemistry of the soils are the same as those of a con-ventional littoral zone with water clearly above the sediment. Likewise the wet grasslands at the edges of floodplains have been called wetlands but are really variants of the swamp communities of flowing waters. There really was no point in introducing the new term 'wetlands'. It gets in the way of understanding how all habitats are naturally connected.

The profundal benthos is the bottom-living com-munity of the deep waters. Its name mixes the Latin for deep (profundum) with the Greek for bottom (benthos) with the lack of respect for the niceties of language that characterizes much technical endeavour. The import-ance of deepness, however, really is that of darkness for the profundal is simply where too little light penetrates for net photosynthesis. This might be in only a metre or two, or much less in very turbid waters, but in a clear, deep lake it might be at several tens of metres. In a clear, shallow lake, plants and algae may cover the entire bottom and there may be no profundal zone at all.

The profundal community, obviously, is only of heterotrophs, animal and microbial, and depends for its energy on organic matter rolling down the slope of the bed from the littoral or falling down from the plankton. Gravity ensures the food supply, but it is sometimes not very nutritious. In a very deep lake the time taken for sinking to the bottom may be so long that micro-organisms in the plankton may have metabolized most of the easily available material on the way; and in a deep, steep-sided lake the extent of the littoral zone may be relatively small so that not much can come from there. In a shallow lake, however, the supply may be copious and very rich so that bacterial activity is so great in the profundal benthos that anaerobic and chemically difficult conditions will be created. The same might be true of a lake with an anaerobic hypolimnion (Chapter 2), for much of the profundal zone will coincide with the hypolimnion. Note, how-ever, that the two concepts of stratification, which determines the extent of the hypolimnion, alternatively called the mixing depth, and the boundary between the littoral and profundal zones, which is determined by light penetration, are independent of one another.

**Fig. 11.3** All lakes are standing waters but all standing waters are not lakes in the sense used by the general public. Standing waters include bogs (upper left), fed by rainwater and covering large areas in the northern hemisphere, fens and marshes (upper right) fed by ground water (the distinction between these and closely similar communities in floodplains is negligible). Bog and fen communities in slightly deeper basins may fringe deeper water, perhaps still entirely occupied by plants and might be recognized as conventional shallow lakes (lower left). Their extent will be proportionately less in much deeper basins where most of the system is open water occupied by plankton and nekton (lower right), but there is no rigid separation. There is a continuum of conditions. Some scientists would regard all but the lower right example as wetlands, but this is to lose the sense of continuity and to think in terms of distinct categories.

This too contributes to an enormous and continuous range of possible structures to the lake community.

Like everything else in ecology, these zones (pelagic, littoral, profundal) are not discrete, isolated things. It is possible to define one boundary, the depth at which light is insufficient to support net photosynthesis, but this boundary changes slightly from day to day because the plankton community and the amount of inborn suspended material in the water change constantly. Where the height of the littoral plants and algae ends and where the plankton community above them begins is even more nebulous, for plankton may live among the plants, receiving some protection there from predators and moving upwards or sideways at night to graze in the open water. There are also problematic animals, such as the phantom midge, a fly whose larva is almost transparent. It lives in the profundal benthos, but as it grows bigger moves at night into the plankton to feed on zooplankters and retreats back to the sediment in daylight, where it is protected from fish predation. Other connections include the passive washing out of fine organic matter from the littoral to the open water, where it may be part of the food of zooplankters, and to the profundal benthos.

Fish also freely move among the three groups of habitats, and with other vertebrates including amphibians, reptiles, birds and mammals are sometimes called the nekton. Nekton compared with plankton, are strong swimmers, rarely at the mercy of water currents but moving where they will. There are patterns of the non-nektonic communities within a lake because not only is the littoral benthos variable among different shore conditions and with depth, so too is the plankton (though much less so because of the mixing of the water). Patterns in the profundal benthos are influenced by stratification and the degree of deoxygenation of the overlying water and by the nature of the sediment. Finer sediments take longer to settle out and are associated with the deep, stiller water, coarser ones settle even in quite strong currents. Fish freely ignore these gradients and boundaries.

They begin life close to where their mothers have laid the eggs, usually on some sort of surface, such as on plants, rocks or debris, or sometimes in gravel on vigorously swashed shores, and for a few species (compared with ocean communities where this is common) in the open water. As they grow bigger they may move offshore and feed on zooplankton and then as adults become again more associated with the benthos where bigger invertebrates, and thus larger meals, are more rewarding for the effort of catching them. The only real barrier is anaerobic water for many fish species.

A final aspect of structure may seem odd, but many small lakes, usually called ponds, but there is no satisfactory distinction to which no exceptions can be found, will dry up every year or in some years. This creates circumstances where particular organisms can thrive when they could not do so in permanent water. Many predators, including most fish cannot survive drying and so pools that are temporary provide predator-free refuges for vulnerable animals. Temperate Amphibia are mostly associated with such habitats. Their eggs and tadpoles are large, and hence otherwise attractive meals for fish, though the thick mucilage covering the former may make eating them difficult. Temporary pools that are also saline, as are many in the warm temperate and tropical regions, add another dimension to this idea of structure, for high and changing salt content also provides different niches.

## 11.4 THE IMPORTANCE OF THE CATCHMENT AREA

It is easy to see a lake as an entity all of its own. From a viewpoint say on a hillside above it, there seems to be a very definite boundary at the water's edge. Put your foot to one side and it gets wet, to the other and it stays dry. When artists paint lake scenes, the reflection of the hillsides or sky seems also to isolate the lake like a mirror on the wall. The idea was reinforced by an early paper in the 19th century by Stephen Forbes, called 'The lake as a microcosm', a microcosm being a miniature version of a bigger whole and indeed understanding of the processes of limnology was crystallized at one stage into the idea of discrete types of lakes, initially oligotrophic (low nutrient) and eutrophic (high nutrient) but blossoming into dystrophic (peaty), argillotrophic (turbid with clay), siderotrophic (iron-stained) and others. The idea was so powerful that it is often still used in teaching limnology. But it is wrong. Lakes do not exist as isolated entities, nor do they form discrete types. There are extremes of particular features but there is continuous variation among them. Sections 11.4 and 11.5 look at the first issue and 11.6 the idea of continuous variation.

The catchment rather than the lake is the discrete entity. The nature of the catchment in determining the chemical quality of the water has already been discussed in Chapters 3 and 4. Easily weathered rocks tend to lead to high conductivities, and relatively higher nutrient concentrations, though these will be still absolutely low in the absence of farming and settlements. Resistant rocks and thin or sandy soils may result in waters little changed from rainfall in composition. But the nature of the catchment has wider consequences. Formally the catchment, or watershed, is the area from which water gathers, and runs into streams and rivers and thence lakes. The area differs depending on the point in the river or lake at which it is measured. This is not much of a problem if the point is the lake outflow, or the place where the river enters the ocean, or even, in defining the subcatchments of a river system, the confluence of a tributary with a bigger stream.

The problems come: where in very flat, swampy terrain lakes may have many connections with one another so that water may flow in different directions at different times depending on the exact location of rainstorms; where the water supply is not a surface flow, but comes from ground water so that the surface terrain gives little clue to its origin; and where the lake is coastal and associated with a river system that has tides so that water may at times be pushed into upstream lakes from downstream river tributaries or other lakes or even the sea. Mostly we tend to gloss over these complications just as we have often sampled only one location in a lake, blissfully ignoring the existence of its internal structure. Moreover we often forget that the atmosphere is a part of the catchment, providing gases and rain that also has a variable composition from place to place. The atmosphere has no relationship whatsoever to the area of the terrestrial watershed. But whatever their delineation, catchment areas and lakes have the same relationship as houses and trashcans (or dustbins or household rubbish bags, or plastic containers on wheels). What goes on the house is reflected in the contents of the trashcan and something of the lifestyle of the inhabitants of the house can be deduced from these. Things can also be brought into the house from other places, making the interpretation of the contents of the trashcan more complicated.

Nonetheless, the prime determinant of activity within the lake, even though the internal processes of the lake are also extremely important, is the immediate surface catchment, its geology, terrestrial ecosystems and land use. This relationship has already been established for rivers from the effect it has through timber debris, leaf litter and eroded sediment. All of these may also move into a lake, but that part of them that has been processed into fine organic particles and dissolved organic matter is the most important. Leaves and big waterlogged debris will be buried in the delta of the inflow or elsewhere on the lake bed, or if fresh, will float through. The dissolved and fine material, however, may have considerable importance.

## 11.5 LAKES AS AUTOTROPHIC OR HETEROTROPHIC SYSTEMS

Lakes have traditionally been considered as autotrophic systems, which means that the total (gross) amount of carbon fixed, or oxygen produced by photosynthesis, is greater than that released or used, respectively, by the total (or community) respiration in the lake. The respirers include the plants and algae that are carrying out the photosynthesis as well as the heterotrophic bacteria and animals. In an autotrophic system, there is thus net production of organic matter, which may be washed downstream through the outflow, or accumulate on the bottom in the sediments. If the system is not autotrophic, that is, community respiration is greater than gross photosynthesis, yet still persists, it is a heterotrophic system and must be being subsidized by organic matter brought in from elsewhere, in other words, from the ecosystems of the catchment. There is increasing evidence that many lakes indeed are

heterotrophic and that the catchment has a greater role than simply the provision of inorganic nutrients. This is, of course, the situation with natural river systems, at least in their erosive stretches.

One indicator is that the carbon dioxide concentrations in river and lake waters are usually well above saturation levels, meaning that a surplus of carbon dioxide is being produced compared with that being taken up in photosynthesis and in turn suggesting a greater rate of respiration than gross photosynthesis. This could be misleading, however, for the surplus carbon dioxide could already be present in the water as it percolates from the soils of the catchments and not reflect the balance of respiration and photosynthesis within the river or lake. In the terrestrial vegetation, oxygen produced will be released to the atmosphere by the plants together with some of the carbon dioxide produced in respiration but the carbon dioxide produced from the intense respiration of fallen organic matter in the litter and soil layers will become dissolved in the soil water and could be washed out to give the supersaturated levels of the freshwaters. The carbon dioxide supersaturation of lake waters is thus consistent with a heterotrophic system but not proof of it. Another problem is that the organic matter that is washed out, both as particles and dissolved, from a pristine terrestrial system has been intensely worked over by the heterotrophs of that system and represents what is no longer easily metabolizable. The dead leaves that are blown into streams in autumn typify this. They require much fungal processing before they can enter the food webs of rivers. Dissolved organic matter has already been processed several times in soils and represents even more refractory material. It is chemically very unreactive and effectively discarded by the versatile microbial communities of the soils as unusable. How can it then be a major source of energy for lakes? One explanation may be that it is chemically changed by the action of ultraviolet light as it passes out of the shade of the forests and into the rivers and there is much evidence from laboratory work of such a change.

A second approach to determining whether lakes are heterotrophic systems is to look directly at the balance of gross photosynthesis and community respiration within the lake. The problem with a real lake is size. Practically the metabolism must separately be measured for each community (plankton, littoral benthos, profundal benthos and associated nekton) and this is difficult to do precisely, given the complexity of the system. It is easiest for the plankton, by incorporating the water in bottles and using the methods of oxygen change described in Chapter 9. The gross production is obtained from the difference in concentration between the light and dark bottles at the end of the experiment and the respiration from the difference between the dark bottle and the initial oxygen concentration. Often when the experiment is carried out over 24 hours, the system is shown to be heterotrophic. Zooplankton in the bottles might be feeding on fine organic particles washed in from the catchment or on bacteria, and dissolved organic matter similarly brought in might support the bacteria.

Doing the experiment for the profundal benthos is also comparatively easy. All that is needed is a set of intact cores of the sediment and its overlying water, sealed from the atmosphere, in which diurnal rates of oxygen uptake can be measured. These are always heterotrophic communities. The problem comes with littoral communities, because release of oxygen direct to the atmosphere from emergent plants has to be measured as well as exchanges within the water and sediment. It is difficult to detect very small changes of oxygen in the air. The problem can be partly solved by measuring changes in carbon dioxide in the air, which, using an infrared gas analyser, is much easier, but then accounting for the carbon dioxide change in the

water and sediment is difficult because of the complex chemistry of carbon dioxide in entering into equilibria with carbonates.

It seems that no-one has yet constructed a complete oxygen or carbon dioxide budget for a real lake. It has been almost done for estuaries using the H.T. Odum diurnal curve method (Chapter 10), with the assumption that emergent plants were minor components of the system and it has been done for mesocosms of lakes with just submerged plants, however. The method allows the determination of gross photosynthesis in the system and community respiration. The state of the system can then be assessed as the ratio of these. Odum generally found for estuaries that it was less than one (heterotrophic systems) and this has been found also for experimental mesocosms of shallow lakes (Table 11.1). An alternative way of looking at the data is to calculate the net ecosystem production ($Ph_g - R_{com}$) simply by integrating the oxygen exchange curve bearing in mind that values above the zero line are positive and those below it negative. This can be done by finding the areas under the curves. Figure 9.6 shows an idealized curve, with the oxygen curve shown by circular symbols. Figure 11.4 shows curves based on actual data.

Heterotrophic systems have negative values for net ecosystem production. A combination of the original

**Table 11.1** Lake ecosystems appear generally to be heterotrophic even when rich in plants. These are some results from an experiment with experimental tanks (Fig. 11.4) in which metabolism of the systems was measured by the Odum method (with some refinements to it) when the tanks were warmed by 4°C and given increased nutrients to simulate ponds affected by global warming and agricultural fertilization. Values are means ± SD in mg oxygen $L^{-1}$ $h^{-1}$ over a 24-hour period in midsummer. P is the probability value for a significant difference (the lower the more likely); ns means no significant difference. The negative net ecosystem production and a ratio of community respiration to gross photosynthesis >1 suggest that the systems were heterotrophic under all circumstances but were increasingly so with warming and fertilization. (Based on Moss (2010). Data of D. Atkinson, B. Moss, U. Noreen and C. Whitham.)

| | Ambient | +4°C | P | No nutrient addition | Added nutrients | P |
|---|---|---|---|---|---|---|
| Gross photosynthesis | 28.3 ± 18.4 | 13.2 ± 10.2 | 0.003 | 23.0 ± 16.0 | 18.4 ± 17.2 | ns |
| Net photosynthesis | 1.15 ± 4.2 | −0.33 ± 2.49 | ns | −0.23 ± 3.54 | 1.05 ± 3.39 | ns |
| Net ecosystem production | −4.08 ± 2.63 | −6.73 ± 1.50 | 0.0004 | −4.84 ± 2.47 | −5.97 ± 2.46 | ns |
| Heterotroph respiration | 5.26 ± 3.83 | 6.41 ± 2.02 | 0.09 | 4.66 ± 3.6 | 7.01 ± 1.92 | 0.044 |
| Plant respiration | 27.1 ± 16.6 | 13.5 ± 8.99 | 0.003 | 23.2 ± 14.8 | 17.4 ± 14.7 | ns |
| Community respiration | 32.4 ± 17.0 | 19.9 ± 9.5 | 0.007 | 27.9 ± 14.5 | 24.4 ± 15.6 | ns |
| Ratio of community respiration to gross photosynthesis | 1.41 ± 0.76 | 1.85 ± 0.6 | 0.047 | 1.40 ± 0.42 | 1.86 ± 0.87 | 0.044 |

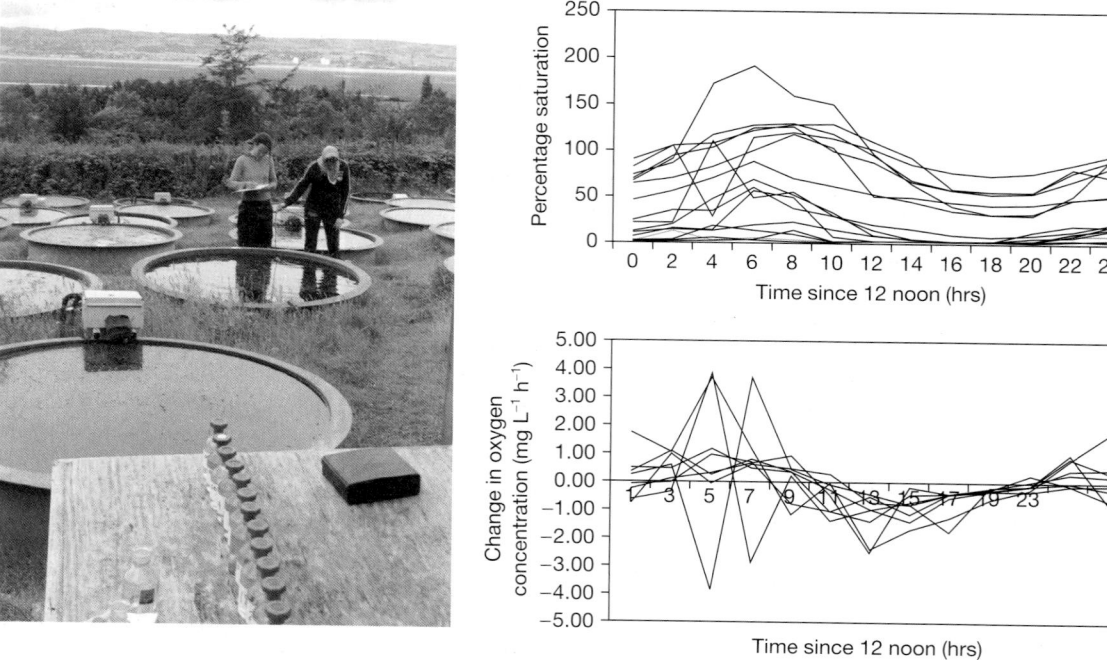

**Fig. 11.4** A set of tanks that can be used for experiments on whole pond systems and some data on changes in oxygen concentrations over 24 hours in them (upper right). The data have been converted to rate of change curves (lower right) from which gross photosynthesis and community respiration rates can be calculated (Table 11.1).

Odum method and calculation of net ecosystem production allows the separate components of heterotroph and plant respiration also to be calculated from the graphs. Even in systems with abundant photosynthetic tissue, the net ecosystem production can be negative in mid-summer, though it is likely to have been positive for a period in spring. Over a year, however, with mostly respiration of organic matter stored in the sediments going on in winter, it is likely to be negative, with the implication that organic matter from outside the lake is being imported and supporting the excess respiration. In experimental mesocosms, the sediment organic matter is put in as part of the experimental system and the experimenter determines its origin. In a natural system, the current general assumption is that it is washed in from the terrestrial vegetation of the catchment, but there is a problem in that although this could be true, it could be provided by surrounding emergent swamp vegetation, which releases oxygen to the atmosphere but of which the decaying biomass collapses into the water and becomes part of the

sediment, creating a respiratory demand not matched by photosynthetic oxygen release into the water. This could give a false impression of the lake as a heterotrophic system, though an indication that the open-water planktonic system might be heterotrophic. The plankton system is only part of the lake, however.

A third way of tackling this issue is to make measurements of the ratio of isotopes of carbon ($^{12}C$ and $^{13}C$) in organic matter of the terrestrial vegetation, in organic matter produced in the lake, and in animals in the lake. The ratio of $^{13}C$ to $^{12}C$ is different in terrestrial plants, taking their carbon dioxide from the atmosphere, from that in aquatic photosynthesizers, taking it from dissolved sources. The ratio is measured as a deviation from a standard ratio (that in a particular limestone rock) and expressed as a change from this, called a delta value. For example a sample relatively lower in $^{13}C$ than the standard might have a delta value of $-30‰$, whereas a sample relatively enriched in $^{13}C$ might have $+10‰$. About 1.3% of all carbon on Earth is $^{13}C$, but plants and algae tend to take up less $^{13}C$ than the lighter $^{12}$C. Expressed as a delta value, air has a value of around 7–9‰, but most plants, because of this discrimination, have values around −26 to −27‰.

Submerged plants and algae take up most of their inorganic carbon from the water and this carbon ultimately comes from limestones or lime minerals in other rocks that were formed on the sea floor from deposits created by marine organisms and inorganic processes. Sea water has a delta $^{13}$C value of 0 to +2 and waters derived from limestones −11 to −12 so that even with some discrimination by aquatic photosynthesizers, the delta $^{13}$C value of aquatically produced material is higher, perhaps −20 to −17 than that produced by most terrestrial plants. Measurement of the $^{13}$C content of aquatic animals often shows them to have relatively more negative values than the primary producers in the water, suggesting that they are feeding on terrestrial material imported into the lake (Fig. 11.5). There is still a snag, however. Since emergent swamp plants in the littoral zone use atmospheric carbon dioxide, they could still be the source rather than the more distant terrestrial plants, so the situation remains unclear.

The issue only assumes any importance if the traditional view of the lake as a separate system is taken. If the unit of study is the catchment, which sees the lake and its influent rivers as part of the catchment system, it is easy to see that different lakes in different situations could have a continuum of degrees of dependence on terrestrial, swamp and submerged plant and algal sources. Those in mountainous terrain, with steep river valleys that allow for much erosion, deep basins with very small littoral zones and a primary production in the lake severely limited by the availability of nutrients could well be strongly dependent on washed in organic matter. Loch Ness, in Scotland is such a case. Those in very flat terrain with extensive littoral zones of reedbeds and very large productivity of emergent plants might appear to be heterotrophic but falsely so. Those in intermediate terrain with moderate nutrient supplies, extensive littoral zones of submerged plants might sometimes be heterotrophic, sometimes autotrophic. The result, and the perception, as often, might simply depend on the choice of lake for study.

What must, however, be true is that the catchment as a whole must be autotrophic (discounting a hypothetical case that it receives quantities of airborne organic dust!). Evidence for this (though it is self-evident if the catchment continues to bear living communities) is that organic matter is stored in soils and sediments to some extent everywhere and this organic matter represents a slight excess of gross photosynthesis over community respiration of the catchment system. Over geological time, this material has accumulated as peat, coal, oil and natural gas and is the reason that oxygen concentrations are so high in Earth's atmosphere and carbon dioxide concentrations relatively low. The implications for this are discussed in Chapter 16, but for the moment, it is worth reflecting that the continents can be divided up completely into catchment areas (or river basins) with their inland water systems. These are the fundamental units for considering ecological processes, and the land mass as a whole can be seen as a single autotrophic catchment with many rivers supplying a single huge endorheic lake, still to be established as either autotrophic or heterotrophic, the ocean.

## 11.6 THE CONTINUUM OF LAKES

A great advance in understanding freshwaters was made in the early part of the 20th century by two pioneers of the subject, Auguste Thienemann, a German very familiar with deep lakes at the foot of the Alps, and Einar Naumann, a Swede equally expert on the shallower lakes scooped out by ice in the glacial plains around the Baltic Sea. These two groups of lakes were apparently very different and shared many characteristics within each group. The deep alpine lakes, studied by Thienemann, were clear with low amounts of nutrients and sparse plankton populations. Their morphometry allowed for only narrow littoral zones and their hypolimnia, being voluminous and supplied with only small amounts of organic matter sedimenting from the sparse plankton, were well oxygenated. Their profundal benthos was typified by the fly genus *Tanytarsus*, which does not survive deoxygenation.

In contrast, Naumann's lakes were shallow, with flatter catchments from which water drained more slowly, picking up more nutrients and supporting a richer plankton. Their hypolimnia were much smaller and prone to deoxygenate in summer and *Tanytarsus* was replaced by *Chironomus* species that could survive deoxygenation. Moreover, the shape of the basin allowed wide littoral zones to develop, though because of the cloudier water, the plants penetrated less deeply. Thienemann and Naumann realized that all of these characteristics were interlinked within each lake group. All things were connected and this was a major advance in understanding. They called the first group

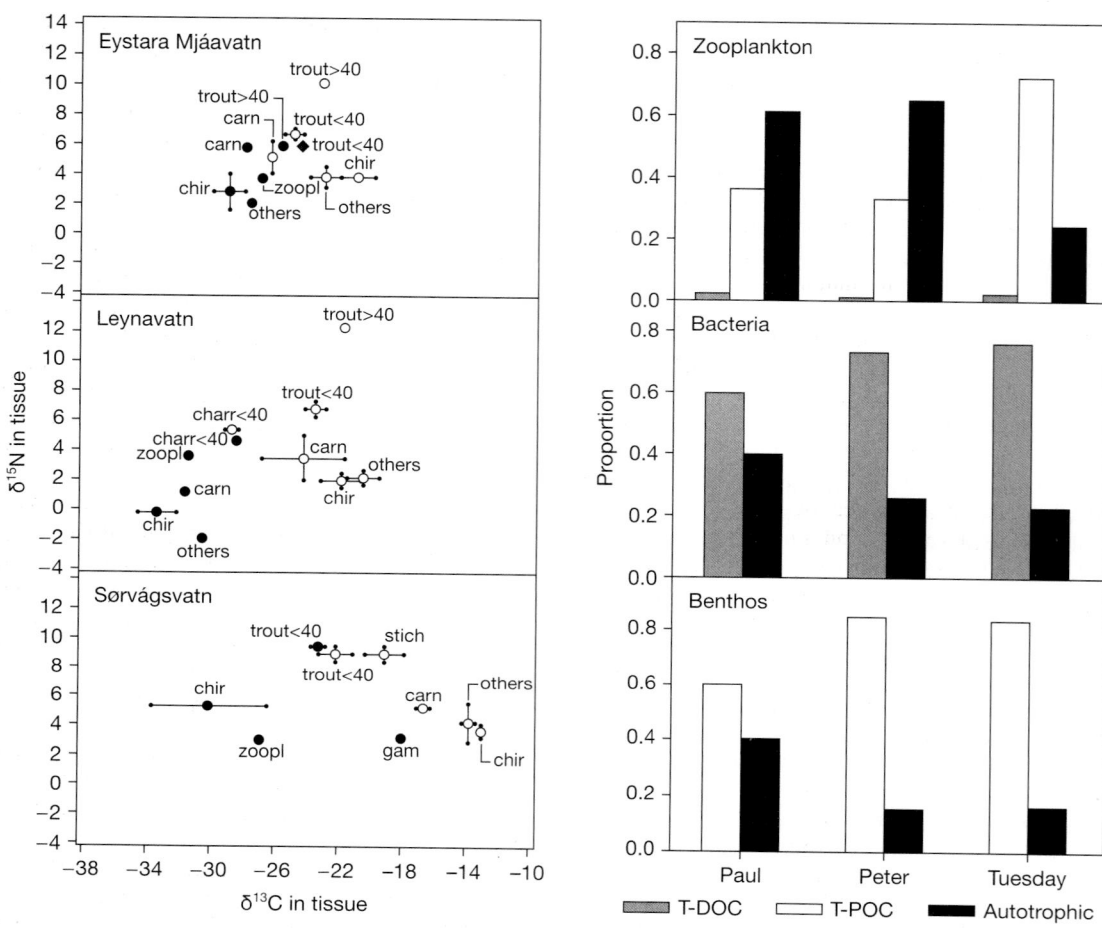

**Fig. 11.5** Evidence that catchment sources of carbon and energy may be very important for lakes is given by studies using the relative amounts of $^{13}$C in organic matter. They are often combined with studies of $^{15}$N to reveal position in the food web. On the left are data from three lakes in the Faeroe Islands (Jeppesen et al. 2002). The lower the value of $\delta^{13}$C, the more likely it is that terrestrial organic matter is being used. Values shown by dots are benthic organisms and their positions lie often towards the left (terrestrial sources). Open circles are planktonic or open-water samples and these often lie within the range that indicates support by terrestrial organic matter. They lie slightly more to the right, however, suggesting a greater component from photosynthesis within the lake. (Abbreviations: chir, chironomids; carn, carnivorous invertebrates; stick, sticklebacks; zoopl, zooplankton; gam, *Gammarus*). Data are given for trout greater or less than 40 cm in length. Values for $\delta^{15}$N tend to increase by 2–4 units for each step in a food chain. On the right are shown data for three lakes in the USA, where the $^{13}$C data have been used in equations to calculate the relative proportions of different food sources from terrestrial (T) dissolved and particulate carbon and from photosynthesis within the lake (autotrophic). The major contribution of terrestrial organic matter for bacteria in the plankton and for the benthic animals can be seen and substantial, though lesser, amounts are taken by the zooplankton. (Based on Cole et al. 2006.)

'oligotrophic', or 'low food' lakes and the second 'eutrophic' or 'high food'. In doing so they created the idea of distinctive lake types and a concept of two main types, oligotrophic and eutrophic that has dominated

the teaching of limnology and thinking within the subject ever since. The problem with it is that although the linkages within a lake perceived by Thienemann and Naumann do exist, they are linked with many other features in much more complex ways than Thienemann and Naumann first thought and if one wishes to think of lakes in groups with particular sets of characteristics, there are many more, indeed thousands more such groups than the two originally described. In fact there is a continuum of variation along many axes, and as more information has accumulated, the idea of lake types has been shown to be wrong. That does not mean that it cannot sometimes be a useful device in teaching and in water management, so long as its limitations are realized. Thienemann and Naumann in fact realized the problem almost immediately.

They knew of small lakes in the middle of peat bogs that had very brown water, coloured with organic matter derived from the surrounding peaty catchment, but with low amounts of nutrients and a sparse plankton. These lakes, set in organic basins, and very shallow, had deoxygenated hypolimnia despite the low plankton production and thus straddled the characteristics of eutrophic and oligotrophic lakes, but note, again with a set of linked characteristics that made logical sense. They solved the problem by creating a third type, the dystrophic lake. Thienemann then went on an expedition to examine the lakes of Indonesia in the tropics. These were often deep volcanic crater lakes and he found that the tropical forested catchments delivered very low loadings of nutrients to the lakes, so that the water was clear, the plankton was limited, as was the extent of the littoral zone, but they had deoxygenated hypolimnia and *Chironomus*. Again there was a mixture of eutrophic and oligotrophic characteristics and a logical explanation. The lakes were more or less permanently stratified under near equatorial conditions so even with a low amount of organic matter entering the hypolimnia each year; the whole oxygen reserve was progressively used up.

Thienemann's response was not to create yet another lake type, but to abandon the concept. Back in Europe, without the benefit of intercontinental travel, Naumann faced the same problem as he studied more lakes, but tried to solve it by creating more and more lake types and thus, in effect, laid the foundation for the idea that there is ultimately an infinity of types, without realizing it. A serious man, his frustrations were perhaps part of the reason why he shot himself in his forties, though nothing is nearly so simple.

Creating lake types is an easy exercise if you consider only a few characteristics that are inevitably closely related in a simple way in a limited geographical region, as Nauman and Thienemann did using nutrients, water clarity, amount of plankton and state of the hypolimnion in the Alps and around the Baltic Sea. Where it becomes meaningless is when you realize that there are actually thousands of characteristics each determining some aspect of the nature of the system. Table 11.2 gives a mere 100 for starters, but hidden within these are many others, particularly where biological variables are concerned. Each catchment and lake is unique, like every individual of a species. They exist in a continuum with as many axes as there are variables and such a hyperspace is difficult to envisage when we can only draw diagrams with three axes.

Modern statistical techniques can, however, take a large number of variables (though even modern computing power cannot cheaply handle thousands, even were the data to exist) from a set of lakes and calculate the similarity of the sets of data from each lake through techniques such as Principal Components Analysis. A two-dimensional diagram is then plotted showing a scatter of points, each of which represents one lake, between two axes, the principal components, which represent the main sources of variation, or determinants of the nature of each lake. The nature of the axes is interpreted from a knowledge of the data, as say, the availability of nutrients or the lake depth. The closer the points are to one another, the greater is the similarity of the lakes, and tight clusters would mean distinctive types. The more lakes and the more variables, the more likely it is that such clusters will not be apparent, however.

In Fig. 11.6 an example is shown for 32 small reservoirs in Ethiopia for which 17 variables were measured in the dry season. There is a little clustering among reservoirs that dry down nearly completely for part of the year, but otherwise no obvious pattern. The arrows are drawn using a second statistical technique, Canonical Correlation Analysis, which calculates the links among the environmental variables measured and shows their relative importance by the length of the arrow (short, relatively unimportant yet still significant, long, a major determinant). The direction of the arrow indicates first any positive correlation among the variables (the angle between the arrow directions is small), any negative correlation (the angle approaches $180°$, or none at all (they point at right angles). An arrow pointing to particular points suggests that the variable concerned is particularly important in determining the nature of these lakes. The set of lakes in Fig. 11.6 that dries down has pH, vegetation cover, suspended matter and conductivity in common.

**Table 11.2** A small selection of the variables that can influence the nature of lakes.

| | Characteristic | Influence |
|---|---|---|
| 1 | Catchment area | Water supply |
| 2 | Catchment shape | Water supply |
| 3 | Range of altitude in catchment | Water supply |
| 4 | Catchment geology | Water chemistry |
| 5 | Catchment soils | Water chemistry |
| 6 | Catchment vegetation | Water chemistry, organic matter supply |
| 7 | Large mammals in catchment | Erosion, edge effects on lake, nutrient input |
| 8 | Migratory birds | Nutrient inputs, grazing of swamps |
| 9 | Proximity to ocean | Water chemistry |
| 10 | Altitude of lake | Weather, accessibility to colonizers |
| 11 | Latitude of lake | Climate, water supply |
| 12 | Annual Precipitation | Water supply |
| 13 | Seasonality of precipitation | Water supply |
| 14 | Percentage of precipitation as snow | Water supply |
| 15 | Balance of groundwater to surface water in lake inflows | Water supply and chemistry |
| 16 | Annual mean temperature | Productivity |
| 17 | Seasonal distribution of temperature | Productivity |
| 18 | Evapotranspiration rate | Water chemistry, biodiversity |
| 19 | Mean wind speed | Stratification, nature of littoral |
| | Between year variability in temperature | Productivity |
| | Between year variability in precipitation | Water supply |
| | Between year variability in many other meteorological variables | Water supply, productivity |
| 20 | Period of ice cover | Growth season, under ice deoxygenation |
| 21 | Depth of snow over the lake ice | Productivity |
| 22 | Prevailing wind direction | Nature of littoral |
| 23 | Presence of natural barriers to fish on outflows | Fish community |
| 24 | Presence of swampy deltas on inflows | Water chemistry, turbidity |
| 25 | Area of lake | Mixing, biodiversity |
| 26 | Mean depth of lake | Mixing, productivity |
| 27 | Contour of the lake bed | Distribution of subhabitats |
| 28 | Shape of lake | Mixing, distribution of subhabitats |
| 29 | Regularity of the shoreline | Variety of littoral habitats |
| 30 | Nature of the shoreline | Variety of littoral habitats |
| 31 | Type of stratification | Productivity |
| 32 | Length of stratified period | Productivity |
| 33 | Stability of stratification | Productivity |
| 34 | Water colour | Productivity |
| 35 | Variety of organic matter entering from catchment | Productivity |
| 36 | Penetration of photosynthetically active radiation | Productivity |
| 37 | Inorganic solids in suspension | Productivity |
| 38 | Amount of incident ultraviolet radiation | Productivity, diversity |
| 39 | Day length | Productivity |
| 40 | Depth of epilimnion | Productivity |
| 41 | Volume of hypolimnion | Fish habitat availability |
| 42 | Degree of deoxygenation of hypolimnion | Nature of profundal benthos, fish habitat |
| 43 | Rate of deoxygenation of hypolimnion | Nature of profundal benthos, fish habitat |
| 44–51 | Content of major ions (H, Na, K, Mg, Ca, $HCO_3$, $SO_4$, Cl | Nature of biological community |
| 51–57 | Nutrient loading (N, P) and different species ($NO_3$, $NH_4$, $N_2$, organic N, organic P) | Productivity, nature of biological community |

**Table 11.2** (*Continued*)

| | Characteristic | Influence |
|---|---|---|
| 58–78 | Content of essential trace elements (about 20 of these) | Productivity, nature of biological community |
| 79 | Natural availability of toxic heavy metals | Nature of biological community |
| 80 | Proportion of lake as littoral zone | Productivity, fish diversity |
| 81 | Area of littoral emergent swamps | Productivity |
| 82 | Variety of dissolved organic compounds produced within the lake | Nature of biological, especially microbial, community |
| 83 | Nature of bed sediment | Nature of littoral and profundal benthos |
| 84 | Relationship of mixing depth to euphotic zone | Productivity |
| 85 | Age of lake | Biodiversity |
| 86 | Continuity of history | Biodiversity |
| 87 | Origin of lake basin | Biodiversity, productivity |
| 88 | Retention time of water mass | Productivity |
| 89 | Horizontal variation in water mass | Productivity |
| 90 | Seasonal variation in lake level | Nature of littoral, productivity |
| 91 | Regional biodiversity | Local biodiversity |
| 92 | Accessibility for colonization | Biodiversity |
| 93 | Floating plant coverage | Nature of littoral and profundal communities |
| 94 | Fish community | Nature of other communities and productivity |
| 95 | Piscivorous birds | Nature and biomass of fish community |
| 96 | Herbivorous birds | Nature and biomass of littoral communities |
| 97 | Available phytoplankters | Productivity |
| 98 | Available zooplankters | Productivity, water clarity |
| 99 | Available benthic invertebrates | Nature of profundal and littoral communities, productivity |
| 100 | Activities of traditional peoples | Nature and diversity of fish and littoral communities |

Lakes are each unique but some order needs to be imposed. Many of the variables given in Table 11.2 group into those linked with climate and weather, those linked with geology and water chemistry and those linked with the morphometry of the basin. A simple three-dimensional continuum can be envisaged using these groups of variables (Fig. 11.7). Sometimes there are distinctive patterns along one of these axes. Thus the nature of thermal stratification is linked with altitude and latitude through their influences on climate (Fig. 2.12) and there is a general gradient of increasing values of many major ions and nutrients along the geological axis, and of size along the morphometric axis. However, those who might like to distinguish say 'tropical' lake types from 'temperate' will have the same problem of Thienemann in Indonesia. Although there is a reasonably clear relationship along the climate axis, with many implications for the nature of the lakes, there is no simple latitudinal relationship with geology or morphometry.

Figure 11.7 embodies the idea of continuous variation. The characteristics of any catchment–lake system can be described by any point in the three-dimensional space and there is an infinity of such points. Drawing a boundary around part of the space is what is done in trying to designate lake types, and this might be useful in emphasizing closeness of relationships among different lakes, so long as it is realized that the boundary can only be drawn arbitrarily. This solves a particular problem in teaching using lake types. A visit to any lake to demonstrate say the characteristics of a 'eutrophic' or 'oligotrophic' lake will reveal some characteristics that do not quite fit the model shown in many text books and the instructor will generally try to rationalize away such difficulties. This can be confusing until it is realized that it is the model that is wrong not the lake.

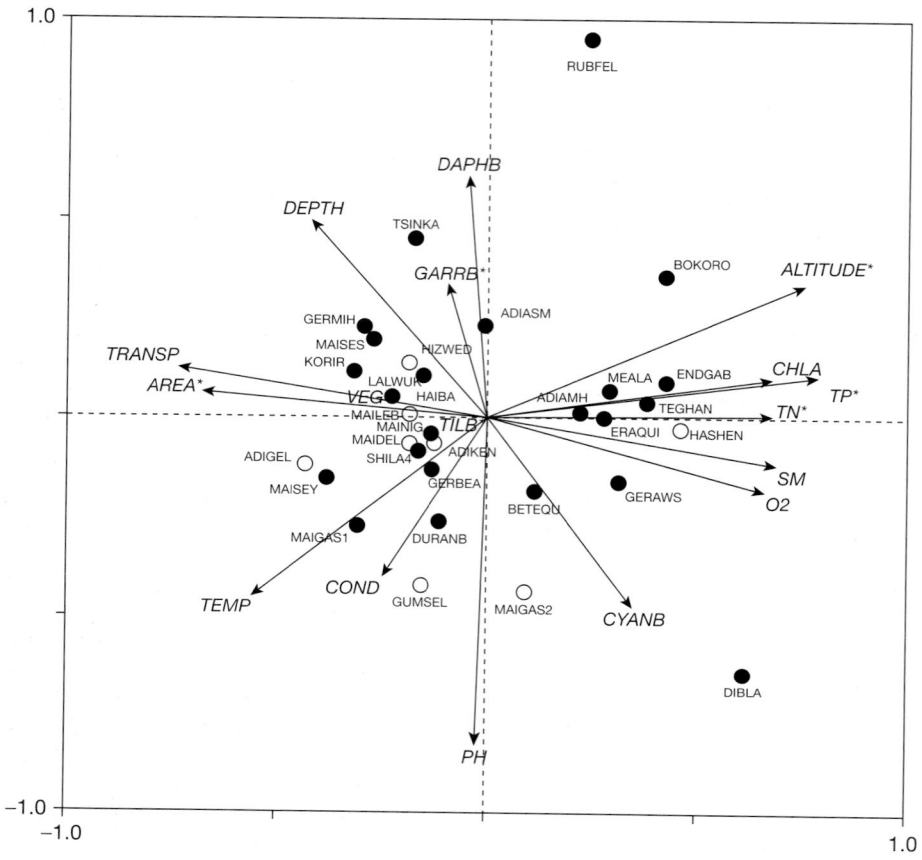

**Fig. 11.6** Data on 17 variables were taken from reservoir lakes in the Tigray District of Ethiopia and used in a principal components analysis that calculates the relationships among the lakes. Solid symbols are lakes with permanent water; open symbols are lakes that tend to dry up in the dry season. The positions of the symbols indicating lakes show their relationships with one another. Clusters would indicate close similarity within the group, but it is clear that they are not greatly clustered and each shows a high degree of individuality. Arrows show the importance of variables in determining the nature of the lakes. The longer the arrow the more important the variable and lakes positioned in the direction of the arrow are most influenced by that variable. Abbreviations: DAPHB, *Daphnia* biomass; CHLa, chlorophyll *a*; TP, total phosphorus; TN, total nitrogen; SM, suspended matter; O2, oxygen concentration; CYANB, biomass of Cyanobacteria; COND, conductivity; TEMP, temperature; TRANSP, transparency. (Based on Dejenie et al. 2009.)

The issue of lake types versus continuous variation has practical consequences. Developed societies have created problems for lakes of nutrient pollution (eutrophication), acidification, toxic pollution, modification of the hydrology and morphometry, overexploitation (overfishing) and introduction of alien species, just as they have for river systems. The European Community Water Framework Directive (Chapter 7) in an attempt to ameliorate this situation uses the concept of types

rather than continua as a framework for action in using typologies (see Section 8.12).

This return to the concept of lake types (the word ecotype is used in the Directive) is so that high quality reference conditions can determined for groups of lakes (and rivers, estuaries and coastal waters) rather than for individual bodies. There is an important difference, however, from the lake types originally envisaged by Nauman and Thieneman. The latter used features that

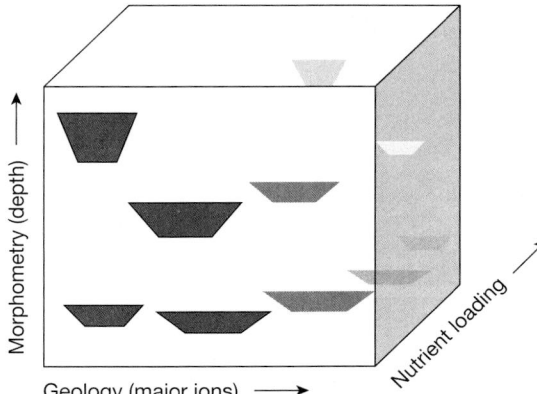

**Fig. 11.7** A simple depiction of the continua among lakes. The thousands of variables that affect lake systems have been condensed into three: one representing size and hydrology (e.g. depth), one representing the catchment geology as the major ion content of the water (Chapter 3) and one the availability of the key nutrients (Chapter 4). Two further equally important dimensions, climate and time since formation or disturbance, cannot be depicted. Each lake is very slightly different from the next and has a unique location within the continuum. There might be some general linkage between the axes such that deep infertile lakes are more likely in igneous terrain, shallow fertile ones in subdued, soft-rock topography.

are influenced by human impact, such as nutrient availability as well as those that are not, such as depth and major ion concentrations. The essence of dealing with the requirements of the Water Framework Directive is that the types should be defined by geographical features that are unchanging and separate from the features that reflect ecological quality. Thus the lake types are to be determined on features such as latitude, altitude, area, mean depth, general geology of the catchment (igneous rocks, sedimentary rocks, peat). The scope of the problem can be illustrated by simply taking four latitude bands of $10°$ covering Europe (though the Directive suggests using over 20 geographic regions), three altitude bands to cover everything from sea level to the high Alps, four areas using a logarithmic scale of 1, 10, 100 and >1000 $km^2$, three depths of 1, 10 and 100 m and the three categories of catchment geology. Even this relatively coarse scheme would give a total of 436 'types', for which reference high-quality conditions must be decided so that standards can be set for good quality. In practice,

many fewer types are being proposed. Table 11.3 gives a proposed system that is likely to be used, but it gives a very coarse separation.

The problem is compounded when the many variables that must be considered in determining ecological quality are considered. The Directive states that for lakes, the general physico-chemical conditions (temperature, nutrients, oxygen), the levels of potential pollutants, the hydrology and morphometry, the nature of the bed and edge, the community compositions and amounts of phytoplankton, larger plants (macrophytes), benthic invertebrates and fish must all be included. Minimally, this means at least 40 variables to be stipulated for each lake type. Not surprisingly, the governments of member states, through their environment agencies are facing many problems in doing this and are attempting to circumvent the stipulations of the Directive to meet the 2015 deadline. They are helped by the fact that water bodies under 50 ha need not be considered, nor do zooplankton, owing to a peculiar omission in the Directive's wording. Unfortunately for the improvement of freshwater habitats in general, most of the water bodies of Europe are probably smaller than 50 ha and they contain a significant proportion of the biodiversity that is supposed to be being conserved; and zooplankton, as will be seen in Chapter 13 are particularly important in determining the ecological nature of lakes. This rather unsatisfactory situation undoubtedly has arisen from a drawing up of the legislation without proper involvement of professional limnologists who could have pointed out the difficulties that would arise and solved many of the problems with a rather different approach.

## 11.7 LAKE HISTORY

We tend to forget that things change; that we will not live forever. So it is with lakes (and rivers too). They are not permanent features of the landscape, and nor is the nature of the landscape unchanging. Each lake had a finite origin, has a history and will eventually disappear. Millions already have gone and have left evidence of their existence in layers of now dry sediment; all existing ones are recording their history in the sediment being laid down in them from materials washed in from their catchments and produced within them. The existence of a lake at a given time and place means that water was then at least sufficiently plentiful; this is obvious, but it is the converse, that its

**Table 11.3** Proposed lake classification system for use in the Water Framework Directive. The system is incomplete as it was still being developed by a working group (ECOSTAT) of the European Union at the time of writing and being arbitrary will be changed as much for convenience as reality, but it gives a flavour of the approach. Country abbreviations are: IE, Ireland; UK, United Kingdom; AT, Austria; DE, Germany; IT, Italy; BE, Belgium; DK, Denmark; EE, Estonia; FR, France; HU, Hungary; LT, Lithuania; LV, Latvia; NL, Netherlands; PL, Poland; RO, Roumania; CY, Cyprus; FI, Finland; ES, Spain; SE, Sweden; NO, Norway.

| Region | Countries where found | Lake type | Altitude (m) | Mean depth (m) | Surface area (km²) | Alkalinity (meq L⁻¹) | Total organic carbon (humic level) (mg C L⁻¹) |
|---|---|---|---|---|---|---|---|
| Atlantic | IE, UK | A1 | 0–200 | 3–15 | <0.5 | >1.0 | |
| | | A2 | 0–200 | 3–15 | >0.5 | >1.0 | |
| | | A3 | 0–200 | 3–15 | <0.5 | >1.0 | 5–15 |
| Alpine | AT, DE, IT | AL3 | 0–200 | >15 | >0.5 | 0.2->1.0 | |
| | | AL4 | 200–800 | 3–15 | >0.5 | 0.2->1.0 | |
| Central Baltic | BE, DK, DE, EE, FR, HU, LT, LV, NL, PL, RO, UK | CB1 | 0–200 | 3–15 | | >1.0 | |
| | | CB2 | 0–200 | <3 | | >1.0 | |
| | | CB3 | 0–200 | 3–15 | | 0.2–1.0 | |
| Mediterranean | CY, ES, IT, RO | M1 | 0–200 | 3–15 | >0.5 | >1.0 | |
| | | M5 | 0–200 | >15 | >0.5 | <1.0 | |
| | | M7 | 200–800 | >15 | >0.5 | <1.0 | |
| | | M8 | 200–800 | >15 | >0.5 | >1.0 | |
| Northern | FI, IE, NO, SE, UK | N1 | 0–200 | 3–15 | >0.5 | 0.2–1.0 | 0–5 |
| | | N2a | 0–200 | 3–15 | >0.5 | <0.2 | 0–5 |
| | | N2b | 0–200 | >15 | >0.5 | <0.2 | 0–5 |
| | | N3a | 0–200 | 3–15 | >0.5 | <0.2 | 5–15 |
| | | N3b | 0–200 | 3–15 | >0.5 | <0.2 | >15 |
| | | N5 | 200–800 | 3–15 | >0.5 | <0.2 | 0–5 |
| | | N6a | 200–800 | 3–15 | >0.5 | <0.2 | 5–15 |
| | | N6b | 200–800 | 3–15 | >0.5 | <0.2 | >15 |
| | | N7 | >800 | 3–15 | >0.5 | <0.2 | 0–5 |
| | | N8a | 0–200 | 3–15 | >0.5 | 0.2–1.0 | 5–15 |
| | | N8b | 0–200 | 3–15 | >0.5 | 0.2–1.0 | >15 |

passing may mean that climate has changed that is of great interest to climatologists who use ancient lake deposits to reconstruct this.

### 11.7.1 The methods of palaeolimnology

Recreating the past history of a lake from its sediments (palaeolimnology, Fig. 11.8) is a fascinating piece of detective work because the evidence is always incomplete. Some things are not preserved, others are abundant, and wisdom has to be applied in interpreting such evidence. A range of new techniques, however, gives more and more sorts of evidence.

Sediment, or mud to most people, does not look very interesting at first. It is grey, black or brown, usually without any obvious layering, though sometimes paired annual layers (varves), one for spring, one for summer may be laid down in anaerobic hypolimnia where there is little disturbance by benthic invertebrates. The spring layer reflects the inorganic material brought in by snow melt, the summer one organic matter and marl laid down by activities within the lake. In shallow, acid lakes with bog vegetation (see Chapter 12) there may be more structured peat, for acid conditions inhibit decomposition of organic matter. Within even the often-amorphous goo, however, is a wealth of organic chemical indicators, including

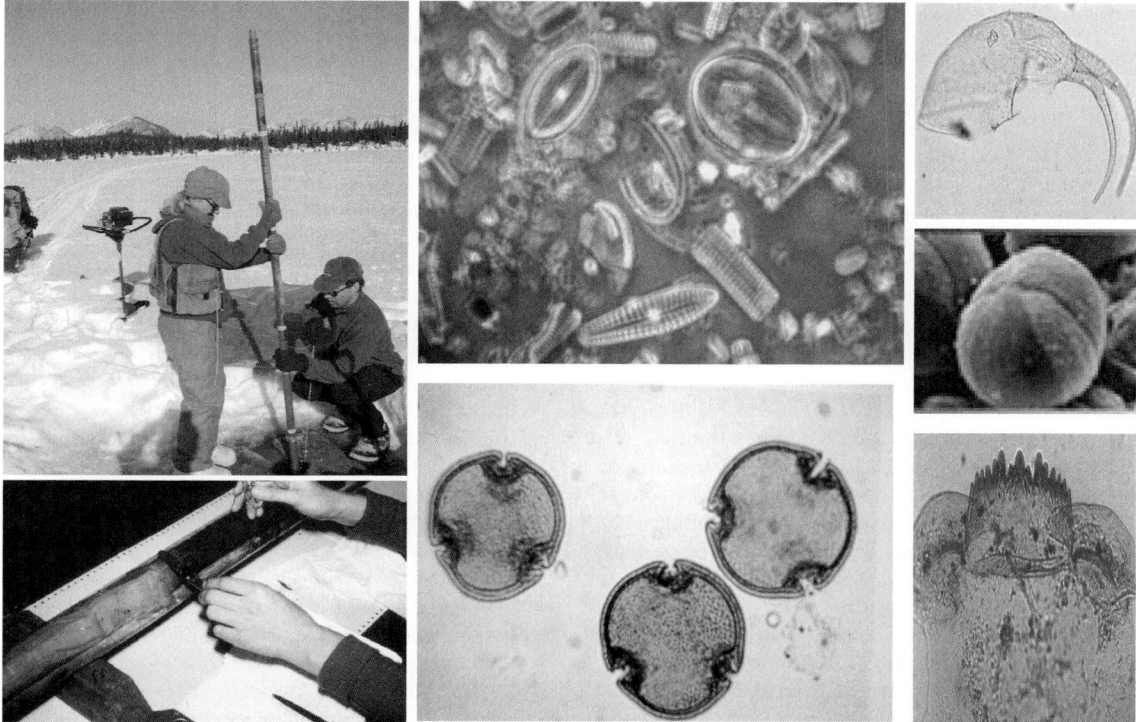

**Fig. 11.8** Palaeolimnology involves first the taking of cores from lakes (left top), the sectioning of the cores (left bottom) then the preparation of the sediment for analysis. Useful fossils are diatoms (middle top), pollen grains, middle lower, and remains of zooplankters, seeds and insect mouth parts (right top to bottom).

photosynthetic pigments that can be traced to different vegetation types and structures of algae, plants and animals. There is also a whole suite of inorganic compounds that can be measured including carbonate, total nitrogen and total phosphorus that may give indications of changing production, and of other elements that may give information on changes in erosion of the catchment or of past pollution by air or water. Carbon particles from power station soots have proved particularly useful in detecting evidence of air pollution.

The first step, however, is to obtain a core of sediment and date representative layers within it. The simplest corer comprises a piece of plastic drainpipe. If the water and mud are both shallow, this can simply be pushed into the deposit until it penetrates the basin material and then pulled up. Success depends on the basin material and sediment sticking in the tube! For deeper water or deeper sediments, more sophisticated

devices are needed that operate by drawing the sediment up against a piston or by forcing the coring tube downwards using compressed air. Very recent, sloppy sediments can be sampled by lowering a freeze corer into them. Freeze corers are boxes filled with solid carbon dioxide and alcohol. The corer is lowered quickly into the surface sediment and the sediment freezes onto the outer faces with its vertical layering intact. It can then be retrieved in an orderly manner whilst still frozen.

Sediment can be dated by several methods, mostly using radioactive isotopes. These usually involve measurement of concentrations of an isotope thought to be produced at a constant rate on Earth and of a derivative formed at a known rate ($a$) from its decay. The time ($t$) during which an amount $A_0$ has decayed to $A$ is the age of the sediment and is given by:

$$A = A_0 e^{-at}$$

and its derivative:

$$t = a^{-1} \log_e (A_0/A)$$

Choice of isotope depends on the estimated age of the sediment. The older the sediment, the longer must the half-life (the time taken for half of a given initial amount to decay) be to ensure that it can still be detected. For sediments up to about 30,000 years old, the $^{14}C$ method can be used and for those up to about 150 years a method using $^{210}Pb$ is useful. Very ancient sediments can be dated using isotopes derived from natural uranium decay.

The $^{14}C$ method is not usable for recent (<200 year) sediments, since the burning of ancient fossil fuels with various and very low $^{14}C/^{12}C$ ratios has upset the previously assumed constant ratio of $10^{-12}$ in the atmosphere. In fact this ratio has never been entirely constant and dates are corrected for this by utilizing an absolute dating method using tree ring counts. By use of a series of fossil, archaeological and recent wood samples, overlapping in age, so that the patterns in thickness of the growth rings can be matched, an absolute chronology has been constructed against which $^{14}C$ dates, which are more easily measured, can be compared over several thousands of years.

Radiometry is expensive. Other methods that are cheaper, if less versatile, are also available. The Earth's magnetic field has changed in both its horizontal and vertical components (declination and inclination) in past times and a record kept in London since before AD 1600 shows a change in declination through some 30° since then. Some minerals, laid down in lake sediments, become magnetized in the direction of the Earth's field at the time they are deposited and some of this magnetization, the remanent, persists, even when the field direction of the Earth changes. The remanent direction of magnetization can be measured in core slices, kept orientated relative to a fixed line on the corer tube, with a sensitive magnetometer and then plotted against depth in the sediment column. An oscillation in recent sediments, from east to west and back, has been discovered and compares well with records kept at the London Observatory. For older sediments, comparison with $^{14}C$ dates shows an oscillation in declination with a period of about 2800 years, with the west and east peaks being contemporary for different lakes. The pattern of remanent magnetization may therefore give a timescale for other lakes where $^{14}C$ dating at frequent positions in the core proves too expensive.

Varves can be simply counted. The paired layers can be shown to be annual from spring and summer tree pollen in the appropriate members of each pair and cores can be dated by counting the pairs. Such visual varving is unusual, however. Varving detectable by more sophisticated methods may be commoner. X-ray photography of thin longitudinal sections of cores from Lake Washington has shown prominent dense bands, which are not themselves annual, but their finer striations may be. Similar examination with a stereo-scan electron microscope has shown fine bands of diatom fossils with pairs of layers characterized by spring and autumn species.

Ash falls (tephra) from volcanic eruptions may result in distinctive sediment layers. If there is a historic record of the eruption, the layer can be dated. A more recent but similar marker comes from the detection in the sediments of radioisotopes that do not occur naturally but which have been made and discharged from human activities. The isotopes, $^{137}Cs$ and $^{241}Am$ were first introduced into the atmosphere in about 1954 from nuclear weapons testing. Their amounts were greatest in 1962–63 then declined. A new peak appeared in 1986 following an accident at Chernobyl, a Russian nuclear reactor, which released isotopes to the atmosphere. Detection of peaks of these isotopes in the sediments thus gives the dates for the 1954, 1963 and 1986 sediment layers.

### 11.7.2 Organic remains

Analysis of the carbon skeletons of sediment organic compounds is useful, because alkanes between $C_{23}$ and $C_{33}$ appear characteristic of higher plants, $C_{31}$ is predominant in acid peat and $C_{27}$ and $C_{29}$ in base-rich forest soils. Changes in the vegetation of the catchment may thus be detected in sediments and the information used to complement or further interpret pollen counts (see later). Pigments are well preserved in anaerobic sediments. Catchment vegetation contributes little pigment to the sediment because the litter has been long exposed to the air before it reaches the lake bed, but pigments produced by lake algae and plants have a greater chance of preservation. Extraction of chlorophyll derivatives and carotenoids with methanol or acetone, chromatography to separate them, and subsequent measurement by spectrophotometry thus helps confirm phases of changing fertility and communities in the lake.

The carotenoids of different algal groups are often specific and indeed are used to help classify the algal divisions. Detection of particular pigments in sediments may then indicate changes in abundance of particular algal groups in the history of a lake. This technique has been applied to myxoxanthophyll and oscillaxanthin, which occur only in the cyanobacteria (blue-green algae). Some pigments are decomposed more rapidly than others, particularly fucoxanthin, diatoxanthin and diadinoxanthin, which characterize diatoms and dinoflagellates. Changes in abundance of these organisms are thus difficult to detect by these methods. But fortunately, diatoms leave morphological fossils. As well as blue-green algal pigments, those of green algae preserve well and β–carotene, which is common to many groups, gives a reasonable overall index of changing photosynthetic production.

Many algal and plant structures are preserved in sediments. They include the heterocysts and sometimes whole filaments of cyanobacteria, colonies of the green algae *Pediastrum* and *Botryococcus*, the silica walls of diatoms and the silicified scales and cysts of Chrysophyta, pollen from higher plants in the lake, its catchment area and perhaps further afield, lignified cells such as sclereids, fibres and xylem vessels, leaf fragments and seeds from aquatic plants. Animal remains include the tests of certain amoebae, sponge spicules, bryozoan statoblasts, exoskeletons of Cladocera and other small Crustacea, mollusc shells, head capsules and mouth parts of dipteran larvae, mite exuviae and even an occasional fish scale. In acid peats, near complete human bodies, sometimes ritually murdered and placed in bogs or bog lakes, where the acid medium preserves all but the bones, have been found, but these are rare.

Because of the closer relationship that algae and plants, rather than animals, have with the physicochemical environment, it is generally easiest to interpret the meaning of fossils of algae, particularly diatoms, and of pollen. The former give information mostly about the lake itself, the latter about its catchment. The occurrence of particular animals reflects to a large extent their competitive and predatory relationships and to some extent these can be reconstructed using knowledge of how predation is size-selective for prey, and the transfer functions described later.

Diatom cell walls have patterns (Fig. 11.8) that characterize particular species. They have been studied for a long time and considerable reconstruction of past environments is possible from an analysis of the diatoms in sediments. Permanent microscope slides of diatom walls can easily be prepared following oxidization of the sediment with hydrogen peroxide or nitric acid. The residual diatoms are resuspended in distilled water before being dried onto a slide and mounted in high refractive index mountant.

From the diatom species, much can be deduced about the balance of planktonic (Chapter 13), and littoral (Chapter 12) communities and hence about changes, for example, in water depth and the abundance of plant beds. Certain genera, such as *Eunotia* and *Frustulia*, are characteristic of base-poor water and some species, such as *Aulacosira granulata*, of more fertile conditions. There are distinct marine and freshwater species and some indicators of brackish conditions. In African lakes, *Navicula elkab* and *Nitzschia frustulum* characterize saline inland waters and may be used in sediment analyses to recognize drops in lake level and periods of endorheicity.

Diatoms have been used to trace changes in the pH of waters believed to have been acidified, and to help distinguish between rival theories of the cause of the acidification (Chapter 8). Careful taxonomy is necessary and study of contemporary lakes suggests that some species are associated with very high (alkaliphilic) or very low (acidophilic) pH. Others are associated with neutrality (circumneutral) whilst intermediates (acidobiontic and alkalibiontic) are also found. An index that compresses information on the characteristics of all the species from a lake can be calculated. For example index B of Renberg & Hellberg (1982) is based on counts of the species present and calculations of the percentages of each group of the total counted:

$$\text{Index B} = \frac{\% \text{ circumneutral} + 5 \times \% \text{ acidophilic} + 40 \times \& \text{ acidobiontic}}{\% \text{ circumneutral} + 3.5 \times \% \text{ alkaliphilic} + 108 \times \& \text{ alkalibiontic}}$$

The index can be related to the pH of lake water by regression of the measured pH against counts made from the diatoms in the contemporary sediment. For example in a series of 33 lakes in southern Scotland:

$$\text{pH (log units)} = 6.3 - 0.86 \log (\text{Index B})$$
$$(r^2 = 0.82, P < 0.001)$$

Changes in pH can then be calculated from measures of the index obtained from a sequence of sediments.

Such indices have recently been refined to remove the partly subjective judgement involved in classifying a species as acidophilous or circumneutral, etc. The new methods do not require such prior ecological classification and can be applied to any variable that influences the occurrence (not necessarily growth) of the species. The method, using weighted averaging, assumes that each species has an abundance that is related to the environmental variable in a Gaussian way. This means that it will be most abundant at some optimal value and decreasingly less abundant with increasing or decreasing values of the variable to each side of the optimum. A large set of lakes is sampled for the variable concerned, and the relative abundance of each species is measured in living samples or contemporary sediments.

The optimum for each species, $U_k$ can then be calculated from:

$$U_k = \Sigma ( y_{ik} \cdot X_i ) / \Sigma y_{ik}$$

where $x_i$ is the value of the variable in lake $i$ and $y_{ik}$ is the abundance of species $k$ in lake $i$. This establishes optima for each of a large number of species in what is called the training set. The diatom assemblage of a particular sediment layer in the same set or a lake broadly similar to those in the set (judged by its sharing a significant number of species) is then determined and the value of the variable, $x_i$, associated with the conditions under which the assemblage was laid down, is calculated from:

$$x_i = \Sigma ( y_{ik} \cdot U_k ) / \Sigma y_{ik}$$

The method, called the transfer function method, can theoretically be used to reconstruct any variable that can be measured and which is somehow linked with a group of fossils. Thus phosphorus and nitrogen concentrations, salinity and pH can be determined from diatoms, and fish stocks (at least in a general way) from the sizes of cladoceran carapaces because fish select the larger individuals of Cladocera when they feed (Chapter 13). Its sensitivity is likely to be greatest with variables such as pH which are well correlated with species distribution and which express a huge range of variation in the variable concerned. A change in one pH unit represents a tenfold change in hydrogen ion concentration. Where variables that have a more limited arithmetic rather than geometric range are concerned, the precision of the calculations possible from weighted averaging is likely to be much lower though still valuable in showing relative changes.

The use of pollen preserved in peat and lake sediments has a distinguished history and has formed the basis for recognition that climate has changed greatly over periods of only thousands of years. The walls of many pollen grains are of resistant waxes ('sporopollenin'). Grains may be concentrated and

separated from sediment samples by digestion with hydrofluoric acid. Genera, and often species, are easily recognizable, though grass pollens, for example, are not easily separable to species. However, major changes in catchment vegetation can be detected. Agricultural activity is recorded by the appearance of the pollen of characteristic annual herbs that accompany cultivation and evidence of deforestation may be found by a complementary decrease in tree pollen.

### 11.7.3 General problems of interpretation of evidence from sediment cores

Jack Vallentyne, in 1969, wrote that 'no anatomist or physiologist in his right mind would ever base a study of the life history of an organism on the analysis of its accumulated faeces. This is, however, precisely the position of a palaeolimnologist with respect to the developmental history of a lake. Sediments are lacustrine faeces, the residue remaining after lake metabolism'. It is therefore wise to examine some of the problems of handling sediment data before considering interpretations from particular lakes.

Sediment is not necessarily deposited uniformly nor are fossils deposited evenly. Benthic animals also may mix the surface sediments as they form, evening out annual variations into a sort of moving average and smoothing long-term trends. In general diatoms are preserved well but there is some selectivity because silicates are more soluble at high pH and thin walls are easily broken by grazers. In deep lakes only a fraction of the diatom wall silica reaches the permanent sediment and dissolution may occur in the surface sediments of shallow lakes, particularly in alkaline waters. The bicarbonate-rich layers of meromictic lakes may allow little or no preservation. Long, thin diatoms, for example *Synedra* and *Asterionella*, break easily by abrasion with inorganic particles or in invertebrate guts, and may then more easily be redissolved. Some thin-walled genera, for example *Rhizosolenia* are rarely preserved at all. Comparisons between the main components of diatom assemblages laid down in dated recent sediments and counts made on the living community for the same period, however, often show a very close correspondence though the correlation might be expected to decrease as the sediments age.

Perhaps the greatest problem, however, is in the way the results are expressed. Early workers often calculated the percentage representation of a particular species or group of fossils in their total count from a sediment sample of undetermined weight. This gave relative changes in frequency. Thus a decrease in frequency of a species A would inevitably result in increases in frequency of other species. The reality, in absolute terms, could have been one of a variety of scenarios in which A may have decreased or increased or stayed the same as others changed. An improvement has been the expression of absolute counts on the basis of per unit weight of sediment, because this gives some indication of absolute changes if the sedimentation rate has been constant.

However, where sedimentation rates have changed, an absolute increase in a species may have been accompanied by a decrease in its numbers per unit weight of sediment, if it has been diluted by sediment from other sources. The only reliable way of expressing results is thus in terms of amount laid down per unit area of lake bed per year which needs a comprehensive dating of the core. This is expensive and has not been done in detail for most cores. All these limitations should be borne in mind in considering results from particular lakes, which will illustrate some of the features of lake development.

### 11.7.4 So what has the history been? Two ancient lakes

In western Egypt, at around 25°30′N, the Dakhleh oasis has seen the presence of man for 500,000 years, at first to hunt prey and to collect particular rocks for tools, later, from around 2300 BC to host settlements of the Egyptian dynasties, then the Romans, Christians and Ottomans. Yet it is presently set, at the foot of the Libyan plateau, in a rocky desert and what agriculture is possible now depends on deep boreholes mining ground water, for the local precipitation is virtually zero. It is unlikely that the oasis would have formed the focus of such settlements had it not previously have been well watered and so it has. Ridges of soft calcareous rocks (Fig. 11.9), called yardangs, formerly laid down in springs deriving water from the local limestones and lake sediments, lie around the basins of

**Fig. 11.9** Yardangs in Libya. The raised features are the remains of lake sediments laid down in past wetter climates, but now left dry and eroded by wind. (Photograph by C.S. Churcher.)

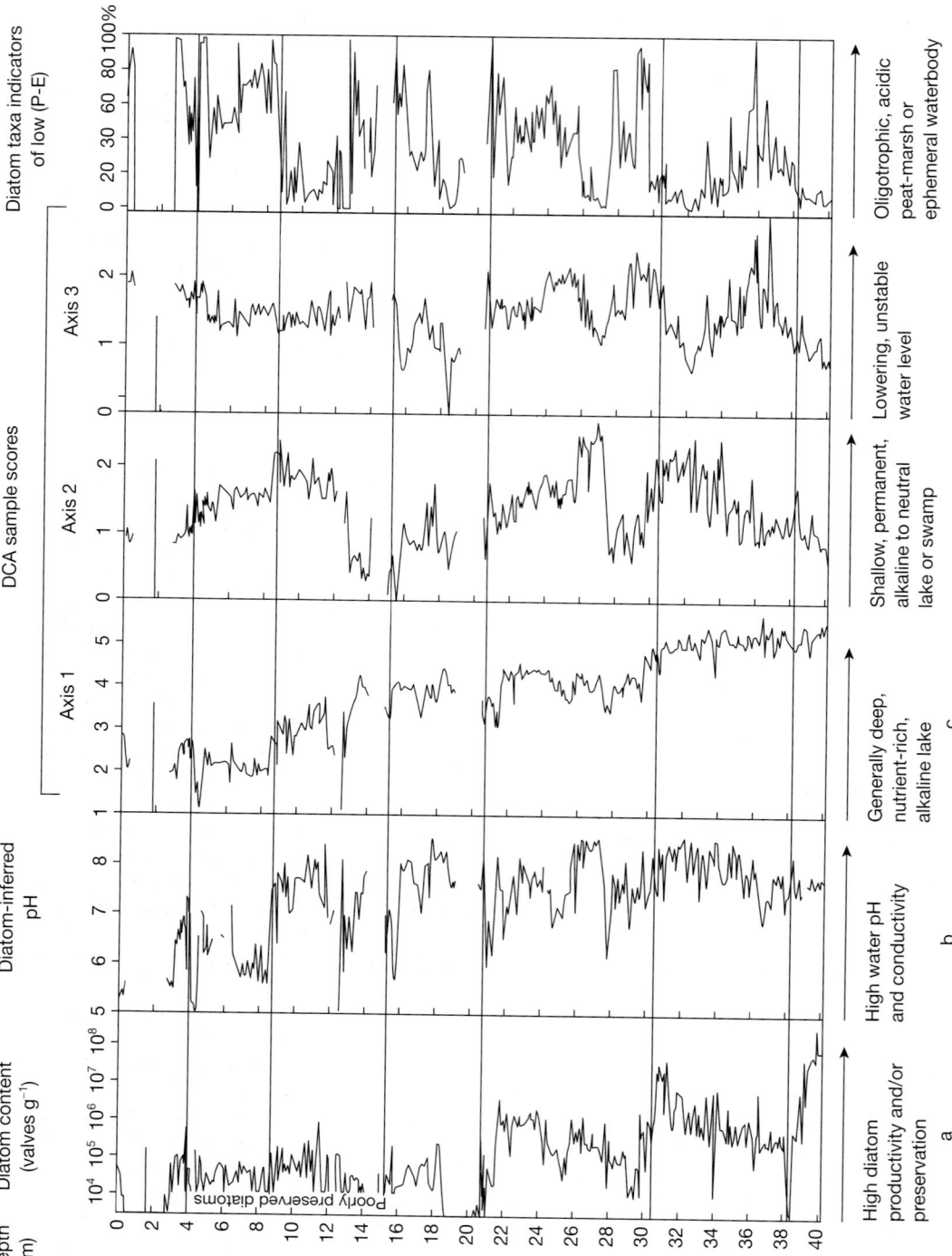

**Fig. 11.10** Lake Tritrivakeley is an ancient lake in Madagascar, whose 40 m of sediments have been examined and the results summarized in this diagram. The labels on the axes indicate the interpretations that can be put on trends in the graphs, which are of statistical treatments to the original data using transfer functions (reconstruction of pH) or detrended correspondence analysis (DCA) to combine the effects of groups of variables, or use of indicator species of diatoms to show the relative wetness (precipitation, P; evaporation, E). Horizontal lines show times of major change, caused by climate cycles, over the general trend of shallowing of the lake as sediments accumulated. (From Gasse & Van Campo 2001.)

the ancient lakes Kellis and Balat. They are now wind eroded and cut about by rare flash floods, but form part of the basins of lakes in the area from around 200,000 to 300,000 to 5000 years ago.

In them are found the shells of two freshwater snails, *Limnaea stagnalis* and *Planorbis planorbis*, much preserved plant matter from reeds or papyrus, and the bones of mammals that require daily or at least very regular supplies of freshwater, including warthog, hippopotamus, extinct species of camel and buffalo, topi, two species of gazelle, Cape zebra, antelopes similar to impala and dik-dik, and hyaena. Remains of mallard, ostrich, crane, turnstone and long-tailed duck, and of monitor lizards and a small turtle, testify to the same conclusion. For millennia, this area was a lake district surrounded by savannahs. Older rocks in the area, including the late Cretaceous Mut Formation of black, leafy shales that collapse to mud with water has revealed lungfish, crocodiles and sharks. And more recent petroglyphs, art inscribed into the sandstone rocks, depict similar water-dependent, savannah animals. The lakes have disappeared by now but the current desert is of recent origin.

In the highlands of Madagascar, in a volcanic crater 1778 m above sea level and now surrounded by cultivated fields and remnants of scrubby forest is a tiny lake, now only 1–2 m deep, Lake Tritrivakeley, but underneath it are 40 m of sediment (Fig. 11.10) accumulated over the past 150,000 years from the catchment, from eruptions of nearby volcanoes and from production in the lake. Analysis of the nature of the sediments and fossil pollen shows that the lake has undergone six cycles of warming and cooling, reflected in changes in vegetation. In each cycle this changed from a heathy vegetation of Ericaceae and arboreal composites, such as the tree *Senecios* now to be seen near the tops of the highest mountains of Africa, to an open dry grassland with scattered fire-resistant trees, to a taller, denser forest, eventually dominated by *Podocarpus* clad in festoons of lichens, and then back to heathy vegetation again, as the cycle went from cool to warm to cool. The cycles reflect small changes in the orbit of the Earth around the Sun that are also linked with the waves of glaciation over the late Pleistocene and Holocene periods of the Earth's recent history.

Over the entire period of 150,000 years, the lake became progressively shallower as sediments accumulated, and changes in the diatom fossils show that the lake moved from a plankton-dominated system, with water up to more than 100 m deep, to a shallow marsh at present. It accumulated the pollen first of submerged plants such as *Aponogeton*, as it shallowed and could support a larger littoral zone, then of emergent bog plants in recent centuries as it became almost entirely covered with vegetation. It also became less productive as each cycle became slightly drier, reflecting a reduction in the amplitude of changes in the Earth's orbit between cycles. This influenced the intensity of the monsoon rains with lesser rains bringing in lower amounts of nutrients. But it reflected each climate cycle too by its own cycle of water-level change, with periods when no diatoms were preserved suggesting that the lake had dried out completely during the hottest periods, when the water also became more saline.

### 11.7.5 Younger lakes

Each of these studies tells of long periods of change and eventually of loss of the lakes, but not a great deal of the first stages; each also is highly localized. But if the deserts of Egypt can have had lakes, almost anywhere on Earth can have had them given sufficiently wet climates in the past, and indeed has had them. At present, our focus tends to be on the recently formed lakes of the north temperate regions, which originated only 10,000 or 12,000 years ago. They too have sediments, though only a few metres, compared with the tens or hundreds of metres of ancient lakes in the subtropics and tropics, but they can give us some insights into what happens as lakes form, and some pointers as to how they develop into changing ecosystems.

Naumann and Thienemann (see above), and many others, were all very much convinced in the early 20th century, that once a lake had formed it not only steadily filled in with sediment, but became more and more eutrophic as it did so. It was a logical view. One might expect nutrients to accumulate with time as more and more water flows in and as the sediments built up and the lake shallowed. The extension of the plants of the littoral zone not only corresponded with Naumann's and Thieneman's concept of a eutrophic lake, but gave the impression of a rising productivity. It was such an attractive idea that it has persisted to the present day. But like the idea of lake types (see above) it was misleading. Lakes do sometimes become more fertile with time, but only if the climate changes in such a way that more nutrients are supplied, or if human activities contribute them. If climate remains steady, the story for pristine lakes is one of an initial fertile phase followed

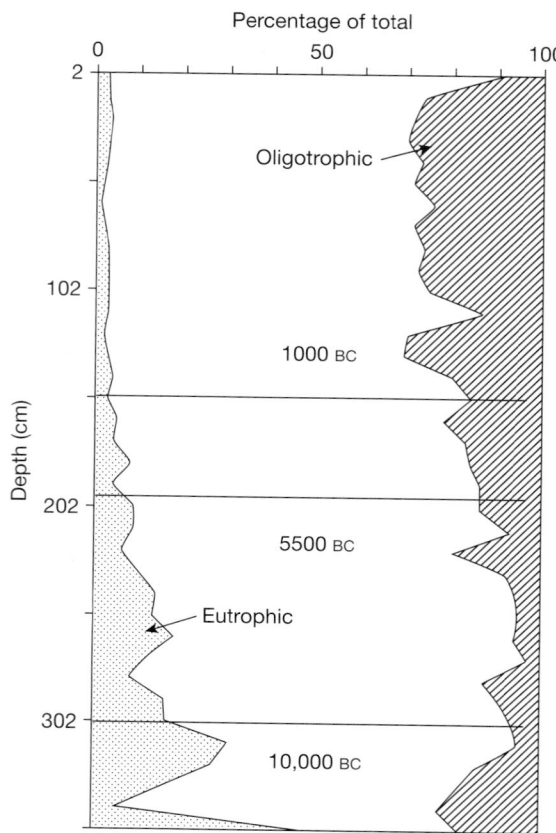

**Fig. 11.11** Blea Tarn is a small lake in the English Lake District that was formed by glacial action. The diatoms in its early sediments suggest fertile, nutrient-rich (eutrophic) conditions, with a trend towards less fertile (oligotrophic) conditions as the soils of the catchment became leached out over time. (Based on Haworth, 1969.)

by a steady decline in nutrients and production: oligotrophication rather than eutrophication, as has already been related in Chapter 3 (Figs 3.6 and 3.7). Figure 3.7 showed the higher concentrations of bases in the earlier sediments of English Lake District lakes as fresh rock debris was available for weathering, but a decline as the surface soils were progressively leached out. This decline is matched by a change in the diatoms in the sediments from those of nutrient-rich waters to those of nutrient-poor lakes (Fig. 11.11).

## 11.8 FILLING IN

Filling in is a parallel but separate natural process from changes in nutrient loading. Stream flow and gravity bring materials from the catchment; organic matter is produced within the lake; some of it is washed downstream but some sinks to the bottom. What is washed downstream eventually settles somewhere, ultimately in the large lake of the ocean. The rate at which sediment builds up depends on the circumstances. It will be higher if the catchment is large in relation to the basin, if it is of easily weathered rocks, or steep, and is usually less than 1 mm to a few millimetres per year other than for short periods in extreme circumstances, such as following a major deforestation or landslide.

In Lake Tritrivakeley, 13 m accumulated in 40,000 years, in the section of the core that could be precisely dated, so the rate of accumulation was about 0.3 mm yr$^{-1}$. Depending on the catchment and the productivity of the lake, the rate varies about ten to twenty fold. In terms of bulk sedimentation, the materials from the catchment will dominate those produced within the lake simply because they will include more indestructible inorganic matter eroded from rocks and soils. Organic matter produced in the lake will tend to be more easily decomposed than that brought in from the land, which represents that which has resisted decomposition by the terrestrial decomposers, but can still be preserved if it reaches the bottom, and is buried rapidly enough. The anaerobic conditions that prevail just below the sediment surface (Chapter 4) will delay decomposition for a very long time. Shallow lakes, in which the passage from water to bottom is short, tend thus to have a greater sedimentation rate than deep lakes. Thus as a lake fills in, the process may accelerate as it shallows. Warmer lakes might be expected to have greater decomposition rates than colder ones and hence fill in less rapidly, but since the rate at which inorganic material weathers may be relatively higher in the tropics, there seems no reason to expect any simple relationship between filling in rate and latitude.

Basins that are very shallow from the beginning may have only a few hundred or thousand years as open-water lakes before they fill in so much that they are completely colonized by emergent vegetation and become swamps, fens and bogs. The process is well shown in many of the shallow basins that were scraped in the land surface as the polar glacier advanced over northern North America and Eurasia. The earliest sediments are derived from open-water conditions and include fine clays from the catchment and a gooey organic matter, often called gyttja, produced from within the lake, or dy when it comes from washed-in peat. As the water shallows and swamp plants encroach, their remains accumulate as a peat or organic soil that retains much fibrousness, because these plants have a lot of resistant, woody xylem tissue. This peat builds up rapidly and eventually is level with the water surface, when a group of plants that prefers slightly drier conditions starts to take over. This group might include trees such as alder, willow, pond cypress or tupelo, ambatch or a variety of species in warmer regions. In the UK this stage is called the fen stage or carr stage if trees are predominant, or more generally a minerotrophic mire. This vegetation may then occupy the basin for as long as the climate favours it and as long as there is a water supply.

In cold conditions, however, there may be a further development. Hitherto, the water will have been derived from the catchment and will have to some extent accumulated some major cations and be relatively base-rich. Warm conditions will exacerbate this by drawing up deeper ground and soil water during the evaporation that occurs in summer. In cold conditions, there is less evaporation, and rainfall may start to leach the bases downwards leaving the surface more acid, rain having a pH of around 5.5 (Chapter 3). Plants that are well adapted to acid conditions, particularly the genus *Sphagnum*, may then colonize or spread from previous small populations and start to form a bog, or in more formal terms, an acidotrophic mire. Because decomposition is inhibited under acid conditions (why else would we pickle cabbage and onions in vinegar?) the peat accumulates rapidly and may even build out to form a floating raft or a dome, giving a *schwingmoor* or raised bog, respectively. If the local geology gives a very acid water, acidotrophic mires may develop from the start, of course, but if the above process, dependent on rain leaching a previously more mineral rich surface, takes place, conditions are said to have become ombrotrophic (Greek *ombros*, rain, as in umbrella) as opposed to minerotrophic.

As a final twist, when conditions move from minerotrophy to ombrotrophy, the supply not only of bases, but of nutrients declines and in first describing this process in the formation of bogs, a German scientist, C.A. Weber first used the terms eutrophic and oligotrophic (in German forms) in 1907. The terms were later adopted by Naumann and Thieneman, but they saw natural processes as moving from nutrient poor to nutrient rich, whereas Weber correctly saw the reverse.

## 11.9 SUMMING UP

I began this Chapter with a suggestion that there are five basic characteristics of lakes: they occupy a basin, a hole in the landscape; they have some sort of structure to the water mass; they cannot be separated from their catchment area; the immense amount of information about them can be ordered by seeing each lake as a product of the age and origin of the basin, the geology and land use of its catchment and the local climate; they are not permanent but have histories that may be studied using the techniques of palaeolimnology. I have demonstrated these but I hope I have also related some greater lessons. First, understanding of a subject changes. The conceptions of the earliest researchers are changed (the ideas of lake types and an inevitable change from oligotrophic to eutrophic conditions, for example) but are still foundations on which better understanding is based. Secondly, a wide appreciation geographically can help liberalize the often narrow and incorrect views that can become fixed if experience is gained only in a limited area. Limnology, like all ecology, is a worldwide subject. And third, the boundaries of limnology are fuzzy. Understanding, as shown also in Chapters 8 and 10, can come from archaeology and anthropology, indeed all aspects of knowledge. Science is not a subject; it is an approach to investigating things that uses all the available information and tests its internal consistency in coming to a conclusion. And the arts have their role to. My first introduction to lakes began the chapter, but my previous background was from a somewhat dirty, industrially polluted northern town. I understand well what the Irish poet W.B. Yeats was saying in *The Lake Isle of Innisfree* (1890).

I will arise and go now, for always night and day
I hear lake water lapping with low sounds by the shore;
While I stand on the roadway, or on the pavements grey,
I hear it in the deep heart's core.

## FURTHER READING

Early ideas on the classification of lakes and lake types appear mostly in the German language, but the history of them can be traced in Brinkhurst (1974), Rodhe (1975) and Talling (2008). Elster (1958) was the last to cling to them in print. Mackereth (1957) and Moss et al. (1994b, 1996a) span the ideas of continua, and partial reversion to types is reflected in the growing literature on the Water Framework Directive (Kolada et al. 2005; Moe et al. 2008). Data for Exercise 12 (Chapter 17) are taken from Moss et al. (1994a).

The new view of lakes as heterotrophic systems is celebrated in a review by Reynolds (2008) and can be traced through Jones et al. (1998), Cole et al. (1994), Carpenter & Pace (1997), Cole (1999) and Sobek et al. (2003). Cole & Caraco (2001) go so far as to suggest that the whole catchment of the Hudson River in New York State is heterotrophic and supported by respiration of ancient stored organic matter, but this cannot be a general phenomenon. Much support for this idea has come from studies on the stable isotopes of carbon, a technique originating with Nier & Galbransen (1939) and Parker (1964) and, together with parallel use of nitrogen isotopes to reveal position in the food chain, are reviewed variously by Peterson (1999) and Hobson (1999). Grey et al. (2002), Post (2002), Oliveira et al. (2006) and Syvaranta et al. (2006) are specific studies in Europe and South America.

The methods of palaeolimnology are exhaustively reviewed in the four volumes of Last & Smol (2001) and Smol (2008) is a fascinating textbook of limnology based on a palaeolimnological approach. Ter Brak & van Dam (1989) and Birks (1998) review the highly numerical methods now used for determining transfer functions that have developed since the use of simple indices by Renberg & Hallberg in 1982 (and others). Haworth (1980) examines the correspondence between the sediment record and contemporary records of diatoms. Mackereth (1958) is an example of corer development and Vallentyne (1969) discusses general issues of interpretation. The original palaeolimnological challenge to the idea that lakes become more eutrophic naturally with time is contained in Round (1961), Haworth (1969) and Mackereth (1966). An instance of natural eutrophication owing to climate change is Haworth (1972).

There are now thousands of examples of the use of palaeolimnology to reveal lake history, particularly to track the effects of natural climate changes (see Gierlowski-Kordesch & Kelts (1994) for a geology perspective) and several specialist journals devoted to this. A smattering of interesting examples is: Bradbury et al. (1981) – Venezuela; Churcher et al. (1999) – Libya; Degens et al. (1971) and Palacios-Fest et al. (2005) – Tanzania; Hutchinson et al. (1970) – a classic from Italy; Lamb et al. (1999) – Morocco; Hodgson et al. (1998) – Antarctica; Richardson & Richardson (1972) – Kenya; and Tibby & Heberle (2007) – Australia.

# Chapter 12

# THE COMMUNITIES OF SHALLOW STANDING WATERS: MIRES, SHALLOW LAKES AND THE LITTORAL ZONE

## 12.1 INTRODUCTION

Imagine you are in a rain forest. There is a huge biomass of trees, which dominate the scene, from short bushy ones to tall slender trunks with most of the leaf canopy high above you. Around your feet are herbs; lichens, ferns and mosses drape the tree branches; creepers dangle from the canopies through the sepulchral half-light. The litter at your feet is rich in organic matter; invertebrates crawl through and over it and swarms of insects hover in sunlit clearings. Monkeys eat leaves high in the canopy, and at night bats and rodents search for insects and seeds whilst snakes and wild cats seek out prey. At dawn many different birds become active for a few hours, then quieten as the day warms. Outside the forest, the winds blow more and a cool night becomes a very hot day, but inside, the shade mutes the heat of mid-day. The air is still and bears the scents of flowers, the stench of rotten fruit fallen to the floor, and the aromas of soil fungi. An occasional large animal, a deer or elephant picks its

way through, avoiding the debris of broken branches where a tree has fallen.

As a composite picture, this will be familiar to many people, yet standing on a lakeshore and looking at the beds of aquatic plants just reaching the water surface, or even seeing the massed stems of a reedswamp, few will be aware that this scene is repeated there at a smaller scale, with different characters but similar roles. Littoral habitats range from the equivalent of the short and scattered scrubby conifers at the Arctic tree line to dense tropical forest. Submerged, floating-leaved, floating and emergent higher plants, and large algae such as the charophytes (collectively called macrophytes) are the equivalents of the tree component, algae on the bottom sediments, attached as epiphytes, or as filaments festooned among the macrophytes mirror the herbs, lichens and creepers. It is dark below the surface canopy. There are insects and worms, mites, snails and Protozoa in and around the sediment and plant debris that lies over it, and at night, free living copepods and cladocerans move around to graze on the periphyton, the community attached to the plants, whilst invertebrate predators, leeches, bugs and beetles, feel for them in the darkness. Larger animals, fish in particular, inhabit the clearings and birds wade through the bottom, picking up prey or pecking plants

*Ecology of Freshwaters: A View for the Twenty-first Century,* 4th edition. By Brian Moss. Published 2010 by Blackwell Publishing Ltd.

to eat. The plants still the water movements as the trees in the forest still the air; the chemical products of metabolism, secreted or released on death, accumulate in the water, and signal information among the organisms, like those of forest plants and carcasses, indicating the availability of pollen or a scavenger's meal.

The littoral zone is ecologically an extension of the floodplain swamps of the rivers and in the shallowest water at the edge of a lake, behaves similarly. As the water deepens and the community becomes dominated by submerged and floating plants it takes on a different aspect that is more associated with lakes and it is this community that will be emphasized in this chapter, though similar communities will also occur in the lagoons of floodplains in yet another example of how things are continuous and not separately distinct in ecological systems. There is another continuity also (Fig. 11.3) and that bridges the swamps and the still, waterlogged mires, such as bogs, marshes and fens that are traditionally considered by terrestrial ecologists, for they are relatively dry in summer. In winter, however, they are very wet, even submerged and equally the province of freshwater ecology.

Just as floodplain swamps and wet grasslands are parts of flowing water systems, extensive areas of bog, freshwater marsh and swamp, hitherto claimed as separate wetlands, collectively called mires, are essentially parts of standing water or lake systems. Lakes are basins where water stands for long enough for its mass to acquire a semi-permanent physical structure, as opposed to flowing waters, where any such structure is very fleeting. Mires are thus logically considered as particular sorts of shallow standing waters. There is then a continuum as the water deepens, with water bodies that have relatively little open water and littoral vegetation over all or most of their area (shallow lakes), negligible pelagic zone and profundal benthos, to deeper lakes where the littoral dwindles (though never entirely disappears, unless the lake is artificial with near vertical concrete sides) and the pelagic and profundal predominate.

The continuity among shallow standing waters is seen in several dimensions and it is useful to illustrate that first before looking at details of processes. To extend the analogy with a forest, with which I began, the parallel is with the whole range of terrestrial vegetation types and just as these vary with light, temperature, water availability, soil and nutrient supply and the nature of the local grazers, so too do mires and the littorals of lakes.

## 12.2 THE SCOPE OF MIRES AND LITTORAL ZONES

If we are to look at the scope of shallow standing waters, the first dimension is that of light, which is related to water depth, and has already been mentioned in the sequence from emergent vegetation, which penetrates above the water surface in very shallow water to fully submerged plants, the lower limit of whose growth defines the point where the littoral changes to the profundal. Light and water depth are closely connected (Chapter 5). If the water surface is, on average for the year, more or less at the soil (sediment) surface, there are mires, distinguished largely by their soil type and nutrient supply as marshes, bogs, fens and carrs. Marshes have largely inorganic soil, the others organic peat; bogs are low in nutrients with the supply directly from rain or rain water that has been little modified by the catchment geology; fens and cars are supplied by more base-rich water; fens are open and grassy, carrs have trees.

As the water deepens, mires merge into swamps, dominated by grasses, sedges or trees, or floating vegetation, but emerging from 1 to 2 m of water (or more for some tropical swamp forests and floating mats) in the wettest periods, but always with water distinctly above the soil or sediment surface. Water down to 2 m will also support emergent vegetation of floating-leaved plants such as water lilies, rooted in the bottom but often with some completely submerged leaves as well as those held floating at the surface. Deeper water, down to the depth of sufficient light has submerged plants, even where there is substantial wave action, but where it is relatively still, often by completely floating plants, which may shade out any underlying submerged vegetation. Water depth and hence light availability thus gives a distinctive sequence of plant form.

### 12.2.1 Temperature

The next dimension, imposed upon the plant form, is that of temperature, reflected in latitude and altitude, and here the distinctions are more subtle and related to length of growth season. This is determined both by temperature and the availability of water. Standing waters may dry down or dry up completely in hot climates. Mires tend to be commonest in cooler climates, for the water balance that keeps them wet will be rare in hotter systems. The extensive mires of the boreal zone in Canada, Scandinavia and Siberia illustrate this. Mires do occur in the tropics, but on mountains and within rain forests, for example in south-east Asia. The polar and cold temperate mires have mainly perennial species, which store energy in their underground stem systems allowing them to use the very short growing season to put on new shoots and flower. Mires in the tropics are structurally like many temperate ones with grasses and sedges on mountains, but are often forests in the lowlands.

Swamp systems also tend to be dominated by perennials and though the characteristic species vary geographically, there are many parallels in appearance irrespective of temperature and latitude. Tree-dominated swamps are lacking towards the Poles, but appear in the cold temperate zones, often with spruces, willows and alders. In the warm temperate regions there are swamp cypresses, tupelos and a much greater range of trees. The wet tropics add hundreds more species and the floodplain forests of Amazonia (Chapters 8 and 9) again illustrate how the flowing systems and lake systems are not distinct, for the high water levels in these are essentially lake-like phases in a big river system. The warm temperate zone and the dry tropics also have swamp systems but they will be of sedges, grasses and trees that can withstand the dry period; nonetheless their appearance to the casual eye is similar to that of swamps elsewhere.

Floating-leaved and submerged communities change perhaps the least with temperature. Evolution of submerged species has been comparatively recent (Chapter 6) and they constitute a small part of plant diversity, still adapting to underwater conditions. Many genera, if not species, are worldwide and the underwater conditions buffer the greater variations in the terrestrial climate as it changes with latitude. Floating plants, however, tend to become bigger in warmer regions, with large genera such as the water hyacinths (Eichhornia spp) supplanting the smaller duckweeds (lemnids, Lemna, Wolffia, Spirodela) of the colder waters, and there are suggestions that the balance between floating and submerged plant communities may favour the floaters in warmer lakes. This may not withstand more evidence, but if it is true it may be a result of calmer weather in the tropics compared with the windier zones of colder regions that break up aggregations of floating plants.

The exception to the relative uniformity of submerged, floating-leaved and floating communities comes in the very cold and in the dry warm temperate and tropical regions. Here the growth period may be very short. In polar lakes only algae and bryophytes may occur in the littorals, in a growing season that is too cool, and underwater too dark, because of the low angle of the Sun and high albedo (Chapter 5) to allow the completion of the life histories of vascular plants, though they are not entirely lacking. In the hot, dry regions it is lack of water that confines the communities to salt-tolerant annual plants and macroscopic algae, such as the charophytes, that can complete their life histories and produce seeds or other propagules that can survive intense drying.

## 12.2.2 Nutrients

Thirdly, there is a dimension of nutrient availability. Aquatic plants largely obtain their nutrients through their roots, though uptake through the leaves is possible in submerged forms. Sediment chemistry is thus important as well as open-water chemistry and the sediment may be self-derived as peat as well as having both mineral and organic components derived from the catchment. Mires come in two general types, minerotrophic and ombrotrophic. Minerotrophic ones have catchment-derived water that is relatively richer in bases, phosphorus and nitrogen than ombrotrophic mires (bogs) that derive most of their base and nutrients directly from rain water. But minerotrophic mires, called poor fens, can be more or less base deficient, depending on the catchment geology. Indeed once again a continuum of variation occurs between the richest minerotrophic and poorest ombrotrophic mires.

Some minerotrophic mires are highly calcareous and floored with whitish soils, rich in marl (Chapter 3), where phosphorus may be very scarce owing to the insolubility of its compounds with calcium. Nonetheless there are many species (called calcicoles, Fig. 12.1) that have evolved efficient enough enzymes to cope with this. Less calcium rich, but still minerotrophic, mires perhaps provide the best conditions for growth and in these high biomasses of sedges, ferns and trees may build up and in turn lay down quantities of peat, thus raising the soil surface and eventually succeeding to drier grasslands or woodlands.

In wet regions, as the minerotrophic mires build up peat layers to above the ground-water table, the surface may become leached by rain, nutrient deficient and acid. The vegetation turns to that of a bog (Fig. 12.2),

**Fig. 12.1** Plants of north-temperate minerotrophic mires (fens and poor fens). Top left, bog bean (*Menyanthes trifoliata*); top right ragged robin, (*Lychnis flos-cuculi*); bottom left, fen orchid (*Liparis loesilii*); bottom right, milk parsley, *Peucedanum palustris*, with swallowtail butterfly, *Papilio machaon*, whose larvae feed on this plant.

often dominated by one genus of mosses, *Sphagnum*, and families of plants such as the Ericaceae, capable, by using mycorrhizae, of gleaning nutrients from the tiny concentrations provided by rain. Insectivorous plants that supplement their nutrient supplies by the capture and digestion of insects and other invertebrates are also prominent. *Sphagnum* has an internal structure of many large empty cells that hold water like a sponge, and properties of ion exchange that absorb cations and replace them in the interstitial water of the bog with hydrogen ions. It thus maintains wet and acid conditions that exclude non-bog plants and also promote the rapid accumulation of peat. Bacterial activity is reduced as pH decreases and the peats laid down under

bog conditions retain the recognizable structure of the living plants. Peats laid down in minerotrophic mires tend to be much more decomposed and amorphous. Bog peat is so highly preservative that occasionally the bodies of people and animals that have died (or been deliberately killed) are preserved: all except the bones, that is, for calcium phosphate is soluble at low pH.

Bogs can develop directly on a rock or mineral soil in the same way as minerotrophic mires if the local geology provides sufficiently acid water (essentially little modified rain water) and frequently do. In the wetter conditions that developed in north-west Europe about 3000 years ago, they began to blanket huge areas of the upland plateaux and to form thick deposits of peat

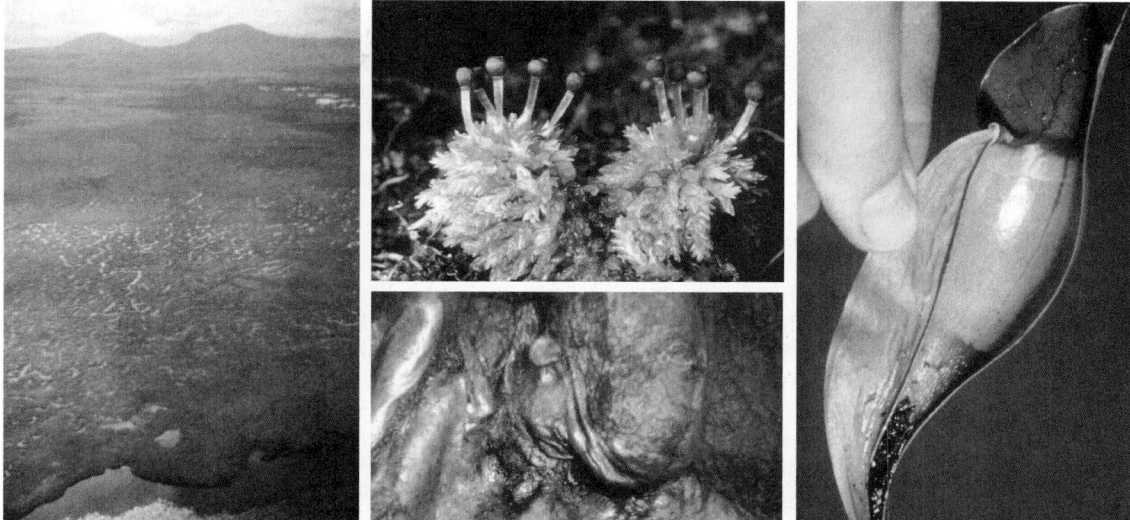

**Fig. 12.2** *Sphagnum* moss (top centre) is the most characteristic plant of bogs (left) in the northern hemisphere. Insectivorous plants, including the pitcher plant (right) are also common. The leaves of pitcher plants are green and photosynthesize but are formed into containers that, in this species (*Sarracenia purpurea*), shown sliced longitudinally, have an upper flange with downwardly directed hairs, then a shiny, slippery upper part and finally a bottom where enzymes are secreted, which digest small invertebrates sliding down the slippery slopes and unable to climb out against the downwardly directed hairs. The low pH and anaerobic peats of bogs readily preserve organic matter, including occasional bodies. Lindow Man (lower centre), aged about 2000 years old, was found in a small bog that had developed on a kettle hole lake in northern England.

over the previously mineral soils, like a layer of icing on a huge cake. Over large areas of the boreal forests, bogs of *Sphagnum* are covered by trees such as the black spruce (*Picea mariana*) in North America, and larches (*Larix* spp), and *Pinus sibirica* in Russia. In the tropics, although conditions in general do not favour peat formation (too dry and too warm), there is one significant exception. Parts of Malaysia and Indonesia, including the world's third largest island, the former Borneo, now Kalimantan, Sabah and Sarawak, have large areas covered by a waterlogged ombrotrophic forest on deep peat. Elsewhere they are smaller, or have been destroyed through logging and deliberate burning.

These tropical peatlands (Fig. 12.3), sometimes underlain by as much as 16 m of peat, are forests with trees up to 40 m high, ancient, very diverse systems where the peat is formed of partly rotted wood of high calorific content. Natural fires are infrequent but have occurred in extreme drought years associated with the climate pattern in the southern hemisphere known as El Niño. The trees occupy hummocks and are supported by stilt and buttress roots in the relatively unstable peat.

**Fig. 12.3** Tropical peat swamps, found most commonly in south-east Asia, are densely forested bogs, with dark, humic stained waters and deep peat deposits. Trees often tilt as they are rooted in insubstantial, sometimes rather sloppy peats and they support a wealth of animals, ranging from the world's smallest fish to elephants and the orang-utan.

Between these mounds, form pools of very brown, almost black, acid (pH sometimes 2.6) deoxygenated water and breathing roots, or pneumatophores rise above the surface like skyscrapers on a city horizon. There are many tree species, including *Pandanus*, the screw pine, and *Shorea* species and others of the family Dipterocarpaceae, which is characteristic of South-East Asia. But many families are present. Sedges, including *Thorachostachyon bancanum* dominate much of the ground flora and there are many species of insectivorous pitcher plants. The pools support communities of air-breathing eels, cat- and other fish, in total some 60 species, turtles, large prawns and a crocodile, *Crocodilus porosus*, whilst the forest is occupied by bats, rodents, wild pigs, elephant, tiger, mouse deer, sambhar, langurs, gibbons, macaques, orang-utan, tree shrews and tarsiers, proboscis monkeys, hornbills and some 200 other bird species.

Compared with the bleak, cold, upland north temperate blanket bogs, and raised bogs developing as mounds of peat at the end of a sequence of filling in of small lakes by minerotrophic then ombrotrophic mire, the south Asian peatlands sound very different. But there are similarities, nonetheless. The tropical peat systems also developed from minerotrophic conditions for they are underlain by podsolized quartz soils, sometimes with the deep ironpans that indicate a long period of leaching of minerals downwards until the initially mineral-rich surface became acid enough for decomposition of organic matter to be inhibited, and peat to accumulate. The peatland then spread like a blanket over large areas and even up modest hills, forming a dome, where the peat is thickest, away from the minerotrophic influence of streams and rivers. Close to these the forest has more *Pandanus* and sedge, but away from them there is a diverse forest of dipterocarps and other tall trees, before eventually an open landscape of much lower stunted trees. At this point, bases and nutrients have been leached downwards through the dome and the surface is very base and nutrient deficient. Much the same pattern is seen in the north temperate bogs with the most extreme, nitrogen-deficient conditions towards the middle.

### 12.2.3 Littoral communities in lakes

The strong contrast between rich minerotrophic conditions and ombrotrophic vegetation becomes muted as water depths increase and the continuum moves through swamps to lake communities, for all such habitats are fed by catchment-derived water. But it is not lost, for some catchments are so poorly weathered as to change the rainwater chemistry very little. Points on the continuum can be seen in the development of acid-water-isoetid communities in sandy or igneous catchments, highly calcareous littorals in limestone regions, and in the middle ground of intermediates between these.

Isoetid communities are named from one particular genus, *Isoetes*, the modern, very small, descendent of huge trees that dominated the swamp forests that laid down the peat, later to be compressed into coal, of the Carboniferous and Pennsylvanian swamp forests, 290–360 million years ago. *Isoetes* shares with *Lobelia*, *Littorella* and a few other genera, a set of characteristics that is well adapted to very soft waters where bicarbonate is scarce and the main source of carbon for photosynthesis is carbon dioxide absorbed through the roots from the sediment (see Chapter 9). Isoetids, as a submerged community in rather nutrient-poor conditions, tend to be backed by emergent swamp communities that share many species with bogs, the genus *Carex* being common in the north temperate region, but many others elsewhere. The biomass may be high in such swamps but not so lush as where nutrients are more plentiful. The productivity is low, so that the turnover time of the vegetation is long. Sometimes, in a continuum with bog vegetation, sticky-leaved insectivorous plants may be found or those whose leaves have been modified into pitchers or bladders in which invertebrates can be trapped. The bigger pitcher plants of the bogs (Fig. 12.2) have their equivalents in the finer submerged bladderworts (*Utricularia*) (Fig. 12.4) growing amid the submerged isoetid communities.

In catchments with waters of greater base and nutrient status, emergent swamps at the edges of lakes become taller and more productive with reeds, cattails (reedmace), or papyrus in central Africa. The submerged littorals have a much greater range of genera of submerged plants than in isoetid waters and leaf uptake of nutrients becomes feasible, though the richer sediments provide for most nutrient needs and the vegetation is denser. Floating plants, dependent on nutrient uptake from the water, become more common. They are scarce in isoetid waters. Overall production is greater although light ultimately will limit the productivity, determines the depth to which the littoral penetrates, and determines a zonation of different species more tolerant or less tolerant of low intensities.

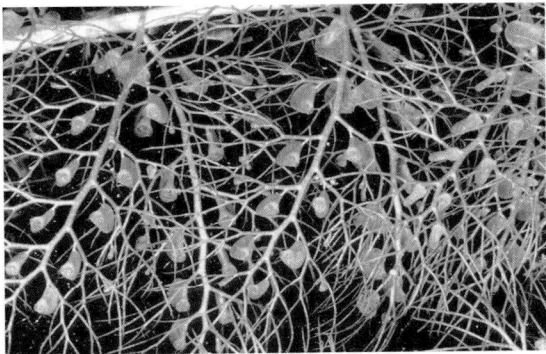

**Fig. 12.4** *Utricularia* is a common submerged plant of fairly acid lakes and bogs, whose green leaves are modified into traps, with a springable lid, in which small invertebrates can be caught and digested. (Photograph by Barry Rice.)

**Fig. 12.5** *Chara vulgaris* is a typical charophyte, a macroscopic alga, sometimes a metre tall, that grows submerged in usually high base status waters. Its 'stem' is a large single cell, with groups of cells at either end from which grow similarly constructed 'branches'. At the tips, sexual organs and eventually oospores are produced. The oospores may remain dormant after release, before germinating to form new plants. Both plant and oospores are typically rough to the touch with marl deposits. Casts of the stems and whole oospores are readily preserved in sediments. (Photograph by Harald Stark.)

The higher nutrient status of the community supports a more intense metabolism than in acid waters, where also brown humic substances may occur in such quantities as to stain the waters like infusions of tea or coffee. The waters of the boreal forests in Finland and Russia and of the tropical peatlands of South-East Asia are particularly coloured, but the phenomenon is general. Littoral zones may reach some tens of metres down the lake profile in very clear waters, with mosses and charophytes the last to persist on the verge of darkness, but a few metres is common to many lakes and less than a metre to those with much plankton or turbidity from other sources or heavily stained water.

The extremes of base status in waters include marl waters on the one hand and highly saline ones on the other. Marl waters tend to have little available phosphate, low phytoplankton densities and be very clear. Coloured organic matter may also be precipitated as well, for much of it is of organic acids. This favours deep littoral zones, but a low production, usually dominated by the smaller species of charophytes, which appear to be able to concentrate phosphorus through their rhizoids and green tissue (strictly they do not have leaves, being algae with a highly characteristic structure of single-celled 'stems' with whorls of similarly structured 'branches'). Other plants do occur but relatively sparsely in swards of *Chara* (Fig. 12.5), which gains its common name of stonewort from the deposits of marl that cover its surfaces and give them a roughness. Sediments formed under charophytes often have rather crunchy calcareous pipe-like structures that formed over the *Chara* stems and are whitish and easily recognized by an experienced palaeolimnologist.

Perhaps by coincidence, charophytes are not uncommon also in saline waters, together with often annual species of plants, which, like the charophytes with their sexually produced oospores are able to withstand drying out through a suitable phased life history. In dry regions of the warm temperate and tropical zones, the littorals will have emergent vegetation which is quite deep rooted and can persist in the annual summer droughts, but a submerged vegetation that is active in winter but gains refuge as seeds when the lake dries down, becoming more saline as it does. Some species will withstand very high salinities during this process.

Thus a geography of littoral zones and conventional wetlands can be created in terms of light (through water depth), temperature and nutrient and base status that emphasizes the continuity among them (Table 12.1) and on which the processes that are common to mires and littoral zones can be superimposed. The dimension of water depth and light availability can also be expressed as the proportion of the water body that is occupied by macrophyte vegetation. This simply

**Table 12.1** General aspects of vegetation in standing waters.

| Water table relative to soil or sediment surface | At the surface | Up to 1 m above | Up to 2 m above | More than 2 m above to euphotic depth | Independent of depth but deeper than euphotic zone |
|---|---|---|---|---|---|
| Base status and pH low (pH <6) | Acid mire (bog) with Sphagnum, sedges, Ericaceae, insectivorous plants. Can be forested. Low diversity. Formation of highly structured peat | Swamp with emergent plants, including many bog plants, cotton grasses and sedges (Carex). Can be forested in warmer climates. Contributions from floating leaved plants but submerged plants scarcer because shaded out and floating plants scarce because of low nutrient content in the water | Emergents become scarce and replaced by small floating leaved plants, with some submerged plants, including isoetids and insectivorous plants like Utricularia | Submerged plants predominant, with isoetids, insectivorous plants and some floating plants, though low nutrient conditions in the water limit these | Very sparse or absent, unless in very sheltered waters when small floaters like lemnids may persist |
| Moderate (6–7) | Poor fen with mixture of fen and bog species and intermediate conditions | Tends to be very diverse with many small species as conditions disfavour vigorous, large competitive plants. Can be forested in warmer climates | Mixture of lilies and isoetids, insectivorous plants, with greater diversity and more floating plants, especially in warmer regions | Greater diversity of submerged plants with a few charophytes and insectivorous plants. Occasional lilies and more floating plants, though tending to be small | Small floating plants, but sparse unless very sheltered |
| High (>7) | Fen (not wooded) or carr (with trees). More diverse, laying down less structured peat because decomposition is more rapid | Vigorous swamp of reeds, large floating plants, trees. Tends to be reduced in diversity, sometimes monospecific | Large and vigorous lilies, greater diversity of submerged plants, including charophytes and floating plants. Occasional tall emergents may persist | High diversity of submerged plants, more floating plants of greater stature, especially in warmer waters. Insectivorous plants scarce, charophytes prominent | Can be very vigorous growth of large floating plants, floating mats of emergents, even forest rooted in floating mats of sedges and gasses especially in warm climates |

increases steadily from mires, where it is 100%, through ponds and pools where it is very high, because they are shallow, to shallow lakes, which intergrade so much with ponds that it is pointless to argue what is the difference beyond area, to deep lakes where littorals may occupy a vanishingly small, but still crucial part of the lake basin. And in reservoirs (Chapter 15), because the changes in water level are human-controlled and do not have the predictability which allows a littoral community to accommodate to seasonal fluctuations as in natural lakes, there may be no littoral zone at all. Because littorals are crucial to the functioning of the whole system, reservoirs are, in effect, disabled lakes.

## 12.3 THE STRUCTURE OF LITTORAL COMMUNITIES

There are always patterns, not necessarily regular repeats as in conventional patterns on wallpaper or carpets, but groupings of organisms that have meaning within littoral communities. The most obvious components of the patterns are usually plants, sometimes tufts or jelly-like lumps of algae in very cold waters. But these harbour complex communities of bacteria, fungi, Protozoa, microscopic and filamentous algae, invertebrates and vertebrates, and doubtless viruses and certainly parasites and parasitoids of all of these. Some are permanent, others appear seasonally and yet others casually visit, but their existence forms patterns and their activities constitute the functioning of the system.

The plant patterns within mires and swamps often follow channels or tracks that represent sources of nutrients as well as supplies of water moving through the mire. Patches of different species may result from slight differences in topography, where a fallen tree trunk has created slightly drier conditions on top of it, or a bushy plant, such as the *Potentilla fruticosa* that grows on calcareous mires in the mid-western USA has accumulated debris around its base that has become leached and more acid and provides the foothold for *Sphagnum* to start growing and a bog to start forming. A patch of nettles might indicate where mammals habitually dung or urinate and a stool, the fibrous mass of old shoot debris protruding above the ground-water surface, of *Carex* might be the base on which alder seedlings can establish and convert a fen to a carr. An enormous effort in plant ecology has been devoted to establishing such patterns and confirming that there is an order, if often changing, to where particular plants

grow. It has also shown that there is also a degree of randomness, that a species grows where its seed happened to land at a time when germination was favoured and no other plant chanced upon that spot. But randomness is the wrong word for there is a reason, if one that cannot retrospectively be discerned. Grazing by wild cattle, antelope or deer might be important in removing competition from large plants so that smaller species can gain a foothold, so some patterns reflect the movements of animals in the past and the frequency of their visits. Hippopotami create obvious channels that influence water movements and the distribution of plants, for example, and effectively engineer some of the structure.

The same subtleties occur in lake littoral zones, superimposed on the greater pattern effected by water depth. There may appear to be a distinct zonation or banding of communities of emergent reeds, floating-leaved lilies, floating and submerged species but this is a trick of the eye. Individual species have distinctive depth ranges, but overlapping of these creates a continuum of community change so that the submerged plants take over gradually from the floating-leaved and these from the emergents rather than there being the abrupt changes often shown in diagrams profiling the littoral as water depth changes. Horizontal patchiness also occurs, with clumps of one species or another, sometimes shifting in position from year to year (Fig. 12.6). Such patterns may result from water movements changing the pattern of sands and finer silts, or of annual differences in weather favouring one species that begins to grow earlier than others and takes over a particular space, or following heavy grazing by swans or other birds the previous season so that propagules, seeds or the vegetative turions were not formed or are scarce in that area for subsequent regrowth. It will generally be very difficult to explain the patterns seen without a knowledge of the history of the precise locations, as a result. Indeed a great deal of effort and a plethora of multivariate diagrams attempting to relate plant occurrence to environmental factors measured only simultaneously are wasted in trying to explain the details of plant distributions. History and also the biological interactions among species are at least as important and usually far more so than the readily measurable variables such as water pH, sediment organic content or temperature.

Depth (vertical) distributions are more amenable to explanation for they depend more on fundamental physiology in relation to light availability, wave

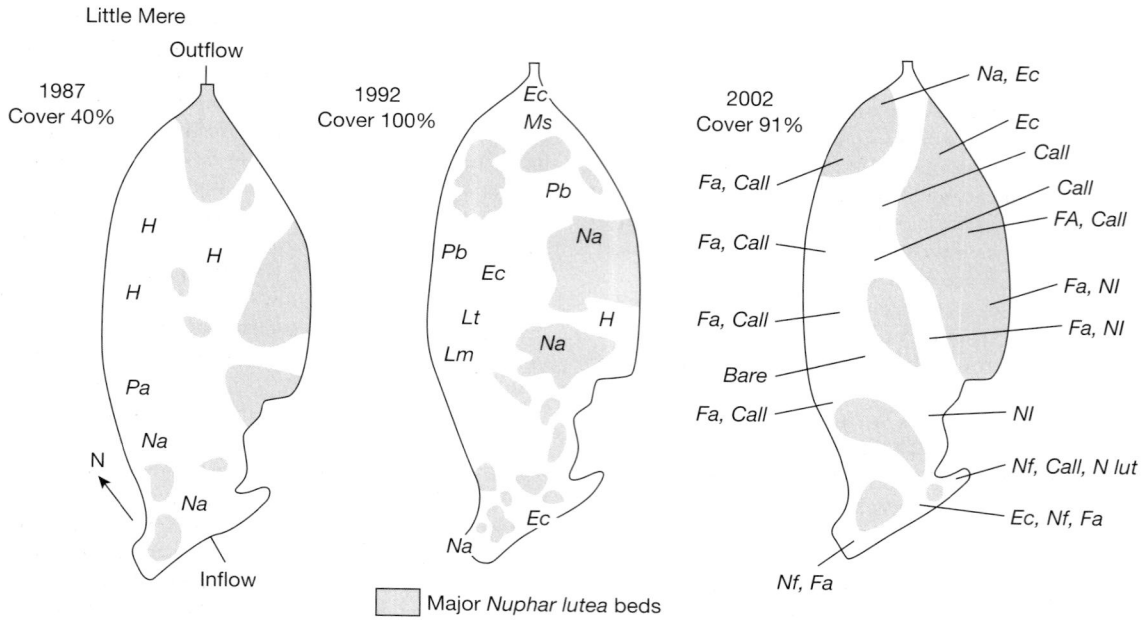

**Fig. 12.6** The pattern of aquatic plants in shallow lakes and littorals typically changes a great deal from year to year. Lily beds remain relatively the same but submerged species show much variation as here at a small lake in north-west England, Little Mere. Abbreviations: H, *Hydrocotyle* (water net, a macroalga); Na, *Nymphaea alba*, the white water lily; Ec, *Elodea canadensis*; Pb, *Potamogeton berchtoldii*; Ms, *Myriophyllum spicatum* (all submerged higher plants); Lm, *Lemna minor* (a floating duckweed); Lt, *Lemna trisulca* (a submerged, but unrooted higher plant) Call, *Callitriche* sp (submerged higher plant with some floating leaves); Fa, *Fontinalis antipyretica* (a water moss); N lut, *Nuphar lutea*, the yellow water lily; Nf, *Nitella flexilis*, a charophyte. (Based on Moss et al. 2005.)

disturbance and water pressure. Emergent plants depend on absorption of carbon dioxide from the atmosphere through surfaces that have stomata and thick cuticles. They cannot easily take up dissolved carbon dioxide or bicarbonate and rely, in the early growth season, on using energy stored in their overwintering rhizomes to produce enough growth to bring the stems above the water surface for the leaves to unfold. There is thus some critical water depth, which can just be crossed before the stored energy runs out. This appears to be around a metre or so for many emergents rooted in the sediment, but the problem can be circumvented by the rhizomes and roots forming a floating mat from which the shoots emerge. In this way water depth becomes immaterial, except that as the floating mat extends outwards to deep water it becomes vulnerable to wave action and rough water and will easily be broken up.

In quiet waters though, floating mats may be extensive and tough, enough to support the weight of large mammals, even elephants in the case of the papyrus swamps of east and central Africa. The problem for floating as opposed to substrate rooted emergents may also be availability of nutrients, for the open water is always less rich than the interstitial water of the sediments. Floating mats cannot grow in very nutrient deficient waters. They may also have a problem in very rich ones too because an abundance of nitrogen seems to encourage more shoot growth and the mat becomes top heavy and may capsize.

Floating leaved plants compromise between the advantages of emergents with their access to sediment nutrients, and submerged plants with their better adaptations to obtaining carbon dioxide from the water. They take most of their carbon dioxide from the air through the top of the leaf, but may have some short-lived thinner submerged leaves, later disadvantaged by shading from the surface canopy of their own leaves, but able to boost growth in spring before the surface canopy has formed. This means that some of these plants can grow down to 2 or 3 m, and therefore extend further down the lake slope than the emergents. The undersides of their leaves may also take up dissolved carbon dioxide, but we do not know whether this is significant given the supply that can diffuse in more rapidly from the air. Submerged plants in standing freshwaters look and behave very like those in running waters for the most part (the podostemonads splayed like green chewing gum over the rocks of tropical streams are the exceptions) and their form is much the same the world over. Their biology was discussed in Chapter 9.

The problems of obtaining enough light by submerged plants seem to be greater than those of gaining carbon dioxide and nutrients. Measurements of the gross production of submerged communities suggest that they are not light saturated and that although the efficiency with which photons are absorbed is high, the shading by both the water and the mass of plants themselves leads to much lower gross photosynthesis than is theoretically possible from the amount of light penetrating the water surface. Of course, the depths to which plants can penetrate in a lake are largely determined by the light availability, but the shading effects occur even in communities in shallow water. Self-shading also limits emergent production but gross production in such communities is much higher because there is no shading by the water once the shoots have emerged above it. Pressure, through collapse of the air spaces that most submerged plants share with emergents for solution of the problem of aerating roots in anaerobic sediment, may also limit the depth of colonization. Mosses and charophytes, which have no such lacunae, penetrate to the greatest depths, some tens of metres in very clear lakes.

Terrestrial plants, in a sense, isolate themselves in a cocoon of cuticle for water conservation. Aquatic plants, to solve the diffusion problem, do the opposite and there is a strong chemical interaction between the plants and the water that is behind some of the complex organic chemistry of natural waters. Substances are absorbed and substances are emitted. Absorption can mean depletion of stocks of ammonium and phosphate in the interstitial water of the sediment in summer. Dissolved inorganic nitrogen becomes very scarce in the littoral water during the growth season, both through plant uptake by the leaves and denitrification deep in the beds where a degree of anaerobiosis, brought about by decomposition of falling dead leaves and the debris of periphyton, encourages bacterial activity. The

uptake creates a pattern in water chemistry (Fig. 12.7) such that the chemistry varies greatly over distances of only centimetres. This has consequences for the distribution of algae and animals in the water.

Periphyton growing on the plants is an important component of lake littoral zones. Its production increases with fertility of the water and it may severely inhibit the growth of the host plant through shading. One device for coping with it is for the host plant to continue to produce new shoots that take time to be colonized and to slough off old, periphyton-covered leaves. Periphyton seems to be an inevitable burden though some large filamentous algae (the Zygnematales, including the common genus *Spirogyra*) appear to avoid it by secreting copious amounts of mucilage. The disadvantage to that, however, may be in increasing the problems of diffusion, but periphyton also competes with the plant for materials at its surface.

Periphyton may have advantages to the host plant by diverting the activities of the invertebrate grazers, snails and mayfly nymphs, for example, that are abundant in the plant beds, from the plant itself. It does not entirely work, however, for plants are grazed, not only by invertebrates but also to a large extent by water birds, fish and some mammals. An older view, which saw the plant communities as essentially static platforms for the activities of periphyton on their surfaces and invertebrates moving within the labyrinths created among them, is being replaced by one in which the plant growth has to be equally dynamic and shifting to cope with its changing environment, not least a much greater damage from grazing than was previously thought.

The plants are not entirely victims, however. Some secrete organic substances (e.g. polyphenols, tellimagrandin II, sulphur compounds, phenylpropanoid glycosides, dithiane and trithiane), a process known as allelopathy, that inhibit the growth of algae, though mostly in the overlying plankton rather than in the immediately more damaging periphyton. It could be that the species of the periphyton have evolved resistance to such substances and that is why they can survive in a habitat, the plant surface, that offers a degree of permanence where they are immune to the effects of water currents, and where plant secretions, or leakages of nutrients where the plant is damaged by grazers, offer compensatory advantages. Other substances produced by plants deter grazing animals. Glucosinolate (which gives water cress its distinctive taste) is an example, and bis-p-hydroxybenzyl-2-isobutylmalate, which deters crayfish.

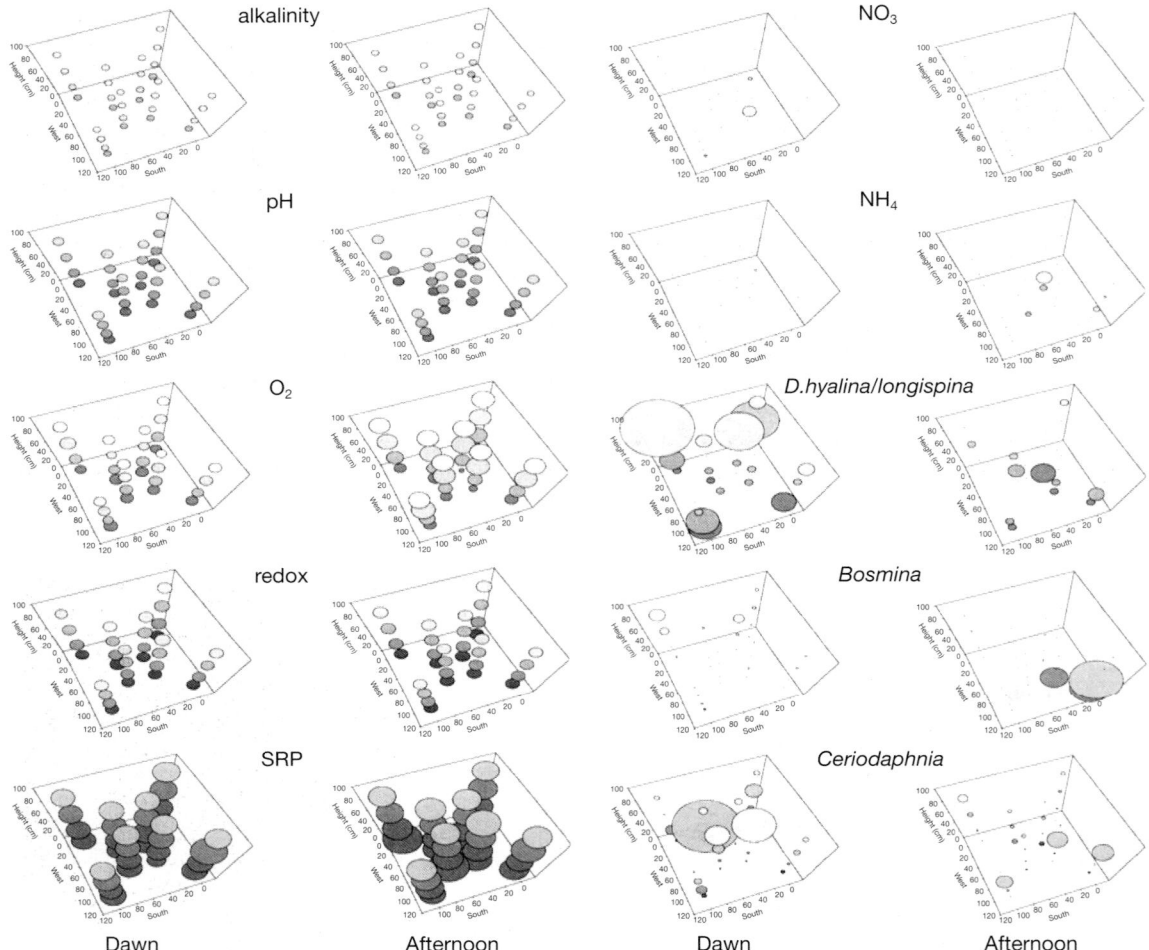

**Fig. 12.7** There is a fine structure within plant beds. These diagrams were based on data from a simultaneous sampling of a cube of water in Little Mere, England, using a vacuum system to take water at distances of about 30 cm in a water depth of about 1 m and an area of 1 m². The view is three dimensional from the top of the cube. Denser shading shows samples towards the bottom and the size of the circles is proportion to concentrations of chemicals or numbers of animals. Samples were taken at dawn (about 0400 hours and in the afternoon (1700 hours). Some variables change a great deal either with depth or time of sampling. (Unpublished data of T. Barker, H. Irfannullah and B. Moss.)

## 12.4 HETEROTROPHS AMONG THE PLANTS

The structure provided, even if shifting, by the plants provides a stage for a much greater diversity of micro-organisms and invertebrates than is found in the plankton of the structurally much more simple open water. As well as the plant surfaces themselves, there are sediments of different particle sizes, organic debris, the water among the plants, which is not uniformly mixed and provides numerous gradients and patches of different chemical quality, and the surface water film, where under still conditions, pollen and trapped aerial insects may subsidize the food source from within the water itself.

The surface sediments have a film of largely motile algae: diatoms, flagellate green algae and euglenoids and filamentous cyanobacteria, huge numbers of bacteria and Protozoa, snails that graze over the surface and oligochaete worms and dipteran larvae that eat the sediment, digesting microorganisms and recycling a stream of faeces that becomes recolonized with bacteria for future assimilation. It may look rather dull seen with the naked eye but a microscope will reveal a constantly shifting world (Fig. 12.8), continually receiving a rain of fine debris from activities going on in the plant canopy as periphyton grazers messily feed, defaecate, and dislodge loose material, and as planktonic organisms washed in from the open-water sink to the bottom. With so much fresh

organic material arriving, a very active chemical industry is maintained. The sediment is anaerobic only a few millimetres below the surface, simply because diffusion cannot bring in oxygen rapidly enough to meet the demand, so anaerobic respiration, based on the succession of substrates described in Chapters 4 and 9 (for sediment processes are common everywhere) of nitrate, manganic and ferric ions, sulphate and the more oxidized of organic compounds, produces nitrous oxide and nitrogen, manganous and ferrous ions, sulphide and methane, respectively. Methane is particularly abundant in mire soils, where the large plant biomass and minimal water movement and mixing leads to severe deoxygenation. Overall, mires and shallow lakes are major net emitters of methane and net storers of organic matter so their future behaviour in relation to climate change (Chapter 16) is of great interest.

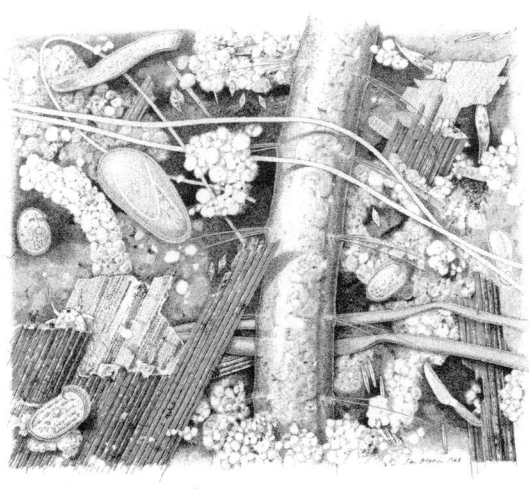

300 μ

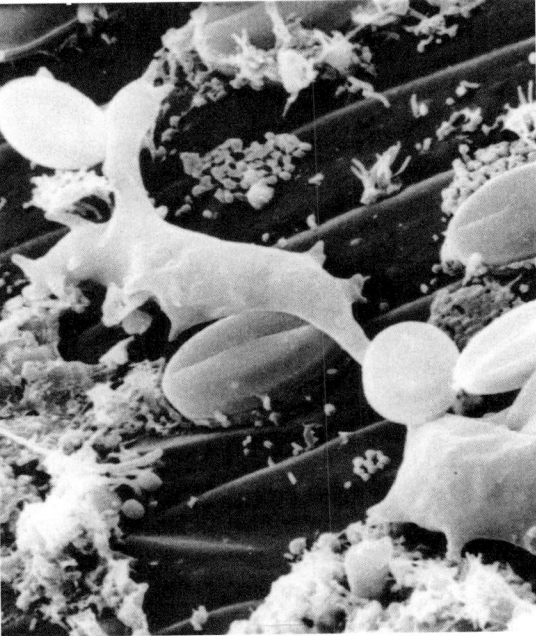

**Fig. 12.8** There is a great deal of complexity at the microscopic level in sediment communities of littoral zones (left, after Fenchel 1969), and associated with the plants (right, electron micrograph by C.J. Veltkamp). On the sediments, part of the body of an oligochaete worm is shown among plant debris (the parallel-celled structures). Diatoms (diamond or boat shaped) and filaments of cyanobacteria crawl through the surfaces. There are several species of ciliates and aggregations of bacteria, mucilaginous material, and inorganic sediment. In the right-hand picture, a background of plant epidermis can be seen with the ovoid diatom cells of *Cocconeis placentula*, colonies of small bacteria and a single amoeba in the centre of the picture. This is a fairly sparse epiphytic community.

At the sediment surface, diffusion and the photosynthetic epipelic (sediment surface) algae maintain oxidized conditions and a brown oxidized layer by day but at night as the algae cease movement and fall back into the sediment, the surface takes on the black appearance of reduced iron sulphide. In warm lakes and in summer in cool ones, it may have this appearance semi-permanently and emits a supply of phosphate into the water because of the breakdown of the precipitation mechanism that otherwise ties phosphate in insoluble complexes with iron and manganese. Both microorganisms and animals at the sediment surface need to be tolerant of deoxygenation, for oxygen is always relatively scarce except in the much disturbed littorals of wave-washed shores where there is bare rock or only gravel and sand can accumulate. The attached algae (epiliths) and the snails, crustaceans and stonefly and mayfly nymphs that graze them resemble the communities of middle reach rivers, though the species are different. Sand and the finer gravels bear some plants, often isoetids if the water chemistry favours them, but they are sparse because of the disturbance, and the sediment algae, mostly diatoms, may be actually attached to the sand grains by short stalks, or lodge in crevices on the grains. They may often be buried for some days and tolerate deoxygenation which does occur in such coarse sediments, but a few centimetres rather than millimetres below the surface.

Meanwhile, activity is just as great on and around the plants (Fig. 12.8). As they grow, they also die, sloughing off dead leaves that fall to the sediments but also creating strong chemical gradients close to their surfaces. A bottle dipped into the open water may give very little clue as to the processes really occurring. It is difficult to sample the periphyton (epiphyte) layers as most methods involve removing the plants and scraping or shaking the organisms off to place them under a microscope. Carefully removing a piece of leaf and direct examination shows much more. There is a layering of the periphyton, which like the sediment communities, is another world within a world. Some algae, including many diatoms, adhere with mucilage secreted through a slit (the raphe) in their cell walls; other organisms are embedded in mucilage and marl, including many bacteria. Above this film, long but anchored filaments of bacteria, cyanobacteria and green algae protrude, together with diatoms on stalks, sometimes complexly branched with a cell at the end of each branch.

Draped among these filaments and stalks are free living cells, sometimes motile by flagella, often not and just held by the structure of the rest, and sometimes, especially when nutrients are abundant, long and robust filaments of green algae: *Spirogyra, Zygnema, Mougeotia, Cladophora, Ulothrix, Bulbochaete,* form cotton-wool-like clouds around the stems and leaves. Ciliate protozoa and heterotrophic nano- (meaning very small) flagellates lumber or scuttle through and over the tangled masses, engulfing smaller animals and bacteria, whilst snails, mayfly nymphs and caddis fly larvae, poking out from their protective cases of leaf debris or tiny twigs, rasp and pick over the periphyton turf like cattle or sheep in a pasture, leaving the more robust, tougher species and those tightly attached, but shaving the rest away and leaving copious faeces to add to the sward or to roll off and fall to the sediment. Other, smaller grazers, including rotifers, copepods, ostracods and cladocerans filter the cloud of free-living cells associated with the sward or may grasp and bite larger cells. Such vigorous grazing increases the amount of light able to penetrate to the plant, for the periphyton burden can become very heavy, sometimes cloaking the plant like a fur coat on a cold Russian in winter.

There are predators too: the large cells of stalked protozoa such as *Vortozoa* such as *Vorticella* and can be extended and retracted on long stalks and *Hydra,* one of the few Cnidaria to inhabit freshwaters, dangles tentacles studded with stinging cells (nematocysts) to trap small animals. It is a world so complex that to obtain manipulable replicate samples for study, many ecologists introduce artificial substrates: glass slides, earthenware tiles, nylon netting or plastic replicas of plants made for domestic aquaria, for colonization. The more complex of these do seem to reproduce the main features of the community quite well, but where the natural substrata, the plants, are living and metabolically active, many subtleties must be missed.

The interstices among the plants, a complex underworld of corridors, caverns and labyrinths are equally busy. There are shoals of small animals, such as the cladoceran *Polyphemus,* a large-eyed predator on large algae and smaller animals that uses chemical substances to hold the shoal together, a device that may reduce the risks, to each individual, of being eaten by a larger predator, such as a fish. Water spiders lurk in silken chambers full of air; damselfly and dragon fly nymphs cling to plants waiting for prey to pass; and water mites, bugs and beetles actively rove. The plant tangles may discourage large predators such as grown fish from hunting, for the light that they need is faded and the plant structure puts obstacles in the way of a darting lunge, but this is still a dangerous place for a small animal. Invertebrate predators are present and mostly rely on contact with their prey, handling it in a particular way to manoeuvre it into their mouths. The prey is not entirely defenceless though. The predators emit substances that belie their presence and the prey, in response to these kairomones, produce young that are slightly differently shaped, confounding the precise handling procedures that the predators must use to manoeuvre prey sometimes not much smaller than themselves. Many examples are now known of such changes (see Chapter 13 for examples in the plankton) though the natures of the substances concerned are not.

Nor are many details of the life histories of many of these organisms beyond a simple knowledge, say, that they produce eggs that overwinter, have several larval stages, emerge as adults to mate then to lay the eggs in some specified location such as on the stalks or leaves of plants or attached to rocks. The risks and mortalities at each stage, the degree to which individuals fly between lakes and thus create metapopulations, and the balance of influences such as the availability and quality of their own food and the losses to predators are usually unknown.

Detailed work on particular groups is instructive. Stoks & McPeek (2003) looked at the life histories of several damselfly species of the genus *Lestes* in central North America, using simple experiments in buckets, or netting cages in ponds. Lestids are slender odonates that hold their wings out when resting, compared with other damselflies that hold them close to the body. The key aquatic parts of their life histories, though, are spent as nymphs. Their occurrence appears to depend on a combination of permanence of the water, the rhythm of their life history, predation on each other and the occurrence of fish and dragonfly predators on the nymphs. *Lestes dryas* is confined to very short-lived vernal (spring) ponds and has a very short life history, completed within the few weeks that water is present. It does not occur in longer lived and permanent ponds, for in these other predatory damselflies can live and it is small and particularly easily caught. Other species (*L. congener, L. disjunctus, L. dryas, L. forcipatus, L. rectangularis, L. unguiculatus*) complete their life cycle within a year, and are confined to temporary ponds of longer duration and yet others (*L. eurinus, L. inaequalis, L. vigilax*) overwinter as nymphs, metamorphosing to adults the following spring and are confined to permanent pools. *Lestes euryinus* and *L. vigilax*, as well as large dragonfly nymphs (*Anax* sp), can be

vigorous predators on the temporary pond group, if given the opportunity, but themselves must have permanent water, so potential prey and predators are kept separate. In the absence of these predators, the temporary pond group could live in permanent waters. In permanent ponds, *L. euryinus* is more vulnerable to fish and *L. vigilax* to dragonfly predation respectively. Since fish eat the dragonfly nymphs, *L. vigilax* tends to predominate in ponds with fish and *L. eurinus* in ponds without them. Such complexities multiplied by several hundred species mean that there is still a very great deal to learn about the workings of littoral communities.

The influence of parasites is also a factor rarely realized. But when one common plant-bed detritivore, *Asellus aquaticus* is carefully examined (Fig. 12.9), it is seen to have ten or more different associated organisms lodging on and in it, and each having some influence on its longevity and reproductive success. There are plenty of lists of species from the littoral, some times linking particular animals to particular plants,

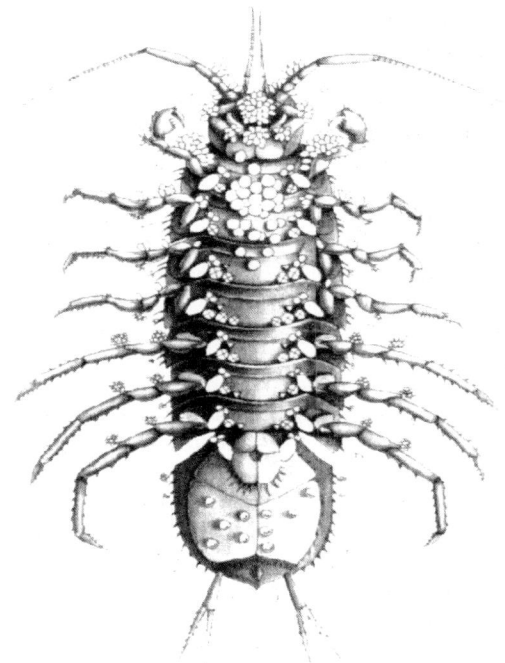

**Fig.12.9** All organisms are associated with a coterie of epibionts and parasites. The underside of a typical *Asellus* is studded with Protozoa, rotifers and bacteria. (From Cook et al. (1998). Drawing by Jane Cook.)

sometimes failing to find any such specificity but demonstrating a greater abundance the denser the plants or the greater surface area of the vegetation. There is also knowledge of a seasonality such that younger plants bear more animals than older, but a really comprehensive understanding often yet stops short of simple description.

### 12.4.1 Neuston

Though they are more easily observed and sampled, these details are equally obscure for the animals that inhabit the surface tension films in the quiet waters of the more sheltered littoral zones. From the air, dust and pollen falls and is trapped on the surface tension layer and dissolved organic matter coalesces into a gel, associated with its underside, that becomes colonized by bacteria. Some species of algae also adhere to the underside. Two groups of animals exploit these food sources. One, the hyponeuston, attaches to the underside and includes the larvae of mosquitoes and specialist cladocerans such as *Scapholeberis mucronata*, the edges of whose carapace are straight and parallel, and allow it to move across the layer as if on a pair of its own rails. The predatory water skaters of the hyperneuston have legs whose distal joints also parallel the film and can exert force against it allowing them to row over the surface. They can move rapidly and sense tiny vibrations when an aerial insect becomes trapped and struggles, attracting the skaters to insert their sucking mouth parts, kill and feed. In the rougher days of winter these animals bury themselves in nearby wet vegetation for they are essentially amphibious. The surface film is an exposed place even for its specialists and organisms that live there are vulnerable to predation. Mosquito larvae will detach and sink rapidly away at the slightest disturbance and the whirligig beetles, roving in swarms to seek prey, have divided eyes, modified for sight in air in the upper part and under water in the lower, the better to detect both prey and their own predators.

### 12.5 LINKAGES, RISKS AND INSURANCES AMONG THE LITTORAL COMMUNITIES

Lake littoral communities are closely linked with both the surrounding terrestrial systems and the open,

plankton-dominated water of the pelagic zone. The land brings nutrients, organic matter and visiting nekton, such as amphibians, birds and mammals; the pelagic contributes fine organic matter in settling plankton and the activities of fish. In turn the littoral provides organic matter to the pelagic and food and nesting sites for the nekton. It can also mean emergence of swarms of flies that provide food for terrestrial birds such as swallows, martins and swifts, and for spiders. The shallow lake Myvatn, in Iceland, contributes up to 2.5 tonnes per year of such terrestrial food from each hectare. But these linkages also mean vulnerabilities from grazing damage and from light interception. The littoral is defined by light availability and the availability of light can be influenced by many factors.

Light for the whole community is vulnerable to development of overlying plankton communities, and for higher plants to large growths of epiphytes or filamentous algae. Insurance mechanisms have evolved, however, that minimize the risk of these in pristine communities (Fig. 12.10). First there are physical mechanisms. The very mass of plants tends to still the water and dampen eddy currents that are needed to keep phytoplankton in suspension. Secondly there are chemical mechanisms, both inorganic and organic. Rooted plants are able to gain nutrients from the sediments; phytoplankton and periphyton are dependent on supplies from the water. Though the mechanisms of release of phosphate from sediments are very active in plant beds where much organic matter falls to the bottom and results in deoxygenation, the same conditions also promote denitrification so that in shallow waters, available nitrogen is often very scarce in summer. Nitrogen deficiency thus limits potentially shading algal growth in a plant bed and may be supplemented as a defence for the plants by production of allelopathic chemicals that inhibit algal growth.

Thirdly there are biological mechanisms involving grazing. The rich diversity of small crustaceans living in the interstices, and loosely attached to plants, is variously able to graze phytoplankton and epiphytes, and larger invertebrates, such as snails and insect larvae and nymphs, very efficiently mow the lawns of epiphytes and periphyton covering the plants and the filamentous metaphyton. All of these animals are vulnerable to predators, however, and experiments have shown that increasing the numbers of their predators leads ultimately to less grazing, more algal growth and reduced or failing plant growth.

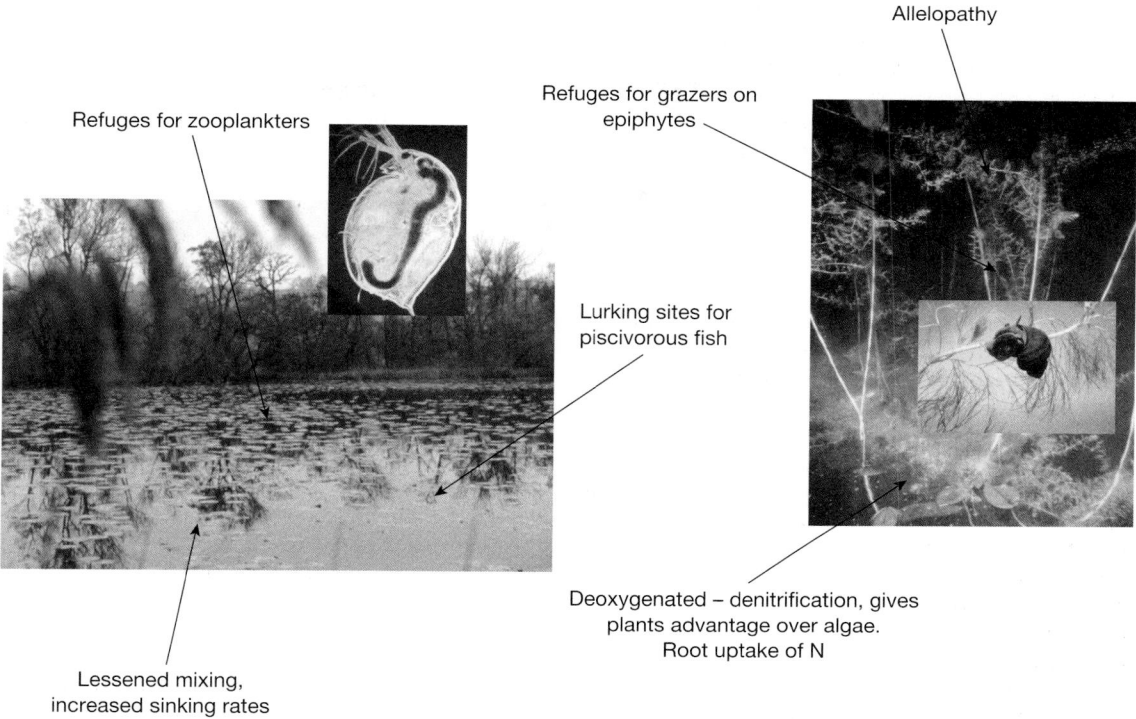

Refuges for zooplankters

Allelopathy

Refuges for grazers on epiphytes

Lurking sites for piscivorous fish

Deoxygenated – denitrification, gives plants advantage over algae. Root uptake of N

Lessened mixing, increased sinking rates

**Fig. 12.10** A variety of mechanisms stabilizes the existence of plant beds in littoral zones (see text).

Invertebrate and vertebrate predation both occur but the latter seems to be most important in general. Vertebrates are visual feeders, needing to see their prey before launching an attack, and space in which to make it without damaging themselves, so the shaded labyrinths among the plants limit this activity, giving a refuge to the grazers. The deoxygenated water at the bottom of the bed is also a deterrent, for in general larger animals require higher concentrations of oxygen than smaller ones. A phalanx of piscivorous fish also forms up around the edges of a bed, where lurking sites are plentiful, also deterring forage fish from entering. Some predation occurs, of course, within the plant beds, but these mechanisms limit it and the preference of visual predators for the largest animals they can ingest (because this represents the best return on the energy invested in capturing them) may mean that the invertebrate predators, being often slightly bigger than their grazer prey, are the more vulnerable.

All of these mechanisms may sometimes fail, though generally not all at once, so the littoral communities are stable. Sometimes, however, several can fail together and the community can be destroyed and switch to a much simpler algal-dominated community of filamentous algae or phytoplankton, or even just muddy water, lacking much plant structure. This is usually the result of human interference (see Chapter 15) but an alternation of the plant-dominated and the turbid-water states can probably occur naturally. Major increases in water level reduce light availability and may eliminate plants, which return as the level decreases, and such alternations have been recorded in Lake Krankeskon in Sweden. In Florida lakes Apopka and Okeechobee, hurricanes can cause immense devastation and simply tear out the plants, replacing them with muddy water and then plankton for a time, but the system then recovers. More usually it is cutting the vegetation too vigorously, use of herbicides, rising salinity, introduction of exotic species that graze heavily, such as common carp, Canada geese, and alien crayfish, or build up of large, artificially fed populations of ducks and geese that displace the plants. Poisoning of the grazers with pesticides or other trace organics present in wastewater effluent can also effect a switch. Removing the cause will allow the plants to recover providing that nutrient levels have not also increased but generally there will have been accompanying eutrophication and this makes restoration more complicated (Chapter 15).

## 12.6 LATITUDE AND LITTORALS

The workings of the littoral may change with latitude. The nature of the plants does not change greatly, except that perhaps floating species are more likely to dominate in warmer climates, perhaps as an adaptation to greatly changing water levels. But algal growth rates and the fish communities change a great deal and these have consequences. If algae grow much faster at higher temperatures, there is a possibility that grazers may not be able to prevent their shading out the slower growing higher plant communities. A set of experiments was made in similar shallow lakes in Finland, Sweden, The Netherlands, UK and Spain, spanning a gradient of about 10° of latitude. Into plastic enclosures (mesocosms) of about 1 m³ volume in the lakes, a submerged plant community was variously exposed to a range of nutrient loadings and fish populations. The consequences of these on the amount of planktonic algae growing in the water were followed. The expectations were that more fish would increase the algal growth and make the water more turbid because they remove grazing zooplankton and that more nutrients would also mean more algae. These effects were found but the particular interest was the relative importance of the fish and the nutrients. In the warmer lakes, the nutrients apparently became more critical because zooplankton grazing activity was negligible because, in turn, the fish predation in the warmer water was more intense (Fig. 12.11). The experiment used only one species of fish, but a general phenomenon of greater fish predation on zooplankton with decreasing latitude is being shown.

Fish communities become richer from the Poles to the Equator, and they become relatively richer in omnivorous species (Fig. 12.12) and poorer in piscivorous species that might control the omnivores feeding on a variety of foods including zooplankton, bottom invertebrates, and sometimes plants and algae. Warmwater fish often reproduce several times per year and populations of small fish can be very large. Sometimes they are ovoviviparous, producing live young that

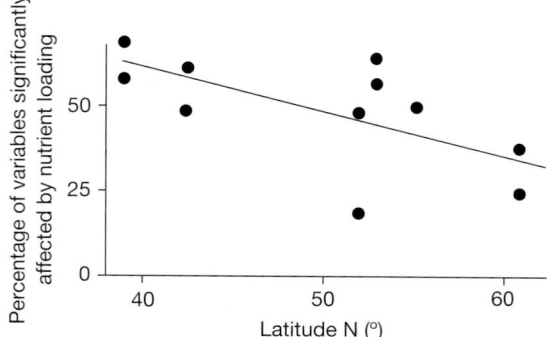

**Fig. 12.11** In an experiment with sets of mesocosms carried out across Europe, the effects of increasing nutrients and fish on the overlying plankton communities of littoral plant beds were studied. This summary of the results shows the proportion of about 30 chemical and biological variables in the systems that were influenced by the nutrient and fish treatments. Strikingly, because fish predation was so great at lower latitudes and eliminated most of the zooplankton, the effects of nutrients became relatively more prominent. (From Moss et al. 2004.)

rapidly become established. Any large, more efficiently grazing zooplankters (see Chapter 13) are rapidly eliminated and algal growth is unhindered.

A comparison of food webs associated with experimental, artificial plants, between paired Danish lakes and lakes in the warm temperate Uruguay (Fig. 12.13) shows clearly how the food webs differ, with maintenance of much higher algal growth in Uruguay. A comparison across 66 lakes from Finland to Spain also showed much higher ratios of fish to zooplankton and lower ratios of zooplankton to algae with decreasing latitude (Fig. 12.14). In the extreme cases of lakes in Greenland, shallow lakes (around 1.5–2 m) have no fish because of winter deoxygenation under the long period of ice cover, whilst deeper lakes do have fish, but only one species, the Arctic charr. The fishless lakes have abundant invertebrates and clear water as the zooplankters keep algal biomass very low. There is more algal turbidity in the lakes with fish as grazing invertebrates are eaten.

## 12.7 THE ROLE OF THE NEKTON

The above sections have emphasized just how important fish can be in regulating the littoral community.

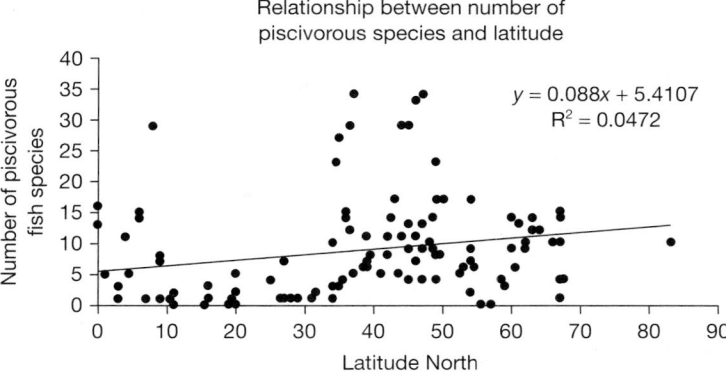

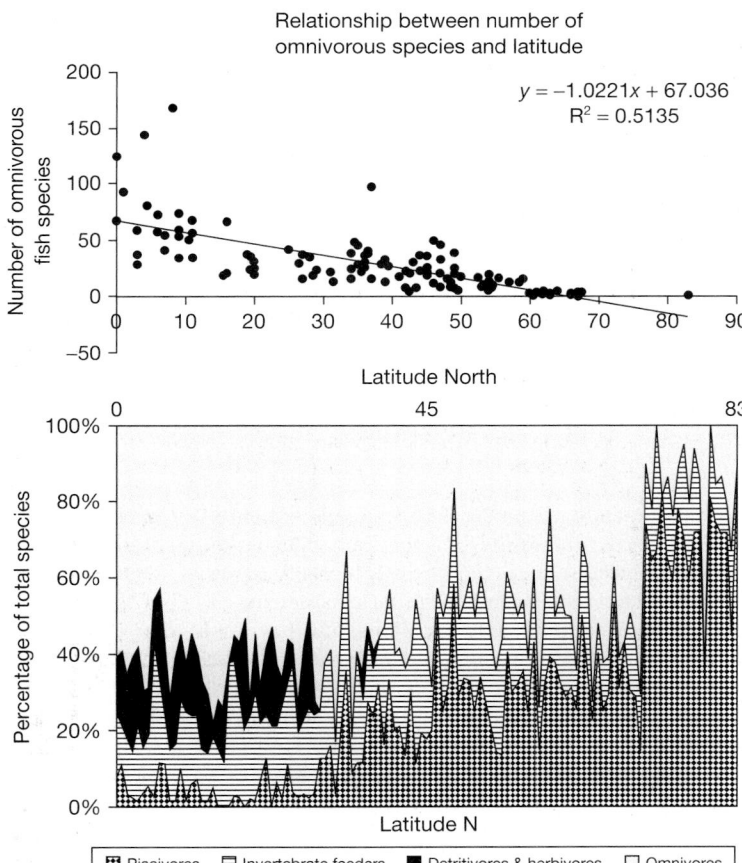

**Fig. 12.12** Changes in the numbers of species of piscivorous fish (top left) and of omnivorous fish (bottom left) and percentage composition of fish communities (right) by trophic category along a latitudinal gradient in South, Central and North America. Species lists were gleaned from the literature for 120 lake and river sites and food preferences allocated from available literature. Trends were very similar for both rivers and lakes so data have been combined. Piscivores means species that primarily feed on other fish as adults; invertebrate feeders feed primarily on benthos or zooplankton, herbivores solely on detritus, plant or algal material. Omnivores take food more or less equally from at least two trophic levels. Trends with latitude for percentage piscivores, omnivores and herbivores but not invertivores are statistically significant at $P < 0.001$ (regression analysis), as is that for actual number of omnivorous species. The trends are not explained by area, altitude, depth or alkalinity (as a surrogate for productivity). (Unpublished data, B. Moss.)

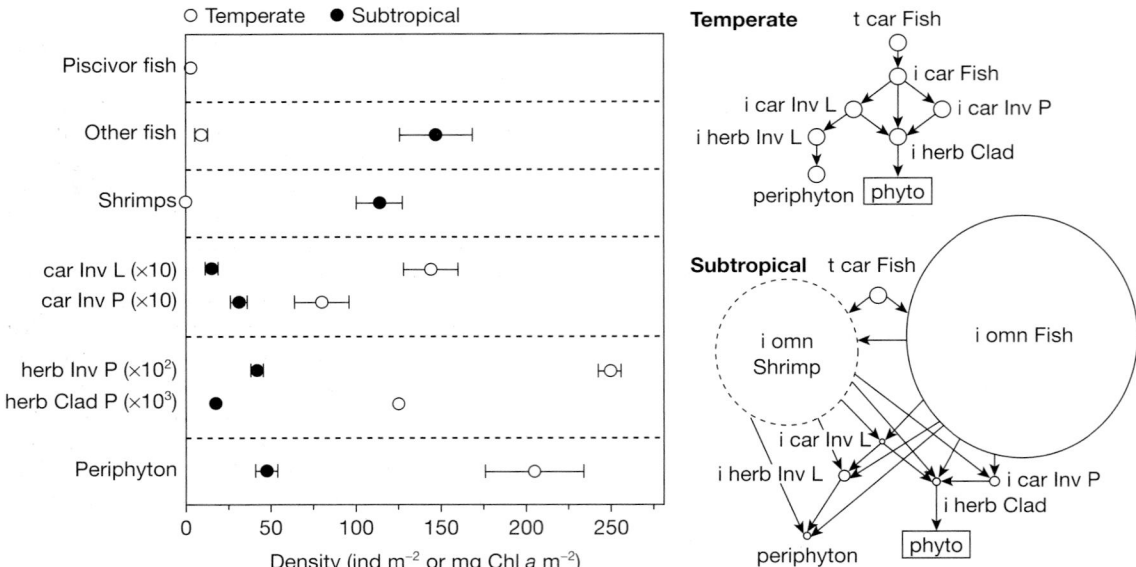

**Fig. 12.13** Experimental systems using artificial plants resembling both submerged and floating species were carried out in six lakes in each of Uruguay (warm temperate) and Denmark (cold temperate). The plants were allowed to colonize and the communities then analysed for numbers of animals and periphyton chlorophyll *a* (left). The two systems were then compared (right) by taking the cold temperate values and plotting them as circles of unit area and plotting diagrams in which the warm temperate values are scaled relative to the cold temperate. There are no shrimps in Denmark, so the circle for these is shown dashed and of notional area. The strikingly greater fish and predatory and herbivorous shrimp populations in the warm temperate lakes are notable as are the lower numbers of other invertebrates and of periphyton biomass. Abbreviations: t, top level of the food web; i, intermediate level of the food web; car, carnivore; inv, invertebrate; L, littoral species; P, pelagic species; herb, herbivore; Clad, Cladocera. (Based on Meerhoff et al. 2007b.) The species richness of the fish communities was also much greater in the warm temperate lakes (Texeira de Melo et al. 2009).

Birds, reptiles and mammals are also prominent parts of the littoral community but they are difficult to investigate because they cannot easily be confined, as fish and invertebrates can be, can for experiments to reveal their roles. Birds may eat plants, but they also eat invertebrates. Many water birds will gather plants as nesting material, as do rodents such as muskrats. Beavers, crocodilians and hippopotami may respectively clear areas of vegetation to make nests, for creating living space in the dry season, or as highways for their nightly movements to graze on land or to bask in the sun by day. In doing so they change patterns of water movement and create niches for other organisms Water snakes eat fish and chicks of water birds. We have very little idea about how all of these animals interact with the plants and invertebrates and water chemistry and this is a fruitful area for future research. The bottom line, however, is that stable littoral and

mire communities are associated with all of these organisms and that it is most unlikely that any bird, reptile or mammal acts independently. The remoteness of the centres of mires and the density of reedbeds provide nesting sites for many birds, but it is unlikely that the plants do not benefit in some way in return or that the functioning of the system does not in some way depend on the birds. It is simply the difficulty of working with large, highly mobile animals that is behind our ignorance of these matters.

Some simple relationships are known, however. The isolation of ponds often means that fish are absent, either because they were never able to invade or became locally extinct when the pond dried out sometime in the past. The tadpoles of amphibian are often attractive, large prey for fish and fishless pools in colder regions are favoured sites for amphibian breeding. The complexities are illustrated, however, by mutual

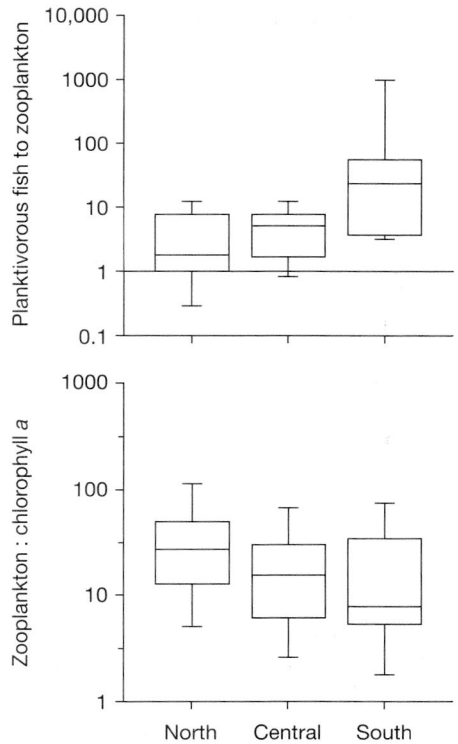

**Fig.12.14** Fish and zooplankton community biomasses, and phytoplankton chlorophyll *a* in 66 shallow lakes across Europe, from Finland to Spain were measured in summer, and the ratios of planktivorous fish to zooplankton and zooplankton to phytoplankton chlorophyll *a* calculated for groups of lakes in north, central and southern Europe. Results are shown on logarithmic scales. The increasing trend of fish to zooplankton and the decreasing ratio of zooplankton to phytoplankton from north to south are clear. In the warmer lakes, the more abundant fish remove so much zooplankton that grazing is limited and algal crops flourish. (Based on Gyllstrom et al. 2005.)

coexistence of much richer amphibian and fish faunas in the tropics, where evolution of predator-deterrent poisons confers immunity on the tadpoles and even adults of many species of frogs.

A second example comes from floodplain lakes in Europe. As the waters rise in spring, many fish move out from lagoons and pools in which they have over-wintered into the surrounding reedswamps where dense cover from the plant debris and perennial stems provides an abundance of safe spawning sites. The piscivorous pike (*Esox lucius*) are prominent among

these fish and there is prolific recruitment. As the water recedes, the fish must move back to the deeper pools and lagoons and the young pike become highly concentrated. There is intense competition among them, reflected in heavy predation on the young of other fish whose food is zooplankton and other invertebrates. In turn numbers of these prey fish are reduced and invertebrate periphyton and phytoplankton grazers and plants benefit at a vulnerable time as the plants are growing up through the water column to reach greater light intensities nearer to the surface. The pike that survive benefit from the lurking sites in the guaranteed plant cover that this mechanism produces. Thus there are hints here of close relationships between the littoral and the plankton, a community to be examined in Chapter 13. And in Chapter 15, a major theme will be the ways in which the littorals of shallow lakes have been damaged or obliterated by a failure of the insurance policies outlined in Section 12.5.

## FURTHER READING

The concept and science of wetlands are exhaustively covered in Mitsch & Gosselink (2007), with Van der Valk (2006) providing a shorter text, though there is a very large literature on mires, particularly their plant ecology and insects. Bradbury & Grace (1983) review productivity, Bedford et al. (1999) nutrient relations, Sraj-Krzic et al. (2006), the importance of mycorrhizae to mire plants, Bouchard et al. (2007) functional traits, and Bodelier et al. (2006) and Bolpagni et al. (2007), the release and storage of methane, a topic of considerable interest where climate change (Chapter 16) is concerned. Adamec (1997, 2008) covers insectivorous plants and Turner & Scaife (1995), bog bodies. Page et al. (1999) and Phillips (1998) describe tropical peat swamps, whilst SheehySkeffington et al. (2006) review the fascinating topic of turloughs, which are shallow lakes on the limestone in Ireland which are full of water for part of the year but dry down, as water tables become lower, to mires and grasslands in summer. They differ greatly from warm country lakes, which evaporate away in summer, becoming more saline, as they remain fresh at all stages.

The plants of lake littorals are reviewed by Spence (1982), isoetid habitats by Smolders et al. (2002) and charophytes by Kufel & Kufel (2002). Spence & Chrystal (1970a,b) is good experimental work on the role of light in determining the occurrence of different species at different depths. The increasing importance of allelopathic chemicals and kairemones can be approached through Burks & Lodge (2002), Mulderij et al. (2007), Van Donk (2005, 2007) and Hilt & Grosse (2008). The topics of the biology of animals and algae associated with lake littorals also have a large literature, of which Reynoldson (1966) is a small gem of how to go about investigating the reasons for the distribution of animals. A flavour of the literature is given by Cyr & Downing (1988), France (1998), Hargeby (1990), Jones et al. (1999), Warfe & Barmuta (2006), Kornijow (1989), Lodge (1985), Theel et al. (2008), Jeppesen et al. (2001), Phillips et al. (1978), Moss (1977), and Schlacher & Cronin (2007). Meerhof et al. (2006, 2007a,b) are beginning to introduce an element of warm temperate biology into this area.

Wider issues of alternative states of plants and turbid water can be traced through Irvine et al. (1989), Scheffer et al. (1993) and Moss (2007), with more detailed studies of regulation and stabilising mechanisms variously covered in Cazzaneli et al. (2008), Timms & Moss (1984), Zambrano et al. (2006), Irfannulah & Moss (2005), Eminson & Moss (1980), Moss (1976, 1995), Moss et al. (1998) and Jeppesen et al. (2001). Hargeby et al. (2007) and James et al. (2008) deal with apparently natural switches between states, the latter concerning the role of hurricanes.

Finally linkages between littoral zones and the catchment and the roles of birds and mammals are variously covered in Gratton et al. (2008), Klaassen & Nolet (2007), Parker et al. (2007b), Hahn et al. (2007, 2008), Schindler & Scheuerell (2002) and Wetzel (1990).

# Chapter 13

# PLANKTON COMMUNITIES OF THE PELAGIC ZONE

## 13.1 KITCHENS AND TOILETS

Lake water sparkling in the sunlight hides a miniscule waterscape that is closer to a slum than a paradise. It contains, in every litre, millions of organisms, passively suspended or sometimes weakly swimming. Some are photosynthetic; others feed on organic matter, live and dead, dissolved and particulate. The water contains their excretions and secretions, faeces and corpses, mixed with debris washed into suspension from the surrounding land. In this melange, chemical and biological changes, both cyclic and irreversible, are taking place very rapidly. The planktonic system has traditionally been seen as the most important system in lakes, probably because of the attraction of big lakes and historical investigations on their open-water fisheries. In big lakes it is the predominant system. But most of the world's lakes are small and shallow and the littoral zones are far more diverse and complex than the open water. The plankton system is, in fact, a highly specialist community, adapted to a habitat of simple structure and scarce resources, and ultimately derived from colonists from the littoral.

Because there is little to see of the plankton community with the naked eye, it is useful to have a scaled up model to be able to imagine its workings. Scaling one of these organisms to human size and considering the rest relative to it will help indicate the structure of this community. The rotifer *Keratella quadrata* (Fig. 13.1), a common zooplankter, has a body about 125 μm long (about half the size of a full stop on this page) with spines, half as long, held out behind. If the body of *Keratella* is scaled to the size of a tall man then the rest of the community ranges from flour grains (for viruses) to peanuts, horses and large houses, and for fish, to the size of leviathans, 50 km long! The water in which the plankton lives is viscous relative to small objects. In the scaled up analogy, the viscosity of the fluid must also be increased, so the community must be imagined as suspended in light oil or glycerol.

Organisms that passively drift, maintained in suspension by water currents, or float or swim weakly, comprise the plankton. They include viruses, heterotrophic bacterioplankton, photosynthetic phytoplankton and the swimming zooplankton, some of which graze on smaller cells and detritus, other of which are predators on smaller zooplankters. The larger, strongly swimming nekton that is not at the mercy of movement by water currents includes fish, and visiting piscivorous birds and bats.

The plankton can also be categorized by size. Sometimes, for the smaller cells, it may be difficult to know whether a cell is photosynthetic or heterotrophic or uses both feeding modes and from the point of view of a grazing zooplankter, size is more relevant than function.

*Ecology of Freshwaters: A View for the Twenty-first Century*, 4th edition. By Brian Moss. Published 2010 by Blackwell Publishing Ltd.

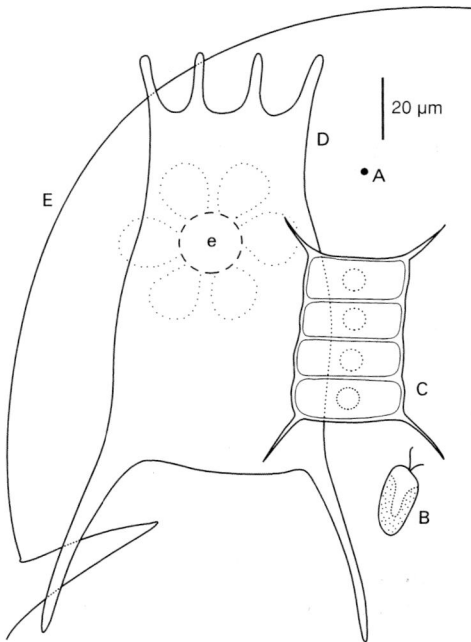

**Fig. 13.1** Relative sizes of some major components of the plankton. (A) a bacterium; (B) *Cryptomonas*, a relatively small phytoplankter; (C) *Scenedesmus*, a moderately large phytoplankter; (D) *Keratella*, a small zooplankter; (E) outline of the head with eye (e), of *Daphnia*, a large zooplankter. The head constitutes about a quarter to a fifth of the total body size.

The non-zooplankters have thus sometimes been divided into ultraplankton (<2–5 μm), nanoplankton (5–20 μm), microplankton (20–60 μm) and net plankton (>60 μm), though there is a continuum of size and these terms mostly reflect the pore sizes of filters and mesh sizes of netting available to separate the organisms. Lately, more terms, femtoplankton (virus-like particles, 0.02–0.2 μm) and picoplankton (0.2–2 μm) have been coined. The latter describes heterotrophic bacteria, and blue-green and eukaryote algae of bacterial size. Indeed almost all of the size categories may contain heterotrophic (bacteria or Protozoa) or photosynthetic organisms (prokaryotes or eukaryotes). Pico- and ultraplankters may carry out a substantial part of the photosynthesis of the plankton community in the oceans and in infertile lakes, though they were unknown until the 1940s when the inverted microscope was invented because relatively coarse nets had been used to concentrate the plankton for study.

In very infertile waters where photosynthetic growth is limited by nutrient shortage, heterotrophic bacterioplankton, feeding on organic matter imported from the catchment or secreted by the phytoplankters, may be as important in providing food to the zooplankters as the photosynthetic organisms. Protozoa (flagellates and ciliates) may then be crucial in converting the smallest bacteria to particles sufficiently large for some zooplankters to feed. It is now usual to distinguish such detrital pathways, or microbial loops, from the more conventional grazing pathways based on photosynthesis *in situ* (see Chapter 11). Carbon dioxide and photosynthetic algae form the bases of the latter and the algae are mostly big enough to be eaten directly by the metazoon zooplankters. Where tiny photosynthetic algae are involved, there may be an intermediate protozoan stage and the detrital and photosynthetic pathways merge. Moreover, some phytoplankton species, particularly chrysophytes, cryptophytes and dinoflagellates, are phagotrophic, consuming bacteria, as well as photosynthesizing and yet others may also absorb dissolved organic matter. The simple concept of a photosynthetic phytoplankton base to a series of herbivorous animals and larger carnivores is still central but garlanded by numerous heterotrophic complications.

But whatever the source of carbon and energy in the productive pelagic kitchen, there are inevitable wastes. Live and dead phytoplankton sink; zooplankton and fish faeces sink; organic particles, washed in from the catchment and littoral zone, studded with colonizing bacteria and Protozoa, sink. They all fall slowly through the water column, perhaps taking only minutes in shallow water, days in deep, to reach the bottom. They fall from the bright upper layers through the diminishing twilight to the dark sediments, where bacteria, Protozoa, invertebrates and fish, if there is enough oxygen, will finally process it, leaving the more refractory molecules to become the organic matter of the sediment. The littoral and pelagic are the kitchens of the lake; the profundal benthos is its lavatory and sewage works, avidly attended by palaeolimnologists seeking its final record of the lake's history.

## 13.2 PHYTOPLANKTON

Phytoplankters are of many species, mostly oxygen-evolving prokaryotic blue-green algae (Cyanobacteria, Cyanophycota) and eukaryotic algae. The eukaryote

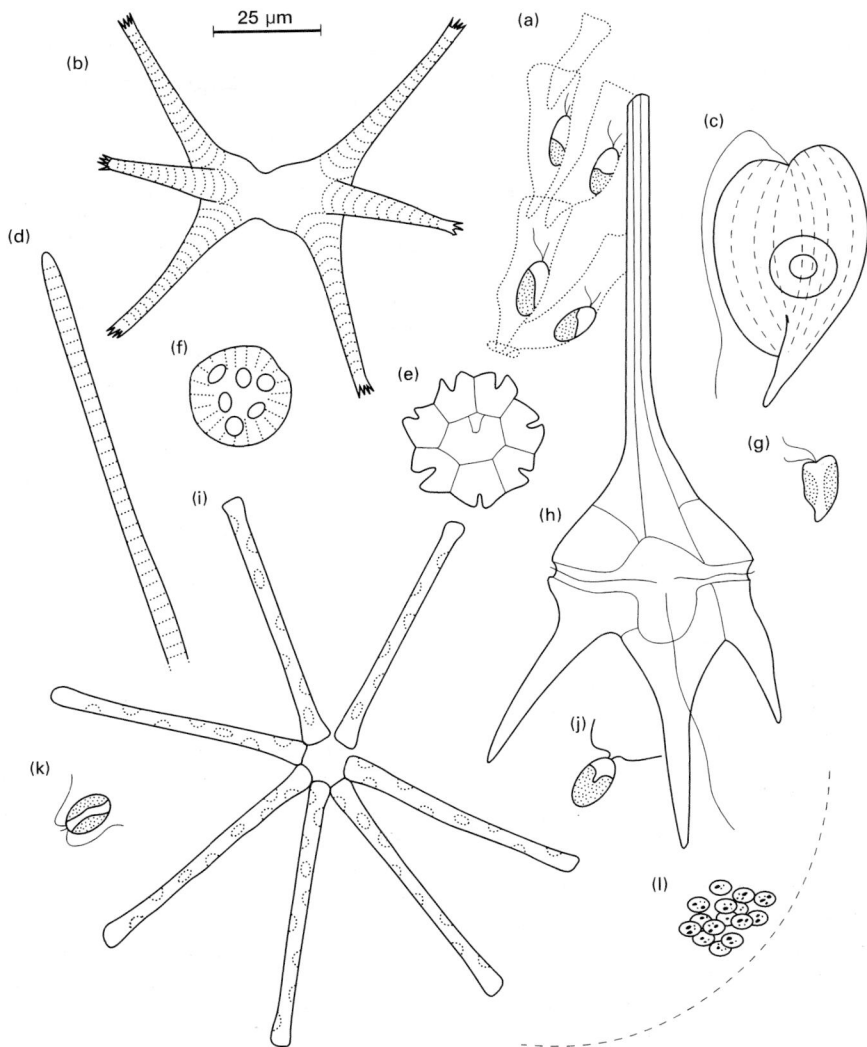

**Fig. 13.2** Some typical phytoplankton algae, drawn to the same scale. Cyanobacteria (blue-green algae): (d) *Oscillatoria*, (l) *Microcystis*. Chrysophyta (yellow-green or golden algae): (a) *Dinobryon*. Chlorophyta (green algae): (e) *Pediastrum*, (b) *Staurastrum* (a member of a group called the desmids), (j) *Chlamydomonas*. Bacillariophyta (diatoms): (f) *Cyclotella*, (i) *Asterionella*. Euglenophyta (euglenoids): (c) *Phacus*. Cryptophyta (cryptomonads): (g) *Rhodomonas*. Pyrrophyta (dinoflagellates): (h) *Ceratium*. Haptophyta: (k) *Prymnesium*. *Microcystis* (l) is a very large alga, of which a diagram of the entire colony could occupy as much as this page. Only a few cells are shown.

groups of greatest importance are the Cryptophyceae (cryptophytes), Dinophyceae (dinoflagellates), Chlorophycota (green algae), Euglenophycota (euglenoids), Bacillariophyceae (diatoms), Chrysophyceae (yellow-green, or golden-yellow algae) and Haptophyceae (Haptophytes). There are several different taxonomic systems, however, that accommodate them. Some examples are shown in Fig. 13.2. In some transparent stratified lakes, light may penetrate to deep layers that have become low in oxygen or anaerobic. Communities of non-oxygenic photosynthetic bacteria (the purple and green sulphur bacteria) may be found there (Chapter 6, Fig. 6.1). In the scaled-up model (Section 13.1), the sizes of unicellular phytoplankters range from those of lentils and peanuts (1–5 μm) to footballs and water melons (50 μm). Some colonies may be visible to the naked eye (several hundred μm) and would be scaled as heavy horses or elephants.

A common misconception is that phytoplankters float. This is generally not so (they are suspended and drift) but certain cyanobacteria (blue-green algae), which are sometimes very abundant in warm or fertile lakes, have organelles called gas vesicles. These comprise masses of protein-bound prisms with conical ends, contain air and give positive buoyancy. Under some circumstances these cyanobacteria may truly float at particular depths in the water column that favour their growth, and in other circumstances may form a paint-like scum or water bloom at the lake surface (see later). Similar gas vesicles are used by the anaerobic photosynthetic bacteria to maintain themselves in the most appropriate part of the redox gradient (Fig. 6.1).

Excepting *Botryococcus braunii*, a green alga, which may remain positively buoyant by storing large quantities of oil, all other phytoplankters are denser than water. Diatoms, which have cell walls of silica, may be considerably more so. Most phytoplankters are kept suspended in the water by wind-generated (eddy) currents that continually lift the sinking cells higher into the water column. Some species have flagella and movement of these may also help counteract the inevitable tendency to sink. Sinking is described, in the simple case of a spherical particle, by Stoke's Law, which states that the rate of sinking (*v*) is related to the acceleration due to gravity (*g*), the radius of the sinking particle (*r*) and the densities of the particle ($\rho_p$) and water ($\rho_w$) and the viscosity of the water ($\mu$) as:

$$v = (0.0222\, g\, r^2\, (\rho_p - \rho_w))\, \mu^{-1}$$

Changing shape from a sphere, without changing density, or increasing the 'radius', the dimension that the cell presents to the water as it sinks, can reduce sinking rates. Flat plates, needle-shapes with curved ends, spines and projections all seem to be advantageous. However, too easy an acceptance of shape as adaptive should be avoided. Envelopes of mucilage, invisible unless the cells are mounted in Indian ink, may be thick enough to give a spiny cell an effectively spherical shape, and may even lubricate passage through the water.

Why do phytoplankters sink? Sinking, with its potential for loss of the organism from the illuminated zone, clearly has disadvantages and some species have evolved buoyancy. Why not all? The answer is that sinking has advantages. Phytoplankters need a supply of inorganic nutrients, which they absorb from the water layer, a few micrometres thick, immediately in contact with the cell. Molecular forces tend to preserve this layer intact and it soon becomes depleted of nutrients, which are not rapidly replaced by diffusion alone from more distant water. Continuous movement of the cell through the water, as it sinks, and is retrieved by eddy currents, sloughs away the depleted nutrient shell and replaces it with a supply of undepleted water. The cells must move relative to the water, if they are not to become nutrient-starved. You might then ask why they do not retain such movement through all having buoyancy. The answer might be that on still days they might get trapped at the surface where high light intensities can be damaging to organisms fitted for photosynthesis in the generally dim environment to which eddy currents can mix them down, or that heavy silica walls confer advantages (less energy to produce) or that oil or protein gas vesicles are costly. But in the end, most phytoplankters sink.

Phytoplankters were once assumed to satisfy their carbon and energy needs through photosynthesis alone. This is true for many but not all. Some require at least one pre-formed organic compound, usually a vitamin, such as cyanocobalamin ($B_{12}$), thiamine or biotin. In general the cyanobacteria, diatoms and desmids (one group of green algae) do not require additional organic compounds, but many algae of other groups are able to take up simple organic compounds heterotrophically. However, the concentrations of such compounds are normally low in natural waters and the many bacteria successfully compete for them. Some plankters, of highly organic sewage oxidation ponds (usually green algae and euglenoids), may depend as greatly on organic uptake for their energy needs as on photosynthesis.

The smaller phytoplankters (up to 10 μm) may occur, during the growth season, in very large numbers: up to $10^6$ mL$^{-1}$ compared with about $10^2$–$10^5$ for the larger phytoplankters. On the scaled-up model, the smaller species would appear as a population of objects the size of tennis balls mutually spaced at distances of about 2.5 m. The larger algae can be imagined as a similar constellation of water melons, 27 m apart. Several species may simultaneously be forming large populations in the water, but there is still a lot of space between the individuals. This might explain why, despite their ubiquity, parasitic fungi (frequently chytrids) and parasitic Protozoa only cause epidemics when algal population densities are very large. Successful infestation of a host cell requires an encounter which may be rare in an environment where hosts are well spaced and both host and parasite are continually moved by turbulence. It is also perhaps why most reproduce vegetatively. Phytoplankters are remarkable (compared with the much more diverse algal flora of the littoral zone) for their near abandonment of sexual reproduction. They live vulnerable lives: most are readily grazed; all may be washed out of their habitat by incoming floods; there is a constant danger of sinking to deep, dark water, where photosynthesis is not possible and where they may be trapped in the sediments; and nutrients are scarce. Their habitat is an extreme one of rarified resources and physical danger. Not surprisingly, there has been selection against sexual reproduction in such a habitat, for death rates are high, sexual reproduction is slow and genetic recombination might disturb the intricate adaptations already developed. Most phytoplankters reproduce only by asexual cell division with generation times of hours or a few days.

The very wide size range of phytoplankters (from lentils to elephants in the model) is also remarkable, particularly because in a nutrient-scarce medium (Chapter 4), small bodies with high surface to volume ratios should be able to compete more effectively for nutrients. Large cells also sink faster and hence are more vulnerable to loss from the epilimnion in stratified lakes. There should thus be selection for small cells. Nonetheless, there are large phytoplankters. The advantage to large size is that big cells are less readily eaten by filter feeding zooplankters, which are mechanically unable to manipulate large cells or colonies into their mouths. There are thus several different risks to balance in surviving as a phytoplankter and the balance may be reached in many ways. A simple equation describes the conditions for increase in a population of a phytoplankter, which means that the risks have been successfully balanced. It will increase its number ($N$) if its growth rate ($b$) is greater than the sum of its rates of loss by sinking and trapping in the sediments ($v$), grazing ($g$) and flushing out of the water body ($w$):

$$dN/dt = bN - (vN + gN + wN)$$

The existence of many thousand planktonic species – with several hundred in almost any lake – means that

this equation has been successfully balanced in thousands of different ways. G.E. Hutchinson long ago pointed out the paradox, or puzzle, that so many species could simultaneously coexist in what appears to be a uniform habitat. The solution is that first it is not entirely structureless at a given time, secondly that it changes rapidly and thriving species and declining species will not keep pace and their populations will overlap, and thirdly that coexistence is possible if the equation is balanced in different ways. The next sections will look at the components of the equation.

### 13.2.1 Photosynthesis and growth of phytoplankton

Photosynthesis, the fixation of light energy into chemical bonds, and growth, the synthesis of new cell material, are different processes. Although the latter requires the former, photosynthesis is not necessarily followed by growth if the necessary materials are not available. Measurement of photosynthesis was discussed in Chapter 9. If water from a well-mixed water column is placed in bottles and resuspended at a series of depths, and the photosynthetic rates measured by the oxygen-release method, a characteristic curve of gross photosynthesis with depth is obtained (Fig. 13.3).

Photosynthesis is often low at the surface, perhaps due to inhibition by ultraviolet light, with a peak at some depth below. This peak is set when the photosynthetic pigments are unable to abstract any more radiation (at light saturation, $I_k$). Its size and position depend on the light saturated rate of photosynthesis per unit of biomass ($P_{max}$) and of the total biomass ($n$) of photosynthesizing cells present. Usually biomass is expressed as chlorophyll $a$. The curve of photosynthesis with depth declines exponentially below the peak. The depth to which photosynthesis extends depends on the surface intensity ($I_0$) and the minimum attenuation coefficient for light absorption in the water ($km_{in}$) (Chapter 5). As the biomass increases it becomes a major contributor to the attentuation and the curve is displaced upwards. Such a curve can be described by an equation for the total photosynthesis per unit area of lake ($\sum a$), which has been determined to be approximately:

$$\sum a = nP_{max}1/1.33\ k_{min}.(I_0/I_k)$$

The value of 1.33 was determined empirically and the term $I_0/I_k$ approximately describes the position of the

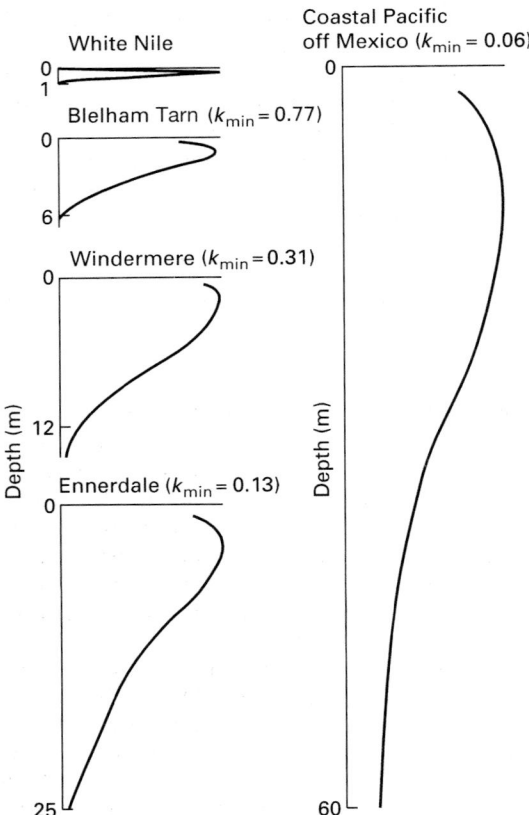

**Fig. 13.3** Examples of gross photosynthesis depth profiles in a series of waters of increasing turbidity as indicated by the value of the minimum extinction coefficient in each case. (Based on Talling 1971.)

varies with the nature of the algae (lower for large cells than for smaller ones) but is often from about 0.008 to 0.021 natural logarithm (ln) units $m^{-1}$ ($\mu g\ L^{-1}$)$^{-1}$. A crop of 100 $\mu g\ L^{-1}$ of chlorophyll $a$, in a lake of background attenuance $k_{min}$ = 0.3 $m^{-1}$, could then reduce the potential euphotic zone (Chapter 5) from 12.3 m to between 3.4 and 0.17 m. At high chlorophyll $a$ concentrations (usually above about 300 $\mu g\ m^{-2}$) the algae can then shade themselves.

Mean values of gross photosynthesis in g $O_2\ m^{-2}\ day^{-1}$ might be 10–30 for temperate lakes and more than 50 for some tropical lakes or in other units, perhaps 800 to 1800 g C $m^{-2}\ year^{-1}$. The actual growth of algae, however, is likely to be much less, for these are values for gross photosynthesis or production. Net production is lower by the amount of respiration of the algal cells and even then may be expressed as carbohydrate or fat storage in the cells, rather than by true growth, the production of new cells.

### 13.2.2 Net production and growth

Algal respiration rates are likely to be high (and net production therefore low) relative to gross photosynthesis in early spring in a temperate lake when the water column is vigorously mixing, and the phytoplankton cells are forced to spend long periods in deeper water at low light intensities. The same is true for longer periods in very deep, well mixed lakes when the cells will also be circulating between the illuminated upper layers and layers below the euphotic zone ($Z_{eu}$). If the mixing depth ($Z_m$; the depth of the epilimnion), a function of wind and weather, is large relative to $Z_{eu}$ they may spend long periods unable to photosynthesize but inevitably respiring. Until, on average, the gross photosynthesis made by the cells when they are in the upper layers exceeds the respiration whilst they circulate throughout the mixed water column, no net production will be possible. This seems to determine the start of growth in spring in high latitudes. For example, in the deeper northern basin of Lake Windermere in the UK, growth starts about 2–3 weeks later than in the shallower southern basin where $Z_m$ is lower. In lakes in arid zones, high concentrations of suspended silt particles may effectively reduce $Z_{eu}$ considerably whilst not affecting $Z_m$. The same will be true of the highly humic stained waters of the peaty regions of the boreal zone and light may limit both gross and net production, even if nutrients are also very scarce. But even under

peak in the water column – the lower the intensity that photosynthesis becomes saturated, the deeper the peak. $I_k$ varies with different algae – it is often low for diatoms and cyanobacteria but higher for green algae, and the value of $P_{max}$ tends to increase with temperature with an approximate doubling for every 10°C.

The effects of the algae in absorbing light can be described by plotting, for a lake, the minimum attenuation coefficient ($k_{min}$) on several occasions against the chlorophyll $a$ concentration. The intercept on the $k$ axis (biomass = 0) gives the attenuation due to the background properties of the water and the slope of the line the attenuation per unit chlorophyll $a$. The value of this transparent conditions, as an algal crop grows and becomes self-shading, the photosynthetic rate per cell, determined by light, may be decreased whilst the respiration rate, determined by temperature does not and net production will then tend to become lower and lower and the nature of the algae will set a limit on their own gross production.

But even if respiratory demands are met, there may still be no growth despite some net fixation of carbon if nitrogen or phosphorus is scarce. Cells may then be forced immediately to respire synthesized carbon compounds, to store them or to secrete them to the water. Sometimes only a few per cent of the carbon fixed in photosynthesis is incorporated into new cell material. In unpolluted freshwater lakes, nitrogen, phosphorus or both are likely to be scarce and the degree of scarcity may determine the rate of growth as well as the potential maximum yield of algae.

### 13.2.3 Nutrient uptake and growth rates of phytoplankton

Phytoplankters need about 20 elements for growth but only C, N and P are likely to limit growth rates on any general basis. All are present in the water at lower concentrations than are required in the cell, so that active, energy-requiring mechanisms, involving enzymes, are needed to concentrate them into the cells. The efficiency of these mechanisms differs between species and can be measured as the half-saturation constant ($K_s$) for uptake rate ($\mu$) in an equation:

$$\mu = \mu_{max} S/(K_s + S)$$

The half saturation constant is the concentration ($S$) of nutrient at which half the maximum rate, $\mu_{max}$ (when the enzymes are saturated to full capacity) can be achieved. Values of $K_s$ should be lower for species growing in infertile lakes than those in fertile ones. Coexistence of two species competing for the same nutrients may also be possible if the first is more adept at taking up one nutrient and the other a second nutrient. For example, David Titman (1976) studied the relationship between two diatoms, *Asterionella formosa* and *Cyclotella meneghiniana*, both of which grew in Lake Michigan, with *Asterionella* more abundant in the open lake and *Cyclotella* near shore. Both species require both silicate and phosphate. Using a continuous culture apparatus in which a nutrient solution of constant composition can be supplied, Titman

determined $K_s$(P) for *Asterionella* to be 0.04 µmol P and for *Cyclotella*, 0.25 µmol P.

This suggests that if phosphate is scarce *Asterionella* will tend to compete favourably with *Cyclotella*. On the other hand if silicate is scarce the reverse is true, for $K_s$(Si) was 3.9 µmol Si for *Asterionella*, and 1.4 µmol Si for *Cyclotella*. For each species in turn, growth rates will be similar when:

$$\mu_{max} S_{(Si)}/S_{(Si)} + K_{s(Si)} = \mu_{max} S_{(P)}/S_{(P)} + K_{s(P)}$$

Hence both nutrients are in balanced supply for growth when:

$$S_{(Si)}/S_{(P)} = K_{s(Si)}/K_{s(P)}$$

For *Asterionella* this ratio is 3.9 : 0.04 or 97, so that at Si : P molar ratios greater than 97 in the water, *Asterionella* will be phosphorus limited. For *Cyclotella* the ratio is 5.6 and above and below this the diatom will be phosphorus and silicate limited respectively. When both species are present, both will be phosphorus limited when the ratio is greater than 97, and *Asterionella* will tend to survive rather than *Cyclotella*. When ratios are below 5.6, both are silicate limited but, being more efficient at silicate uptake, *Cyclotella* will predominate. But between 5.6 and 97, each diatom's growth rate is limited by a different nutrient and they should be able to grow together. In Lake Michigan, the Si : P ratio is between 200 and 500 in the open lake but is between 1 and 10 near the shore. The general predominance of *Asterionella* offshore and *Cyclotella* inshore is consistent with the laboratory findings.

This somewhat detailed example serves two functions. First it suggests that a high degree of explanation is possible in interpreting events in the open water, because, despite its complexities, the open water is a much simpler, less structured medium than the littoral zone. In the history of limnology there has perhaps always been more attention given to the plankton than the littoral perhaps because of this advantage, but much greater mechanistic explanation than in the example (two species, two nutrients) is not easy when more variables are introduced.

The second role served by the example is to emphasize the importance of availability of silicate, phosphate (and in other cases, inorganic nitrogen) in determining phytoplankton behaviour. A variety of indicators and tests may be used to demonstrate this. For nitrogen, high rates of ammonium uptake in the dark and increases in the ratio of carotenoids to chlorophylls suggest nitrogen deficiency. (Chlorophylls

**Table 13.1** Phytoplankton associations commonly encountered under various general conditions. Code letters are arbitrary and as used in Reynolds et al. (2002), on which the table is based.

| | Deep | | | | | | Shallow | |
|---|---|---|---|---|---|---|---|---|
| | **Mixed** | | | **Stratified** | | | | |
| | Low nutrients | Medium | High nutrients | Low nutrients | Medium | High nutrients | Clear water, low nutrients | Turbid water, high nutrients |
| | A Urosolenia, Cyclotella comensis (diatoms) Z Synechococcus, prokaryote picoplankton E Dinobryon, Mallomonas (yellow–green algae) | B Aulacoseira subarctica, A. islandica (diatoms) | C Asterionella formosa, Aulacoseira ambigua Y Cryptomonas, Rhodomonas (cryptomonads) | F Colonial chlorophytes, Botryococcus | N Tabellaria, (diatom) Cosmarium, Staurodesmus (green algae) T (very deep epilimnia) Geminella, Mougeotia, Tribonema (green algae) $L_o$ Peredinium, Woronichia, (dinoflagellates Merismopaedia (cyanobacterium) | P Fragilaria crotonensis, Aulacoseira granulata, (diatoms) Closterium aciculare, Staurastrum pingue (green algae) H Anabaena flos-aquae, Aphanizomenon, Anabaena lemmermanni, Gloeotrichia echinulata (cyanobacteria) U Uroglena (yellow green alga) $L_m$ Ceratium (dinoflagellate), Microcystis (cyanobacterium) | X3 Kolliella, (green alga) Chrysococcus (yellow–green alga) X2 Plagioselmis, (cryptomonad) Chrysochromulina (yellow–green alga) E Dinobryon, Mallomonas (yellow green algae) | D (riverine) Synedra acus, Nitzschia (diatoms) S (cool waters) Planktothrix agardhii, Limnothrix redekei, Pseudanabaena, (warm waters) Spirulina, Arthrospira, (saline waters) Raphidiopsis, Aphanothece (cyanobacteria) $S_N$ (in warm waters) Cylindrospermopsis, Anabaena minutissima (cyanobacteria) X1 Chlorella, Ankyra (green algae) G (where grazing intense). Eudorina, Volvox (green algae) J (ponds) Pediastrum, Coelastrum, Scenedesmus (green algae) M Microcystis (cyanobacterium) |

W small organic ponds, Euglenoids, Synura, (yellow green alga) Gonium (green alga) Q Small humic lakes Gonyostomum are nitrogen-containing compounds, which the cell may be unable to synthesize if nitrogen is scarce). For phosphorus an increase in the activity of acid phosphatase enzymes (which can break down organic phosphorus compounds), a high rate of isotopic $^{32}P$ uptake and an absence of free phosphate in the cells suggest scarcity. Nutrient limitation is frequently demonstrable. The interesting question, raised in Chapter 4, is whether this is normal, or whether it is an artefact of human activities changing the loading rates of different nutrients in different ways and altering the natural Redfield ratio.

## 13.2.4 Distribution of freshwater phytoplankton

Land vegetation obviously differs from place to place, both in its appearance and species composition. Many algae are cosmopolitan and among the freshwater phytoplankton genera, at least, such major latitudinal differences are not found. There are some climatic effects, however, with Cyanobacteria tending to be commoner in warm lakes. But this may reflect secondary effects such as less intense zooplankton grazing (see Chapter 12). The substantial differences in phytoplankton communities among different lakes (Table 13.1) for the most part reflect the depth and presence of absence of stratification, the nutrient loading and the ways in which the survival equation has been balanced under different conditions.

Diatoms, with their relatively heavy cells, are most common in vigorously mixed waters, such as those of deep lakes in spring, or in shallow waters (though not so shallow that the diatoms too readily settle out). The stabler waters of the summer tend to support less dense green algae, flagellates, such as dinoflagellates, and cyanobacteria, especially those with gas vesicles. Nitrogen-fixing cyanobacteria tend to develop in the late summer waters, when nitrogen has been depleted and supplies from the catchment have become low as evaporation exceeds rainfall. Daily movements up and down the water column by motile organisms such as large dinoflagellates may then give access to greater nutrient supplies at the top of the hypolimnion. Vesiculate blue-green algae also may migrate to gain access to nutrients, and the paint-like scums or blooms that are sometimes seen at the surfaces of fertile waters (see below) may reflect breakdown of this mechanism.

The phytoplankton of infertile lakes is likely to be of small organisms with high surface to volume ratios. These are readily grazed so scarce nutrients might be rapidly recycled by excretion from the grazers instead of the cells being lost to the sediment and their nutrients removed from use. Unicells are more likely to dominate than colonies or filaments. Fertile waters, on the other hand, may be able to sustain greater proportions of larger organisms. Nutrient supply is easier and the organisms may invest more energy in avoiding grazing, any loss of nutrient through sinking to the sediments being met by renewed supplies from the catchment or even return from the sediment (Chapter 4).

Small green algae with low sinking rates and euglenoid or green algal flagellates are characteristic of small ponds, with well-mixed shallow lakes often having growths of buoyant filamentous cyanobacteria. All generalizations are breached somewhere, however, so Table 13.1 should be taken as a general scheme that might not be a good guide in individual situations. There are, in any case, frequent transitions between the associations as conditions change seasonally and many more genera and species are involved than those listed in the table. Nonetheless there is some pattern and predictability

## 13.2.5 Washout

Phytoplankton communities are influenced by washout, the rate of replacement of the water mass, as well as by mixing and stratification and water chemistry. The effects of vigorous washout are to favour diatoms and can be demonstrated in the Norfolk Broads, a series of shallow riverine lakes. These waters can be arranged in a gradient from rapidly flushed (say once every 2 weeks or less), as with Wroxham Broad, to poorly flushed (every two months or so) (Ranworth Broad). In the most flushed, the phytoplankton is dominated by centric (radially symmetrical) diatoms (*Stephanodiscus, Cyclotella, Aulacoseira*)), which have heavy cells requiring much turbulence to maintain them in suspension. Where lowland rivers develop phytoplankton it is also usually diatom-dominated. As the flushing rate decreases, small, bilaterally symmetrical pennate diatoms such as *Synedra* and *Diatoma* join the centric diatoms, together with filamentous cyanobacteria (*Oscillatoria*) (Fig. 13.4). These have longer generation times or lower sinking rates, requiring less water movement to keep them in suspension.

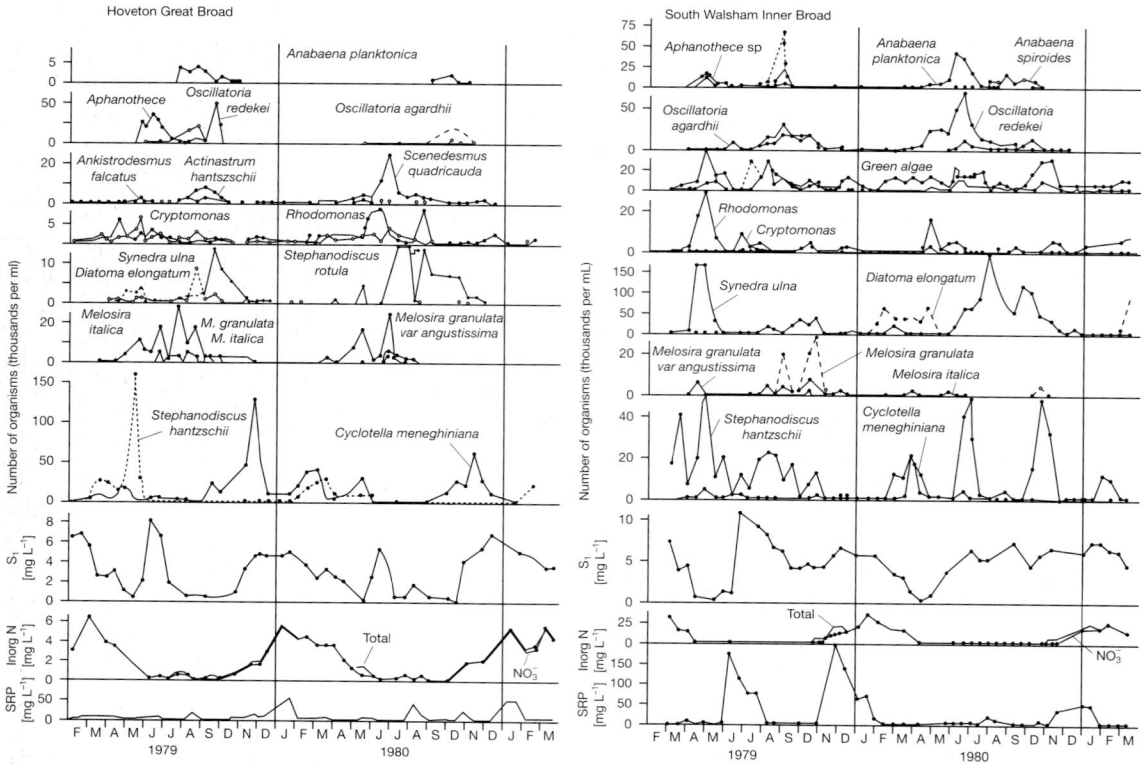

**Fig. 13.4** Seasonal succession of the main species of algae in two of the Norfolk Broads. The Broads are ancient artificial lakes set in river floodplains. Hoveton Great Broad (left) is set close to a river and is completely flushed about once per three weeks. Its phytoplankton is dominated by diatoms (*Stephanodiscus hantzschii, Cyclotella meneghiniana, Melosira (Aulacoseira) islandica, M. granulata, M. italica, M. granulata var angustissima, Synedra ulna, Diatoma elongatum, Stephanodiscus rotula*) with few cyanobacteria (*Anabaena planktonica, Oscillatoria agardhii, O. redekei, Aphanothece*). Other algae include green algae (*Ankistrodesmus falcatus, Actinastrum hantzschii, Scenedesmus quadricauda*) and cryptomonads (*Cryptomonas, Rhodomonas*). The same species, plus *Anabaena spiroides*, occur in South Walsham Broad, which lies away from the same river and is flushed about once every three months, but Cyanobacteria are proportionally much more abundant and form dense growths (blooms) at the surface in summer. The patterns of available nutrients show a build up of silicate in winter, then a spring depletion (by the diatoms) and some regeneration, followed by further depletion in autumn. Nitrogen builds up in winter but is severely depleted in summer. The lower values in South Walsham Broad reflect the lower inflow from the river. Soluble reactive phosphorus (SRP) is generally low as it is taken up rapidly, but increases in winter and through release from the sediments, especially in South Walsham Broad, in summer. (Based on Moss and Balls 1989.)

## 13.2.6 Cyanobacterial blooms

Cyanobacteria can form surface aggregations (blooms) (Fig. 13.5), when they float to the surface, and are often associated with production of toxins of considerable potency. These include nerve and liver toxins, capable of killing a large mammal in hours. The neurotoxins are often anatoxins (secondary amine alkaloids) or saxitoxins (cyclic polypeptides). The hepatotoxins come

in over 70 variants, commonly microcystins, each a related cyclic polypeptide. Also produced are cyto-toxins, dermatoxins and lipopolysaccharide irritant toxins. Why they are produced and what their natural role might be are still unsatisfactorily answered questions. There is increasing evidence that they may be passed into food webs, though they do not bioaccumulate by increasing their concentration in successive trophic levels, as fat-soluble pollutants do, and hence

**Fig. 13.5** Gas vesicles appear as black dots in the cells of some Cyanobacteria (top left) and are revealed as prismatic structures occurring in bundles by electron microscopy (bottom left). Aggregation at the surface can cause nuisances, as at this resort on Hartbeespoort Dam in South Africa (top right). In the UK, in summer, activity in many lakes is banned or discouraged by local authorities because of the risk of cyanobacterial toxicity, though sometimes the risk is overrated.

may have effects on, for example zooplankton grazers, but they seem not to have allelopathic effects (see Chapter 12) on other algae. A study in Lake Constance, where cyanobacterial blooms have increased in the 20th century, showed that *Daphnia* has evolved increased resistance to the effects of the toxins. *Daphnia* from former periods were cultured from ephippia (resting eggs, see below) from the sediments and their growth rates measured in the presence of increasing concentrations of cyanobacteria. Recent animals proved to be much more tolerant than earlier ones. Mass deaths of flamingo in some of the East African saline lakes have been attributed to cyanobacterial toxins, but only by inference. Cyanobacteria are the

normal main food of some flamingo species, so the linkage seems odd. Furthermore, the genes for toxin production appear to have evolved very early and before the evolution of the organisms on which the toxins now have major effects.

The presence of blooms is often associated with eutrophication. Blooms, however, can be natural phenomena and found in relatively undisturbed lakes in the tropics. There is evidence also of them from the ancient sediments of temperate lakes (Fig. 13.6). The word 'bloom', unfortunately has been misused recently to mean any very large (or not even very large) growth of algae (or indeed of other organisms) and is rapidly losing precision. It is used here with the original meaning

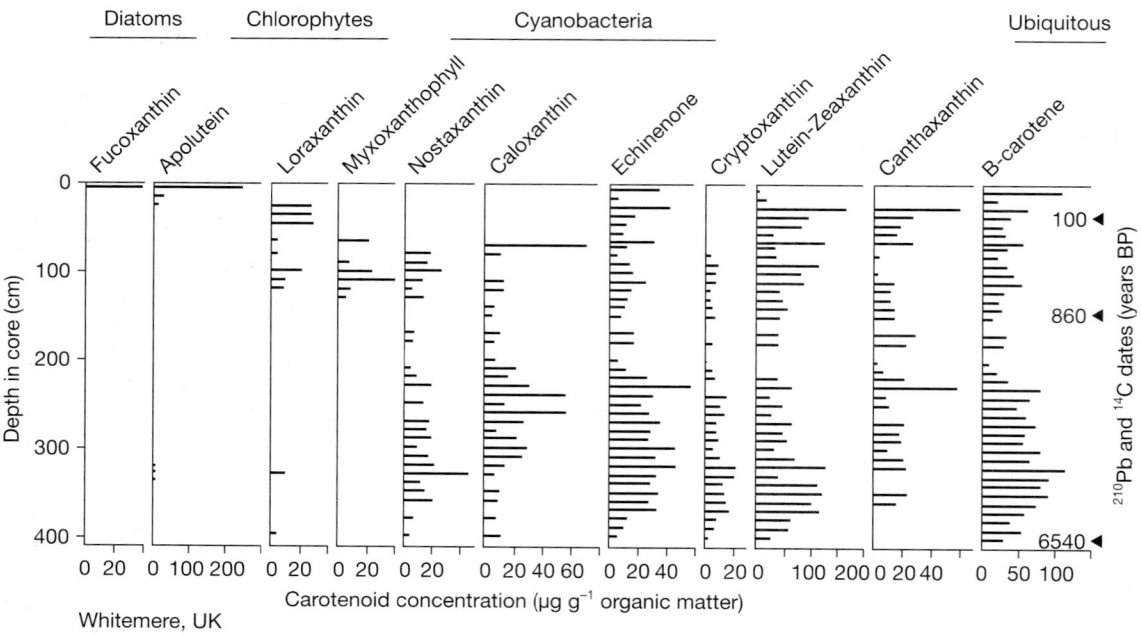

**Fig. 13.6** Pigments preserved in sediments can be extracted, separated by high pressure liquid chromatography and identified. In this core from a kettle hole lake, Whitemere in Shropshire, UK, pigments characteristic of Cyanobacteria are abundant from at least 6000 years ago. The lake currently has cyanobacterial blooms and there is a historic tradition of blooms in lakes in this area. This suggests that blooms can be natural phenomena although their size is no doubt exacerbated by human activities such as eutrophication. (Based on McGowan et al. 1999.)

of a surface aggregation of cyanobacteria. The organisms concerned include, among others, species of *Aphanizomenon, Anabaena, Microcystis* and *Oscillatoria*, which can regulate their buoyancy with gas vesicles. The protein walls of the vesicles are permeable to atmospheric gases but not to water, and contain air. Some vesicles are weaker than others and can be collapsed by pressure (about 7 atmospheres). If the vesicles are first removed from the cells, rather more pressure (about 11 atmospheres) is needed to collapse them. This is because in the cell they are already subjected to considerable internal osmotic pressure.

Because they may occupy up to 30% of the cell volume, gas vesicles can make the cells buoyant so that they float upwards. This movement, like sinking, has advantages in promoting nutrient uptake. However, as the cells rise into regions of higher light intensity in the water column, their photosynthetic fixation of carbon increases and the concentrations of soluble organic substances, such as sugars, rise in the

cell. This is accentuated if phosphorus and nitrogen supplies are low and new cell growth is prevented. As the concentration of soluble organic substances rises, so also does the osmotic (turgor) pressure in the cell. The weaker vesicles may collapse. The cell may then become denser than water and starts to sink. This mechanism prevents the cells moving into the highest light intensities at the water surface, which, in summer, may be lethal for these organisms.

As the cells sink into the darker, deeper waters, the rate of gas vesicle formation is greater than that of cell division. The concentration of gas vesicles in the cells increases, the cells become positively buoyant again, and start to float upwards. The cycle apparently keeps them in water layers most suitable for their survival and gains them access to nutrients at the top of the hypolimnion where the sinking detritus is decomposing. In extremely fertile water, the phytoplankton crop may, in summer, reach such a concentration that the euphotic zone is much shallower than the epilimnion.

The cyanobacterial cells may then spend much time at very low light intensities and the differential rates of gas vesicle synthesis and cell production may lead to formation of cells so buoyant that they rise to the surface very rapidly on calm days. The mechanism by which increased turgor pressure bursts the weaker vesicles is unable to operate, for photosynthesis is inhibited at the high extreme surface light intensity and the cells are trapped at the surface forming the characteristic scum. This may cause smells as it decays especially if it is later windrowed at the lake edge. On some lakes the blooms are dramatic indeed, forming thick porridges and clogging the cooling water intakes of boat motors.

At least that is one explanation of how algal blooms form, and in support of it, it is claimed that cells from the bloom are not viable if attempts are made to grow them in culture. Others claim that this is not so and that surface bloom formation is a device by which the algae cope with high pH and a shortage of $CO_2$ in very fertile waters packed with algae. Increasing the pH of suspensions of the algae caused movement to the surface and closest access to the supply of atmospheric $CO_2$, for example. It may be that there are different sorts of blooms with different explanations. Joseph Shapiro, in 1990, indeed synthesized much information pointing to carbon availability as the master variable controlling blue-green algal abundance. This followed his experiments in polyethylene bags suspended in a lake, in which adjustment of $CO_2$ concentrations downwards by increasing the pH led to predominance of cyanobacteria, whilst the reverse led to green algal dominance. Shapiro linked other features of cyanobacterial abundance (association with stratified conditions and deoxygenated hypolimnia; with low N to P ratios; with long residence time; with grazer removal of competing algae; and with relatively high temperature) to $CO_2$ availability. In general the larger genera of cyanobacteria are associated with high nutrient loading (though at the very highest loadings they may give way to green algae). This may be because in heavily eutrophicated lakes, there is frequently a large amount of organic matter produced and consequently a high availability of carbon dioxide following its decomposition. However, experimental attempts to stimulate blue-green algal populations by adjusting the pH do not always succeed and different explanations for blooms seem to be more convincing in different situations. Perhaps because many species are concerned, no single, simple story has emerged.

## 13.3 HETEROTROPHS IN THE PLANKTON: VIRUSES AND BACTERIA

Heterotrophy is the sole source of energy for most bacteria in lakes and some evidence suggests that large proportions of the organic matter produced by the algae, and secreted into the water for lack of nutrients to turn it into new growth, may be used by the bacterioplankton. There is also a considerable supply that comes from the littoral and the catchment. The bacterioplankters are about the size of lentils (equivalent to about 1 μm) in the model outlined earlier, though with shapes varying from rods and cocci to filaments and branched (prosthecate) forms, square cells, star shapes and stalked forms. They are suspended freely in the water as cells or small colonies and commonly are studded onto a nucleus of detritus. Some are as small as 0.1 μm.

It is difficult to know their population densities because methods of study are unsophisticated. The best methods of estimating their numbers or biomass use counting, after fixation with glutyraldehyde in the field then filtration on to very fine black filters followed by staining with fluorescent substances specific to each main group, and examination with a fluorescence microscope. Determination of adenosine triphosphate (ATP) after separation of the bacterial size fraction by screening and filtering is also useful. Traditional ways of characterizing medical bacteria by counts of and tests on colonies, each derived from a single cell on a plate inoculated with a diluted suspension, have been replaced by detection of DNA sequences from environmental samples. Most freshwater bacteria are difficult to culture and it is estimated that less than 0.1% have been cultured. The 6000 or so bacteria species from all sources, formally described after culturing, is dwarfed by the $10^6$–$10^7$ that probably exist. There is a problem though of what constitutes a species in bacteria. They are morphologically often very similar and they exchange genes freely. Molecular methods are able to describe small differences in DNA sequences and thus arbitrary definitions of bacterial species have to be used: for example that members of the same species have >70% of their DNA base sequence in common, that the melting point of their DNA differs by <5% and that there is a >97% similarity in the sequences of their 16S ribosomal RNA.

Bacterial diversity is currently measured by a barrage of molecular techniques. Nucleic acid is extracted from environmental samples and particular parts of it, usually the 16S ribosomal RNA, which is possessed by all organisms and tends to have base sequences that change only slowly, are separated into differing batches which can each be proliferated using the polymerase chain reaction. The different batches can then have their bases sequenced and compared with known sequences or recorded as new, or more likely be compared with primers of known sequence by hybridization experiments. The greater the hybridization ( joining up of the strands), the greater the similarity. Other techniques such as fingerprinting can be used where properties of the sequences are measured, such as size and melting temperature. Terminal restriction fragment length polymorphism (T-RFLP) is one such currently popular technique, but new approaches are being rapidly developed. Figure 13.7 shows a phylogeny, based on molecular studies, with the major

known groups of freshwater bacteria indicated. There is a lesser diversity than in soils though soil bacteria may wash in from the catchments and proliferate, but there does seem to be a distinctive freshwater bacterial flora and although certain groups (Proteobacteria, Actinobacteria, Bacteroidetes, Verrucomicrobia and Planctomycetes) are common everywhere, there seems to be a great deal of local variation as the flora becomes adapted to local conditions. The idea of 'everything is everywhere, the environment selects' (Chapter 6) may be truest for bacteria, though bacteria in Antarctic lakes, for example, show their greatest similarities with those in other cold lakes and not with bacteria from elsewhere.

Numbers or biomass or genetic diversity, however, are not good measures of activity because the turnover of the populations may be rapid. Also and unfortunately,

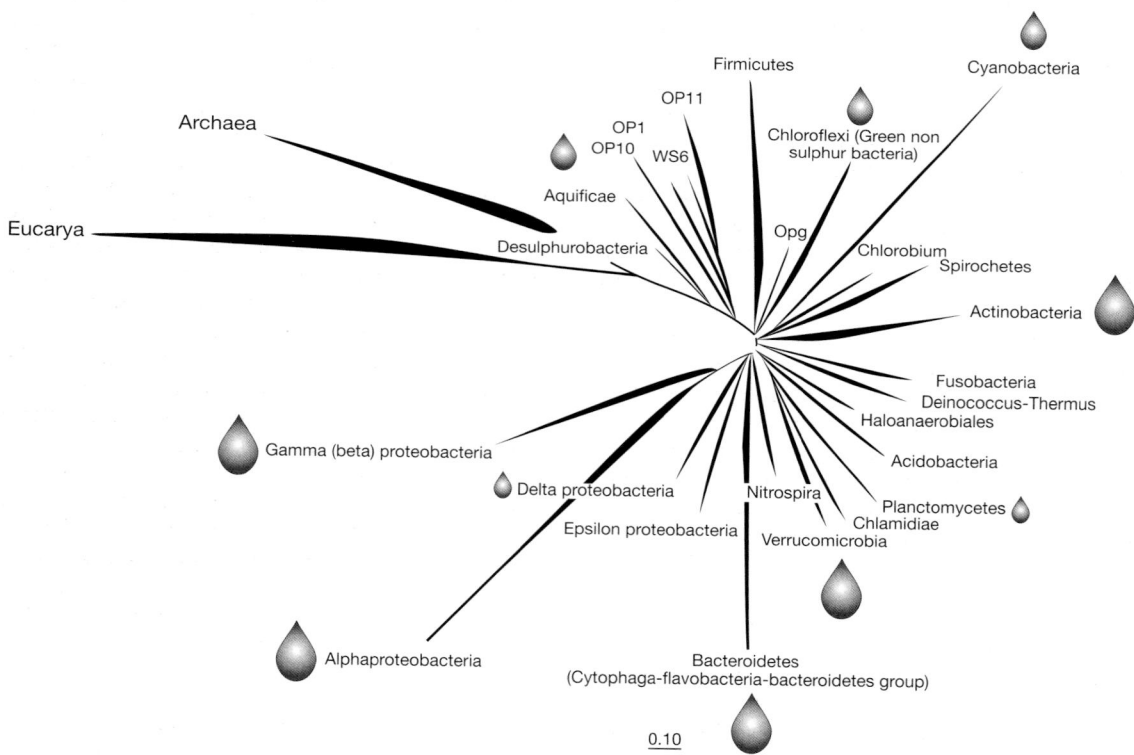

**Fig. 13.7** Molecular methods are revealing much diversity in planktonic bacterial communities. Based on differences among the nucleotide sequences of 16S ribosomal RNA, relationship trees can be constructed in which evolutionary linkages can be demonstrated relative to a common ancestor. Distance from the centre and from branch points indicate greater differences. Groups very common in freshwaters are shown by large symbols, those that are scarcer by smaller ones. (Based on Logue et al. 2008.)

there is little connection between taxonomic groups and function. Genes, for example for nitrogen fixation or denitrification, are not confined to particular groups but occur across several groups. Particular genes can be detected that signify the potential for a particular process to occur (e.g., *nifH* for nitrogen fixation, *nirS*, *nirK* and *nosZ* for denitrification, *amoA* for nitrification, and *pmoA* for methanogenesis). But detection of the gene does not necessarily mean that the process is actually occurring or, even if it is, to what extent.

Measures of activity of the whole community can be made from uptake of tritiated ($^3$H) thymidine into the cells. Thymidine is a component of DNA and the method must be calibrated against some other measure of cell production. Using this method in Lake Michigan, Scavia et al. (1986) showed that secondary bacterial uptake of carbon in a North American lake accounted for more than the current fixation of carbon by photosynthesis. The bacteria were presumably drawing on previously produced reserves in the water or derived from the catchment.

The activity of the bacteria feeding on particular organic compounds, such as the glycolic acid the phytoplankters often secrete when their growth is inhibited for lack of nutrients, can be measured by separation of the bacterial cells from the water using fine filters and then measurement of uptake of the radioactively labelled substance. The concentrations of such substances are often too low for convenient and precise chemical analysis. The life of a given molecule may be only seconds and the entire pool of some dissolved substances may be turned over every few minutes in summer. The problem, however, remains that many processes may be going on simultaneously and individual bacteria may be doing several things simultaneously. Techniques using microarrays, which are glass slides printed with gene sequences from hundreds of processes, are being developed. Nucleic acid extracts from samples are applied to the slides along with fluorescent substances that fluoresce where active DNA has hybridized with the material on the slide. Thus it can be seen which processes are switched on and which are inactive. Relating this to the rate of the process as opposed to its existence remains a difficulty. Paradoxically, the older approach of culturing is gaining new impetus, using new techniques such as low nutrient media and abandoning the traditional media of medical microbiology, use of specific signalling molecules, such as vitamins, to stimulate growth and long incubation times, to get over these problems and early methods that employ enrichment of the cultures with particular substrates to isolate bacteria with particular functions are also being used again, coupled with molecular techniques to better characterize the bacteria concerned.

The amounts of bacteria and their activity are one aspect of freshwater microbiology; their fates are another. They are grazed by animals (see below) and viruses lyse them. Viruses are everywhere. About 20 years ago they were first investigated in the ocean and interest has now turned to freshwaters. It is too early to make broad generalizations about their role, but it is unlikely that they are of minor importance. They infect all organisms, but most emphasis has been placed on the viruses of heterotrophic bacteria, where there are about 10 virus particles in the water per bacterium, with totals of $10^9$ to $10^{11}$ viruses per litre for $10^7$–$10^9$ bacteria. Some 5–25% of bacteria are infected at any one time, and burst sizes (the number of viruses produced per host cell) are perhaps 10–40 for bacteria, ten times as many for phytoplankton cells and there is probably a complete turnover of both bacterial and viruses populations every day or two, so that nutrient turnover may be high in the water. In the north-temperate Lake Erie, it has been estimated that the stock of carbon contained in viruses and bacteria is about the same as that in fish (8 ± 4, 41 ± 14, and 12–64 Gg, respectively), though ten or a hundred times lower than those of zooplankton and phytoplankton. An even greater relative abundance of bacteria is found in the tropical lake Tanganyika with the stock of bacteria about 60% of that of the phytoplankton. It is the relative turnover that gives importance, however. Sometimes it seems that viral-caused death of bacteria is as great or greater than that caused by zooplankton grazing. At present it seems that the genetic diversity of aquatic viruses, as measured by DNA sequences, is lower than expected and that viruses may be less important in freshwaters than in the ocean, but every new study adds to the apparent complexity and variability of virus behaviour in freshwaters, and it is too early to be certain of anything

## 13.4 PROTOZOA AND FUNGI

Nearly 50 years ago, working with inshore sea water, R.E. Johannes (1965) suggested that the hitherto ignored protozoans might be important. This was by grazing bacterial cells and detritus and regenerating

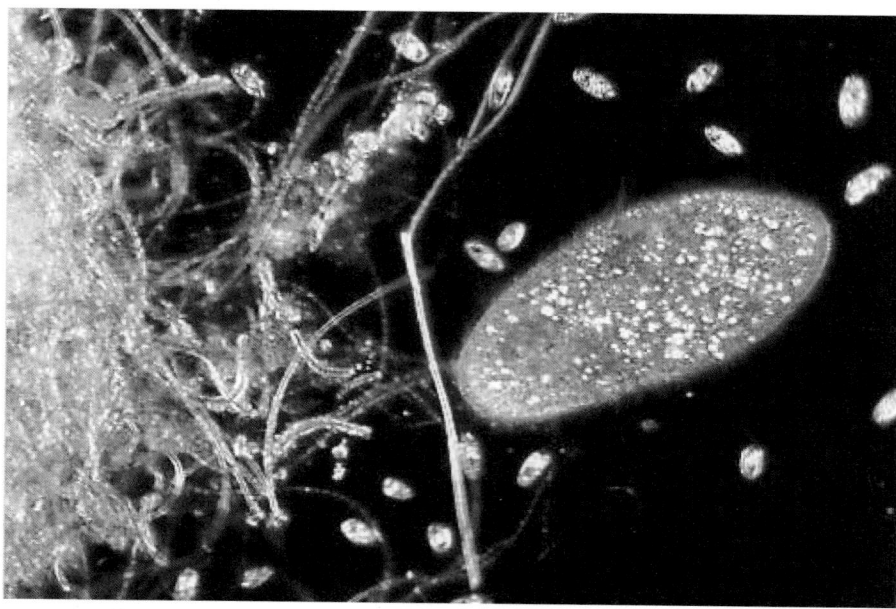

**Fig. 13.8** In freshwaters, organic detritus becomes colonized by bacteria (the long filaments), flagellates (the small oval cells), and ciliates (the large cell, *Paramecium*), to form microscopic aggregates. Such aggregates are then readily available to zooplankters, particularly those that feed raptorially.

their contained nutrients at much higher rates than bacteria or the larger zooplankters alone could do. Since then, much work has accumulated suggesting that bacteria and the smallest phytoplankton cells are fed upon largely by ciliate, amoeboid and flagellate (heterotrophic nanoflagellate) Protozoa. In doing so they form larger aggregates, which may be more easily ingested by the zooplankton grazers than freely suspended cells only 1 μm or so in size.

This microbial complex (Fig. 13.8) is now thought to have a major role in regenerating nutrients for the marine phytoplankton, and in many lakes to account for as much carbon and energy as the traditional food chain involving photosynthesis of phytoplankton. Protozoa are common in fresh waters and *inter alia* have been shown to eat small diatoms, cyanobacteria, and heterotrophic bacteria. Even the distinction between autotrophs and phagotrophs is not clear in many algal groups. Some chrysophytes, for example, can themselves feed on bacteria as well as photosynthesize.

Heterotrophic flagellates may number up to $3 \times 10^5$ L$^{-1}$ and ciliates usually a few hundreds. Both groups are most abundant in spring and summer and there is often a link, sometimes weak, with photosynthetic

algal production or biomass. Correlations of ciliates with algal chlorophyll *a* are often stronger, as are those of heterotrophic flagellates and bacteria. In Loch Ness, a highly infertile lake, most of the organic matter comes from the catchment and numbers of bacterioplankton and Protozoa are linked with wet periods when more water enters from the streams. Elsewhere, in more fertile (though still infertile) lakes, correlations between algal and bacterial biomass may be poor and bacterial production may sometimes be several-fold greater than that of the photosynthetic algae, which certainly suggests a major external source of carbon to support the bacteria (see Chapter 11). It is likely that this is generally true in pristine lakes, where natural nutrient inputs to support much algal biomass are very low. The lower bacterial biomass, turning over more rapidly, requires less nitrogen and phosphorus to process as much or more carbon and energy. Where there has been eutrophication (Chapter 15), the balance may turn in favour of autochthonous production of the phytoplankton.

Perhaps the extreme case of the importance of heterotrophic pathways is that of the dry valley lakes in Antarctica (e.g. Lakes Bonney, Frixell and Joyce), which lie in an arid rocky landscape, and are covered by clear ice but not by snow, which is swept away by strong winds. The light intensity below the ice is very low but there are photosynthetic flagellates, some of them mixotrophic, viruses, bacteria, ciliates, including the mixotrophic (part photosynthetic) *Mesodinium rubrum* and a few zooplankton grazers (*Daphniopsis studeri*). Nutrients are very scarce and the lakes are strongly chemically stratified with deep saline layers. They are cold endorheic lakes. The system appears heterotrophic and has very low productivity, though the remarkable thing is that there is any growth at all under such conditions. Recycling of nutrients by viral attack on the bacteria appears to be very important for 22–34% of bacteria are infected (cf. up to about 5% in warmer waters) but burst size is low (4 compared with more than 20). The system is heterotrophic but the source of the extra organic matter is not clear. It may be stored in the water from some previous more productive warmer phase or it may come from dust that is deposited on the ice or on the feeder glaciers and works its way into the water. Rather similar small standing waters develop in tubes called cryoconites in the ice of glaciers, with a similar microbial system.

Fungi and Protozoa also attack phytoplankters as parasites. Many of these are specific to single species of algae or groups of them, and there is usually a degree of infestation in any population. Infected cells become part of the detrital aggregates of organic matter, bacteria and Protozoa, which, with the phytoplankton, form the food of the herbivorous zooplankters.

## 13.5 ZOOPLANKTON

Rotifers and crustaceans are the major groups of freshwater zooplankters (Fig. 13.9) other than Protozoa. Freshwater jellyfish, flatworms, gastrotrichs and mites, all carnivorous on other zooplankters, may be common in particular lakes, especially in the tropics, but are scarce in temperate regions. Rotifers are man-sized to horse-sized on our scaled-up model and are mostly suspension feeders. Their name comes from the rhythmically beating, ostensibly rotating 'wheel' of cilia close to the mouth. The cilia direct water, with its suspended fine particles, into the gut. Although some rotifers are predatory grasping feeders, most take particles from about 1–20 μm, a range shared with the filter-feeding Cladocera (Crustacea) which can also take food a little larger, perhaps 50 μm.

The crustacean zooplankters include the Cladocera, most of which have a carapace covering the body and giving a smooth outline. The group includes herbivores (water fleas, *Daphnia* and *Bosmina* among others) and carnivores on smaller zooplankton (*Leptodora* and *Polyphemus*), which are raptorial (actively grasping their prey). The small-particle feeders have thoracic limbs bearing hairs (setae) on which are closely spaced (a few μm) setules that retain small particles as the limbs beat, and eventually convey food to the mouth. There is controversy about whether the action is a simple filtering one or one in which the creation of small currents pushes particles of food towards the mouth. A correlation between the sizes of particles taken and the spacing of the setules supports the former case but theoretical considerations suggest that the water is too viscous to allow simple filtration. Direct impaction of particles on the limbs may be important and the organisms can also reject unsuitable food – that which is toxic or too large to ingest. A claw on the lower abdomen can be used to prise out unsuitable food from the feeding groove between the limbs, along which food must pass to reach the mouth. Cladocera move through the water more actively than rotifers, rowing with their large, branched second antennae. On the scaled model, cladocerans, at most a few millimetres in length, would be as tall as church steeples in some cases.

The third important group of zooplankters, also crustacean, is the Copepoda, whose adult members are usually a little larger than Cladocera. They may be small-particle feeding (mostly the calanoid copepods, such as *Diaptomus*) or raptorial, the cyclopoid copepods, which include *Cyclops*. The prey of these may be smaller zooplankters, larger colonies, or aggregates of phytoplankton and detritus. The copepods can tackle a wider range of bigger food particles (5–100 μm) than the non-raptorial Cladocera and rotifers. The calanoid copepods do not filter particles but actively select from those brought near the mouth by the movements of the limbs.

Life histories vary among the zooplankton. Although the cytological mechanisms differ, both rotifers and Cladocera are parthenogenetic. Females asexually produce broods of eggs, which hatch into more females. This allows rapid replacement of populations that are especially vulnerable to predation (see later). The eggs are born in sacs at the base of the body by rotifers and in pouches within the carapace in Cladocera, and young are released which resemble the adults and

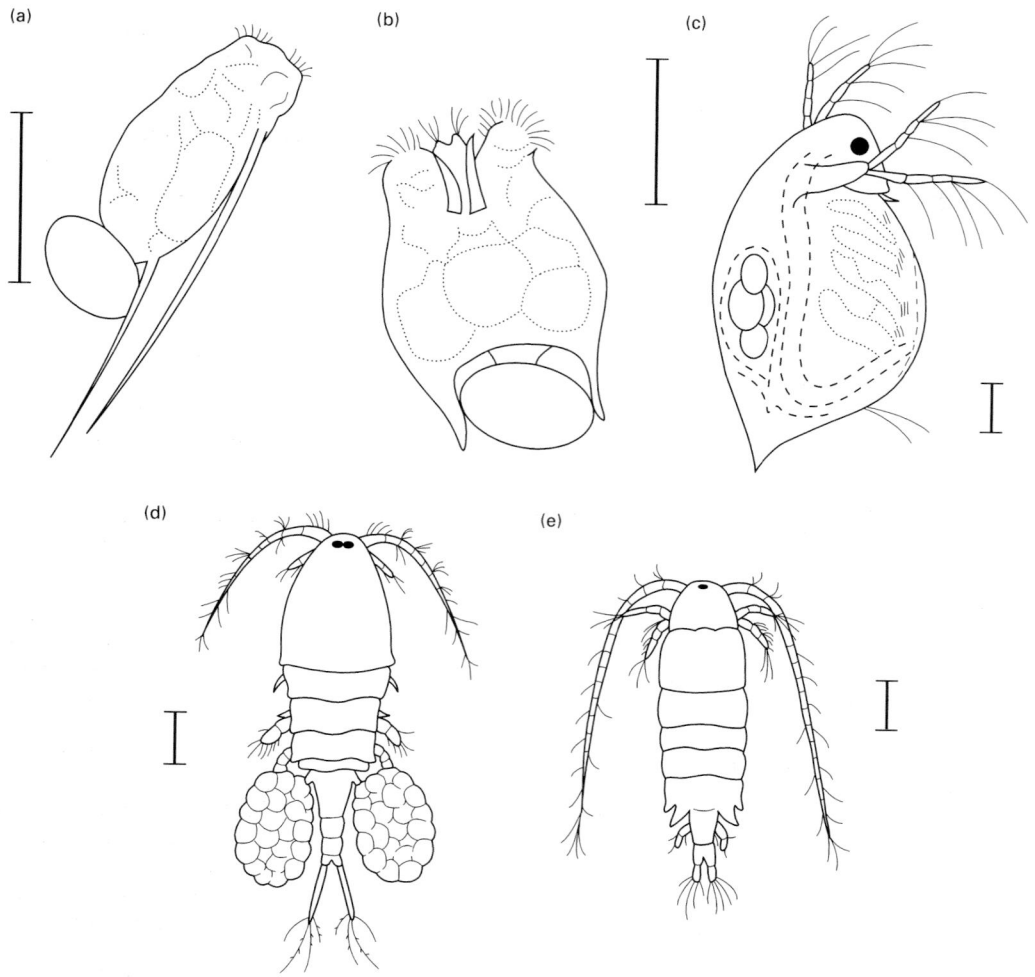

**Fig. 13.9** Some representative zooplankters. In all cases the length of the scale lines represents 100 µm. Rotifera: (a) *Filina*, (b) *Brachionus*. The corona of cilia can be seen in each case and at the rear, a single egg. Crustacea (Cladocera): (c) *Daphnia*. The filtering limbs are enclosed by the carapace, which also contains the egg pouch containing a few eggs. Crustacea (Copepoda): (d) *Cyclops*. The egg sacs are paired and the antennae, the lower pair of appendages on the head, are not branched; (e) *Diaptomus*, a calanoid copepod, in which the antennae are branched. When the animal is carrying eggs these are contained in a single egg sac, in contrast to the paired sacs of the cyclopoid copepods.

soon grow large enough to reproduce. The rate of egg production is high, for a new generation of rotifers is produced in only a few days and each female produces up to 25 young in her lifetime of 1–3 weeks. Cladocerans take longer per generation (1–4 weeks), but each have a longer life expectancy (up to 12 weeks or so) and may produce up to 700 young per lifetime. The genetic advantages of sexual reproduction are not lost in these animals because most produce males during times of food shortage or other inclement conditions. Eggs are then fertilized, become thick walled and do not hatch immediately. In some Cladocera they are held in thickened egg pouches called ephippia, which fall to the sediments. Eventually the eggs hatch to form a new season's parthenogenetic females.

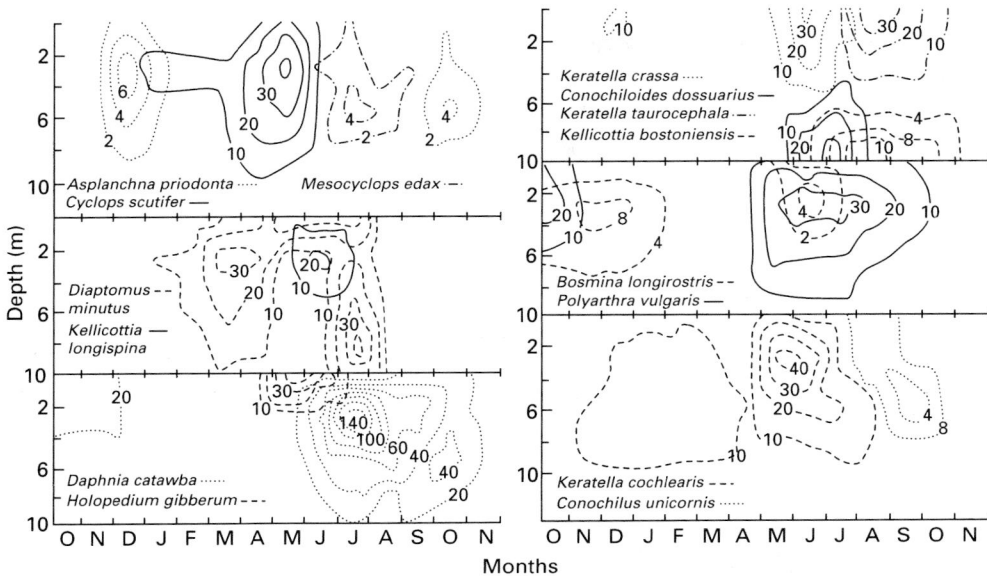

**Fig. 13.10** Distribution of zooplankton species with depth and season in Mirror Lake, New Hampshire, USA. Values are mean monthly production ($\mu$g L$^{-1}$ month$^{-1}$). *Cyclops*, *Mesocyclops* and *Diaptomus* are copepods; *Daphnia*, *Holopedium* and *Bosmina* are cladocerans. Other species are rotifers. Further niche separation, where distributions overlap, is given through food selectivity and vulnerability to predation. (From Makarewicz & Likens 1975.)

The Copepods are different. Each generation is sexual, and before the new mature adults are formed, there are eleven successive moults. The first six, after the egg hatches, are of juveniles called nauplii, which look quite different from the adults. The next five, the copepodites, do look like the twelfth stage, which is the reproductive adult. In terms of their longevity and fecundity the copepods are similar to the cladocerans. Cyclopoid copepod females carry two eggs at a time, calanoids only one. The mysids are a further group of shrimp-like animals, including the genera *Mysis* and *Neomysis* which are omnivores or predators on other zooplankters, relatively large (up to 2 cm), and which have sexual life histories.

The zooplankton community thus includes a variety of forms and activities, much of which is ultimately related to the effects that predation, among themselves, or by vertebrates, has upon their numbers (see later). They are also much more heterogeneously distributed (Fig. 13.10) than the phytoplankters. Zooplankters move actively, may shoal both vertically and horizontally and often go through diurnal vertical migrations, reaching the water surface by night and moving down by day. The shoals may partly be due to water

movements; there is a shifting structure of parcels of water of slightly different temperature generated by wind and differential heating at the edges and middle of the lake. But biological factors, ranging from the effects of differential feeding by predators and the production of signalling substances are equally important. Nets have been traditionally used for sampling, because the concentration of zooplankters (at most 1–2 mL$^{-1}$ for the larger ones) is small. Some of the larger, faster-moving copepods and mysids may be able to detect the shock wave that precedes a net as it is drawn through the water and avoid being caught. The use of acoustic methods has now made it much easier to see patterns of zooplankters and of their fish predators.

### 13.5.1 Grazing

The herbivorous zooplankters feed on phytoplankton, bacteria and detritus, discriminating more by size than taxonomy. Most of the bacteria and bacterial/ Protozoa-studded detritus seem readily available, but phytoplankters pose more problems. Some are inedible, usually the larger forms and often the larger cyanobacteria, and the proportion tends to increase with increasing lake fertility. Particles smaller than about 30 μm are most vulnerable. The quality of the food material may also be important. It is not uniform. And the concentration of food particles may be too low at times to support the zooplankters, which may then become food limited. In Lake Constance the rate of egg production of *Daphnia* depends on food concentration (measured as carbon in particles <50 μm in size), with no eggs produced when food is <0.2 mg C L$^{-1}$ and a rise in production as food increases, to about 0.7 mg C L$^{-1}$, when egg production increases no further. Lake Constance has less than 0.7 mg C L$^{-1}$ for much of the year. However, apparently full guts at all times in the animals of some lakes may mean that temperature, food quality and other factors, rather than food availability, are more important.

There is a danger in generalizing from lake to lake and from species to species for, particularly in the latter case, marked selectivity of food occurs. Some zooplankters are very fussy eaters. Tests by Bogdan & Gilbert in 1982 with bacteria, a yeast, and three small algae showed that among three rotifer species, *Keratella cochlearis* would take all, but preferred *Chlamydomonas* (an alga), whilst two *Polyarthra* species would take only *Chlamydomonas* and *Euglena* (both algae). A cladoceran, *Bosmina longirostris*, also preferred *Chlamydomonas* and other workers showed that it exerted up to a 13.7 times preference for *Chlamydomonas* over *Aerobacter* (a bacterium), whilst another cladoceran, *Daphnia rosea* showed no preference at all.

Some animals prefer live food (e.g. *Bosmina longirostris* and *Diaptomus spatulocrenatus*), others dead detritus (*Keratella cochlearis*), and others (*Conochilus dossuarius*) have no preference. Bacteria may be more readily taken, particularly by the larger animals, if they are attached to detritus. Among the algae, the assimilability of different species, and hence their ability to support growth and egg production, varies greatly and is not just a function of size. For *Daphnia* species in Lake Washington, the greatest egg and biomass production occurred when the flagellate *Cryptomonas erosa* and a small diatom, *Stephanodiscus hantzschii*, were the main foods, lower with larger diatoms, *Asterionella formosa* and *Aulacoseira italica*, and lowest with the small-celled *Chlorella* and a thinner variant, *tenuissima*, of *Aulacoseira italica*.

Cyanobacteria can be poor food, though this is not universal. Part of the problem may be due to the size and difficult handleability of the larger forms, but sometimes they may be toxic, reducing feeding rates even if given as separated cells rather than as colonies. Picophytoplanktonic cyanobacteria appear to be readily eaten by ciliates and the ciliates thence by copepods. Filaments of cyanobacteria may be too large or awkward (too stiff) for ingestion. Some cladocerans may not have wide enough gaps between the edges of the carapace that cloaks their limbs to bring the filaments or colonies onto the limbs and, if the filaments reach the feeding groove, rejecting them with the abdominal claw may pose heavy energy demands. More palatable foods may be rejected at the same time so that growth of the animal is further compromised. This may give an advantage to small animals (which cannot take in the large cyanobacteria at all so do not have to reject them from the feeding apparatus). It may be why small species are often predominant in mid-summer in fertile lakes when such large algal forms are common, but there are other reasons, connected with fish predation (see later).

*Aphanizomenon* is a cyanobacterial genus with stiff filaments, which sometimes bundle together in parallel to form 'flakes' visible to the naked eye. Often there is an association between such flakes and an abundance of *Daphnia*. *Daphnia* can feed on single filament *Aphanizomenon* and even sometimes on small colonies. Larger colonies are not ingested and interfere slightly with feeding on small green algae such as *Ankistrodesmus*, which *Daphnia* assimilates more efficiently than *Aphanizomenon*. At high population densities (say 10–15 L$^{-1}$) *Daphnia* may cause selection in favour of flake *Aphanizomenon* by removing potential algal competitors with it for nutrients.

In Lake George, Uganda, the major zooplankter, *Thermocyclops hyalinus* assimilates between 35 and 58% of ingested *Microcystis*, the major phytoplankter present, which is a cyanobacterium. On the other hand, in experiments in netting enclosures in two contrasted lakes along the same river in the UK, *Daphnia hyalina* alone survived, but not for long, in one whilst it and two larger species persisted in large numbers in the other. The latter lake was dominated by diatoms with only a few cyanobacteria, whilst the former, with a longer retention time, had few diatoms but many cyanobacterial filaments (Fig. 13.11). Reports of inabilities of temperate zooplankters to assimilate cyanobacteria may reflect the present state of flux in many temperate lakes due to eutrophication. This has stimulated growth of previously less common cyanobacteria, for which the zooplankters may not yet

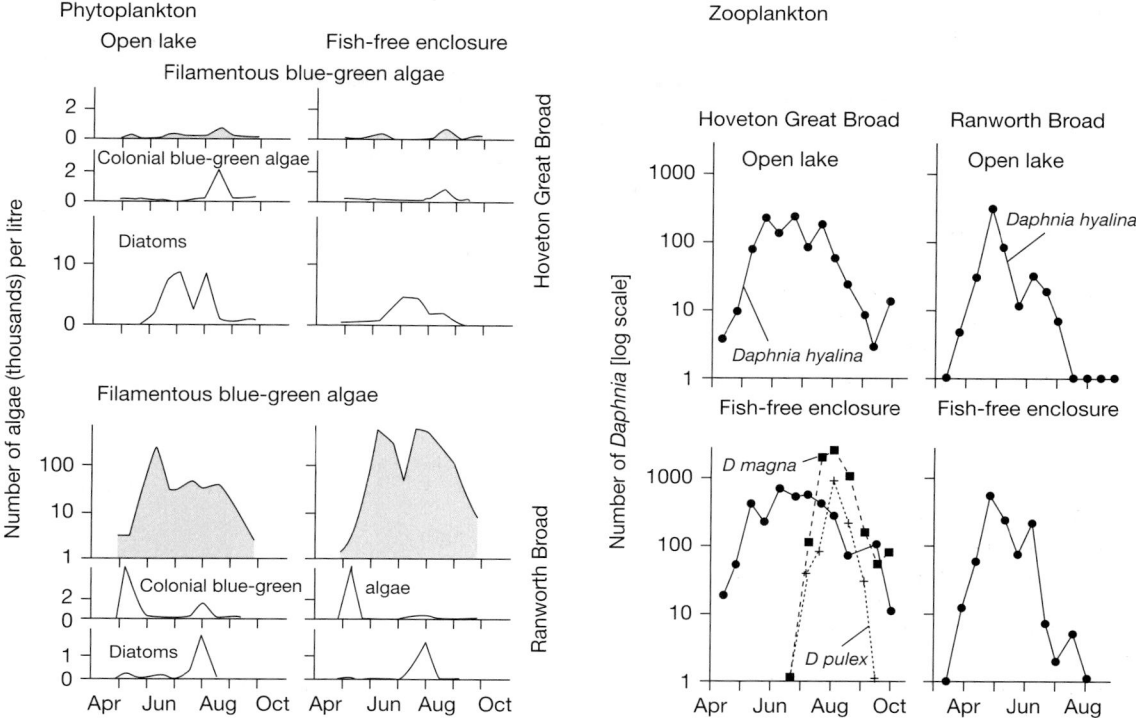

**Fig. 13.11** Hoveton Great Broad has a phytoplankton rich in diatoms; Ranworth Broad is dominated in summer by Cyanobacteria. Water from each Broad was simultaneously enclosed by netting that allowed free movement of algae (left) but minimized exchange of zooplankters and kept fish out. In Hoveton Great Broad, with a very palatable food source, a small *Daphnia* species, *D. hyalina* grew well in spring in the open lake but was decimated by fish predation in early summer. In the enclosures, protected from this, it remained abundant and was joined by two much larger species, *D. pulex* and *D. magna*. In Ranworth Broad, although *D. hyalina* grew in spring, when diatoms were present, it collapsed in summer as cyanobacteria took over and keeping fish out did not obviate the decline. Predation thus limited *Daphnia* in Hoveton Great Broad and food quality in Ranworth Broad. (Based on Moss et al. 1991.)

have evolved suitable means of coping. Lake George is not a recently polluted lake, but has had a naturally large crop of cyanobacteria, presumably for a very long time.

Studies in enclosures in lakes give clues as to how selective grazing may help to determine the composition of phytoplankton communities. Karen Porter, in 1973, enclosed 500-L samples of lake water in large polyethylene bags, which she sealed and resuspended for several days in the lake. From some bags she had removed the larger zooplankters (crustaceans) by filtering the water through a 125-μm mesh net. In others she increased the zooplankton population several-fold by adding animals. The major effect of grazers, which included small-particle feeding (*Daphnia*

*galeata mendotae* and *Diaptomus minutus*) and raptorial (*Cyclops scutifer*) herbivores, was to suppress small flagellates, nanoplankters and large diatoms. Large colonial green algae were not affected or even increased. They were ingested but not digested and may even have benefited from passage through the guts. Phosphate released there by digestion of other species was taken up by the colonial green alga *Sphaerocystis schroeteri* as it passed through undigested and emerged growing healthily on copepod faecal pellets.

In another example, from a very fertile Scandinavian lake, existing fish and zooplankters were asphyxiated in plastic enclosures by adding solid $CO_2$. *Daphnia galeata mendotae* was then added to some enclosures and *Bosmina longirostris* to others. The latter is small and unable to handle large filaments or colonies. In its enclosures the algal crop increased, higher total phosphorus concentrations were maintained in the water, the pH was forced upwards by $CO_2$ uptake and the proportion of cyanobacteria in the phytoplankton community was increased. The *Daphnia*, however, kept the water clear, the phosphorus concentrations and pH low, and reduced the cyanobacterial component of the algal biomass. Phosphorus was kept low perhaps by sinking of phosphorus-rich faeces to the sediment. *Daphnia* may have directly grazed the cyanobacteria (*Microcystis*) or, by grazing the other species, may have created conditions (lower pH, higher transparency, lower phosphorus availability) less favourable to cyanobacterial growth. The potential impacts of grazing on the phytoplankton are thus varied and depend very much on the species present, both of animals and algae.

### 13.5.2 Feeding and grazing rates of zooplankton

Ingestion rate, or feeding rate, depends on the volume of water handled per unit time (the grazing rate) and on the food concentration. It can be measured by feeding a radioactively labelled ($^{32}$P) yeast to an animal and then, after a few minutes anaesthetizing it in saturated $CO_2$ solution, which prevents defaecation. The radioactivity incorporated into the animals is measured and grazing rate ($G$) calculated as:

$$G \, (\text{mL animal}^{-1} \, \text{h}^{-1})$$
$$= \frac{\text{radioactivity per animal}}{\text{radioactivity per mL yeast suspension}}$$
$$\times \frac{60}{\text{time (min) of feeding}}$$

Ingestion rate is then calculated as grazing rate times the concentration of yeast cells as cells, organic matter or C animal$^{-1}$ h$^{-1}$. Grazing rates tend to decrease almost exponentially as food concentrations increase, for example in *Daphnia rosea*, from about 1.5 to 2.0 mL h$^{-1}$ at 25,000 cells mL$^{-1}$ to about 0.2 mL h$^{-1}$ at 500,000 cells mL$^{-1}$. They increase with body length and temperature (up to a temperature limit) whilst ingestion rates increase with food concentration up to a plateau that is quite high relative to natural concentrations. In general grazing rate seems to decline above a threshold food concentration so that there is

an upper level of feeding rate dependent on species and conditions. Laboratory experiments under ideal conditions, however, tend to give values several times higher than those carried out with radioactively labelled natural phytoplankton in lake water in chambers suspended in a lake, because of shortage of food or low food quality.

Measures of the grazing rates of complete communities, using radioactive tracers or by feeding suspensions of tiny plastic beads of known size, suggest that rotifers filter up to 1 mL$^{-1}$ day$^{-1}$, whilst *Daphnia* species may filter 5–30, and *Diaptomus* about 35. This means that the crustaceans, if abundant (say 10–50 L$^{-1}$), may filter all of the surrounding water every day and this suggests a major potential impact of grazing. Size of animal is an important determinant of grazing rate, which usually increases by some power of the body length:

$$G = K \, \text{length}^b$$

where $b$ tends to be between 1 and 3, depending on species. Direct measurements of grazing rates are rarely now made and size distribution and density of the community are used as surrogates in equations to calculate the impact of grazing.

### 13.5.3 Competition among grazers

The open water of a lake is a relatively unstructured environment. Usually, however, several zooplankton species occur together and competition for what may become a limiting food resource, as grazing proceeds, might be expected. To some extent this may be offset by differences in food particle size taken and occurrence of different species at different times and places in the lake (Fig. 13.10). Rotifer populations, however, are often sparse in the presence of large (>1.2 mm) *Daphnia* species, even at low densities. When *Daphnia* is removed by fish predation (see below) rotifers usually increase and in laboratory cultures rotifers die in the presence of the bigger animals. This may follow from simple contest competition, the diets of both groups overlapping considerably, but the larger *Daphnia* being able to filter more efficiently. There may also be interference competition with small rotifers swept into the feeding chamber created by the limbs of *Daphnia*. Some may be ingested, and others damaged before rejection, and eggs may be torn off to face predation as free-living bodies. Smaller cladocerans, such as *Bosmina* may coexist with rotifers because they also are not powerful feeders and are too small to sweep rotifers into their feeding baskets. Small cladocerans may also be more vulnerable to invertebrate predation by insect larvae emerging from the benthos, which prevents rises in populations to competitive levels.

### 13.5.4 Predation in the zooplankton

Herbivorous zooplankters inevitably consume protozoons as well as algae and bacteria. In truth they are omnivores and the strict separation of herbivory and carnivory is not possible at this level. However, these animals become prey to stricter carnivores, both invertebrate and vertebrate. The vertebrates, including amphibians such as salamanders, wading birds in shallow ponds, and especially fish, are always much bigger and more mobile than the invertebrates. They often have such overriding importance in determining the nature of zooplankton communities that the significance of invertebrate predation may be overlooked. The effects of predation can be easily investigated in experiments in which predators are present or excluded, but the simple life histories of rotifers and cladocerans allow a closer understanding through demographic analysis of the populations of prey, in which birth rates and death rates can be separately estimated. The method is applicable to any zooplankter, and depends ultimately on finding the birth and death rates of the animal as the year progresses.

The rate of change of numbers over a short time, $t$, is given by:

$$N_t = N_0 e^{rt}$$

where $N_0$ and $N_t$ are the numbers at the beginning and end of the period, e is the base of natural logarithms and $r$ is the intrinsic rate of natural increase: $r$ equals $(b - d)$ the difference between instantaneous birth and death rates. Death may come from predation, parasitism and washout. If, by regular sampling, the numbers of animals are established, estimates of $r$ can be obtained for the periods between samplings, at times $t$ and $(t + 1)$ from integration of the above equation:

$$r = 1/t \cdot (\log_e N_{(t+1)} - \log_e N_t)$$

To understand the dynamics of the population $b$ and $d$ must be estimated. The instantaneous birth rate, $b$, is defined by:

$$N'_{t+1} = N'_t e^{bt}$$

$N'$ represents a potential population size in the absence of deaths and cannot be estimated. Hence $b$ cannot be directly measured. However, a finite approximation to birth rate, $B$, can be defined as:

$$B = \frac{\text{number of newborn (during interval } t > t + 1)}{\text{population size at } t}$$

$$B = (N'_{t+1} - N'_t)/N'_t$$

and because

$$b = 1/t \cdot (\log_e (N_{t+1}/N'_t))$$

for each time interval

$$b = \log_e [1 + ((N'_{t+1} - N'_t)/N'_t)] = \log_e (1 + B)$$

$B$ can be independently estimated from the number of newborn per individual per day. Those about to be born are carried as eggs or embryos by the female until they are released when the female moults.

$$B = \frac{\text{number of reproductively mature adults } (N_A)}{\text{total population } (N_t)}$$

$$\times \frac{\text{number of eggs and embryos carried per adult (brood size, } E)}{\text{number of days for egg to mature from production release } (D)}$$

$N_A$, $E$ and $N_t$ are readily estimated from sampling of the natural population. $D$ depends on temperature and is measured in laboratory cultures. Typically it might be 20 days at 4°C to 2 days at 25°C. From the lake temperature at the time of sampling, an appropriate $D$ value is selected. $b$ and $r$ can then be used to calculate $d$, the instantaneous death rate:

$$d = b - r$$

Figure 13.12 gives these data for *Daphnia galeata mendotae* in Base Line Lake, Michigan, together with changes in population. From March to early June the population increased and death rates were low. In midsummer the population remained steady but low, yet birth rates (and therefore production) were high. Death rates, however, were then also high. There was no evidence of large losses through parasitism or washout and the main mortality followed fish predation after young zooplanktivorous fish hatched in May and June. Although the population could double itself every 4 days, predation accounted for almost all of the production

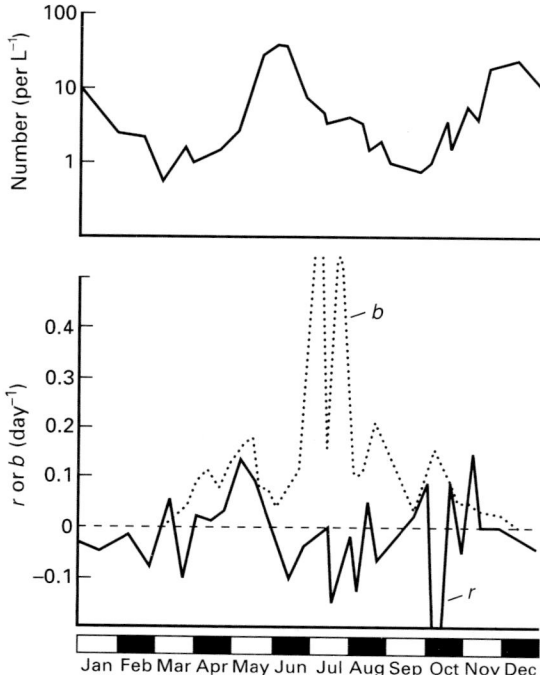

**Fig. 13.12** Population changes of *Daphnia galeata mendotae* in Base Line Lake, Michigan. Upper graph shows changes in the total population, and the lower one the observed intrinsic rate of increase (*r*) and the calculated birth rate (*b*). The difference between the graphs gives *d*, the instantaneous death rate. (After Hall 1964.)

and kept the population low. This approach assumes that all the mortality is of adults but this is probably not so. Eggs, carried by the adults when they were eaten, are also eaten, so that the method overestimates birth rates and therefore death rates. Eggs carried may not always develop and invertebrate predators might also eat newly hatched *Daphnia*. More sophisticated analyses taking these factors into account are available, but the principles remain the same.

### 13.5.5 Predation on zooplankters by zooplankters

Invertebrate predators of and among the zooplankton are rotifers (*Asplanchna*), Cladocera (Fig. 13.13) (*Bythrotrephes*, *Leptodora* and *Polyphemus*), cyclopoid copepods (*Cyclops*, *Mesocyclops*), mysids (*Mysis*, *Neomysis*)

(Fig. 13.13), larvae of the fly genus *Chaoborus* (Fig. 14.5), coelenterates including free living *Hydra*, water mites (*Hydracarina*) and free living flatworms, the rhabdocoeles, such as *Mesostoma* (Fig. 13.13). The cladocerans and mysids appear to be confined to temperate lakes, the coelenterates and rhabdocoeles are more common in the tropics and cyclopoid copepods and chaoborids are worldwide.

Predator–prey relationships can be examined as a sequence of detection (encounter), attack, capture and ingestion or escape. Detection for invertebrate predators is usually by sensing small tremors in the water. Water mites, for example will assume an attacking position in response to vibrating glass fibres but not to still ones. They rely also on chemical signals, remaining motionless in water conditioned by the previous presence of prey but moving around in unconditioned water. The crustaceans and *Chaoborus* probably rely on random encounters, dependent on frequent movement. *Leptodora* has mechanoreceptors on its first thoracic limbs, which detect the prey and the large eye of *Polyphemus* suggests that it may use visual cues. *Mesostoma lingua*, a tropical flatworm, uses several methods of encounter. It may trap prey in mucus, sit and wait for it to arrive, secrete neurotoxins into the water or actively search, especially in the surface tension film.

Attack generally involves grasping and biting the prey by the predator and its effectiveness means the difference between ingestion and escape. The pattern of bite damage to the prey (all of which is usually not eaten) is often consistent suggesting a particular way of attack. The production of spined or distorted (exuberant) forms (Fig. 13.14) may interfere with the handling mechanism of the predators and allow prey to escape. Mechanisms may involve genetic selection of different clones, but such forms are often produced in parthenogenetic species in response to the presence of chemicals (kairemones) incidentally released into the water by the predator. The rotifers *Keratella tropica* and *Brachionus* spp produce longer spines when their populations are declining and their predator, another rotifer, *Asplanchna*, is present. *Chaoborus* induces the production of a pedestal with extra spines (neck teeth) in *Daphnia pulex*, which increase the likelihood of escape, but have a cost in that less energy is available for reproduction. Small *Daphnia* species may produce elongated heads (helmets) in response to predators whilst large species, too big to be handled by invertebrates, may not. The substances concerned are yet

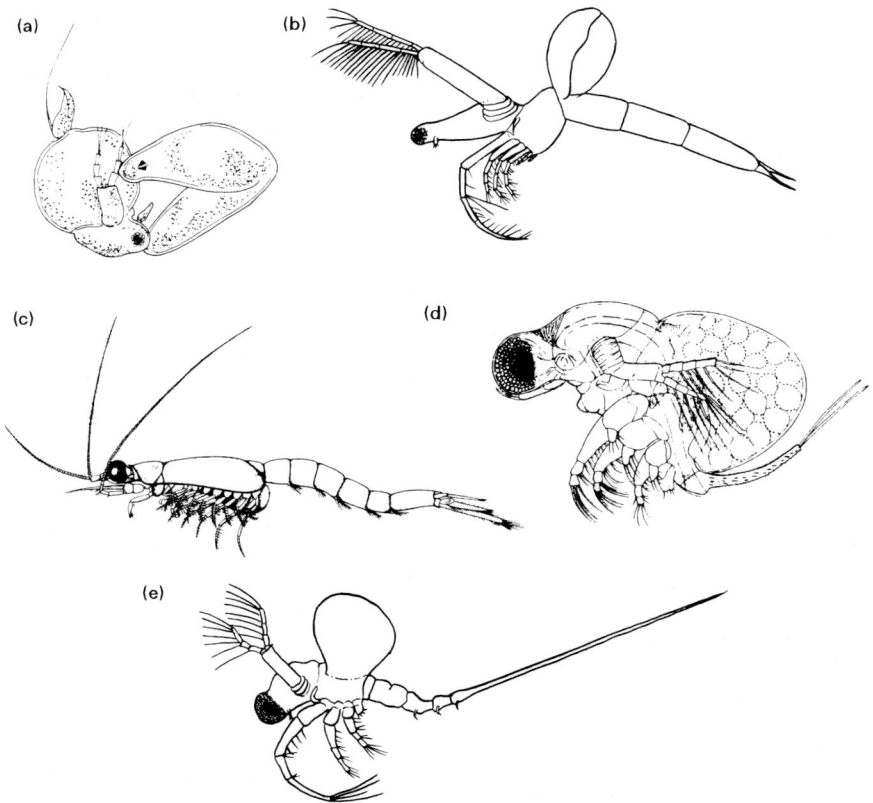

**Fig. 13.13** Invertebrate predators on zooplankters include flatworms, such as *Mesostoma*, here (a) enveloping its prey, *Moina micrura*, in mucilage, and raptorial crustaceans, such as *Leptodora kindtii* (b), *Mysis relicta* (c), *Polyphemus pediculus* (d) and *Bythotrephes cederstroemi* (e). *Mesostoma* is about 1.5 mm long, the others are between 3 and 7 mm.

unidentified, though the neck-tooth inducing substances from *Chaoborus americanus* are known to be polar organic molecules, stable to heat and peptidase, destroyed by acid and base digestion and containing hydroxyl groups.

The impact of invertebrate predation on zooplankton communities is often difficult to establish, especially where vertebrate predation is also occurring. There are several approaches. The first is to examine gut contents, and to look for inverse correlations in numbers of predator and prey in the lake. The second involves laboratory experiments in which single prey or a choice is fed to the predator, and the third is to carry out manipulative experiments in containers, from which vertebrate predators have been removed. Advantage can also be taken of favourable circumstances, where

fish predation is absent or invertebrate predators have newly invaded.

Gut analyses demonstrate the existence of a relationship but not its extent. Inverse correlations give that additional insight. For example, in Lake Michigan, a new predatory zooplankter, *Bythotrephes cederstroemi*, achieved prominence in the 1990s. It is a palaearctic species whose introduction to this North American lake, in the mid-1980s, is obscure. Several *Daphnia* species were formerly common and the smaller herbivorous *Bosmina longirostris* was scarce. The daphnids and *Bosmina* were preyed upon by the native *Leptodora kindtii*. *Bythotrephes* increase in the lake from 1987 onwards was associated with a decline in *Leptodora* and two of the *Daphnia* species and an increase in *Daphnia galeata* and *Bosmina*. This suggests a release

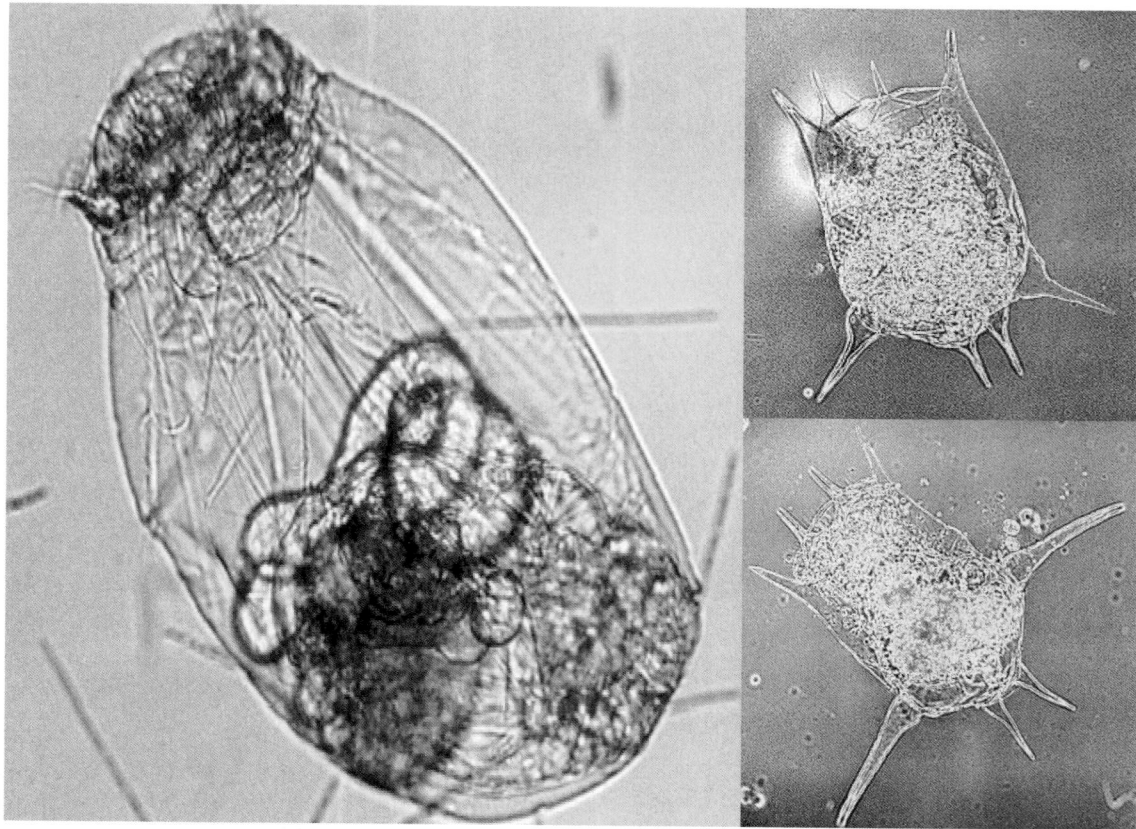

**Fig. 13.14** Predators secrete substances into the water that act as unintended signals to potential prey. The rotifer *Brachionus calyciflorus* (right) produces exaggerated spines (lower right) in response to a predatory rotifer (*Asplanchna*, left), that impede the handling of the prey so that it stands a greater chance of escape.

from *Leptodora* predation of *Bosmina* and possibly the daphnids and a possible predation of *Bythotrephes* on *Leptodora*. Vertical movements (see later) of the daphnids following *Bythotrephes* introduction changed so as to bring them into lesser contact with the *Bythotrephes*.

A clear example of the potential importance of invertebrate predation comes from the fishless Great Salt Lake in the USA (Fig. 13.15). A single zooplankton grazer, the brine shrimp, *Artemia franciscana*, feeds on a green alga, *Dunaliella viridis*, for part of the year and on a variety of other algae that are attached to cast off *Artemia* exoskeletons in the remainder. The Great Salt Lake varies in salinity as rainfall changes and was only half as salty in 1985–86 as it had been

before or afterwards. The decreased salinity allowed a predatory bug, *Tricorixa verticalis* to invade. The bug sucks fluids from its prey and attacked the *Artemia*, whose abundance was reduced, and other grazers (*Diaptomus*, *Cletocampus*, rotifers) appeared. The grazing efficiency nonetheless declined and algal concentrations markedly increased. With the rise in algal population there was an uptake of the remaining soluble nutrients in the lake and a decrease in transparency. This was a very clear demonstration of what are known as top-down effects operating through the food web from the predator to the producer level, a theme which gains even greater predominance with a consideration of fish predation in the open water.

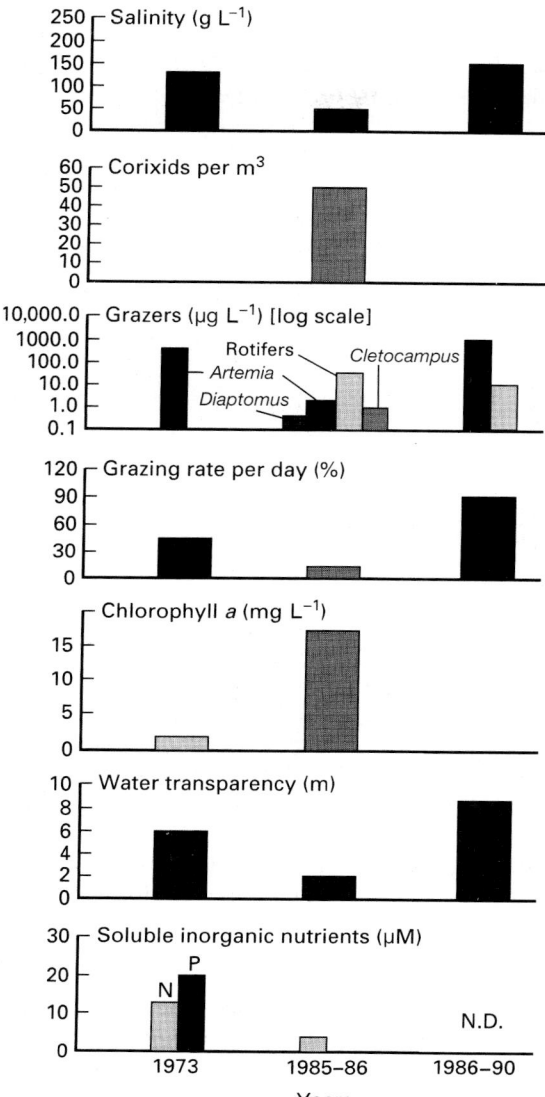

**Fig. 13.15** Changes in the Great Salt Lake, Utah, USA, resulting from changing rainfall and salinity and the consequent increase in corixid (bug) predation on the zooplankton. (Based on Wurtsbaugh 1992.)

## 13.6 FISH IN THE OPEN-WATER COMMUNITY

Fishes are very diverse. They include omnivores eating a range of foods from invertebrates to plants, and specialists on diets such as the eggs of other fishes. Adult size ranges from the 7.9 mm of *Paedocypris progenetica*, which was recently discovered in Indonesian peat swamps, to the (sometimes) 5 m of the European catfish, or wels (*Siluris glanis*). Big fish, however, grow from little fish. Diets and behaviour change as fish grow from tiny larvae to fingerlings to adults, and the fish may move between littoral and pelagic habitats as they grow. Table 13.2 lists some major freshwater fish orders with some indication of their distribution.

Newly hatched fish depend on the remains of the yolk sac for food, but then feed on organisms of a size appropriate to their mouth gape. These may be algae or rotifers. Later in their first year the fish will move to larger prey: bigger zooplankters such as Cladocera or clumps of filamentous algae. Perhaps in their second year they will need even larger items to meet their metabolic requirements. These items will be more varied (insect larvae, molluscs, other fish, filamentous algae, higher plants, for example) and reflect specialization in the species. As they grow, many fish move from the shelter they may find as larvae among the plant beds of the littoral zone to the open water. As adults they may favour particular parts of the lake, may move around a great deal in search of food or may be constrained to certain areas by the behaviour of their own predators, which include other fish, birds, and reptiles. Fish are notoriously difficult to sample well because of their movements. The most representative methods involve fleets of different-mesh sized gill nets, but these kill the fish. Trawls, seines, and non-return traps give selective live samples and are better suited to the littoral zone or profundal. Electrofishing, in which the fish are stunned by an electric field generated between electrodes in the water can be used non-destructively but only very locally. Increasingly, acoustic methods are used but these do not easily distinguish among species.

### 13.6.1 Predation on the zooplankton and fish production

Almost all freshwater fish feed on zooplankters at some stage. This may be for a few weeks immediately after the fry have used up their yolk sacs, for a year or so,

**Table 13.2** Some major orders of freshwater fish.

| Order | Freshwater spp (% of total) | British spp | Temperate US spp | Tropical African spp |
|---|---|---|---|---|
| Lepidosireniformes (Air breathing lung fish) | 5 (100) | 0 | 0 | 4 |
| Polypteriformes (Bichirs) | 11 (100) | 0 | 0 | 6 |
| Acipenseriformes (Sturgeons with primitive, partly cartilaginous skeleton) | 15 (60) | 1 | 14 | 0 |
| Semionotiformes (Gars) | 7 (100) | 0 | 7 | 0 |
| Mormyriformes (Elephant snout fish; snout is often elongated and proboscis-like) | 101 (100) | 0 | 0 | 101 |
| Clupeiformes (Herrings, shads; often plankton feeders with long gill-rakers) | 25 (9) | 2 | 5+ | 2+ |
| Salmoniformes (Salmonids, pike, ciscoes, coregonids, grayling, smelt; believed ancestral to many other orders; often anadromous, breeding in freshwaters but spending most of life in the sea) | 80 (16) | 14 | 70 | 0 |
| Cypriniformes (Cyprinids [coarse or pan fish], carps) | 3000 (100) | 20 | 209 | 180 |
| Siluriformes (Catfish with sensory barbels on head and no scales) | 1950 (98) | 1 | 37 | 345 |
| Atheriniformes (Killifish, guppies) | 500 (60) | 0 | 186 | 0 |
| Perciformes (Percids, centrarchids, cichlids; extremely diverse, with spiny fins) | 950 (14) | 11 | 55 | 700+ |
| Anguilliformes (Eels, often catadromous, breeding in the sea but living in freshwaters) | 15 (3) | 1 | ?10 | 0 |
| Total | 6559* (45) | 50 | 583 | 1338 |

*Total freshwater fish species is about 6850 or about a third of all fish

with switches to benthic invertebrates or other fish as they grow, or, for many shoaling open-water species, for their lifetime. Overall fish production is thus unlikely to be precisely related to zooplankton production, but there should be some general link, as demonstrated by the small mouth yellowfish, *Barbus aeneus* in Lake Le Roux, South Africa.

The small mouth yellowfish is endemic to the Orange River system, which drains an arid land, subject, even in the absence of human activity, to much erosion in the wetter months. The river, and the lakes formed by dams along it, including Lake Le Roux, are turbid with suspended clay and silt. Depending on rainfall, Lake Le Roux may have a secchi disc transparency varying from only 80 cm to less than 30 cm. The silt absorbs light and the phytoplankton crops and their dependent zooplankton stocks are correspondingly low in turbid years (Fig. 13.16). The yellowfish population (measured as catch per unit effort of fishing) is correspondingly low in these years as also is its growth

rate (Fig. 13.16) which depends on the availability of suitable zooplankton food but also on temperature. The turbid years are also ones in which heat radiation is intercepted higher in the water column, giving a lower water temperature because more heat is radiated back to the atmosphere instead of being mixed down into the water column and this too may slow the fish growth.

Beyond general links among fish production and amount of zooplankton, the zooplankton community composition is often shaped by predation and vertebrate effects seem to be more extensive than those of invertebrate predators. The first clues came from Hrbacek et al. (1961) and since then there have been many confirmations that fish will preferentially take the larger, slower moving zooplankton species, notably *Daphnia*, leaving the faster copepods, which can evade attack, and the smaller Cladocera, and particularly rotifers that would provide less rewarding meals. Effects of fish predation are clearly shown when fish have

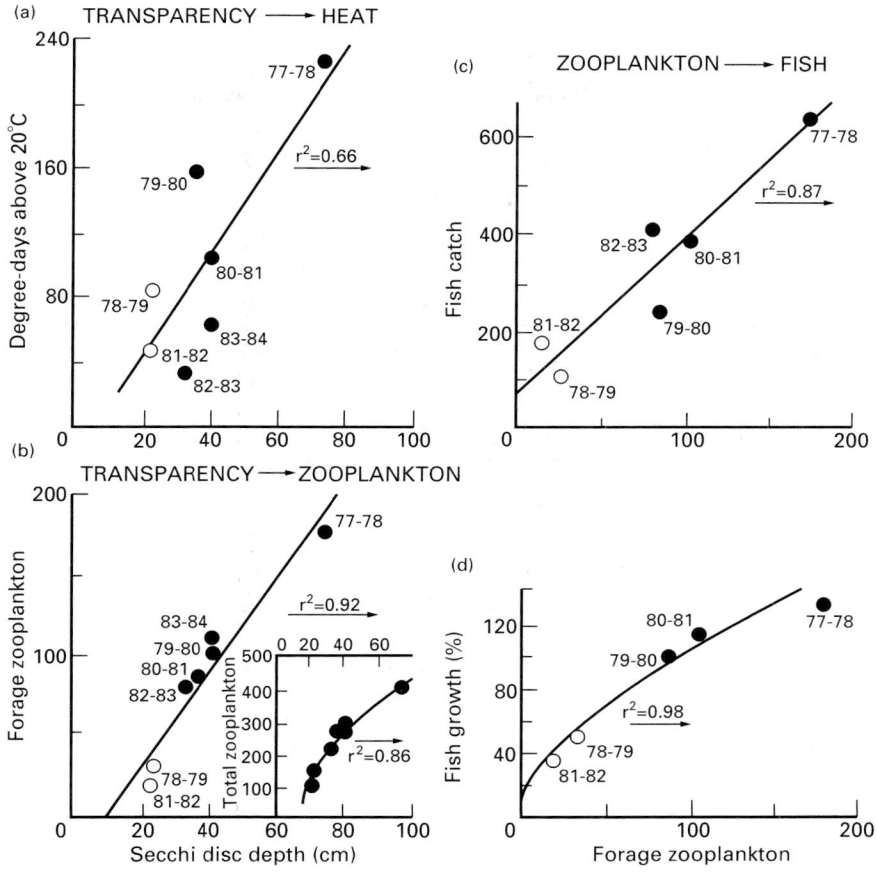

**Fig. 13.16** Relationships between: (a) summer heating and transparency (the greater the penetration of longwave radiation, the warmer the water; (b) zooplankton available to fish and transparency (the greater the transparency, the greater the phytoplankton and consequently the greater the zooplankton production, either of foraging herbivores or (inset) total zooplankton); (c) fish catch and (d) fish growth and available zooplankton, in Lake Le Roux between 1977 and 1984. Open symbols show relatively wet years. (After Hart 1986.)

been introduced into lakes that previously lacked them. Figure 13.17 shows the marked shift in zooplankton species and sizes that followed introduction of the planktivorous fish *Alosa aestivalis* into Crystal Lake in Connecticut, which previously lacked such a planktivore. The zooplankton community was changed from one of *Epischura*, *Daphnia* and *Mesocyclops*, all usually more than 1 mm in size, to one of *Ceriodaphnia*, *Tropocyclops* and *Bosmina* which are all smaller than 1 mm. *Cyclops*, at just under 1 mm, persisted in both situations.

This work led to development of the size-efficiency hypothesis to explain the size ranges of crustacean zooplankton communities. It proposes that all zooplankters compete for particulate matter in the water but that the larger animals are most efficient. Small animals are thus excluded by starvation if large ones are present. Vertebrate predators (largely fish), however, select the larger Crustacea (cladocerans, calanoid copepods), and, depending on the intensity of predation, allow smaller zooplankters (smaller Crustaceans, rotifers) to coexist up to the state of complete elimination of the

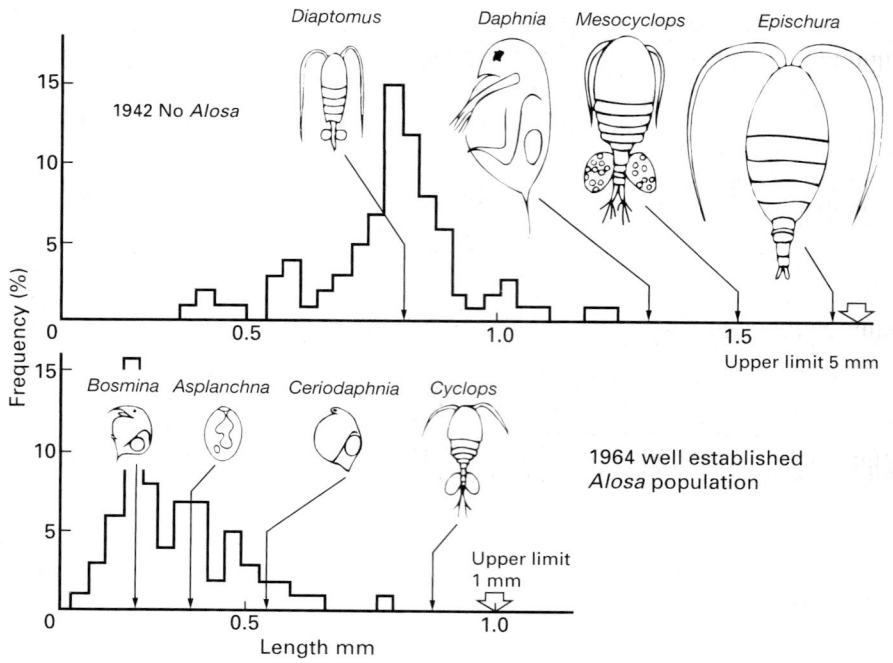

**Fig. 13.17** Composition of the mainly crustacean zooplankton of Crystal Lake, Connecticut before (1942) and after (1964) introduction of a planktivorous fish, *Alosa aestivalis*. Planktivorous fish had previously not been present. Specimens are drawn to scale and represent mean size for each species. The arrows indicate the size of the smallest mature instar of each species. The effect of the fish has been to replace a community of large species with one of much smaller organisms. (From Brooks and Dodson 1965.)

large forms where predation is intense. At this stage the fish may then take whatever is left and in warmer lakes, where seasonal changes do not intervene, frequently do. Zooplankton populations at low latitudes are frequently small (see Chapter 12).

Fish do select the largest prey that they can catch and ingest. The larger the prey, the greater is the return of energy for that invested in catching it. They must see their prey to catch it but objects smaller than about 1 mm are not readily seen. Rotifers, small Cladocera such as *Bosmina*, nauplii and early copepodites will thus escape. The larger Cladocera are most vulnerable. They move slowly and probably do not have sensory mechanisms capable of detecting the shock wave of an approaching fish. In contrast the copepods have sensory hairs on their antennae. With a flick of their abdomens they can move away from the line of attack by the fish with great speed.

### 13.6.2 Avoidance of vertebrate predation by the zooplankton

As with invertebrate predation, zooplankters have evolved ways to minimize the risk of being eaten by fish. Cladocera frequently produce individuals that are smaller, thinner and more translucent during the summer when fish feeding is intense (Fig. 13.18). These forms may be less visible but may have smaller brood chambers and produce fewer eggs. Within a lake, where predation is concentrated, for example, at the margins where fish may find refuges against their own predators, the larger, or sometimes just different, forms may persist offshore and the smaller ones survive more readily inshore. Faced with intense predation, the cladocerans of warm lakes tend to be smaller, and reproduce more rapidly than those of cooler lakes.

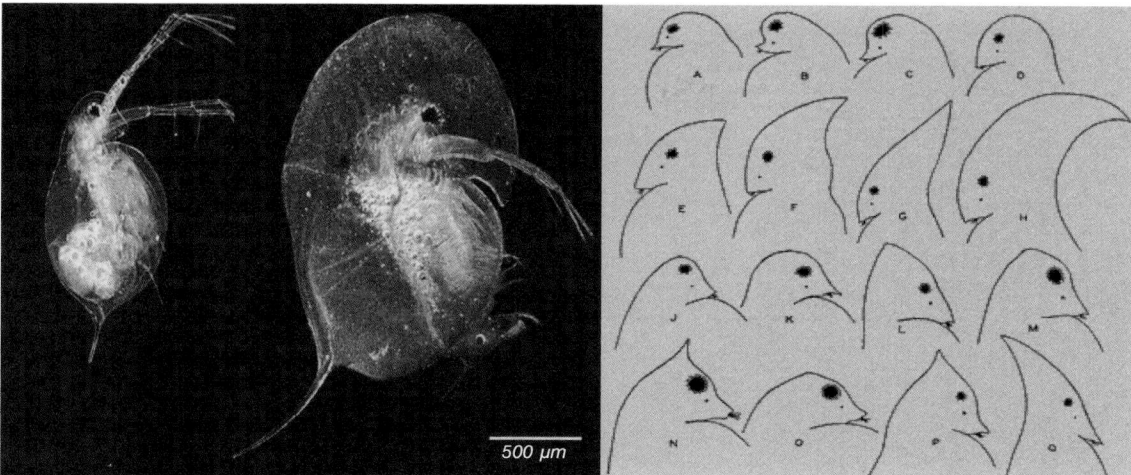

**Fig. 13.18** *Daphnia* responds to predators by changing its form. To the left (courtesy of University of Alaska), *D. longiremis* produces small forms in ponds with fish and large forms in ponds with only invertebrate predators. Changes can occur within the same lake throughout a season. As fish predation becomes more intense, thinner more transparent helmeted forms are found. Right upper (a–h), *Daphnia pulex*; lower (j–q), *Daphnia longispina*. (After Robert Pennak.)

The smaller, thinner animals produced apparently in response to fish predation (though there is evidence that physical factors such as temperature and turbulence may also stimulate increase in their numbers) often have protruberances such as long spines or, in Cladocera, extensions of the head (helmets). This is called cyclomorphosis for the occurrence of these forms is often seasonal in response to the production of large numbers of young fish in spring. The protruberances may, as suggested above, be devices largely to minimize predation by invertebrates, particularly for the rotifers and smaller Cladocera. Fish suck in their food and the shape of it seems not to matter very much, but many zooplankters may be coping with threats from both invertebrate and vertebrate predation.

There are also behaviours that minimize contact between the prey and the predator. Vertical migration has long been known in zooplankters, with the animals remaining at depth, in the dark, by day, and moving to the surface at night to feed. Many explanations have been put forward for this. It might be most economical, for example, to grow at low temperatures, which minimize respiration rates, and to spend time in the warmer surface waters only when it is necessary to feed. However, the hypothesis that diurnal vertical migration is a way of avoiding fish is now widely accepted.

Zooplankters are more likely to show vertical migration in the presence of fish predators than in their absence. By remaining in deeper darker waters by day, they avoid being seen by the fish but invoke certain costs because the deeper water is often cooler and poorer in food so that their growth and reproduction are inhibited. These costs are apparently balanced by the greater benefit of predator avoidance. The zooplankters become vulnerable only late in the day when they must use light cues to move upwards to graze during the ensuing night. They may then become outlined against the twilight sky to fish lurking below.

An experimental investigation of vertical migration is shown in Fig. 13.19. *Daphnia* were placed in thermally stratified tubes, through which there was a constant drip of water. Some tubes received water that had had zooplanktivorous fish swimming in it; others had water that had not been exposed to fish. In the fish-conditioned water, the *Daphnia* migrated between the top and bottom of the tubes, whilst in the fishless water, they remained permanently in the warm surface waters. Growth rates were twice as high in the non-migrating animals suggesting a major cost to migration, but in turn there would be at least as high a cost of being exposed to predation.

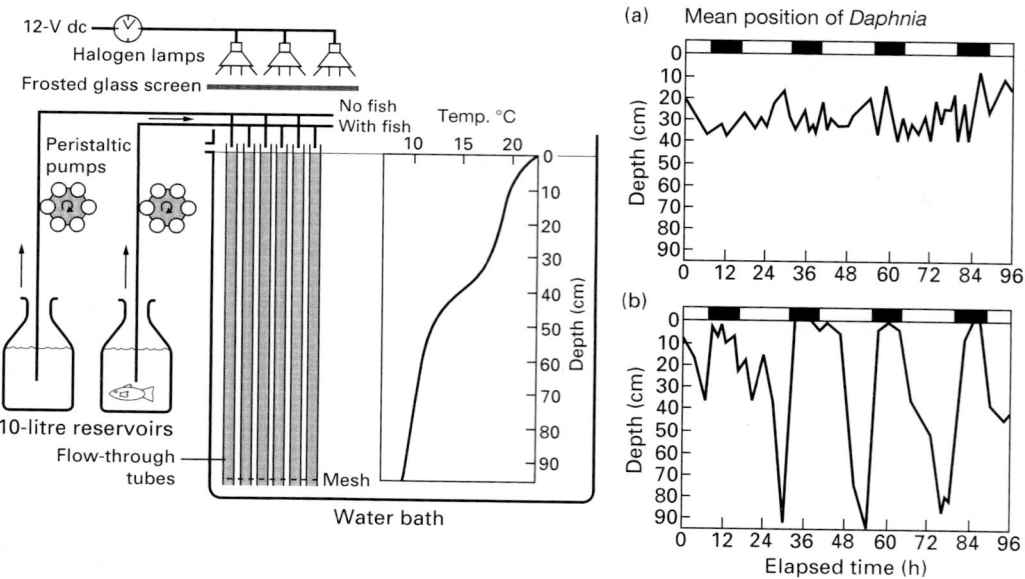

**Fig. 13.19** Arrangement and results of an experiment in which a *Daphnia* population, contained in thermally stratified water columns, was exposed to water from which fish had been excluded, or in which they were living. With the influence of fish (b), the *Daphnia* migrated vertically each day (and also grew less rapidly, through being exposed to lower temperatures (inset graph). In the absence of fish kairemones (a) they did not migrate, and grew more quickly. (From Dawidowicz & Loose 1992.)

## 13.7 PISCIVORES AND PISCIVORY

A further complication in interpreting the processes going on in open water (and even more so in the littoral zone, Chapter 12) is that fish themselves have predators. Their activities cause changes in the community, numbers, size distribution, habitat occupied and behaviour of their prey, and sometimes cascading consequences for the zooplankton and thence the phytoplankton. Piscivores include many other fish, reptiles (turtles, snakes and crocodilians), birds such as grebes, mergansers, herons and cormorants, and mammals such as fish-eating bats, otters and freshwater seals.

Piscivorous fish may be so voracious that small bodied fish cannot coexist with them, and take refuge among structures such as plant beds, where the predators may be less effective. In a Norwegian lake, when piscivorous pikeperch were introduced, the previous large roach population of the open waters (12,000–15,000 fish ha$^{-1}$) was reduced to only 250 ha$^{-1}$, largely by movement into the littoral. Discovering the effects of piscivores is difficult because they are wide ranging. Whole lake experiments, where they are introduced or removed, give valuable but unreplicated information. In experimental enclosures, they may not necessarily behave as they would in the entire lake, and the enclosures need to be very large.

One good example (Fig. 13.20) is from Wintergreen Lake in Michigan. The lake is small and in a bird sanctuary with large numbers of geese, which strongly fertilize it, so that under the winter ice, decomposition of organic matter can lead to deoxygenation. In the very long cold winters of 1977 and 1978 the main piscivorous fish, the largemouth bass, *Micropterus salmoides*, was eliminated. There followed an eruption of small zooplanktivorous fish that in turn reduced the populations of large Cladocera and their individual size, and led to increased phytoplankton and turbidity, and a community of small Cladocera. When bass were eventually reintroduced, there was a reversal of these changes, planktivorous fish declined, large bodied *Daphnia* increased and the water became much clearer. This is another good example of a 'trophic cascade' the effects of a change at the top end of the food web in a particular 'keystone' species having cascading effects down to the producer levels.

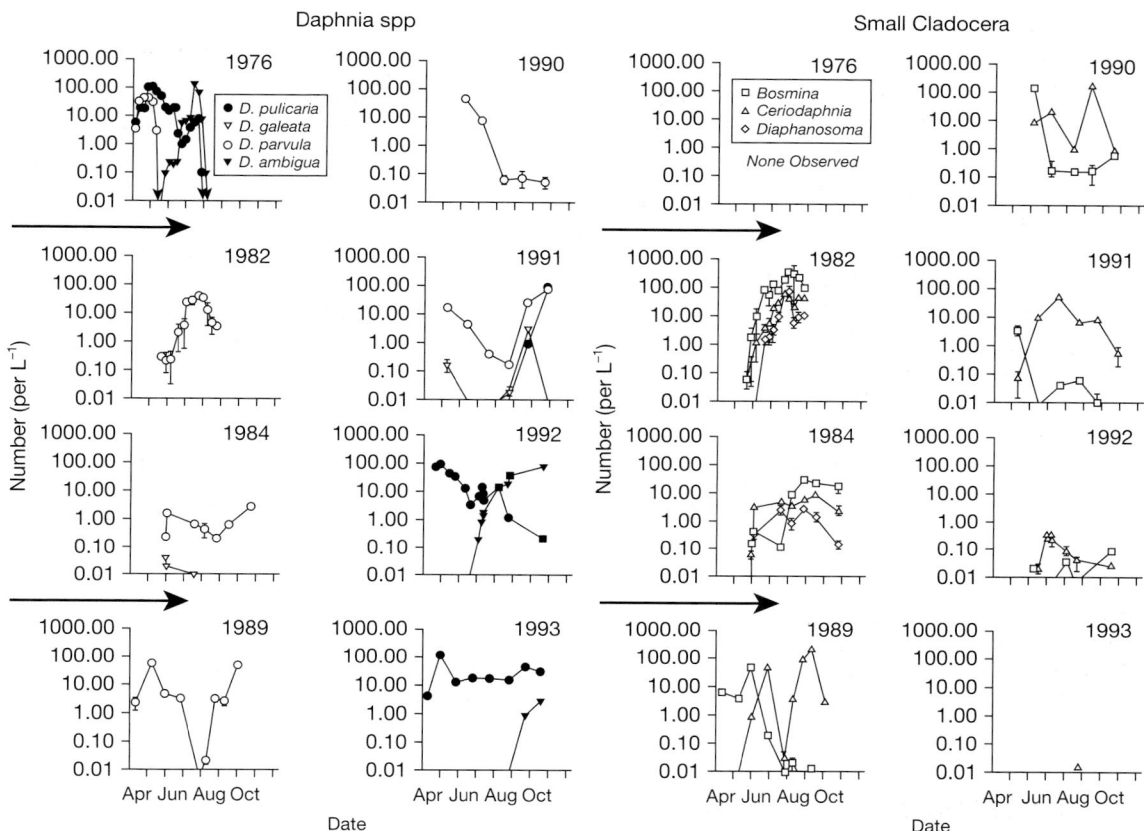

**Fig. 13.20** Natural experiments can provide useful information about whole lake systems. In Wintergreen Lake, Michigan, a severe kill of fish (particularly the piscivorous small-mouthed bass) in 1978 (upper arrows) led to loss of large daphnids and a rise in small Cladocera (*Bosmina, Ceriodaphnia, Diaphanosoma*) for several years, until bass were restocked in 1988 (lower arrows). It took some time for the bass stock to reduce the stock of zooplanktivorous fish after 1988 and for effects to be reflected in the zooplankton community (return of large numbers of *Daphnia*, reduction in small Cladocera). Immediate responses are not to be expected with ecological changes. Patience is necessary. (Based on Mittelbach *et al.* 1995.)

## 13.8 FUNCTIONING OF THE OPEN-WATER COMMUNITY

The plankton community is very dynamic. So are all ecosystems, but whilst the movement of animals and the growth of plants are obvious in terrestrial and littoral systems, a large block of water may give the impression of very little happening. That is not so. Not only is the relative position of every particle, live or dead, changing from second to second, but dozens of chemical changes are simultaneously going on. A fish swimming will emit a plume of urine containing ammonium that will be snapped up immediately by phytoplankton cells that seconds later might benefit from the excretion of phosphate by *Daphnia*, which the next minute is part of the fish's dinner as it turns back to distance itself from a cruising piscivore. Just as the zooplankton may filter the entire lake every day, many phosphorus atoms may cycle through water to fish and back in hours. The picture will change as the seasons change, and from year to year as the average weather changes and more, or less, inflow water comes in, or stratification or ice cover lasts longer than usual. There is a link, for example, between the depth of the thermocline in some English lakes and the annual position of the Gulf Stream in the Atlantic Ocean. When the Gulf Stream penetrates far to the north, English summers are calm and warm, the thermocline forms at shallow depths and the zooplankton production is reduced in early spring, probably because calmer conditions and reduced mixing lead to fewer highly edible diatoms being available.

There are patterns, but there will also be a great deal of chaos. Chaos has a special meaning in ecology. It is not a complete and totally random separation of happenings and events, causes and consequences. It is the phenomenon of so many events occurring simultaneously that the consequences cannot be separated. From a single starting point, differences in the next step, real but too small to see or measure, can eventually build, through chains of steps to very different final outcomes. In one experiment using a large mesocosm containing a plankton community monitored over several years, it was found impossible to predict events beyond about 15–30 days. The plankton system itself behaved much like the weather. Strong seasonal changes controlled by the Earth's movements, however, do give a general pattern and some idea of how the planktonic system continually juggles the many balls of physics, chemistry and biology, can be gained from considering it, as I have done before in general scenarios for different climate systems. Of course, no individual lake will behave entirely like the scenario and the scenario will be unable to include every detail of every lake. But I have tried to distil some of the essence. The details of your particular lake will be many and fascinating and your intellectual reward for detailed study. Eventually they may prove general enough to change the scenario and that is the nature of how understanding advances.

### 13.8.1 Polar lakes

The simplest of lake ecosystems are in the continental Antarctic and were discussed above. Somewhat more complex are those of the maritime Antarctic and of the extensive polar landscapes around the Arctic Sea, which form the basis of this scenario. Spring comes late, perhaps in May or June when the ice has finally melted over most or all of the lake. During the winter, the plankton community experienced inverse thermal stratification and if the ice was covered with snow, almost no light penetrated to the underlying water. But often the strong winds sweep the snow clear for long periods and a twilight penetrates to support a phytoplankton of small green flagellates, often mixotrophic and depending on both dissolved organic matter washed in or produced the previous summer. The

algae, being motile will tend to migrate to form a dense green layer just below the ice–water interface where there is most light.

Some of the Arctic pools are very shallow and may freeze to the bottom. The few species of fish, often only a single species, have a difficult time: they cannot survive at all in the shallower pools, and may not even persist in the deeper ones if deoxygenation under the ice is severe. There are large Arctic lakes also, however, and these are the main strongholds of the fish communities. Nutrient concentrations will generally be very low for the frozen landscape delivers little water, in the short spring, from vegetation that tends to retain what supplies there are, though lakes fed by glaciers may be a little richer. As the lake ice melts and more light penetrates, the waters mix for the summer. It is rarely calm or warm enough for direct thermal stratification and so the phytoplankton is dominated by diatoms, cryptomonads chrysophytes, dinoflagellates and green flagellates and apart from picoplankton, cyanobacteria are scarce. Chrysophytes often form siliceous cysts in which they may overwinter, and the flagellates can persist in the water column, but the ways of winter survival of the diatoms are not well known. They may simply rest in a quiescent state on the bottom.

As in almost all lakes, there will be a succession of algal species with diatoms declining as silicate and inorganic nitrogen concentrations fall. Mixotrophic flagellates and a few dinoflagellates become more abundant as bacteria multiply in the warmest period. A zooplankton community manifests itself as the waters warm a little, hatching from resting stages or growing from overwintering individuals. Large Cladocera may dominate where fish have been eliminated and in the shallower tundra ponds, species that are quite large and feed on benthic detritus may become abundant. The migratory waders, ducks and geese that have overwintered in central Europe will now have returned to breed on the Arctic tundra. They may be major predators on the larger zooplankters of ponds shallow enough for wading (Fig. 13.21), whilst fish, notably the Arctic charr, make inroads on the daphnids in the deeper lakes, so that copepods and rotifers come to dominate, whilst in the intermediately deep lakes, without fish, large zooplankters may maintain very clear water, all of the algal groups able to grow being easily vulnerable to grazing.

Roosting and excreting birds, especially geese, will bring nutrients in from their feeding on the tundra, and in the Antarctic, seals, finding basking sites on lakeshores

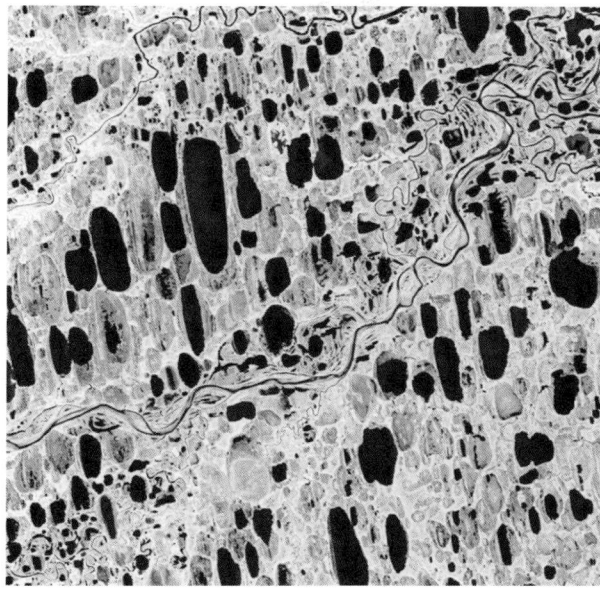

Significant declines in:
Daphnia middendorfiana (1.2–3.4 mm)
Eurycercus lamellatus (0.6–2.3 mm)
Daphnia pulex (0.8–2.9 mm)
Diaptomus bacillifer (1.5–1.8 mm)
No decline in small Cladocera (0.2–0.4 mm),
cyclopoid copepods (0.5–3.4 mm)
or fairy shrimps (1.1–17.6 mm)

**Fig. 13.21** Red phalaropes (*Phalaropus fulicarius*) are waders that selectively feed, like fish, on zooplankters in shallow tundra ponds (left) near Point Barrow in Alaska. Large shrimps are able to avoid predation by rapid movement but large daphnids are easily caught. (Photographs, NASA, R. Griffith. Data from Dodson & Eggar 1980.)

close to the ocean may create quite naturally, with their faeces and urine, what would be regarded as heavily polluted conditions elsewhere. Benthic invertebrates, notably chironomids and mosquitoes complete a life history that may span several years and emerge in swarms over a short period, giving dense black clouds that misleadingly suggest high productivity. The summers are short, however, and by August, perhaps only after a two-month growth period, temperatures are again falling and ice is starting to form for the long winter. The birds begin to move southwards in September and will not return until April or May. Gradually the landscape whitens with snow, and the waters, sealed in by ice, begin to lose oxygen, so that there may be a build up of phosphate and ammonium from the deoxygenated sediments, which, along with supplies brought in by the snow melt will support the initial algal growth of the next spring.

### 13.8.2 Cold temperate lakes

Matters get more complicated as climate warms and a landscape less frozen, or not frozen at all, offers a greater range of catchments. Some of the lakes are close to the ocean in generally maritime climates with freezing only occasional in winter and a long mixing period from say November to April (in the northern hemisphere) of cool water, and a direct summer stratification often disturbed by summer storms. Others are deep in the continents and covered with winter ice and strongly stratified in hot summers (see Chapter 2). Under the ice the plankton community will have similar features to those described for polar regions, whilst in the maritime lakes, populations established the previous autumn may overwinter, marking time or growing a little, depending on the wash through of water in what are often wet winters. Ice melt and the lengthening day in spring start a growth typically of diatoms.

Usually several species are involved, multiplying up from small residual populations that overwintered at low densities in the water column and forming distinct 'spring peaks' (Fig. 13.22), whose eventual decline may follow from depletion of available nutrients, the onset of direct stratification reducing the vigour of mixing, or from grazing by daphnids multiplying up again from overwintering animals or hatching from ephippia. There may be a brief clear water period as the daphnids clear the diatoms, but phytoplankters do not entirely disappear. Chrysophytes, often *Dinobryon*

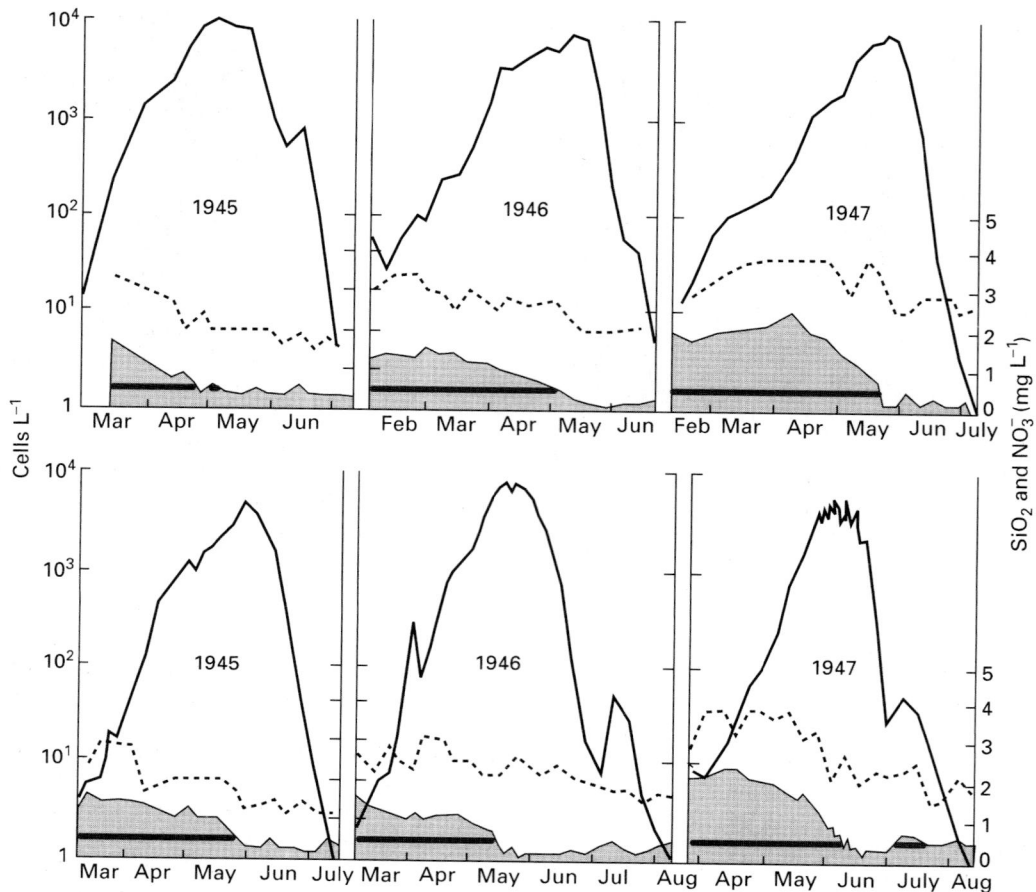

**Fig. 13.22** Annual cycles in the spring growth of *Asterionella formosa* in the north (lower) and south (upper) basins of Lake Windermere. Because of the lesser depth of the south basin and thus the greater exposure to light during the mixing period, growth begins earlier in the south. Interrupted lines show nitrate concentrations (×10) and the shaded areas show silicate concentrations. Growth becomes limited at around 0.5 mg $SiO^2$ $L^{-1}$ (dark line). Monitoring of Windermere phytoplankton, begun by John Lund in the 1940s (Lund, 1949, 1950, 1964) has continued until the present day and forms a unique long-term set of data of great value in retrospectively looking at effects of climate and other changes. Elsewhere, counting of phytoplankton has become less popular, for it is tedious and often replaced simply by determination of phytoplankton pigments, which can be semi-automated. A great deal of valuable information is thus lost in the interests of speed and the decline of patience.

species, which have high affinities for nutrients, are able to grow, perhaps helped by some phagotrophy as they not only photosynthesize but can also ingest bacteria. Cryptophytes are similar and also abundant. Meanwhile, water is still flowing in from the catchment, to some extent replenishing nutrients that have been removed by the diatoms, which now, their growth rates much reduced, sink to the hypolimnion and sediments. As the water column stratifies, young

fish, spawned in the littoral for the most part, move offshore to find larger meals than the rotifers and littoral microalgae on which they grew after their yolk sacs ran out. Large Cladocera become scarcer in the open water as fish predation intensifies, and copepods and rotifers more abundant. By now however, piscivores have discovered the bonanza of young fish and there follows an uneasy coexistence in which all the devices for minimizing predation risk in both the zooplankters and zooplanktivorous fish are brought to bear. Relieved a little of grazing pressure and benefiting from some recycling of nutrients arising from it, the phytoplankton community develops a mixed nature. Some slower growing species, small desmids (green algae) that began growth earlier, now become more prominent. Dinoflagellates appear and a few summer diatom species, usually very small ones with low sinking rates.

Bacterial activity has increased with some products such as vitamins secreted into the water that chrysophytes and green algae can use. There may be some layering in the epilimnion with cryptophytes taking advantage of the detritus, whose rate of sinking lessens when it meets the density gradient around the thermocline. Some cyanobacteria, such as the filamentous *Planktothrix*, may also grow at the bottom of the epilimnion where low light levels favour them. As the summer progresses, large cyanobacteria may become more abundant, together with large colonial green algae. The latter may be the outcome of prolonged grazing removing small algal competitors. The onset of the cyanobacteria has many explanations, some or other of which may be correct in some lakes, others in others. They may have benefited from grazing loss of small competitor species, as do the colonial green algae and the big dinoflagellates such as *Ceratium*, which become common alongside them. They may be favoured by rising pH as other algae photosynthesize. Cyanobacteria have high affinities for carbon dioxide at low concentrations. Nitrogen-fixing species may be favoured as other algae deplete inorganic nitrogen and supplies from the catchment have dwindled as summer evaporation reduces inflow streams to trickles. Nitrate is the major nitrogen form brought in from the catchment and cyanobacteria cannot take it up but take up ammonium regenerated by zooplankton grazing and fish excretion. Ammonium thus dominates summer nitrogen supplies. Phosphorus is also scarce in deeper lakes, but, because of sediment release is often abundant in summer in shallow ones and low N : P ratios are thought to favour some cyanobacteria.

Conditions in late summer often become calmer and the mechanisms that lead to surface bloom formation come into play. Deep below, in the hypolimnion, regeneration of ammonium, phosphate and even nitrate (if oxygen is plentiful) will have increased their concentrations to values much higher than in the epilimnion, but, except for species able to move up and down the water column (dinoflagellates, some Cyanobacteria),

this has no benefit to the nutrient-starved community above. If the hypolimnion is small or if large amounts of organic matter are falling into it, and usually both, oxygen may by now have run out and the redox sensitive reactions, described in Chapters 4 and 9, will have taken over. Nitrate will be absent, but ammonium, phosphate, reduced iron and manganese, sulphide and methane will have created a rather noxious and smelly water, though none of this is perceived at the surface. Some photosynthetic bacteria may have established pink water with their populations at the top of the hypolimnion if there is enough light and the anaerobic bacteria and tolerant Protozoa will burgeon throughout. In maritime lakes, with less strong stratification, summer storms may shave some water from the top of the hypolimnion, as may the internal waves or seiches induced by strong unidirectional winds that travel, in big lakes, along the metalimnion, giving a small shot of nutrients to a slightly deepened epilimnion.

From August, however, the waters start to cool, and the wind is able to deepen the epilimnion. Diatom populations return as cooling begins to disfavour the mixed community of the summer. Nutrient supplies from the catchment resume as the streams rise. Eventually, during a storm, perhaps in October or November, a northern hemisphere lake will overturn, the stratification being finally destroyed and mixing restored to the entire water column. The exact timing of this may mean that phosphate and ammonium from the former hypolimnion boost the autumn diatom growth, but it may come too late as the daylength shortens and light becomes limiting. Reoxygenation of the water will quickly remove phosphate, as oxidized iron and manganese compounds re-form and precipitate, and sulphide is reoxidized to sulphate. In a mild winter in maritime lakes, however, a small amount of growth of phytoplankton may still be possible, and with the help of some heterotrophy, the water under the winter ice will, as in Arctic lakes, bear some flagellates. The system settles into a period of limited activity for the winter, awaiting the lengthening and warming days of the spring when the diatoms grow again and the adult fish move to spawn in the littoral.

### 13.8.3 Warm temperate lakes

Standing waters are scarcer in the warm temperate zone than in the other regions considered here. Most of any size are artificial reservoirs; the natural basins

**Fig. 13.23** Severe drying down is normal in many warm temperate lakes, though in recent years climate changes have led to more severe conditions, even complete drying out in some lakes of the Mediterranean climate zones.

tend to be small and shallow or coastal lagoons and prone to drying out in summer, often with a marked rise in salinity. Lake Kinneret in Israel, Lake Tahoe in California/Nevada and the Great Salt lake of Utah are among the most thoroughly studied, but it is the shallow lagoons that epitomize the unpredictable state of many Mediterranean zone lakes.

Water supply is the key to how warm temperate lakes function (Fig. 13.23). Most rain falls in winter and evaporation rates can then still be high for the winters are mild. The amount of run-off tends to be very variable from year to year and the lake may veer from being a few metres deep to bordering on drying out late in the subsequent summer. Conductivities tend to be relatively high, even in winter, for evaporation in the catchment produces saline soils that leach into the lake. The vegetation of the catchment is also vulnerable to drought and fires, so natural soil erosion may bring in relatively turbid water in winter. There is usually a short period of winter mixing and diatom populations may reach their peak then, more or less disappearing as stratification begins early and becomes stronger. The pulse of winter nutrients may be quite

high from the bare soils, but the relatively large algal production in sunny, warm conditions will generally keep available nutrients at low concentrations.

Stratification brings an algal community that is comparable with that in mid-summer in cooler climates, with a mixure of green algae, dinoflagellates, and an increased occurrence of large cyanobacteria. Zooplankton grazing is spasmodic, for the richer fish communities of warm lakes, coupled with invertebrate predation from a more diverse assemblage, remove both large Cladocera that sometimes thrive for a short period in the cool season and their smaller sisters, leaving mostly copepods and rotifers. As evaporation raises the salinity, water levels fall and conditions favour flagellates. Some, typical of coastal seas or brackish waters, such as *Prymnesium parvum*, a haptophyte species that produces a fish toxin, may develop and there may be fish kills, though the fecundity of the fish and frequent reproduction will rapidly compensate. By late summer, the littoral zone will be dry and the water mass dwindling. This will not be disastrous because the littoral organisms will compensate by producing resting stages in the drying mud. The plankton may also be using this strategy, with ephippia, spores and cysts. Even cyanobacteria can produce akinetes, single large cells that persist on damp mud. The fish may be less fortunate and become locally extinct if the lake dries out entirely. In consequence, amphibians may be a more prominent part of the system, retreating to shaded, damp refuges in the surrounding vegetation or stream valleys if the water gives out. The late summer can be a quiescent period until new rains, if they come, regenerate the system during the winter.

### 13.8.4  Very warm lakes in the tropics

Conditions in lowland tropical lakes were once described as 'endless summer', for year-around the water is warm and the processes characterizing summer in cooler lakes are permanently present. But there is a seasonality in most tropical lakes, with only small ones right on the Equator lacking it. Tropical climates vary a great deal and the drier ones will have systems not unlike those described above for the warm temperate zone. Where water supply is available year around, they take on different properties. The extreme case of a small lake straddling the Equator is Lake George in Uganda, though it is influenced by water moving between it and Lake Edward, a larger lake just off the Equator, through the Kazinga Channel, by a climate of alternating dry and wet seasons and by a degree of seasonality in the amount of water that supplies it from the Ruwenzori Mountains of the Moon, which

to some extent compensates for local supplies in the dry season.

Lake George (Fig. 13.24), nonetheless has a very steady climate. Incident radiation, although irregularly intercepted by cloud, varies within a range of only +13% of the annual mean, and the water temperature is always about 30°C. This constancy is reflected in the low diversity of the plankton. Over 99% of the plankton biomass is phytoplankton (though heterotrophic bacteria have not been measured), and of this, six species of Cyanobacteria comprise 80%. Only a dozen or so other species have been recorded, compared with hundreds in more seasonally variable lakes. There is a great seasonal stability in phytoplankton biomass and species composition, and also in zooplankton biomass, which is dominated by only two copepod species, with *Thermocyclops hyalinus* comprising 80% by weight. It is likely that the copepods do feed on the cyanobacteria, as do some of the fish. Herbivorous fish form part of freshwater communities below about latitude 20°, when algal populations become more or less seasonally permanent. High fish populations reduce cladoceran communities to a very small size. Lake George is, however, likely to be unusual in the stability of its plankton communities. Away from the Equator, tropical lakes show as much seasonal variability as temperate ones.

Diatoms are common in many tropical lakes and again their growth coincides with turbulent conditions generated in the cooler seasons when stratification is weakest. In the deeper tropical lakes, stratification

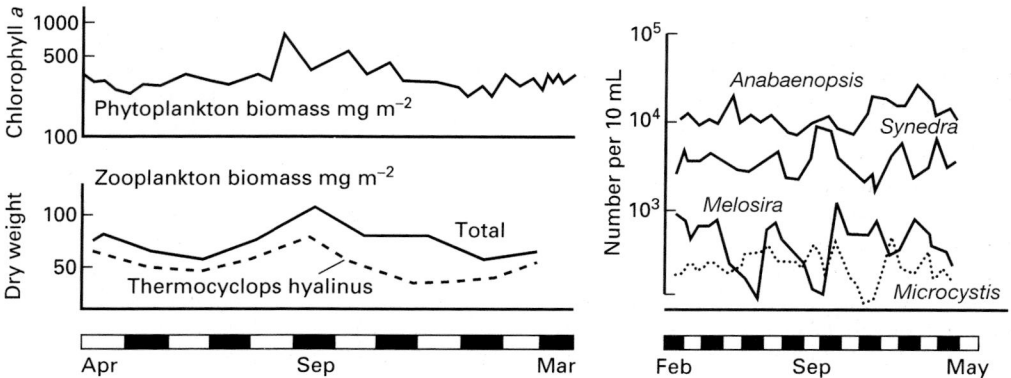

**Fig. 13.24** Seasonal changes in the plankton of Lake George, Uganda. Details are given of the major zooplankter and four of the most abundant phytoplankters. *Melosira* (*Aulacoseira*) and *Synedra* are diatoms, the others are Cyanobacteria. From Ganf & Viner, 1973.

is weakened but persists all year, with the thermocline deepening or shallowing from time to time. In periods of strongest stratification, cyanobacteria become commoner and a host of other species have a more or less constant presence. Intense predation on zooplankton is usual and fish communities may also specialize a great deal on particular foods, notably in the bigger, more ancient lakes. Nitrogen fixation by cyanobacteria may be very important because denitrification rates are high and supplies from the catchment are often low. Tropical climates may be wet but the high temperature means also high evaporation so that run-off bringing in nutrients may be low. The fluctuations in level between hot and cool, wet and dry seasons mean that sediments at the edge are often exposed to drying and rewetting, generating phosphates, so nitrogen supplies often become limiting by default. Endorheic tropical lakes (Fig. 13.25) may be very extreme, with dense,

permanent cyanobacterial growths, often of *Spirulina*, and very low diversity of both phytoplankton and zooplankton. Concentration of salts means that production can be very high, that sediments are permanently deoxygenated at the surface, and phosphate freely released from the sediment in large quantities. There tend to be very few, highly specialist osmotolerant fish species and large flocks of flamingo, filtering the cyanobacteria and the copepods that graze on them. A white crust of salt lines the edge and covers the sediments, which may be intensely black from reduced iron sulphide precipitation.

To some extent, these patterns are recognizable, which is why Table 13.1 could be drawn up. Polar lakes might move from winter communities like X2, X3 or E to summer ones like A, E or Z. Cold temperate lakes have sequences B or C to Y to P to Lm or H. In the warm temperate lakes, Lo in winter and spring may

**Fig. 13.25** Lake Nakuru is an endorheic lake in Kenya with dense growths of planktonic Cyanobacteria (mostly *Spirulina*, lower left) and large flocks of lesser flamingo (*Phoeniconias minor*). Linkages back to the land system are illustrated by frequent predation of the flamingo by hyaena.

be succeeded by Sn, X1 or M in summer. Lakes like George and endorheic lakes have permanent communities of M and H or S respectively and more seasonal tropical lakes may alternate between B or C when they mix a little and Lm, M or Sn when they are very strongly stratified. But individual variations are very common.

## FURTHER READING

An excellent set of recent reviews of aspects of lakes, including the plankton, is O'Sullivan & Reynolds (2004), *The Lakes Handbook*, Vol. 1. The expanding work on viruses is covered by Clasen et al. (2008), Middleboe et al. (2008) and Wilhelm & Matteson (2008). The similarly rapidly expanding field of lake bacteriology can be approached through Scavia et al. (1986), Weisse (2006), Van der Gucht et al. (2007), Corno & Jurgens (2008), Descy & Sarmento (2008), Logue et al. (2008, a particularly readable review), Logue & Lindstrom (2008) and Romina-Schiaffino et al. (2009). Laybourn-Parry (1992) is a good book on freshwater Protozoa and two ends of the microbial loop pathway are Fogg & Westlake (1955) and Laybourn-Parry (1997). Canter-Lund & Lund (1995) is a beautifully illustrated book on phytoplankton and Lund's work on seasonal changes in diatoms (1954, 1964, 1971) is classic literature. Litchman & Klausemeier is a recent review on phytoplankton, Talling (1976) and Zonneveld (1998) analyse depth profiles of photosynthesis, Tilman (1977) and Titman (1976) examine nutrient competition and Infante & Litt (1985) and Porter (1973, 1976) are examples of the literature on palatability of different species to zooplankters.

Cyanobacteria, at least partly because they produce poisons and everyone has some fascination with death, or at least avoiding it, are well covered. Reynolds & Walsby (1975) is still the most interesting review on blooms, Sivonen et al. (2007) bring molecular and other aspects up to date, Shapiro (1990), Hanson et al. (2007) and Jensen et al. (1994) look at various ecological aspects and Wiegand & Pflugmacher (2005), Babica et al. (2006) and Ballot et al. (2004) specifically review the toxins. A new area is the rate (rather rapid) at which organisms can evolve to meet changes in the environment. This has been studied with respect to tolerance of Daphnia to toxins (Hairston et al. (1999) and is expanding (Hairston & De Meester (2008).

There is no shortage of zooplankton literature either. Analysis of population dynamics began with Edmondson (1960) and was developed by Hall (1964). Complications were sorted out by Taylor (1988) and Threlkeld (1979). Methods for feeding rates were pioneered by Burns & Rigler (1967), and Folt & Burns (1999) review the factors influencing zooplankton distribution within lakes. Recent decades have shown greatest emphasis on cyclomorphosis, predator avoidance, kairemones and vertical migration. Interest began in Europe with the classic paper of Hrbacek et al. (1961) and then rapidly developed. A selection of interesting papers is: Lampert (2006), Havel (1987), Hall et al. (1976), Green (1967), Parejko & Dodson (1990), Jeffrey & Gilbert (1997), Gliwicz (1986), Gilbert (1988), Hanazato & Ooi (1992), Lehman & Caceres (1993), Zaret (1969) and Lazzaro et al. (2009). For clarity in thought and writing I have long admired papers by M. Gliwicz and W. Lampert. The particular linking role of nekton is emphasized by Vander Zanden & Vadeboncour (2002), but fish will be more comprehensively treated in the next Chapter.

The contrast between chaotic effects in plankton and a degree of order imposed by weather patterns can be seen in Beninca et al. (2008) on the one hand and George & Taylor (1995) and George (2002) on the other. A modelling approach to revealing some order in complicated data sets is shown by Gal et al. (2009) for Lake Kinneret in Israel. Lean (1973) and Lehman & Scavia (1982) demonstrate the importance of very fast processes in the plankton. Arctic and Antarctic lakes are interesting for their comparative simplicity and extreme conditions. Green & Lyons (2009), Laybourn-Parry (2009) and Van Geest et al. (2007) provide recent insights. Beklioglu et al. (2007) do likewise for Mediterranean lakes. Talling contributed a great deal to fundamental understanding of tropical lakes (1966, 1969 and 1986); Lake George was the site of intensive study (Moriarty et al. (1973), Ganf & Viner (1973)) until it was disturbed by political changes in Uganda in 1971. Melack (1979) demonstrates the strong seasonality of tropical lakes, Sarma et al. (2005), the particular stresses on their zooplankters and Hurlbert et al. (1986) record an interesting system in Peru.

# Chapter 14

# THE PROFUNDAL ZONE

## 14.1 THE END OF THE LINE

The plankton is a busy community; the littoral even more so, but all things must end. As the cycles of production and consumption and nutrient regeneration turn, some material is lost, sometimes to the overflow, but commonly to the hypolimnion and benthos. There is a steady rolling, under gravity, of particles downhill from the edge to the depths of the lake and a steady rain of particles falling through the water column. As they fall, colonizing bacteria and Protozoa will continue to metabolize them so that in a deep lake with a deep epilimnion and much activity from wind generated eddy currents, material may take some time finally to pass through the one-way gate of the metalimnion and into the hypolimnion, where the near lack of currents means that their journey to the bottom will accelerate and they will become part of the colder, dark, profundal realm. A suitably small submarine probing with its lights in the gloom (indeed such vehicles do exist (Fig. 14.1)) would see a flat, black or brown plain of mud, with clumps of dead branches and leaf litter sticking out of it. There are swarms of white ciliates cruising over the surface and perhaps settling around the carcase of a fish. From small burrows, tubes protrude,

*Ecology of Freshwaters: A View for the Twenty-first Century*, 4th edition. By Brian Moss. Published 2010 by Blackwell Publishing Ltd.

and the insect larvae that built them, from sediment and secretions, sway out to feed, whilst the siphons of bivalves suck in mud, and motile crustaceans seek larger debris. Fine pink, hair-like oligochaetes protrude into the water–mud interface and move below it together with large numbers of nematode worms. Everywhere, but unseen, are huge numbers of bacteria. An occasional fish will probe the bottom and suck in worms and larvae.

The profundal benthos is much less structured, nonetheless, than the bottom communities of the littoral. To a casual observer its existence is suggested only by the clouds of midges (chironomids) which emerge from the bottom through the water column to swarm and mate around the lake and which can sometimes be a problem for local amenity. They can be so dense on Lake Malawi (Fig. 14.2) that they have choked and killed fishermen paddling through the swarm and breathing them in. And I remember nights in July next to Gull lake in Michigan, where every surface was covered with large mayflies briefly resting on their one night of adulthood before they laid their eggs on the lake surface to fall to the bottom, hatch and continue the Sisyphean task of processing the wastes.

A comparison between littoral and profundal sediment macroinvertebrate communities recorded at the peaks of their development in the same lake illustrates just how less diverse is that of the profundal. At 2 m water depth in Lake Esrom, in Denmark, the littoral plants and their underlying sediment provide habitat

**Fig. 14.1** In marine work, autonomous underwater vehicles (AUV) are frequently used for scanning the sea bed and taking continuous readings of water properties. They are less frequently used in freshwaters, though one called Tantan is used in Lake Biwa in Japan. In the picture a manned small submarine and an AUV, owned by Woods Hole Oceanographic Institution, are shown. (Pictures WHOI.)

for at least 40 macroinvertebrate species including oligochaete worms, caddis-fly and dipteran larvae, gastropod and bivalve molluscs. A comparable sampling of sediment from under 20 m of water, in the hypolimnion, revealed only five species: an oligochaete worm, three dipteran larvae, and a bivalve mollusc.

The diversity found in the profundal much depends on the oxygen status of the hypolimnion. In some of the big, ancient deep lakes of the world, with well oxygenated hypolimia, the profundal benthos is rich and holds many endemic species that have evolved in this somewhat terminal of habitats. Lake Biwa in Japan has 28 endemic molluscs, many of them profundal bivalves, and four crustaceans, including the wonderfully named shrimp *Jesogammarus anandalii*, which at night moves to the top of the hypolimnion to prey on zooplankters and supplement its diet of falling detritus. Likewise lakes Fuxian in China, Ochrid in Macedonia, Khubsugul (Khovsgol) in Mongolia, Balkash

in Khazakstan and Baikal in Russia all have notable collections of endemic benthos.

## 14.2 THE IMPORTANCE OF OXYGEN

There are strong correlations between the occurrence of particular species in the profundal benthos and the lowest oxygen concentration reached at the surface of the sediments in summer. Figure 14.3 contrasts the respiration rates of four littoral animals from Lake Esrom and four profundal species. In the limpet, *Theodoxus*, which grazes algae from the rocks of the wave-disturbed littoral, respiration rate is maximal only at full saturation and steadily falls with decreasing saturation. With littoral species from progressive depths, rates at saturation are lower, then fall with decreasing saturation to 40–60% before plunging to around 20 or 30%. In the profundal species, the rates

**Fig. 14.2** Swarms of midges, particularly of *Chaoborus*, are common on Lake Malawi. The midges aggregate from a large area in mating swarms.

are low, even at saturation, but are largely maintained as saturation decreases until a final drop-off at saturations as low as 10%.

Frequently, profundal animals are rich in haemoglobin, which allows continued respiration at very low external levels, by concentrating oxygen within the organism, thus allowing the animal to continue feeding. The low diversity of the profundal benthos, compared with the littoral, might thus be attributed simply to oxygen stress. It lives also at lower temperatures, for the deeper waters of many temperate lakes remain at 4–10°C year around. Temperature is not crucial in reducing diversity, however. The hypolimnia of tropical lakes can be very warm (Chapter 2) yet are also species poor. They are often severely deoxygenated.

Even so there is a wide range of animals that can cope with deoxygenation and other factors may be important. Reduced diversity in the profundal is a feature of very infertile lakes with well oxygenated bottom waters, such as Thingvallavatn in Iceland (Table 14.1). The clue may be in the relatively simple habitat structure of the profundal and in the relatively low quality and short supply of food that eventually reaches the bottoms of deep lakes.

## 14.3 PROFUNDAL COMMUNITIES

Many profundal communities are dominated by chironomid larvae (Diptera) and oligochaete worms, with sometimes some small bivalve mollusc species. Attempts have been made to classify lakes on the basis of their benthic invertebrates and although these have been completely successful only for limited regions or purposes (Chapter 11), a general trend in benthic fauna related to lake fertility can be seen. Well-oxygenated hypolimnia have a variety of larvae of *Chironomus*, *Tanytarsus* and other chironomid species, *Pisidium* spp (bivalve molluscs), some Crustacea, such as the amphipod *Pontoporeia* and sometimes insect larvae lsuch as *Sialis* (alder-fly), and oligochaetes.

At the other extreme of sediments covered by anaerobic water for part of the year, the chironomid fauna is reduced first to one or two detritivorous species, for example *Chironomus anthracinus*, and about the same

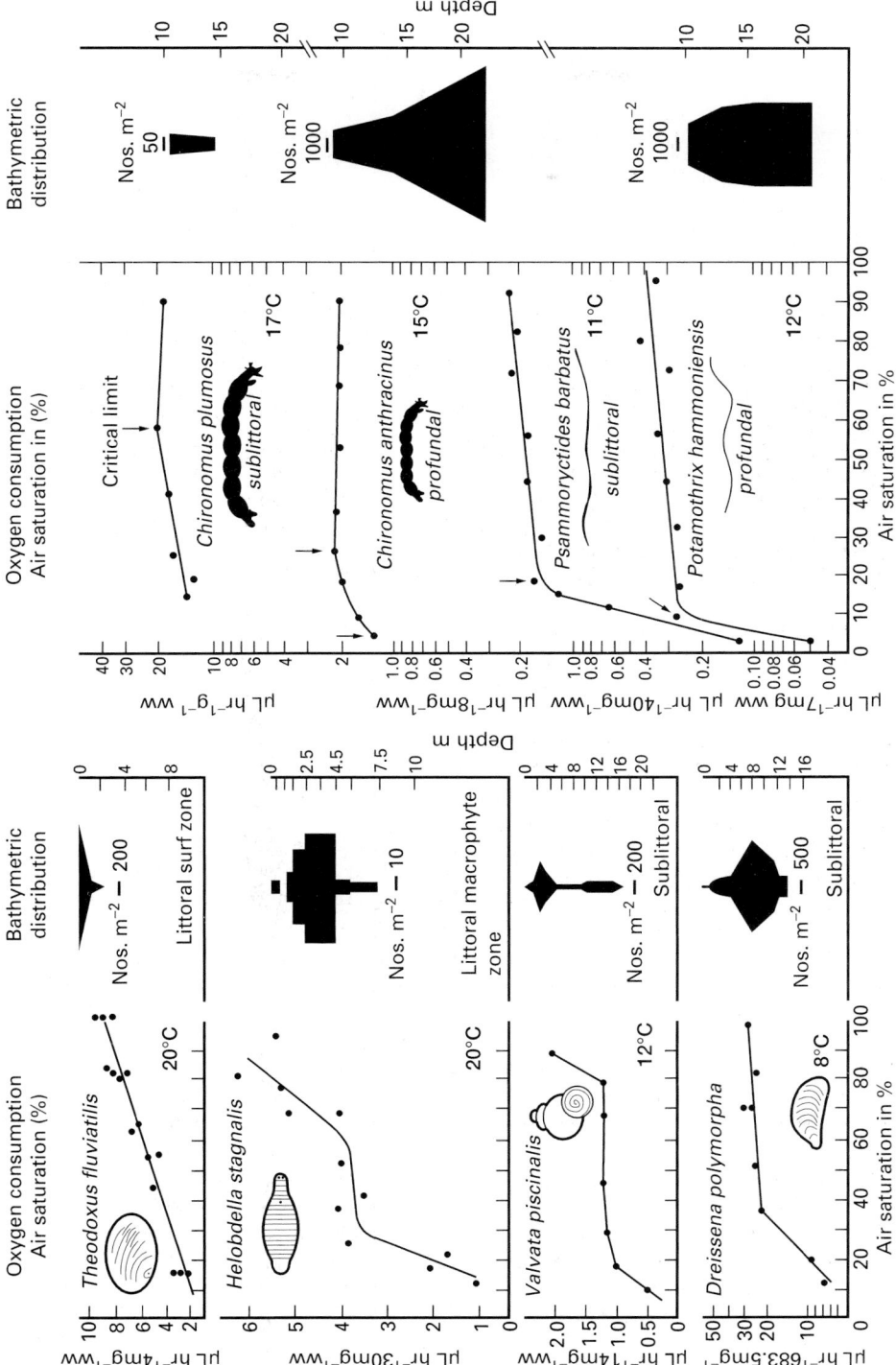

**Fig. 14.3** Respiration rates of benthic animals that are common in Lake Esrom, Denmark. Values are given on a per animal (mean weight) basis and are collected from various sources. The key differences are in the shapes of the curves as respiration declines with decreasing saturation with oxygen. (From Jónasson 1978.)

**Table 14.1** Number of bottom living animals, their biomass, annual production, turnover ratio (production : biomass) and species diversity in successive depth zones of Lake Thingvallavatn in Iceland. Biomass and production are given as ash-free dry weight per $m^2$. Turnover ratio is given in parentheses in the production column. (Based on Lindegaard 1992.)

| Depth (m) | Nature | Species richness | Number of animals $m^{-2}$ | Biomass (mg $m^{-2}$) | Production (mg $m^{-2}$ $yr^{-1}$) | Turnover (yr$^{-1}$) |
|---|---|---|---|---|---|---|
| 0–2 | Littoral surf zone, rocks and boulders | 36 | 21,000 | 3900 | 14,000 | 3.6 |
| 2–6 | Littoral rocks and boulders | 41 | 18,000 | 3500 | 11,500 | 3.3 |
| 6–10 | Littoral rocks and boulders | 39 | 10,400 | 2600 | 8000 | 3.1 |
| 10–20 | Littoral rocks, sand and aquatic plants (*Nitella* sp) | 35 | 3500 | 1400 | 3600 | 2.6 |
| 20–114 | Profundal bare rock and sediments | 18 | 3900 | 850 | 1200 | 1.4 |

number of species of larval predators. These often include *Chaoborus*, the translucent 'phantom larva', which migrates to the epilimnion to hunt zooplankton at some stages of its life history (Chapter 13). There is usually also a much greater biomass of oligochaete worms such as *Tubifex* and *Ilyodrilus*. The profundal benthos of such a lake, Lake Esrom, has been studied in some detail and will illustrate the biology of these organisms.

## 14.4 BIOLOGY OF SELECTED BENTHIC INVERTEBRATES

### 14.4.1 *Chironomus anthracinus*, a detritivore

*Chironomus anthracinus*, a gnat, starts life in Lake Esrom as an egg mass deposited on the lake surface in May between sunset and darkness (Fig. 14.4). Mated female gnats dip their abdomens into the surface water film. The egg masses are about $2 \times 2.5$ mm in size when dry but swell a hundredfold when wetted, and are deposited in the lee of beech woodlands on the western shore. These create the calm conditions necessary for the flight of the gnat, but water currents subsequently distribute the eggs throughout the lake and they sink to the bottom.

By June the eggs have hatched into instars less than 2 mm long, the first of four stages which precede pupation and emergence of the adult some 23 months later from populations in the profundal. Growth is rapid and the third instar is reached in July. The growth coincides with a ready supply of food falling from the epilimnion where a major population of diatoms has dominated the spring growth and is now dying (see Chapter 13). The first instar is transparent and probably moves along beneath the sediment surface, swallowing sediment as it moves. The second has heavier musculature and some haemoglobin. It builds a tube, open at the surface and tapering at the base. In this it lives, pumping a current of water past its mouth by undulations of its body. The larva may also emerge partly from the tube to gather sediment encircling it. The third instar larvae build tubes, lined with salivary secretions, which project a little way above the sediment surface, and feed on the deposits around the tube. They spread a net of salivary threads over the mud, to which particles stick, then drag the net down into the tube to eat it.

Lake Esrom is fertile and the dissolved oxygen concentrations fall rapidly in its hypolimnion. By July the lower few metres are almost deoxygenated and at around 1 mg $O_2$ $L^{-1}$; growth of the *Chironomus* larvae stops (Fig. 14.4). This may be because only limited respiration is then possible, or because the supply of sedimenting food has changed in quality or amount as the overlying plankton community processes it first. On the other hand, if growth of *Chironomus* stops, so does predation on it by bottom-feeding fish, which

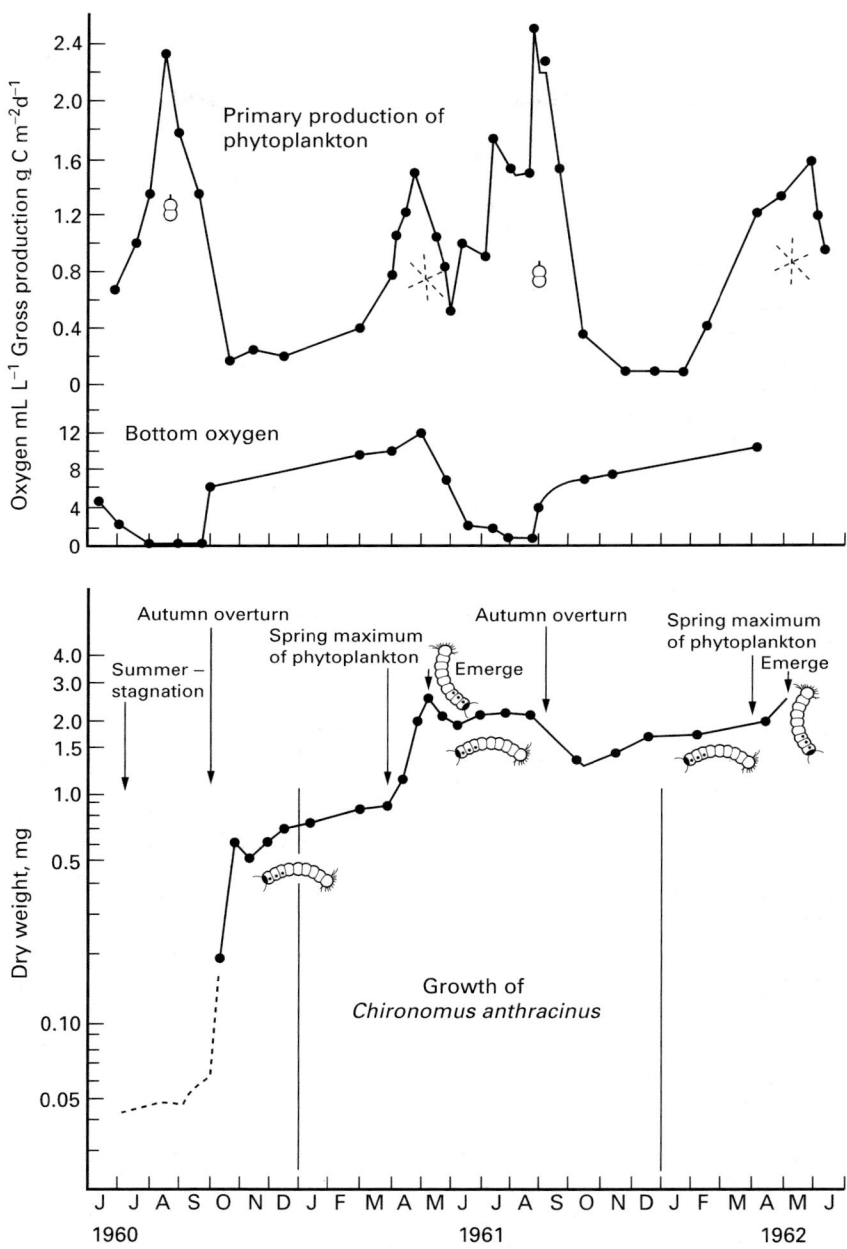

**Fig. 14.4** Events in Lake Esrom and the development of the *Chironomus anthracinus* population. (Redrawn from Jonasson 1978.)

cannot tolerate the deoxygenation and move to shallower waters.

After the overturn of stratification in Lake Esrom in September, and reoxygenation of the water, growth of *Chironomus* resumes and the third instar larvae moult and change into fourth instar larvae. These are bigger, over 1.5 cm, heavily muscled and bright red in colour. They produce tubes of sediment particles glued with salivary secretion, which have 'chimneys' projecting 1–2 cm above the mud surface. The height of the chimney may be sufficient to reach water only a few millimetres from the sediment surface that is better oxygenated than that immediately in contact with the sediment.

Growth of the fourth instar larvae depends on the supply of phytoplankton and detritus reaching the bottom in autumn, but is soon reduced as the shortening days diminish plankton production. Growth resumes the following spring, but most of the larvae are not mature enough to pupate and form adults. They must therefore remain as fourth instars to make further growth in the spring and autumn of the second year. Pupation follows in the succeeding spring when the pupae emerge from the tubes and float to the water surface. This happens in the evening. Within about 35 seconds of reaching the surface, the pupal skin splits and the adult emerges, turning from the pupal red to black. The adults (imagos) rest on the surface until sunrise when the rising warmth quickens their metabolism sufficiently for them to fly away and later to mate and lay eggs on the water. The adult life of the midge is very short, only a few days, compared with the 23 months spent as a larva in the profundal.

At lesser water depths, where there is no summer deoxygenation, *C. anthracinus* is able to grow sufficiently in one year to emerge the next. The shallow-water populations also have higher respiratory rates, which probably also accelerate development of the larvae. A few of the deep-water population do manage to emerge after only 12 months, in the spring following their birth, but they do not contribute any young to the population. Their eggs are mostly eaten as they reach the sediment by the large population of remaining fourth instar larvae.

### 14.4.2 *Chaoborus flavicans*, a predator

Carnivores in the profundal benthos of Lake Esrom are few (about 10%) compared with detritivores. There are

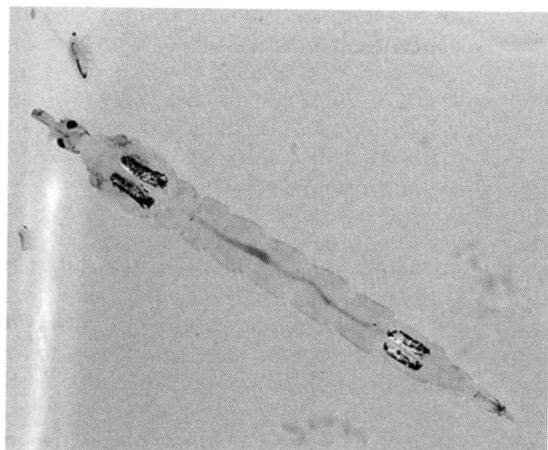

**Fig. 14.5** *Chaoborus*, the phantom midge, is a common predator in the profundal benthos, moving up at night to feed on zooplankton in some of its instars. It is so called because of its transparency, only the eyes and air sacs being easily visible. A 0.75 mm daphnid, one of its potential prey, is shown.

two main species, both larvae of dipteran flies. *Chaoborus flavicans* (syn. *C. alpinus*) feeds mainly on the plankton and only partly on the sediment community, and little is known about the other, *Procladius pectinatus*. Both species ultimately emerge for brief adult lives in which they lay eggs.

*Chaoborus*, the phantom-midge (Fig. 14.5), is so called because of its transparent body, punctuated only by its dark eyes and apparently black (an optical effect) air sacs at the hind end. These possibly allow it to regulate its buoyancy when it moves between the epilimnion and the sediment. Eggs are laid in late summer by the adult midges and first instar larvae appear in the plankton in September. Zooplankters, on which *Chaoborus* mainly feeds after seizing them with its prehensile antennae, are reasonably abundant in autumn and the *Chaoborus* larvae quickly pass into their second and third instars. These spend some time in the plankton, particularly during overcast weather when their visibility to prey is least, and some in the sediment. Fourth instar larvae are generally produced the following spring, and these migrate nightly from the sediment to the surface water, where zooplankters are again abundant. In winter, *Chaoborus* spends most of the time in the sediment, possibly feeding on oligochaete worms. Pupation and emergence are in July.

## 14.5 WHAT THE SEDIMENT-LIVING DETRITIVORES REALLY EAT

In relatively shallow water, much of the organic matter arriving at the sediment surface is quite rich in energy and nutrients. In deeper water, processing by the planktonic community may have reduced this richness, leaving particles lower in nitrogen and energy content. Thus the overall production of the benthos in Lake Thingvallavatn (Table 14.1) shows a lower biomass, a lower annual production and a lower turnover rate with depth. Partly this is due to lower average temperature with depth but it is also probably due to the reduced quality of food reaching the bottom.

There is some order to where animals live in apparently structureless sediment. Those organisms living closest to the sediment surface, such as *Chironomus anthracinus* and *C. riparius* have the advantage of better food quality, though the disadvantage of greater exposure to predators. This is also true of those filtering the particles out just before they can be sedimented, such as *Chironomus plumosus* and *Glyptotendipes paripes*. The surface deposit feeders often construct U-shaped tubes in the sediment from which they rarely emerge, whilst the filter feeders construct J-shaped tubes from which they protrude. Animals deeper in the sediment, such as the oligochaetes, have to process material that has already been ingested by the surface-dwellers and defaecated, but are least vulnerable to foraging fish searching through the surface sediment.

The faeces of the surface-feeders are still rich in carbon but not in other elements and the remaining carbon compounds are likely to be refractory. It seems likely that processing by bacteria is important in converting this material into usable food. Studies in the invertebrate community of a bog lake in Northumberland, UK have uncovered a story paralleling that of the feeding of shredders in streams (Chapter 7).

Blaxter Lough is a shallow basin set in the peat of an extensive blanket bog. Erosion of the peat by waves at the windward edge provides a ready source of organic matter but the major detritivore, *Chironomus lugubris*, is conspicuously distributed at the opposite side of the basin. The eroded peat is washed by water movement across the lake bottom to the leeward shore and as it moves it is broken down into smaller particles. However, although *C. lugubris* has some restrictions on the size of particles it can eat, these do not explain why it does not colonize the area where the peat is freshly eroded. Suitably sized particles sieved from eroding or *in situ* peat would not support its growth.

On the other hand, if fresh peat was allowed to become colonized by microorganisms over a few days, it would support growth of *Chironomus*, whether in the laboratory or in chambers placed in any area of the lake. The natural distribution of the chironomids in the lake reflects the distance travelled by suitably fine peat particles in order for them to become colonized by palatable bacteria and fungi. The microorganisms absorb nitrogen compounds from the water and, by the time they become palatable, the peat particles have increased in calorific content per unit weight by only 23%, but have doubled in protein content.

Peat ingested by *Chironomus lugubris* contains more bacteria than fungi but the balance changes as the microorganisms pass through the gut. The faecal pellets are relatively large, coherent and dominated by fungi. They form the food source of a small cladoceran, *Chydorus sphaericus*, which can rasp material from them, presumably digesting most of the microorganisms, and producing fine faeces of its own. These are small enough to be nutritious again to *Chironomus*, once recolonized by bacteria. A reciprocal relationship exists between the two animals, resulting, with the help of microorganisms, in the ultimate breakdown of the peat. Initially peat is poor food, much like the sediment of the profundal following a long passage through the plankton system, or after it has been worked over by the surface feeders. The bacteria produced on such material are nonetheless unlikely to be as rich a food supply as fresh algal material. *Hieronymus plumosus*, another chironomid, in a Swedish lake selectively fed upon bacteria, cyanobacteria and diatoms (*Microcystis* and *Aulacoseira*) from the sediment, but assimilated five times as much carbon from the diatom, *Aulacoseira*, as from the bacteria and did not readily digest the cyanobacterium, *Microcystis*. In infertile lakes, where algal material reaching the sediment is scarce, bacteria, however, are likely to be a major source of carbon for the benthic animals.

Studies on the carbon isotope signature of chironomid larvae in such lakes suggest that methane-producing or metabolizing bacteria are a major food source (Fig. 14.6). Carbon signatures of the larvae resemble those of methane, but it is not yet clear how the mechanisms work and whether it is the methane-producing bacteria, methane-oxidizing bacteria or protozoa that have eaten these bacteria that are the immediate sources for the chironomids. It is unlikely that it is

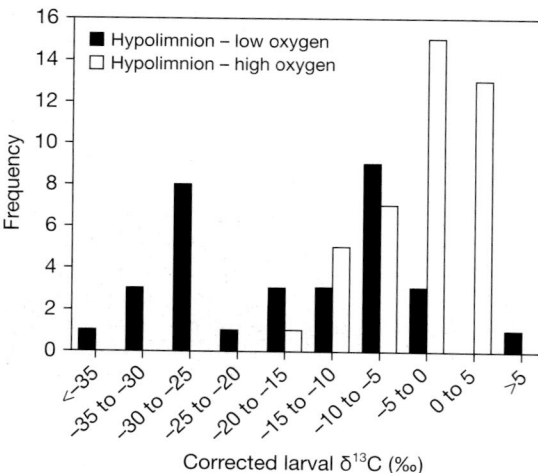

**Fig. 14.6** The δ¹³C signature of biologically produced methane is very low and transmitted to organisms feeding on the bacteria processing methane. The signatures of profundal chironomids separate into those with very low values taken from hypolimnia where oxygen is very scarce and those with higher values from better oxygenated hypolimnia. The implication is that in deoxygenated hypolimnia and sediments, methane-producing or -consuming bacteria are the major sources of food. (Based on Jones et al. 2008.)

symbiotic methane producing bacteria in the chironomid guts. The bacterial communities of sediments have not been investigated in the detail of the planktonic bacteria, but sediments being anaerobic only a little way below the surface, it is likely that most bacteria are anaerobes, and carbon compounds being the most abundant substrates, that most of these are methanogens. In fertile lakes, which are often also shallower, the abundance of algal material, and its entry, barely degraded, to the sediment, mean that bacteria may account for only a few per cent of the invertebrates' food. This then places some importance on the nature of the sedimenting material in the relationship between the planktonic community and the underlying benthos.

## 14.6 INFLUENCE OF THE OPEN-WATER COMMUNITY ON THE PROFUNDAL BENTHOS

Activity in the profundal zone is influenced by all of the catchment, the littoral and pelagic zones, but the

relative importance of each will vary in different lakes and even in different parts of the profundal in the same lake. The growing realization that in many lakes, and particularly in pristine ones, allochthonous organic matter may be a major source of carbon and energy, and the consequent net heterotrophy of the whole lake system (Chapter 11), has made understanding of the profundal of great interest. Current approaches involve dosing whole lakes with sodium bicarbonate labelled with ¹³C and following changes in the δ¹³C values of various components. Calculations can then establish what proportion of the carbon metabolism in the lake comes from autochthonous processes (in which ¹³C levels are enriched by the addition made) and allochthonous supplies. In one study in mid-western USA, at Crampton lake, damselfly and dragonfly nymphs sampled at 1.5 m in the littoral zone derived 75% of their carbon from autochthony within the lake, but chironomids from 1.5, 3.5 and 10 m depths took 43, 39 and 17% respectively from this source. The remainder came from allochthonous sources or old autochthonous production. Stable isotope studies are increasingly used and give a snapshot of the system but not a profound understanding of the processes going on. To obtain this is more time consuming and the best such study is still that carried out by Johnson & Brinkhurst (1971a,b,c) in the Bay of Quinte, on the northern shore of Lake Ontario.

The Bay of Quinte (Fig. 14.7) is long, narrow, and winding. It is shallow (about 5 m deep) at its inner end, where several towns enrich it with sewage effluent, and opens out, over 100 km distant, into the 30-m-deep waters of inshore Lake Ontario, where depth and dilution have reduced the fertility of the water. At four stations (Big Bay, Glenora, Conway and Lake) along this gradient, the amount of sedimenting material and its fate were followed as the bacteria, benthic invertebrates and fish processed it. The results emphasize both quantity and quality of the sedimenting material as important in determining the productivity of the benthic animals.

In the inner bay, Big Bay, station was a benthic community dominated by chironomids, while the third station, Conway, had a rich association of bivalve molluscs (*Sphaerium*), oligochaete worms, chironomids and crustaceans with an intermediate community at the second station, Glenora. In Lake Ontario, the fourth station, there was a more diverse community of *Sphaerium* spp., Crustacea, and many other species. In general, the diversity increased towards the main lake,

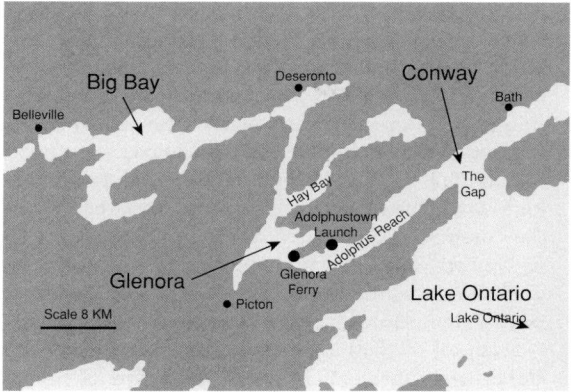

**Fig. 14.7** The Bay of Quinte, a long winding side shoot of Lake Ontario.

along with the gradient of decreasing fertility and a gradient of summer bottom-water temperatures, which were above 22°C at Big Bay, but around 10°C in Lake Ontario.

The first task was to determine the rate of supply of materials to the bottom communities. The sedimenting seston was collected in 20-cm-diameter funnels fitted into bottles to retain it and suspended about 1.5 m above the bottom. 'Seston' includes all the fine particulate matter suspended in the water. The traps were emptied weekly and the inorganic and organic parts of the sediment measured. Bacteria colonize seston while it is still suspended and these bacteria continually decompose it, even in the traps. The rate of this decomposition was found to be a few per cent per day and appropriate corrections were applied to correct for this for the four stations.

Sedimentation rates decreased from the inner bay to the lake, though not steadily, for Big Bay had a much

greater rate of sedimentation of organic matter than the others. The overall rate of processing of this material after it reached the bottom was measured as the community respiration, the sum of bacterial, invertebrate and fish respiration. The first two components were measured together as the rate of oxygen uptake from water overlying the sediment in small cores. The sediment and its overlying water were sealed from the air by a layer of oil and incubated in the laboratory at the appropriate natural temperature. The respiration rates of fish feeding on the benthic community could not be directly obtained. They were estimated from studies elsewhere as about 50% of the total invertebrate respiration (see below), and this was added to the measured sediment core respiration to give total community respiration. Although community respiration decreased from Big Bay to Lake Ontario (Table 14.2), it did not do so to the same extent as sedimentation rate. This point will be returned to later.

**Table 14.2** Mean sedimentation rates and community respiration rates at four stations in the Bay of Quinte.

| Station | Organic matter sedimented (g m$^{-2}$ day$^{-1}$) | Community respiration (g O$_2$ m$^{-2}$ day$^{-1}$) | Mean temperature (°C) |
|---|---|---|---|
| Big Bay | 3.01 | 0.35 | 17.1 |
| Conway | 0.71 | 0.25 | 11.8 |
| Glenora | 0.29 | 0.22 | 10.8 |
| Lake Ontario | 0.28 | 0.15 | 9.1 |

It was then necessary to separate the activity of the benthic microorganisms from that of the macro-invertebrates (those larger than about 1 mm and therefore not the protozoa and organisms such as nematodes which had to be included with the micro-organisms). This was done by measuring the respiration rates of invertebrates separately. Representative animals were placed in small jars with a substratum of sand, almost free of microorganisms, and their rates of oxygen uptake measured at a variety of temperatures. Numerous experiments produced equations relating respiration rate to size (as dry weight) of animal and temperature for all of the major species. This meant that from routine samplings in which temperature was measured, and animals were counted and weighed, respiration rates for the whole macro-invertebrate community could be calculated.

It was also possible to find net production, the increase in amount of animal tissue per unit time, by keeping representative animals in small mud cores, freed of other animals by previous heating or freezing, and by measuring by how much their weight increased over several days or weeks. The method has the disadvantage that growth rates may be altered in the absence of competition with other species. Growth rates were expressed as percentage increases in weight of animal per unit time, and allowed extrapolation to the natural community using the relationship:

production = growth rate × biomass

Production of animals that formed distinct cohorts in their life histories was determined by a variant of the Allen curve technique (Chapters 9 and 15).

Assimilation rates, approximately the sums of respiration rates and net productivities, were then calculable and these are given in Table 14.3. Biomass

of the macroinvertebrates increased towards the outer lake – this contrasts with sedimentation rate and community respiration – and assimilation, production and respiration all reached peaks at Glenora, the second station, and were generally similar or lower among Big Bay and the outer two stations. The high sedimentation rate at Big Bay, therefore, did not support comparably high invertebrate production. The turnover rate of the community, measured by the yearly production to biomass ratio did, however, follow inversely the gradient outwards, probably reflecting the decrease in mean temperature.

From all of these data, the diagrams in Fig. 14.8 could be constructed. They show the flow of energy through the sediment community (bacteria, invertebrates and fish) at the four stations, and all quantities have been converted to cal m$^{-2}$ day$^{-1}$ for rates, and to kcal m$^{-2}$ (in brackets) for the standing biomass of the various components. $IM$ is the incoming organic matter, the amount of sedimentation.

Community respiration ($R_{COM}$) degrades less than a quarter of incoming organic matter, and animal production alone less than a twentieth at Big Bay, so that much of it is not utilized ($NU$) and forms the permanent sediment. It is not used because it is refractory and difficult even for bacteria to degrade. Its low quality probably reflects the nature of the cell walls of cyano-bacteria, which are abundant in the phytoplankton there, but also the large import of fibrous organic matter left after terrestrial decomposition and timber processing and washed into the Bay.

The amount of unutilized matter is small at the other three stations. This is reflected in the low organic content of the sediment at the Lake Ontario station, 3–4%, compared with 32% in the sedimenting material. The organic content of sediment has, in

**Table 14.3** Productivity of the benthic macro-invertebrate community in the Bay of Quinte. All rates are in kcal m$^{-2}$ yr$^{-1}$, and biomass in kcal m$^{-2}$.

| Station | Biomass (B) | Assimilation | Production (P) | Respiration | Turnover (P/B) (yr$^{-1}$) |
|---|---|---|---|---|---|
| Big Bay | 5.45 | 108.7 | 74.3 | 34.3 | 13.6 |
| Glenora | 29.9 | 368 | 233 | 136 | 7.8 |
| Conway | 25.6 | 142 | 65.8 | 75.8 | 2.6 |
| Lake Ontario | 38.0 | 165 | 51 | 115 | 1.3 |

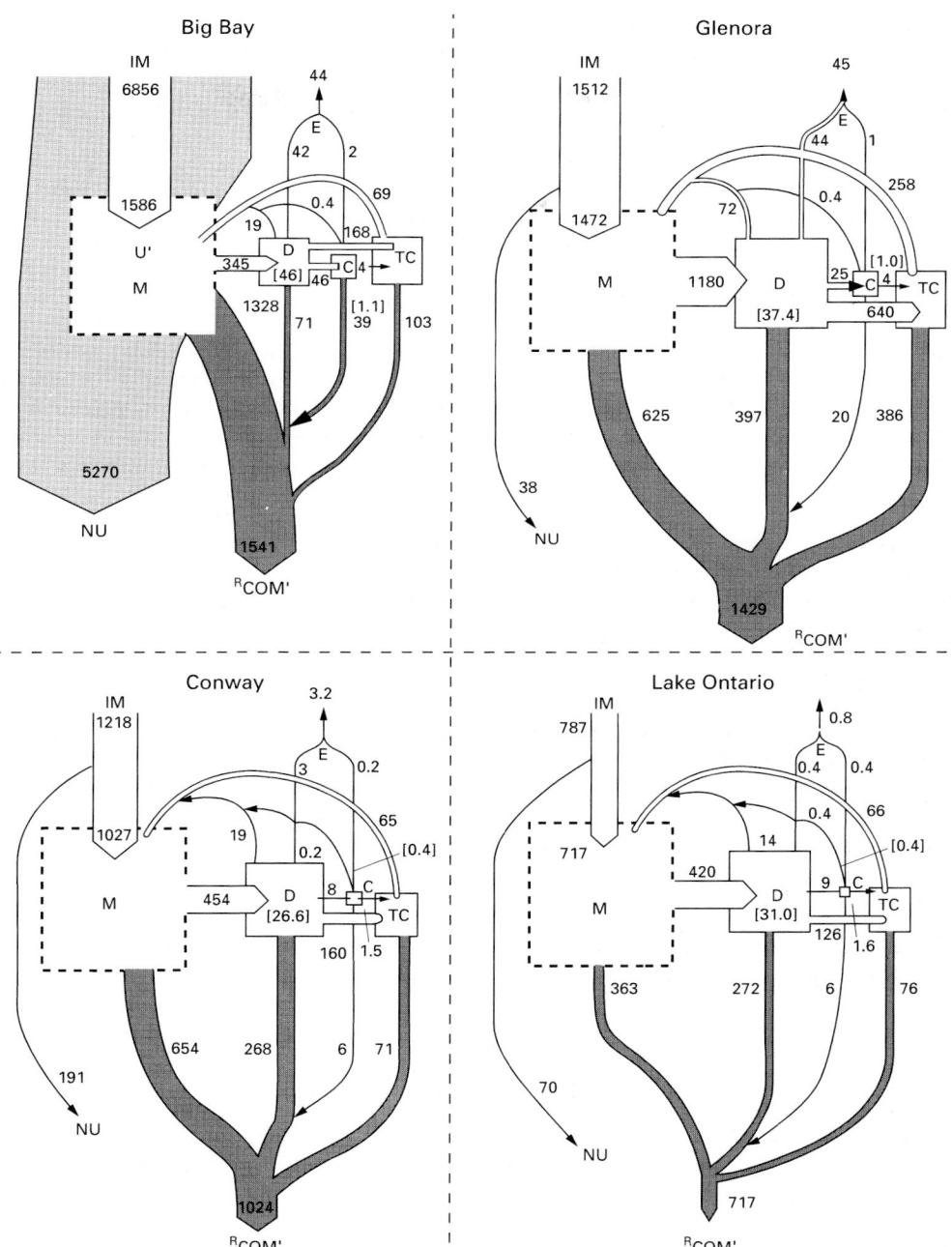

**Fig. 14.8** Mean rates of energy flow at four stations in the Bay of Quinte. Boxes represent standing crops and stocks (kcal m$^{-2}$) and pipes the rates of flow in cal m$^{-2}$ d$^{-1}$. IM: incoming organic matter; M: microorganisms; U: amount utilized; NU: not utilized and stored in permanent sediment; E: emerging insects; D: detritivores; C: carnivores; TC: top carnivores (fish); $R_{COM}$: community respiration. Black pipes show respiratory losses. (Redrawn from Johnson & Brinkhurst, 1971c).

the past, been used as an indicator of potential benthic animal production in lakes. These studies indicate that it represents the net result of several processes of accumulation and degradation and its use as such an indicator may be misleading.

These processes are amenable to a general treatment, which may have implications wider than those for the Bay of Quinte. First, several measures of the efficiency of energy use may be deduced for the benthic community. The proportion of incoming energy used by the whole community (microorganisms, invertebrates and fish) is:

$$a = (R_{COM} + E)/IM = U/IM$$

where $E$ is the energy lost in the emergence of adult insects that fly away, and $U$ is the energy used, i.e. not stored in permanent sediment.

The proportion of usable energy channelled through the macroinvertebrates is:

$$b = (R_D + R_C + E)/(R_{COM} + E)$$

where $R$ is the respiration of detritivores, D, and carnivores, C.

Thirdly, $E_{gc}$, the net growth efficiency of the invertebrates, is defined as:

$$E_{gc} = [A_D - (R_D + R_C)]/A_D = P_{D+C}/A_D$$

where $A$ is assimilation and $P$ is production of both detritivores and carnivores.

Table 14.4 gives these quotients for the four Bay of Quinte stations. They show clearly the lower utilization of incoming matter at Big Bay ($a = 0.23$), and that the microorganisms at Big Bay take a greater proportion of the utilized material (($100 - b$) = 90%) than they do at the other stations (61–73%). This depends on the quality of the sedimenting seston. If it is difficult to

degrade, a greater investment of its contained energy must be made by bacterial activity to convert it to a form (bacterial cells) usable by the invertebrates.

The product of $a$ and $b$ gives the proportion of incoming energy usable ($U$) by the invertebrates, and is very low at Big Bay, 2.3%, and 23–25% at the other stations. A general equation for utilization by the animals is:

$$U = a \cdot b \cdot IM$$

$a$ probably decreases with increased allochthonous import of material (usually of a low quality, refractory nature) from the catchment, while $b$ reflects the cost of processing the material and is low when allochthonous matter, or tough-walled algae, particularly cyanobacteria, are present.

$E_{gc}$ can now be incorporated into the model. Production of macroinvertebrates bears some relationship, $c$, to their utilization of organic matter:

$$P = c(U)$$

and

$$U = R_{D+C} + E$$

E, the insect emergence, is generally only a small proportion of the total energy flow and may be neglected so that:

$$P = c(R_{D+C})$$

Because

$$E_{gc} = P_{D+C}/R_D = P_{D+C}/(P_{D+C} + R_{D+C})$$
$$R_{D+C} = P_{D+C}[(IM - E_{gc})]/E_{gc}$$

Also, because

$$P = c(R_{D+C})$$
$$c = P/R_{D+C} = E_{gc}/(IM - E_{gc})$$

and because

$$U = a \cdot b \cdot IM$$

therefore,

$$P = a \cdot b \cdot c \cdot IM$$

This is now a relationship that describes how production of invertebrates is related to the supply of incoming organic matter. The two quantities would be directly dependent only if $a$, $b$ and $c$ were constants, which they are not. They all decrease as $IM$ increases; $a$ and $b$ decrease for the reasons stated above, $c$ does so because as the import of organic matter increases,

**Table 14.4** Efficiency of energy use in the benthic communities of the Bay of Quinte.

| Station | a | b | Egc |
|---|---|---|---|
| Big Bay | 0.23 | 0.1 | 0.68 |
| Glenora | 0.97 | 0.31 | 0.64 |
| Conway | 0.84 | 0.27 | 0.40 |
| Lake Ontario | 0.91 | 0.39 | 0.34 |

the rate of deoxygenation in the surface sediment and the water just above it also increases. Animals must then use more energy in obtaining oxygen (in body movements to keep water circulating over the animal's surface or in production of haemoglobin). Or, like *Chironomus anthracinus* in Lake Esrom, they may have periods when they lie quiescent, respiring, albeit at a low rate, but probably not feeding. This means that a smaller proportion of their energy supply is available for growth. *c* should also be low at low levels of import because of the extra activity then necessary in seeking food. The relationship between benthic invertebrate production and import of organic matter to the community may then have a maximum at intermediate import levels flanked by minima due to food scarcity on one side, and to low food quality and to deoxygenation on the other.

The material not used by the invertebrates and micro-organisms forms the permanent sediment. It contains a record, albeit a strongly distorted one, of activities in the lake and can be used to discern the lake's history, a topic covered in Chapter 11. The recent history of many lakes, recorded in the sediments or in contemporary data is one of considerable change through human use (Chapter 15). The sediments are the books that record the sins and ambitions of the human state.

## FURTHER READING

The use of stable isotope measurements has brought new interest to work on the profundal benthos, which has been relatively ignored in the past decades. Classic work is reviewed by Brinkhurst (1974) and was carried out particularly by Jonasson (1972, 1977, 1978, 1996), Johnson (1985) and Lindegaard & Jonasson (1979). Community structure has long been studied, with particular interest on ancient deep lakes and their endemics, by Ishikawa et al. (2004), Nishino & Watanabe (2000), Sugina (2006) and Yong-De et al. (2008). The smaller animals of the profundal, particularly the nematodes, tend to be ignored for they are difficult to identify. Traunsperger (1996) and Michiels & Traunsperger (2005) give some insights. Johnson & Brinkhurst (1971a,b,c) is a particularly satisfactory study which moves from community composition to productivity and functioning of the profundal benthos. McLachlan et al. (1979) and Johnson et al. (1989) began to look at the nature of food sources and recent work using carbon-13 additions includes Solomon et al. (2008). The role of methane processing bacteria was introduced by Jones & Grey (2004) and is developing apace (Deines et al. (2007), Eller et al. (2007), Jones et al. (2008)).

# Chapter 15

# THE USES, ABUSES AND RESTORATION OF STANDING WATERS

## 15.1 INTRODUCTION

'Wherever his thoughts wandered, they could not get beyond the circle of his beloved lake; indeed I never knew them aberrant but once, when he informed me, with a doubting air, that he had sent his wife and his two eldest children to a fair at a country village two miles off, that their ideas might expand by travel; as he sagely observed, they have never been away from 'our broad'. I went into his house at the dinner hour, and found the whole party going to fall most thankfully upon a roasted herring gull killed of course on 'our broad'. His life presented no vicissitudes, but an alternation of marsh employment. In winter, after his day's reed cutting, he might regularly be found posted at nightfall, waiting for a flight of fowl, or paddling after them on the open water. With the first warm days of February, he launched his fleet of trimmers, pike finding a ready sale at his own door to those who bought them to sell again in the Norwich market. As soon as the pike had spawned, and were out of season, the eels began to occupy his attention and lapwings eggs to be diligently sought for. In the end of April, the island in his watery domain was frequently visited for the shooting of the ruffs which resorted thither on their first arrival. As the days grew longer and hotter, he might be found searching, in some smaller pools, near his house, for the shoals of tench as they commenced spawning. Yet a little longer and he began marsh mowing – his gun always laid ready upon his coat in case flappers should be met with. By the middle of August, teal came to a wet corner near his cottage, snipe began to arrive, and he was often called upon to exercise his vocal powers on the curlews that passed to and fro. By the end of September, good snipe shooting was generally to be met with in his neighbour-hood, and his accurate knowledge of the marshes, his unassuming good humour, and zeal in provid-ing sport for those who employed him, made him very much sought after as a sporting guide by snipe shots and fishermen; and his knowledge of the habits of different birds enabled him to give useful information to those who collected them'.

Revd Richard Lubbock. Diaries. (1798–1876)

The Revd Lubbock's view, no doubt through rose-tinted spectacles, for damp and ague had their toll, nonetheless pictures a family that essentially lived on the natural products of a lake in the 19th century. It was a lake that doubly illustrates human dependency of standing waters, for it was a Broad, a shallow lake in

*Ecology of Freshwaters: A View for the Twenty-first Century*, 4th edition. By Brian Moss. Published 2010 by Blackwell Publishing Ltd.

**Fig. 15.1** P.H. Emerson, a pioneering photographer who, in the late 19th century, was one of the first to work in the open air as opposed to a studio, used the Norfolk Broads as his main subject and left us with a record of traditional activities. His subjects had to remain very still for long periods as exposure times for the film were several minutes, but we have records of fishing for eels (upper left), wildfowl shooting (upper right), cutting and bundling reed for thatching roofs (lower left) and stripping the bark from osiers to produce the material for basket making.

East Anglia, dug out of the floodplain peat some 1000 or so years previously, when the climate was drier, and then flooded and connected to the river when matters got naturally wetter in the 13th century. Small hamlets and villages had found a living by the broads for centuries (Fig. 15.1). They grazed cattle on the fens surrounding the Broads, cut fen hay for the wintering stock, cut reed (*Phragmites australis*) and sedge (*Cladium mariscus*), to roof their houses, poles of alder (*Alnus glutinosa*), for fencing and fuel, excavated still some peat to dry for burning, fished, shot birds for the pot or to sell and would no doubt eat anything they could catch that was large enough to make a meal.

Modern aspirations have destroyed both the richness that made such a life possible and the tolerance of the vicissitudes, to which the more privileged Lubbock was blind. The Broads also epitomize a transition from a relatively sympathetic use, which conserved much of the biodiversity, to a current exploitation that leaves only a fragmented and damaged ecosystem (Fig. 15.2). Drainage for agriculture has converted most of the mires to grassland and isolated the waterway behind floodbanks; intensification of agriculture and a rise in population has increased the loading of phosphorus and nitrogen and favoured a switch from a plant-dominated, clear-water community to one turbid with phytoplankton; exotic species (Canada geese, coypu, zebra mussel) have colonized, though their damage has been lower than elsewhere; motor boats cause physical damage to the lake edges and river banks; pesticides

**Fig. 15.2** By the late 20th century, almost everything damaging that can happen to a freshwater system had happened in the Broads. There was widespread eutrophication from sewage effluent and agriculture, so that most of the submerged plant community had been lost (left). A tourist industry based on boats and an even larger fleet of private boat owners had caused widespread erosion to river banks and the fringing reeds of the lake edges (upper middle). Coypu (*Myocaster coypus*), a South American rodent, introduced in the 1930s to fur farms, had escaped and were damaging reedbeds (lower centre); and the fens and other wetlands that had surrounded the Broads, and which to some extent had been drained for several centuries, were suddenly threatened by deep drainage for conversion to arable land, as a result of the vagaries of government policies on agricultural subsidy (right). Much has been done to halt these trends and the coypu has been eliminated, but a great deal of residual damage and a pervadent eutrophication problem remain.

and antifouling paints have had subtle effects on community composition; migratory fish that once travelled the rivers up to the Broads, the salmon and burbot, no longer appear. Rarely is one out of hearing by day of the sound of a vehicle engine. Of the five main ways in which human communities damage standing waters (engineering, eutrophication, acidification, toxic pollution and exotic species), only acid precipitation has no detectable effect for the land is chalky and the waters well buffered.

Yet all is not lost (Fig. 15.3), for thousands of people still enjoy a holiday in boats in a landscape that is less frenetic than most, or race their yachts, or angle for coarse fish. The conservation organizations have preserved a fraction of the area and slowly restore some of the plant and bird diversity. It is not easy; the pressures that have degraded the system are still there, sometimes lessening a little, sometimes worsening or joined by new ones.

## 15.2 SERVICES PROVIDED BY STANDING WATERS

Leaving aside the global regulatory services of climate regulation, such as carbon storage, to be considered in Chapter 16, fisheries, both for recreation and for food, drinking water storage and improvement, and amenity and recreation are the three groups of services now most commonly provided by standing waters to human societies and these form the basis for the first part of this chapter. Each is marred by negative impacts, including overfishing, eutrophication, poor reservoir design and operation, introduction of alien species, drainage and toxic pollution. But there are remedies and restoration that can be applied. The sequence of sympathetic use to abuse to attempts at repair, seen above for the Broads, gives a structure to this chapter.

**Fig. 15.3** Despite the severe ecological problems, the Broads provide the highest concentration of aquatic nature reserves in the UK, a reed cutting industry (left) that helps maintain the characteristics of the landscape and an income for nature conservation, a valuable boating holiday industry that gives pleasure to a large number of people, and varied angling, though the pike no longer come as large as this one photographed in the 1960s.

## 15.3 FISHERIES

For many people, fish and fisheries are the reasons to study freshwaters. In the developed world recreational fisheries are prized, and in the developing world freshwater fish are the most important protein source for a billion people. Freshwater fish may be crucial to health, not only in diet, but also through the worm parasites (Chapter 10) to which fish play intermediate host, particularly in the Far East. Fisheries for wild fish have a history that is frequently shown in archaeological excavations and they generally show that the fish were steadily overexploited. The preserved fish bones, or shellfish shells, excavated from successively more recent levels in kitchen middens are of smaller and

smaller animals. And that is still true. Most world fisheries are now overfished and yields have fallen greatly. As a result there has been an upsurge in fish culture, especially in Asia, particularly China, and Africa. The share of fish production provided by aquaculture was 29% in 2001 and by now has likely overtaken the yield from the wild catch.

Fish yields (the crops taken by man) are broadly related to fish production in a lake, which in turn is related to the overall productivity of the system. The yield is always lower than the total production because some fish are unsuitable biologically for sustained fisheries, and others may be difficult to catch or unacceptable as food for sociological reasons. Maintenance of a fishery, without overfishing, when more fish are taken than are replaced by birth and sub-sequent new fish recruitment and growth, ideally requires three things. The biology of the fish should be understood; only those species whose populations will stand up to fishing should be taken; and there should be monitoring of the catch and imposition of regulations on the fishery to protect the stocks.

These requirements are not always achieved, particularly in the developing world. Unwritten knowledge of the fish biology is often extensive among the fishermen, but not seen in a context of long-term conservation of the stocks and simple collection of monitoring statistics from fishing villages widely spaced around a big lake may be impossible. Rough and ready methods of regulation may be more practicable than the statistical models developed for marine fisheries, where single species of shoaling fish are often targeted and models are highly sophisticated. Such models have not usually been able to guarantee protection of the stock, however, for they require rigorous enforcement of regulations on net sizes and number of fishermen (fishing effort). The latter is particularly difficult to control. A bonanza attracts more in and the bonanza soon turns to a dearth. Population and economic pressures now demand increased fish yields. Often these have involved fishing for inappropriate species or introduction of supposedly high-yielding exotic species. The problems that these have caused, and the subsequent solution of pond culture to the need for increase in fish yield, are considered later. Finally the impacts and issues of recreational angling are discussed. One estimate is that 12% of all fish yield comes from recreational fisheries and that 11% of the world's human population goes fishing.

### 15.3.1 Some basic fish biology

Fascinating differences are found among fish, with great implications for the suitability or otherwise of a species for a fishery. I have chosen, from the 13,000 or so known freshwater species, the brown trout (*Salmo trutta*), the Nile perch (*Lates niloticus*), a 'tilapia' (*Sarotherodon niloticus*), the walleye, *Sander vitreus*, and the grass carp (*Ctenopharyngodon idella*) (Fig. 15.4) to illustrate the variety among fish because of the ranges of their reproductive biology, diet and zoogeography. The website 'Fish base' (www.fishbase.org/home.htm), is a comprehensive source, internationally maintained, of information on these and the rest.

Brown trout are carnivores, eating mostly benthic invertebrates; they are indigenous to Europe, North Africa and western Asia, but have been introduced to suitable waters elsewhere for their sporting qualities. Nile perch are voracious piscivores in the River Nile and its associated, or formerly associated, great Lakes Albert and Turkana. They are valued food fish in some places, being large (specimens weighing over 45 kg are common and lengths may be 2 m or more) and have been introduced to other African lakes (see later).

'Tilapia' is a name given to cichlid fish of the genera *Tilapia*, *Sarotherodon* and *Oreochromis*. *Sarotherodon niloticus* feeds on fine bottom detritus and phytoplankton, is also native to the Nile watershed and widely introduced to other African lakes and rivers. Walleye are North American piscivores, which feed on zooplankton when young. Some comparison will be made between walleye and their close European relatives, the pike-perch or zander, *Stizostedion lucioperca*. Last, the grass carp is an avid feeder on submerged and even emergent aquatic plants. It is endemic to the River Amur and parts of eastern Asia but has been widely introduced to other areas of Eurasia for control of nuisance aquatic plants and pond culture.

### 15.3.2 Eggs

Fish eggs are mostly released into the water for their development. *Sarotherodon* species are exceptions for the male or female may gather them, once fertilized, into its mouth for brooding. With such close protection, few eggs are needed. *Sarotherodon niloticus* protects the young fish in this way when predators approach, but may merely guard them, as eggs, in a shallow depression scraped on the sandy bottom by sweeping movements of its tail. Trout also carefully excavate a nest or redd in gravel, much as described already for salmon (Chapter 7).

The Nile perch and grass carp take little or no care of their eggs and must produce large numbers to ensure survival of enough young to maintain the population. The eggs of both species are planktonic and kept floating in the water by incorporation of oil in the former and a water-filled cavity between the egg membranes in the latter. While *S. niloticus*, which guards its eggs, may produce only a few thousand, the Nile perch releases several millions to the open water. Walleye also take no care of their eggs. They are scattered onto gravel in well-oxygenated water having been fertilized

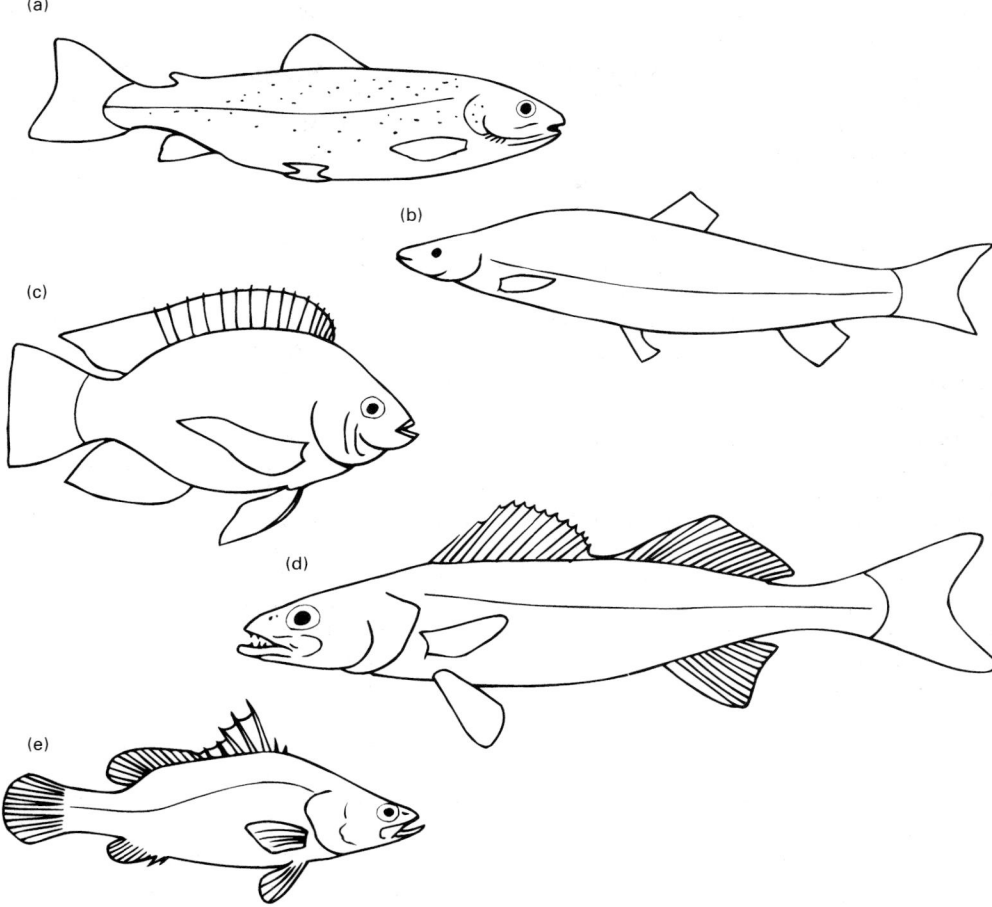

**Fig. 15.4** Five fish species of contrasted biology (see text). (a) Brown trout, *Salmo trutta*; (b) Chinese grass carp, *Ctenopharyngodon idella*; (c) 'tilapia', *Sarotherodon niloticus*; (d) pike-perch, *Stizostedion lucioperca* (the walleye is a similar though stockier fish); (e) Nile perch, *Lates niloticus.*

during release from the female. The walleye's European relative, the pike-perch, is similar in morphology, but quite different in spawning behaviour. The male pike-perch excavates a nest on a muddy organic bottom, around the exposed roots or rhizomes of aquatic plants, to which the sticky eggs adhere. The female guards them and fans water over them with her tail – this may increase the rate of survival in a habitat generally unsaturated with oxygen. Many temperate fish attach their eggs to stones or weeds in lowland rivers and shallow lakes, and often these eggs are unguarded.

Large numbers of small eggs tend to be produced by those species that do not hide or guard their eggs and smaller numbers of larger eggs by those that do. In the latter, the individual probability of survival is doubly enhanced, for a larger egg contains more yolk for sustenance of the fry. On the other hand, the spawning requirements of the 'protective' type may be more stringent and less easily available whilst the larger egg, with its smaller surface-area : volume ratio may require greater external concentrations of oxygen to survive.

The general trend is not always followed. The eggs of the pike-perch, which are guarded, are smaller (0.8–1.5 mm diameter) than those of the walleye (1.4–2.1 mm), which are not. Furthermore, the walleye produces only 30,000–65,000 eggs per kilogram of body weight, compared with 110,000–260,000 in the pike-perch. This reversal of the expected trend is probably related to the contrasted habitats in which these fish live. The walleye inhabits well-oxygenated waters, the pike-perch stagnant or slow-moving productive ones with low oxygen concentrations and high turbidity, where the nesting habitat is frequently associated with very organic sediments. The large numbers of eggs produced, even though guarded, may be necessary in a fertile habitat containing many cyprinid fish, which prey on eggs to a greater extent than the species coexisting with walleyes.

### 15.3.3 Feeding

Fry hatch from the eggs after varying periods of development, dependent on temperature, among other factors. Trout spawn in autumn, walleye between March and June, the tropical Nile perch and tilapia probably throughout the year. The grass carp spawns in rising flood waters in spring when increased turbidity may camouflage the eggs against predators. Hatching occurs at times – spring and summer in temperate regions – when food is available for the fry. The egg yolk is only sufficient to feed the fry for a short time and any increase in the amount of yolk produced per egg would mean a corresponding decrease in the number of eggs produced.

Small fish can eat only small portions; large fish can eat bigger items. Less energy is needed to find a given amount of food as large items than as small ones. The diets of fish thus often change markedly as the fish increase in size. Trout fry (alevins) dart from their shelter in the gravel to take small chironomid larvae and Crustacea in the weeks after their yolk is used up. When they have grown to about 4 cm they station themselves in the water about 8 cm apart, defending their 'water-space' against neighbours by aggressive darts. They then feed on invertebrates moving past them in the drift (Chapter 7).

Older trout actively hunt food along the bottom, and, at lengths >30 cm, may take fish fry and larger fish. Trout have wide mouths and many backwardly-directed teeth, which efficiently hold prey once it is grasped. Other fish species feeding in mid-water, but on smaller items such as zooplankton, have a much narrower mouth, protrusible into a lengthened tube with which they suck up prey, like a vacuum cleaner.

The tropical elephant snout fish (Mormyridae) are good examples.

The adult Nile perch is a voracious feeder even on other piscivorous, but smaller, fish such as the tiger fish (*Hydrocynus vittatus*). When it is younger, however, it takes invertebrates. The fry in Lake Chad, 0.3–1.35 cm in length, feed on planktonic Cladocera and inhabit shallow, weedy areas. At about 20 cm they begin to take larger invertebrates, a bottom-living prawn (*Macrobrachium niloticum*), snails and some small fish. As they grow they take larger fish. Nile perch have large heads, widely gaping mouths and serried ranks of backwardly directed teeth; they vigorously chase their prey. The dorsal and anal fins are situated well back (see Fig. 15.4), giving the fish a powerful tail thrust, which, as in the trout, allows bursts of high speed.

Newly hatched walleye, only 6–9 mm long, feed in protective schools on plankton – large diatoms, rotifers, nauplii of copepods (Chapter 13). Progressively, they eat larger zooplankters and *Chaoborus* larvae (Chapter 14). Finally they become piscivorous, seizing their prey then manoeuvring it until it can be swallowed head first. Some favoured prey species, such as yellow perch (*Perca flavescens*), have spiny pectoral fins, which would lodge in the throat were the prey swallowed tail first. Walleye have elongate gill rakers (the strips of bone which protect the delicate gills from damage by large particles pulled in with the respiratory water current) and it is on these that spiny fins could catch. The pike-perch does not have such elongate rakers and is able to swallow at least some of its prey tail first. Spiny fins have some advantage for the prey, because in the time taken for a fish, seized usually at the tail, to be manoeuvred into a head-first position for swallowing, there is a greater possibility of escape. Spines also may be used by a fish to avoid capture if they can be jammed into rock crevices.

The grass carp becomes predominantly vegetarian at lengths above about 30 mm. As fry, it eats rotifers and crustaceans, occasional chironomid larvae and perhaps some filamentous algae. Between 17 and 18 mm it takes more chironomids and fewer of the smaller zooplankters. By 27 mm, higher plant food becomes prominent in the diet. Although thereafter it unavoidably takes invertebrates associated with water plants, the grass carp is well adapted to a plant diet. Like other Cyprinidae (its Family) the grass carp is toothless, but has strong projections of the pharyngeal bones, which line the region between the mouth, and the entrance to the oesophagus. These 'pharyngeal teeth' are serrated in younger fish but become flattened, with both cutting and rasping surfaces, with age. Young fish eat only the softer, submerged plants, whereas older ones can tackle more lignified emergent plants. The pharyngeal teeth tear and rasp the plant food into particles 1–3 mm in diameter. Only the cells that are rasped and ruptured are digested and half of the food passes out, undigested, as faeces. The pH of the gut secretion is quite high: 7.4–8.5 in the anterior part, around 6.7–6.8 in the rectum, and such values are not particularly noteworthy. They provide a comparison with *Sarotherodon niloticus*, which, perhaps because of its extremely low gut pH, between 1.4 and 1.9, is one of the few fish yet examined that can digest even the cyanobacteria (Chapter 13).

Fry of this tilapia may feed on insect larvae but the fish soon turn to an algal diet. For example in Lake Volta (Ghana), *S. niloticus* eats the weft of algae loosely hanging from submerged dead trees, and bottom detritus is also taken. In Lake George, Uganda, it takes cyanobacteria, but whether from the water column or dense aggregations on the bottom, is not clear. Feeding makes little use of the teeth or jaws. Algae are sucked in with the respiratory current and entangled with mucus secreted by glands in the mouth, then passed back into the pharynx. The food is thus not filtered out, as it is in many other plankton feeders, by fine projections on the gill rakers.

*Sarotherodon niloticus* shows some selectivity in its food. A comparison between the percentage representation of different foods in the gut ($r$) compared with that in the external environment ($p$) may be used to calculate an electivity index:

$$\text{electivity} = (r - p) / (r + p)$$

In Lake George, *S. niloticus* showed a positive selection for *Microcystis*, *Lyngbya* (cyanobacterium) and *Melosira* (a diatom) but discriminated against the smaller species, *Anabaenopsis* (cyanobacterium) and *Synedra* (diatom).

### 15.3.4 Breeding

Changes associated with spawning are major events. The gametes alone may constitute a quarter of the body weight and the energy demands in producing them, and in the act of spawning, may be very great. A 'spent' fish (one that has just spawned) is weak and more vulnerable to predation, and the extensive migrations, which some fish undertake before spawning, may have exhausted them so much that bacterial and fungal infections are common. Nonetheless, most fish spawn in several successive years after reaching maturity.

Breeding occurs at different ages in different fish, at a time that represents, for each, a compromise between several factors. If left too late there is a high chance of failure to breed through early death. If attempted too early the fish may be too small and unable to cope with the energy demands. Trout first breed when they are 3 or 4 years old, walleye from 2 or 3 years and *S. niloticus* at only a few months. This reflects high growth rates at higher water temperatures and lack of seasonal food scarcity in tropical freshwaters.

In the main part of Lake Albert (Uganda, Zaire), *S. niloticus* reaches a size of 50 cm and breeds when it has attained 28 cm. In the Bukuku lagoon, a part of the lake now completely isolated by a sandbar, it breeds at 10 cm and achieves only 17 cm at most. This appears to be a response to the extreme environment of the lagoon, which is very saline and must dry out almost completely from time to time. A fish able to mature earlier and therefore produce more frequent generations may have a greater chance of survival there than one whose breeding cycle is longer than the persistence of its environment.

Breeding rituals are common in fish. They preserve adaptive differences between closely related species and may need specific environmental conditions. Examples are provided by the European three-spined stickleback (*Gasterosteus aculeatus*) and the African *Haplochromis burtomi*, a cichlid fish. Sticklebacks are small and silvery-brown (5–8 cm). They eat small invertebrates. Sometimes they winter in estuaries. In spring, the males leave the mixed shoals and take on breeding colours: bright blue and red underparts and a translucent appearance to the scales on the back. Each male chooses a small territory on a sandy or silted bottom, and defends it against other males. He excavates a depression by sucking up sand or mud and expelling it some distance away. He then collects strands of aquatic plants or filamentous algae and, with the help of a secretion from the kidney, forms them into a tunnel-shaped nest about 5 cm long and broad, which lies in the depression. At this stage he becomes responsive to swollen, gravid (bearing ripe eggs) females, though not to thin, spent ones. If a suitable female enters the territory, he first creeps through his nest and then performs a 'courtship' dance in which he zigzags towards the female, then turns towards his nest. This may not immediately attract the female, though she may swim nearby, adopting a characteristic posture with the head up. The male may then dart at her with his spines raised and usually she will then be led down to the nest. By inserting his snout the male points at the nest entrance, then backs off and swims on his side with his back towards the female. She appears to inspect the nest opening, and then may retreat to the water surface. The courtship process may be repeated several times before the female enters the nest, with something of a struggle, for the opening is narrow.

Eventually her head is well in and her tail sticks out of the entrance. The male then puts his snout against the base of her tail and quivers violently. The tail begins to rise as the male continues quivering and when it is raised high the female releases a stream of 50–100 eggs into the nest. When the last egg is laid, the female, now much thinner, rushes out of the nest as the male bursts in and releases a cloud of spermatozoa quickly over the eggs. Thereafter the female is chased away, the male prods the fertilized eggs deep into the nest, adds sand to reinforce and camouflage it and wafts water over the eggs with his fins. He remains guarding the fry until about 10 days after hatching when his breeding colours have also faded.

Spawning behaviour in *Haplochromis burtomi* in Lake Tanganyika is equally complicated. Little is known of the preliminaries of courtship but at its culmination the female lays a very small batch of quite large eggs on the lake bed while the male courts attendance. When she has laid the eggs she quickly turns and scoops the unfertilized eggs into her mouth. Then the male sweeps past the female, displaying his anal fin as he does so. On it are light, circular markings, which, against the darker fin background, resemble eggs. These deceive the female who moves to pick up what she thinks are eggs. In doing so she sucks in water from near the male's genital aperture from which he has just released sperm and the eggs are fertilized in the female's mouth. The process is repeated several times until her mouth is full of fertilized eggs where they are protected until hatching.

These rituals appear often to have evolved to minimize the chances of hybridization in fish communities where specialization and speciation have resulted in minimization of competition for food or space. Unless each sex recognizes particular attributes in the other, mating does not occur. These colour and behavioural features are genetically linked with gene combinations that code for the particular specializations that promote

the chances of survival. In ancient lakes, such as those of East Africa, flocks of closely related species, particularly among the Cichlidae, have evolved (see Chapter 6) high degrees of specialization and endemicity. Even in temperate and near polar lakes, something of the same process can be seen, for example in brown trout.

Techniques that extract particular enzyme proteins and then characterize differences (polymorphisms) in the same enzyme have been used to distinguish differences between individuals or species in different individuals and populations by their electrical properties (electrophoresis). These studies have shown great variation in brown trout, with 54% of enzymes studied being polymorphic. This is consistent with the considerable colour and behavioural variation known from this widely distributed species. Indeed, since 1755, variants of the brown trout have been described as 50 different species. Variation is inevitable in a species spanning Iceland, arctic Norway, the Atlas Mountains of Morocco and the eastern region of Afghanistan, but it may be just as great within a single lake. Lough Melvin, in Ireland, for example is only 22 km² but contains three brown trout populations that are genetically distinct and do not interbreed. The gillaroo feeds on benthic organisms and spawns on the lake shores and outflow river. It has strongly marbled flanks. The sonaghen (or sonachen) is a mid-water feeder and spawns in the smaller inflow streams. Its back is bluish and its marbling is less pronounced than that of the gillaroo. Third the ferox trout becomes piscivorous after its third year, lives longest and in males often retains, for all the year, the hooked jaw of its spawning period. It is redder in colour and spawns in the deeper waters of the main inflow to Lough Melvin.

These distinctive fish may have arisen from separate natural introductions, differentiation of some ancestral form by breeding isolation, or artificial stocking. The latter is unlikely because the forms have been known for the two centuries that pre-date stocking operations. Evidence suggests a differentiation within the lough, based on the availability of different habitats and the custom of salmonids to return to spawn on the grounds of their own birth. Such local variation is a valuable resource for fishery management and breeding programmes but has been greatly eroded in many parts of the trout's range by habitat deterioration and interbreeding with stockings of farm-raised fish.

A second example of such rich variation is in the two genetic morphotypes, each with two subsidiary phenotypic morphs of the Arctic charr, *Salvelinus*

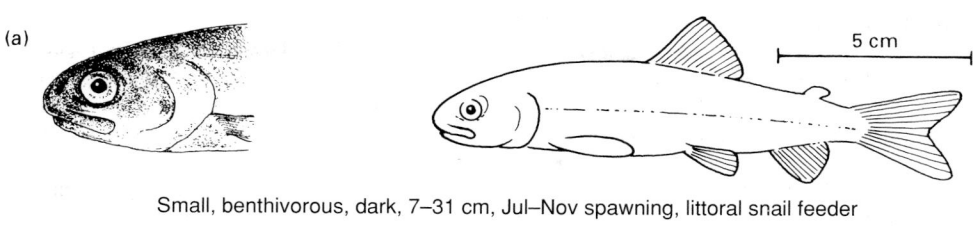

Small, benthivorous, dark, 7–31 cm, Jul–Nov spawning, littoral snail feeder

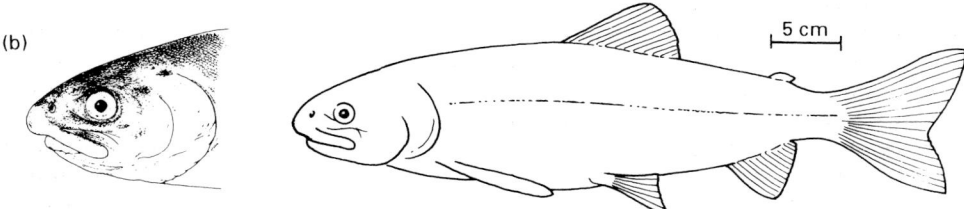

Large benthivorous, dark, 9–55 cm, Jul–Aug spawning, littoral snail feeder

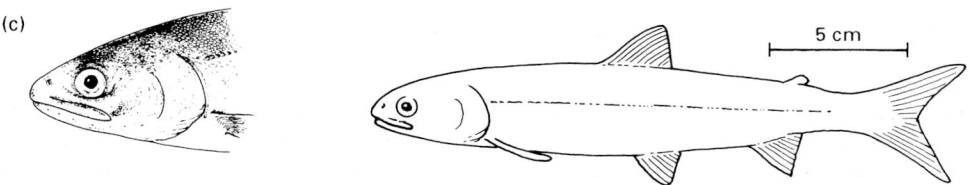

Planktivorous , Silvery, 13–26 cm, Sept–Oct spawning, whole lake, zooplankton feeder

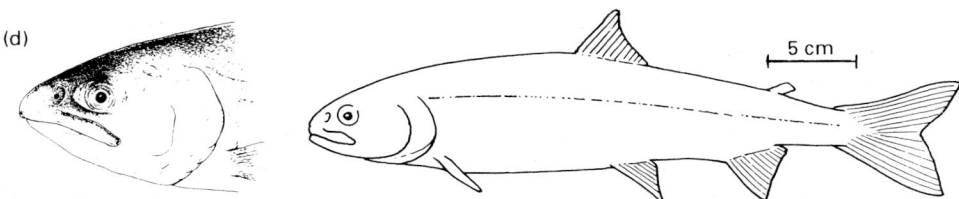

Piscivorous, Light silvery, 23–65 cm, Sept–Oct spawning, whole lake, fish feeder

**Fig. 15.5** Morphotypes of Arctic charr found in Lake Thingvallavatn, Iceland with details of the heads. The small benthivorous form (SB) is at the top, then the large benthivorous (LB), the planktivorous (PL) and the piscivorous (PI) at the bottom. (Based on Sandlund *et al.* 1992.)

*alpinus* in Lake Thingvallavatn, Iceland (Fig. 15.5). One morphotype is a littoral, benthic feeding fish with small and large variants, all with overshot mouths and large pectoral fins, which aid in manoeuvring over the bottom. The larger form cruises over the bottom whilst the smaller lives in interstitial spaces among the stones. The other morphotype is planktivorous in one morph and piscivorous in the other. All four types spawn in the littoral zone and feed on chironomid larvae at first. They avoid competition and remain distinct, however, because they spawn at different times.

### 15.3.5 Choice of fish for a fishery

Knowledge of the natural history of fish is essential for wise choice of species for a sustainable fishery. In such a fishery, annual mortality due to natural causes and fishing combined should be no greater than annual growth of the stock plus recruitment of new fishes to it. A high-yielding fishery is thus one that uses fishes of prolific growth and recruitment matched by high natural mortality. Ideally the natural mortality is replaced by removal in the fishery. A second requirement is that the fishery methods should not damage the habitat and hence interfere with spawning and recruitment.

Where only subsistence fisheries are concerned, with individuals or very small groups using relatively inefficient methods such as spears or hooks and lines, almost any fish species will sustain a limited amount of hunting. Where more people, using intensive methods such as large nets, in a commercial fishery, are involved, the most suitable fish are those of the open water (pelagic fish), followed by the bottom-living (demersal) fish of the profundal. Fish of the littoral zone are usually quite unsuitable.

Pelagic fish live in an unstructured habitat where, like the zooplankton (Chapter 13) they are continually at risk from their own predators. Many drifting eggs are usually produced and mortality at all stages is high. The fish tend to spawn early and grow fast. The 'structure' of the open water is not damaged by fishing methods. In contrast, the littoral habitat can be severely damaged by trawled nets, which as well as disrupting nesting sites, may also wreck the habitat of fish feeding on specialist food sources (e.g. the rock dwelling fish of Lake Malawi, Chapter 6). Egg-guarding, and hence low egg production and mortality, mean low recruitment rates, and the cover provided by a well-structured habitat limits natural mortality rates. Demersal fish form an intermediate case with a much less vulnerable habitat than the littoral, but one that nonetheless can be destroyed by too frequent disturbance.

Suitable fisheries fish should thus be adapted to a relatively unpredictable habitat in which risks of natural death are high. Whole lakes, littoral zone included, may sometimes fall into this category if they are subject to such disturbances as frequent drying out.

Lake Chilwa (Chapter 6), in Malawi, is one such. It has limited fish diversity, with species that are omnivorous and unfussy about their conditions for breeding. They are capable of living in a variety of habitats, and of growing fast and reproducing quickly when they recolonize the lake from the rivers after a drying phase. Fishes such as these have been naturally selected for $r$ (high growth rate) as opposed to $K$ (stable population) characteristics. These terms come from the logistic growth equation:

$$dN/dt = rN \cdot (K - N)/K$$

where $N$ is number, $t$ is time, $r$ is the intrinsic rate of natural increase and $K$ is the 'carrying capacity' of the environment. $r$-selected fish tend to invest much energy in growth and reproduction. Examples are the five main fish compared in Fig. 15.4. $K$-selected ones make efficient use of the resources to which they are closely adapted. Examples are the littoral fish of Lake Malawi and the other African Great Lakes, discussed in Chapter 6. Fisheries may easily damage $K$-selected populations.

### 15.3.6 Measurement of fish production

Production is estimated as the increase in weight of the population per unit time and usually per unit area. The first problem is to estimate the absolute population size per unit area of waterway. The most widely used method of sampling fish is to net or trap a sample of the population. These fish are then marked (by dyes or fin clipping) or tagged in some way to make them identifiable, then released again. After a period to allow them to mix randomly (it is assumed), the population is again sampled and the number of marked and unmarked fish counted. The ratio of recaptured marked fish ($n_{rm}$) to the total number recovered in the second sampling ($N'$) is taken to be equal to the ratio of the number of fish originally marked ($n_m$) to the total population ($N$):

$$N = (n_m \cdot N')/n_{rm}$$

$N$ may be expressed per unit area of the lake. In a big lake, however, the population may move over only part of it, which must be determined by tagging fish with radio-trackers and following their movements. Practical problems of the mark–recapture method are in ensuring that the samples are not selective of particular fish sizes, and that the marking technique does not alter fish behaviour or increase the chance of death. These ideals are probably never attained.

Mark–recapture techniques are most suitable for small water bodies where there is a reasonable chance of recapturing sufficient of the marked fish. In larger lakes, it is more usual to estimate the stock either by relative methods (catch per unit effort of fishing, see below) or by fishing of representative areas to depletion. An area is isolated by nets then repeatedly fished in a standard way until no more fish are caught. The cumulative catch is then plotted ($x$ axis) against the sequential number of fishings ($y$ axis). The inflexion of the asymptote of this curve gives an estimate of the total stock.

In capturing inshore fish for marking or depletion estimates, beach seine nets may be useful. These involve the laying out of a small-meshed net in a wide arc with the start and end of the arc on the shoreline of a shelving beach. The top of the net has floats to keep it at the surface and the bottom is weighted to keep it down. After setting, the net is hauled in to concentrate the fish. Seines may also be set in the open water, but must have a rope threaded into the bottom so that as the net is drawn in, it is closed at the bottom into a 'purse'. This requires a mechanical winch on the boat used. Fish escape around the seine nets but this may be minimized by an elongated sock of netting bulging out at the centre and called a cod end. The fish tend to move into this as the net is hauled in. Trawling is also a relatively non-selective method for bottom-living fish. The trawl is a bag of netting, kept open either by its resistance to movement through the water or by a wooden beam across its entrance, and pulled by a sufficiently powerful boat.

Gill nets kill the fish and thus cannot be used for mark–recapture estimates but can be used for depletion fishing of limited areas. The net is floated passively in the water at a desired depth and fish encountering it may move through its meshes and pass out the other side, or they may be too big to penetrate it at all. Particular size groups, however, move part through it until the widest part of their body becomes jammed and their gill covers catch on the netting as they try to move back. Such nets, dependent on their mesh size and the slackness with which the net is set, are very selective for particular size ranges. A set (or fleet) of different mesh sizes may be used for experimental fishing to obtain an estimate of the balance of different-sized fish in the population and a relative estimate of the size of the fish stock.

Finally, but also destructive, depletion fishing has been used in delimited bays in some lakes by use of the fish poison, rotenone. This is extracted from particular leguminous plant species (*Derris, Lonchocarpus, Tephrosia*) whose dried roots may contain up to 5% of the poison. It acts by constricting the blood vessels of the fish when applied at about $0.05–0.1$ mg L$^{-1}$, and has a short half-life once in the water. The fish can be revived using antidotes once caught, if the technique is carefully used. However, not all fish affected by the poison come to the surface for weighing and rotenone may have long-term effects on other organisms, particularly invertebrates.

### 15.3.7 Growth measurement

The individuals of most temperate fish species spawn over a limited period and the newly spawned generation or cohort can be treated as a unit, often recognizable in successive years because of the annual or other periodic rings laid down in the skin scales or in the otoliths (the ear bones) (Fig. 15.6). When a population is sampled it is held in an aerated tank while each individual, or a random sample if there are many, is weighed and its length measured. A length/weight graph may be used to avoid the need to weigh as well as measure in future samplings. The fish are usually lightly anaesthetized to calm them during these measurements.

Scales are removed from a part of the body, often high on the back just below the dorsal fin, where their rings are known to be clear. If this is done carefully, with blunt forceps, the fish should suffer little damage, though its chances of becoming infected by fungi, protozoa or bacteria subsequently may be increased. Removal of otoliths requires dissection and is fatal. The scales may be used simply to age the population and identify separately the different cohorts (often called year-classes) or they may be used on an old fish to estimate the growth in previous years. The distance between the rings is approximately proportional to the growth in the year the ring was laid down. Rings, however, may be reabsorbed during periods of starvation.

For a given cohort, an Allen curve may be plotted relating the mean weight of fish (on the vertical axis) to the numbers remaining in the cohort for a sequence of sampling occasions (Fig. 15.7). At first there are many small fry, but as individual weights increase, the numbers decline. The area under the curve as it approaches the abscissa, when the last survivor dies,

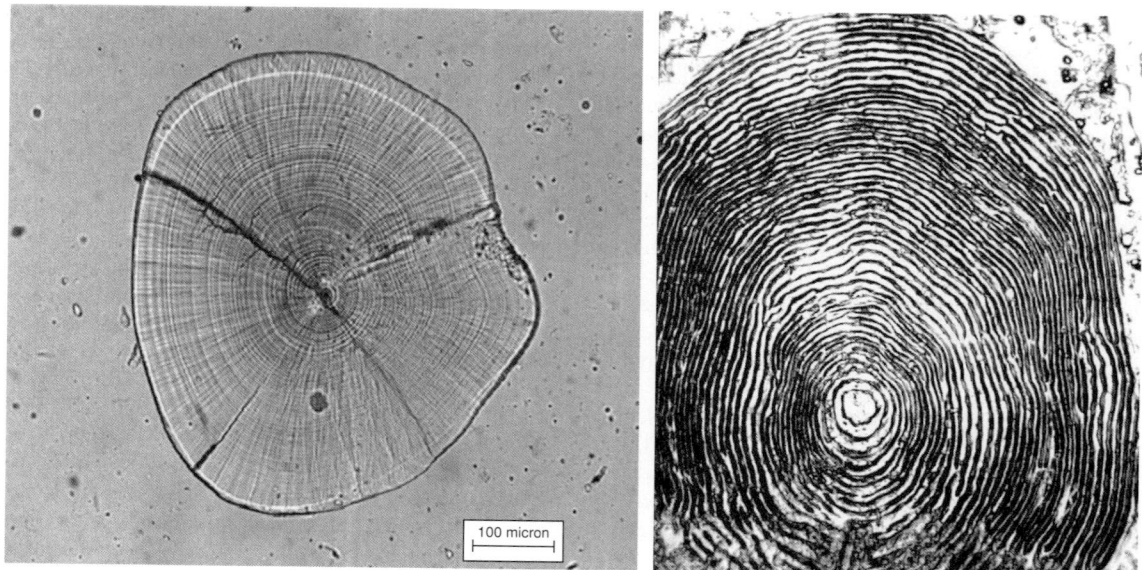

**Fig. 15.6** Ear bones (otoliths, left) and scales (right) may provide ways of determining the age of fish and thence of providing some of the basic data needed for stock management. Otoliths are very small (the scale is one tenth of a millimetre) and may need special treatment to reveal growth rings, which in this very young, native Australian smelt are laid down daily (photograph by Zeb Tonkin). In the Chinook salmon scale, about 50 mm long (photograph by Oregon Department of Fisheries and Wildlife), rings are laid down less regularly but are wider in summer than in winter. A bunching of rings thus indicates a year's growth. This fish has two such bunches and is now in its third year.

gives the total production. Production in a given year can be found by determining the area under the curve between points representing the times in question. The curve is roughly hyperbolic, but has irregularities – numbers decline in winter in temperate lakes, though the increase in weight of the survivors may be negligible. Weight change may even be negative as fat stores laid down the previous summer are used up. A similar loss of weight occurs during spawning when the weight converted to gametes can be determined from the area under the curve, as it reverses direction during the spawning period. By adding up the production of each of the several year classes present in a given year, and by doing this for each species, a measure of the total fish production may be obtained.

## 15.3.8 Fish production and commercial fisheries in lakes

Sufficient estimates are now available to draw some generalizations about fish production. In both rivers and lakes it bears a general relationship to nutrient loading or concentration (Fig. 15.8). This suggests that the community as a whole is controlled by bottom-up mechanisms, reflected in the amount of primary productivity in lakes and perhaps the rate of processing of allochthonous detritus in rivers.

Fisheries are ultimately limited by this natural productivity but do not differ from any other commercial venture in that they must maximize the yield of their product, harvestable fish. The particular problem of fishing, however, is to sustain the yield from year to year. No more must be harvested than the equivalent of the annual increment of fishes becoming large enough to be worth catching, plus the annual growth of those already fishable. It is relatively easy for fishermen, when not subject to control, to remove more than this annual recruitment and growth, in which case the fishery will eventually fail.

Figure 15.9 shows the increase in biomass of a newly hatched cohort of fishes. The rate of increase is at first high but declines as the maximum potential biomass, represented by the curve's asymptote, is reached.

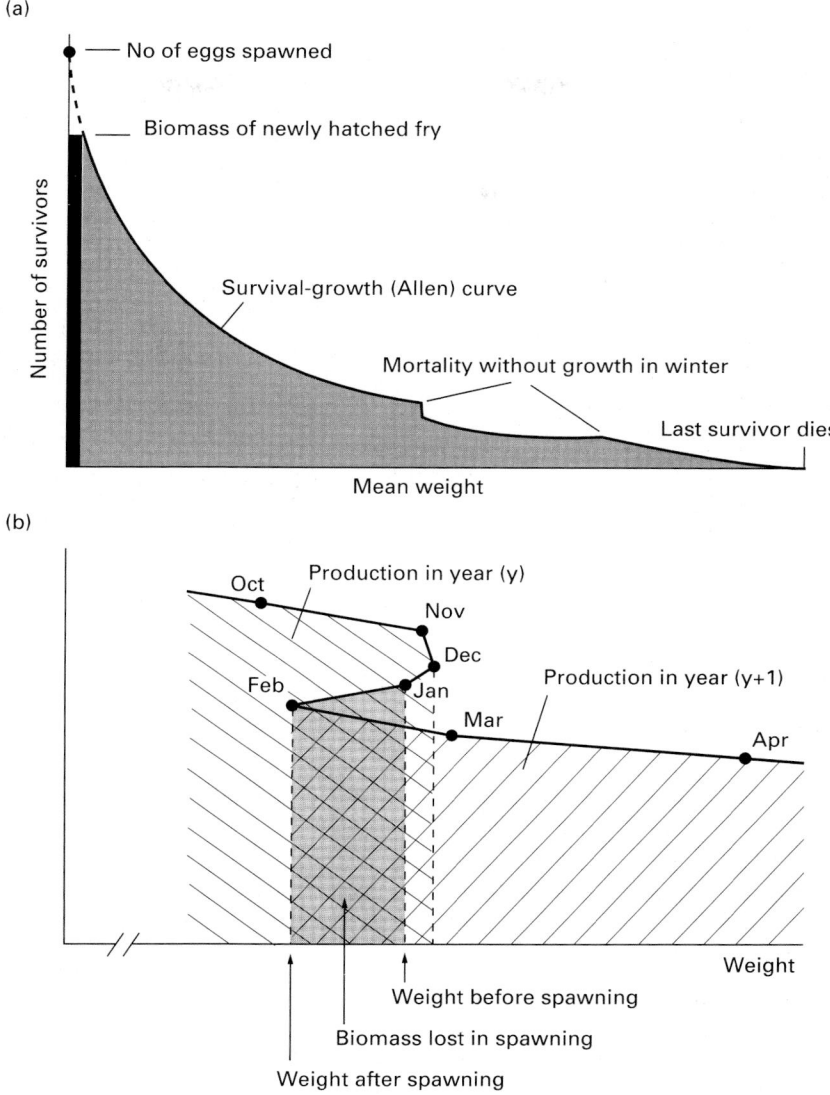

**Fig. 15.7** Allen curve for fish. Number of animals in a given cohort is plotted against mean weight for a series of dates throughout the life of the cohort (a). The area under the curve gives the total net production. Irregularities in the curve arise from mortality without growth in winter, and from spawning. (b) shows detail of this. Spawning results in loss of weight between December and February, which reduces the total production and must be allowed for in the calculations. (Based on Le Cren 1972.)

Simultaneously some members of the cohort die and the rate of mortality is at first high, but declines as the fishes become older, bigger and less vulnerable to predators. The net effect of growth and death is to create the biomass curve; growth exceeds death in the early part of the cohort's existence, and total biomass increases, but eventually mortality predominates and the biomass falls. There is a point at which the biomass of the cohort is maximal. The aim of a fishery is to catch that portion of the biomass that, after the maximum

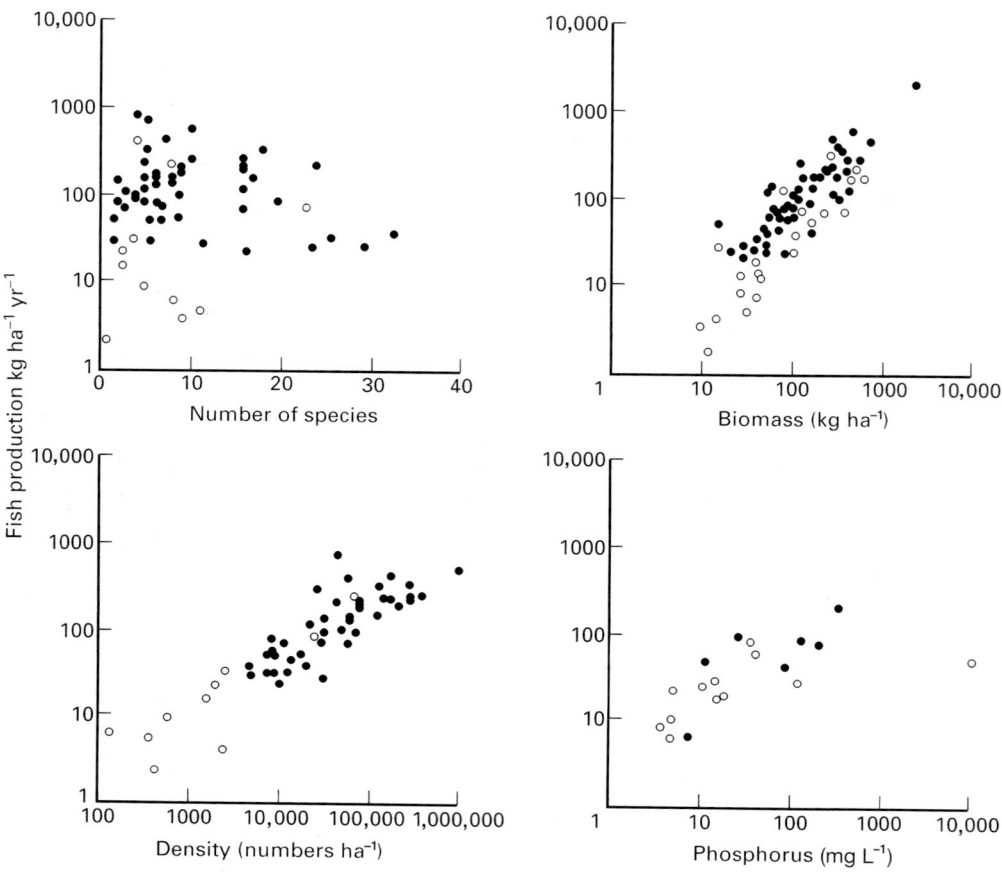

**Fig. 15.8** Correlations between fish production, and number of species, density and biomass in a series of lakes (open symbols) and rivers. Number of species seems to matter little, but number of fish and the nutrient status that supports the system are positively correlated with production. (From Randall et al. 1995.)

has been attained, would be lost to natural mortality. The more rapidly the fish can be removed after the maximum the better. The intention is to replace the natural survival curve *ab* with the fishing mortality curve *ac*, the area between the curves representing the yield. It is important that fishing does not remove fishes of an age at which growth exceeds natural mortality, for this will reduce the potential yield and may also remove fish that have not spawned.

Removal of pre-spawners may reduce the potential recruitment to the next season's fishery and is called recruitment overfishing. It is also important that fishing mortality should only ever replace natural mortality, and never exceed it. Fish that can safely be removed are thus mature and should not be allowed

to grow to their potential maximum individual size, by which time most of the biomass of the cohort will have been lost by natural mortality.

The year-to-year changes in a fish population can be represented by an equation drawn up by Sir Frederick Russell in 1931:

$$P_2 = P_1 + (R + G) - (F + M)$$

where $P_1$ and $P_2$ are the fish stocks (biomass) in two successive years, $R$ is the annual recruitment of mature fishes to the fishery, $G$ is the growth made by those already fishable but not yet removed, $F$ is the annual mortality due to fishing and $M$ the natural annual mortality. In a well-run fishery, $P_1$ is equal to $P_2$ and $M$ is zero, but this is never achieved, for natural

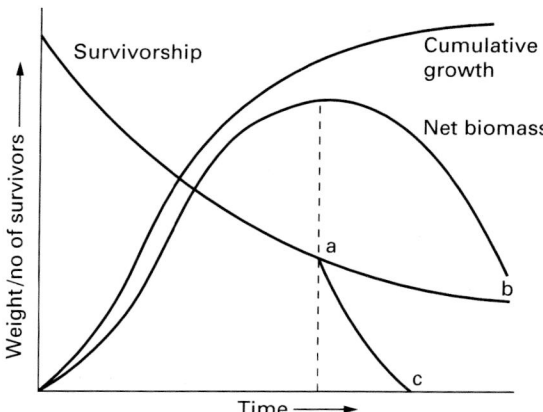

**Fig. 15.9** Ideal exploitation of fish stock. The net biomass of each generation (cohort) represents the balance between cumulative growth and death, and at some time reaches a peak. Provided spawning has by then occurred, the peak represents the time from which most efficient removal of fish can take place. The natural survivorship curve, *ab*, is replaced by the steeper fishing mortality curve, *ac*, as fishing ideally removes biomass before it can be further diverted to disease organisms, parasites or predators other than man. (Based on Fryer & Iles 1972.)

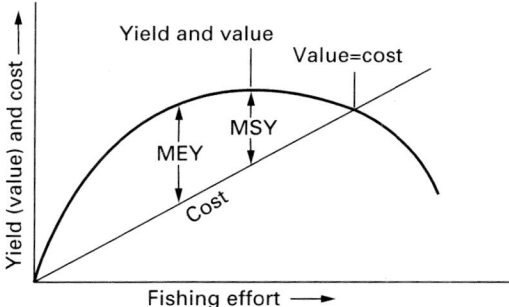

**Fig. 15.10** Relationship between yield of a fishery (also its commercial value) and fishing effort (the curved graph) and costs of a fishery and fishing effort (straight line graph). MEY is maximum economic yield, MSY is maximum sustainable biological yield. The MSY varies from year to year, depending on conditions for growth and recruitment and previous fishing effort, and is no longer regarded as a useful fixed parameter, as it once was. The point of the graph, however, is that fishing below what appears to be the maximum possible is always more profitable for the fishery as a whole, as well as being better for the stock.

environmental fluctuations will alter *R* and *G* in ways that a fisheries manager cannot predict in time for him to regulate the amount of fishing (*F*). *P* should, however, fluctuate around a mean without showing a general tendency to increase (underfishing) or decrease (overfishing). The year to year changes in a fishery can be monitored and fishing methods regulated through devices such as controls on net mesh size, number of nets allowed, and season for fishing, to keep *F* at the desired level. *F* is theoretically the maximum sustainable yield, if *P* is stable and *M* is minimized, but the concept is outmoded not only for the reasons given above that *P* and *M* will be affected by natural environmental changes and are not constants, but also for economic reasons.

Figure 15.10 shows the relationship between yield of a fishery and fishing effort – the amount of fishing carried out. As the latter increases, the yield reaches a peak (the maximum yield) above which the yield is reduced as overfishing interferes with recruitment or growth by removing spawning fish or fish not yet growing at their maximum rates. The yield curve is also a curve describing the value of the catch, assuming the sale price of the fish remains steady. As fishing effort

increases, so proportionately does its cost (the straight line graph in Fig. 15.10).

Overfishing eventually leads to cost being greater than value and some fishermen go out of business. This is the usual state of an unregulated fishery. At an earlier stage, however, the greatest profit (value minus cost) is reached at a lower yield, the maximum economic yield (MEY), than the supposed maximum sustainable biological yield (MSY). A well-run fishery, in the interests of both fishermen and fish will thus attempt to keep yields around this point. What usually happens, however is that such management is impossible and that the larger fish species, which are those most prized, become over fished (Fig. 15.11). The fishermen then seek smaller species, which also become overfished and finally the smallest species, whose overfishing brings about a final collapse. During this process, called 'fishing down', lower and lower levels of the food web are taken, for the larger fish tend to be piscivores.

Such a collapsed mixed fishery may or may not recover as fishing ceases. The fishing methods may have irreversibly damaged the habitat or even a small amount of fishing remaining on depleted stocks may prevent recovery. Other stresses on the fish, such as water pollution may also have got worse. At this stage there will be social disruption, demands that natural

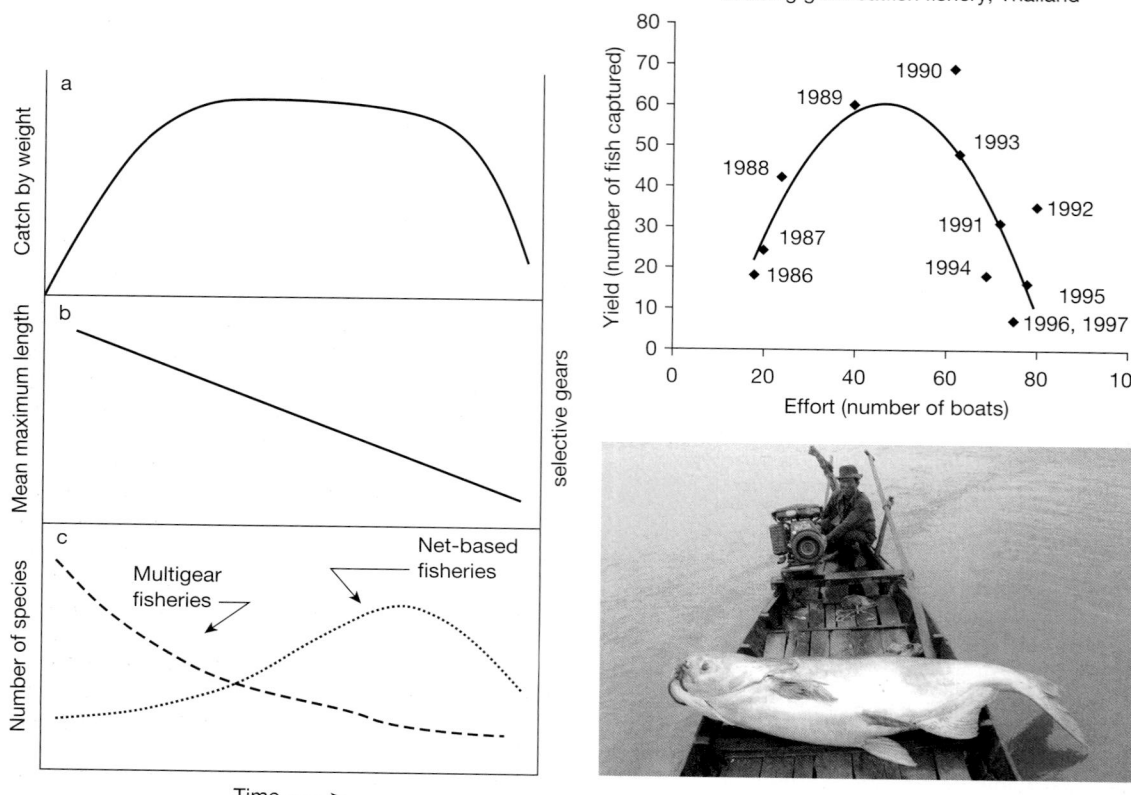

**Fig. 15.11** At the left is shown a notional set of curves characterizing the process of fishing down a mixed stock with time. The catch at first increases, several species are fished and a variety of techniques (gears) is used. Because the yield is high, more fishermen enter the fishery and the bigger species become very scarce. The mesh size of nets then is reduced to catch smaller fish and the fish community becomes less diverse so that most fishing is concentrated on nets of smaller and smaller mesh. The yield, even of small fish, eventually declines. On the right are shown data on yield and fishing effort from the Mekong giant catfish (photograph by Zeb Hogan) fishery in Thailand, which shows the classic symptoms of overfishing as more fishermen enter the fishery. (Based on Allan et al. 2005.)

fish predators such as fish-eating birds or seals be culled, arguments for artificial restocking with exotic species supposed to grow better than the native fish, and demands that mesh regulations be relaxed even further. In the past these demands have often been acceded to and many species have been introduced, particularly Pacific salmonids (*Onchorhyncus* spp), which have been introduced to two-thirds of the world's countries, and tilapias. In turn, the introduced species are also overfished but not before they may have caused many problems for the native biodiversity of the lakes concerned. In Finland, in particular, approaches have been made to preserve fisheries and

biodiversity that involve extensive discussions and negotiations among the fishermen, local communities and national interests. The point is made that all the science necessary is known. The problem is a social one. Negotiation with education is obviously the sensible approach, but often it will come too late.

## 15.4 CHANGES IN FISHERIES: TWO CASE STUDIES

Management of any fishery is vulnerable to the fact that fish growth and recruitment are subject to natural environmental change particularly of climate. More often, however, problems are caused by changes wrought by human activities. These may be indirect, having an ultimate effect on the fishery, or they may be deliberate, but unsuitable manipulations of the fishery itself. An example of the interaction of both kinds is that of the North American Great Lakes, and of the latter, some of the East African Great Lakes.

### 15.4.1 The North American Great Lakes

The North American Laurentian Great Lakes (Ontario, Erie, Huron, Michigan, Superior) stretch almost half-way across the continent, and are among the largest lakes in the world. They drain a huge area, originally of conifer forest to the north and deciduous forest to the south, and were once probably all well oxygenated, clearwater lakes with maximum total phosphorus concentrations probably lower than $2\ \mu g\ P\ L^{-1}$, very much towards the lower end of the fertility continuum (see Chapter 4).

The waterway they provided, from the Atlantic Coast to the mid-west and plains region of the USA and Canada, was a main route by which the continent was explored by Europeans in the 17th and 18th centuries. The discovery of minerals and cultivable land led to great increases in population. For example, the catchment of Lake Erie, which in 1750 was a largely unexploited wilderness supporting perhaps 100,000 people, now contains some 12 million people with their associated industry and agriculture. Lake Superior has changed the least in 200 years – its catchment still contains much intact forest. Changes in the lakes have been greatest around the shallow Lake Erie, and intermediate in the other three Great Lakes, Michigan, Huron and Ontario. The most apparent change in the 20th century has been eutrophication (see below), though other changes have been equally significant and began in the 18th and 19th centuries. These changes are reflected in the commercial fish catches of the waterway.

Commercial fish yields in the 20th century remained relatively constant in Lakes Superior, Michigan and Erie, but declined in Lakes Huron and Ontario. The data mask the fact, however, that great declines in yields of prized salmonid, coregonid and other fish have been compensated by catches from a much less diverse fish community supported by increased fertility and production in the water. The reasons for the changes, in the order in which they became significant were:

intensive selective fishing, modification of the tributary rivers, invasion or introduction of marine species, and last, eutrophication.

The changes began in Lake Ontario, the lowest basin on the waterway and have spread upstream so that the state of the upper Great Lakes fisheries in 1970 was approximately that of Lake Ontario in 1900. Atlantic salmon, *Salmo salar*, were only ever present in Lake Ontario in the Great Lakes system, for upstream movement was blocked by the Niagara Falls. Fishing for salmon began in the 1700s, was in decline by 1880, and had ceased altogether by 1900. The fishing was intensive, but the species survived it for many decades, and seems to have disappeared because of clogging of its spawning sites in tributary streams. In the 19th century, forests were cleared over much of the catchment, and dams were built on the streams to power sawmills. Waterlogged sawdust increasingly covered the stream gravels. Clear felling has two effects on drainage streams, other than chemical ones (Chapter 4). It reduces flow in summer because more water evaporates than previously, and it increases temperature, because the streams are no longer shaded. Repeated attempts to re-establish an Atlantic salmon fishery in Lake Ontario have failed because the spawning stream waters are now too warm and the flows insufficient to maintain the cool, oxygenated water and gravel bottom which the salmon require.

In the upper lakes, and in Lake Ontario, after the salmon declined, whitefish (*Coregonus clupeiformis*) and lake trout (*Salvelinus namaycush*) were both heavily overfished, though additional factors contributed to their decline, and fisheries for them had declined in Lake Erie by 1940 and Lake Huron by the 1950s. A trout fishery is now maintained by annual stocking. Gradually, however, after these fisheries became less profitable, lake herring, or cisco (*Leucichthys artedi*) and deep-water ciscoes (*Leucichthys* spp) were subsequently fished out. Currently, the lake fisheries depend on percids and other fish that have been favoured by different changes taking place in the lake.

The sturgeon (*Acipenser fulvescens*), although a valuable commercial fish, was deliberately removed because of the damage it did to nets. By 1890–1910 it had almost disappeared, partly from overfishing, as its valuable by-products (gelatin, isinglass, a bladder extract used in clarifying beverages and sizing textiles, and caviar) were prized, and partly from ruination of its spawning habitat (see below). It is particularly vulnerable, with a low growth rate and late sexual maturity. Even following a ban on commercial fishing, it is now common only in parts of Lake Huron. (In most of Europe sturgeon were made locally extinct for much the same reasons by AD 1500).

The changes in tributary streams, which affected salmon reproduction in Lake Ontario, became widespread elsewhere in the late 19th and early 20th centuries. Most of the commercially exploited fish were those of shallow water, which entered streams to spawn. Congregation of sturgeon, coregonids and percids in the water below mill dams provided easy fishing with seines, dipnets, and even spears. Drainage of swamps and marshes, associated with the headwaters, removed a favoured breeding habitat for sturgeon.

Between 1860 and 1880, two marine species, the sea lamprey (*Petromyzon marinus*) and the alewife (*Alosa pseudoharengus*) entered Lake Ontario. They may have come up the St Laurence River, which opens out at the northern edge of their ranges, or via the canal built in the early 1880s between the Hudson River and Lake Ontario. The Hudson River enters the sea at New York and had been connected to the lake by canals to aid navigation. The lamprey feeds by rasping fish flesh with a tongue after it has attached by a sucker, which forms its jawless mouth. Both species could have entered Lake Ontario at any time in the previous centuries, but if they did, they were unable to establish significant populations. Possibly the community changes caused by fishing and stream modification provided suitable niches for them. The Erie and Welland canals, both of which, for navigation purposes, by-pass the Niagara Falls, removed an otherwise impassable barrier to migration of these species upstream to the upper lakes. The lamprey reached Lake Erie by 1921, Lake Huron and Lake Michigan in the early 1930s and Lake Superior in 1946. The alewife generally lagged behind, reaching Erie and Huron in 1931–1933, Michigan in 1949, and Superior in 1953.

Both immigrants like deep water, and are neither abundant nor problematic in the relatively shallow Lake Erie. In the other lakes they have caused major changes. The pattern appears to have been one of parasitism by the lamprey, firstly of the larger deeper-water carnivores, such as lake trout, burbot (*Lota lota*), and deep-water ciscoes, then of smaller species, until the lamprey population itself declined. Reduction of the large piscivores then apparently allowed increase of the alewife, which feeds aggressively on large zooplankters and benthic Crustacea, such as *Pontoporeia*. These are also the main food sources of the young piscivores,

whose populations cannot then recover from the lamprey depredations. Alewives may even increase their competitive advantages by feeding on the young of the large piscivores, and have been among the commonest Great Lakes fish.

With all of these influences it is difficult to separate the effects of progressive eutrophication this century. The mechanisms by which certain species disappear on eutrophication are not fully known. They may involve loss of gravel spawning habitat as increased sedimentation covers it with organic deposits. The burbot, which has commonly disappeared, lives and spawns in the deepest parts of well-oxygenated lakes, from where hypolimnial deoxygenation may force it at an early stage. Extensions of marginal plant-beds, in providing cover, spawning habitat and abundant invertebrate food may favour some species unable previously to compete successfully. Conditions leading to summer total phosphorus or chlorophyll *a* concentrations in the epilimnion of the order of $20–30 \ \mu g \ L^{-1}$ have led, in Lake Erie and in similar large lakes such as the European Bodensee, to predominance of percid and cyprinid fish.

Attempts to limit eutrophication by use of phosphate stripping (see below) have been successful in many areas of the Great Lakes. Some fish are being restocked and lampricide use has helped. Restoration of the former fish communities, however, is complicated by continuing changes. The introduction of Pacific salmonid game fish, including coho (*Onchorhynchus kisutch*) (Chapters 7 and 8) is apparently reducing the alewife population and may have yet unforeseen effects on other fish. These introductions have proved very popular with recreational anglers. The introduced salmonids are not as productive as formerly, however, because control of eutrophication, at least in the lower lakes, is reducing lake productivity overall and this is causing concern among angling lobbies.

### 15.4.2 The East African Great Lakes

Tropical Africa has undergone many geological and climatic changes. Yet none has been so devastating and widespread for the freshwater fauna as the glaciations that completely removed the freshwater habitat from much of the temperate land surface. African fish communities have thus had a long period of development and speciation has occurred to a high degree (Chapter 6). The East African lakes have been formed in a variety of ways (Chapter 11) and their fisheries have developed from the technically crude but biologically sophisticated to the commercially advanced but ecologically unwise.

Initially the subsistence fisheries depended on one of five main methods: addition of natural plant poisons to the water; spears and harpoons; hooks and line; non-return basket traps; and baskets scooped through the shallows. Sometimes these methods have been very cleverly used. On Lake Albert, the Banyoro tribe collected grass or brushwood and tied it into bundles, which they lowered to the lake-bed in 6–10 m of water attached to a line buoyed by pieces of ambatch (*Aeschynomene profundis*), a light corky wood. Overnight the bundles became colonized by fish, mainly the cichlid *Haplochromis* species, taking cover from predators. The bundles were hauled up and the *Haplochromis* baited alive on small hooks on lines with which the larger tiger fish (*Hydrocynus vittatus*) were caught. In turn, the tiger fish were used to bait large barbed hooks to catch Nile perch, the ultimate quarry.

Baskets, woven from papyrus, reeds or pliant tree branches were widely used. Women of the Jaluo on north-eastern Lake Victoria moved into shallow water in groups of seven or eight, each with a small basket on her head and a much larger, wide-mouthed basket to hand. The women converged in a circle and simultaneously swept the large baskets through the encircled water, scooping out the fish and depositing them in the head baskets. Pelicans feeding in the same area employ similar methods, driving fish into a small area that they surround before scooping with their mouths.

Such methods are now rarely to be seen for the demands of increasing population have brought about an expansion of artisanal fisheries, largely based in shallow water and catching the readily filleted and tasty tilapias. The keys to development of these fisheries have been the introduction of gill nets and sailing boats by Arab traders in the 19th century. Nets were at first of twine and then flax or cotton, but rotted easily. Rayon, laboriously picked from the linings of old car tyres, provided a more durable material, eventually to be replaced by custom-made monofilament nylon nets. These gill net fisheries have been extremely successful. They employ cheap gear and a large number of people, and exploit a group of fish which has many of the characteristics of the ideal fishery fish in the offshore open water down to about 20 or 30 m. Artisanal fisheries are suited to the local conditions, though they too expand and fish down the community until yields are small compared with when the fishery began.

However, commercial ambitions, resulting initially from European colonists, have led to mechanized fishing. Greek settlers brought the skills of Mediterranean purse-seining to exploit the fish at the centres of the large lakes, where the bigger boats were less vulnerable to storms than canoes and sailing dhows. Species of sardine-like fish (Clupeidae), particularly *Limnothrissa miodon* and *Stolothrissa tanganyikae* are successfully fished in this way in Lake Tanganyika. The sardines eat zooplankters, moving to the surface to do so. Predators (*Lates* spp) of the sardines move with them and are also caught. Lights are used to attract the fish towards the boats, which use large nets closed and drawn in by power winches. Such a fishery is very efficient but also liable to overfishing; catches of four species of the predators were halved over 7 years.

The main problem with mechanized fisheries, however, is that because catches are large, big boats, large-scale docking, cold stores onshore, roads and fuel are all needed. This means investment of capital and also considerable unemployment of fishermen. A large boat, run by a crew of six, can catch as much fish as a fleet of over 100, three-man canoes. Because two different groups of fish are usually concerned, however – the tilapias inshore and the sardines offshore, it is possible for both fisheries to coexist.

Mechanized fishing by power trawls, however, is probably much more damaging than purse seining. It destroys the littoral zone and takes species that are unsuitable for a fishery as readily as those that are. It was introduced to Lake Malawi in 1968 and took as many as 160 species, 80% of them small haplochromines. Many of these are endemic and highly specialized and have a very restricted distribution, perhaps over as little as 3000 m$^2$ of lake bottom in the cases of some species. Significantly 20% of them disappeared from the catches in one 3-year period and there is a real danger that many have become extinct. If trawling is allowed to continue, extensive conservation areas will need to be set aside if this fish community is to retain its diversity. However, the sustainable yield cannot remain more than modest and a better policy would be to abandon trawling and to support the artisanal fisheries very strongly. The same problem occurred in Lake Victoria in the 1960s and 1970s where bottom trawling made many littoral species scarce and may have driven some to extinction. The underlying problem was with attitudes that regarded the small species as 'trash fish' to be removed so that they did not compete for food with bigger, more valuable species. Understanding of the ecology of the systems has nearly displaced such ignorance but not entirely.

If mechanized fishing poses severe problems, a possibly worse aspect of the moves to intensify fishing in the African lakes is that of introduction of alien species. Fish introductions on a world scale have been extensive in the past 50 years, with perhaps 250 species being transferred, *inter alia* among 130 different countries. Fishery officers have sometimes had the misconceptions of those agriculturalists who believe that natural communities can be improved upon. The introduction of the Nile perch to Lake Victoria has, in some senses, been a disaster, which was foreseen at the time by scientists who were simply ignored, and in other senses as an economic triumph, though a possible short-lived one.

The Nile perch was once a member of the Lake Victoria fish fauna, but this was in the geological past. Its bones are fossilized in sediments some hundreds of thousands of years old. It has been absent from the lake for a long interim in which evolution has produced a remarkable flock of highly specialist small fishes of the genus *Haplochromis*. The argument for introduction of the Nile perch was that it would feed on the small fish, which were not marketable, and would package their flesh into its own very large and easily catchable body. At the stage when it was introduced, the tilapia fisheries (based also on introduced species, were overfished, mostly through use of illegal small-meshed nets, and there was pressure to improve the fish yield from the lake (Fig. 15.12).

After an alleged illegal introduction by the Uganda Game and Fisheries Department, probably around 1954, followed by legal ones in the 1960s, the Nile perch took a little time to expand its population and was not a problem even by 1971. Since then, however, it has become distributed throughout the lake perhaps due to other changes, including effects of littoral

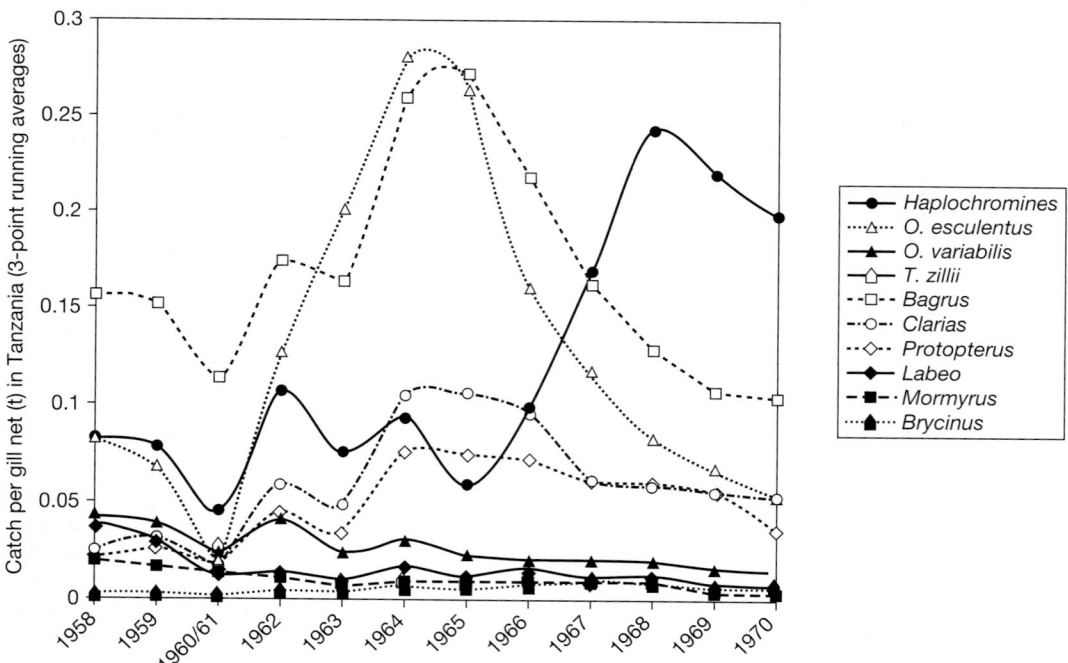

**Fig. 15.12** During the 20th century the stock in Lake Victoria was progressively fished down. Some species became scarce quite early, but *Oreochromis esculentus*, an introduced tilapia and a catfish, *Bagrus docmac*, became mainstays in the 1960s. As these were fished down, trawling was introduced for small haplochromine fish in the late 1960s, but this fishery also eventually declined. (Based on Kudhongania & Cordone 1974.)

trawling in removing competitors with its young, and eutrophication. It has demonstrated its voraciousness by eating not only the small haplochromines but also other commercially valuable fish, such as the tilapias, and has apparently reduced the fish stocks so much that it is now forced to take its own young and prawns (*Caridina*) as a major food.

Catching Nile perch, which may typically weigh 35–50 kg and has reached 179 kg, requires large boats so that some of the artisanal fishermen on tilapia have been put out of business. At first it was disliked locally and less valued at the lakeside (1 shilling per kilo) than the tilapia (30 shillings per kilo). However, the mechanization it has brought has provided new

jobs and the total yield of the fishery increased five times between the 1970s and the 1990s to 500,000 t yr$^{-1}$. Frozen fillets find a good market in the large towns and substantial processing plants have been built. It is an oily fish, which, for rural storage and distribution in an equatorial climate, needs to be smoked, which requires fuel (the less oily tilapias can simply be sun-dried). There is evidence of consequent deforestation, with its attendant erosion and other problems in the area.

The fish fauna of Lake Victoria has been greatly changed (Figs 15.13 and 15.14). Samplings in the Mwanza Gulf at the south end of the lake suggest that two-thirds of the small haplochromine species have

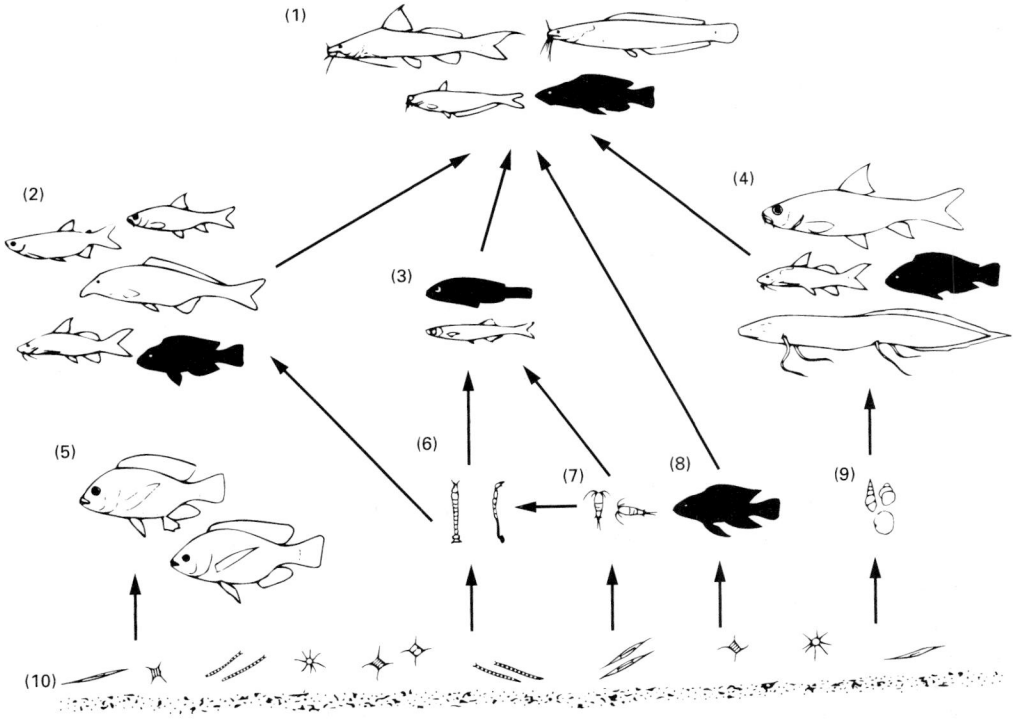

**Fig. 15.13**  Food web in Lake Victoria prior to the introduction of the Nile perch. (Based on Witte et al. 1992.) Key for Figs 15.13 and 15.14  (haplochromid fish are shown shaded in black): 1, piscivores – *Bagrus docmac, Clarias gariepinus, Schilbe mystus* (all catfish) and haplochromine cichlid fish; 2, insectivores – *Alestes* spp, *Barbus* spp (sardines), mormyrid fish, *Synodontis afrofischeri* (a catfish) and haplochromids; 3, zooplanktivores – *Rastrineobola argentea* (also 13) and haplochromines; 4, molluscivores – *Barbus altianalis, Synodontis victoriae*, haplochromines and *Protopterus aethiopicus* (lungfish); 5, algivores – *Oreochromis variabilis* and *O. esculentus*; 6 and 15, chironomids; 7, zooplankton; 8, detritivorous and phytoplanktivorous haplochromids; 9, molluscs; 10, phytoplankton and detritus; 11, adult Nile perch; 12, juvenile Nile perch; 14, introduced Nile tilapia, *Oreochromis niloticus*; 16, prawns (*Caradina nilotica*). (From Witte et al. 1992.)

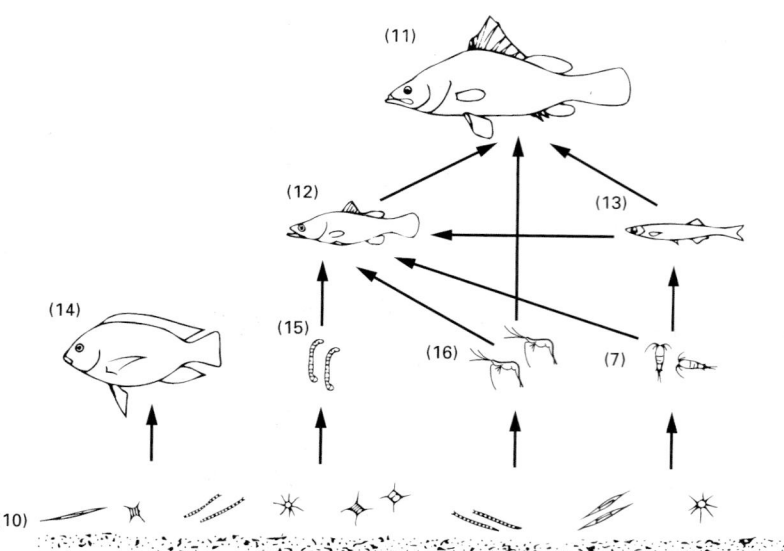

**Fig. 15.14** Food web in Lake Victoria following the introduction and expansion of the population of Nile perch. For key see Fig. 15.13. (From Witte et al. 1992.)

been made extinct. The endemic *Oreochromis* species, whose fishery was once a mainstay, have also been replaced by introduced species (*Oreochromis niloticus* and *Oreochromis leucostictus*). These changes were reflected in the fish landings around the lake (Fig. 15.15) by the late 1990s.

The increased yield (Oguta Ohwayo 1996) by the 1990s was variously attributed to several factors and it is difficult to separate them. There was a change in fishing methods coupled with an increased fishing effort; eutrophication of the lake will have increased the fish production; and the main caught fish are now three *r*-selected species, Nile perch (60%), the introduced Nile tilapia, *Oreochromis niloticus* (14%) and the endemic open-water *Rastrineobola argentea* (Fig. 15.15). Economically the countries bordering the lake benefited greatly from the changes. However, rather more processing capacity than is required by the present yields has been built, and this has encouraged overfishing. A fishery dependent on a species that is a top predator whose current production depends on cannibalization of its own young and relatively few other prey is also inherently unstable, especially when imposed chemical changes to the lake are probably continuing. As a top predator its yield must inevitably become lower than that which its prey previously provided. Evidence from the first decade of the 21st century is that the lake is now being overfished. It shows the

classic symptoms of a decline in catches (Fig. 15.15) from the peaks of the 1990s, a shift to more of the yield coming from lower trophic levels, a marked increase in the number of fishermen and boats (doubling between 1990 and 2000 and as much again by 2003, an increase in the number of gears used and in illegal gear, and a drop in catch per unit effort from 80 kg to 45 kg per boat-day. On the positive side there has been some recovery in species that had been thought extinct, as Nile perch predation on them is reduced.

With this example and others like that of *Cichla ocellaris* in Lake Gatun (Panama Canal zone) it seems odd that introductions to the African lakes are still being mooted. *Cichla ocellaris* was introduced to ponds as a sport fish but escaped to the main lake in floods. One of its consequences, apart from a major simplification of the food web, has been an increase in malaria carrying mosquitoes, whose larvae were eaten by one of the fish that *Cichla* has almost eliminated.

The problem is that some introductions have proved useful, though these have been usually to man-made lakes (see below) where a previously riverine fish fauna did not have species capable of exploiting the open-water plankton. *Limnothrissa miodon*, for example, was introduced to Lake Kariba (formed in the 1960s) without problem, and even to the older, but still comparatively recent, Lake Kivu, formed perhaps 20,000 years ago. Almost half the British fish fauna

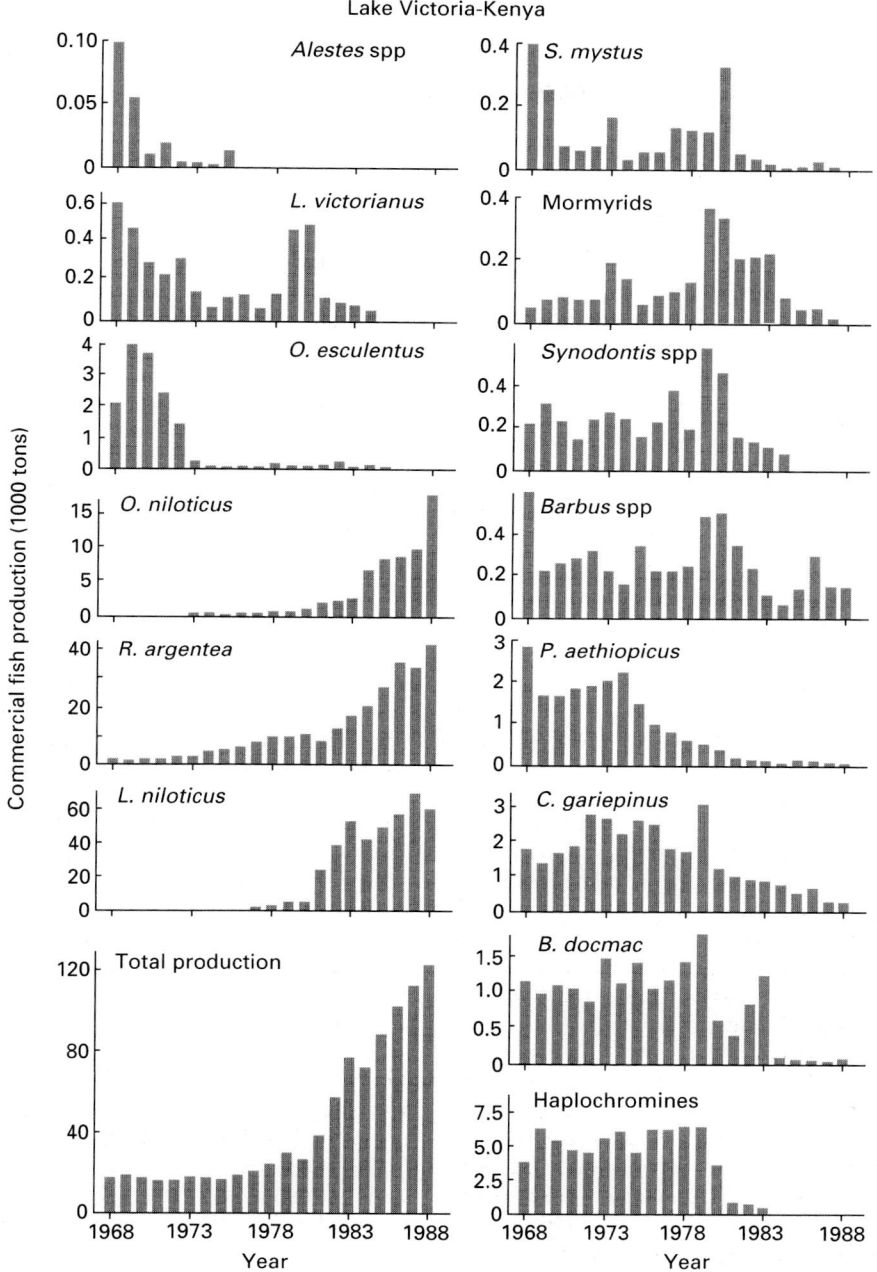

**Fig. 15.15** Fish landings by the 1990s and fish yields of particular fish from Lake Victoria. Abbreviations: L., *Lates*; O., *Oreochromis*; R., *Rastrineobolus*; S., *Schilbe*; P, *Protopterus*; C, *Clarias*; B, *Bagrus*. (Based on Oguta Ohwayo 1992.)

is also introduced and there have been few problems. The British fauna was severely depleted by glaciation and an early isolation of the islands by the English Channel prevented much recolonization from Eurasia.

It is a quite different matter to propose introducing the Lake Tanganyika clupeids to Lake Malawi, however, as has been suggested. Lake Malawi has its own open-water sardine, *Engraulicypris sardella*, which some fishery biologists have claimed to be 'inefficient' because *Chaoborus* larvae, a potential prey of the fish, persist in the lake but are absent from Lake Tanganyika. The alleged inefficiency may be grossly misplaced. The large swarms of *Chaoborus* (Chapter 14) represent not a huge unused production but an aggregation from small populations over the whole lake area for the very necessary mating! Once a species is introduced it becomes exceptionally difficult, if not impossible to eradicate.

We are left, however, with a quandary. There is a problem of high population, short of protein, in Africa, as elsewhere in the developing world. In their attempts to meet this problem, fishery officers and government officials have doubtless felt that they have been doing the right thing in encouraging mechanized fishing or making introductions. Yet most of the wild fish populations of such ancient lakes are unsuitable for much increased exploitation. A better solution perhaps is an expansion of pond culture and this is vigorously underway, but it too has its drawbacks.

## 15.5 FISH CULTURE

Pond and cage culture of fish (Fig. 15.16) is an ancient art. The Egyptians were culturing tilapia in 200 BC and the Chinese have cultured fish from at least 500 BC. Common carp were retained in ponds in mediaeval Europe to provide winter protein. More recently there has been interest in the culture of valuable marine and game fish in the developed world. Trout and salmon farms have increased markedly in number in Europe and North America in the past 30 years to produce fish that can be sold for a high price (by Third World

**Fig. 15.16** Pond and cage culture of fish is expanding rapidly. Cage culture, in which the cages are established on rivers or in lakes, as here in Sabah, is especially prone to escape of fish. If alien species are used, as often they are, this can have widespread consequences.

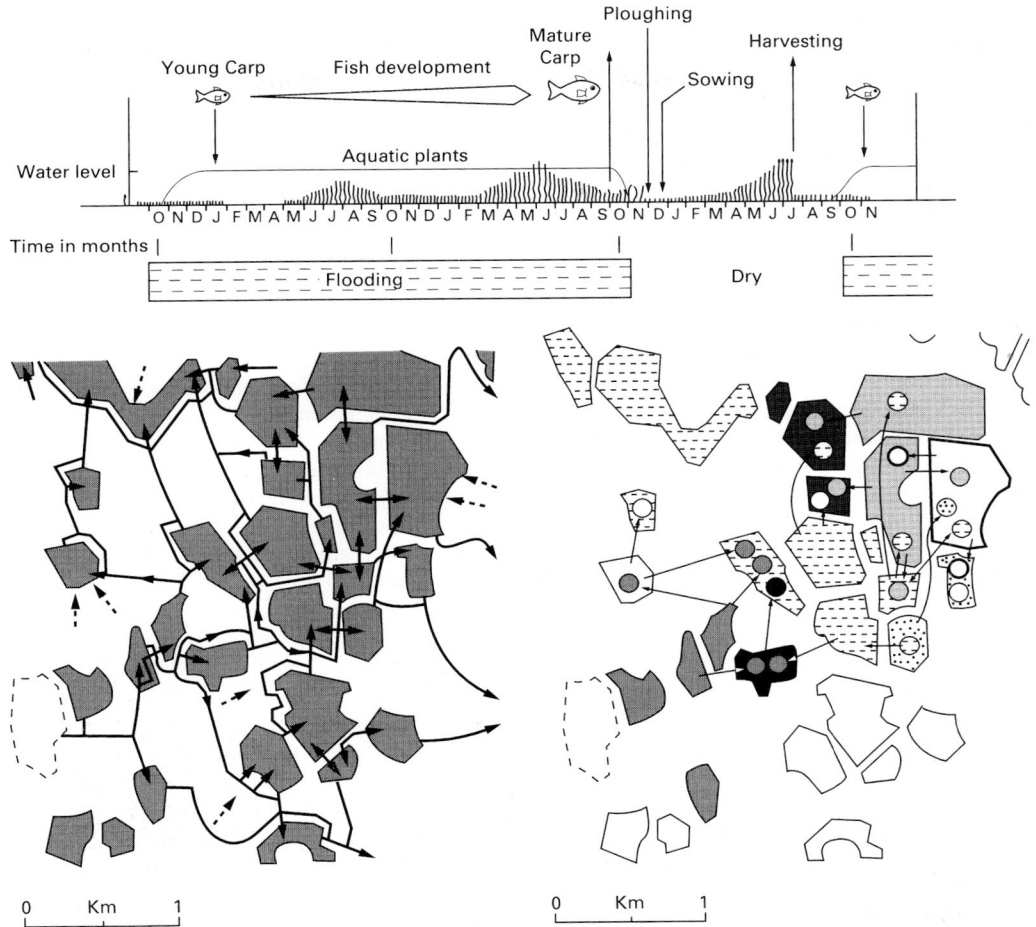

**Fig. 15.17** The many ancient shallow ponds of La Dombe in southern France have been traditionally managed to give alternate yields of fish (mostly carp) and cereals (formerly oats or wheat, now mostly maize) with little or no input of fertilizer. (Upper diagram) Transfer of water between ponds is governed by traditional custom enforced by honour, rather than a formal legal system. The lower diagram shows something of the system near Le Boucheaux and the complex and confusing pattern of water transfers, shown by arrows and different shading. Those who operate it understand the system perfectly.

comparisons) to offset the high costs of production. Such farms depend on feeding high protein food (generally of fish meal made from small marine fish) and are net users of protein and energy. They provide no solutions to food problems though they may be very important as sources of employment in areas such as Western Scotland and Norway. La Dombe (Fig. 15.17), in south-east France, near Lyon is an ancient series of ponds that can be flooded and dried out by a series of sluices. The water regime is controlled by local custom

and law and allows a system of carp cultivation and maize growing to exist. The maize stubble, after flooding and stocking provides initial food for the carp and as the stocking rates are not excessive, an aquatic plant community can develop. The carp turn over the soil and mobilize nutrients so that when they are big enough to harvest and the pond is drained, the maize benefits from an initial flush of nutrients, though some fertilizer is eventually needed. Carp is a prized food fish in mainland Europe.

Greater fundamental significance attaches to fish farming in the developing world. Here there are two trends: one towards high-technology culture of tilapia, which could become a luxury industry serving rich subtropical countries such as the Gulf States, and the other towards low-technology culture on a village basis. The latter is far more important for it not only helps preserve the wild fisheries, but also provides protein to those who are really short of it. Asia now accounts for 90% of global aquaculture, marine and freshwater, finfish and shellfish, with the mainstay being finfish, and by 2004, aquaculture had accounted for 43% of aquatic food consumed, and had a growth rate of 8.9% per year between 1950 and 2004.

About 250 species are cultured, the most common being the carps (silver (*Hypophthalmichthys molitrix*), grass (*Ctenopharyngodon idella*), common (*Cyprinus carpio*), bighead (*Hypophthalmichthys nobilis*), crucian (*Carassius carrasius*)) then tilapias (*Oreochromis, Tilapia, Sarotherodon*), roho (*Labeo rohita*), catla (*Gibelion catla*), mringal (*Cirrhinus mrigala*), white amur bream (*Parabramis pekinensis*) and channel catfish (*Ictalurus punctatus*). Only two species have been truly domesticated, and then only 10,000 years later than dogs, cats and farm stock. Domestication means that breeding is subject to human control, that behaviour and appearance differ greatly from those of wild stock and that survival of at least some varieties would no longer be possible in the wild. The two species are common carp and crucian (golden) carp (goldfish), though a few others are virtually domesticated. Wild type common carp is now virtually extinct in its native range in eastern Europe and western Asia. Its domestication began with the Romans 2000 years ago and it was spread rapidly in mediaeval times and is now ubiquitous. Goldfish were bred in China largely for ornamental purposes.

Tilapia are ideal fish for both high- and low-technology culture. They taste good, have no fine intramuscular bones, breed early and easily, thrive on cheap plant and algal food and hence produce high yields. They are tolerant of wide temperature and salinity ranges, are relatively free from parasites and diseases and hybridize readily. This latter helps breeding programmes. Suitable species include *Oreochromis andersonii, O. macrochir, O. niloticus* and *O. aureus*. Because they breed frequently, large populations of small fish may result. This can be avoided by stocking predators such as *Channa striata* with them, and by culturing first generation hybrids which are almost entirely male and do not breed further. Males also grow faster than females.

Crosses between female *O. nilotica* and male *O. aureus* produce more than 85% males and if *O. urolepis hornorum* is used as the male parent, 100% males can be almost guaranteed in the first generation. Treatment of the fry with androgenic steroids can also turn all the fish into males but this increases the cost.

Cyprinid fish are used for culture in India and China, often in mixtures that allow a very full exploitation of the available food supply. For example, the major carps, catla, rohu, and mrigal will take zooplankton and other invertebrates, the white amur, bighead or silver carp eat phytoplankton, the grass carp eats plants, and the Chinese black roach (*Mylopharyngodon piceus*) and the common carp will eat benthic invertebrates. Stocked in combination in ponds that can be cheaply fertilized with cow dung, grass cuttings, by-products of agriculture such as rice bran, or even cheap artificial fertilizer, high yields can be obtained.

Even raw human sewage can be used if diluted and the ponds stocked with air-breathing fish such as catfish and murrel (*Channa striata*) originating from deoxygenated swamp habitats (Chapter 9). Fish from such ponds must be well cooked because of the presence of various trematode parasites and tapeworms for which the fish form an intermediate host. Pigs may be penned over ditches leading to such fish ponds, which they fertilize and ducks may also be used to provide continuous fertilization. Rice fields, after the rice has been harvested and the stubble left, can also be used for culture though in recent years the use of pesticides to improve rice yields has prevented many fields from being used.

Low-technology culture of mixed species is very valuable and poses few problems *per se*, beyond those of parasite transmission. Some of the Indian major carps will not spawn easily but can be induced to do so by a simple injection of ground-up pituitary gland preserved in alcohol from a wild fish that was just about to spawn. There is a vast number of small ponds and ditches in the developing world that can be used – those created for irrigation, stock watering, water chestnut cultivation and flood control, for example. Yields, particularly where the ponds are fertilized with village wastes, are much higher than those of wild fisheries. The latter might produce, in the tropics, up to a few hundred kg ha$^{-1}$; intensive pond culture can realize as much per m$^2$, though this requires expertise and heavy feeding. On a village scale yields 10–100 times those of wild fisheries would not be unreasonable, however. Such village polyculture represents a sensible and helpful approach to the problems of the poor, whilst complementing the wise management of lakes and their fisheries. The major reservation about aquaculture is that it almost always uses alien species, not native ones, though frequently native species are just as productive. In every case of introductions, fish have escaped from farms and established in the natural waterways, often suppressing the native species and although there are codes of practice to try to avoid this, they have everywhere been breached. Escape of the bighead and grass carp to the Donghu Lake in Wuhan, China has displaced some 60 native species and use of the North American crayfish (*Pacificastus leniusculus*) in Europe has decimated the native *Astacus astacus* through co-introduction of a fungal disease (*Aphanomyces astaci*) to which it is tolerant and the European native not. In Australia and New Zealand, introductions of alien salmonids have severely threatened the future of the entire group of galaxioid fishes that are endemic to the region.

## 15.6 STILLWATER ANGLING

Recreational fishing (angling) divides itself into game or fly-fishing and coarse fishing. Game fishing is usually for salmonids (Atlantic and Pacific salmon, brown trout, rainbow trout, and sometimes grayling (*Thymallus thymallus*)), uses active techniques in which a replica fly is cast at the surface of the water to lure the fish, and is associated more with flowing waters than lakes. Trout are frequently sought by such techniques from the edges of upland lakes and from artificial lakes stocked with rainbow trout. Coarse fishing, for pike, perch (*Perca fluviatilis*) and cyprinid fish such as roach (*Rutilus rutilus*), tench (*Tinca tinca*), bream (*Abramis brama*) and common carp in Europe and many species elsewhere, is a more sedentary occupation, not confined to lakes, for it is practised also on slow-flowing rivers and canals, but often a feature of them, in which baits of worms, maggots or nutritious pastes are dangled in the water for the fish to come to them.

The game fish/coarse fish distinction is peculiarly British, and carries certain social cachés because game fishing is much more expensive than coarse fishing. Elsewhere, there is little distinction and, in the North American Great Lakes, anglers will cheerfully pursue salmonids from boats using baits rather than flies. In most western countries, recreational angling involves many people and substantial funds. Fishing in the UK attracts upwards of 2–3 million people, rather more than attend football matches. In Finland, there are 2.1 million people who fish regularly for recreation, compared with 1200 commercial fishermen from a population of around 5 million.

Such angling is only partly about catching fish. In the UK they are thrown back anyway and not eaten. Social surveys have shown that some anglers enjoy the sense of freedom, the relaxation, and the opportunity to reminisce as much as the excitement of catching a fish. The surroundings are important; anglers regard themselves as natural historians, sensitive to the state of the water and have traditionally been seen as allies of the conservation bodies in lobbying for higher quality waters and reporting pollution incidents that might otherwise have gone uninvestigated.

For such anglers, the management of the fishery is essentially that of managing access to the site, the number of anglers, and their activities and gear so as to minimize stress to the fish. Such management is regulated legally, for example by the Salmon and Freshwater Fisheries Act (1975) in the UK, by-laws set by the regulatory authority, and the rules of the owner of the fishery or angling club. The law bans certain gears, such as foul hooks, barbed gaffs and knotted keep nets, gives the opportunity for setting of a closed (close) season when fishing is not allowed, and bans the transfer of fish, without licence, from one water body to another so as to minimize the spread of diseases and parasites. The regulatory authority can set a close season during spawning, authorizes fish transfers, and may prescribe that a fisherman use no more than one or two rods at a time. Local rules may determine the number of anglers by confining fishing to a fixed number of places, or pegs and by banning certain baits and practices.

Though angling has come under scrutiny as potentially a cruel sport, especially when the fish are put back, often damaged, after being kept for some hours in a submerged net, angling as described above is compatible with many other water uses and the maintenance of attractive habitats. Anglers, but no more than walkers and boaters, disturb birds and are as prone to leave litter. Sometimes the litter can be damaging to wildlife – lead shot for weighting lines, lengths of discarded monofilament nylon line, often with hooks still attached, as well as the drink cans and broken glass, sandwich wrappings and expanded polystyrene containers that mar many places. New laws have resolved the shot problem by replacing lead with heavy steel and educational campaigns about the effects of tangling line on birds are likely to have some effect.

There are developing problems, however. The increasing demand for angling, which can be inexpensive in a society where increasing numbers are unemployed, or needing relief from a worsening work environment, leads to needs to accommodate more angling. This may mean habitat modifications – the provision of platforms and car parks, for example, which destroy natural habitat. It may mean damage to bankside vegetation as anglers cut reed that is in the way of their casting, trample the surroundings, dig turf for worms, even light fires to keep warm. These problems can be controlled by local rules and sensitive design. More insidious and very damaging, however, are changes in attitudes to angling, as, like many other sports in recent decades, it has become a competitive activity, with sponsorship money pandering to an apparently insatiable need to inflate male egos.

Competitive angling, in which he wins who catches the most or the biggest fish, or the heaviest bag of them, now threatens the coexistence of angling with other water uses, not least wildlife conservation. It has brought with it increased demands to stock waters with more or different fish, practices such as live baiting, demands for removal of piscivores and competitors of target fish and a reduced sensitivity to the quality of the habitat and the needs of other users. There has always been demand for stocking of waters because freshwater fish recruitment in the UK is annually very variable, being dependent on temperature in the early summer and other weather-related factors. Some cohorts of fish are thus naturally poor, others very strong. On average the carrying capacity of a water will be achieved through a mixture of species of varying annual strengths. Stocking will simply lead to greater mortality of one component or another, unless it is to replace fish lost after a pollution incident. Regulatory authorities in the UK, which have carried out much stocking in the past in response to anglers' demands, have largely ceased this practice. Anglers themselves, however, are responsible for thousands of fish transfers each year, many of them illegal. Sometimes they involve fish brought in from mainland Europe, a practice which can introduce new diseases and parasites.

Most problematic has been the spread of common carp, an alien fish that is extremely damaging. It is omnivorous, feeding as an adult particularly on bottom invertebrates, for which it forages in the sediment. In doing so it disturbs the sediment, creating turbidity and destroys rooted aquatic plants. Together with other bottom-feeding fish such as bream it can transfer considerable amounts of phosphorus to the overlying water. It has been identified as a significant forward switch agent (see below) in the conversion of plant-dominated shallow waters to algal-dominated ones. Carp are particularly prized by match anglers and those who seek fish of record size. They grow large and attempt to resist capture. Since the 1980s in the UK there has been a trend for competitive carp fishing in heavily stocked ponds typically with 1500 kg ha$^{-1}$ and even up to 14,000 kg ha$^{-1}$ (a natural fish community might have 50–100 kg ha$^{-1}$). Fish kills due to bacterial and other disease are not uncommon and large fish for stocking are sold for many thousands of pounds each. In the UK, carp do not breed very successfully because of the low temperatures. This has confined the problem to some extent. In Australia, however, where carp have also been introduced, they now predominate to the detriment of native fish in many river systems and are a major problem.

Live baiting is inherently a cruel practice. It can also lead to the discarding of unused fish into a lake from which they were naturally absent. The most notorious example is the introduction of ruffe into Loch Lomond in 1980, where it is now very common and predatory on the eggs of the powan, a rare native fish near confined to the loch. The pressures for predator control from anglers and fishery managers are persistent. Birds such as cormorants (Fig. 15.18), herons, grebes, goosanders and mergansers take 0.3 to 0.5 kg of fresh fish per day and have been seen as competitors by the fishermen. Red kite and osprey populations were markedly reduced towards the end of the 19th century and the early decades of the 20th century, as were those of otters, by the demands of fishery owners, but there is little evidence that the fishing is improved by predator control. The piscivores take mostly small, diseased or damaged fish, or those reared in farms and stocked in reservoirs to which they are ill adapted. In one loch, where there was pressure for control of cormorants, which were believed to be feeding on trout, it was found that they were feeding on perch, for which there was also a control programme because the perch were believed to be competing with the trout!

Predation can improve fisheries by skewing the size of the fish towards the larger end, and in any case

**Fig. 15.18** Fish–eating birds are often thought to be detrimental to fisheries. Cormorants are efficient predators (right, photograph by B. Hackett). In China cormorants have traditionally been used for fishing (the bird is prevented from swallowing its catch by a ligature tied around the neck (lower left). In Europe cormorant numbers have been increasing owing to protection by conservation legislation and some large roosts now occur, for example at Nardermeer in The Netherlands (top left). There is little evidence that bird predation makes great inroads on fisheries and the point is often unappreciated that predators are likely to have regulatory effects on ecosystems that ultimately benefit the whole system, including the fishery.

shooting some predators at a site rich in prey merely creates an opportunity for more of the same or different ones to move in. Fortunately the high intrinsic value of such birds and mammals in the public perception has swung fishery management opinion away from predator control and towards a broader view of conservation. The pressures generated by injections of large sums of money generally undermine the balance of any endeavour, however, and should be resisted in angling, particularly because of the many other uses of the waters and the otherwise very positive social benefits of a pastime that has very ancient origins.

## 15.7 AMENITY CULTURE AND THE AQUARIUM TRADE

Of the two truly domesticated fish species, goldfish were first bred in China from the torpedo shaped, grey-green, wild *Carassius auratus* about AD 960 as aquarium and ornamental pond fish. The range of varieties now available worldwide, including veiltail, eggfish, telescope, calico, celestial, lionhead, tumbler, comet, water bubble eye, brocade, pompom, and fantail, gives some idea of the monstrosities available (Fig. 15.19) to a lucrative aquarium trade. In Japan and now elsewhere, common carp have been similarly converted to

**Fig. 15.19** Goldfish have been so extensively bred for the aquarium trade that few now resemble the original wild species (approximated by the photograph upper left). Many varieties are monstrosities (bubble eye, upper right; black moor, lower left, pearl scale, lower right) that are highly valued by some aquarists, but have none of the fundamental beauty of a species tempered by natural selection.

the garish and highly expensive varieties of koi for garden ponds. But these are simple commercial enterprises that have little consequence for aquatic ecosystems. Predators rapidly take any escapes of such self-advertising forms. What is of greater concern is the taking of wild fish for sale in the aquarium trade. Little is known about the extent of this and of the balance between captive breeding of tropical fishes and wild capture. The Peruvian Amazon is exploited to support a large trade in the USA, with about 28 firms supplying nine million fishes worth 2.5 million dollars in 2001. The trade supports 10,000 people in Peru. Fish are the most common pets kept in the developed world and 96% of them are freshwater species. There appear to be two aspects to the trade: high volume, low value characin and callichthyd species, such as the cardinal tetra (*Paracheirodon axelrodi*), exported via Miami, probably with high mortalities in transit; and

individual provision of very expensive species, such as silver arawana (*Osteoglossum bicirrhosum*), stingrays (*Potamotrygon* sp) and red tail catfish (*Phracteocephalus hemioliopterus*), often to Asian collectors. It seems unlikely that this trade is a major threat to conservation of the species or ecosystem and for a parallel trade from the African Great Lakes, the high costs of transport have lead to its substantial replacement by captive breeding. But it is yet another route by which potentially damaging alien species may invade.

## 15.8 DOMESTIC WATER SUPPLY, EUTROPHICATION AND RESERVOIRS

Industrialization in the 18th century in Europe, the 19th in North America and the 20th in Asia needed labour. It led to population increase, crowded conditions, poor sanitation and epidemics of diseases such as cholera and typhoid. It created a need to grow more food on rural land worked by fewer people. It also created a need for power to drive machinery. The solution to these problems was to use natural lakes and artificial reservoirs to store water ready for drinking and irrigation and to generate power. The saviour of the poorer peoples of the cotton and wool processing cities of Lancashire and Yorkshire in the UK was the building of reservoir dams for drinking water on the rivers of the Pennine Hills lying between them.

There can be no objection to the use of natural lakes for storage of drinking water and only a little to raising of their levels to increase capacity. This might alter their outline unaesthetically and for a time might upset the processes of the littoral zone or impede migration upstream of salmonids, but these are trivial problems that can be solved. The net benefit is often great. But the creation of new lakes poses more complicated issues. They destroy a whole section of a river system, may create problems both upstream and downstream and may not be without internal problems. As to whether a particular dam is for good or ill will depend on the particular site and the person being asked. There are nearly a million sizeable dams, 45,000 of them very big (greater than 15 m or storing more than three million m$^3$ of water) indeed, affecting 60% of the world's rivers, as well as millions of small dams holding ponds for village purposes.

Beyond such issues are those of management of the lake or reservoir, for the ideal undisturbed catchment that delivers water of high quality that needs minimal treatment is hard to find. Agriculture, forestry and urbanization have affected most, and the world's commonest water quality problem is eutrophication caused by disruption of nutrient retention in the catchment. Eutrophication affects natural lakes and reservoirs alike, so a logical progression is to look at the problem and its consequences first and then to examine the pros and cons of reservoir construction.

### 15.8.1 Eutrophication – human induced changes in the production of lakes

Artificial eutrophication (abbreviated here to eutrophication, for 'natural eutrophication' is very rare) includes any increase in nutrient loading, either by phosphorus or nitrogen, or more usually both. The term is sometimes used to indicate the problems arising

from the increase in loading, with the ugly neologism 'nutrification' created to describe the increase in loading, irrespective of any detected problem. The original definition is used here.

Increased loading of phosphorus comes from wastewater treatment works, discharge of raw sewage (including that from stock and fish farms) and, increasingly, from arable land. Soils have traditionally been thought to retain phosphorus quite efficiently but recent evidence suggests that this capacity is now being exceeded following decades of fertilization in some areas. Nitrogen is also derived from excretal sources, but greater amounts come from cultivated land where soil disturbance and fertilization mobilize the very soluble nitrate ions to the watercourses. Nitrate may also enter from the atmosphere, following oxidation of nitrogen oxides produced by vehicle engines and, in the tropics from burning of vegetation to clear land for agriculture or to promote new growth for grazing. Table 15.1 shows that almost all lakes in the USA have excessive amounts of TP and TN compared with reference standards derived from pristine systems. TP values are on average three times, and TN values five times higher. Similar problems occur everywhere in the developed world and increasingly in the developing countries.

Eutrophication in rivers was dealt with in Chapter 8, where problems of increasing aquatic plant and filamentous algal growth were discussed. In lakes, the problem is reflected sometimes in increased plant growth but usually in increased phytoplankton growth. In shallow lakes, there may be eventual complete loss of all submerged aquatic plants, and sometimes also the regression of marginal reedswamps, but these are issues more for conservation (see below) than water supply. Increased phytoplankton crops may make water turbid and unattractive; they increase the costs of filtration for domestic supply, and may cause tastes and odours through secretion of organic compounds and substances toxic to mammals and sometimes fish. Fine organic detritus from plankton crops passing through the waterworks' filters may support clogging communities of nematode worms, sponges, hydrozoans, zebra mussels and insects in water distribution pipes. Dissolved organic matter secreted into the water by the algae may make subsequent chlorination to disinfect the water more costly, or produce astringent-tasting chlorinated phenolic substances in the domestic water supply.

Increased phytoplankton crops increase the rate of hypolimnetic deoxygenation. Anaerobic, sulphide-rich

**Table 15.1** Nutrient status of USA lakes, compared with target reference values. [n] is number of observations. (Based on Dodds et al. 2009.)

| Ecoregion | Name | Reference TP (µg L⁻¹) | Current median TP (µg L⁻¹) [n] | % > reference target | Reference TN (µg L⁻¹) | Current median TN (µg L⁻¹) [n] | % > reference target |
|---|---|---|---|---|---|---|---|
| I | Willamette and central valleys | 7 | 38 | 91 | 122 | 305 | 77 |
| II | Western forested mountains | 14 | 19 [296] | 61 | 147 | 249 [45] | 65 |
| III | Xeric west | 11 | 29 [170] | 75 | 39 | 537 [24] | 100 |
| IV | Great Plains grass and shrublands | 26 | 50 [127] | 70 | 126 | 1489 [2] | 100 |
| V | Central cultivated Great Plains | 23 | 85 [213] | 85 | 211 | 1416 [2] | 100 |
| VI | Corn Belt and Northern Great Plains | 25 | 80 [393] | 87 | 159 | 1708 [3] | 100 |
| VII | Mostly glaciated dairy region | 10 | 38 [787] | 85 | 120 | 800 [35] | 100 |
| VIII | Nutrient poor glaciated Upper Midwest and Northeast | 7 | 12 [1238] | 76 | 91 | 330 [159] | 100 |
| IX | South eastern temperate forested plains and hills | 24 | 40 [727] | 68 | 52 | 537 [24] | 100 |
| X | Texas–Louisiana coastal and Mississippi alluvial plains | 16 | 61 | 92 | 241 | 725 | 100 |
| XI | Central and Eastern forested uplands | 18 | 19 [267] | 53 | 124 | 593 [14] | 100 |
| XII | Southern coastal plain | 5 | 20 [692] | 93 | 318 | 743 [545] | 94 |
| XIII | Southern Florida coastal plain | 16 | 35 [10] | 81 | 340 | 1435 [7] | 100 |
| XIV | Eastern coastal plain | 3 | 17 [280] | 98 | 218 | 460 [120] | 94 |
| Mean | | 15 | 39 | 80 | 165 | 809 | 95 |

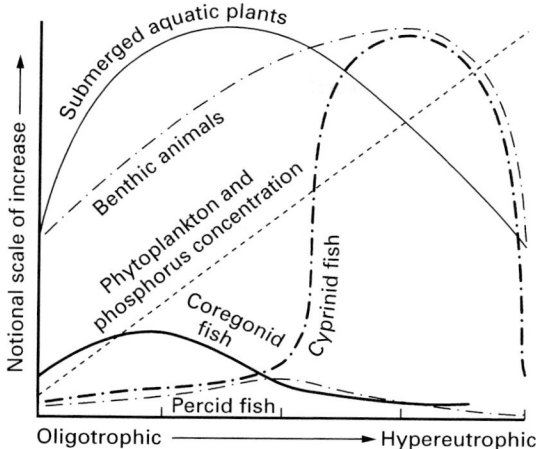

**Fig. 15.20** General changes in north temperate lakes as they become eutrophicated. Eventual collapses in aquatic plants may require additional factors (see text). In general, though yields of fish may increase, cyprinids are less desirable as a commercial catch than coregonids. (Based on Hartmann 1977.)

hypolimnion water is unsuitable for water supply, putting much of a lake or reservoir out of use for a long period in summer, when, in many areas, water is short. A deoxygenated hypolimnion also excludes some fish groups, particularly the coregonids (white fish) and salmonids. They may then be unable to live in the lake at all or to pass through it to up-river spawning grounds because they are also intolerant of the high temperatures in the epilimnion. Such fish depend on cool, well-oxygenated hypolimnia for their summer survival, and frequently support valuable fisheries.

Fish tolerant of lower oxygen concentrations may increase in production as the coregonids and salmonids disappear (Fig. 15.20) but in extreme eutrophication, when dense algal growth outcompetes the marginal aquatic plant beds, the major loss of structure in the ecosystem may have severe effects. There is a loss of spawning and living habitat for the fish, some of which attach their eggs to aquatic plants or their detritus. Large plant-living invertebrates such as snails and insect nymphs are much reduced in numbers and this may lead to declines in the growth and survival of larger fish that depend on them for food.

Fish-eating (e.g. bittern, heron) and plant-eating (swan, coot) bird populations may consequently decline

so that the entire conservation value of a habitat deteriorates. The loss of plants may also make bank edges more vulnerable to erosion by waves or boats so that banks may have to be expensively and unaesthetically protected by metal or wood piling.

The degree to which eutrophication is considered a problem depends on place and people. A small lake heavily fertilized by the village sewage in south-east Asia may be a valuable source of protein in the form of deoxygenation-tolerant cultured fish, feeding on thick algal soups. A very modest degree of eutrophication by perhaps the effluent from a couple of holiday cottages in Canada or Sweden may be a serious problem because it has decreased the transparency of the lake from 5 to 3 m, reduced the values of the property, and has been associated with a reduction in lake trout catches. Water supply companies have seen eutrophication as a problem only when its symptoms in a drinking water reservoir cannot be treated in some chemical or mechanical way and there is plenty of available technology to do this. More fundamental solutions have not been thought worthwhile unless they significantly reduce filtration costs. The threshold loading for this is far above that needed to provide a quality associated with high biodiversity but sensitivity to the problem has increased following the deaths of dogs and sheep from drinking water containing large concentrations of cyanobacteria in the UK in 1988 and from deaths of dialysis patients in Brazil. Some estimates of the costs per year of eutrophication are shown in Table 15.2.

Eutrophication of temperate lakes is very familiar. Virtually all of the lakes of the agricultural and populated lowlands have been eutrophicated to some extent. In a survey of English lakes even in protected areas – nature reserves of various kinds – Carvalho & Moss (1995) found that three-quarters were damaged by nutrient pollution. It has been thought, however, that lakes in the tropics were not seriously affected because of less intensive agriculture and a more diffuse distribution of excretal wastes. The case of the East African Lake Victoria suggests that this is no longer so (Fig. 15.21).

Lake Victoria is one of the world's largest lakes (69,000 km²; maximum depth 79 m). J.F. Talling studied it in the late 1950s and early 1960s and published data on its annual cycles of thermal stratification, oxygenation and phytoplankton seasonal succession. It then showed little deoxygenation of the bottom waters. Diatoms dominated the phytoplankton,

**Table 15.2** Costs in the USA and in England and Wales of eutrophication. (Based on J.L. Pretty et al. (2002) and Dodds et al. (2009).)

| | USA million dollars (2009) per year | England and Wales million pounds (2002) per year |
|---|---|---|
| Fisheries | 189–589 | 0.04–0.17 |
| Recreational boating | 82–567 | 13.5–47 |
| Other tourism | na | 4.1–16.3 |
| Lakeside property values | 4500† | 13.8 |
| Biodiversity and conservation (costs of recovery plans) | 44 | 10.3–14.2 |
| Water treatment | 813+* | 54.7** |
| Industrial (abstraction, irrigation, livestock, navigation) | na | 0.7–1.4 |
| Clean-up costs (e.g. fish kills, weed cutting) | na | 0.7–1.4 |
| Gas emissions ($NO_x$, ammonium) effects | na | 7.17–11.19 |
| Sewage effluent treatment (removal of P) | na | 70.4 |
| Treatment of algal blooms | na | 0.7 |
| Cost of adoption of new farm practices to reduce nutrient losses | na | 4.8 |
| Monitoring and investigation of incidents | na | 0.9 |
| Cost of new policy development to cope with the problems | na | 0.28 |
| Total | 5728–6513 | 183–238 |

na, not assessed
†Housing on lakesides is much more common in the USA than in England and Wales, mostly because of the great difference in numbers of lakes.
*Underestimated because water treatment costs could not be apportioned between eutrophication related problems and other costs so some costs are not allowed for. The value given is the cost of buying bottled water where the supply was unacceptable for taste and odour reasons.
**Underestimated as does not include the cost of replacement bottled water.

with some cyanobacteria; nitrogen supply limited the phytoplankton growth. By the early 1990s the phytoplankton crop had increased tenfold, and the primary productivity fivefold. There was a switch to dominance by cyanobacteria, many of them nitrogen fixing, with diatoms much reduced, a depletion of silicate from the epilimnion, widespread deoxygenation of the hypolimnion, and frequent fish kills, associated with the deoxygenation. The phytoplankton, in bioassays, still shows evidence of nitrogen limitation; phosphorus concentrations in the water have changed little from the 1960s, but sediment core analyses suggest an increase in phosphorus loading to the lake during the last century.

Water enters the lake from direct rain on the surface (83%) and inflow from the catchment (17%). The concentration of combined nitrogen in the rain has not increased much, but the clearance of woodland from about 1920 onwards, and increasing local populations, which have risen by about 3–4% per year, have resulted in enough run-off of nitrogen to have caused the changes. Leaching of nitrogen from the catchment may have initially stimulated diatom production, which led to loss, by sedimentation, of the soluble silica, with only slow current replacement from the catchment. The diatom growth maintained nitrogen-limited conditions, and increased run-off of phosphate decreased the nitrogen to phosphorus ratio in such a way as to favour nitrogen-fixing cyanophytes. The increased phytoplankton production led to deoxygenation of the hypolimnion.

Rival explanations involve changes in the food web of the lake, following introduction of the Nile perch, and climate change. The symptoms could be explained without any increase in nutrient loading if the water column has ceased to mix as freely as it did as a result

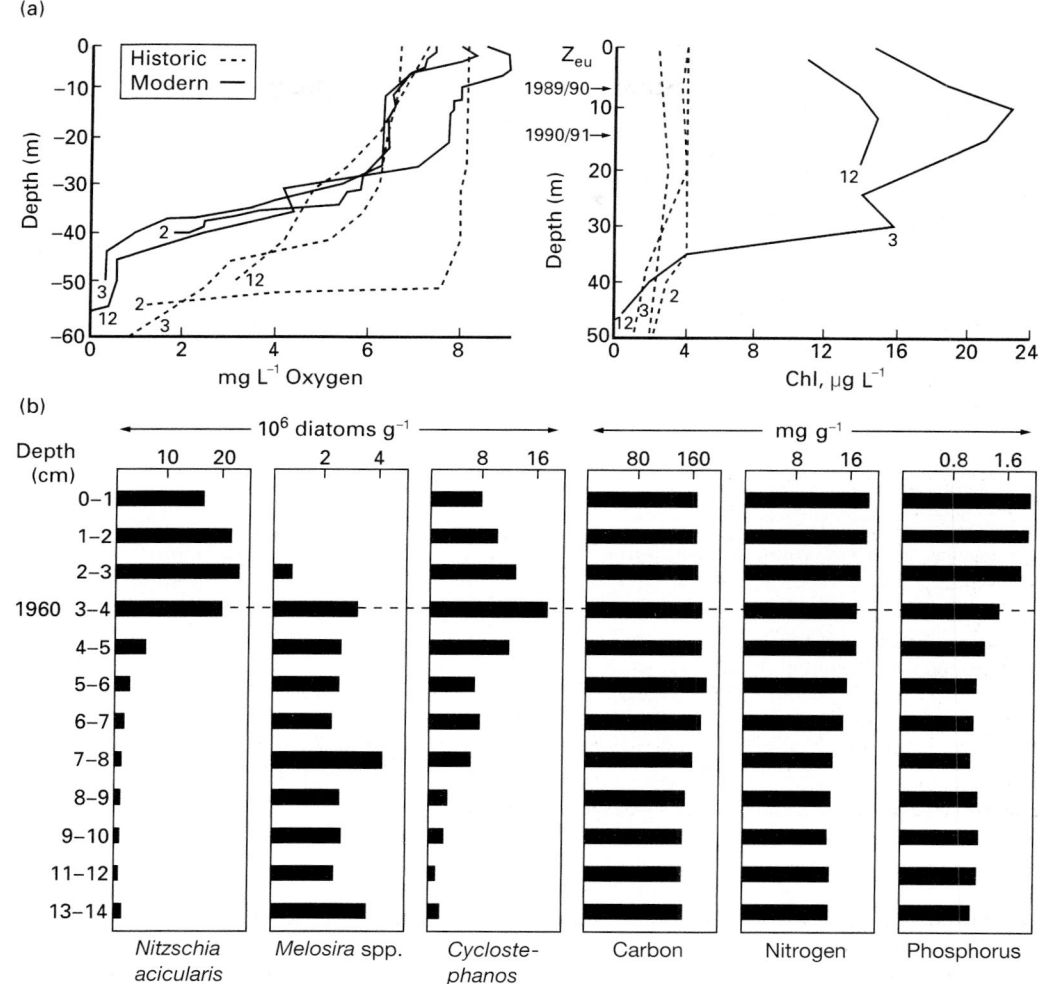

**Fig. 15.21** Changes in Lake Victoria shown by (a) analyses made in 1960–61 and 1989–90 of oxygen and chlorophyll *a* concentrations with depth in comparable months (numbered) and (b) changes in diatoms and chemistry in a sediment core (see Chapter 11 for methods of palaeolimnology). Major changes in planktonic diatoms (*Nitzschia, Melosira, Cyclostephanos*) occurred after about 1960 and are matched by increases in carbon, nitrogen and phosphorus contents. The bottom of the core is dated at about AD 1800. (Based on Hecky 1992.)

perhaps of a warming climate trend. There is some evidence for this but it involves comparison of conditions over only one year in the 1960s and one year in the 1990s. Mixing in such a large and relatively shallow lake may vary from year to year as a result of random vagaries of weather, without any underlying trend. Greater stability of the water column would lead to loss of diatoms, failure of silica to be returned

to the surface layers, greater denitrification and hence decreased N to P ratios, which favour cyanobacteria. Mixing disfavours cyanobacteria (Chapter 13) and stabler conditions might lead to their greater success with increased nitrogen loading to the lake through nitrogen fixation. Only data over several years on the temperature stratification will determine if this explanation has value.

## 15.8.2 Dams and reservoirs

In the 1960s and 1970s, several very large lakes were created in Africa, and much information resulted from the early stages of these. Previously there were big dams in North America, Europe and Russia and subsequently there has been much building in South America and Asia, with Brazil, China and India now among the most active. The water rising behind a newly closed dam is often turbid with suspended sediment in the river and from erosion of the newly flooded soils at the water's edge. The turbidity prevents much phytoplankton growth but as the new lake becomes larger the shoreline stabilizes and the river silt is deposited in deltas as the flow is halted by the water mass. In Lake Kariba (Zimbabwe–Zambia) there was no early turbid phase, for river silt is deposited in swamps just upriver from the lake; elsewhere it has been prominent.

Flooding kills the river valley vegetation, which rots underwater, with two consequences. First, there may be deoxygenation of the bottom water with production of $H_2S$. In Lake Volta in Ghana, the entire water mass was deoxygenated for a time, as flooded softwood forests decayed. Secondly, the waterlogging and decomposition of the soils release ions. The rise in Lake Kariba was from 26 mg $L^{-1}$ total dissolved solids in the river to 67 mg $L^{-1}$ in the early lake and high levels of ammonium and phosphate may be found for a time. This in turn may stimulate increased growth of phytoplankton, aquatic plants and fish. Lake Kainji (Nigeria), which is frequently flushed out, consequently did not undergo these stages, nor did Lake Nasser-Nubia, where 80% of the basin was desert.

In Lake Kariba, however, there was a spectacular colonization and spread of a floating fern, *Salvinia molesta* (Fig. 15.22). It is a robust plant, up to 30 cm long with overlapping leaves densely covered with hairs. These prevent wetting and waterlogging. *Salvinia* spp can normally reproduce sexually – sporocarps are produced on trailing underwater stems – but *S. molesta* produces stolons and quickly builds up a dense mat. This floating mat may support other species, such as *Scirpus cubensis*, rooted in it. *Salvinia molesta* sporocarps are mostly sterile. It seems to be a pentaploid hybrid of two related South American species, *S. biloba* and *S. auriculata*, perhaps of horticultural origin.

*Salvinia molesta* was a problem in the new Lake Kariba in the early 1960s for it impeded navigation and the use of fishing nets. It also created anaerobic conditions in the shallow margins of the lake. *Salvinia* spp do not form such monospecific stands in South America, where they are endemic, and it is a mystery how the hybrid has reached East and Central Africa and now also Sri Lanka and Indonesia, where it is also a problem. Probably botanists, aquarists or water gardeners introduced it, as they did other noxious floating plants, like the water hyacinth, *Eichhornia crassipes* (Fig. 15.22). Removed from contact with their endemic competitors and grazers, such plants have frequently become problems demanding expensive control. *Salvinia* was known in the River Zambezi before the Kariba Dam was built but the river flow presumably prevented build up of large populations until the lake started to form. By 1962 *Salvinia* covered a quarter of the (4400 km$^2$) lake.

Around 1962 it seemed that *Salvinia* might permanently hinder navigation and fishing on Lake Kariba, and might damage the turbines of the power station built underground next to the dam. At the Gebel Auliya dam, built in the 1930s on the River Nile, *Eichhornia crassipes* has continually to be controlled to prevent its spread into irrigation ditches below the dam. It is very bulky and would rapidly block the water flow in them. Masses of the South American *Eichhornia*, originally introduced as business gifts to Louisiana farmers (it has beautiful flowers), now clog canals in the southern USA. Their control, to which an entire scientific journal is devoted, costs large sums.

Fortunately *Salvinia* declined in Lake Kariba in the mid-1960s, as the initial burst of nutrients was flushed out. Its growth is now limited by the availability of nitrogen and it covers less than 10% of the lake, mainly in sheltered inlets. Wind disturbance may, in any case, have prevented its covering the entire lake and it is fortunate that plans to spray it with arsenate, and thus contaminate the lake, were abandoned. It now provides an extra habitat for wildlife, particularly wading birds, such as the jacana, which wander over it.

Serious aquatic weed problems arise from availability of a fast-growing, usually exotic species, lacking its natural competitors, and a copious nutrient supply. Because aquatic plants frequently reproduce rapidly by vegetative means, problems caused by introductions may be very severe. Apart from the water hyacinth, the spiked water milfoil, *Myriophyllum spicatum*, a native of Europe, has caused clogging of ditches and littoral zones in the USA, the pond weeds *Elodea* and *Egregia* have caused similar problems in the reverse direction. Currently Great Britain is facing an increasing problem

**Fig. 15.22** *Salvinia molesta* (top right) and *Eichhornia crassipes* (top left) have been notorious in causing problems in warm water lakes and reservoirs where they have been introduced. *Salvinia* covered nearly a quarter of the area of Lake Kariba (lower left) within a few years of closure of the dam in 1958, but, with declining nutrients as the initial flush of decomposition was washed through, is no longer a problem and the littoral zone is now varied (lower right).

from the introduction, long ago, of the Australian swamp stonecrop, *Crassula helmsii*.

### 15.8.3 Fisheries in new lakes

The filling of a man-made lake creates an extended period of rising river level for the original river fish fauna (Chapter 9), and not surprisingly most of the river species flourish initially. Production in the early, nutrient-rich phase may be very high. As the lake level stabilizes some of these fish become confined to the river mouths, if they need flowing water for spawning. In Lake Volta the mormyrids (elephant snout fish), which were important river species, are examples. In contrast, species which feed on submerged plants,

detritus and periphyton, such as *Sarotherodon galilaeus*, *Tilapia zillii* and *Oreochromis niloticus*, have much increased their proportion of the total fish population in the new Lake Volta.

Some niches in the lake may be unoccupied because there are no appropriate species to exploit new food sources. No zooplanktivore was present in Lake Kariba until *Limnothrissa miodon* and *Stolothrissa tanganyicae* were introduced from Lake Tanganyika in 1965. These introductions might be seen as unwise especially in view of the initial problems caused by *Salvinia molesta* but seem not to have been retrograde. The fish are eminently suitable for a commercial fishery and were introduced to a relatively depauperate local fish fauna (28 species). The original riverine habitat was subject to severe draw downs that undoubtedly favoured rather generalist fish. As far as is known none of these have been greatly affected by the sardine introductions and most grow better than they did in the river.

The early high fish production of new lakes has been supported by high production of invertebrates in the littoral zone, where many of the original trees may remain, dead but standing, for several years. The submerged branches became covered with abundant periphyton, stimulated by the high nutrient levels, which in turn supported grazing invertebrates. Notable among these in Lake Kariba and Lake Volta was a mayfly, *Povilla adusta*. Its larvae burrowed into the bark and rotting wood of the softwood trees flooded in the southern part of Lake Volta, and took advantage of holes bored by beetles (*Xyloborus torquatus*) in the hardwood trees around Lake Kariba.

About a fifth of the future basin of Lake Kariba was cleared mechanically of trees and bushes before inundation, and the debris burned. This was to create areas free of snags for the nets of a future fishing industry. At Lake Volta there was no clearance, because of cost and because it was thought that the softwood vegetation would soon rot down. Artisan fishermen in Lake Kariba have found it most profitable to fish where submerged trees still remain because fish production is apparently higher there. The submerged trees are an ephemeral habitat, however, which must eventually disappear under the action of wood borers, bacteria and water movement. The production they foster is a vestige of the initial productivity surge, which gives way, after a few years, to a less productive, relatively stable ecosystem.

The experiments unwittingly carried out in the creation of a new lake are of great significance. According to long-held ideas on lake fertility, the initially fertile water should have remained highly productive and gradually increased in fertility, as nutrients from the catchment area were presumed to accumulate in the basin. The fact that these lakes became less fertile as an initial supply of nutrients was washed out or fixed in sediments is further evidence that most lakes do not maintain their fertility unless an external loading of nutrients is continually applied.

### 15.8.4 Effects downstream of the new lake

Once a new lake has filled, the total river flow below the dam may be about the same as it was before. If water is removed from the lake for irrigation, the flow may be lower at some times but greater at others – in the dry season when the irrigation network drains to the river. The seasonal pattern of flow is, in most cases, considerably changed with consequences for the lower river ecosystem.

First, the silt carried previously by the river is deposited in the lake, and the turbidity of the outflowing water is reduced. In the River Nile this silt fertilized the delta lands and provided a detrital food source for a valuable inshore sardine fishery in the Mediterranean Sea off the Nile delta. This fishery has declined greatly since the closure of the Aswan High Dam, which impounds Lake Nasser-Nubia, and agriculture on the delta now requires increased use of artificial fertilizers. The delta is also eroding back rapidly partly from lack of silt to feed it, partly from sea-level rise. The consequences for farmers are considerable not least because the soils are being infiltrated with sea water and progressively becoming uncultivable. The now regulated River Niger, below the Kainji Dam, no longer drains some of the downriver swamps at times essential for rice cultivation in them. Indeed the entire floodplain system below the dam (Chapters 9 and 10) is severely disrupted with flood regimes often bearing little resemblance to the natural cycles on which the system depends.

### 15.8.5 New tropical lakes and human populations

The creation of new lakes in the tropics has led to some new human problems and intensified some pre-existing ones. River valleys in the tropics are relatively densely populated and the new lakes have displaced as many as 50,000 people (Kariba), 42,000 (Kainji), 80,000 (Volta) and 120,000 (Nasser-Nubia). It is estimated that some 40 million people all told have been displaced by dam building, a million by the Three Gorges Dam in China alone. Although the moving of the villages to be flooded is planned in advance, the modification of a culture closely geared to the seasonal flooding and shrinking of the river, and the fishing and farming opportunities presented by this, is no easy matter. During the period after such moves there was increased mortality, not all of it attributable to infectious disease, but linked with the stress involved with a major change in lifestyle. Water-borne diseases were, of course, features of the rivers before inundation. But the increased shoreline of the lakes and particularly the networks of irrigation channels which are associated with some, for example, Lake Nasser-Nubia, have exacerbated locally what is a widespread and serious problem of malaria and schistosomiasis.

## 15.8.6 Man-made tropical lakes, the balance of pros and cons

The larger projects have attracted much criticism, and scepticism that their overall costs would exceed the benefits they would confer. Some of this, based on the early 'problem' period after formation of the lake, has not been borne out once the lake has reached some sort of equilibrium. Other criticism has been well founded, particularly that concerned with the problems of people displaced from their traditional homelands. There is often a general insensitivity on the part of governments to real human needs. Dams are usually justified on a balance of the costs of building against the commercial benefits. Properly constructed analyses should include also the social, environmental and health costs. Frequently these are 'paid' by the local rural populations whilst the benefits accrue to multinational companies gaining cheap electricity in return for capital invested in the dam, and to urban elites in the country concerned.

The Volta scheme, for example, could provide abundant cheap electrical power for Ghana. Its effects have been felt only in a minor way, however, for the loans of about US $170 million necessary to build the dam in the 1960s are yet being paid off, and the non-Ghanaian Kaiser Aluminium, a company which financed the associated aluminium smelter and which uses much of the generated power, will enjoy a pre-agreed low cost for its power for several decades. Nonetheless, Tema, where the smelter is situated, has established some new industry to supplement the national income and to reduce dependence on imported goods. It was expected that the annual fish harvest would be 20,000 t but this was pessimistic for catches ran for some years at 40,000 t yr$^{-1}$ after the peak of 60,000 t yr$^{-1}$ in the late 1960s. It was 28,000 t yr$^{-1}$ in 1998, suggesting overfishing but recent data are not available. At first the catch compensated for the reduced imports of beef protein from countries to the north affected by the Sahelian drought, but fish prices have now risen, most of the fish are exported and the local populations benefit much less.

In the long-term, the costs of the Volta scheme should decrease as the industrial benefits flourish. For the moment the huge lake has disrupted land communications, and water transport has yet to replace them. A planned irrigation scheme has not yet been constructed, but cultivation of the wet mud flats left on drawdown of the water level allows cropping of maize, tomatoes, cow peas, and sweet potatoes at times when lack of rain prevents growth elsewhere in the country. Schistosomiasis has certainly increased, and it is yet difficult to justify a case that the dam has been beneficial to the people of Ghana as a whole.

The Aswan High Dam in Egypt has provoked the greatest controversy and its advantages and disadvantages are on a large scale. It has provided a constant supply of energy that has allowed industrial development, and also supplies annually an extra $19 \times 10^9$ m$^3$ of irrigation water for crops in a country otherwise only 3% cultivable. The Aswan scheme has increased cultivation in the valley by a factor of 1.6, though the richer delta farmland now seems doomed. Early fears that the lake would result in a net loss of water by seepage and evaporation have not been borne out.

The drawbacks of Aswan are more serious than those of the Volta, which may largely be those of delays in being able to take advantage of the opportunities offered. Egypt is arid and the evaporation of irrigation water is leading to increased soil salinity, which could threaten yields. Lake Nasser produces 10,000–13,000 t of fish annually, but the detritus carried to the sea by the unimpeded Nile supported a sardine fishery of 15,000 t yr$^{-1}$. The sardine fishing has declined completely, and the lake fish must be transported long distances to the centres of population near the coast. The fishery balance is certainly negative. Then there are the problems of the Nile delta and the need for artificial (and expensive) fertilizers to replace the once free silt.

Big dams are often heralded as triumphs of engineering. They may be anything but. A recent account from an engineering viewpoint notes the progressive loss of capacity through sediment accumulation behind the dam, the onset of coastal erosion as sediment is denied to the river and the local coastline, erosion of the downstream channel and bank collapse, increased flood risk due to alterations in the natural flooding regime and risks of failure due to ageing of the materials used to build the dam. As much land is taken out of production each year through salinization as is brought under irrigated cultivation; many dams are unsafe due

**Table 15.3** Impacts of dams on river systems and possible ways of mitigating such impacts.

| General impact | Specific effects | Mitigation |
|---|---|---|
| Flow regime | Seasonal differences evened out. Too little flow. No flood pulse. Abrupt changes in flow downstream as water is released to increase power generation. Sometimes virtually no downstream flow in dry periods | Agreement on minimum flows and seasonality of flow. Intentions to mimic natural pattern as greatly as possible. Phased changes in flow regime to allow downstream communities to adjust |
| Temperature regime | Outflow water warmer in winter, cooler in summer. May be very cold if hypolimnion water released. Abrupt changes in temperature if water suddenly discharged from different levels | Mixing of reservoir water by aerators or pumps. Release only of surface water |
| Water chemistry | Some ions reduced. Conductivity tends to increase through evaporation in the reservoir. Hypolimnion water, if discharged may be low in oxygen, high in ammonia and reduced iron and manganese | Mixing of lake water by aerators. Release only of epilimnion water. Clearing of lake basin previous to flooding can minimize problems of deoxygenation and nutrient release |
| Sediment | Retained in dam. Downstream flow with low sediment may erode river bed and banks | Sedimentation of dam can be minimized by pre-dam smaller reservoirs that can be periodically dug out. Disturbance of bottom sediment close to dam and flushing out may help maintain downstream supplies |
| Phytoplankton | Increases in dam over upstream water. Outflow may contain large amounts of phytoplankton | Minimize nutrient supply to dam by pre-clearing and maintenance of natural vegetation in remaining catchment. Establishment of waste water treatment in urban catchments. |
| Plants | Major increases in dam, often of floating species. Littoral zone may not develop if water level changes are random. Plants may develop downstream because of reduced flows and higher nutrient levels derived from decomposition of former land vegetation within the dam | Initial large growths in dam will decline as nutrients decline. Meanwhile mechanical removal is superior to chemical treatment |
| Invertebrates | Community in downstream river tends to have more filter feeders (on phytoplankton) and fewer shredders. Irregular flow regime may leave communities dry or wash them away | More sensitive flow regime |
| Fish | Spawning and return runs of anadromous fish blocked. Irregular flow regime and lack of flood pulse upset spawning rhythms. Fishery in dam may be poor if lake fishes not present. Vulnerability to introduced species. Distant fisheries may be ruined for lack of supply of organic silt | More sensitive flow regime. Fish passes and ladders, hatcheries and road transport to deliver young fish to river below dam. Introduce suitable pelagic fish for lake fishery |
| Birds and mammals | Lack of flood pulse may upset migratory movements in and out of the flood plain | Negotiate a more sensitive regime of water release |
| People | Displacement to other, less favoured areas. Increase in stress and disease | Better planned transfers with food and financial compensation |
| Overall | Consider cost/benefit analysis in a much wider arena than usual. Include costs in loss of ecosystem services, costs to traditional peoples, costs of mitigation | More thorough appraisal of whether the scheme is truly beneficial to society as a whole |

to poor construction or human error in operating spillways; dams are associated with increasing local incidence of earthquakes. The power benefits and the food produced by irrigation usually go elsewhere than to the local population; the insensitive displacement, and, it is alleged, destruction of rural people and cultures cannot be regarded as a tolerable snag to the fuelling of international industrial markets but only as an outrage. Climatic changes and almost universal underestimation even of identifiable costs have made many projects economic banes rather than boons.

Nonetheless, despite the clearly documented problems of the past, schemes for damming of even greater scope have been prepared. The Grande Carajos scheme is intended to industrialize one-sixth of Brazil, with parts of it flooding up to a third of a million hectares of Indian land, displacing 50,000 people. And the Three Gorges Dam across the Yangtze River in China is 100 m high, 2 km long, consumed the equivalent of 44 Great Pyramids of material and displaced more than a million people. In the late 1990s, a World Commission on Dams was set up by the United Nations to investigate the benefits and disbenefits. It proposed a series of recommendations to maximize the former and minimize the latter, recognized that some dam schemes should never have been built, that the promises made for many were not fulfilled, that others have been highly beneficial. It proposed sensible systems for assessing proposed schemes. Alas, its findings, rejected by major dam-building countries such as China and India, were not formally adopted by major funding agencies such as the World Bank, and appear to have been almost completely ignored. Table 15.3 shows a summary of problems caused by dams and measures that can be taken to mitigate them, for inevitably with a need for greater water storage in the face of climate change, dam building will continue apace.

## 15.9 AMENITY AND CONSERVATION

Big deep lakes have their own, special values. There is the attraction of diverse fish faunas and endemic species, such as the Baikal seal, the long vistas to distant mountains, and the delights of boat journeys along the coastline. Who cannot be inspired by the nocturnal escape by row boat of Ernest Hemingway's Lieutenant Henry and his lover, Catherine Barkley, across Lago Maggiore, from war-torn Italy to neutral Switzerland for the birth of their baby (*A Farewell to Arms*, 1929) or

John Hillaby's 1000 mile trek to Lake Turkana (*Journey to the Jade Sea*, 1964)? William Wordsworth, Henry Thoreau and countless other writers and artists have been inspired by lakes. Wildlife holidays, cruising, sight-seeing and SCUBA diving all are now part of a tourist industry based on large lakes. But, like the floodplain systems described in Chapter 9, with which they merge and from which they differ little, it is the shallow standing water systems that contribute hugely to freshwater biodiversity and for which conservation issues are most pressing. Mires, shallow lakes and ponds are particularly threatened, by drainage, eutrophication and introduced species. They cover a much larger area than the big, charismatic lakes, and they are vulnerable because they often share the lowlands with large human populations that have traditionally exploited them or who now need the fertile soils that their drainage might produce.

Table 15.4 lists some of the world's major temperate mire areas, their particularly valuable features and the threats to them. Increasingly, parallel threats are now occurring in the tropics. Notable is the frequent threat of water withdrawal and drainage, and then conversion to agricultural land. It is the same threat as happens to floodplain wetlands. What is not mentioned, though it may be increasingly important, is the damage that nitrogen oxides from vehicles, rained down as nitrate may also do to mire communities whose diversity rests on parsimony of nutrients. Increased nitrogen loading favours vigorous, large competitive species that crowd out smaller ones. In the traditional management of fens in Europe, the removal of hay, and of grazing animals as meat, helped maintain low nitrogen levels and high diversity, but the reduction in traditional usage coupled with the increased nitrogen load in the rain means that many of them are losing diversity and being taken over by rank grasses, nettles and willows.

Nutrients are also one key to changes in shallow lakes. The natural condition of most shallow waters is to be dominated by diverse littoral communities, the exception being those Boreal and other peatland lakes where brown organic substances stain the water and reduce light penetration. Many shallow lakes, however, are now devoid of aquatic plants and dominated by phytoplankton or suspended sediment or their levels of brown substances have increased in recent decades. In the first instance it is widely believed that this is a eutrophication problem; in the second that it results from a change in balance of the fish

**Table 15.4** Some major world mire systems, with particular characteristics and current threats from human activities.

| Region | Location | Nature | Particular characteristics | Threats |
|---|---|---|---|---|
| North and South America | Central California marshes and vernal pools | Arid landscape with depressions with pools and mires | Many endemic species | Water diversion, drainage |
| | Alpine meadows of the Rocky and Sierra Mountains | Wet high grasslands, strong connections with native forests | Endemic species | Timber harvest, ski runs |
| | Nebraska prairie potholes | Part of a large complex of glacial pothole lakes located on bird migration pathways | Waterfowl wintering and breeding | Groundwater withdrawal, conversion to agriculture and rangeland |
| | Depressional wetlands and seeps of New England and south-east Canada | Generally wet area with large variety of bogs, marshes and fens | Amphibian breeding | Urban development |
| | Marginal marshes of the St Laurence Great lakes | Extensive fringes to the big lakes, lagoons and embayments | Waterfowl and fish habitat | Shoreline development, industrial contamination, invasive species |
| | Wet pine savannahs of the south-eastern coastal plain | Pond pine and sweet bay wet savannahs, controlled by fire with rich bird and plant communities, reptiles and amphibians. Insectivorous plants. Still occasional black bears | Fire-dependent plants, endangered species | Suppression of fire. Conversion to agriculture and forest plantation |
| | Puna lakes and peatlands | High Andean plateau in Peru | High altitude waterfowl and flamingos. Water storage | Overgrazing, mining contamination |
| | Ibera marshes and Pantanal | Argentina and Brazil. Extensive, rich in wildlife (storks, jacare, capybara, jaguar) | High biodiversity | Partial drainage for agriculture. Large dams |
| | Swamps and swamp forest of the wet Chaco | Brazil and Paraguay. Open wet savannah with palm and quebracho trees (used for tannin extraction) | Water storage, high biodiversity | Cattle grazing, fire |
| | Humid meadows of Patagonia | Argentina & Chile. Previously glaciated flat plains with many wet depressions. Some areas quite arid with saline basins | Wildlife habitat, water storage | Cattle overgrazing, water withdrawal |
| | Peatlands of the Magellanic complex and Tierra del Fuego | Ombrotrophic, extensive Sphagnum peatlands | Water storage | Drainage, peat and placer (sand deposits with precious metals) mining, overgrazing, forestry |

| Region | Wetland | Description | Features/values | Threats |
|---|---|---|---|---|
| Eurasia | Scandinavian peninsula wetlands | Extensive boreal forested and tundra wetlands | Shallow lakes, wildlife and fish | Acid deposition, agriculture and hydropower generation |
| | Norfolk and Suffolk Broads | Ancient (13th Century) man-made lakes in floodplain system. Small system but highly valued in UK | High diversity, long historic use | Drainage, agriculture, eutrophication, salt water intrusion, recreational damage |
| | Danube Delta | Bordering the Black Sea in Roumania. Very extensive and on bird migration routes | Reedbeds, canals, bird habitat | Impoundments and levees, industrial and agricultural pollution |
| | Baltic Sea wetlands | Finland, Latvia, Estonia, Sweden. Previously glaciated region still emerging after glaciation | Extensive, diverse, birds and fish | Drainage for agriculture, peat mining, oil shale mining |
| | Neusiedlersee | Austria/Hungary. Large shallow lake, partly in arid area with high salinities. Huge beds of reed | Migratory waterfowl, rare plants | Drainage and agricultural eutrophication. Pumping groundwater |
| | Guadiana high basin (Tablas de Daimiel) | Spain. High plateau water collecting areas of the river | Birds, water conservation | Pumping of ground water for agriculture |
| | Camargue, Rhone Delta | France. Part freshwater, part salt marsh and lagoon with brine pools | Waterfowl, wild bulls and horses. Allegedly ferocious mosquitoes | Rice cultivation |
| | Middle eastern wadis, Azraq Oasis, Jordan | Azraq is set in the middle of the desert as a wetland of marshes and pools, fed by wadis and ground water | Birds | Water diversion for agriculture. Large dams |
| | Southern Siberian lowlands | Russia and Kazakhstan. Extensive forested wetlands with largely intact ecosystems in many areas | Waterfowl | Forestry, mining, oil and gas |
| | Blanket bogs of Scotland, Ireland and English Pennines | Formed about 3000 years ago in climatic wet phase helped by deforestation for grazing. Thick peat deposits. Ombrotrophic | Carbon storage, long history of traditional use. Grouse shooting | Industrial pollution (metals, acidification in England), burning for grouse habitat, drainage, peat mining for power generation in Ireland |
| | Three rivers plain (Sanjiang) | Far east Russia, north-east China. One of the biggest Chinese mires. Cranes, whooper swans, white storks | Cranes, waterfowl, traditional reed production | Poaching, wildlife trafficking, water diversion, conversion to agriculture and forestry |
| | Yangtze and Chaingjiang Valleys | China | Chinese alligator, waterfowl | Multiple human activities |
| Oceania | Eastern Hokkaido Marshes | Very varied ombrotrophic and minerotrophic mires in Northern Japan. Volcanic area | Waterfowl and waders, salmon fishery | Channelization, sedimentation, loss of traditional use and spread of willows |
| | Murray-Darling system | Major river system of Australia. Numerous lakes and mires on the floodplains | Closed and open forested wetlands, fish birds and marsupials | Overgrazing, diversion of water, salinization, introduced species, dams |
| | Alpine and subalpine Bogong High Plains | Australia. Great Dividing range. Alpine area with peat forming vegetation | Endemics | Cattle grazing and trampling |
| | Wakaia Ecological region | New Zealand. Tussocky upland wetlands | Indigenous vegetation | Overgrazing |

community towards benthic fish that disturb the bottom in feeding; and in the third either from changing climate or chemical changes in rainfall consequent on reduction of sulphate in solution of the acid precipitation problem. In this latter case, conditions may simply be returning to those of a previous less polluted era, but in the former two, we are dealing with continuing severe effects of human activities, and the two are related.

Increasing nutrient loading will be resisted by littoral communities by the buffer mechanisms discussed in Chapter 12. More nutrients will promote better plant growth, greater provision of refuges for grazers and denser plant beds. It will change the community of plants, with competitive, vigorous species taking over as they do in fens (see above) and with floating species growing more vigorously, but there is little evidence that nutrient increase alone will cause the loss of plants in cool lakes. In warm-water lakes, where zooplankton grazing is suppressed by intense fish predation, it is common to find a coexistence between quite large phytoplankton populations and aquatic plants that can cope with the reduced light conditions through a year-round growth season, and life forms that keep them towards or at the surface. In cool lakes, however, there tends to be either a community of plants and clear water, or few plants and water turbid from phytoplankton or suspended sediment.

Where phytoplankton has taken over, and plants have disappeared, the buffer mechanisms have been disrupted. Plants may have been excessively cut or treated with herbicides. Vertebrate grazers, either native, such as ducks and mute swans, may have been multiplied by artificial feeding to damaging levels, or aliens such as Canada geese may have been introduced. Stocking of common carp is frequently associated with loss of plants and there are numerous instances of loss of plants coinciding with introduction of alien crayfish. The activities of invertebrate grazers on phytoplankton and periphyton can also be impeded by pesticide residues, rising salinity or some of the huge range of trace organic substances that are released in wastewater effluents. Frequent coincidence of loss of plants with rises in amounts of wastewater effluent are usually attributed to the nutrients in the effluent, but this may not be the reason.

Nutrients are involved, however. The higher the nutrient loading, the greater the potential for phytoplankton and periphyton growth, and the harder the invertebrate grazers have to work to counteract this, so that any temporary reduction in their populations, owing to a particularly good forage fish recruitment in a warm year for example, may cause the buffer mechanisms to fail and a switch to phytoplankton dominance to occur. Higher nitrogen loads also result in a loss of plant diversity. Diversity gives an insurance policy to the plant community stability. In a mixed community, damage to one species, by chance overgrazing by birds in a cool spring when growth is slow, for example, can be compensated for by growth of others. In a simple community, such damage may not be compensated for and a switch might occur.

Once the plants have disappeared, or their growth seriously reduced, the stability of the newly established phytoplankton may be ensured by a replacement set of buffer mechanisms. The phytoplankton begins growth earlier in the year, is more efficient at uptake of nutrients from the water, and provides no refuge for its own grazers, particularly the large daphnids, against fish predation. Filamentous algae sometimes substitute for the phytoplankton and may inhibit the growth of seedlings or the expansion of aquatic plant turions on the bottom. The sediment produced under algal communities is less structured, more amorphous, and may also overwhelm the plant propagules. Loss of plants means also loss of a mechanism that promotes rapid sedimentation of mud and thus material, stirred by fish such as carp and bream feeding in the bottom, remains suspended, especially in large, windy lakes. If, as is usually the case, nutrient increase has accompanied the various other mechanisms that destroy the plants or their buffers, there will have been increased production and greater night-time deoxygenation, so that piscivorous fish will have declined, leaving greater stocks of zooplanktivorous fish to prevent much zooplankton grazing of the algae. A syndrome thus sets in that keeps the lake turbid with reduced diversity. Loss of plants will mean loss of visiting birds and mammals associated with the plants. The only positive effects might be to human communities using the lake for activities such as competitive sailing. Yachtsmen do not like plants.

Ponds are obviously important in rural economies in the tropics for fish culture and stock watering (see above). They are usually man-made, though many are natural and in the developed world also were dug with a distinct function in mind, as listed in Chapter 11. Often these functions have become redundant but ponds still have a role in conservation and in the appearance of the landscape. There is no formal definition of a pond, but they are usually small (<2 ha), shallow and potentially completely littoral in nature. They need not necessarily be permanent. There are plenty of invertebrates that thrive in temporary waters and some are unusual and of great interest. Though each pond represents only a small part of the landscape, the tendency for them to occur in clusters, linked formerly by only lightly used land, created a distinctive 'patch' ecology, particularly valuable for amphibians. Many ponds, being isolated, are fishless and amphibian tadpoles do not easily coexist with predatory fish.

The number of ponds present in the 19th century in the UK has now been more than halved and at present rates of loss, there will soon be few left. The reason is partly that they have been filled-in because farming practices have become more intensive, and cattle grazing has been replaced by arable cultivation. Partly it is because stock are now watered through pipelines to drinking troughs and the ponds have not been maintained. With time they inevitably silt up. The distribution of newts and frogs in the UK closely echoes the distribution of ponds and their loss is one of the reasons for declining amphibian populations. Paradoxically, voluntary conservation bodies may also be something of a problem for existing ponds. They lend themselves to 'management', which amounts to a sort of gardening. Common myths are: that the bigger the better; ponds should not be shaded by trees; ponds need to be dredged to keep them from being choked by vegetation but must have 'oxygenating' plants; new ponds need to be planted because natural colonization is slow; water level fluctuations should be minimized; livestock should be denied access; there should be an inflow to prevent them becoming stagnant and that ponds are self-contained islands in a sea of dry land. Conservation of biodiversity benefits from having a range of sorts of ponds, and so long as noxious water, for example from stockyards, and other pollutants and invasive species are kept out, ponds are best left to develop their own characteristics.

## 15.10 RESTORATION APPROACHES FOR STANDING WATERS: SYMPTOM TREATMENT

As with river and floodplain restoration, there is a similar range of approaches to mitigate the damage done to standing water systems. They range from management and treatment of symptoms to more fundamental approaches of nutrient control and, when all else fails, to creation of new habitats, usually ponds. The creation of new large reservoirs might also sometimes be seen in this light.

Problems with fisheries are often dealt with at the symptom level. Overfishing can be controlled by enforcement of proper regulations and by creation of reserved areas where fishing is banned to allow reproduction to take place unhindered. In recreational fisheries, stocking from hatcheries is very common. It is ultimately futile but nonetheless temporarily alleviates the problem. Management of recreational fisheries is often targeted at single, prized species and not at the condition of the ecosystem as a whole. Fishermen want many, large, hungry specimens to catch and these are mutually incompatible requirements on any sustained basis.

For water supply and storage, especially in the face of eutrophication, many problems are solved by technologies of filtration and chemical treatment at the waterworks. Flocculation with aluminium salts, sand filtration, chlorination, passage through activated charcoal and ultraviolet treatment can easily convert a turbid, smelly water rich in pathogens to a clear sparkling product, but costs can be reduced by a degree of lake or reservoir management. It is still not unknown for algicides, both copper based and organic, to be used to curb the symptoms of large algal growths and for aluminium hydroxide or ferrous sulphate to be used to precipitate phosphorus and algae from the water. More subtle is to use mixing devices or aerators to favour diatoms and green algae over the cyanobacteria, which, being gelatinous, are often slow to filter and have the risk of toxins. In New Zealand in particular, a gelatinous diatom, *Didymosphaenia geminata* has recently started to grow abundantly on rocks in rivers and at lake edges, giving a somewhat unaesthetic appearance, referred to as rock snot, though control methods have not yet been developed.

Reservoirs pose particular problems for amenity and conservation values. Their general lack of a littoral zone, when the water level usually fluctuates irregularly, means that they will lack many of the features that natural lakes have. It is often difficult to negotiate environmentally sensitive management regimes with hydroelectric and irrigation companies who see their commercial activities as paramount, but proper evaluation of the economic losses of ecosystem services lost in the downstream floodplain in the future may change this position as compensation rights will become important. A sensitive regime (see Table 15.3) is one that mimics the natural pattern as far as possible and that therefore has a degree of predictability for the lake community. In such circumstances, species selection will produce a shoreline community of some interest and value, instead of the sterile ugly fringes of reservoirs managed without consideration for other water users.

In shallow lakes, the problem of loss of aquatic plants has recently been cleverly tackled by a technique called biomanipulation. Piscivorous fish are stocked, or zooplanktivorous fish and benthic feeders are removed to reduce their stocks from say $20 \text{ g m}^{-2}$ to $1–2 \text{ g m}^{-2}$. Stocking of piscivorous fish had previously been used in German reservoirs quite successfully but rather expensively, for continued restocking was necessary, and piscivores are expensive to rear in hatcheries. The effect is to encourage the growth of zooplankton, particularly the efficiently feeding large daphnids, which can clear the water quite rapidly. Sometimes, on large lakes, the zooplanktivorous fish can be removed through a commercial fishery, an instance of deliberate overfishing. In ideal cases, after the water clears, aquatic plants, perhaps following reintroduction, begin to establish and re-create the stabilizing mechanisms that ensure their persistence. In theory, biomanipulation should be successful without any control of nutrients (see below) but in practice, nutrient control always helps because it reduces the risk of a new switch flipping the system back to algal dominance. It is of course necessary to remove any existing or potential switch mechanism before biomanipulation will work. It is no good removing the effects of predation if pesticides prevent the redevelopment of *Daphnia* or herbicides the growth of plants.

There are now numerous instances of the use of biomanipulation since it was suggested by Jurgen Benndorf (1992) and Joseph Shapiro in the 1970s. When it fails it is usually because insufficient fish have been removed or because the algal population, perhaps dominated by large cyanobacteria, is inedible to the developing zooplankton. Timing may be important. *Daphnia* can often control small, early spring populations of cyanobacteria, but not the massed numbers of mid-summer. It is usually impossible to remove all the fish and in warm lakes the populations may re-grow so rapidly that there are only transient effects.

Sometimes spectacular improvements can be short-lived because the scheme is too small. A classic instance is Zwemlust in The Netherlands.

Zwemlust is a small isolated lake, a remnant of the floodplain system of the River Vecht, used for the past 76 years for swimming. It was full of aquatic plants in the 1960s. These were disparaged so the lake was treated with herbicide and very soon was equally full of the cyanobacterium. *Microcystis*. The turbidity was such that the swimmers could not see their feet in 1.5 m of water, a situation that fell foul of health and safety regulations in the 1970s. The water had to be cleared. The lake could be drained down and the fish were removed and replaced with a much smaller stock of rudd, with the intention of controlling snails that harboured a trematode parasite causing irritation to the swimmers' skins. After the lake refilled, zooplankton developed abundantly, the water cleared and large growths of a few species of aquatic plants, particularly *Elodea*, appeared. For a few years they remained, but eventually, because the lake was small and isolated, they attracted in large numbers of coot, which, together with the rising numbers of rudd, grazed them so severely that the lake switched back to algal dominance. It has since been biomanipulated again and zebra mussels are being used to clarify the water.

Zwemlust was a very important example in improving our understanding of the processes. Where bigger schemes have been carried out they have had more permanent success, though recovery of the fish stocks means repeated biomanipulation every few years. One spectacular scheme was at Lake Veluwe, also in The Netherlands, where extensive beds of charophytes slowly developed following flushing with low phosphate water and biomanipulation (Fig. 15.23). On balance, however, the results of biomanipulation have rarely been as good or long-lasting as hoped. One response to this has been to propose additional manipulations, for example the building of baffles or islands in large lakes to minimize wind mixing and reduce resuspension of bottom sediment or to use zebra mussels (though an introduced species outside the Black Sea area), as now at Zwemlust, to clarify the water. Zebra mussels graze cyanobacteria more effectively than *Daphnia*. Ultimately, however, it seems that results will always be unsatisfactory without nutrient control and indeed if nutrients are reduced enough, internal changes in the fish community will render biomanipulation unnecessary (see below).

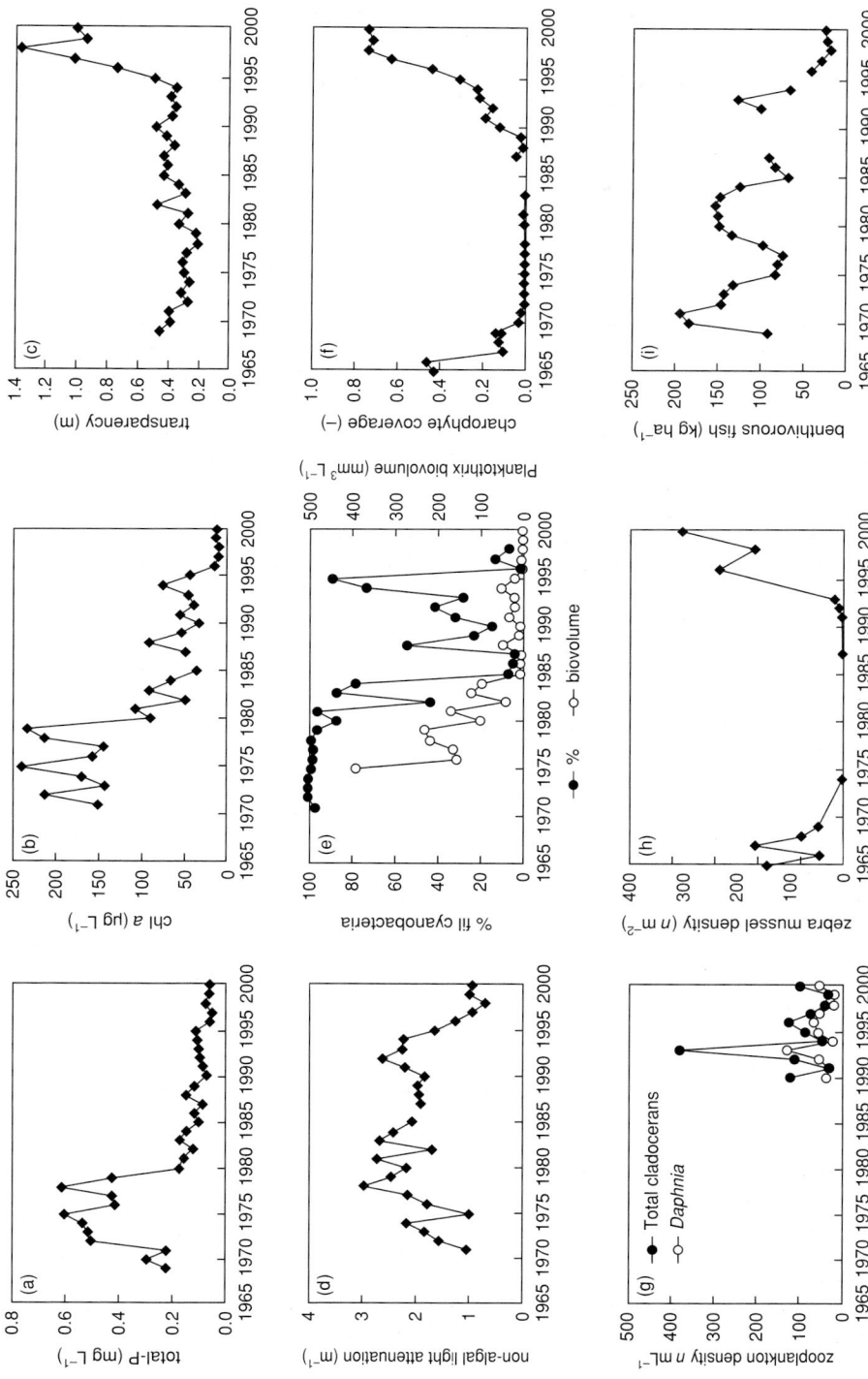

**Fig. 15.23** Changes in Lake Veluwe, The Netherlands. As in many damaged lakes, managers attempt all sorts of remedial work without the rigours of experimental controls so that it is often difficult to interpret what happened and why. Lake Veluwe offers a more straightforward case than many. Before 1970, the lake was reasonably clear with charophytes and introduced zebra mussels. It became eutrophicated in the 1970s and lost its plants. In 1980, lower phosphorus water was pumped into it from elsewhere. This reduced the algal populations, but did not restore clear water, for there was a great deal of sediment disturbance. The lake is large and windswept. There were no plants to secure the sediment and a large stock of bottom feeding fish, particularly bream, stirred it up. In 1990–91 a commercial fishery was used to reduce the fish stock and there was an eventual clearance of the water and return of charophytes and zebra mussels, which expanded their ranges and are maintaining the water in a clear state. (Based on Ibelings et al. 2007.)

## 15.11 TREATMENT OF PROXIMATE CAUSES: NUTRIENT CONTROL

Eutrophication problems are those of increased nutrient loading and although the symptoms can be treated temporarily, the ultimate need is to reduce the loading. The first steps are relatively easy, where point sources are involved but matters become difficult where the sources are diffuse. Some approaches were discussed in Chapter 8 for rivers and these of course apply to lakes also, for rivers supply lakes. But lakes illustrate the complications. There is first the question of which nutrient or nutrients should be removed. Greatly increased algal production usually needs increase in both nitrogen and phosphorus because even if phosphorus is currently limiting the potential crop, the nitrogen supply is generally not greatly in excess of algal need. To reduce the algal crop of a lake, however, should require reduction, if it is severe, in only one nutrient. An analogy might be drawn with motor cars, which require lubricating oil, fuel and coolant to keep them moving, but which stop if they run short of any one of these.

Phosphorus can be most readily controlled, nitrogen less easily. Its compounds are very soluble, they enter waterways from many diffuse sources (every field seep) and there is a potential but uncontrollable supply from the atmosphere through nitrogen-fixers. Phosphorus is readily precipitated, enters mostly from a relatively few 'point' sources – large stock units and wastewater treatment works – and has no atmospheric reserve. It is thus usual to attempt to control phosphorus. This may seem pointless if the limiting nutrient is nitrogen. However, in many cases nitrogen is limiting because phosphorus has been artificially increased to a greater extent, and phosphorus control will ultimately restore the former state. In other cases, where phosphorus has naturally accumulated and where nitrogen increase has driven eutrophication, it may be necessary to control nitrogen.

This will be difficult and, although there can be legislative provision for removal of nitrogen from sewage effluents, most control will have to come from changes in agricultural practice. The leaving of wide bands of natural vegetation (buffer zones) alongside the channels of inflowing streams can lead to some nitrate removal by plant uptake and denitrification. Constructed wetlands (Chapter 10) can also be effective. But ultimately changes from the present intensive farming practices will be necessary and these need to be far-reaching to be effective.

Where phosphorus control is the sensible option, the questions to be asked are: what are the present supplies of phosphorus and how do these contribute to the total in the water; how is the total P concentration related to the algal crop; what size of algal crop is tolerable in the restored lake; is it possible to achieve a low enough phosphorus concentration to achieve that crop; how shall it be done; and what will be the complications? Governments and regulatory authorities will never wish to do more than the minimum, because of the costs involved, so the answers to these questions are important. For conservation purposes, however, even the most stringent control will be far short of achieving the very low concentrations of the pristine state and management can never do enough.

### 15.11.1 Present supplies of phosphorus, their relative contributions and how they are related to the algal crop

Most sources of phosphorus are easy to identify though some may be cryptic. Survey of the catchment will reveal obvious ones but it may be expensive to measure them directly. An approximate budget may, however, be drawn up, as a desk-study, using export coefficients (Chapter 4). The calculated loadings from various sources can then be inserted in the Vollenweider equation (Chapter 4) to relate loading to mean concentration and therefore to calculate what the reduction in loading should be to attain a desired concentration in the lake. The problems of measuring true loading, let alone those of measuring the retention coefficient have meant that this approach has not been widely used, however.

The concentration of phosphorus in the lake can be related readily to the expected mean or maximum chlorophyll *a* concentrations from relationships obtained from a large number of lakes (Fig. 15.24). These relationships are used as a basis for planning the reduction in loading which will give a desired chlorophyll *a* concentration. What this target should be, however, is a problem not easily solved, for it concerns human perceptions. Some limnologists divide temperate lakes into trophic categories: ultra-oligotrophic, oligotrophic, mesotrophic, eutrophic, hypertrophic, which form a series of increasing fertility. Ultra-oligotrophic lakes

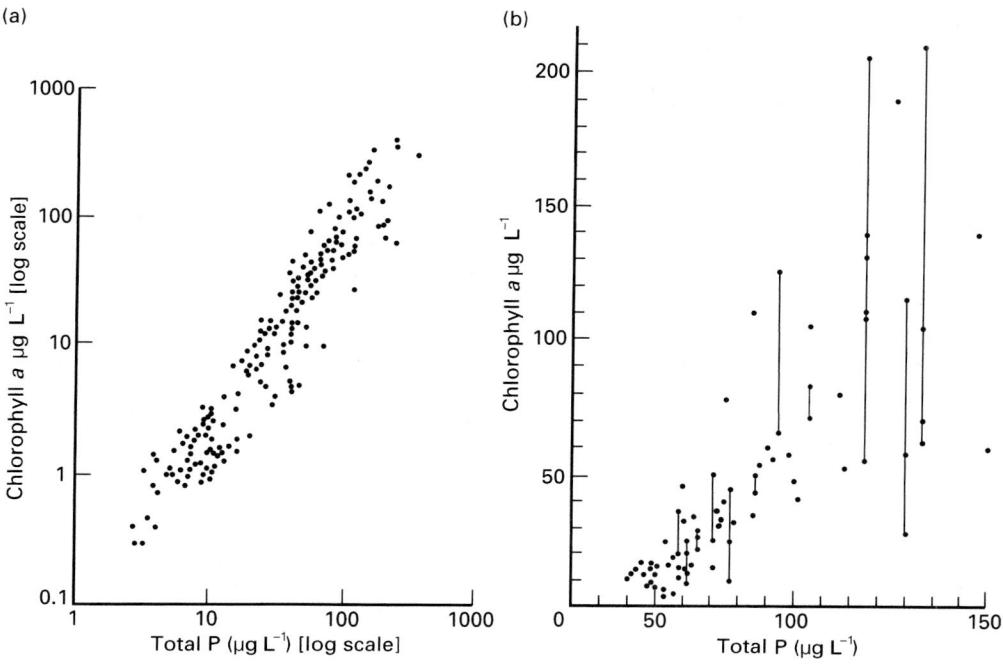

**Fig. 15.24** Relationship between summer chlorophyll *a* concentration and total phosphorus concentration in lakes, with data plotted (a) on log scales and (b) on linear scales. (Based on Shapiro 1980.)

have very clear water, little phytoplankton, hypolimnia saturated with oxygen and coregonid and salmonid fish; hypereutrophic lakes have turbid water, dense algal growths, anaerobic hypolimnia (if they are deep enough) and cyprinid fish. Defining the intermediate categories of such a multivariate continuum, however, is much more difficult and not really sensible. But lake restoration has political as well as scientific aspects, and politicians and administrators need definitions for the proscribing of law. A working party of the Organization for Economic Co-operation and Development therefore gathered views on the definitions of the above trophic categories in terms of phosphorus and chlorophyll *a* concentrations. It was then possible to decide modal chlorophyll *a* and total phosphorus concentrations for each trophic category and then to relate these (Fig. 15.25) to combinations of inflow phosphorus concentration and $T_w$, the water replacement time. The degree to which the inflow concentration needs to be reduced to achieve a particular target for chlorophyll concentration can then be estimated.

### 15.11.2 Methods available for reducing total phosphorus loads

The best methods are those that act at source. These include diversion of sewage effluent to the sea where it is diluted, and precipitation (stripping) of phosphorus from the effluent before it is discharged. Less fundamental or effective are the precipitation of phosphate by adding chemicals to the lake, aeration of the hypolimnion, or removal of phosphorus-containing biomass, though these are really symptom treatments.

Diversion of effluent is only possible where a lake lies near the sea because pipelines are expensive. The effluent should not itself constitute a large part of the water supply to the lake, or water residence times will be increased. Lake Washington (Fig. 15.26) is a well-known example of this method. Around the lake lie Seattle and its metropolitan suburbs. In 1955 a cyanobacterium, *Oscillatoria rubescens*, became prominent in the plankton, signalling a series of changes consequent on the progressive development of the area.

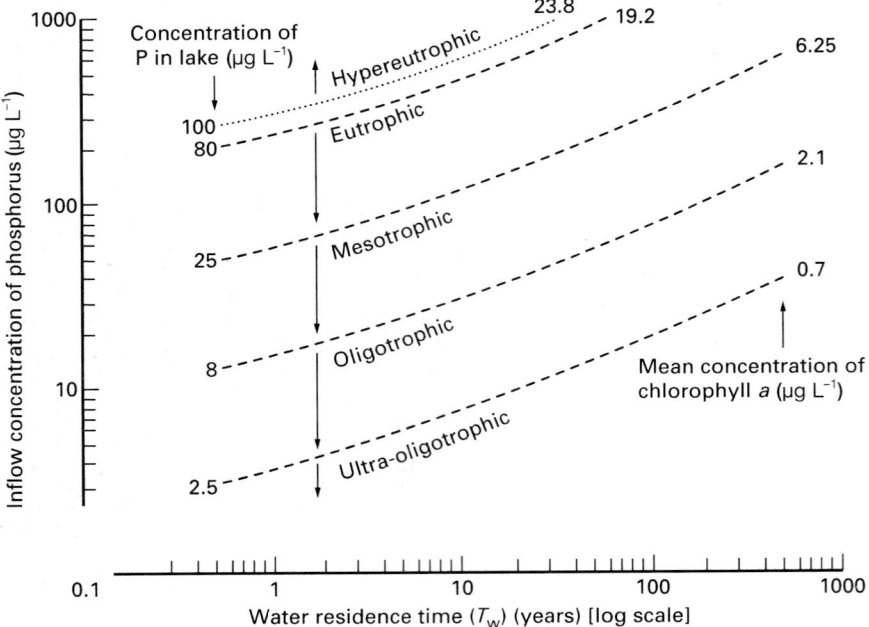

**Fig. 15.25** Relationships among inflow phosphorus concentration, water residence time and the consequent most likely phosphorus and chlorophyll $a$ concentrations in a given lake. The longer the residence time, the more it is likely that phosphorus will be deposited in the sediment so that lower in-lake phosphorus and chlorophyll $a$ concentrations will be obtained for a given inflow concentration. The terms 'hypereutrophic', etc., are placed arbitrarily on the basis of a consensus determined by the Organization for Economic Co-operation and Cultural Development. (Based on Vollenweider & Kerekes 1981.)

The lake was receiving sewage effluent (24,200 m³ per day) from about 70,000 people and the effluent was providing about 56% of the total P load to the lake. By 1967 almost all of the effluent had been piped to the ocean in Puget Sound. The transparency of the lake quickly increased from about 1 m to 3 m and chlorophyll $a$ concentrations decreased from 38 to about 5 µg L⁻¹. Since the early 1980s (Fig. 15.27) the lake improved even more. This was due to a resurgence in *Daphnia* populations as the quality of the phytoplankton changed away from dominance of cyanobacteria, and because a predator of the *Daphnia*, a mysid shrimp, *Neomysis mercedis* decreased. *Neomysis* decreased because a specialist fish predator on it, the long-fin smelt (*Spirinchus thaleichthys*) had increased, probably as a result of engineering operations extending its spawning habitat in streams entering the lake.

Diversion of effluent is not always practicable but all sewage treatment works can use phosphate stripping.

The effluent is run into a tank and dosed with precipitant. Aluminium salts work well but disposal of the precipitate in the works' sludge as farm fertilizer may be precluded because aluminium salts are poisonous. Iron salts are not and ferrous ammonium sulphate is frequently the precipitant chosen. The costs of the process are largely in chemicals rather than installations, and up to 95% of the phosphate can be easily removed, and more with greater difficulty. The USA and Canadian legislatures require that effluents discharged to the St Lawrence Great Lakes should contain less than 1 mg L⁻¹ of PO₄-P, compared with 10–20 mg L⁻¹ previously and similar standards have been adopted in Europe.

Results of phosphate stripping have not always been so dramatic as those of complete diversion for Lake Washington, but it is an effective approach. Even after the effluent has been dealt with, however, the lake water may still contain a substantial background

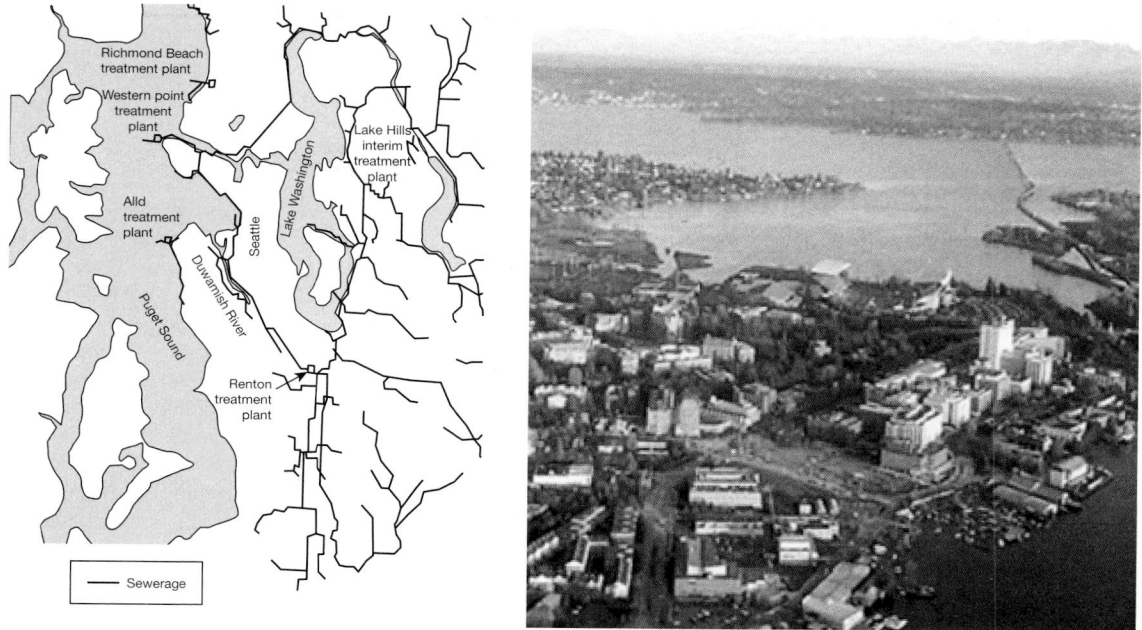

**Fig. 15.26** Map of Lake Washington and the sewer system designed to remove effluent away from the lake and discharge it to Puget Sound.

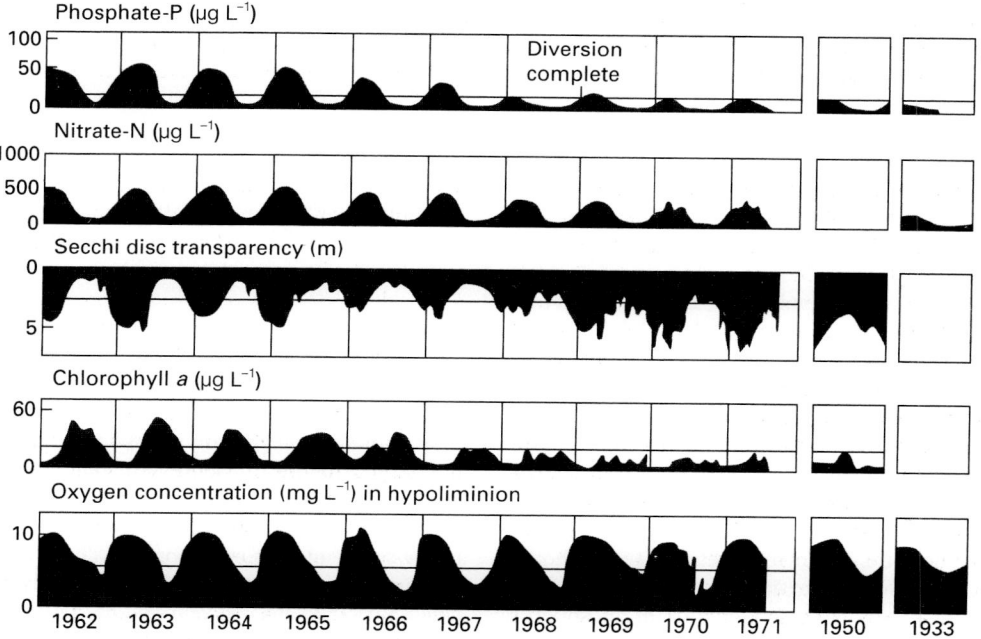

**Fig. 15.27** Changes in Lake Washington between 1962 and 1981. Data for two earlier years are placed at the right-hand side to suggest the possible end point of the changes. The lines are smoothed to emphasize long-term trends. (After Edmondson 1991.)

concentration from agricultural activities, and in lakes with a long water residence time it might take many years to obtain a marked improvement. Comparisons across a series of attempts suggest that sometimes 5–20 years may be needed for significant results because of internal release of phosphorus from the sediments. But during that period, a series of mutually helpful changes may take place. As the phosphorus is slowly reduced, production decreases and oxygen concentrations may rise. In turn, the piscivorous fish community may increase and eat more zooplanktivorous fish. In turn the zooplankton grazers will increase and the phytoplankton decrease, so that alongside the nutrient control, an internal, spontaneous biomanipulation may take place.

Reducing the amount of phosphorus reaching the sewage treatment works by concerted public campaigns can reduce the costs of stripping. Australia has been prominent in encouraging desirable practices. It emphasizes six main themes: wash vehicles on porous surfaces (e.g. lawns) away from drains and gutters; fertilize lawns and gardens sparingly; compost all garden and food waste; use zero or low phosphorus detergents; wash only full loads in washing machines; collect and bury pet faeces. Among these, the promotion of non-phosphate detergents (Chapter 8) is a contentious issue for a huge market is involved.

Even with phosphate-free detergents, the phosphate remaining in the effluent (from food excretion) would still need removal by precipitation. The costs of precipitation increase greatly as the concentration decreases, so that complete removal of detergent phosphate would not reduce the costs of stripping proportionately. Hence, why should we not continue to use *ad libitum* a substance whose properties are well known, for which the technology of removal is efficient, and which is acknowledged to be an ideal product? The problem is that not all sewage is treated in wastewater treatment works. Some is allowed to decompose in septic tanks, from which an effluent trickles. Often these are in remote areas where watercourses are of high quality and thus very vulnerable. And phosphorus stripping is not yet a widely used process in the treatment works of some countries, including the UK. In some remote areas, removal of detergent phosphorus might obviate the need to carry out stripping for a considerable time; and because reduction of phosphorus concentrations in lakes is proving more difficult than at first thought, any reduction must be deemed ultimately sensible.

### 15.11.3 In-lake methods

Once phosphorus is in the lake, three main methods have been used to remove it. The first is to treat the lake with a solution of aluminium or ferrous salt to precipitate the phosphate; the method may also coagulate particulate matter. Results may be immediately very good with a clarification of the water but ultimately negligible if the treatment is not repeated periodically so long as external inputs of phosphate continue.

A second method depends on the premise that entrainment of hypolimnion water contributes significant amounts of P to the epilimnion and involves hypolimnetic aeration. Air is bubbled into the hypolimnion in such a way that the hypolimnion is oxygenated without mixing its water with the surface waters during summer. This technique increases the volume of water available to fish but its use in reducing the phosphorus content of the lake in its productive upper layers is equivocal because little phosphorus may pass to the epilimnion in summer.

A third potential way of reducing the phosphorus content within the lake itself is to remove biomass that has accumulated in it. The problem is that, compared with the sediment, the biomass accumulates very little of the total load. Organisms such as fish, at the top end of the food web, accumulate only small quantities and smaller organisms such as invertebrates and algae, which accumulate more, are uneconomic to remove from the water. Removal of aquatic plants is easier but they are bulky and accumulate phosphorus mostly from the sediments whose reserves are very great. Substantial improvement in a lake must not be expected by biomass removal for several to many years, and only then if external supplies are also reduced.

### 15.11.4 Complications for phosphorus control – sediment sources

There are few cases where phosphorus control alone has been dramatically successful. One reason is that inevitably it has been tried on the most severe examples of lake eutrophication, where sources of phosphorus in the sediment may be important. The Swedish Lake Trummen, for example, had become highly eutrophicated by 1981 after 30 years of discharge of sewage effluent into it. It was accumulating 8 mm year$^{-1}$ of black, sulphurous mud and during ice cover in the winter its water column (2 m) became deoxygenated with consequent fish kills. The sewage effluent and some industrial discharges were diverted in 1958, but by 1968 the lake was still suffering high algal crops, low transparency, deoxygenation and fish kills. Much of the algal crop was being supported by phosphate released from the sediment. There was an internal load of 177 kg P $yr^{-1}$ compared with the external one which had been reduced to 3 kg P $yr^{-1}$.

In 1970 and 1972 surface sediment was sucked from the lake, settled in a lagoon and later disposed of as fertilizer, whilst the water, after treatment with aluminium salts, was run back to the lake. Following sediment removal, phosphorus concentrations decreased, the water cleared, and winter deoxygenation no longer occurred, though in recent years there has been some regression towards the former state. This suggests that the sediment was a major supplier of phosphorus. Further evidence for a major role of sediment sources comes from lakes where the nutrient content of the water has been greatly reduced by sediment sealing.

A technique called the Riplox process has been tried at Lake Lillesjon near Varnamo in Sweden. Diversion of sewage failed to restore the lake because of phosphate release from a sediment rich in P but not in Fe. The Riplox process injected concentrated solutions of calcium nitrate, ferric chloride and lime from a specially designed harrow into the sediment. The nitrate acted as a substrate for denitrifying bacteria, which oxidize organic matter in the sediment, thus creating conditions for the oxidized microzone to strengthen or re-form. The lime adjusted the pH to the optimum (7–7.5) for denitrification and the iron chloride precipitated phosphate. The transparency of the lake subsequently increased from 2.3 to 4.2 m; total phosphorus concentrations fell significantly. The treatment appears to have been successful but, perhaps for reasons of cost, has not been widely used elsewhere. It will only work in the longer term, of course, where external nutrient supplies are also reduced.

There are snags to any presumption that the removal or sealing of sediment will inevitably restore a lake from eutrophication where external phosphorus control has failed. Sediment is variable and complex. Generalizations about its behaviour are premature. Current understanding is: that most sediments will release phosphorus under both aerobic and anaerobic conditions to some extent, though to a much greater extent in the latter circumstances; that this release is unlikely to be important in a deep, well flushed lake

but significant in a deep, poorly flushed lake; and that it is likely to be a normal feature of even pristine very shallow lakes. Rarely is all the sediment removed and sealed sediment surfaces are soon buried by new sediment. Phosphorus may diffuse upwards to the sediment surface from remaining deeper layers and release may resume after a period of reduction. A clever idea to remove, progressively, the phosphorus stored in the sediments has been to siphon out hypolimnial water, loaded with phosphorus, into the outflow stream over a number of years. The water is replaced by inflow water that has had its phosphate content reduced.

### 15.11.5 Nitrogen reduction

In many mires and in some, perhaps many, lakes, nitrogen reduction may be a greater priority than phosphorus reduction. In the traditional management of fens, removal of hay accomplished this, but hay is no longer so widely used for feeding stock in the developed world. Much nitrogen comes to ombrotrophic mires through rain and there is no solution to this problem short of reduction in vehicle usage and intensive stock husbandry. Those are unlikely without major changes in lifestyles and come under the heading of ultimate solutions, discussed in the final Chapter 16. Where nitrogen comes in from the land, more can be done through subsidy and encouragement of less intensive cultivation and the use of buffer zones. There is yet, however, no really convincing evidence that these have made much difference, though they are widely touted.

The reasons are clear. First intensive arable cultivation is always leaky of the very soluble nitrate and as much as 25% of the applied fertilizer directly or indirectly is leached out, giving concentrations entering water courses from 5 to 10 mg $NO_3$-N $L^{-1}$. If the diversity of aquatic plants is a measure of effects of nitrogen (Fig. 15.28), maximum values for the year (those in winter) should be lower than 1 mg $L^{-1}$. This is still much higher than in pristine waters (Chapter 4), whose values are only a tenth of this. If a buffer zone is completely efficient at removing nitrogen, to reduce concentrations from a catchment of 5–10 mg $L^{-1}$ to 1 mg $L^{-1}$ will take a land area of 80–90% of the catchment. Similar calculations pertain to diffuse phosphorus sources because although the percentage reduction in concentration needs to

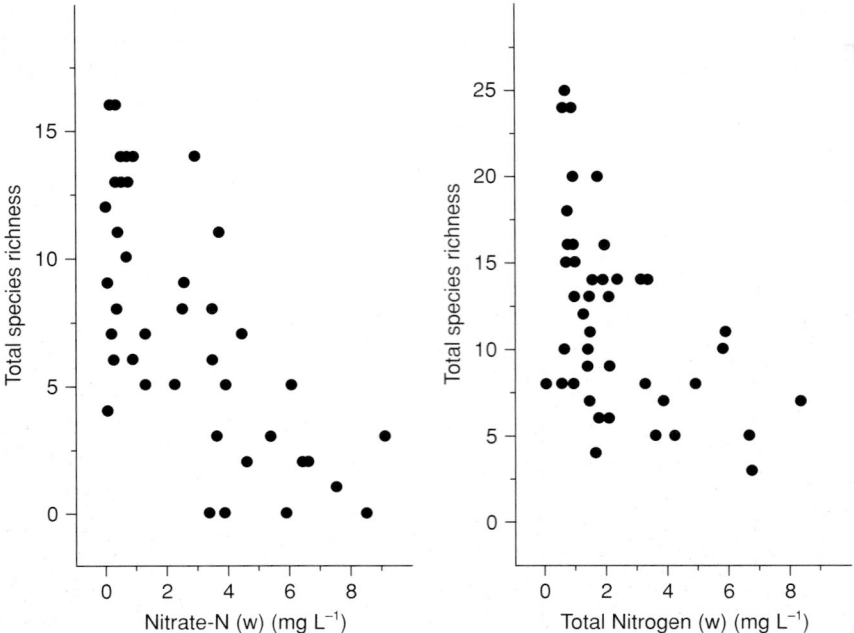

**Fig. 15.28** Nitrogen may be a limiting nutrient but it may also control the species richness of aquatic systems. Maximal nitrate or total nitrogen concentrations are found in winter or the wet season. Here winter concentrations for a series of shallow lakes in the UK and Poland have been plotted against submerged, floating and floating-leaved plant species richness. The greatest richness is found at the lowest nitrogen concentrations, below about 1–2 mg N L$^{-1}$. (Based on James et al. 2005.)

be much less, the efficiency of buffer zones in fixing phosphorus is lower. It may be that we have to accept that eutrophication control of diffuse nutrient sources is incompatible with modern agriculture and that a new approach to landscape and environmental quality is necessary (Chapter 16). Indeed very fundamental changes will be needed to solve the problems indicated in this chapter for standing waters and in Chapters 8 and 10 for flowing ones.

## 15.12 HABITAT CREATION

A last resort in rehabilitation of standing water habitats is to create new ones. Frequently these are dug out by enthusiasts in local nature reserves in unsuitable places where the water table is too deep and some sort of impermeable liner of puddled clay or butyl rubber has to be used to hold the water. Inevitably the pond then does not look or feel 'right' in its landscape and may be too regular in shape, either erring in roundness

or squareness. It is very difficult to get a natural look, with sensitivity to the to lie of land and direction of prevailing wind. There is a tendency to try to put in all possible features from islands for birds nesting (artificial islands erode away if not protected with rock or concrete edges, which look odd) to shallow edges for ducklings to walk in and out, and steep banks for nesting holes for kingfishers and martins. The most sensitively constructed ponds have gently sloping edge slopes (less than 1 in 15) for a natural looking littoral. Excavated spoil is used to give irregular surrounds with temporary puddles and there are interconnected swampy areas for animal cover. Groups of ponds of varying size and depth in a naturally waterlogged area give the greatest diversity, when natural colonization is allowed and the lure of garden centres with their cultivars of water lilies and various exotic species is avoided. Such an approach is least expensive and what grows is what will grow naturally with no need for the meddling management of periodic dredging, vegetation clearance and general tidying up.

**Fig. 15.29**  The London Wetland Centre (right) was created from the disused Barn Elms reservoirs (left) with very little transfer of materials on or off site. It now forms a very rich nature reserve in the centre of London.

On a bigger scale, there are opportunities to create ponds and lakes, often of several hectares, from exhausted gravel workings. About 100 million tonnes per year of gravel are extracted from floodplains in the UK for the construction industry and 1500 ha of worked out excavations become available each year, 500 ha of which are floodable. There are also about 60,000 ha of exhausted workings, 15,000 ha of them already flooded. This does not compensate for the rate of loss of other ponds but it is a valuable contribution. New gravel workings can become extremely valuable wildlife habitats, particularly when the gravel is removed 'dry' from a pumped pit. If it is extracted from a flooded pit, the water tends to be turbid from disturbed clays and when the pit is abandoned often remains turbid, because aquatic plants cannot colonize because of the poor light climate. Where it is kept dry but later flooded, aquatic plant colonization and clear water may be achieved. More than 20% of the populations of several ducks species depend on flooded gravel pit lakes. Perhaps the *piece de resistance*, however, was the conversion by the Wildfowl and Wetlands

Trust of the abandoned concrete Barn Elms reservoirs in central London to a lake and mire area now extremely rich in wildlife (Fig. 15.29). It was remarkable because the project had to be completed, under the planning controls imposed, without substantial import of materials or removal of waste from the site, and was very skilfully completed to have an extremely natural look. It is a project on the sort of scale that is now needed to compensate for the damage done to freshwaters, but, as Chapter 16 will show, our endeavours for the future may need to be even more ambitious.

**FURTHER READING**

The area with which this Chapter began, the Norfolk and Suffolk Broads in the UK has been discussed in Moss (2002), and a subsequent useful paper on part of it is Barker et al. (2008a), which illustrates the conflicts between maintenance of an ecosystem and its use, in this case by yachtsmen. Fish and fisheries have an extensive and specialist literature, as, for many years, fisheries were treated separately from the rest of freshwater management. General works on fish biology are Nelson (2006) and Wooton (1998), whilst evolutionary and genetic issues are covered in Ferguson (1989) and McGinnity et al. (1997).

Fish production is reviewed in Downing et al. (1990), and general fisheries management in Cowx & Gerdeaux (2004), Pitcher & Hart (1982), and a major text book, Guy & Brown (2007). Garrod (1961a,b) is notable for a clear exposition of the use of statistics in managing the *Oreochromis* fishery of Lake Victoria. As often, the well-developed science was ignored and the fishery became seriously overfished. Tropical fisheries in general are lucidly described by Lowe-McConnell (1975, 1987). Salmi et al. (2000) explain the role of negotiation and compromise in managing Finnish inland fisheries and Hickling (1961) is a readable gem of a book, containing much personal knowledge of fisheries the world over. Issues of birds and fisheries are introduced in Harris et al. (2008) and Winfield (1990). Fish, being relatively oily, accumulate non-polar persistent organic pesticides and other chlorocarbon compounds. There is a toxicological literature on this, e.g. Kiviranta et al. (2002) and Turunen et al. (2008). Finnish fishermen have high body loads of such compounds, but, because of their otherwise healthy lifestyle, have lower mortality rates than non-fishermen.

Hoffman (2005) interestingly traces overfishing in the mediaeval period and Allan et al. (2005) give a modern update for freshwaters. Pauly et al. (1998, 2002) are classic expositions on fishing down and the general collapse of wild fisheries. Fish introductions are so widespread that case studies and reviews of their effects are legion. Cadwallader (1978), Canonico et al. (2005), Crawford & Muir (2008), Cruz et al. (2008), De Silva et al. (2009), Gozlan (2008), Hobbs et al. (1989), Pister (1985), Rowland (1989), Shearer & Mulley (1978) and Zaret & Paine (1973) are examples. McDowall (2006) is a thorough account of how introduced north temperate salmonids are undermining whole families of southern hemisphere fish in Australia and New Zealand. Introductions and other threats to fisheries in Africa are covered in Allison et al. (1996), Barel et al. (1985), Balon & Bruton (1986), Chapman et al. (2008), Coulter et al. (1986), Odada et al. (2003) and Pitcher & Hart (2007). Welcomme (2002) discusses the use of fish parks in the tropics. Parks are structures of brushwood or floating plants that draw in

fish from a wider area and improve fishing efficiency but may also increase the risk of overfishing.

Fisheries in the St Lawrence Great Lakes are described and discussed by Christie (1974), Beeton (2002) and Smith (1972). Lake Victoria now has an extensive literature because of the introduction of the Nile perch. The circumstances of the introduction are explored by Pringle (2005a,b) and the consequences by Balirwa et al. (2003), Goldschmidt (1996), Goldschmidt & Witte (1992), Goudswaard et al. (2008), Matsuishi et al. (2006), Mugidde (1993) and Lowe-McConnell (1992), Witte et al. (1992). Hecky (1992) introduced the idea that eutrophication may be an important part of the story.

Fish domestication is interestingly covered by Balon (2004) and pond culture by Hickling (1961) and Jhingran (2002). The ethics of recreational angling have been much discussed recently. Arlinghaus et al. (2007) and Huntingford et al. (2006) give contrasted points of view. Management of angling can be approached in Bell et al. (1985), Cooke & Cowx (2004), Hewlett et al. (2009), Hickley et al. (1995), Maitland (1995), Morrison (1987) and Templeton (1995). The latter is a comprehensive text book. The Peruvian aquarium trade is described in Moreau & Coomes (2002).

Since 1947, when the term 'eutrophication' was first used, some 11,000 papers have been published with this word in the title or abstract. Hutchinson (1973), Hutchinson et al. (1970), Jeppesen et al. (2005) and Pickering (2001) are good starting references. The eutrophication and other problems of large lakes are reviewed by Beeton (2002), of standing water wetlands by Brinson & Malvarez (2002), Fraser & Keddy (2005), Matthews (1993) and Moore, P.D. (2002), of shallow lakes by Carvalho & Moss (1995). The Aral Sea is a notorious case of a huge lake much reduced in size by diversion of its inflow waters for irrigation and is discussed in Williams (2002) and Williams & Aladin (1991). The new problem of rising dissolved organic carbon concentrations in lakes is introduced in Forsberg & Petersen (1990) and Monteith et al. (2007).

The pros and cons of building large dams are continuing controversies. See Fujikura & Nakayama (2009), Scudder (2005) and World Commission on Dams (2000) for the issues. New reservoirs, however, provided opportunities to study the early stages of lake development and many lessons have been learnt. See Harding (1966), Lowe-McConnell (1966), McLachlan

(1974), Armitage (1978), McCartney (2009) and March et al. (2003) for some of them.

Reservoir management is unfortunately seen mostly from an engineering point of view, but the Water Framework Directive, in Europe, now demands a more enlightened view to include the ecological consequences. Abrahams (2005), Moss (2008b) and Schilt (2007) discuss some of these. Models for biological management are now becoming more sophisticated (Hakanson, 2004).

General lake restoration reviews and manuals are Cooke et al. (2005), Gulati et al. (2008), Moss et al. (1996b) and O'Sullivan & Reynolds (2005), and nutrient planning is used in Dillon & Rigler (1974) and Vollenweider (1975). Alternative states and biomanipulation are increasingly interlinked. Balls et al. (1989) began the recent exploration of this, though Uhlmann (1980) had the original idea. The literature on biomanipulation is now extensive and can be traced through Mehner et al. (2004), Meijer & Hosper (1997), Meijer et al. (1999), Shapiro (1980), Shapiro et al. (1975), Shapiro & Wright (1984), Sondergaard et al. (2008). Moss et al. (2002) is an amusing read on this topic. Fanslow et al. (1995), on filtration capacity in zebra mussels, has renewed relevance because The Netherlands is now very keen to use these mussels in reducing algal crops. Much literature on P and N has already been referred to in previous chapters, but Foy (1985) is interesting on the subject of P inactivation and Boar et al. (1989) on consequences of nitrogen loading.

Finally, ponds and gravel pits, their management and creation, are covered in Andrews & Kinsman (1990), Biggs et al. (2005), Cereghino et al. (2008), Williams et al. (1999, 2008) and Giles (1992). Moore, N.W. (2002) is a fascinating account by a prominent conservationist of his retirement project in creating a pond to encourage dragonfly breeding.

# Chapter 16

# CLIMATE CHANGE AND THE FUTURE OF FRESHWATERS

## 16.1 THE MERCHANT OF VENICE

In 1653 Thomas Harvey discovered that the blood circulated in the body. But this was merely a formal demonstration of something that had been instinctively known for some time. Fifty years earlier, William Shakespeare had published his play, *The Merchant of Venice*. In the play, Antonio, a merchant, needs to borrow a large sum of money to help his friend Bassanio. As his own money is currently tied up in a fleet of ships trading across the sea, he borrows from a moneylender, Shylock, who, because of a deep dislike between them, insists that if the ships do not return, the loan must be redeemed by a pound (about 2.25 kg) of Antonio's flesh. The ships are delayed and Shylock seeks, at the court of the Duke of Venice, to redeem the loan in flesh. Antonio is defended by a young lawyer, a woman, Portia, dressed as a man, for women were not permitted in mediaeval Venice to partake in affairs of state. The Duke, representing authority, was keen that the laws of contract be upheld and that the bargain be completed, for otherwise the commercial system of Venice, on which its vast wealth depended, would be undermined. Portia argues that this should be so but that in taking his pound of flesh,

which would, of course kill Antonio, not one drop of blood must be spilt for the bargain was for flesh alone. Shylock is exposed as a potential murderer and the Duke, sensing political advantage, switches sides and banishes him.

The relationship between marine and fresh waters and the rest of the planet, the land, is very like the blood and the flesh. Fresh waters move materials around, bring nutrients, remove 'waste', the millions of small headwater streams coalescing into the veins and arteries of the rivers and the circulation being maintained by the energy of the Sun with a reservoir in the ocean at the heart of the system. It is not possible to maintain any component, freshwaters, land or ocean separately. The blood and flesh are one. And like Antonio and Shylock, in their commercial dealings, we have held this system to ransom, risking its future for the sake of our immediate gain. And the State has upheld this, because it, too, thinks only of the present, and rather little of the future, until the intellectual climate, represented by Portia, changes and the State sees the need to change too if it is to survive. Not only are the freshwater system and the planet inseparable, but we are playing a dangerous game with them, and like Portia we need to sway the state with intellect. The information is already all there within the scientific community, but its acceptance means a severing of long-held beliefs about human relationships with the planet. It was the revealing of the knife in the court of Venice that focused the issue there. For us, the knife may be our seeing how

---

*Ecology of Freshwaters: A View for the Twenty-first Century*, 4th edition. By Brian Moss. Published 2010 by Blackwell Publishing Ltd.

the continuing effects of environmental damage and climate change come together to threaten our entire culture and existence.

## 16.2 CLIMATE CHANGE

Climate has changed continually during the history of the Earth, from when a very hot ball of gas and dust cooled and condensed. As the atmosphere grew, differential absorption of radiation from the Sun, and the properties of matter in radiating back the absorbed radiation at slightly longer wavelengths than they were absorbed, established a natural greenhouse effect. This has maintained conditions at the planet's surface that allow liquid water to persist and thus also our particular biochemical system to survive. Within this permissible range of conditions, there have been hotter and colder periods, for the orbit and energy output of the Sun, and the tilt of the Earth change and combine to make some periods ice ages and others much warmer. The movements of the Earth's plates across the plastic inner mantle also alter the patterns of land and ocean, so that the ocean currents, which redistribute heat as part of the circulatory system, also change, and local climates with them. All these changes happen slowly, over tens of thousands, if not sometimes millions of years, and there is ample time for ecosystems, through movement and evolution of their organisms, to adjust. But at present, climatic change is happening much more rapidly than at any time in the past for which we have records in changing fossils, rock chemistry, the composition of gas bubbles in ancient polar ice, or the balance of oxygen isotopes in carbonates preserved in chalks and limestones, all of which can allow us to reconstruct past temperatures.

World average temperature has increased by about 0.76°C in the past 150 years and the rate of increase has accelerated in the past 20 years. This period coincides with a major change in the composition of the atmosphere (Fig. 16.1) with increases in the greenhouse gases, carbon dioxide, methane and nitrous oxide. Carbon dioxide concentrations, in particular, have been directly monitored for some decades and there has been a steady increase from 280 ppm before the industrial revolution to more than 379 ppm by now. This is greater than any concentration measured (in preserved gas bubbles in cores of Antarctic ice), over the past 650,000 years (range 180–300). The increase can be explained by the burning of carbon stores, fossil

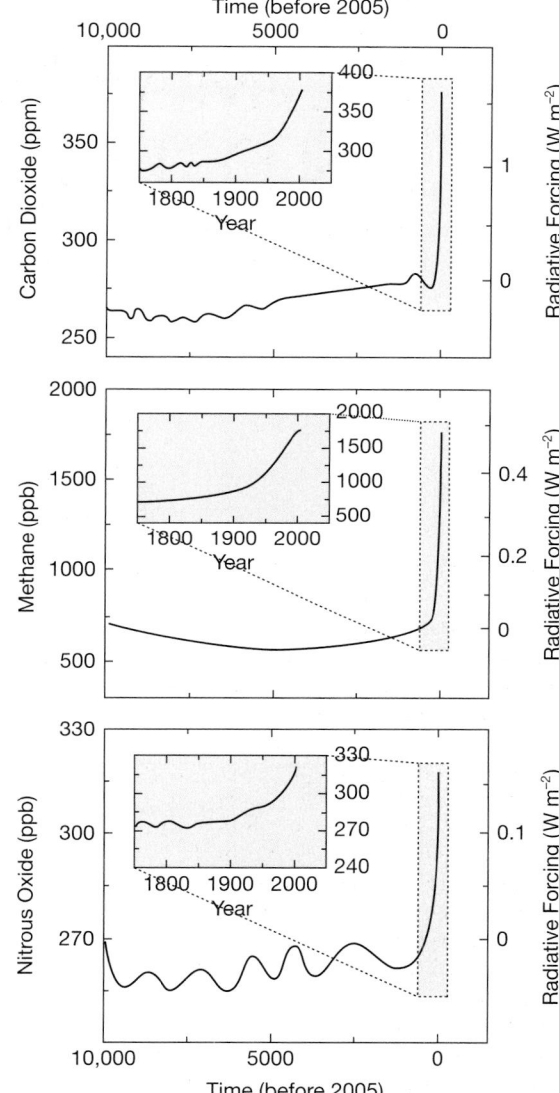

**Fig. 16.1** Changes in atmospheric concentrations of the three most significant greenhouse gases. Data are derived from analyses of bubbles in ancient Antarctic ice cores and from modern measurements (insets). The radiative forcings (effectively the heating effects) are also shown. (Based on IPCC 2007.)

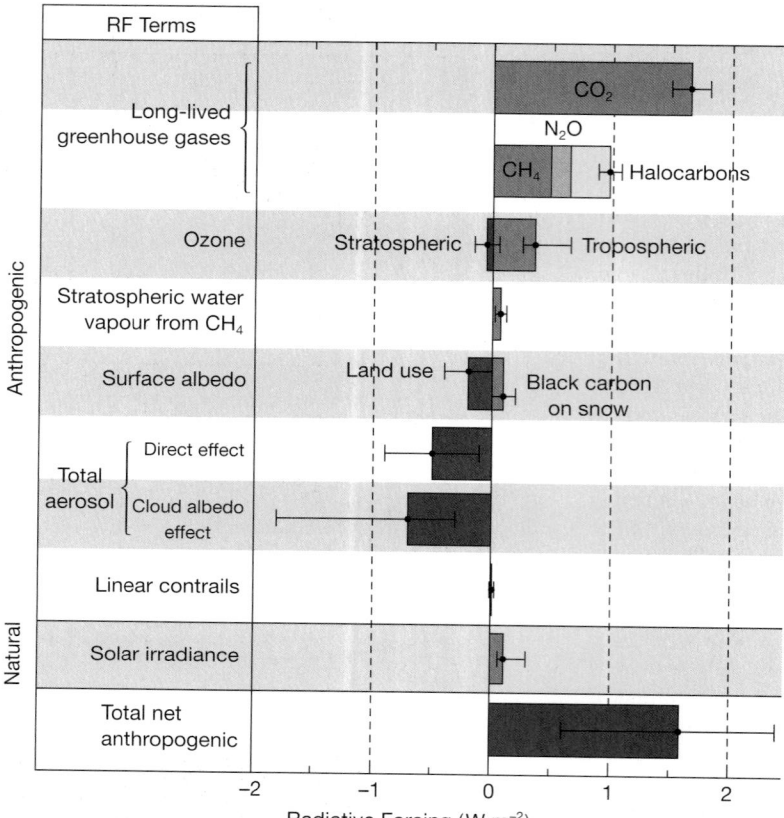

**Fig. 16.2** Components of radiative forcing for 2005. Some tend to increase temperature (positive values), others decrease it, for example changes in land use, atmospheric aerosols from industry and increased cloudiness, but the net effect is positive. The total net anthropogenic effect is shown. (Based on IPCC 2007.)

fuels, laid down by past freshwater ecosystems, but there is an additional source from forest clearance and drainage and oxidation of wetland soils. We know how much coal, oil and natural gas has been burned over the past two centuries and it more than accounts for the atmospheric increase. Currently between 6.9 and 7.5 Gt are burnt per year and land-use change contributes between 1.8 and 9.9 Gt. About half of it has not appeared in the atmosphere but appears to have been precipitated as carbonate in the ocean or taken up into peat deposits by wetland and other soils.

Methane concentrations have increased from a number of sources. Methane is emitted from waterlogged soils, and rice cultivation in wet paddy fields has expanded greatly; there are leaks of natural gas from oil drilling; and there have been forest clearances by burning, in which the fires become so fierce that they are starved of oxygen and some of the carbon escapes as methane. Concentrations have risen from 715 ppb to 1774 ppb. Nitrous oxide emerges also from waterlogged soils but its main source seems to be from agriculture and to a lesser extent the burning of fuels in vehicle engines. Recent decades have seen large increases in agricultural intensification and in motor transport. Concentrations are now 319 ppb; previously they were below 270 ppb. There are also other greenhouse gases. For example ozone produced at ground level from photochemical smog in which nitrogen oxides from car exhausts react with oxygen in bright sunlight, and halocarbons, developed as refrigerants and propellant gases for spray cans, both act as greenhouse gases. Paradoxically, halocarbons in the stratosphere react with ozone and have eroded the layer of ozone that filters out ultraviolet radiation, and this is an additional problem.

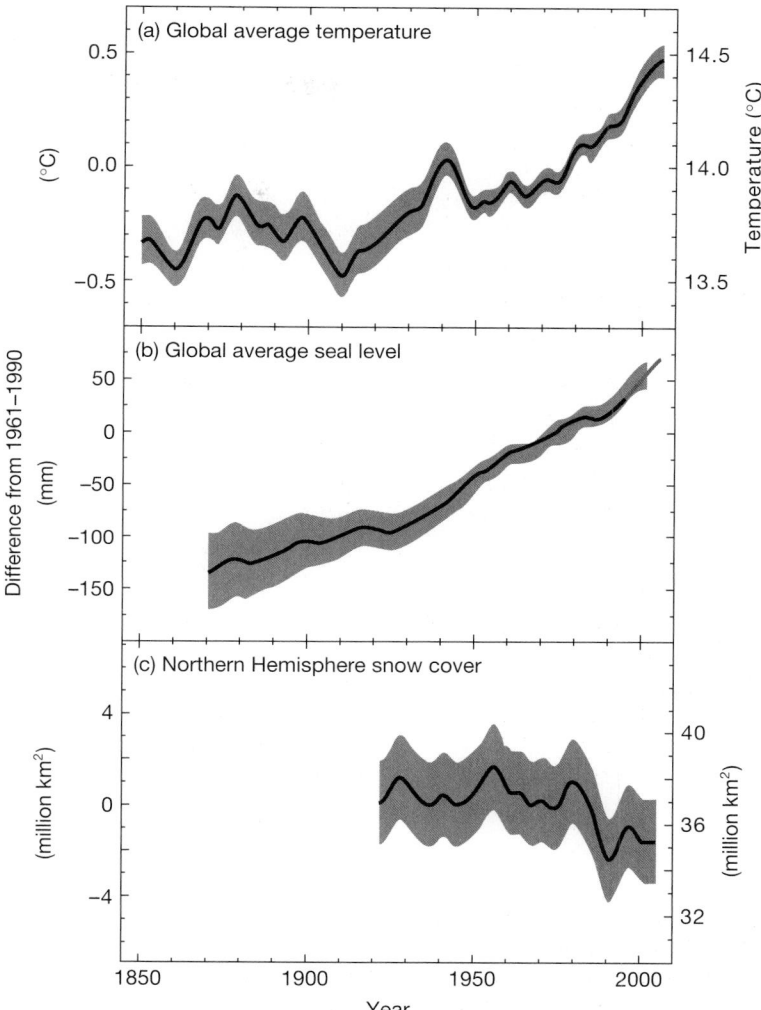

**Fig. 16.3** Changes in northern hemisphere temperatures, global average sea level and northern hemisphere snow cover since 1850. Solid line shows the mean and the shaded areas the range of uncertainty. (Based on IPCC 2007.)

There are some processes that tend to cool the planet, as the increase in greenhouse gases tends to warm it. Smoke particles and the ash from volcanic eruptions intercept heat radiation and the Sun's activity also varies a little. On balance, however, taking all these things into account, there is now a net heating effect and most of it comes from human activities (Fig. 16.2). There have been several main consequences (Fig. 16.3), summarized in rising temperature, rising sea level and decline in the area of polar ice, but the ramifications of each of these are many.

## 16.3 EXISTING EFFECTS OF FRESHWATERS

Changing temperature means also changing water balance. More warming means more melting of ice, greater evaporation rates and greater storage of water vapour in the atmosphere to fall eventually as rain. There are many local effects but on average, this means retreat of glaciers almost everywhere (Fig. 16.4) and higher summer river flows in polar and high mountain regions with glaciers, and in winter almost

**Fig. 16.4** The Muir glacier in Alaska in 1941 (upper) and 2004. It is obvious that there has been a major melting back and this is typical of the worlds' glaciers.

**Table 16.1** Observed effects of current climate warming on freshwater systems.

| | Observed change | Time span | Location |
|---|---|---|---|
| Run-off/ streamflow | Annual increase 5%, winter increase 25–90% | 1935–1999 | Arctic rivers in Russia and Canada |
| | Earlier peak snowmelt flow | 1936–2000 | Western North America, New England, northern Eurasia |
| Floods | Increasing catastrophic floods (1 in 100 year) due to earlier break up of river ice and rain | Recent years | Russian Arctic rivers |
| Droughts | 29% decrease in annual max daily streamflow due to evaporation with no change in precipitation | 1847–1996 | Southern Canada |
| | Due to unusually warm summers | 1998–2004 | Western USA |
| Water temperature | 0.1–1.5°C increase in lakes | 40 years | Europe, North America, Asia |
| | 0.2–0.7°C increase in deep water in lakes | 100 years | East Africa |
| Stratification and water chemistry | Decreased available nutrients in summer from stabler stratification or longer growing period | 100 years | North America, Europe, East Africa |
| | Increased catchment weathering | 10–20 years | North America, Europe |

everywhere. Net flows are lower year around in warm regions and in cool regions, in summer. River flows overall are several per cent higher than previously. These changes, and adjustment of the atmosphere to greater heating, means also a more vigorous movement of air masses and greater incidence of extreme weather events, such as hurricanes, storms and droughts. Hitherto, as well as the temperature rise, there has been a rise in sea level of about 17 cm, about 60% of it due to simple thermal expansion of the ocean water mass and 40% to melting of the mountain and Greenland glaciers. The Arctic is warming twice as fast as the global average. The area of permafrost in the Arctic has decreased by 7% since 1900 and the area of Arctic sea ice has shrunk by 2.7% per decade since 1978 (Fig. 16.3). There has been increased rainfall in the eastern parts of North and South America, northern Europe and north and central Asia and reductions in the Sahel, Mediterranean region, southern Africa and parts of southern Asia. The area of land classed as very dry has doubled since the 1970s. The last time the polar regions were warmer than now was 125,000 years ago when sea level rose 4–6 m in response to a temperature rise of 3–5°C.

All of these effects have consequences for the freshwater system (Table 16.1) and water availability for people. The retreat of the glaciers has meant the formation of increasingly large lakes at their toes, so that the moraine deposits that hold them back are close to being overtopped in many cases, with threats of a breach and catastrophic surges of water to flood villages further down the valley. Enormous piles of loose rock, previously held stable by ice have become unstable and have begun to slip, delivering also meltwaters high in nitrate and heavy metals from leaching of the fresh rock surfaces and previously frozen soils. The permafrost melting means a longer growth season for wetland plants but difficulties in communication as roads and railways sink into the mire. Of some 29,000 long-term records of temperature from lakes, 89% show warming in recent decades (Fig. 16.5). There has been a shift in the timing of spring events in lakes and rivers, such as the spring diatom growth and the rise in daphnids that graze it (Fig. 16.6). Organisms that have aerial stages, such as dragonflies, have shifted their ranges northwards and upwards in Europe (Fig. 16.7). The timing of fish movements has changed. And warming has extended the stratification period in many lakes and made the stratification more stable (Fig. 16.8). This has had the effect of reducing nutrient availability in summer as mixing is reduced and may have reduced fish and other production.

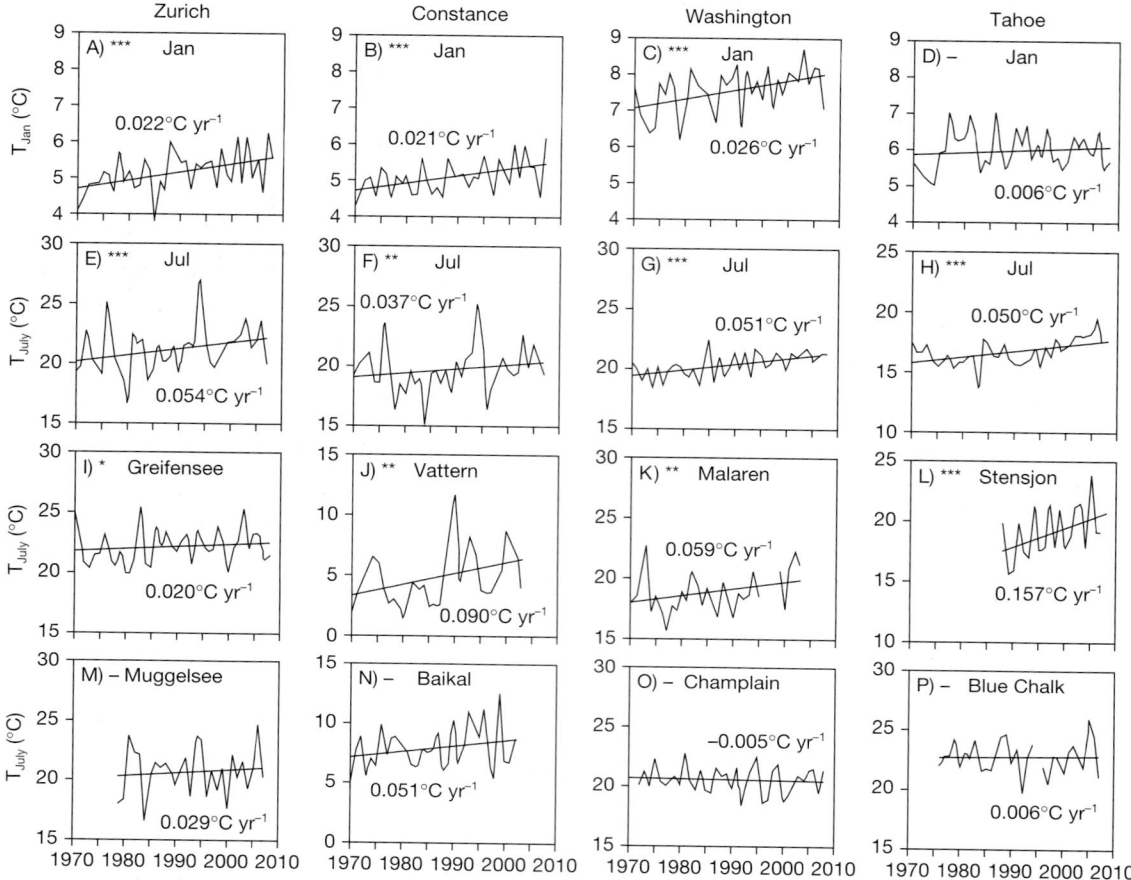

**Fig. 16.5** Long-term records of lake temperature for lakes in Europe, North America, and Russia. Asterisks indicate probability of change (*<0.1, **<0.05, ***<0.01): – means no significant change statistically detected though there are clear trends. The rate of change in temperature per year is also shown. Many world lakes are now showing trends in increasing temperature. (Based on Adrian et al. 2009.)

Effects on floodplain systems are particularly evident on the big river deltas, where the land surface is very close to sea level and where, especially in Asia there are large human population densities, up to 500 km$^{-2}$ in the delta of the Ganges–Brahmaputra in Bangladesh. Seven major deltas that receive water from the Tibetan plateau have huge cities on them, including the Zhujiang, Changjiang and Huanghe in China and the Mekong in Vietnam and Cambodia. Not only have catastrophic river floods increased in intensity but sea-level rise causes erosion of the delta with retreats of several metres per year, currently 3.6 to 4.5 in the

Lena delta in northern Russia, which does not have engineered protection, and salt water penetration into the deposits and up river, where it may affect freshwater fisheries. Forty million people are involved one way or another in fisheries in the Mekong.

## 16.4 FUTURE EFFECTS

Given that climate change is already occurring and has had demonstrable effects, emphasis has shifted to what might happen in the future. Prediction is very difficult

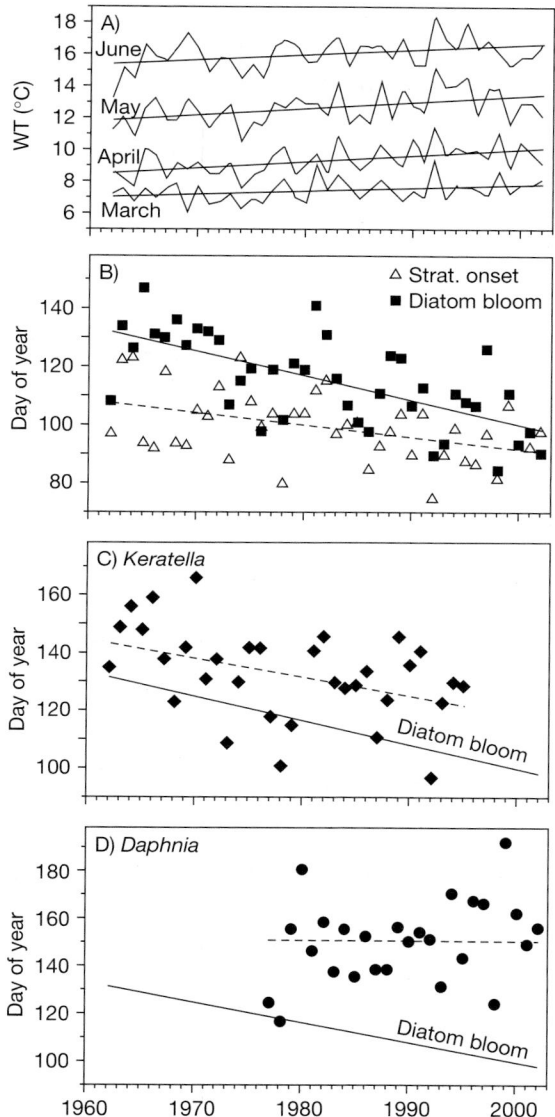

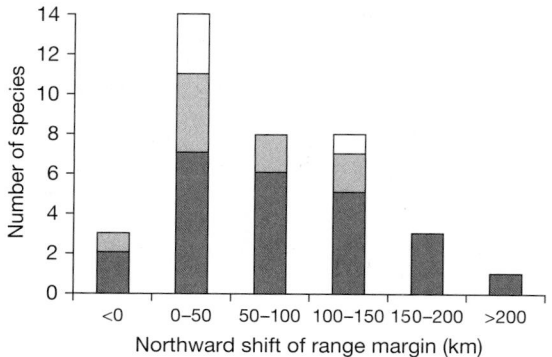

**Fig. 16.7** Northward shift of range margins of British dragonflies and damselflies between 1960–1970 and 1985–1995. Northern species (white), ubiquitous species (hatched) and southern species (dark shading) are shown, with more southern species moving relatively further northwards. (From Hickling et al. 2006.)

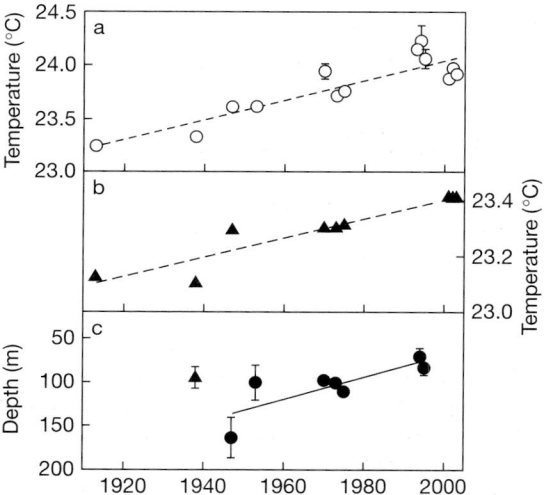

**Fig. 16.8** Temperature in the surface waters (150 m) (top), and deep waters (600 m) (middle) in Lake Tanganyika since 1920. The bottom panel shows the depth of the layer below which oxygen declines, which effectively marks the bottom of the epilimnion. This has halved and is believed to have led to reduced nutrient availability at the surface and to decreased productivity. (Based on O'Reilly et al. 2003.)

**Fig. 16.6** Changes in the plankton of Lake Washington, USA. The top panel shows the increase in water temperature in spring and early summer. Panel B shows the earlier and earlier dates of onset of thermal stratification and of the peak of the spring diatom bloom. The trend in the latter is repeated in Panels C and D, which show the dates of peak populations of a rotifer, *Keratella*, and *Daphnia*, which fed on the spring diatoms. These also show trends to earlier onset, but at different rates so that the food and feeders are becoming mismatched. This has implications for zooplankton and thence fish production. (From Winder & Schindler 2004.)

and very tempting. It is always interesting to try to foresee the future. There are several problems, though. The first is that there are many possibilities. Especially where human activities are concerned; the second is that prediction depends on things behaving in an orderly, linear way, with consequence proportionate to cause; and the third is that some of the actions might have feedback effects that act as brakes (negative feedback) or accelerators (positive feedback) on further change.

The first step in prediction is to create a model (essentially a set of linked equations) that successfully relates variables such as atmospheric carbon dioxide concentration, changes in the Earth's orbit and other factors contributing to radiative forcing (the heating effect if positive, cooling if negative), thence temperature and precipitation. If the model explains past carbon dioxide and climate data well, it is considered to be able to explain the consequences of putting in future higher greenhouse gas levels. There are many such global circulation models, each giving broadly the same predictions for the consequences, in different parts of the world, of different future levels of carbon dioxide concentration, but also having some differences that are

sometimes quite large. Thus we are able to state that a rise to 480 ppm $CO_2$ equivalent by volume (including the effects of other greenhouse gases normalized to carbon dioxide) in the atmosphere will give an overall increase (over pre-industrial levels) of about $2°C$, 650 ppm of $4°C$, and so on, but whether the levels will rise to these concentrations, and how rapidly, depends on the assumptions made about the way the world population and its political systems will operate in future.

The Intergovernmental Panel on Climate Change (2007) has used four scenarios (Table 16.2), each of which assumes different economic and population conditions. A1 assumes that the current market-driven economic system will prevail and has three sub-scenarios in which fossil fuel continues to be burnt at current or increasing rates, in which energy is no longer generated by fossil fuel use and in which there is a balance between fossil fuel and non-fossil fuel generation. In this scenario, population reaches a peak in 2050, then declines. B1 assumes the same population change, is no less aggressive about economic growth but assumes that it will use cleaner technologies and be more service-orientated rather than manufacturing-based. A2 and B2 assume more regional determination

**Table 16.2**  Scenarios (storylines) used for prediction by the IPCC (2007).

| A1 Storyline. Global economy, business as usual | A2 Storyline. Regional, reduced economy, increasing population | B1 Storyline. Global, reduced economy, eventually declining population, more technology development | B2 Storyline. Regional, reduced economy, increasing population, more technology development |
|---|---|---|---|
| Market orientated with high economic growth Population peaks in 2050 then declines Strong regional governance Rising incomes, converging among countries A1F1 Fossil fuel intensive **Business as usual** A1T no fossil fuel use **Business as usual with greatly reduced carbon emissions** A1B **Business as usual with reduced carbon emissions** | Regional economy with low growth Continuously increasing population Strong preservation of local identity and self reliance Low technology development | Convergent economy, service and information based with low growth Population peaks in 2050 then declines Global solutions to economic, social and environmental sustainability **Clean and resource efficient technology** | Local economies with intermediate growth Continuously increasing population at lower rate than A2 Local and regional solutions to environmental protection and social equity **More rapid technology development than A2, less rapid, more diverse than A1/B1** |

and B2 especially the preservation of local identity rather than the rampant globalization of A1 and B1 and assume a steadily increasing global population. There are of course an infinite number of scenarios that can be designed and no-one knows which may prevail, but a start has to be made somewhere.

We thus begin with two major sources of variation: the design of the global circulation model and the scenarios that it uses. Such models then predict future temperature, precipitation, and evapotranspiration and plot the results on a world map typically at a resolution of $100 \text{ km} \times 100 \text{ km}$. They can be downscaled to smaller areas by using local weather data, but the uncertainties then increase, for the variability of weather and the microclimatic effects of local topography must be included. The models can predict physical and chemical effects and feedbacks, for example the increased warming effect of decreasing albedo as the polar ice melts. But they cannot yet predict ecological consequences. And one problem with ecological change is that it is rarely linear and frequently has step changes or switches in which an abrupt change can occur when some threshold is reached. There are also potential positive feedbacks, for example if warming increases the carbon dioxide or methane release from soils and sediments through changes in bacterial activity. Analysis of long-term data of physics, chemistry and biology from the Muggelsee, a shallow lake in Berlin, illustrates this. There were three sorts of change: abrupt permanent change, gradual permanent change and abrupt temporary change (Fig. 16.9). Most changes recorded were abrupt, that is non-linear (Table 16.3). This makes future prediction very uncertain.

The sorts of global maps and graphs now frequently produced to show predicted changes in temperature or precipitation under various scenarios (Fig. 16.10) are thus not possible for biological phenomena, though gross changes in potential major vegetation types controlled by climate can be shown. Nonetheless it is very important to understand biological consequences, not least because of the potentially dangerous effects of positive feedbacks affecting the storage or release of carbon and the need to have arrangements in place to cope with the effects of climate change. Table 16.4 gives some expected effects of general trends under all the scenarios considered by the IPCC. Different scenarios give different timing and intensity for the consequences. Figure 16.11 links the intensity of these consequences to carbon dioxide concentrations and calculated temperature rises. Currently it is thought

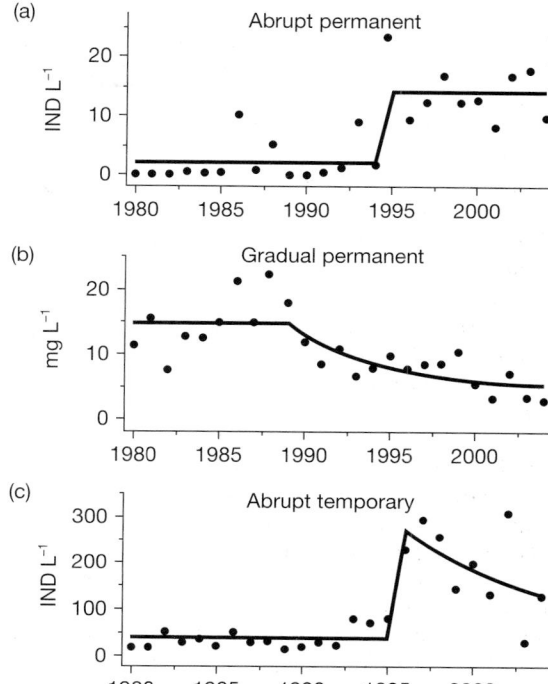

**Fig. 16.9** Changes in the Müggelsee, Berlin, since 1980, illustrating abrupt permanent change (peak abundance of the copepod, *Thermocyclops oithonoides*), gradual permanent change (mean summer total algal biomass) and abrupt temporary change (summer abundance of zebra mussel larvae). Dots are actual observations and lines are fitted from mathematical models. (Based on Wagner & Adrian 2009.)

that it is unlikely that a rise of 2°C can be avoided and that a 4°C rise is very likely because fossil fuel use is still rising and current policy attempts to prevent it are inadequate.

### 16.4.1 Future effects on freshwaters

There are four approaches to predicting future effects on freshwaters. These are direct experimentation, space-for-time studies, paleoecological reconstruction and dynamic modelling. Direct experimentation might involve investigation of temperature increase on aquarium systems in the laboratory. These are easy to do and inexpensive and can use very high replication using microbial communities of bacteria, protozoa,

**Table 16.3** Changes in the Muggelsee in the past 30 years. Changes are categorized as ap, abrupt permanent, gp, gradual permanent, at, abrupt temporary (see Fig. 16.9 for examples). Probabilities are *, <0.05, **, <0.01 and ***, <0.001. (Based on Wagner & Adrian 2009.)

| Variable | Year of change | Direction of change | Type of change | Initial level | Current level | % variance explained by time and probability |
|---|---|---|---|---|---|---|
| Spring | | | | | | |
| March temperature | 1989 | Increase | ap | 2.7 | 4.5 | 36* |
| Spring temperature | 1989 | Increase | ap | 8.5 | 10.1 | 40* |
| Weeks with silicate limitation | 1996 | Decrease | ap | 3.4 | 0 | 39** |
| Biomass of cyanobacteria | 1991 | Decrease | gp | 2.9 | 0.2 | 47*** |
| Biomass of cryptophytes | 1993 | Decrease | ap | 1.5 | 0.8 | 42* |
| Total algal biomass | 1993 | Decrease | gp | 14.4 | 4.4 | 64*** |
| Abundance of *Codonella cratera* (Tintinnid protozoon) | 1991 | Increase | ap | 339 | 3039 | 80*** |
| Timing of peak of *Daphnia galeata* | 1992 | Earlier | at | 11.8 | – | 44** |
| Peak abundance of *Daphnia galeata* | 1991 | Decrease | gp | 87 | 1.7 | 47*** |
| Abundance of *Cyclops kolensis* | 1994 | Increase | gp | 0.1 | 9.7 | 90*** |
| Abundance of cyclopod copepods | 1994 | Increase | ap | 4.2 | 11.0 | 64*** |
| Summer | | | | | | |
| August Temperature | 1994 | Increase | ap | 18 | 20.0 | 22.0* |
| Number of weeks of stratification | 1992 | Increase | ap | 9.6 | 13.8 | 32* |
| Biomass of cyanobacteria | 1990 | Decrease | ap | 8.7 | 3.2 | 45** |
| Total algal biomass | 1990 | Decrease | gp | 14.9 | 5.0 | 60** |
| Abundance of *Codonella cratera* | 1992 | Increase | ap | 60.8 | 309 | 53** |
| Abundance of *Daphnia galeata* | 1994 | Decrease | gp | 27.1 | 2.0 | 56*** |
| Abundance of *Leptodora kindtii* | 1988 | Decrease | ap | 1.4 | 0.3 | 56*** |
| Abundance of *Dreissena polymorpha* larvae | 1995 | Increase | at | 37.9 | – | 74*** |
| Timing of appearance of *Diacyclops bicuspidatus* | 1994 | Later | ap | 10.4 | 14.4 | 36* |
| Abundance of Thermocyclops oithonoides | 1994 | Increase | ap | 0.6 | 4.2 | 72*** |
| Abundance of daphnids | 1992 | Decrease | ap | 66.1 | 36.3 | 32** |
| Abundance of copepods | 1988 | Increase | ap | 139 | 297 | 57** |

algae and rotifers to reveal possible shifts in herbivores and predators, but these are of most interest to theoreticians and give only remote clues as to what might happen to ponds, lakes and rivers. Equally there have been many studies on the influence of temperature on behaviour, growth, respiration and reproduction on individual species. Some of these, particularly on fish are necessary for predicting future effects because individual species have very different tolerances. Studies on very resilient species, such as the three-spined stickleback (Fig. 16.12), however, give indications of what might happen to less tough species. A species in isolation, however, may behave differently in a community, where influences of competition, food scarcity or predation will affect its performance. Generally it will be more vulnerable.

More realistic are experiments in replicated mesocosms, several metres cubed in volume, which can contain a nearly complete pond system (Fig. 16.13). Such studies are rare, however, for they are expensive

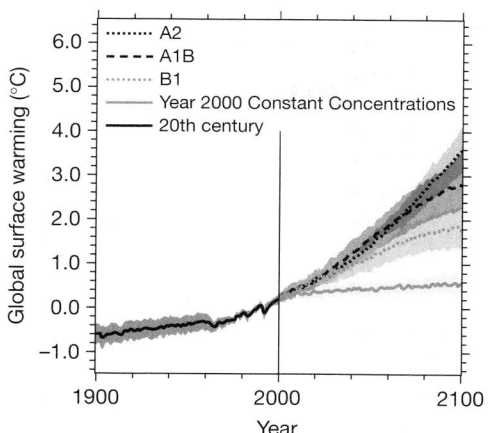

**Fig. 16.10** Temperature predictions for scenarios A2, A1B and B1 used by the IPCC to predict mean average global temperature. The existing trend is shown and then the predictions with their ranges of uncertainty shaded. The trend that would occur if concentrations were held at those in 2000 is also shown. (Based on IPCC 2007.)

to set up and maintain. Energy costs to warm the system are very high. It is possible, however, using suitable experimental designs to investigate the interactions of warming and other influences such as nutrient supply and the presence or absence of fish. Arrangements can also be made for water replacement (and hence simulation of the hydrological effects of climate change) and major variables such as pH and oxygen concentration as well as temperature can be monitored continuously, giving very full data. Table 16.5 summarizes some effects of 3°C and 4°C warming at different nutrient loadings in a set of such mesocosms. The problem is, however, that the results might be different if, for example, different species of plants, different compositions of sediment, different nutrient regimes or different fish were used. There is an almost infinite set of combinations of these in the lakes of the world! It is also not possible to use more than one trophic level of fish in practicable mesocosms, for the volumes are too low to support piscivores. But if relevant conditions

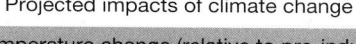

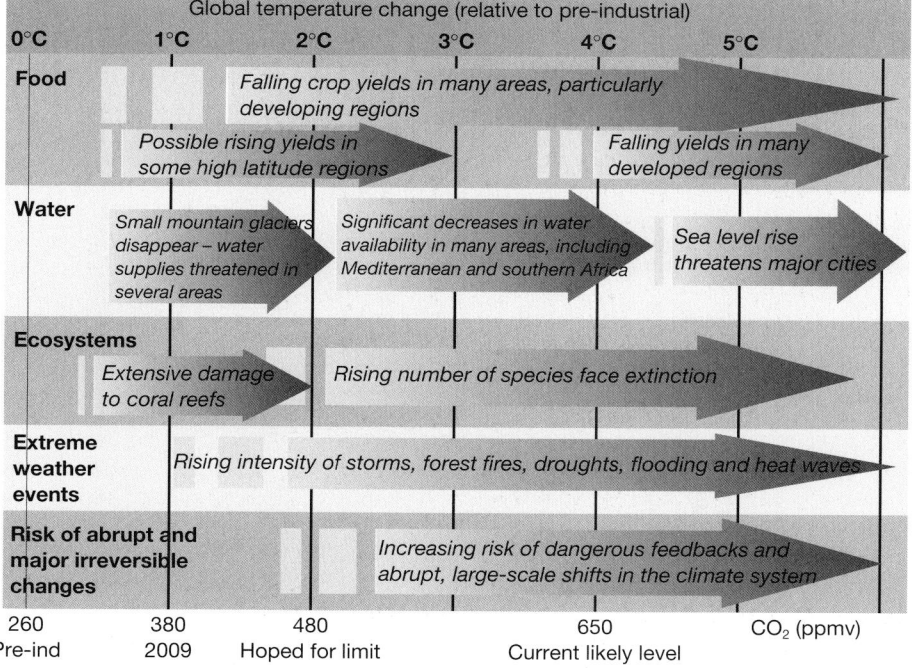

**Fig. 16.11** Expected effects of progressively increasing global temperature, linked with carbon dioxide equivalent concentrations of greenhouse gases. Increased shading indicates increased intensity of effect. (Drawn from IPCC data.)

**Table 16.4** General consequences of predicted climate change.

| | Likelihood in future | Freshwater ecosystems | Land ecosystems, agriculture & Forestry | Water resources | Human health | Industry and society |
|---|---|---|---|---|---|---|
| Increased precipitation and heavy precipitation events | Very likely | Washout of headwater streams, movement of woody debris, creation or erosion of salmon spawning grounds. Reduced residence time in lakes. Greater diffuse nutrient loading, more dilution of point sources | Community change towards more water-tolerant species, greater growth in summer. Crop damage, inability to cultivate land due to soil waterlogging | Greater supply but lesser quality owing to soil erosion and diffuse pollution | Increase in respiratory diseases and water born infections owing to flooding of areas with poor sanitation | Disruption of settlements and commerce due to flooding. Loss of property |
| Increased area affected by drought | Likely | Longer periods of drying out of small streams and pools. Loss of species particularly fish from previously permanent systems. Increased symptoms of eutrophication as residence time increases | Land degradation, lower yields/crop damage and failure; increased livestock deaths; increased risk of wildfire | Water scarcity, lower quality | Food and water shortage. Increased risk of enteric diseases and malnutrition | Water shortages for settlements, industry and societies; reduced hydropower generation potentials; potential for population migration |
| Intense tropical storm activity | Likely | Major damage in shallow lakes; loss of plants, switch to turbid conditions | Crop damage, wind throw of trees | Power failures and disruption of supply | Accidental deaths; stress from loss of shelter, food. Water born disease increase | Disruption by flood and high winds; withdrawal of risk coverage in vulnerable areas by private insurers; potential for population migrations; loss of property |

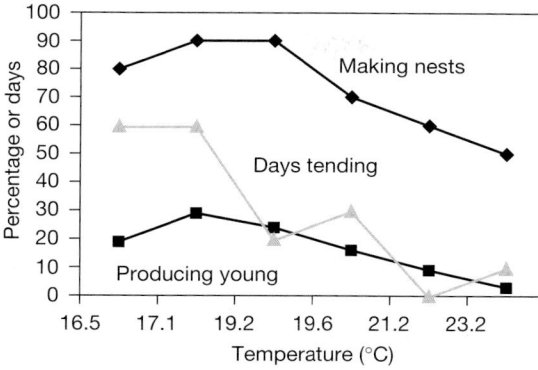

**Fig. 16.12** Effects of warming on the breeding behaviour of male three-spined sticklebacks (*Gasterosteus aculeatus*). Males make nests and take over all parental care of the offspring, but modestly rising temperatures result in fewer males making nests, and less time spent tending the nests (by fanning oxygenated water through them) by those that make them. As a result fewer young are produced with more than a 2°C rise in temperature over current values. (Data of K. Hopkins, A.B. Gill & B. Moss.)

are used, mechanisms can be understood through experiments and the results can definitely link causes and effects. Small streams can also be investigated with this approach using heated, recirculating channels, though this has not yet been done. Large lakes and rivers cannot.

For these bigger systems, space-for-time studies may be used. The space is a latitudinal or altitudinal gradient of temperature, changes along which are assumed to reflect the effects of future changes in temperature in time. Thus, conclusions drawn in Chapter 12 about changing fish communities and their effects with different latitudes might be used to predict effects of future warming. Cold temperate communities might be expected to lose piscivores and gain omnivores, with greater predation on zooplankton, lesser grazing and higher phytoplankton crops, thus an increase in intensity in the symptoms of eutrophication. In an extensive study of Danish lakes (Fig. 16.14), temperature was found to correlate negatively with some algal groups, such as diatoms and positively with others, particularly cyanobacteria, so that with

**Fig. 16.13** Experimental mesocosms established at the University of Liverpool, UK for determining the effects of raised temperature. The 48 tanks can be heated by a piped hot water system and are big enough (3 m³) to contain a reasonably complete shallow lake ecosystem. See Table 16.5 for results.

**Table 16.5** Summary of effects of warming in two experiments in which temperature rises of 3°C and 4°C were applied to shallow lake communities that were eutrophicated to modest levels. Numbers are probability values for significant changes. ns, no significant effect. (Based on Moss 2010.)

| | Warming by 3°C, low nutrient loading | | Warming by 4°C, moderate nutrient loading | |
| --- | --- | --- | --- | --- |
| | **Effects of warming** | **Effects of nutrients** | **Effects of warming** | **Effects of nutrients** |
| Total plant biomass | No effects on biomass but increase in proportion of an alien species, *Lagarosiphon major* | ns | Increased floating plants, <0.001; no change in submerged biomass | Increased floating plants, <0.001; decrease in submerged biomass, <0.001 |
| Planktonic chlorophyll *a* concentration | ns | <0.001 increase | <0.0001 decrease | <0.0001 decrease |
| Gastropod number | 0.003 increase | <0.001 decrease | <0.01 decrease | ns |
| Cladocera number | ns | <0.001 increase | <0.01 decrease | <0.001 increase |
| Ostracod number | <0.001 increase | 0.011 increase | <0.001 increase | <0.001 increase |
| TP concn | 0.018 increase | <0.001 increase | ns | ns |
| SRP concn | 0.04 increase | <0.001 increase | <0.03 increase | ns |
| pH | 0.017 increase | <0.001 increase | <0.004 increase | ns |
| Conductivity | <0.001 increase | <0.001 increase | <0.001 increase | <0.0001 increase |
| Oxygen (%) | 0.036 decrease | 0.005 decrease | <0.0001 decrease | <0.0001 decrease |

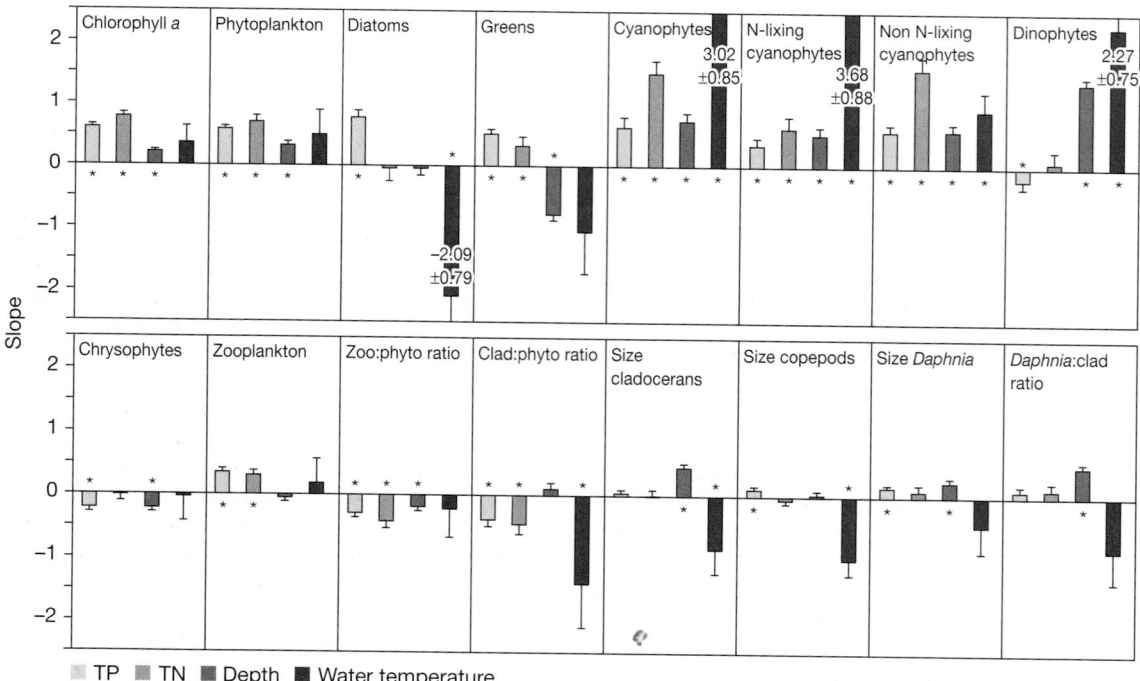

**Fig. 16.14** Slopes of multiple regressions relating plankton variables (log-transformed) to concentrations of total phosphorus (TP) and total nitrogen (TN) in surface water, mean lake depth, and surface water temperature (all log-transformed) measured in August in 250 lakes and over 800 lake-years in Denmark. Significant ($p < 0.05$) slopes are indicated by asterisks. Major reductions in diatoms and green algae with temperature are shown, whilst in contrast, cyanobacteria tend to increase with temperature. Effects of increased fish predation with rising temperature are shown by reductions in the Cladocera: phytoplankton ratio, the proportion of Daphnia and the individual sizes of the zooplankters. (Based on Jeppesen et al. Chapter 6 in Kernan et al. (eds) 2010.)

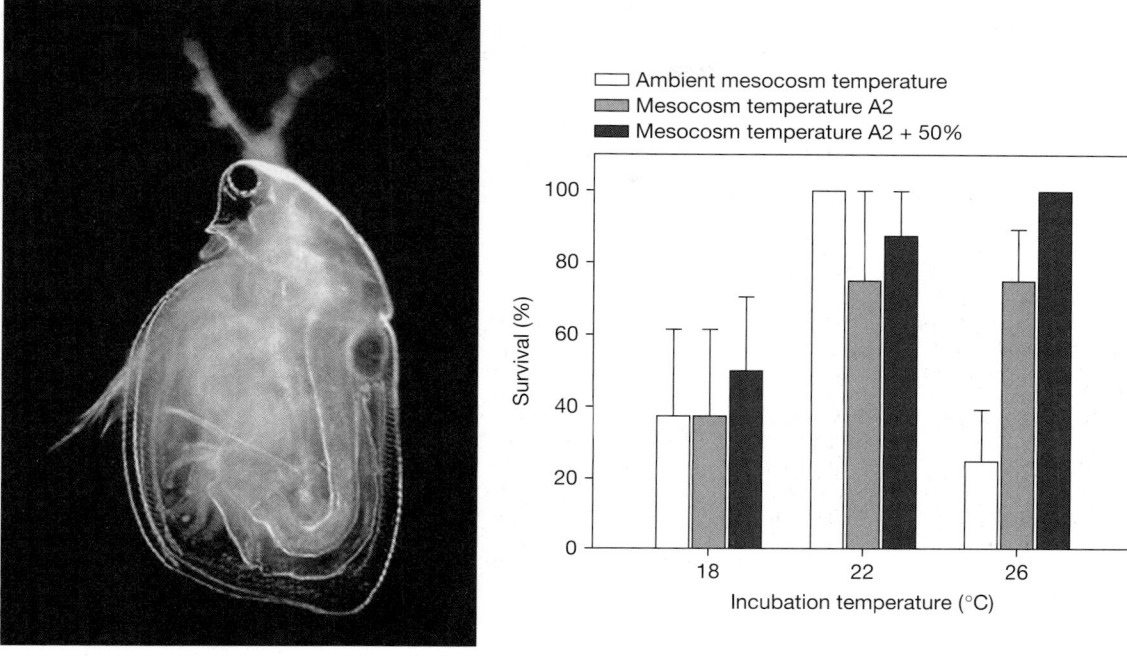

**Fig. 16.15** *Simocephalus vetulus*, a littoral zooplankter, can adapt evolutionarily quite quickly to increased temperature. The animals were exposed in mesocosms held at ambient temperature, at about 4°C above ambient (IPCC scenario A2) and at about 8°C above ambient (IPCC A2 + 50%). They were then grown in the laboratory at 18, 22 and 26°C. At 26°C, survival of the warm-reared clones was much greater than for those reared in cooler mesocosms. (Based on Van Dorslaer et al. 2007.)

increasing temperatures in the future we might expect a greater incidence of the latter and possibly more problems with toxicity.

The drawback of space-for-time studies lies in the fact that ecosystems are not just determined by temperature or even climate as a whole. Consultation of Table 11.2 shows that climate is just one of hundreds of factors involved. If temperature increases, a whole ecosystem does not shift with it. Many freshwater organisms do not migrate easily and those that do, move at different rates. Remnants of the lower-temperature community will also persist and the ultimate consequences of interactions among the old and the new are impossible to predict. There is also the probability of evolutionary change in some organisms, especially the smallest, to the new conditions. Even zooplankters can accommodate, through genetic change, a several degree change within a growth season (Fig. 16.15). The problem for prediction, however, is that not all will do this rapidly enough and it will be especially

unlikely for larger species, such as fish, that can have major effects in structuring the ecosystem. Thus although some general features, such as a greater incidence of cyanobacteria might be predictable, most of the details, such as actual species, or even whole groups will not.

Some of the change that might occur as temperatures rise could be in relative abundance of species already present. Minority species might become more abundant; present dominants might decline. Some insight into this can be obtained from palaeoecological studies of sediments, at least in lake systems, and theoretically some of the difficulties of space-for-time comparisons can be avoided, as it is the same location that is being studied. If indicators of past temperature are available, or actual records from the lake concerned, the fossil sequence in the sediments can be matched up and if there have been warmer or wetter periods in the past, predictions can be made for a future in which these conditions might occur. Probably

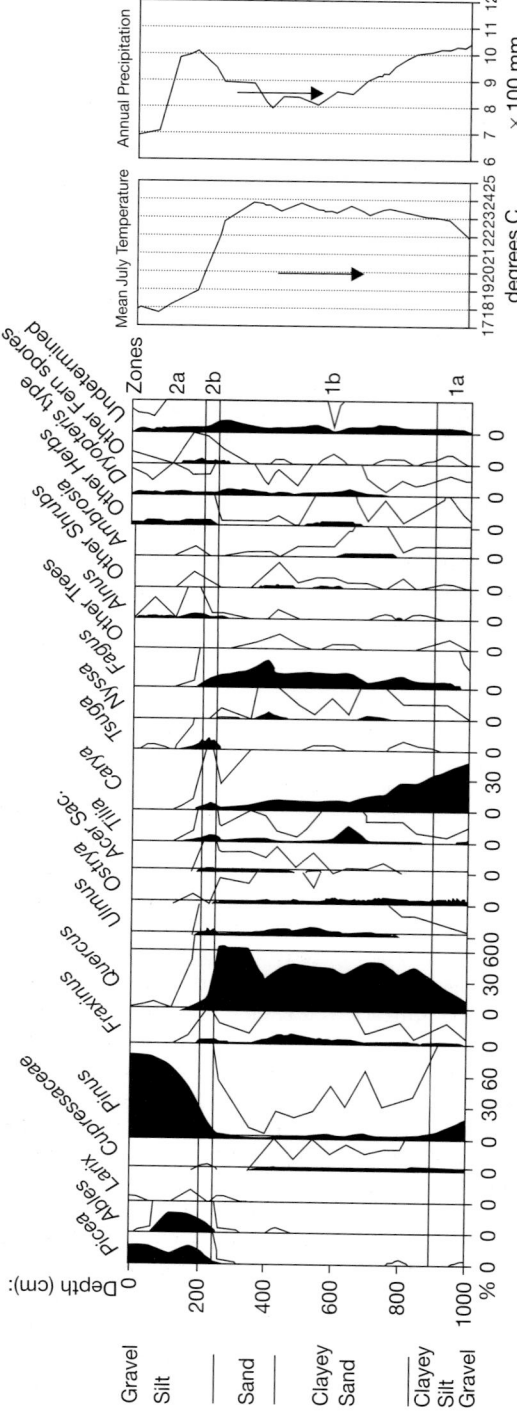

**Fig. 16.16** Lake sediments from the warm interglacial periods still persist despite the erosive effects of subsequent icy periods. Sediments at Fernbank in New York State date back to around 50,000 years in a brief interglacial and contain a wide range of mollusc, ostracod and plant remains. Here are shown data on plant pollens as percentages of the total assemblages. Shaded areas show actual percentages and lines the same data on a one-hundredfold expanded scale to show more detail. Transfer functions (Chapter 11) have been used to reconstruct the temperature and rainfall at the time. Arrows show the current temperature and rainfall of the area. From such data, predictions of plant communities for a warmer 21st century might be derived. Zone 1b represents a rise of about 4°C over the present. The rapid change from oak to pine forest as the next glacial period (2a) set in was quite abrupt. (Based on Karrow et al. 2009.)

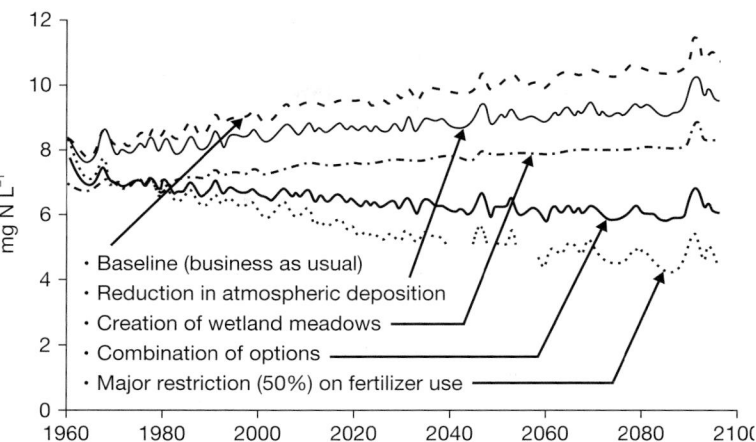

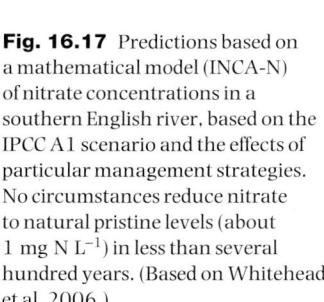

**Fig. 16.17** Predictions based on a mathematical model (INCA-N) of nitrate concentrations in a southern English river, based on the IPCC A1 scenario and the effects of particular management strategies. No circumstances reduce nitrate to natural pristine levels (about 1 mg N $L^{-1}$) in less than several hundred years. (Based on Whitehead et al. 2006.)

changes in precipitation can be traced best in this way and tropical lakes offer good sites. In the temperate latitudes there has been a very significant temperature change since the glaciation, but this provides less useful information for a warming trend than conditions in sediments in the warm interglacial periods. There are some such sediments in northern regions though many were obliterated by the subsequent glaciations (Fig. 16.16). Mathematical models also offer an approach to prediction especially valuable where physics and chemistry are to be predicted, though it is much more difficult to incorporate meaningful details of biology. Figure 16.17 shows how climate change is likely to affect the nitrate concentrations of a southern English river, with various management and mitigation techniques incorporated.

Overall, however, it will be impossible to predict very closely what climate change will bring to freshwaters and the uncertainties of the general circulation models and the future scenarios of human reaction compound this uncertainty. Nonetheless general trends derived from all these approaches are summarized in Table 16.6. Many other impacts on freshwaters have already occurred and climate change does not replace these. They are already serious and climate change in general will make them somewhat worse.

### 16.4.2 Switches and feedbacks

The second and third things that make accurate prediction of the future very difficult are switches and

feedbacks. Many, perhaps all, ecosystems can exist relatively stably in different states. The shallow lake system with its turbid and clear-water states is perhaps the most investigated, but flips between bare rocky intertidal shores and dense kelp forests, conditioned by the presence or absence of the sea otter, which preys on the sea urchin grazers of the kelp, are also well known. Forests in tropical regions may also have grassland alternatives switched by elephants and other grazers. A feature of such alternatives is that once a change has occurred, driven by a particular factor, the system cannot be switched back by a simple reversal. It is often necessary to reduce the intensity of the driver to a much lower level than caused the forward switch to reverse it. Thus, if climate change flips the world's ecosystems into a new state, as a result of build up of carbon dioxide beyond some threshold, reduction of the carbon dioxide concentration to just below the threshold will not necessarily reverse the change. A much more substantial reduction will be needed. The Gaia hypothesis (Chapter 6) suggests that living systems have kept conditions for the biosphere within a band in which water can persist as a liquid, but it does not mean that fairly substantial swings in conditions cannot occur within this band, resulting in major changes in the balance of different sorts of organisms. Thus, Peter Ward (2009) invokes a pessimistic Medea hypothesis (Medea, in Greek mythology, killed her children) in which organisms change things so as to become self-destructive and suggests that present human activities are a good example of this. One of the ways in which such a switch could occur is in

**Table 16.6** Expected consequences of current rates of climate change on features of freshwater systems. (Modified from Kernan et al. 2010.)

| | River and floodplain | Lake | Standing mire |
|---|---|---|---|
| Ice cover | Reduced period of cover. Earlier melting. Changes in ice–dam regime in Arctic | Shorter period | Shorter period. Earlier melting. Loss of permafrost |
| Stratification | | Earlier onset of direct stratification, prolonged stratification. Change from dimictic to monomictic. Stratification in very deep lakes may persist over winter and become permanent | |
| Water level | Reduced in summer | Reduced in summer. Possibility of complete drying out in arid areas | Lowered water table in summer and increased evaporation |
| Permanence | Possibility of conversion from permanent to temporary stream in arid regions and elsewhere in some summers | In arid areas some lakes will dry out in summer | Possibility of conversion from mire to damp grassland or dry land. Desiccation of peat surfaces |
| Flood pulse | More variable and less predictable timing | | |
| Sediment regime | Extreme events bring in more fine sediment, clogging gravel bottomed rivers | Greater turbidity from washed in sediment as a result of increased soil erosion in catchment and extreme rainstorms | |
| Oxygen | Greater amplitude. Night-time depletion | Increased as a result of plankton growth at surface. Reduced in hypolimnion. Night-time depletion in shallow lakes | Greater deoxygenation of soils if habitats remain wet, leading to species changes and greater emission of methane and possibly nitrous oxide. In drier mires, increased oxygenation, greater decomposition rates and carbon dioxide release, lowered methane production |
| Sulphate concentration | Extreme rainfall events will flush out sulphate from soils causing acidification episodes | Sulphide in surrounding wetland sediment will oxidise to sulphate and hydrogen ions, increasing acidification | In drier mires greater oxidation of sulphide and production of sulphate and acid |
| Dissolved organic carbon | May increase owing to greater leaching in winter. May decrease owing to higher soil respiration | Difficult to predict as some processes will tend to increase the input, whilst greater metabolism at higher temperatures will tend to decrease it | |
| Acidification | | Will increase due to drought oxidation and pulses in heavy rainfall events | |
| Eutrophication | Greater winter run off will increase nutrient levels. Faster mineralization of organic matter washed in will increase available amounts | Symptoms will increase owing to food web changes and increased retention time. Increased denitrification may mitigate | Greater mineralization may mean community change towards larger more competitive species |

| | | | |
|---|---|---|---|
| Effects on algae | Greater and earlier growths on rocks in headwater rivers. Reduced summer flows will increase phytoplankton growth in larger rivers | Increased cyanobacteria, decreased diatom contributions. Longer growth season. Lesser grazing pressure leads to greater crops | |
| Effects on aquatic plants | Greater growth owing to longer season and accumulation of fine sediments | Reduced submerged communities owing to greater phytoplankton shading. Increased crops of floating species, sometimes leading to decreased oxygen under the mats and effects on fish communities | Considerable change. In sites that remain wet, there may be succession to forest and conversion of bog to poor fen as nutrients become concentrated by evaporation and surfaces dry in summer. In dry sites there will be loss of fen vegetation and conversion to scrub and forest. Small species will be lost |
| Particulate organic matter input | Greater wash through and decreased retention of leaves in winter. Temporary increases in large timber following extreme storms. More rapid mineralization | Difficult to predict as subject to conflicting processes | |
| Zooplankton | Increase in large rivers in summer | Earlier spring growth in cool lakes, but greater predation by fish and reductions in community, unless fish kills occur, in which case there will be greater zooplankton numbers and more grazing on phytoplankton | |
| Bottom invertebrates | Changed community in headwater streams as oxygen levels are reduced and fine deposits accumulate. Fewer mayflies/stoneflies/caddis flies, more diptera/oligochaetes. Selection for species with resting stages when rivers become temporary | Changes in littoral zone consequent on plant changes. Decreased diversity or even extinction in profundal as hypolimnion oxygen declines. Possible elimination of endemics in large deep, especially tropical, lakes if stratification becomes permanent | Considerable change dependent on plant changes |
| Fish | Reduction in cold-requiring species such as salmonids. Increase in cyprinids | Reduction in piscivorous species. Increase in omivores and herbivore/detritivores | |
| Birds | Affected by changes in invertebrate communities but dependent on species | Affected by changes in invertebrate communities but dependent on species | Communities will change dependent on plant changes but also on alteration of migratory behaviour and changes in migration routes |
| Mammals | Difficult to predict | Difficult to predict | Difficult to predict |
| Alien species | High risk of spread of algae, plants, invertebrates and fish | High risk of spread of algae, plants, invertebrates and fish | High risk of spread of algae, plants, invertebrates and fish |

the operation of a positive feedback in the Earth's carbon cycle.

Much of the carbon released from fossil fuel burning has not accumulated in the atmosphere but has been fixed as peat or organic matter in soils or as carbonate in the ocean sediments. Warming will influence both these processes. It will increase the rate of respiration of microorganisms within the organic deposits, and in summer, drying may result in greater penetration of air and also accelerate their oxidation. Warming and higher carbon dioxide levels should also increase the growth of land vegetation and that should result in greater organic storage. The two processes might balance, which would give a neutral effect, or warming might enhance photosynthesis over respiration, which would act as a check on carbon dioxide levels. There is, however, no indication that either of these possibilities has prevented build up of carbon dioxide in the atmosphere. On the other hand, the expectation that respiration will increase more than photosynthesis as temperatures rise, and also in many areas as water availability limits plant growth, is being borne out by experimental evidence and there is a distinct risk that the mires and the lake sediments will become sources of carbon dioxide, or even greater sources, if they are already sources.

Such an effect could result in a positive feedback of carbon dioxide concentrations and a runaway heating effect. The mires also contain large quantities of dissolved methane from anaerobic respiration in the waterlogged soils. Being a covalent compound, less methane can be held in warm water than cool (Chapter 2) and amounts may diffuse into the air that could also result in feedback effects. The situation in the oceans is different but equally threatening. Increased concentrations of carbon dioxide in the air have led to greater dissolution in the ocean and adjustments in the inorganic carbon equilibria (Chapter 3) such that the equilibria are pushed to the right, hydrogen ions are formed and pH falls. As pH falls it resets the equilibria so that less carbon dioxide can be absorbed and a major sink for carbon dioxide released from fossil fuel burning is blocked. This too could have positive feedback effects. But again we cannot be certain what will happen as experimentation is not possible at the global scale. The risks are such that, as is widely realized, something major has to be done to curb the rate and eventually direction of emission of greenhouse gases.

## 16.5 CONTROL AND MITIGATION OF GLOBAL WARMING

As the use of scenarios for prediction shows, there are very different approaches in society to slowing or eventual reversing of climate change but all currently depend on maintenance of an economic system that rests on an expanding economy and whose success is measured as gross domestic product, GDP. Gross domestic product is the sum of consumer expenditure, social and welfare costs and the costs of repair of environmental damage. Thus the more damage that is done and needs to be cleaned up, the greater is the GDP and the healthier the economy is considered to be. Currently, the mitigation of climate change is seen as an economic opportunity to increase GDP by all governments.

The idea that it has been a relentless pursuit of GDP that has caused the problem, through increased consumption, has not been embraced, nor have the findings of the Millennium Ecosystem Assessment been taken on board that 70% of natural ecosystems will have been lost or seriously damaged by 2050. The significance of loss of ecosystems is that they are major regulators of the Earth's carbon balance. Loss of them means that less carbon is stored, more appears in the atmosphere and the risks of runaway warming increase. The pursuit of rising GDP, climate change and the loss of ecosystems are all interconnected. An ultimate advance will be a replacement of GDP with a better index of the human state that does not actively promote environmental damage and ecosystem destruction. Current attempts at valuation of ecosystem services (Chapter 9) draw attention to the costs of environmental damage but, though they need not, still operate within the classic economic system. They might influence the cost–benefit analysis of whether a large project, such as forest conversion to agriculture or a new large dam should go ahead, but ultimately the approach is subservient to promotion of GDP.

There are better indices of societal wealth, including the Index of Sustainable Economic Wealth (ISEW), also called the Genuine Progress Index (GPI). This equals Consumer expenditure + Human-made capital + Household labour − Environmental damage − Income distribution. It takes into account contributions to society, that are considerable but ignored by GDP, and places the costs of environmental damage, including

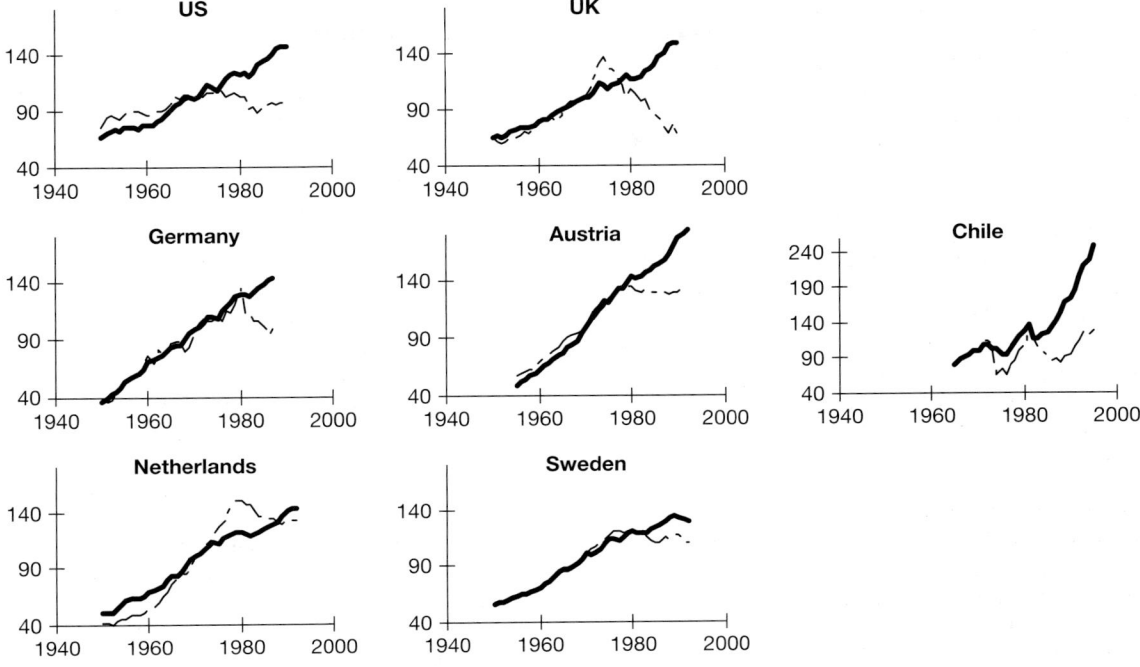

**Fig. 16.18** Changes in Gross Domestic Product (GDP) and Genuine Progress Index (GPI) in the 20th century. Values are normalized to a value of 100 for 1970. GDP is shown as a solid line and GPI as a dashed line. In most countries shown, GPI declined after the 1970s as GDP continued to rise.

the loss of ecosystem services, and the promotion of poverty through vastly different incomes to individuals, as a debit not a credit. In the developing world, as more damage has been done to the environment, GDP has steadily risen, but GPI has flattened or fallen (Fig. 16.18).

Other indices try to take into account additional measures of human welfare. The Happy Planet Index uses (Life satisfaction × Life expectancy) divided by Ecological footprint and measures the ecological efficiency by which human well-being is delivered (http://www.happyplanetindex.org). Life satisfaction is measured through questionnaires and ecological footprint is measured as the equivalent area of land needed to support the food, material and energy consumption per person in a given country. An even allocation over the world's population would give about 1.9 ha per person. Highly consumptive countries such as those in the United Arab Republics (9.57 ha), North America (8.56–9.57), Europe (up to 8.17, in Norway), Japan (3.91) and Australasia (8.15) have high ecological footprints. The world mean is now 2.1, above the 1.9 ha considered indefinitely sustainable. The five least demanding countries, Congo DR, Haiti, Nepal, Mozambique and Bangladesh use around 0.5–0.6 ha per person. A plot of HPI versus GDP shows that the index rises steeply with GDP from very low to modest GDP, then falls rapidly as GDP increases (Fig. 16.19). Simple measures of human state, such as the proportion of a nation's population that considers itself (in questionnaires or interviews) to be content or happy, also show a similar pattern. Pushing GDP to high levels does not improve the human lot any more than it maintains an environment likely to support a large human population indefinitely into the future.

Despite all this, there is a near universal addiction by governments to increasing GDP, for the minority who gain individually from this are also those with the greatest power and influence. Most of the world's population continues to suffer from the minority gain.

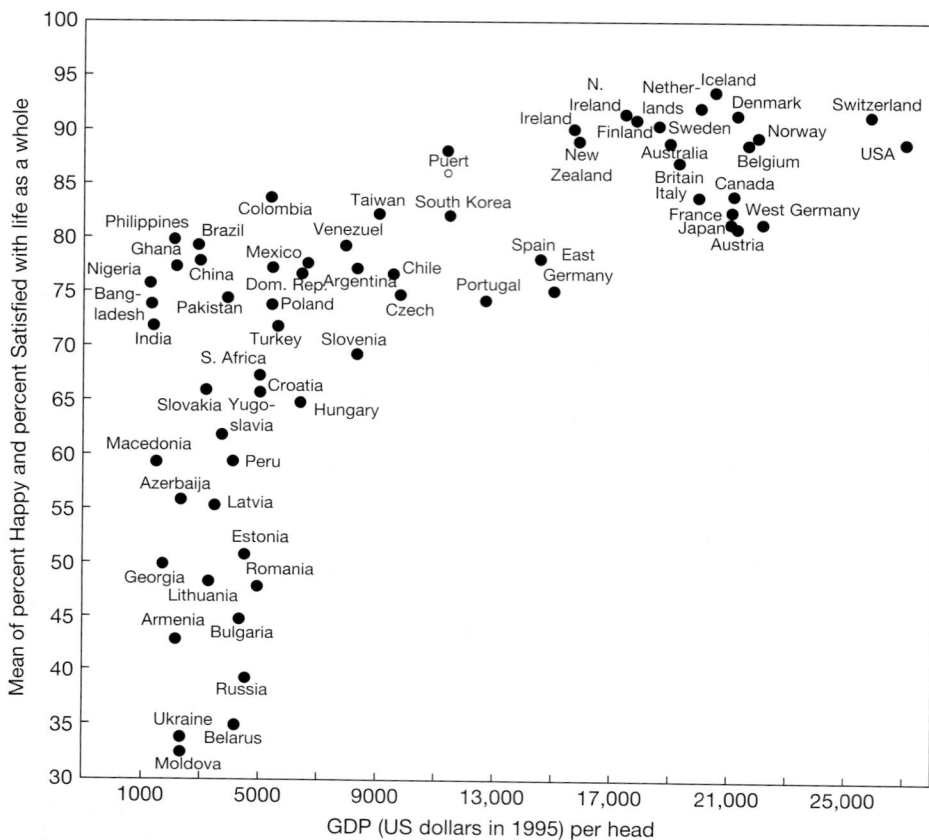

**Fig. 16.19** Relationship between percentage of the population declaring itself happy or satisfied with life as a whole in various countries compared with GDP. Happiness and satisfaction rise rapidly with GDP up to a plateau, situated at about half of the GDP of the developed world, but then rise little if at all. (Based on data from the World Bank 1997.)

Temperatures will continue to rise in the immediate future by at least another half degree simply because of the amount of carbon dioxide already in the atmosphere. Emissions are still rising, however, and none of the provisions being made by the world's governments will yet prevent a rise of at least 2°C or are likely, even without allowance for biological positive feedbacks, to prevent at least a 4°C rise. Radical action is needed. Table 16.7 lists some ideas for radical action recently considered, with their pros and cons. No one knows if many will have much effect or how many will be needed to prevent a rise above 2°C, which is seen as a threshold between a manageable if uncomfortable increase and the possibility of widespread disaster. Some of them could be very dangerous in creating more

problems than they solve. But none of them recognize that the climate problem is not isolated from other problems and most, if not all of them, are designed to fit in with current philosophies of economics. It is these that are the ultimate cause of a plethora of related problems.

## 16.6 THE REMEDY OF ULTIMATE CAUSES

Our ultimate problem is that we cause all sorts of environmental damage that is likely to undermine our future. They will not destroy the planet or life upon it. Bacteria and other microorganisms are extremely

**Table 16.7** Potential solutions to reducing carbon emissions to the atmosphere considered in an exercise sponsored by 'The Guardian' newspaper (UK) in 2009 plus some others.

| Proposal | Advantages | Disadvantages | Overall conclusion |
|---|---|---|---|
| Generation of solar power in deserts | No shortage of solar energy, large deserts available | Deserts provide ecosystem services, for example provision of iron rich dust to support oceanic production. Very large solar arrays would be needed with large mirrors to concentrate the energy, so local wind climate would be altered. Large remote installations are vulnerable to terrorism and the energy costs of building and maintaining them could be large. | Possibly feasible |
| Using geothermal heat to generate steam for driving turbines | Already used in Iceland where hot lava is close to the surface. Takes up little space: boreholes for pumping water down and retrieving steam | Little problem on a small scale. If used on a large scale might have consequences in causing earth movements, including greater frequency of earthquakes in areas where it would most conveniently be used | Feasible |
| Domestic fuel cells. Generation locally of electricity, rather than centrally to reduce transmission losses | Large power stations waste a lot of energy (about 55%), including 5% in transmission | Fuels cells are large batteries that require materials for manufacture (mineral oxides) and hence would mean more mining damage to ecosystems. They also require a fuel (natural gas, ethanol) and produce carbon dioxide, thought this can theoretically be captured and stored. There would be energy costs in provision of the fuel and land costs if ethanol is generated from plant crops | Possibly feasible |
| Cheap biomass cooking stoves. | Efficient stoves for wood and dung burning replace open fires in developing world, and need less fuel and produce less smoke, methane, carbon monoxide and soot | None, provided a way can be found to finance the purchase of the stoves by a poor rural population | Highly feasible |
| Marine turbines to extract energy from currents and tides and wind turbines to capture wind energy | Abundant energy in water movements can be exploited with no carbon dioxide generation. Some devices do not require barrages, but operate only for limited periods during the day. Wind turbines individually generate very little and are visually intrusive where huge numbers are built | Large-scale generation needs barrages that strongly affect coastal ecosystems and the services they provide. Only some regions have suitable large tides | Locally highly feasible |

**Table 16.7** (*Continued*)

| Proposal | Advantages | Disadvantages | Overall conclusion |
|---|---|---|---|
| Biochar. Charcoal is produced from wood or crop wastes. Gases released in production are used in further production or elsewhere as fuels. The charcoal is buried in soils where it is relatively inert | A way of storing carbon that is removed from the atmosphere by photosynthesis. Incorporation in soils may improve soil structure, water retention and nutrient retention and result in greater productivity | To make much difference, a lot of organic matter must be used. This may impact on food production or promote forest destruction. Charcoal does oxidize eventually | Feasible |
| Carbon capture and storage using coal and wood | Carbon dioxide is taken from the exhaust gases of power stations, compressed and pumped underground into depleted oil or gas fields, where it is stored under pressure or dissolved in underground water. If wood rather than coal is used carbon dioxide could be net removed from the atmosphere | Very expensive and takes much energy to compress the carbon dioxide. Risks of escape of stored carbon dioxide. Does nothing to reduce mining damage to ecosystems and if wood is used encourages deforestation | Feasible, but encourages continued consumption and damage |
| Nuclear power generation using thorium rather than uranium | Overcomes some objections to nuclear power generation (long-lasting plutonium waste. Thorium more abundant than uranium | Technology already developed but abandoned as it offered no potential for producing nuclear weapons. Still some risks from reactor accidents. Increased mining damage | Feasible |
| More efficient motor vehicles, using electricity or hydrogen as a fuel | Reduces immediate carbon dioxide production | The electricity or hydrogen must be generated and this may still involve fossil fuels unless there is complete conversion to generation by wind, tide, solar and nuclear sources. Does nothing to reduce the other impacts of motor vehicles (ecosystem destruction through road building, encouragement of transfer of food over large distances) | Highly feasible |

| Proposal | Positive aspect | Analysis | Verdict |
|---|---|---|---|
| Liming oceans to absorb carbon dioxide | Increases the pH of the ocean so allowing more absorption of carbon dioxide and loss to sediments | Colossal amounts needed. Lime has to be produced by burning limestone, thus producing carbon dioxide so unworkable without capture and storage of this carbon dioxide. Adding lime in quantity will change ocean albedo and could result in unpredictable changes to ocean ecosystems | Probably infeasible and too risky |
| Cloud seeding ships to increase cloudiness and reflect sunlight. Wind propelled ships spray aerosols of sea water | Uses wind energy to power the process | Natural processes already produce clouds and no guarantee that cloudiness would be increased. Even if it did there would be other consequences, for example on marine production, that could be detrimental | Probably infeasible and too risky |
| Conversion of power station carbon dioxide into algal biomass for biofuels or into methanol by chemical processes for fuel | Gains more usable energy per unit carbon dioxide. Essentially a recycling process | Earth already has recycling processes that do this, except that the natural systems previously doing it have been destroyed. Algae culture requires space and energy is needed to concentrate the algae into fuel or process them into fuel products, as it is for chemical methanol production. There seems to be no net gain and it would be better to re-establish ecosystems that are more efficient at recycling, having been subjected to the continual testing of natural selection over millions of years | No major gain and detracts from the need to restore natural ecosystems that have been lost |
| Increasing energy efficiency of buildings by better insulation and better design and use of solar panels | Entirely positive | Needs financial incentives from government as can initially be costly. Will take a long time to achieve on a wide scale and needs legal provisions to ensure completion | Highly feasible |
| Increasing ocean phytoplankton production by fertilization to produce more sedimenting organic matter or by seaweed farming | Theoretically attractive since ocean phytoplankton already sediments a great deal of carbon. Sea weed farming is carbon neutral unless the seaweed is digested and the carbon dioxide permanently stored | Increasing algal stocks increases absorption of solar radiation and physical warming. Fertilization changes the composition of the ocean phytoplankton from calcium carbonate depositing species to others whose organic matter is more readily recycled within the surface layers, so there could be a net detrimental effect | Highly dangerous |
| Artificial photosynthesis; development of a chemical replacement for natural photosynthesis that more efficiently uses carbon dioxide, thus allowing release of land for other purposes, such a energy generation | Ostensibly attractive in terms of production of more and cheaper food or of hydrogen as a fuel, thus increasing the energy to carbon dioxide ratio | Unlikely that such a process can be developed. Natural photosynthesis has evolved over a very long period and subjected to natural selection so that it is very likely to be the most efficient possible process under earth conditions. Artificial photosynthesis if developed would encourage greater exploitation of the planet's resources and compound the problems overall | Probably infeasible and very dangerous |

resilient and the mechanisms that stabilize the biosphere within limits for life and have carried it through major extinction events in the past will undoubtedly continue to operate, but for large organisms, particularly ourselves, the future is far from certain. To guarantee a human future we have to solve two equations satisfactorily. Paul Ehrlich drew up the original version of the first:

Environmental damage = Population size
    × resource use × waste (pollutant) production
    × power of technology

The second equation is that:

Environmental value (or negative damage, if you like)
    = (Ecosystem size × structure
        × connectivity)/available nutrients

Moving into these areas takes us to the margins of the scope of this book, but they nonetheless are the contexts for looking after freshwater habitats and water resources. Environmental repair from the Ehrlich equation increases if reductions are made in any of the four components, but the emphasis on GDP makes this much more difficult than if human welfare was measured with more comprehensive indices. Populations will inevitably rise to about 9 billion, from the present 6 billion, because the parents of the extra 3 billion are already born. However, by changes in social and economic structures, notably the disparity of power and wealth in many developing countries, which gives the poor very little security over the land they rent to farm, and hence means that security in old age has to be provided by working children, birth rates can and have been reduced. Working against this is the current distasteful and cynical buying up of land in the developing countries by developed countries to attempt to ensure their own food supplies and biofuels with expected global warming.

Reducing resource use, be it energy, water, food or industrial materials is also difficult for countries of the west, already indulging a large ecological footprint and inured to a profligate lifestyle. All current indications, not least those that deal with carbon dioxide emissions by attempting simply to replace energy from fossil fuels by equal or greater amounts from other sources, are that this has still to be taken on board. Although warming will increase river flows on average, by about 10%, this will be matched by a 30–50% population increase and much of the 'new' water will be in remote regions, including the Arctic, away from the centres of population growth. Food and industrial materials might be the lesser problems, though an impending shortage of oil (it will run out eventually) will undermine the plastics industry. In the western world, much of the food that is produced is wasted as a consequence of how the supply chain operates; some estimates are that only 15–20% of what is produced is actually eaten; strong government can reform supplier activities through legislation.

Waste production is easier to reduce as waste has a commercial value as a raw material and recycling schemes have been readily adopted. It is possible that carbon dioxide, also a waste material, will be similarly dealt with to some extent. Technology tends to become more powerful and there is little that will stop this. The key to reducing its impact on the environment is to use it in constructive rather than destructive ways: efficient stoves rather than huge machines to drain wetlands. If some of the four components of the equation cannot be reduced much, then others have to be reduced even more. There are plenty of examples in past cultures where overpopulation, overconsumption or the increasing technology of warfare have led to collapse.

It is in the second equation that greater difficulties lie. The perception of most humans is that they are the most important components of the Earth and that the rest of the planet can be indefinitely bent to their service. The reality that humans depend on ecological services for maintenance of a liveable environment and that these services can be seriously damaged, has not yet been realized or accepted by most, and there are powerful exploitative lobbies that do their best to obfuscate the truth. It may take the consequences of some major catastrophe, rather than logical argument to tip the balance but the truth will eventually prevail.

Environmental damage is now global. The possibilities of moving elsewhere following a collapse, or simply the rise of a new society elsewhere as an old one fails, a common theme of human archaeology, are no longer options for continued comfortable human existence. The indications of the Gaia theory are that there must be repair of ecosystems on a global scale and where repair is not possible, replacement with semi-natural systems that provide more of the services than a wasteland of concrete or an intensive farming system can do. That greenhouse gases are accumulating implies that the systems are being overstretched and that substantial repair of what has been damaged is needed. Natural ecosystems have evolved over a very long period and been tempered by natural selection of their components to an efficiency that it is inconceivable can be improved upon, given the need to incorporate resilience to change. Our problem is that we do not know how much repair is necessary to guarantee a future, but it would be prudent to attempt as much as possible.

The Millennium Ecosystem Assessment attempted a scoping of the problem of ecosystem loss to match the approach of the IPCC on climate change. It too used scenarios to predict future trends (Table 16.8). Its four scenarios paired combinations of global versus regionally based economies with greater or lesser attention to repair of ecosystem services and it used rather fanciful names to describe them. Human welfare, in its predictions, increases more where ecosystems are given their due value (Fig. 16.20) and as in the IPCC scenarios. The business as usual scenario (Order from strength) is most damaging. The TechoGarden scenario, in which it is accepted that restoration of many existing ecosystems may be impossible but that replacements can be designed and managed that replicate some of their features, tends to perform well. But the Assessment overall was pessimistic. Problems still flourish in all the scenarios. Ecosystem destruction, overfishing, population increase and damage from invasive species all increase whatever policy is selected. The Assessment perhaps was too cautious in accepting the political realities of the moment. But these are not fixed and history has many examples of sweeping and rapid change.

We have many techniques for patching up parts of ecosystems. For freshwaters, they are described in Chapters 7, 9 and 15, but the results have been generally temporary and unsatisfactory. This is because they have treated only small components of a much larger damaged whole and have been concerned only with symptoms and proximate causes. If we are seriously to attempt ecosystem repair, and really solve the second of the equations above, we have to be much more ambitious and tackle ultimate causes: the nature of ourselves and our societies, and their political and economic systems. We have to manage whole catchments to minimize nutrient loss to freshwaters; we have to restore the structure that is characteristic of them, be it large timber debris in headwater rivers, the natural flood regime and the undrained floodplain in rivers, the plant-dominated littoral zone and fringing swamps in lakes. We have to reinstate food webs that include not only fish and invertebrates but also the birds and mammals that make linkage with the land systems as well. And we have to reconnect systems. We have to convert the sort of landscape shown in the left of Fig. 16.21 to that on the right and we have to think not in terms of a few hundreds of metres of river stretch or a single small lake or a pond but in terms of entire river systems and catchments.

Above all, we must believe that we can solve the problems, for apathy and self-interest will undermine us all. We have the advantage of large brains with cerebral hemispheres that can foresee consequences but we currently use them, like other apes, in scheming and

**Table 16.8** Millennium Ecosystem Assessment scenarios for predicting future trends.

| *Global orchestration* Global economy, subservient ecology | *Order from strength* Regional economy, subservient ecology | *TechnoGarden* Global economy, pervadent ecology | *Adapting mosaic* Regional economy, pervadent ecology |
|---|---|---|---|
| Globally connected society, focusing on trade. Reactive approach to ecosystem problems, but takes strong steps to reduce poverty and inequality and to invest in infrastructure and education | Regionalized and fragmented world, concerned with security and protection. Emphasizing regional markets, paying little attention to public goods and taking a reactive approach to ecosystem problems | Globally connected world, relying on environmentally sound technology, using highly managed, often engineered ecosystems to deliver ecosystem services and taking a proactive approach to ecosystem problems | Focus on regional, watershed scale ecosystems. Strong local management of ecosystems and proactive approach to problems |

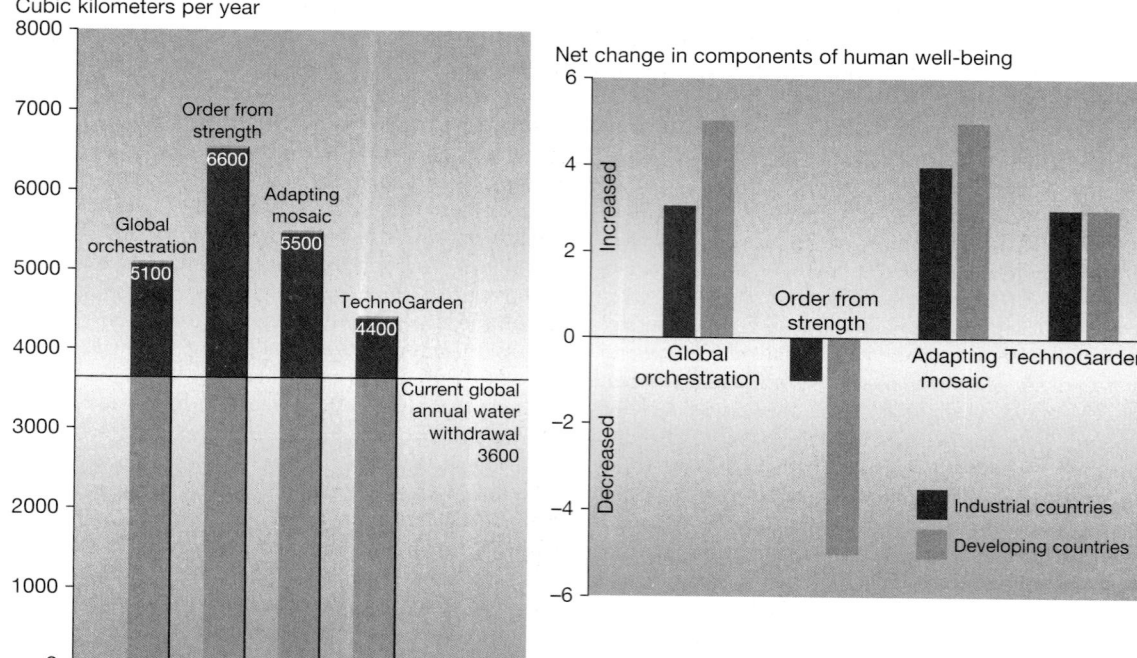

**Fig.16.20** Predictions for the four Millennium Ecosystem Assessment scenarios of water needs (withdrawal by human populations) in 2050 (left). All scenarios predict increased demand, hence decreased availability per person. On the right are predictions of general human well-being in industrial and developing countries. There are increases for three scenarios but marked declines in the Order from Strength scenario. (Based on Millennium Ecosystem Assessment (http://www.millenniumassessment.org/en/index.aspx) 2004.)

deception to selfish advancement. Our future might demand all sorts of revolution. It certainly demands removal of the curse of GDP and its not-so-innocent perpetrators. I will leave the last word to the brilliant, but very human, John F. Kennedy, who as President of the USA said in 1965: 'The problems of the world cannot possibly be solved by sceptics or cynics whose horizons are limited by the obvious realities. We need men who can dream of things that never were'.

## FURTHER READING

The web now has thousands of sites, informal, scientific and governmental, covering climate and environmental change. The two to start with are those of the Intergovernmental Panel on Climate Change (http://www.ipcc.ch/) and the Millennium Ecosystem Assessment (http://www.millenniumassessment.org/en/index.aspx),

from which all reports can be freely downloaded. The key summary documents are IPCC (2007) for physical climate changes and Bates et al. (2008), for water resources. A selection of the many papers giving evidence of existing climate change in freshwaters includes: Adrian et al. (2009) on lakes, Austin & Coleman (2007) for Lake Superior, Baron et al. (2009) on increases in nitrate in headwater streams, Beebee (1995) on amphibian life histories, George et al. (2004) on the effects of changes in the North Atlantic Oscillation on English lakes, Heino et al. (2009) on northern Scandinavia, O'Reilly et al. (2003) for Lake Tanganyika, Parry et al. (2007) for a variety of case studies, and Winfield et al. (2008a,b) for fish communities in Lake Windermere.

Predictions for the effects on freshwaters of climate changes in the future are equally prolific. Graham & Harrod (2009) deal particularly with salmonid fish, Guinotte & Fabry (2008) with ocean acidification,

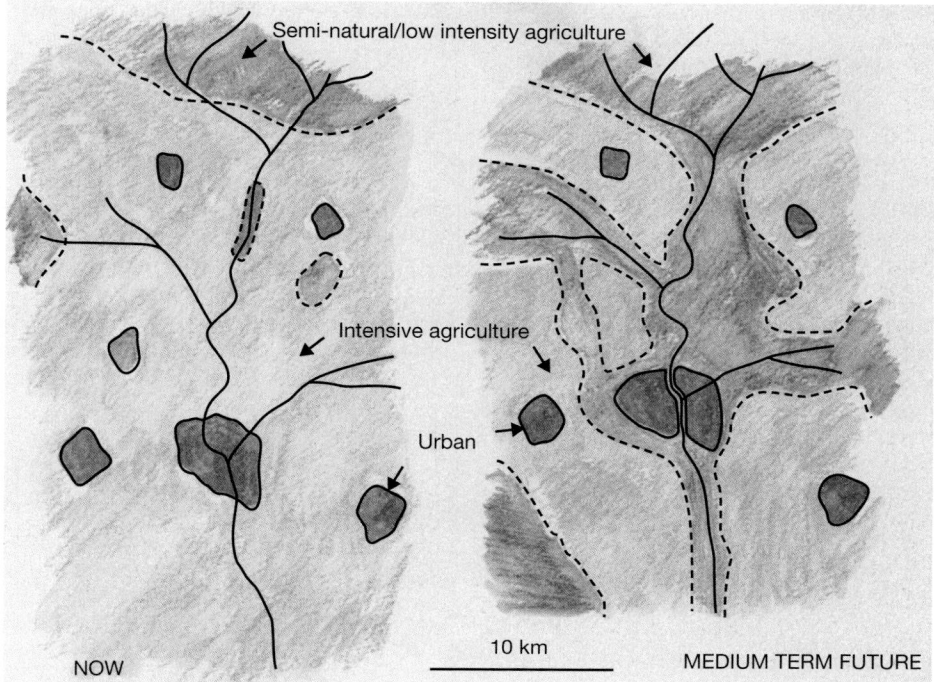

**Fig. 16.21** Current landscape (left) and the sort of landscape (right) that will be needed in industrialized countries in the future. There will need to be a much greater proportion of natural and semi-natural ecosystems to continue to provide ecosystem services, coupled with a much greater connectivity between them.

Jackson et al. (2001) with water resources, Johnson et al. (2009) with British rivers, Johnson et al. (2005) with the prairie pot holes of middle North America and their importance for bird migration, Mooij et al. (2005) for shallow Dutch lakes, Sahoo & Schladow (2008) for lake and reservoir management, Rouse et al. (1997) and Prowse et al. (2006) for Arctic North America. Palmer et al. (2008) make the point that unmodified rivers will be more resilient than tamed ones and Poff (2002) deals with flooding effects.

Previous chapters have listed work concerned with the many other influences of human activities on freshwaters, but particularly relevant to the points made in this one are ones on linkages between systems, where birds and mammals transfer nutrients (Crait & Ben-David (2007), concerning otters and Kameda et al. (2006) about cormorants) or structure the habitat (Naiman & Rogers 1997). Policy makers often question the relevance of maintaining biodiversity, though it is patently obvious to biologists. Hooper et al.

(2005) review the important link between diversity and ecosystem functioning. In contrast, Gherardi (2006) and Pimental et al. (2002) review the severe and increasing problems of introduced species. Many introductions are from relatively warmer climates and may thus be expected to thrive more readily with climate change.

Carbon balance is an important issue, with carbon credits proposed as a currency with which to regulate carbon emissions. In theory, emissions from one country might be compensated for by planting trees or conserving carbon stores about to be damaged, in another. It is a cynical economic approach that will do little but make money for speculators, but it emphasizes the importance of carbon storage. Freshwater lakes and mires are particularly important (Kling et al. 1991; Downing et al. 2006, 2008) and emit more carbon if damaged (Jauhiainen et al. 2005). Ehhalt & Schmidt (1978) review methane movements and Piao et al. (2007) is one of several papers now beginning to question the previous belief that warming would increase the productivity of forests and thence storage of organic matter in their soils.

Concern about the effectiveness of current policies on reducing carbon emissions is given detailed quantitative treatment in Anderson & Bows (2008), who show that a rise to lower than 650 ppm carbon dioxide (about 4°C) is very unlikely on any current policy. Arguments that the situation is retrievable, but the problems are political, not technical, are made by Monbiot (2007) and the Netherlands Environmental Assessment Agency (2008). Ehrlich & Pringle (2008) point out strategies that will also help. Lenton et al. (2007) warn of the risk of precipitous change in the state of the climate and Moss (2008b) notes the current dangerous conservatism in water management.

Ehrlich & Holdren 1971 widen the issue of human futures by considering population, resource use and technology. Diamond (2004) is a fascinating account of how many cultures have collapsed in the past through combinations of climate change, overexploitation of natural resources and pig-headed adherence to established practices. These clearly form models now for a global society. The allusion to ourselves as scheming and deceptive apes comes from Rowlands (2008), who is also not optimistic about our future. Ward (2009) thinks all is lost unless major engineering schemes are put into place to counteract climate change. It seems to me that that will be to compound the errors of the past. It is time to listen to ecologists, not technologists.

# Chapter 17

# PROBLEM EXERCISES

The problems below illustrate some of the intricacies of interpreting freshwater data. They can all be done with basic knowledge and common sense and there are not necessarily simple and single answers. But that is the nature of real problems. If you can work out a satisfying answer, you will have learned a lot.

## EXERCISE 1. STRATIFICATION

Figures 2.10 and 2.11 in Chapter 2 are called depth–time diagrams. To construct them, a series of temperatures is measured at regular intervals during a year at a series of depths in the water column. This can easily be done using a thermistor probe. The probe is part of an electrical circuit with a control box in the boat. A small current is passed through the circuit into the probe, which contains a metal alloy, whose resistance changes rapidly with temperature. The control box measures this resistance and converts it directly to a temperature, read on a screen.

The temperatures are written at their appropriate coordinates of depth and time on a piece of graph paper with depth as the vertical axis and time as the horizontal. Lines, called isotherms, are then drawn among the temperature readings joining up positions of equal temperature. Generally these are drawn at intervals of 1° or 2° but for tropical lakes it may be necessary to use intervals of 0.5° or even 0.1°. Mixing periods will be revealed by the lines being vertical or near vertical, stratified periods by their having a strong horizontal component.

Sketch a likely depth–time diagram for water temperature over a year for a deep, small lake in a volcanic crater in equatorial Africa, where the surface temperature is high (around 30°C all the year round) and there is little seasonality, only brief mixing affecting just the surface layers. Then imagine that there has been heavy rain and a large quantity of rock and soil has plunged from the crater wall in a landslide into the depths of the lake causing considerable mixing. Sketch the depth–time diagram that covers the week before the rains, the following week and then the week after that when normal hot weather has re-established.

The following report appeared on the front page of 'The Guardian' on 26 August 1986:

VOLCANIC GAS KILLS 1500 VILLAGERS

A gas bubble disaster which has killed 1500 people, believed to have been overwhelmed and 'drowned' by gas released from a volcanic crater lake in Cameroon will prompt an international aid effort today. The gas rolled over a six square-mile

*Ecology of Freshwaters: A View for the Twenty-first Century*, 4th edition. By Brian Moss. Published 2010 by Blackwell Publishing Ltd.

area around Lake Nyos, north-west Cameroon, catching villagers unaware and giving them no chance to escape.

Further information subsequently came to light:

'On 21 August at about 21.30 hours a series of rumbling sounds lasting perhaps 15 to 20 seconds caused people in the immediate area of the lake to come out of their homes. One observer reported hearing a bubbling sound, and after walking to a vantage point he saw a white cloud rise from the lake and a large water surge. Many people smelled the odour of rotten eggs or gunpowder, experienced a warm sensation and rapidly lost consciousness. Survivors who woke 6 to 36 hours later felt weak and confused. Many found that their oil lamps had gone out although they still contained oil and that their animals and family members were dead. Birds were not seen in the area for at least 48 hours after the event. The plant life was unaffected. When Swiss missionary helicopter pilots flew into the area on 24 August the lake surface was calm but it was littered with floating mats of vegetation and had turned from its normal blue colour to a rusty red. Vegetation damage showed that a water surge had washed up the southern shore to a height of about 25 m. A water surge 6 m deep had flowed over the spillway at the northern end of the lake'

Lake Nyos (also called Nios) (altitude about 1200 m above sea level) is about 2000 m × 1000 m in dimensions and has a steep-sided basin with a maximum depth of 200 m. The release of gas does not appear to have been from volcanic eruption for there was no heat release with it. It appears to have come from within the lake itself and followed very heavy rain. In a rather similar nearby lake there is a fish, *Konia dikume*, called the bleeding fish because of its tendency to haemorrhage all over the body when caught. Its blood has double the concentration of haemoglobin of other fish. Concentrations of bicarbonate and other ions in the waters of Lake Nyos under normal conditions increased steadily with depth.

Write a short article reconstructing the limnological changes that might have occurred during the events of August 1986, and giving the reasons for your deductions. Include also information (from the internet) on what measures have been taken to avert a future similar disaster.

## EXERCISE 2. CATCHMENTS AND WATER CHEMISTRY

The English (Cumbrian) Lake District offers a splendid example of how the local geology affects the composition of natural waters. It is an area of low mountains (up to about 1000 m) highest at the centre, with lakes radiating out from the centre like the spokes of a wheel. These were formed by glaciers gouging out the valleys, then leaving moraines to act as dams at the feet of the valleys, when the ice melted back. There are also many small mountain lakes or tarns at the heads of the valleys in basins, called corries or cwms, gouged out by ice, and a few lakes, also formed by ice action in the lowlands surrounding the mountains. The highest central part of the area is craggy and formed from igneous rocks of the Borrowdale Volcanic Series whilst the northern part, of smoother hills, is of metamorphic rocks, the Skiddaw Slates, which are slightly more easily weathered. To the south, in a more subdued landscape of low hills, are sedimentary rocks formed in the Silurian Period and these are often sandstones. Surrounding the upland area are more recent, softer rocks in lowlands of soft sandstone and limestone. Figure 17.1 shows the geology of the area and the total ionic composition of many of the lake waters, expressed as the conductivity. This is a measure of the ability of the water to conduct an electric current and depends on the amounts of ions dissolved in it. It is measured in μSiemens cm$^{-1}$. Conductivity is the reciprocal of the more familiar resistance, measured in ohms. Note how the conductivities are generally related to the nature of the local geology. Then examine Table 17.1, which shows some basic data for some of the bigger lakes, which are identified on Fig. 17.1. How and why are the various characteristics related? Consider the ratios of values (Na : Ca for example) as well as their absolute values and plot scatter diagrams. If you are familiar with statistics, try using regression analysis to reveal the relationships.

## EXERCISE 3. THE VOLLENWEIDER MODEL

You are a water quality planner for a national environmental agency. Use equation 4.1 to estimate the relative effect on concentration of a substance in a small lake, of a climatic change that increased the rate of run-off of water from the catchment by 30%. Assume

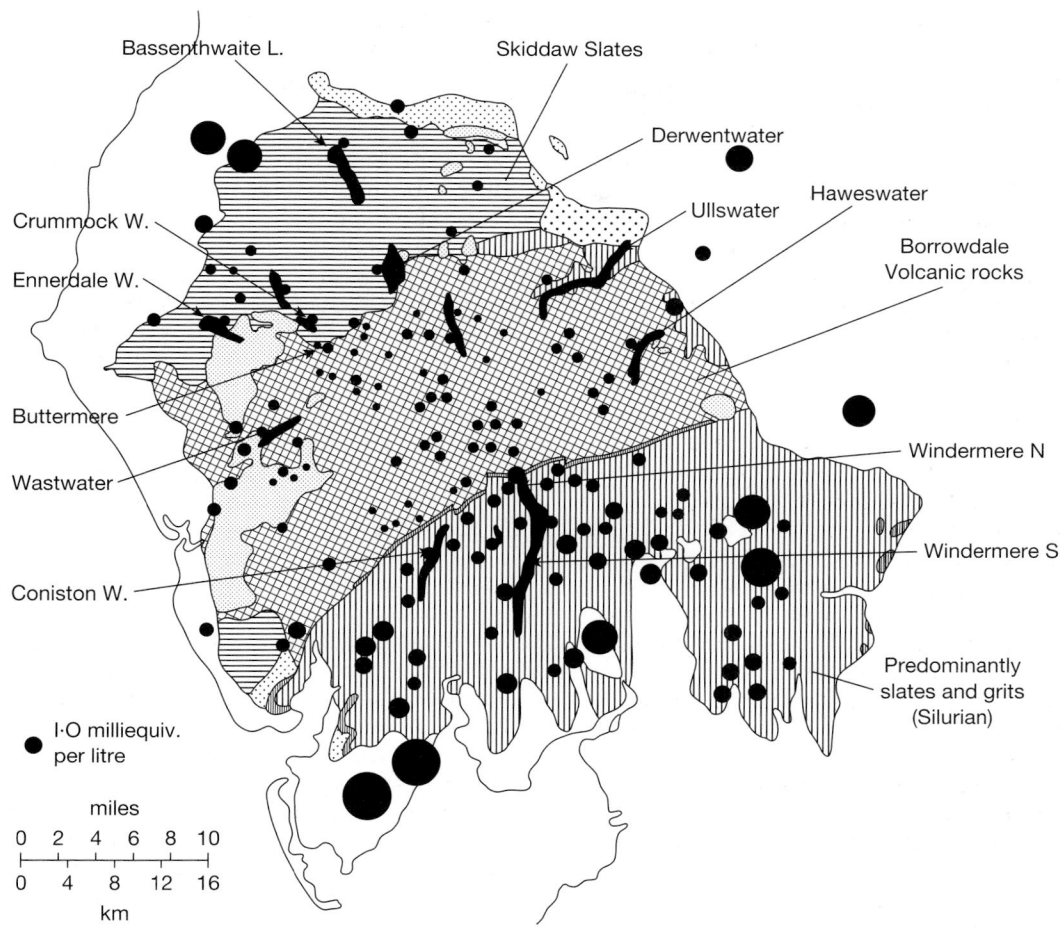

**Fig. 17.1** The total ion content, measured as conductivity, of the waters of the English Lake District, reflects the nature of the underlying rocks. The larger the symbol, the greater the conductivity (data from Mackereth 1957). Borrowdale volcanic (igneous) and Skiddaw slate (metamorphic) rocks weather slowly and give low ion waters; sedimentary rocks in the southern part give higher values, but the highest conductivities come from limestones on the fringes. Some of the major lakes, for which data are given in Table 3.2, are shown. The lakes radiate outwards from the central, highest mountains, like the spokes of a wheel. They were formed as river valleys were dammed by glacial moraines when the last glaciation ended about 12,000 years ago.

the lake has no point sources of this substance, only soil-derived diffuse ones and that the concentration in the inflow water is not altered by the rate of run-off. Now make a similar estimate for a second lake that has a major, steady point source of the substance (e.g. a sewage treatment works or a herd of hippopotami), providing half of the total load prior to the climate change. Now consider how the estimate might change for extremely large lakes rather than small ones. The

equation was derived for exorheic lakes with a flow-through. How might the equation change for endorheic lakes?

## EXERCISE 4. NUTRIENT BUDGETING

In considering management of water bodies in which the loads of elements such as nitrogen and phosphorus

**Table 17.1** Characteristics of some of the major English Lake District lakes.

| | Altitude (m a.s.l.) | Geology of catchment | Mean depth (m) | Percentage of catchment cultivable | Na$^+$ (mg L$^{-1}$) | Ca$^{++}$ (mg L$^{-1}$) | Maximum nitrate (mg N L$^{-1}$) | Dissolved vitamin B$_{12}$ (ng L$^{-1}$) | Phytoplankton biomass (µg L$^{-1}$) |
|---|---|---|---|---|---|---|---|---|---|
| Wastwater | 61 | Igneous | 39.7 | 5.2 | 3.6 | 4.4 | 0.14 | No data | 23 |
| Buttermere | 110 | Igneous | 16.6 | 6.0 | 3.6 | 4.3 | 0.11 | 2 | 70 |
| Ennerdale Water | 120 | Igneous | 17.8 | 5.4 | 3.8 | 4.9 | 0.13 | No data | 93 |
| Crummock Water | 107 | Igneous | 26.7 | 8.0 | 3.8 | 4.2 | 0.14 | 1.8 | 110 |
| Haweswater | 241 | Igneous | 23.4 | 7.7 | 3.0 | 9.6 | 0.14 | No data | 370 |
| Coniston Water | 50 | Igneous/ sedimentary | 24.1 | 21.8 | 4.3 | 11.6 | 0.25 | No data | 790 |
| Windermere (north basin) | 39 | Igneous | 25.1 | 29.4 | 3.5 | 11.3 | 0.28 | 6.12 | 1400 |
| Derwent Water | 50 | Igneous | 5.5 | 10.0 | 4.9 | 8.9 | 0.10 | 2.78 | 1800 |
| Windermere (south Basin) | 39 | Sedimentary/ igneous | 21.3 | 29.4 | 3.8 | 12.4 | 0.25 | 7.94 | 2800 |
| Ullswater | 145 | Igneous | 25.3 | 16.6 | 3.3 | 11.3 | 0.15 | No data | 3800 |
| Bassenthwaite Lake | 75 | Igneous/ metamorphic | 5.8 | 29.4 | 5.1 | 10.8 | 0.25 | 6.56 | 4200 |

have been increased, with the creation of eutrophica-tion problems (e.g., increased algal growth and prob-lems for the filtration of the water for the drinking water supply), the first step is to compile a budget to work out the sources and sinks of the substance. The following gives you experience of doing this for phosphorus in a shallow lake in eastern England. Phosphorus comes from point (discrete) sources and diffuse sources. The point sources are the sewage treatment works; the diffuse sources are agricultural (arable and some stock). The task is to construct a balance sheet, like a bank account, with Inputs on one side and Outputs on the other. It helps if you first construct a flow diagram showing the inputs and outputs of water and then work out where the phosphorus sits in this. You need to be very careful about units. The ultimate balance sheet, which should account for all inputs and outputs so that inputs = outputs, should be in grams of P per m$^2$ of lake per year (g P m$^{-2}$ yr$^{-1}$). You will need to use ALL the data given in Table 17.2.

What source(s) deliver most of the phosphorus, control of which should therefore take priority in restoring the lake from eutrophication? Use equation 4.1 to calculate the mean annual concentration in the lake. A pristine lake in this situation would have about 25 µg P L$^{-1}$. How do present concentrations relate to this?

## EXERCISE 5. LIGHT PENETRATION

A photometer was lowered into Wet Lake in June. Measurements of light intensity at different depths were made with its photoelectric cell variously covered with filters that selectively passed blue light (460–500 nm), green light (500–580 nm), yellow light (580–590 nm) and red light (640–720 nm). The light intensities at particular depths in the water column, normalized to constant surface light intensity, are shown (in arbitrary units) in Table 17.3.

Plot these data in a form that will give straight-line graphs and then calculate the extinction (absorption) coefficients in m$^{-1}$ for each waveband and comment on their relative sizes, and the likely reasons for the differences. Explain precisely what an extinction coefficient is and why it has the units that it has. In Wet Lake, net phytoplankton photosynthesis was detectable at 11 m and microscopic algae were found growing on the bottom mud at this depth also. However, bulky aquatic plants (macrophytes) were found in water no deeper than 8 m. Why do you think this was so? How would you expect the relative magnitudes of the extinction coefficients for red, blue, green and yellow light to change in a peat-stained brown water in a lake in the Boreal forest, surrounded by thick peaty deposits, given that Wet lake has water that has only moderate amounts of coloured organic matter dissolved in it?

**Table 17.2** Data necessary for calculation of the nutrient budget of Barton Broad. Based on Osborne (1980). Broad is a local term for a shallow lake in eastern England.

| | |
|---|---|
| Area of catchment (km$^2$) at the outflow from the Broad | 118 |
| Area of Broad (ha) | 63.4 |
| Mean depth of Broad (m) | 1.0 |
| Annual rainfall on catchment (cm) | 50 |
| Annual evaporation from catchment (cm) | 45 |
| Number of people served by sewage works | 8000 |
| Annual phosphorus excreted and used by one person each year (g yr$^{-1}$) | 800 |
| Mean concentration of phosphorus in water running from the land in the catchment (agricultural sources) (µg P L$^{-1}$) | 50 |
| Phosphorus concentration in rain falling directly on the Broad (µg P L$^{-1}$) | 10 |
| Current sedimentation rate (of wet sediment) (cm yr$^{-1}$) | 1.12 |
| Density of wet sediment (g cm$^{-3}$) | 1.12 |
| Water content of sediment (%) | 80 |
| Phosphorus content of dry sediment (mg P g$^{-1}$) | 1.8 |

**Table 17.3** Penetration of light of different wavebands into Wet Lake. Values are arbitrary units.

| Depth (m) | Blue | Green | Yellow | Red |
|---|---|---|---|---|
| 0 | 120 | 96.3 | 191 | 79.8 |
| 0.1 | 104.8 | 91.2 | 168.9 | 69.8 |
| 1 | 76.1 | 67.9 | 95.5 | 47.9 |
| 2 | 64.2 | 53.7 | 67.3 | 28.2 |
| 3 | 38.7 | 42.6 | 37.7 | 18.0 |
| 4 | 33.0 | 34.5 | 31.7 | 12.0 |
| 6 | 22.5 | 18.7 | 15.1 | 4.9 |
| 8 | 9.3 | 9.8 | 10.3 | 2.8 |
| 10 | 4.4 | 4.7 | 4.4 | 1.3 |
| 12 | 1.3 | 1.8 | 1.9 | 0.35 |
| 14 | 0.53 | 0.71 | 0.80 | 0.14 |
| 16 | 0.20 | 0.32 | 0.60 | 0.06 |
| 18 | 0.10 | 0.14 | 0.13 | 0.03 |
| 20 | – | 0.09 | 0.08 | 0.01 |
| 22 | – | – | 0.02 | – |

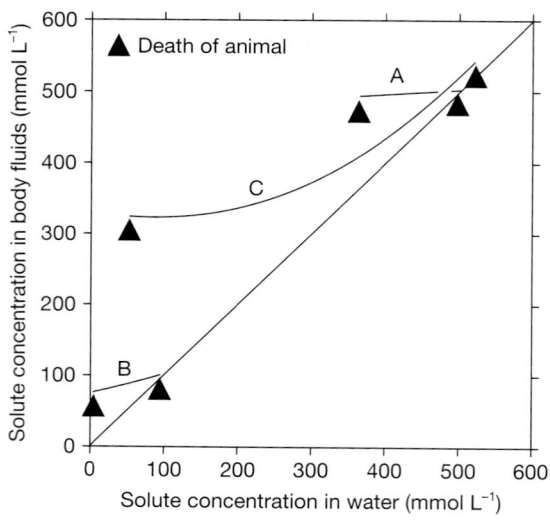

**Fig. 17.2** Salinity tolerances of three species, A, B and C from a little explored island.

## EXERCISE 6. BIODIVERSITY

Comment on the following data (Table 17.4) on number of species of phytoplankton algae and fish in four different lakes, making hypotheses to explain the differences in species richness, drawing your interpretation from your knowledge of these and other lakes.

## EXERCISE 7. PROBLEMS WITH A FROG

Scientific notebooks have just been discovered with information about aquatic invertebrates from three

different habitats on a remote island. This information was first about the concentrations of body fluids (vertical axis) in three animal species, A, B and C, when they were placed in waters of different salinities (horizontal axis) (Fig. 17.2). A 45° line has been drawn also showing points where external and internal salinities would be equal. Secondly, there was information about the number of species found in the open water and in the sediments of the three habitats, 1, 2 and 3 from which A, B and C separately came (Table 17.5). Third, the main animal groups found in each of the three habitats were indicated (Table 17.6) as lists X, Y and Z.

**Table 17.4** Characteristics of four contrasted lakes.

| | Wroxham Broad | Lake Victoria | Lake Superior | Lake Chilwa |
|---|---|---|---|---|
| Locality | UK | East Africa | USA/Canada | Central Africa |
| Nature | Small, shallow, nutrient-rich, exorheic | Large, deep, moderately nutrient-rich, exorheic | Large, deep, nutrient-poor, exorheic | Large, shallow, nutrient-rich, endorheic |
| Number of species of phytoplankton algae | 112 | 120 | 170 | 56 |
| Number of species of fish | 8 | 700 | 131 | 12 |

**Table 17.5** Number of species recorded of invertebrates greater than 1 mm in size in the three habitats 1, 2 and 3.

| Number of species | Habitat 1 | Habitat 2 | Habitat 3 |
|---|---|---|---|
| Open water | 10 | 126 | 20 |
| Sediment | 22 | 138 | 46 |

**Table 17.6** Dominant groups of invertebrates in Communities X, Y and Z.

| Community X | Community Y | Community Z |
|---|---|---|
| Oligochaetes | Polychaete worms | Polychaete worms |
| Triclads | Crustacea | Crustacea |
| Gastropods | Bivalve molluscs | Gastropods |
| Chironomid larvae | | Echinoderms |
| Crustacea | | Bivalve molluscs |
| Mayfly nymphs | | Nemertean worms |

Fortunately or unfortunately, the scientist who wrote the notebooks concerned found a frog, which she kissed and which turned into a handsome prince. She then abandoned her work to live happily ever after without giving a key to the codes A, B and C, 1, 2 and 3 and X, Y and Z. We wish to salvage whatever information we can from this hitherto unexplored island. Please attempt, setting out your logic and reasons, to make what you think might be the proper connections among species physiology, habitat and community. Also explain how animals A, B and C might maintain the concentrations of the body fluids that they do.

## EXERCISE 8. PREDATION IN STREAMS

Cages were created enclosing the bottom gravel and overlying water in a Swedish stream with a water depth of about 30 cm. The cages were 1.5 m long and 0.5 m high and wide, and made of plexiglass, except that the upstream and downstream ends were of 6 mm mesh plastic netting. There were 16 such cages and into a random four of them were placed two brown trout (*Salmo trutta*), about 12 cm long. To another four were

added two bullhead (*Cottus gobio*), about 11 cm long. A further four had one trout and one bullhead and the remaining four were kept free of fish. The cages were placed in the stream one month before the experiment began, and ceramic tiles were placed on the bottom for biofilm colonization.

The experiment lasted for the month of July and after two weeks the fish were removed briefly, anaesthetized, and their stomach contents gently removed by suction. The fish were then replaced. All lived. At the end of the experiment, the gut contents were again measured and the bottom invertebrates remaining in the cages were sampled by disturbing the bottom and catching the animals in a fine net held downstream. The tiles were also removed and chlorophyll *a* in the biofilms extracted and measured. Figure 17.3 shows the two fish species, Table 17.7 shows the results of a statistical analysis on the invertebrate populations left after the experiment ended, and Table 17.8, the results of examining the stomach contents of the fish in terms of the numbers of different groups of invertebrates eaten. Figure 17.3 also shows the results of measuring the chlorophyll *a* on the ceramic tiles at the end of the experiment. What might be concluded from these data?

## EXERCISE 9. DEFORESTATION AND TROPICAL STREAMS

The island of Borneo was once almost entirely covered by primary tropical rain forest, but much has been removed in recent years, at first by increasing populations of slash and burn cultivators, who moved on after a period and allowed a secondary forest to recover. Commercial deforestation in recent years has been much more extensive. Eight streams in primary forest and eight in secondary forest, following slashing and burning, 9–21 years previously, were examined. Some of the data are shown in Table 17.9. Comment on these data. Are the communities of the secondary forest inferior to those of the primary forest?

## EXERCISE 10. SWAMP HABITATS AND INSECT ADAPTATIONS

Figure 17.4 shows measurements made of the water chemistry along a transect through a floating swamp of papyrus on a river delta at the edge of Lake Victoria in Uganda in 1929. Explain the patterns found and the

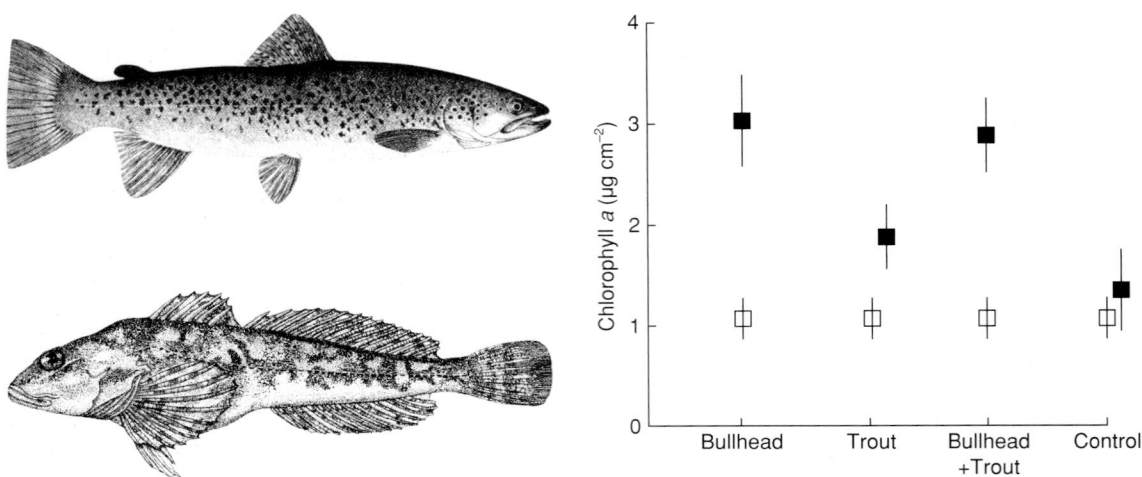

**Fig. 17.3** Trout, bullhead (from Maitland, 1972) and the results of an experiment where these fish were placed in cages in which ceramic tiles had been placed. The chlorophyll $a$ in the algae on the tiles was measured at the beginning (open symbols) and end (closed symbols) of the experiment. (From Dahl 1998a).

**Table 17.7** The results of an experiment in which the bottom invertebrates were counted following exposure in cages in a stream to bullhead (B), trout (T), both bullhead and trout (B+T) or no fish at all (C). The second column shows the relative numbers in terms of whether they were greater in some treatments than others. The third column shows the statistical significance or probability that the results were obtained by chance as calculated from a one-way Analysis of Variance. The smaller the probability, the more likely it is that the result is a real rather than a random effect. A value of 0.05 or 1 in 20 is conventionally taken as being the threshold of real significance, but values of up to 0.1 (1 in 10) are often recognized.

| Taxon | Result | Probability |
|---|---|---|
| *Baetis rhodani* (mayfly nymph) | C greater than all others, which did not differ | 0.004 |
| *Ephemera danica* (mayfly nymph) | No differences | 0.66 |
| *Gammarus pulex* (freshwater shrimp) | C and T did not differ but were greater than B or B+T | 0.004 |
| Orthocladiinae (two-winged fly larvae) | No differences | 0.52 |
| Tanypodiinae (two-winged fly larvae) | No differences | 0.8 |
| Chironomid pupae (two-winged fly pupae) | No differences | 0.52 |
| Simuliidae (blackfly larvae) | C and T did not differ but were greater than B or B+T | 0.07 |
| Tipuliidae (cranefly larvae) | No differences | 0.1 |
| *Pacificastacus leniuscullus* (crayfish) | C, T and B+T did not differ but all were greater than B | 0.014 |
| Limnephilidae (caddis fly larvae) | C and T did not differ but were greater than B or B+T | 0.07 |
| *Polycentropus* sp (caddis fly larvae) | C and T did not differ but were greater than B or B+T | <0.001 |
| *Leuctra* sp (stonefly nymph) | C and T did not differ but were greater than B or B+T | 0.003 |

links among them. Figure 17.5 shows the results of experimental work with nymphs of a damselfly (*Proischnura subfuscatum*, Zygoptera) that is common in pools among Uganda floodplain papyrus swamps, where it occurs in water with an average oxygen concentration of 0.85 mg L$^{-1}$ (or in terms of partial pressure, 14 mm Hg). Like all zygopterans it has three flat plates or tail fans or gills at its rear, which are variously used for absorption of oxygen, exchange of ions, movement and signalling between individuals.

**Table 17.8** Prey consumption of bullhead and trout measured from their gut contents.

| Prey | Number of prey eaten per fish | |
|---|---|---|
| | **Bullhead** | **Trout** |
| Aquatic | | |
|   *Gammarus pulex* | 2.17 | 0.19 |
|   *Pacificastus leniusculus* | 0.5 | 0 |
|   *Baetis rhodani* | 1.08 | 0.44 |
|   *Leuctra* sp | 0.17 | 0 |
|   *Polycentropus* sp | 0.25 | 0 |
|   Tanypodiinae | 0.08 | 0.06 |
|   Orthocladiinae | 0.17 | 0.69 |
|   Simuliidae | 0.08 | 0 |
| Terrestrial | | |
|   Coleoptera (beetles) | 0 | 0.12 |
|   Diptera (two-winged flies) | 0 | 1.0 |
|   Arachnida (spiders) | 0 | 0.38 |
|   Trichoptera (caddis flies) | 0 | 0.06 |
|   Formicidae (ants) | 0 | 0.06 |

These gills are often broken off when predators, such as beetles, attempt to capture the nymph by grasping them.

Experiments were carried out on groups of nymphs that had their gills intact or had lost them. In all graphs, the gilled group is shaded. Upper left (Fig. 17.5) shows the rate of oxygen consumption with standard deviations, measured in closed containers (respirometers). The difference is significant at $P < 0.05$. Lower left (Fig. 17.5) shows the percentage of time the nymphs spent submerged on the bottom of containers in which they also had access to air (through being able to climb out of the water on a twig) over a range of oxygen concentrations, expressed as partial pressures. Right (Fig. 17.5) shows some behaviour over a range of oxygen partial pressures. The upper panel shows percentage of time spent out of the water, the middle panel shows the percentage of time the animals spent lifting their wing buds away from their bodies and the lower panel the percentage of time spent spreading the wing buds widely away from the body. Probability values are shown for the differences between the gilled and non-gilled groups. Explain the meaning of these data.

**Table 17.9** Characteristics of streams ($n = 8$) in primary and secondary forest in Sabah, north-west Borneo. Mean values are shown with the statistical probability of difference between them. For small invertebrates, values are numbers per $m^2$ and for crabs, shrimps and fish they are catch per unit effort, using standardized methods within each group.

| Characteristic | Primary forest | Secondary forest | Probability |
|---|---|---|---|
| Maximum water temperature (°C) | 25.8 | 25.8 | 0.917 |
| Channel slope (%) | 2.0 | 0.9 | 0.067 |
| Mean width (m) | 5.2 | 4.4 | 0.385 |
| Particle size (log units) of sediment | 3.9 | 1.8 | <0.001 |
| Area of sediment (%) | 57.6 | 86.2 | 0.002 |
| Overhang of forest (%) | 27.3 | 6.9 | <0.001 |

| | Density | Species richness | Density | Species richness | Density | Species richness |
|---|---|---|---|---|---|---|
| Ephemeroptera | 581 | 14 | 187 | 11 | <0.001 | 0.01 |
| Plecoptera | 54 | 4 | 7 | 4 | <0.001 | 0.89 |
| Trichoptera | 266 | 11 | 39 | 8 | <0.001 | 0.01 |
| Odonata | 29 | 4 | 11 | 4 | 0.07 | 0.91 |
| Diptera | 1191 | 11 | 733 | 10 | 0.12 | 0.56 |
| Coleoptera | 174 | 12 | 112 | 13 | 0.22 | 0.45 |
| Palaeomonidae + Atyidae | 1.6 | 8 | 2.1 | 8 | <0.01 | 0.88 |
| Potamonidae + Parathelphusidae | 0.11 | 2 | 0.01 | 2 | <0.001 | 0.88 |
| Open water fish | 0.86 | 6 | 0.74 | 6 | 0.36 | 0.57 |
| Benthic fish | 0.51 | 11 | 0.23 | 9 | 0.05 | 0.02 |

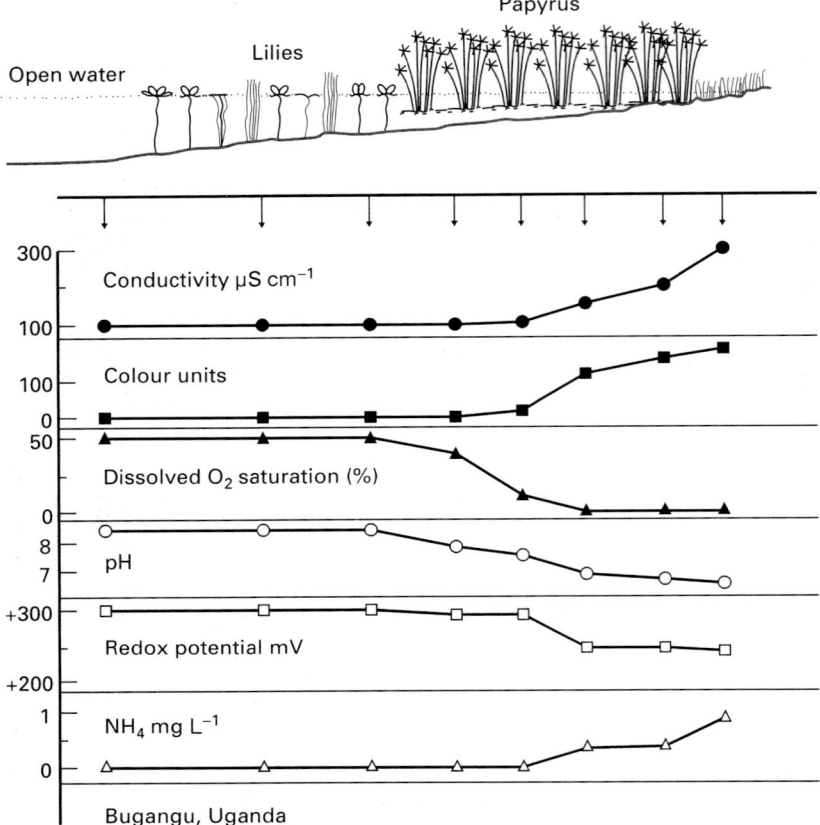

**Fig. 17.4** Water chemistry of a transect through a Ugandan papyrus swamp. (Based on Carter 1955.)

## EXERCISE 11. ECOSYSTEM VALUATION IN A FLOODPLAIN

Various ways are being explored to justify the maintenance of natural systems in a social and political system that has traditionally seen them there for exploitation rather than as a basic life-support system. One of these is through economic valuation of the services they provide. This is relatively easy if the services are traded (e.g., the renting of grassland for grazing, the sale of timber, the cost of fishing licences, the value of sold fish and the receipts of tourism through entry fees to parks and reserves). It is least easy for cultural and spiritual services and for the regulatory services such as regulation of atmospheric composition and maintenance of water quality. Cultural services can only be estimated by asking a wide range of people how much they would be willing to pay for them if they

had to, and the numbers given depend on who is asked, when they are asked and how they are feeling at the time. Regulatory services can only be assessed by calculating the cost of producing and operating a machine that would replace these services. In general such costs turn out to be infinitely high for such services are irreplaceable. Existing examples of valuations thus tend to be partial and limited, but they illustrate the principle.

The town of Wareham in Dorset, UK lies between the floodplain sections of two rivers, the Frome and the Piddle, which have been embanked within the town and will remain so. But below the town, the former floodplain, bordering the estuary, has also been enclosed by banks, which keep out the sea and river floods and are now grazing marshes (400 ha with some 26 properties). They are of some nature conservation value because they are quite wet, but are less valuable

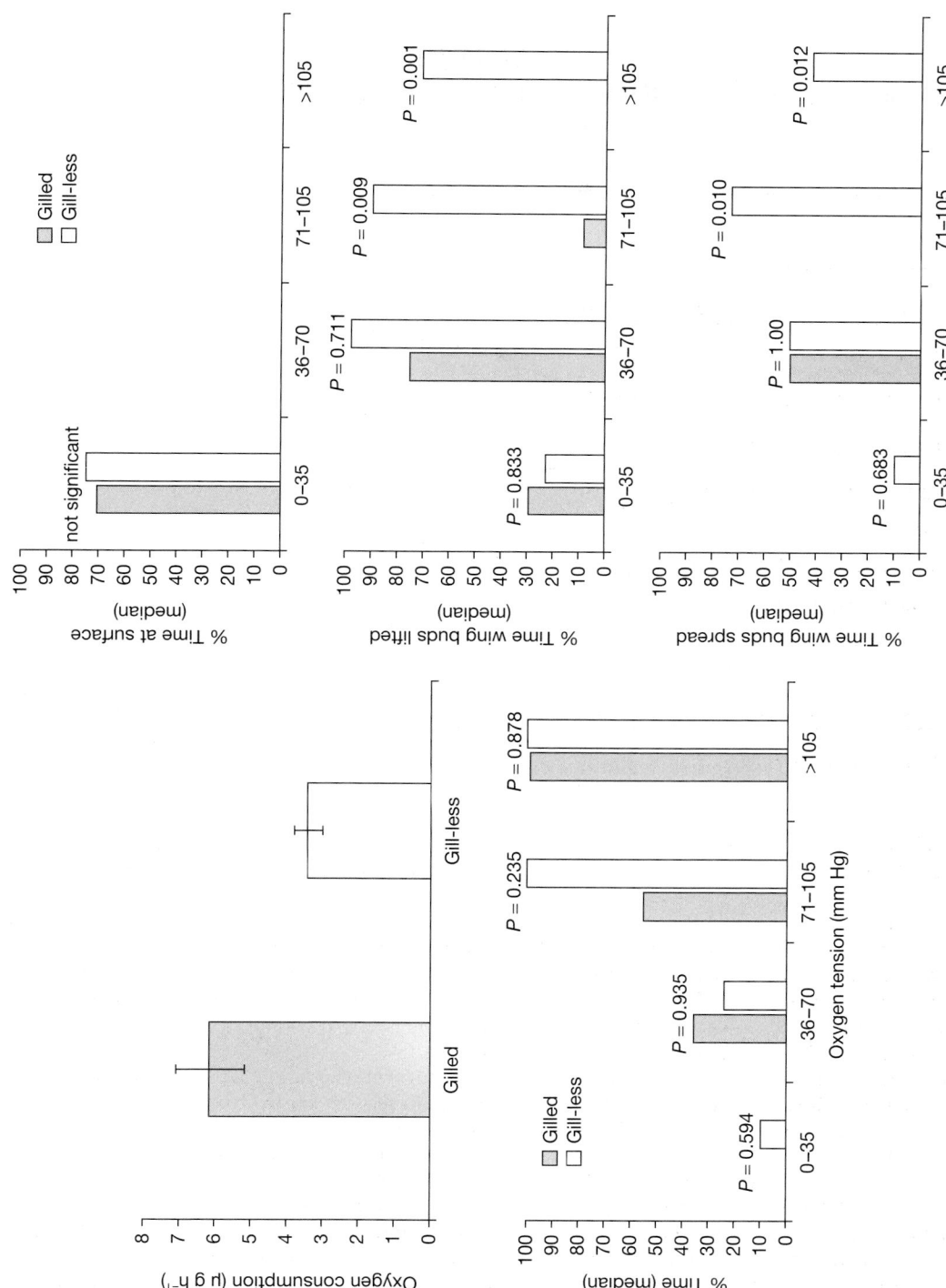

**Fig. 17.5** Results of experiments with nymphs of a damselfly from swamp waters. (Based on Apodaca & Chapman 2004.)

**Table 17.10** Estimated values for all ecosystem services other than carbon storage, denitrification and phosphorus fixation in soils and sediments, which are shown collectively, for component habitats of the former floodplain below Wareham under various options for managing the floodbanks or breaching them. Values are means over the next 100 years and are in millions of pounds at 2005 prices.

| Option | Value of component for the whole scheme | | | | | | | | | Total |
|---|---|---|---|---|---|---|---|---|---|---|
| | Saltmarsh | Mudflat | Reedbed | Woodland | Heathland | Grazing marsh | Carbon storage | Denitrification | P control | |
| Present | 0.69 | 5.68 | 1.66 | 2.04 | 1.39 | 0.26 | 0.47 | 0.2 | 0.12 | 18.01 |
| 1. Do nothing | 1.41 | 9.36 | 4.29 | 1.36 | 1.12 | 0.25 | 0.99 | 0.43 | 0.26 | 21.75 |
| 2. Minimal repairs | 1.32 | 9.52 | 2.65 | 1.36 | 1.12 | 0.27 | 0.83 | 0.36 | 0.21 | 20.77 |
| 3. Rebuild to higher standard | 0.69 | 5.56 | 1.36 | 2.04 | 1.39 | 0.23 | 0.44 | 0.19 | 0.11 | 17.51 |
| 4. Limited breaching | 1.44 | 9.41 | 3.16 | 1.38 | 1.35 | 0.26 | 0.89 | 0.38 | 0.23 | 21.39 |
| 5. Complete breaching | 1.37 | 9.31 | 4.29 | 1.36 | 1.35 | 0.25 | 0.99 | 0.42 | 0.25 | 21.89 |

than the reedswamps, saltmarshes and mudflats, which formerly occupied this area. The floodbanks are old and weak, and cost a great deal to maintain. They are also likely to be increasingly ineffective as sea levels rise and summer rainfall increases.

The British Government is also obliged, under European legislation, to create saltmarsh and reedswamp habitats that might be lost elsewhere with sea-level rise. A decision has to be made about future management of the area. The options are: (1) to do nothing and allow the floodbanks to erode, resulting in re-establishment of the floodplain in time but possibly with very severe flooding in the interim; (2) to carry out minimal repairs, again with the possibility of severe flooding in a high flood, but possibly delaying such an event; (3) to rebuild the banks completely to higher levels to cope with increased sea level and river flows. This would be expensive and give no increase in habitat but maximal protection to agricultural grazing marsh and property; (4) to breach the banks in some places and allow reestablishment of part of the floodplain, and some valuable habitat, whilst putting in extra protection for the more valuable properties and land; (5) to breach the banks extensively to reconstitute the downstream floodplain, giving maximal new habitat, but with greater flooding of grazing marsh and agricultural properties.

For the 400 ha as a whole, present or future ecosystem services include grazing land, freshwater and marine fisheries and fish nurseries, carbon storage in soils, denitrification of water entering the estuary, fixation of pollutant phosphate from the river, recreation (boating, angling, bird watching, shooting (of duck and other wildfowl) and tourism (walking, aesthetic backdrop to an attractive town). The problem lies in which option would give greatest benefit. Table 17.10 shows estimated total values of provisioning and cultural ecosystem services of various habitats within the 400 ha and of three regulatory services (carbon storage, denitrification, phosphorus removal) for the whole area. On the basis of these data, which option would you choose and why?

## EXERCISE 12. TOP DOWN AND BOTTOM UP CONTROL IN SHALLOW AND DEEP LAKES

Table 17.11 gives data on nine variables for each of 24 lakes, formed as kettle holes on the formerly glaciated north-west midlands plain in the UK. Using whatever graphical or statistical techniques are available to you, establish whether there are any patterns or groupings among these lakes. Can you classify them or find continuous trends among them? What controls the amount of phytoplankton chlorophyll *a* in these lakes?

## EXERCISE 13. PALATABILITY OF AQUATIC PLANTS TO FISH

For a long time it was thought that grazing on submerged plants was negligible and that they became available to the littoral animals as food only as dead detritus. There is now evidence that they are grazed no less than plants in other habitats and interest has turned to why some are grazed more than others. There are several ways in which a particular species might reduce grazing losses. In a set of experiments, vulnerability to grazing by common carp *Cyprinus carpio*, was tested on five aquatic plants. Table 17.12 shows some characteristics of these species. Figure 17.6 shows the amounts taken by the fish under standard conditions when whole plants were offered and when the plants had been ground up and made into pellets of the same size and shape. Figure 17.6 also shows results of an experiment in which extracts of each plant were made with ethanol (water soluble) and diethyl ether (non-water soluble) and the extracts mixed into pellets with ground lettuce and broccoli, which were shown otherwise to be palatable to the carp. Comment on the relative vulnerabilities and defences of the five aquatic species to grazing by carp.

## EXERCISE 14. THE PLANKTON OF PADDLING POOLS

A most revealing experiment on lake function was carried out in children's plastic portable swimming pools placed on the roof of San Diego State College in California (Hurlbert et al. 1971). The pools were given a standard sediment of chopped alfalfa, filled with water and inoculated with algae and animals from local ponds. An omnivorous fish, *Gambusia affinis*, was added to half of the ponds, the remainder being fishless, and the consequences were followed over several weeks. Table 17.13 gives some of the main data. Interpret them as fully as you can and create a scenario of how the contrasted systems were functioning.

**Table 17.11** Data from a series of small kettle-hole lakes in the north-west Midlands of the UK. G, ground water; S, surface water.

| Lake | Area (ha) | Maximum depth (m) | Thermal stratification in summer | Source of water | Plant cover (summer) (%) | Conductivity ($\mu$S cm$^{-1}$) | NO$_3$-N in winter (mg L$^{-1}$) | Mean annual total P ($\mu$g L$^{-1}$) | Chlorophyll a (summer) ($\mu$g L$^{-1}$) | Zooplankton biomass (summer) ($\mu$g L$^{-1}$) |
|---|---|---|---|---|---|---|---|---|---|---|
| Betley Mere | 9.3 | 1.8 | Y | S | 100 | 659 | 1.85 | 506 | 80.1 | 97.7 |
| Berrington Pool | 2.5 | 12.2 | Y | G | <10 | 392 | 0.72 | 113 | 20.4 | 35 |
| Betton Pool | 6.4 | 10.9 | Y | G | <20 | 356 | 0.64 | 113 | 13.8 | 75 |
| Bomere | 10.3 | 15.2 | Y | G | <10 | 132 | 0.60 | 67 | 13.9 | 293 |
| Chapel Mere | 6.5 | 2.4 | N | S | >75 | 721 | 0.65 | 1267 | 13.9 | 4910 |
| Colemere | 27.6 | 11.5 | Y | G+S | <10 | 239 | 1.27 | 400 | 29.7 | 740 |
| Cop Mere | 16.8 | 2.7 | N | S | >75 | 457 | 2.34 | 315 | 55.2 | 704 |
| Combermere | 51.5 | 11.8 | Y | G+S | <10 | 513 | 0.9 | 362 | 20.5 | 1203 |
| Crosemere | 15.2 | 9.3 | Y | G | <10 | 474 | 0.6 | 214 | 9.2 | 2047 |
| Fenemere | 9.4 | 2.2 | N | G+S | 10–20 | 756 | 2.8 | 487 | 52.8 | 912 |
| Hatchmere | 4.7 | 3.8 | Y | G+S | 20 | 484 | 1.32 | 85 | 30.5 | 160 |
| Little Mere | 2.5 | 2.6 | N | S | >50 | 523 | 1.91 | 1510 | 13.1 | 7640 |
| Mere Mere | 15.8 | 8.1 | Y | G+S | <20 | 523 | 1.01 | 54 | 20.1 | 228 |
| Oakmere | 18.3 | 8.0 | Y | G | <10 | 188 | 0.33 | 61 | 8.4 | 378 |
| Ossmere | 9.5 | 3.0 | N | G | <10 | 491 | 0.15 | 296 | 31.7 | 2520 |
| Petty Pool | 11.7 | 3.0 | N | S | 10–20 | 465 | 1.03 | 261 | 52.7 | 470 |
| Quoisely Big Mere | 4.0 | 2.4 | N | G+S | 10–20 | 611 | 1.54 | 404 | 11.0 | 3070 |
| Quoisely Little Mere | 2.2 | 1.8 | N | G+S | 100 | 639 | 2.13 | 264 | 10.5 | 4430 |
| Rostherne Mere | 48.7 | 31.0 | Y | G+S | <5 | 523 | 0.84 | 439 | 22.6 | 340 |
| Tabley Moat | 2.0 | 1.5 | Y | S | 100 | 632 | 3.87 | 720 | 21.4 | 7010 |
| Tabley Mere N | 5.0 | 3.0 | N | S | >75 | 701 | 3.74 | 323 | 13.3 | 7210 |
| Tabley Mere S | 14.4 | 3.0 | N | S | >75 | 707 | 5.28 | 326 | 19.9 | 1960 |
| Tatton Mere | 31.7 | 11.0 | Y | G+S | 10–20 | 518 | 0.75 | 263 | 10.1 | 256 |
| Whitemere | 25.5 | 13.8 | Y | G | 10–20 | 309 | 0.91 | 1456 | 16.7 | 430 |

**Table 17.12** Characteristics of five plants used in feeding assays with common carp and of pellets made of broccoli and lettuce. Phenolic compounds are often bitter tasting substances, produced as deterrents to grazing, particularly by invertebrates. Soluble protein is that which can be easily extracted with water. Values are means plus or minus standard deviation for $n$ replicates.

| Plant | Habit | Relative mechanical toughness ($n = 15$) | Carbon (% of dry mass) ($n = 5$) | Nitrogen (% of dry mass) | C:N ratio | Phenolic content (% of dry mass) ($n = 10$) | Soluble protein (% of dry mass) ($n = 3$) |
|---|---|---|---|---|---|---|---|
| Ceratophyllum demersum | Submerged, coarse-leaved | 299 ± 75 (stems); 76 ± 19 (leaves) | 37.2 ± 0.17 | 3.5 ± 0.08 | 10.6 | 4.3 ± 1.3 | 0.1 ± 0.04 |
| Potamogeton pectinatus | Submerged, fine-leaved | 362 ± 90 (s); 63 ± 16 (l) | 34.8 ± 0.29 | 1.3 ± 0.11 | 27 | 4.9 ± 1.5 | 0.2 ± 0.12 |
| Scirpus validus | Large emergent | >500 ± 125 (s and l) | 38.6 ± 0.33 | 1.3 ± 0.11 | 28.9 | 6.7 ± 2.0 | 0.19 ± 0.11 |
| Typha latifolia | Large emergent | >500 ± 125 (s and l) | 38.9 ± 0.29 | 0.8 ± 0.11 | 47.1 | 7.0 ± 2.1 | 0.15 ± 0.08 |
| Chara aspera | Submerged charophyte, with rough texture and marl deposits | 0.1 ± 0.02 | 20.7 ± 0.13 | 1.1 ± 0.07 | 18.3 | 3.3 ± 1.0 | 0.13 ± 0.06 |
| Broccoli/lettuce | | Not applicable | 39.5 ± 0.1 | 4.1 ± 0.01 | 9.6 | 10.3 ± 3.1 | 0.28 ± 0.17 |

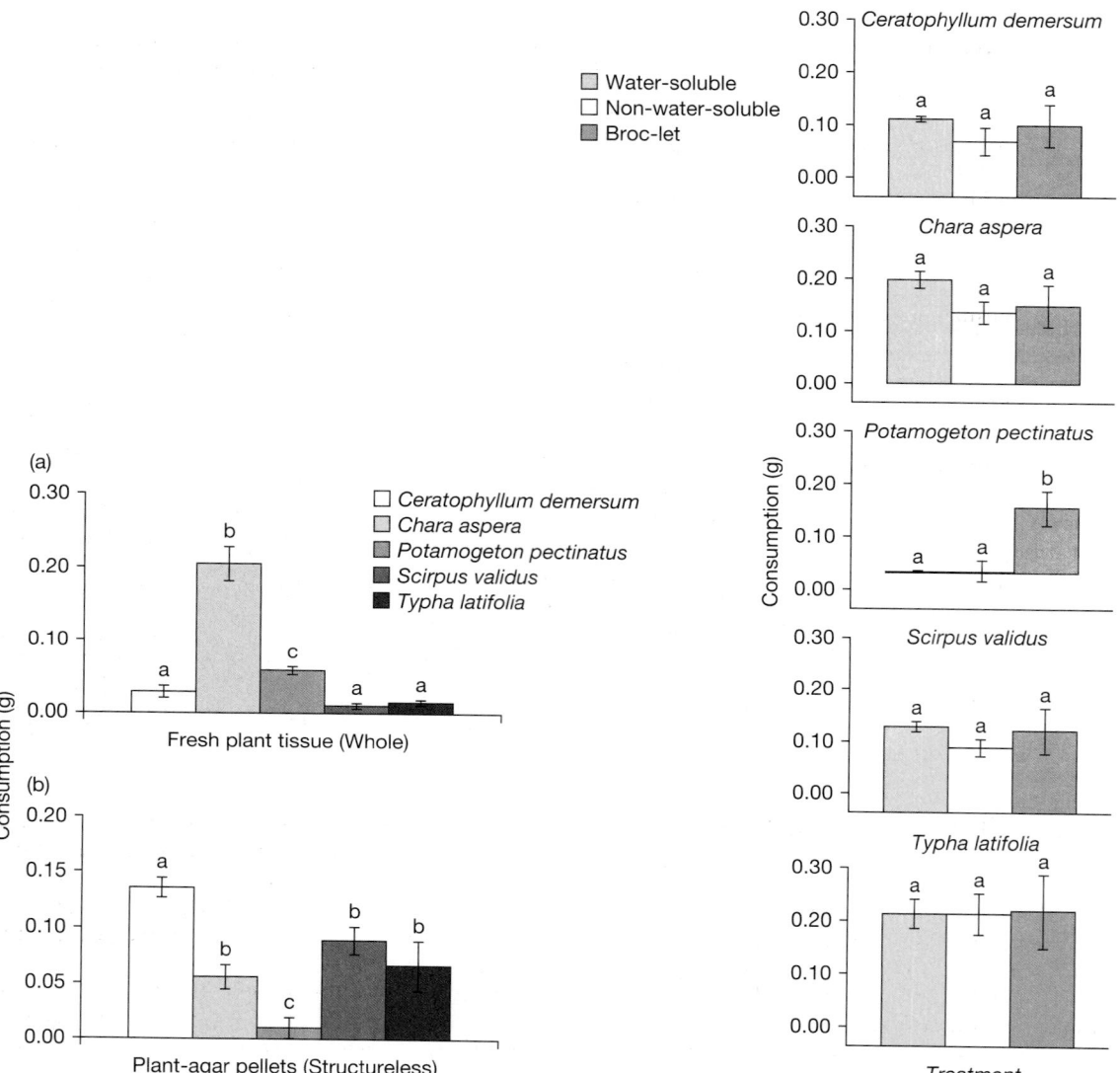

**Fig. 17.6** Common carp were fed pieces of intact plant and ground fresh plant incorporated into pellets of agar of constant size (left) and the amounts eaten under standard conditions recorded. Letters that differ for comparisons between intact or pelleted plants indicate significant differences in the amounts taken. On the right, the plants and a standard food of lettuce and broccoli were extracted in methanol and ether and purified to give extracts of water soluble and non-water-soluble compounds. These were then dried into pellets of the broccoli–lettuce mixture and presented to the fish under standard conditions with a broccoli–lettuce control to which nothing had been added. The amounts taken are shown and different letters again indicate significant differences. (Based on Miller & Provenza 2007.)

**Table 17.13** Effects of *Gambusia affinis* on pond ecosystems established in late November. (After Hurlbert et al. 1971). *Cochochloris peniocystis* is a small cyanobacterium. All differences were significant at the 0.1 level or better, except where indicated with an asterisk.

| Ecosystem component | Variable measured | Without fish | With fish |
|---|---|---|---|
| Zooplankton (N per10 L) | *Daphnia pulex* (2 Dec) | 92 | 0.3 |
|  | (3 Feb) | 1840 | 0 |
|  | Total rotifers (2 Dec) | 1130 | 5930 |
|  | (3 Feb) | 32* | 4* |
| Phytoplankton (millions of cells per mL) | *Coccochloris peniocystis* (10 Jan) | 0 | 117 |
|  | (2 Feb) | 0 | 220 |
|  | Colonial algae (2 Feb) | 79* | 52* |
| Macroscopic bottom algae (g per tank) | *Spirogyra* (6 Feb) | 312 | 29 |
|  | *Chara* (6 Feb) | 24* | 31* |
| Phosphorus concentration (3 Feb) (mg L$^{-1}$) | Inorganic phosphate-P | 10 | 0.33 |
|  | Organic phosphate-P | 18 | 55 |
|  | Particulate-P | 12 | 271 |
|  | Total-P | 41 | 326 |
| Benthic invertebrates (number per cm$^2$ of tank bottom) | Chironomid larvae (3 Feb) | 25 | 0 |
|  | Oligochaete worms (7 Feb) | 14 | 0.7 |
|  | Emerging insects (5 Nov and 7 Feb) | 486 | 0 |
| Light extinction coefficients (m$^{-1}$) | Blue (425 nm) | 5.1 | 64 |
|  | Red (680 nm) | 0.8 | 12 |

## EXERCISE 15. PROBING THE PROFUNDAL

All the data obtained in the understanding of lake systems have to be collected from instruments or samples. Instruments can be automated but biological sampling still takes hard work and is not necessarily straightforward. One difficulty, if you can see what you are sampling, is avoiding bias as to where the sample is taken. On the other hand, you can see if the sampler is working properly and how it is working. Sampling the profundal benthos has the opposite problem. You cannot see what you are sampling (unless you are a diver using a light and taking samples in comparatively shallow water, say down to 30 m for safety) but you cannot see how the sampler is working. There are many designs for samplers, generally based on the principles of closing jaws, either operated by springs (Ekmann dredge) or by simple leverage (Ponar or Shipek sampler), around a portion of the bottom, or on thrusting a tube into the sediment and then closing the top of the tube with a plug so that the water and sediment do not run out on retrieval (Kajak–Brinkhurst corer, or if several are mounted together, Multiple corer). All of these are shown in Fig. 17.7. Figure 17.8 shows their (and others') comparative performance in sampling the profundal benthos of Lake Winnipeg (Flannagan 1970) in comparison with cores taken by divers. Elliott & Drake (1981) report a parallel rigorous analysis of sampling efficiency of similar grabs in gravel-bottomed rivers. Figure 17.9 shows relative performance for three groups of profundal invertebrates.

The multiple corer performs best, but is heavy and needs a mechanical winch to bring it back to the surface. The Ekman dredge performs nearly as well, in fact better for chironomids, and takes more sediment on a single sampling. Single Kajak–Brinkhurst corers can be hand-hauled, but take only about a third as much sediment as an Ekman dredge. Hand winching takes time and even a very muscular person might find difficulty in raising an Ekman dredge or Kajak–Brinkhurst corer to the surface faster than 0.1 m per

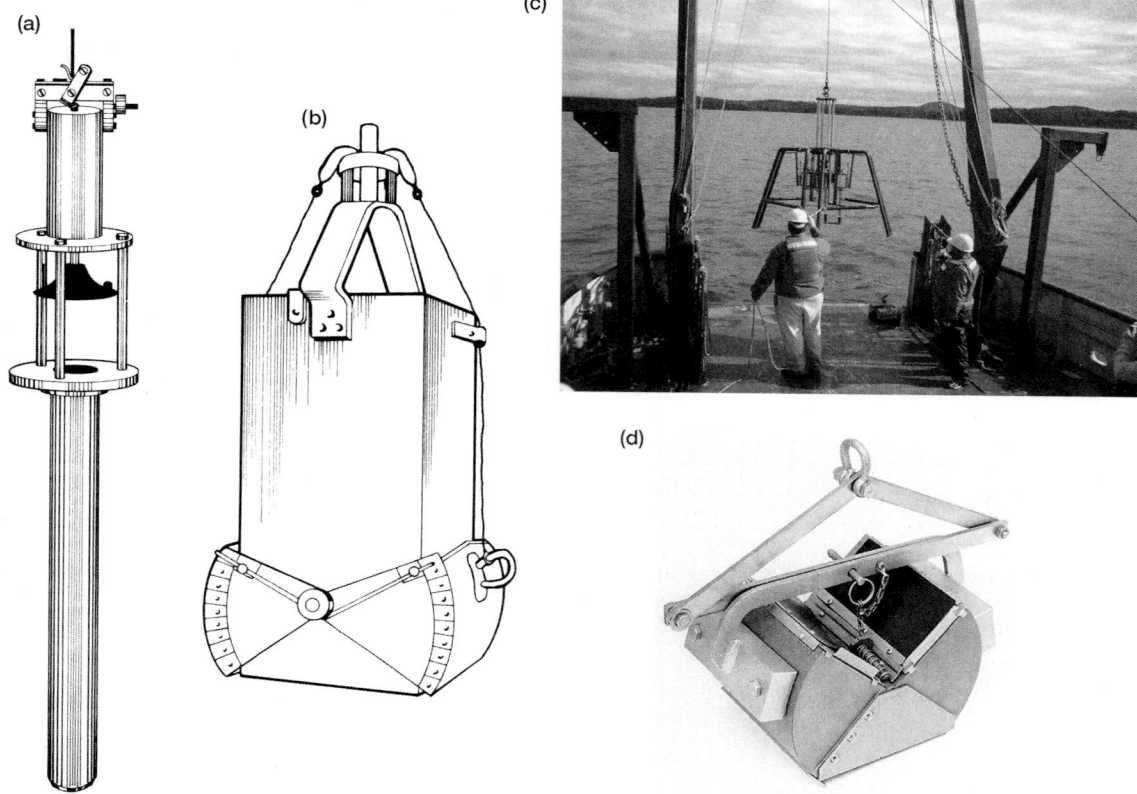

**Fig. 17.7** Some of the several kinds of samplers designed for the profundal benthos. (a) A Kajak–Brinkhurst sampler, named as often, for its inventors. It is dropped vertically and takes a core of surface sediment. The stopper is then released using a weighted messenger dropped down the line, and blocks the top of the tube as the sampler is hauled to the surface. (b) An Ekmann dredge, whose jaws are held apart by springs, which are also released by a messenger weight when the sampler is positioned in the sediment. The vigorous snap of the jaws is useful if there is vegetable debris or plants to cut through. (c) A multiple corer, a series of Kajak–Brinkhurst samplers mounted together. (d) A Ponar grab, in which the jaws are held open by a catch, which falls off when the sampler rests in the sediment. Pulling the sampler up then closes the jaws around the sample.

second, even at the beginning of a day's work. When the sample is brought to the surface, you need to sieve it through a net to isolate the animals otherwise you will have to carry a huge weight of sediment back to your laboratory. This can take 5–10 minutes per sample. You are working on the benthos of a lake 90 m deep, in a remote location, with only a partner and a rowing boat and no mechanical power. The statistical advice you receive is that you need to take 20 samples each with about as much sediment as taken by an Ekman dredge at each of five different depths (90, 70, 50, 30, 10 m) to obtain a reliable sample of the profundal benthos. Give a rationale for the equipment you would choose and the plans you would make to carry out this task. About how many days will you need?

## EXERCISE 16. THE CURSE OF BIRDS FOR LAKE MANAGERS

A small lake in Florida is a bird sanctuary. The birds are protected against any disturbance by State legislation. However, the lake is greatly eutrophicated by bird guano. The mean total phosphorus concentration in

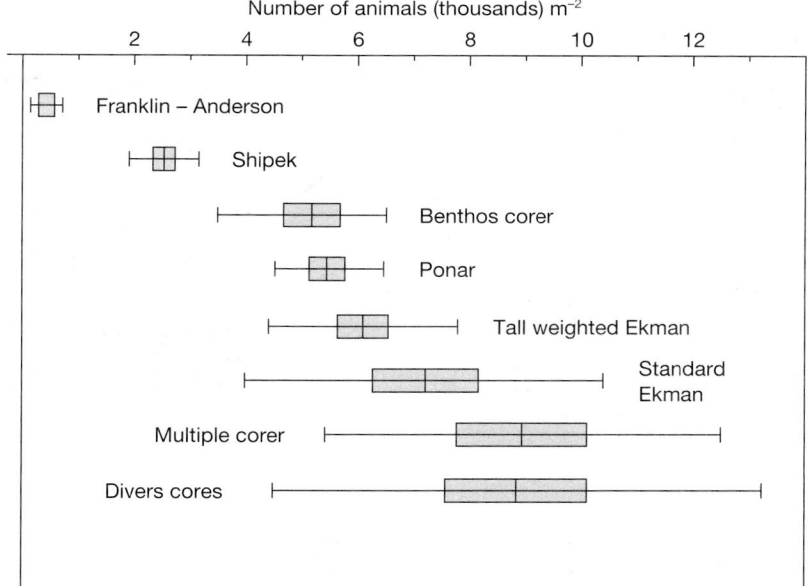

**Fig. 17.8** Results of a trial in which the same benthos community in Lake Winnipeg, Canada, was sampled with different samplers. Results are shown as means and standard deviations (the box) and standard errors (the whiskers). Cores taken directly by divers were used as an absolute control. (From Flannagan 1970.)

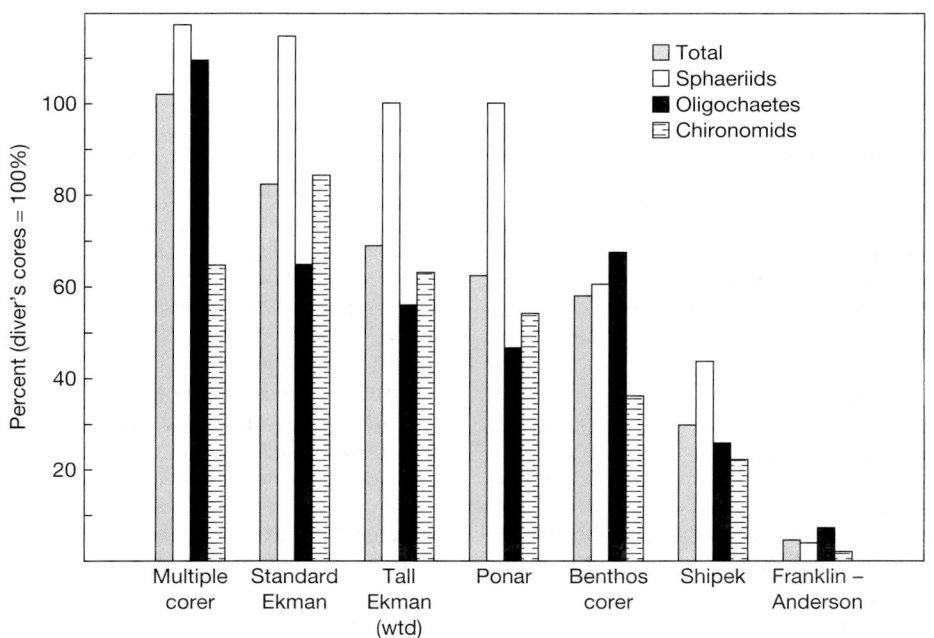

**Fig. 17.9** Relative efficiencies of the samplers tested in Fig. 17.8 in sampling three groups of profundal benthos. Values are shown as percentages of the sample obtained directly by SCUBA divers. (Based on Flannagan 1970.)

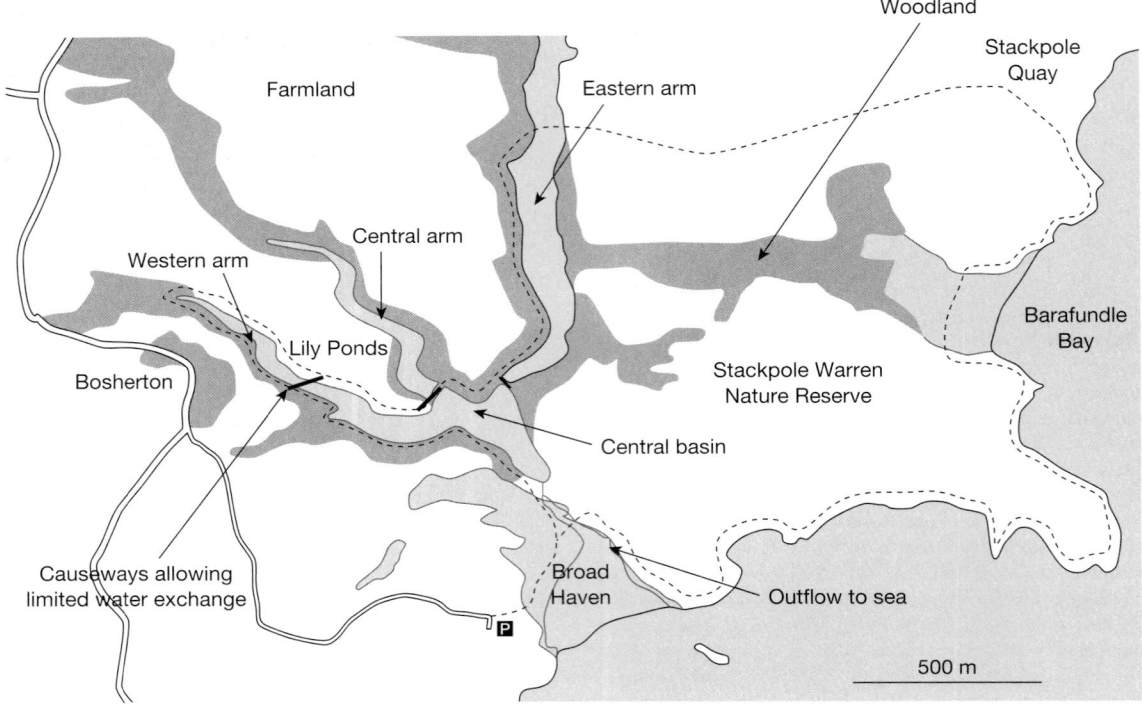

**Fig. 17.10** Bosherston Lake.

the water in winter is 400 μg P L$^{-1}$, of which about 300 is due to bird excreta and 100 to various diffuse sources in surrounding agricultural land and from urban development. Moreover, there is substantial release of phosphorus from the sediments in summer and concentrations may then reach 1000 μg P L$^{-1}$.

The outflow stream has the same water quality as the lake, is only 5 km long, and discharges to the Gulf of Louisiana. Federal legislation requires that streams entering the Gulf shall have only 20 μg P L$^{-1}$. You have been asked to solve the problem of meeting this standard. What would you do?

## EXERCISE 17. NUTRIENT PROBLEMS IN TRICKY SITUATIONS

In western Wales is a lake that was formed by the damming, close to the sea, of a stream system in the 17th century so that it has three arms and a common central basin (Fig. 17.10). The local geology is

of Carboniferous Limestone and the valleys in which the arms are formed are steep and covered with ash woodland. On the plateaux between the valleys is agricultural land, supporting a large herd of dairy cattle. The western and central arms are supplied by spring water filtered through the limestone and have clear water with a diverse community of plants, particularly charophyte species. Causeway dams separate them from the central basin but water can pass through gaps in the causeways, though mixing is impeded. The central basin has charophytes but a greater proportion of vascular plants.

The eastern arm is somewhat different. It has a community of more nutrient tolerant plants, heavy growths of filamentous algae and not infrequent algal blooms. Formerly sewage effluent was discharged to it from a village, but has now been diverted. Extensive reedbeds occupy the top of this arm and act as nutrient filters. However, the arm has much higher phosphorus concentrations than the west and central arms and it would appear that these arise from release from the stores in the sediments accumulated during the period when effluent was discharged into the lake. A causeway, with sluices in it, separates the eastern arm from the central basin but the poor water quality discharged into the central basin from it is jeopardizing the charophyte communities of the central basin. The problem is to reduce the threat of increased nutrient loading from the eastern arm to the central basin (and

by backflow in dry summers to the central and western arms). The area is a National Nature Reserve and there is no land available for dumping sediment, nor is it possible to gain access to the site using trucks or tankers. The adjoining sea supports lobster fisheries, and has very high amenity value. Tourism is the major industry of the area. How might you sensitively solve this problem?

# REFERENCES

Abdallah, A., de Mazancourt, C., Elinge, M.M., et al. (2004) Comparative studies on the structure of an upland African stream ecosystem. *Freshwater Forum*, **21**, 27–47.

Abrahams, C. (2005) The ecology and management of draw-down zones. *British Wildlife*, **August**, 395–402.

Adamec, L. (1997) Mineral nutrition of carnivorous plants: a review. *Botanical Review*, **63**, 273–299.

Adamec, L. (2008) Mineral nutrient relations in the aquatic carnivorous *Utricularia australis* and its investment in carnivory. *Fundamental and Applied Limnology*, **171**, 175–183.

Adrian, R., O'Reilly, H., Zagarese, S.B., et al. (2009) Lakes as sentinels of climate change. *Limnology and Oceanography*, **54**, 2283–2297.

Alin, S.R. & Johnson, T.C. (2007) Carbon cycling in large lakes of the world: a synthesis of production, burial, and lake-atmosphere exchange estimates. *Global Biogeochemical Cycles*, **21**, Article GB3002, 1–12.

Alix, C. (2005) Deciphering the impact of change on the drift-wood cycle: contribution to the study of human use of wood in the Arctic. *Global and Planetary Change*, **47**, 83–98.

Allan, J.D. & Castillo, M.M. (2009) *Stream Ecology. Structure and Function of Running Waters*, 2nd edn. Springer, Rotterdam.

Allan, J.D., Abell, R., Hogan, Z., et al. (2005) Overfishing of inland waters. *BioSciences*, **55**, 1041–1051.

Allison, E.H., Irvine, K., Thompson, A.B. & Ngatunga, B.P. (1996) Diets and food consumption rates of pelagic fish in Lake Malawi, Africa. *Freshwater Biology*, **35**, 489–515.

Andersen, J.M. (2005) *Restaurering af Skjern Å*. Report 531 of the Danish Environmental Ministry, Copenhagen. (In Danish, English summary.)

Anderson, K. & Bows, A. (2008) Reframing the climate change challenge in light of post-2000 emission trends. *Philosophical Transactions of the Royal Society A*, doi:10.1098/rsta.2008.0138.

Anderson, S. & Moss, B. (1993) How wetland habitats are perceived by children: consequences for children's education and wetland conservation. *International Journal of Science Education*, **15**, 473–85.

Andrews, J. & Kinsman, D. (1990) *Gravel Pit Restoration for Wildlife*. Royal Society for the Protection of Birds, Sandy.

Andrews, J.E., Brimblecombe, P., Jickells, T.D., Liss, P.S. & Reid, B. (2004) *An Introduction to Environmental Chemistry*. Blackwell Science, Oxford.

Apodaca, C.K. & Chapman, L.J. (2004) Larval damselflies in extreme environments: behavioural and physiological response to hypoxic stress. *Journal of Insect Physiology*, **50**, 767–775.

Arco, L.J. & Abrams, E.M. (2006) An essay on energetics: the construction of the Aztec chinampa system. *Antiquity*, **80**, 906–918.

Arlinghaus, R., Cooke, S.J., Schwab, A. & Cowx, I.G. (2007) Fish welfare: a challenge to the feelings-based approach with implications for recreational fishing. *Fish and Fisheries*, **8**, 57–71.

Armillas, P. (1971) Gardens on swamps. *Science*, **174**, 653–661.

Armitage, P.D. (1978) The impact of Cow Green reservoir on invertebrate populations in the River Tees. *Annual Reports of the Freshwater Biological Association*, **46**, 47–56.

Austin, J.A. & Colman, S.M. (2007) Lake Superior summer water temperatures are increasing more rapidly than regional air temperatures: a positive ice-albedo feedback. *Geophysical Research Letters*, **34**, doi:10.1029/2006GL029021.

Babica, P., Blaha, L. & Marsalek, B. (2006) Exploring the natural role of microcystins – a review of effects on photoautotrophic organisms. *Journal of Phycology*, **42**, 9–20.

Balian, E.V., Lévêque, C., Segers, H. & Martens, K. (2008) The freshwater animal diversity assessment: an overview of the results. *Hydrobiologia*, **595**, 627–637.

Balirwa, J.S., Chapman, C.A., Chapman, L.J., et al. (2003) Biodiversity and fishery sustainability in the Lake Victoria basin: an unexpected marriage? *BioScience*, **53**, 703–711.

Ball, P. (1999) *H₂O. A Biography of Water*. Weidenfeld and Nicholson, London.

Ballot, A., Lothar Krienitz, L., Kotut, K., et al. (2004) Cyanobacteria and cyanobacterial toxins in three alkaline rift valley lakes of Kenya – Lakes Bogoria, Nakuru and Elmenteita. *Journal of Plankton Research*, **26**, 925–935.

Balls, H., Moss, B. & Irvine, K. (1989) The loss of submerged plants with eutrophication. I. Experimental design, water chemistry, aquatic plant and phytoplankton biomass in experiments carried out in ponds in the Norfolk Broadland. *Freshwater Biology*, **22**, 71–87.

Balmford, A., Bruner, A., Cooper, P., et al. (2002) Ecology – economic reasons for conserving wild nature. *Science*, **297**, 950–953.

Balon, E.K. (2004) About the oldest domesticates among fishes. *Journal of Fish Biology*, **65**, Suppl A, 1–27.

Balon, E.K. & Bruton, M.N. (1986) Introduction of alien species or why scientific advice is not heeded. *Environmental Biology of Fishes*, **16**, 225–230.

Barel, C.D.N., Dorit, R., Greenwood, P.H., et al. (1985) Destruction of fisheries in Africa's lakes. *Nature*, **315**, 19–20.

Barker, T., Hatton, K., O'Connor, M., Connor, L., Bagnell, L. & Moss, B. (2008a) Control of ecosystem state in a shallow brackish lake: implications for the conservation of stonewort communities. *Aquatic Conservation: Marine and Freshwater Ecosystems*, **18**, 221–240.

Barker, T., Hatton, K., O'Connor, M., Connor, L. & Moss, B. (2008b) Effects of nitrate load on submerged plant biomass and species richness: results of a mesocosm experiment. *Fundamental and Applied Limnology*, **173**, 89–100.

Barko, J.W. & Smart, R.M. (1980) Mobilization of sediment phosphorus by submersed freshwater macrophytes. *Freshwater Biology*, **10**, 229–238.

Barko, J.W., Murphy, P.G. & Wetzel, R.G. (1977) An investigation of primary production and ecosystem metabolism in a Lake Michigan dune pond. *Archiv fur Hydrobiologie*, **81**, 155–87.

Baron, J.S., Schmidt, T.M. & Hartman, M.D. (2009) Climate-induced changes in high elevation stream nitrate dynamics. *Global Change Biology*, doi:10.1111/j.1365-2486.2009.01847.x

Bates, B.C., Kundzewicz, Z.W., Wu, S. & Palutikof, J.P. (Eds) (2008) *Climate Change and Water*. Technical Paper of the Intergovernmental Panel on Climate Change, IPCC Secretariat, Geneva.

Baxter, C.V., Fausch, K.D. & Saunders, W.C. (2005) Tangled webs: reciprocal flows of invertebrate prey link streams and riparian zones. *Freshwater Biology*, **50**, 201–220.

Beadle, L.C. (1981) *The Inland Waters of Tropical Africa*, 2nd edn. Longman, London.

Bêche, L.A., McElravy, E.P. & Resh, V.H. (2006) Long-term seasonal variation in the biological traits of benthic-invertebrates in two Mediterranean-climate streams in California, U.S.A. *Freshwater Biology*, **51**, 56–75.

Bedford, B.L., Walbridge, M.R. & Aldous, A. (1999) Patterns in nutrient availability and plant diversity in temperate North American wetlands. *Ecology*, **80**, 2151–2169.

Beebee, T.J.C. (1995) Amphibian breeding and climate. *Nature*, **374**, 219–220.

Beebee, T. & Rowe, G. (2007) *An Introduction to Molecular Ecology*. Oxford University Press.

Beeton, A.M. (2002) Large freshwater lakes: present state, trends, and future. *Environmental Conservation*, **29**, 21–38.

Beklioglu, M., Romo, S., Kagalou, I., Quintana, X. & Bécares, E. (2007) State of the art in the functioning of shallow Mediterranean lakes: workshop conclusions. *Hydrobiologia*, **584**, 317–326.

Bell, D.V., Odin, N. & Tornes, E. (1985) Accumulation of angling litter at game and coarse fisheries in South Wales, UK. *Biological Conservation*, **34**, 369–379.

Beltaos, S. (2008) Progress in the study and management of river ice jams. *Cold Regions Science and Technology*, **51**, 2–19.

Beninca, E., Huisman, J., Heerkloss, R., et al. (2008) Chaos in a long-term experiment with a plankton community. *Nature*, **451**, 822–826.

Benke, A.C., Chaubey, I., Milton, W.G. & Lloyd, D.E. (2000) Flood pulse dynamics of an unregulated river floodplain in the southeastern U.S. coastal plain. *Ecology*, **81**, 2730–2741.

Benndorf, J. (1992) The control of indirect effects of biomanipulation. In *Eutrophication: Research and Application to Water Supply*, Sutcliffe, D.W. & Jones, J.G. (Eds). Freshwater Biological Association, Ambleside; 82–93.

Bergstrom, A-K. & Jansson, M. (2006) Atmospheric nitrogen deposition has caused nitrogen enrichment and eutrophication of lakes in the northern hemisphere. *Global Change Biology*, **12**, 635–643.

Beschta, R.L. & Ripple, W.J. (2008) Wolves, trophic cascades, and rivers in the Olympic National Park, USA. *Ecohydrology*, **1**, 118–130.

Biggs, J., Williams, P., Whitfield, M., Nicolet, P. & Weatherby, A. (2005) 15 years of pond assessment in Britain: results and lessons learned from the work of Pond Conservation. *Aquatic Conservation: Marine and Freshwater Ecosystems*, **15**, 693–714.

Bilton, D.T., Freedland, J.R. & Okamura, B. (2001) Dispersal in freshwater invertebrates *Annual Review of Ecology and Systematics*, **32**, 159–181.

Birks, H.J.B. (1998) D.G. Frey & E.S. Deevey review No. 1 – Numerical tools in palaeolimnology – Progress, potentialities, and problems. *Journal of Paleolimnology*, **20**, 307–332.

Boar, R.R., Crook, C.E. & Moss, B. (1989) Regression of Phragmites australis reedswamps and recent changes of water chemistry in the Norfolk Broadland. *Aquatic Botany*, **35**, 41–55.

Bodelier, P.L.E., Stomp, M., Santamaria, L., Klaassen, M. & Laanbroek, H.J. (2006) Animal–plant–microbe interactions: direct and indirect effects of swan foraging behaviour modulate methane cycling in temperate shallow wetlands. *Oecologia*, **149**, 233–244.

Bogdan, K.G. & Gilbert, J.J. (1982) Seasonal patterns of feeding by natural populations of *Keratella*, *Polyarthra* and *Bosmina*: clearance rates, selectivities and contributions to community grazing. *Limnology and Oceanography*, **27**, 918–934.

Bohonak, A.J. & Jenkins, D.G. (2003) Ecological and evolutionary significance of dispersal by freshwater invertebrates. *Ecology Letters*, **6**, 783–796.

Bolpagni, R. et al. (2007) Diurnal exchanges of $CO_2$ and $CH_4$ across the water-atmosphere interface in a water chestnut meadow (*Trapa natans* L.). *Aquatic Botany*, **87**, 43–48.

Boston, H.L. & Adams, M.S. (1983) Evidence of crassulacean acid metabolism in two North American isoetids. *Aquatic Botany*, **15**, 381–386.

Boston, H.L. & Adams, M.S. (1986) The contribution of crassulacean acid metabolism to the annual productivity of two aquatic vascular plants. *Oecologia*, **68**, 615–622.

Bouchard, V., Frey, S.D., Gilbert, J.M. & Reed, S.E. (2007) Effects of macrophyte functional group richness on emergent freshwater wetland functions. *Ecology*, **88**, 2903–2914.

Boulton, A.J. (2003) Parallels and contrasts in the effects of drought on stream macroinvertebrate assemblages. *Freshwater Biology*, **48**, 1173–1185.

Boulton, A.J. & Brock, M.A. (1999) *Australian Freshwater Ecology. Processes and Management*. Gleneagles Publishing, Mt Osmond.

Bouwman, A.F. et al. (2002) A global analysis of acidification and eutrophication of terrestrial ecosystems. *Water, Soil and Air Pollution*, **141**, 349–382.

Boycott, A.E. (1936) The habitats of fresh-water Mollusca in Britain. *Journal of Animal Ecology*, **5**, 116–186.

Bradbury, I.K. & Grace, J. (1983) Primary production in wetlands. In *Ecosystems of the World 4A: Mires: Swamp, Bog, Fen and Moor*, Gore, A.J.P. (Ed.). Elsevier, Amsterdam; 285–310.

Bradbury, J.P., Leyden, B., Salgado-Labouriau, M., et al. (1981) Late Quaternary environmental history of Lake Valencia, Venezuela. *Science*, **214**, 1299–1305.

Brewin, P.A., Buckton, S.T. & Ormerod, S.J. (1998) River habitat surveys and biodiversity in acid-sensitive rivers. Aquatic Conservation. *Marine and Freshwater Ecosystems*, **8**, 501–514.

Brinkhurst, R.O. (1974) *The Benthos of Lakes*. Macmillan, London.

Brinson, M.M. & Malvarez, A.I. (2002) Temperate freshwater wetlands: types, status and threats. *Environmental Conservation*, **29**, 115–133.

Brito, E.F., Moulton, T.P., De Souza, M.L. & Bunn, S.E. (2006) Stable isotope analysis indicates microalgae as the pre-dominant food source of fauna in a coastal forest stream, south-east Brazil. *Austral Ecology*, **31**, 623–633.

Brittain, J.E. et al. (2009) Arctic rivers. In *Rivers of Europe*, Tockner, K., Uehlinger, U. & Robinson, C.T. (Eds). Academic Press; 337–379.

Brock, T.D. (1967) Life at high temperatures. *Science*, **158**, 1012–1019.

Brock, T.D. (1978) *Thermophilic Microorganisms and Life at High Temperatures*. Springer-Verlag, New York.

Bronmark, C. & Hanssen, L.-A. (2005) *The Biology of Lakes and Ponds*, 2nd edn. Oxford University Press.

Brooks, J.L. & Dodson, S.I. (1965) Predation, body size and composition of plankton. *Science*, **150**, 28–35.

Brookes, A. (1995) Challenges and objectives for geomorphology in U.K river management. *Earth Surface Processes and Landforms*, **20**, 593–610.

Buckton, S.T. & Ormerod, S.J. (2002) Global patterns of diversity among the specialist birds of riverine landscapes. *Freshwater Biology*, **47**, 695–709.

Buckton, S.T., Brewin, P.A., Lewis, A., Stevens, P. & Ormerod, S.J. (1998) The distribution of dippers, *Cinclus cinclus* (L.), in the acid-sensitive region of Wales, 1984–95. *Freshwater Biology*, **39**, 387–396.

Burgis, M.J. & Morris, P. (2007) *The World of Lakes: Lakes of the World*. Freshwater Biological Association, Windermere.

Burks, R.L. & Lodge, D.M. (2002) Cued in: advances and opportunities in freshwater chemical ecology. *Journal of Chemical Ecology*, **28**, 1901–1917.

Burns, C.W. & Rigler, F.H. (1967) Comparison of filtering rates of *Daphnia rosea* in lake water and suspensions of yeast. *Limnology and Oceanography*, **12**, 492–502.

Cadwallader, P.L. (1978) Some causes of the decline in range and abundance of native fish in the Murray-Darling river system. *Proceedings of the Royal Society of Victoria*, **90**, 211–224.

Calow, P. & Petts, G.E. (Eds) (1992) *The Rivers Handbook*, Vols 1 and 2. Blackwell Scientific, Oxford.

Canonico, G.C., Arthington, A., McCrary, J.K. & Thieme, M.L. (2005) The effects of introduced tilapias on native biodiversity. *Aquatic Conservation: Marine and Freshwater Ecosystems*, **15**, 463–483.

Canter-Lund, H. & Lund, J.W.G. (1995) *Freshwater Algae*. Biopress, Bristol.

Caraco, N.F., Cole, J.J. & Strayer, D.L. (2006) Top-down control from the bottom: Regulation of eutrophication in a large river by benthic grazing. *Limnology and Oceanography*, **51**, 664–670.

Cardinale, B., Hillebrand, H. & Charles, D.F. (2006) Geographic patterns of diversity in streams are predicted by a multivariate model of disturbance and productivity. *Journal of Ecology*, **94**, 609–618.

Caro, P. (1993) *Water*. McGraw Hill, New York.

Carpenter, S.R. & Pace, M.L. (1997) Dystrophy and eutrophy in lake ecosystems: implications of fluctuating concepts. *Oikos*, **78**, 3–14.

Carter, G.S. (1955) *The Papyrus Swamps of Uganda*. Heffer, Cambridge.

Carvalho, L. & Moss, B. (1995) The current status of a sample of English sites of special scientific interest subject to eutrophication. *Aquatic Conservation: Marine and Freshwater Ecosystems*, **5**, 191–204.

Casey, H.C. & Downing, A. (1976) Levels of inorganic nutrients in *Ranunculus penicillatus* var. *calcareus* in relation to water chemistry. *Aquatic Botany*, **2**, 75–80.

Caulfield, P. (1971) *Everglades*. Sierra Club, Ballantyne, New York.

Cazzaneli, M., Warming, T.P. & Christoffersen, K.S. (2008) Emergent and floating-leaved macrophytes as refuge for zooplankton in a eutrophic temperate lake without submerged vegetation. *Hydrobiologia*, **605**, 113–122.

Cereghino, R., Biggs, J., Oertli, B. & Declerck, S. (2008) The ecology of European ponds: defining the characteristics of a neglected freshwater habitat. *Hydrobiologia*, **597**, 1–6.

Chambers, P.A., Lacoul, P., Murphy, K.J. & Thomaz, S.M. (2008) Global diversity of aquatic macrophytes in freshwater. *Hydrobiologia*, **595**, 9–26.

Chapin, M. (1988) The seduction of models. Chinampa agriculture in Mexico. *Grassroots Development*, **12**, 8–17.

Chapman, L.J., Chapman, C.A., Kaufman, L.S., Witte, F. & Balirwa, J. (2008) Biodiversity conservation in African inland waters: Lessons of the Lake Victoria region. *Verhandlungen internationale der Vereinigung theoretische und angewande Limnologie*, **30**, 16–34.

Cheshire, K., Boyero, L. & Pearson, R.G. (2005) Food webs in tropical Australian streams: shredders are not scarce. *Freshwater Biology*, **50**, 748–769.

Churcher, C.S., Kleindienst, M.R. & Schwarcz, H.P. (1999) Faunal remains from a Middle Pleistocene lacustrine marl in Dakhleh Oasis, Egypt: palaeoenvironmental reconstructions. *Palaeography, Palaeoclimatology, Palaeoecology*, **154**, 301–312.

Christie, W.J. (1974) Changes in the fish species composition of the Great Lakes. *Journal of the Fisheries Research Board of Canada*, **31**, 827–854.

Clarke, A., MacNally, R., Bond, N. & Lake, P.S. (2008) Macroinvertebrate diversity in headwater streams: a review. *Freshwater Biology*, **53**, 1707–1721.

Clasen, J.L., Brigden, S.M., Payet, J.P. & Suttle, C.A. (2008) Evidence that viral abundance across oceans and lakes is driven by different biological factors. *Freshwater Biology*, **53**, 1090–1100.

Cole, J.J. (1999) Aquatic microbiology for ecosystem scientists: new and recycled paradigms in ecological microbiology. *Ecosystems*, **2**, 215–225.

Cole, J.J. & Caraco, N.F. (2001) Carbon in catchments: connecting terrestrial carbon losses wit aquatic metabolism. *Marine and Freshwater Research*, **52**, 101–110.

Cole, J.J., Caraco, N.F., Kling, G.W. & Kratz, T.K. (1994) Carbon dioxide supersaturation in the surface waters of lakes. *Science*, **265**, 1568–1570.

Cole, J.J., Carpenter, S.R., Pace, M.L., Van de Bogert, M.C., Kitchell, J.L. & Hodgson, J.R. (2006) Differential support of lake food webs by three types of terrestrial organic carbon. *Ecology Letters*, **9**, 558–568.

Cole, J.J., Prairie, Y.T., Caraco, N.F., et al. (2007) Plumbing the global carbon cycle: integrating inland waters into the terrestrial carbon budget. *Ecosystems*, **10**, 171–184.

Cook, C.D.K., Gut, B.J., Rix, E.M., Schneller, J. & Seitz, M. (1974) *The Waterplants of the World*. Junk, The Hague.

Cook, J.A., Chubb, J.C. & Veltkamp, C.J. (1998) Epibionts of *Asellus aquaticus* (L.) (Crustacea, Isopoda): an SEM study. *Freshwater Biology*, **39**, 423–438.

Cooke, G.D., Welch, E.B., Peterson, S.A. & Nichols, S.A. (2005) *Restoration and Management of Lakes and Reservoirs*, 3rd edn. Taylor & Francis, New York.

Cooke, S.J. & Cowx, I.G. (2004) The role of recreational fishing in global fish crises. *BioScience*, **54**, 857–859.

Corno, G. & Jurgens, K. (2008) Structure and functional patterns of bacterial communities in response to protist predation along an experimental productivity gradient. *Environmental Microbiology*, **10**, 2857–2871.

Costanza, R., d'Arge, R., de Groot, R., et al. (1997) The value of the world's ecosystem services and natural capital. *Nature*, **387**, 253–260.

Coulter, G.W., Allanson, B.R., Bruton, M.N., et al. (1986) Unique qualities and special problems of the African Great Lakes. *Environmental Biology of Fishes*, **17**, 161–184.

Cowx, I.G. & Gerdaux, D. (2004) The effects of fisheries management practices on freshwater ecosystems. *Fisheries Management and Ecology*, **11**, 145–151.

Crait, J.R. & Ben-David, M. (2007) Effects of river otter activity on terrestrial plants in trophically altered Yellowstone Lake. *Ecology*, **88**, 1040–1052.

Crawford, R.M.M. (1989) *Studies in Plant Survival*. Blackwell Scientific, Oxford.

Crawford, S.S. & Muir, A.M. (2008) Global introductions of salmon and trout in the genus *Oncothyncu*: 1870–2007. *Reviews in Fish Biology and Fisheries*, **18**, 313–344.

Croll, D.A., Maron, J.L., Estes, J.A., et al. (2005) Introduced predators transform subarctic islands from grassland to tundra. *Science*, **307**, 1959–1961.

Cruz, M.J., Segurado, P., Sousa, M. & Rebelo, R. (2008) Collapse of the amphibian community of the Paul do Boquilobo Natural Reserve (central Portugal) after the arrival of the exotic American crayfish *Procambrus clarkii*. *Herpetological Journal*, **18**, 197–204.

Cyr, H. & Downing, J.A. (1988) The abundance of phytophilous invertebrates on different species of submerged macrophytes. *Freshwater Biology*, **20**, 365–374.

Dacey, J.W.H. (1980) Internal wind in water lilies: an adaptation for life in anaerobic sediments. *Science*, **210**, 1017–19.

Dahl, J. (1998a) Effects of a benthivorous and a drift-feeding fish on a benthic stream assemblage. *Oecologia*, **116**, 426–432.

Dahl, J. (1998b) The impact of vertebrate and invertebrate predators on a stream benthic community. *Oecologia*, **117**, 217–226.

Darby, H.C. (1983) *The Changing Fenland*. Cambridge University Press, UK.

Davies, B. & Day, J. (1998) *Vanishing Waters*. University of Cape Town Press.

Davies, B.R., Thoms, M. & Meador, M. (1992) An assessment of the ecological impacts of inter-basin transfers, and their threats to river basin integrity and conservation. *Aquatic Conservation: Marine and Freshwater Ecosystems*, **2**, 325–350.

Davis, S.M. & Ogden, J.C. (Eds) (1994) *Everglades, the Ecosystem and its Restoration*. St Lucie Press, Delray Beach, FL.

Dawidowicz, P. & Loose, C.J. (1992) Metabolic costs during predator-induced diel vertical migration of *Daphnia*. *Limnology and Oceanography*, **37**, 1589–1595.

Dawson, F.H. (1976) The annual production of the aquatic macrophyte. *Ranunculus penicillatus* var *calcarcus* (R.W. Butcher) C.D.K. Cook. *Aquatic Botany*, **2**, 51–74.

Dawson, F.H. (1978) Aquatic plant management in semi-natural streams: the role of marginal vegetation. *Journal of Environmental Management*, **6**, 213–21.

Dawson, F.H. & Haslam, S.M. (1983) The management of river vegetation with particular reference to shading effects of marginal vegetation. *Landscape Planning*, **10**, 149–158.

De Silva, S.S., Nguyen, T.T., Turchini, G.M., Amarasinghe, U.S. & Abery, N.W. (2009) Alien species in aquaculture and biodiversity: a paradox in food production. *Ambio*, **38**, 24–28.

De Waal, L.C., Large, A.R.G. & Wade, P.M. (Eds) (1998) *Rehabilitation of Rivers. Principles and Implementation*. John Wiley & Sons, Chichester.

Decamps, H., Pinay, G., Naiman, R.J., et al. (2004) Riparian zones: where biogeochemistry meets biodiversity in management practice. *Polish Journal of Ecology*, **52**, 3–18.

Degens, E.T., Von Herzen, R.P. & Wong, H-K. (1971) Lake Tanganyika: Water chemistry, sediments, geological structure. *Naturwissenschaften*, **58**, 229–41.

Deines, P., Grey, J., Richnow, H-H. & Eller, G. (2007) Linking larval chironomids to methane: seasonal variation of the microbial methane cycle and chironomid $\partial^{13}C$. *Aquatic Microbial Ecology*, **46**, 273–282.

Dejenie, T., Asmelash, T., De Meester, L., et al. (2009) Limnological and ecological characteristics of tropical highland reservoirs in Tigray, northern Ethiopia. *Hydrobiologia*, **610**, 193–209.

Dellapenna, J.W. (2007) Ecocide and genocide in the Iraqi marshlands. In *River Basin Management IV*, Brebbia, C.A. & Katsifarakis, K.L. (Eds). WIT Press, Southampton; 401–409.

Denny, P. (1980) Solute movement in submerged angiosperms. *Biological Reviews*, **50**, 65–92.

Descy, J-P. & Sarmento, H. (2008) Microorganisms of the East African Great Lakes and their response to environmental changes. *Freshwater Reviews*, **1**, 59–73.

Diamond, J. (2004) *Collapse. How Societies Choose to Fail or Succeed*. Penguin, Kansas City, MO.

Dillon, P.J. & Rigler, F.H. (1974) A test of a simple method for predicting the capacity of a lake for development based on lake trophic status. *Journal of the Fisheries Research Board of Canada*, **32**, 1519–1531.

Dobson, M., Magana, A., Mathooko, J.M. & Ndegwa, F.K. (2002) Detritivores in Kenyan highland streams: more evidence for the paucity of shredders in the tropics? *Freshwater Biology*, **47**, 909–919.

Dobson, M.J. (1980) 'Marsh fever' – the geography of malaria in England. *Journal of Historical Geography*, **6**, 357–389.

Dodds, W.K. et al. (2009) Eutrophication of U.S. freshwaters: analysis of potential economic damages. *Environmental Science and Technology*, **43**, 12–19.

Dodson, S.I. & Egger, D.L. (1980) Selective feeding of red phalaropes on zooplankton of Arctic ponds. *Ecology*, **61**, 755–763.

Douglas, M.M., Bunn, S.E. & Davies, P.M. (2005) River and wetland food webs in Australia's wet–dry tropics: general principles and implications for management. *Marine and Freshwater Research*, **56**, 329–342.

Douglas, M.S. (1947) *The Everglades: River of Grass*. Ballantine, New York.

Downing, J.A., Plante, C. & Lalonde, S. (1990) Fish production correlated with primary productivity, not the morphoedaphic index. *Canadian Journal of Fisheries and Aquatic Sciences*, **47**, 1929–1936.

Downing, J.A., Prairie, Y.T., Cole, J.J., et al. (2006) The global abundance and size distribution of lakes, ponds, and impoundments. *Limnology and Oceanography*, **51**, 2388–2397.

Downing, J.A., Cole, J.J., Middelburg, J., et al. (2008) Sediment organic carbon burial in agriculturally eutrophic impoundments over the last century. *Global Biogeochemical Cycles*, **22**, GB1018, doi:10.1029/2006GB002854.

Driscoll, C.T., Lawrence, G.B., Bulger, A.J., et al. (2001) Acidic deposition in the northeastern United States: sources and inputs, ecosystem effects, and management strategies. *BioScience*, **51**, 180–198.

Dudgeon, D. (1994) The influence of riparian vegetation on macroinvertebrate community structure and functional organisation in six New Guinea streams. *Hydrobiologia*, **294**, 65–85.

Dudgeon, D. (2000) The ecology of tropical Asian rivers and streams in relation to biodiversity conservation. *Annual Reviews of Ecology and Systematics*, 31, 239–263.

Dudgeon, D., Arthington, A.H., Gessner, M.O., et al. (2006) Freshwater Biodiversity: importance, threats, status and conservation challenges. *Biological Reviews*, **81**, 163–182.

Dugan, P. (Ed.) (1994) *Wetland Conservation: a Review of Current Issues and Required Action.* IUCN, Gland, Switzerland.

Dussart, G.B.J. (1976) The ecology of freshwater molluscs in north west England in relation to water chemistry. *Journal of Molluscan Studies,* **42**, 181–198.

Edmondson, W.T. (1960) Reproductive rates of rotifers in natural populations. *Memoria del Istituto Italiano del Hydrobiologia,* **12**, 21–77.

Edmondson, W.T. (1991) *The Uses of Ecology, Lake Washington and Beyond.* University of Washington Press, Seattle and London.

Ehhalt, D.H. & Schmidt, U. (1978) Sources and sinks of atmospheric methane. *Pure and Applied Geophysics,* **116**, 452–464.

Ehrlich, P.R. & Holdren, J.P. (1971) Impact of population growth. *Science,* **171**, 1212.

Ehrlich, P.R. & Pringle, R.M. (2008) Where does biodiversity go from here? A grim business-as-usual forecast and a hopeful portfolio of partial solutions. *Proceedings of The National Academy of Sciences,* **105**, 11579–11586.

Eller, G., Deines, P. & Kruger, M. (2007) Possible sources of methane-derived carbon for chironomid larvae. *Aquatic Microbial Ecology,* **46**, 283–293.

Elliott, J.M. & Drake, C.M. (1981) A comparative study of seven grabs used for sampling benthic macroinvertebrates in rivers. *Freshwater Biology,* **11**, 99–120.

Elser, J.J., Bracken, M.E., Cleland, E.E., et al. (2007) Global analysis of nitrogen and phosphorus limitation of primary producers in freshwater, marine and terrestrial ecosystems. *Ecology Letters,* **10**, 1135–1142.

Elster, H.J. (1958) Das limnologische Seetypensystem, Ruckblick und Ausblich. *Verhandlungen internationale der Vereinigung theeoretische und angewande Limnologie,* **13**, 101–120.

Eminson, D.F. & Moss, B. (1980) The composition and ecology of periphyton communities in freshwaters. I. The influence of host type and external environment on community composition. *British Phycological Journal,* **15**, 429–46.

Engelhardt, K.A.M. & Ritchie, M.E. (2001) Effects of macrophyte species richness on wetland ecosystem functioning and services. *Nature,* **411**, 687–689.

Engstrom, D.R., Fritz, S.C., Almendinger, J.E. & Juggins, S. (2000) Chemical and biological trends during lake evolution in recently deglaciated terrain. *Nature,* **408**, 161–166.

Evans-Pritchard, E.E. (1940) *The Nuer.* Oxford University Press, Oxford.

Fanslow, D.L., Nalepa, T.F. & Lang, G.A. (1995) Filtration rates of the zebra mussel (*Dreissena polymorpha*) on natural seston from Saginaw Bay, Lake Huron. *Journal of Great Lakes Research,* **21**, 489–500.

Fenchel, T. (1969) The ecology of marine microbenthos. IV Structure and function of the benthic system, its chemical and physical factors and the microfauna communities with special reference to the ciliated Protozoa. *Ophelia,* **6**, 1–182.

Fenchel, T. & Finlay, B.J. (1995) *Ecology and Evolution in Anoxic Worlds.* Oxford University Press, Oxford.

Fenchel, T. & Finlay, B.J. (2004). The ubiquity of small species: Patterns of local and global diversity. *BioScience,* **54**, 777–784.

Fenchel, T., Esteban, G.F. & Finlay, B.J. (1997) Local versus global diversity of microorganisms: cryptic diversity of ciliated Protozoa. *Oikos,* **80**, 220–225.

Ferguson, A. (1989) Genetic differences among brown tout, *Salmo trutta*, stocks and their importance for the conservation and management of the species. *Freshwater Biology,* **21**, 35–46.

Finlayson, C.M. (2005) Plant ecology of Australia's tropical floodplain wetlands: a review. *Annals of Botany,* **96**, 541–555.

Fisher, S.G. & Likens, G.E. (1973) Energy flow in Bear Brook, New Hampshire: an integrative approach to stream ecosystem metabolism. *Ecological Monographs,* **43**, 421–439.

Fitkau, E.J. (1970) Role of caimans in the nutrient regime of mouth-lakes in Amazon effluents (a hypothesis). *Biotropica,* **2**, 138–142.

Fitkau, E.J. (1973) Crocodiles and the nutrient metabolism of Amazonian water. *Amazoniana,* **4**, 101–133.

Flannagan, J.F. (1970) Efficiencies of various grabs and corers in sampling freshwater benthos. *Journal of the Fisheries Research Board of Canada,* **27**, 1691–1700.

Fogg, G.E. & Westlake, D.F. (1955) The importance of extracellular products of algae in freshwater. *Verhandlungen internationale der Vereinigung theoretische und angewande Limnologie,* **12**, 219–232.

Folt, C.L. & Burns, C.W. (1999) Biological drivers of zooplankton patchiness. *Trends in Ecology and Evolution,* **14**, 300–305.

Forsberg, C. & Petersen, R.C. Jr (1990) A darkening of Swedish lakes due to increased humus inputs during the last 15 years. *Verhandlungen internationale der Vereinigung theoretische und angewande Limnologie,* **24**, 289–292.

Fortey, R. (2008) *Dry Store No. 1: The Secret Life of the Natural History Museum.* Harper Perennial.

Foy, R.H. (1985) Phosphorus inactivation in a eutrophic lake by the direct addition of ferric aluminium sulphate: impact on iron and phosphorus. *Freshwater Biology,* **15**, 613–630.

Foy, R.H. & Lennox, S.D. (2006) Evidence for a delayed response of riverine phosphorus exports from increasing agricultural catchment pressures in the Lough Neagh catchment. *Limnology and Oceanography,* **51** (1, part 2), 655–663.

France, R.L. (1995) Stable isotopic survey of the role of macrophytes in the carbon flow of aquatic food webs. *Vegetatio,* **124**, 67–72.

Fraser, L.H. & Keddy, P.A. (2005) *The World's Largest Wetlands: Ecology and Conservation.* Cambridge University Press.

Fryer, G. (1991) *A Natural History of the Lakes, Tarns and Streams of the English Lake District.* Freshwater Biological Association, Ambleside.

Fryer, G. & Iles, T.D. (1972) *The Cichlid Fishes of the Great Lakes of Africa*. Oliver and Boyd, Edinburgh.

Fujikura, M. & Nakayama, M. (2009) Lessons learned from the World Commission on Dams. *International Environmental Agreements*, **9**, 173–190.

Gal, G., Hipsey, M.R., Parparova, A., Wagnera, U., Maklerc, V. & Zohary, T. (2009) Implementation of ecological modelling as an effective management and investigation tool: Lake Kinneret as a case study. *Ecological Modelling*, **220**, 1697–1718.

Ganff, G.G. & Viner, A.B. (1973) Ecological stability in a shallow equatorial lake (lake George, Uganda). *Proceedings of the Royal Society, B*, **184**, 321–346.

Garrod, D.J. (1961a) The rational exploitation of the *Tilapia esculenta* stock of the North Buvuma island area, Lake Victoria. *East African Agriculture and Forestry Journal*, **27**, 69–76.

Garrod, D.J. (1961b) The history of the fishing industry of Lake Victoria, East Africa, in relation to the expansion of marketing facilities. *East African Agriculture and Forestry Journal*, **27**, 95–99.

Gasse, F. & Van Campo, E. (2001) Late Quaternary environmental changes from a pollen and diatom record in the southern tropics (Lake Tritrivakely, Madagascar). *Palaeography, Palaeoclimatology, Palaeoecology*, **167**, 287–308.

Gaston, K.J. & Spicer, J.I. (2004) *Biodiversity: An Introduction*, 2nd edn. Wiley-Blackwell, Oxford.

George, D.G. (2002) Regional scale influences on the long-term dynamics of lake plankton. In *Phytoplankton Production*, Williams, P.J., Le B., Thomas, D.N. & Reynolds, C.S. (Eds). Blackwell Scientific, Oxford; 265–290.

George, D.G. & Taylor, A.H. (1995) UK lake plankton and the Gulf Stream. *Nature*, **378**, 139.

George, D.G., Maberly, S.C. & Hewitt, D.P. (2004) The influence of the North Atlantic Oscillation on the physics, chemistry and biology of four lakes in the English Lake District. *Freshwater Biology*, **49**, 760–774.

Gersberg, R.M., Elkins, B.W. & Goldman, C.R. (1983) Nitrogen removal in artificial wetlands. *Water Research*, **17**, 1009–1014.

Gherardi, F. (2006) Bioinvasions in fresh waters and the Nero dilemma. *Polish Journal of Ecology*, **54**, 549–561.

Gibbs, R.J. (1970) Mechanisms controlling world water chemistry. *Science*, **170**, 1088–1090.

Gierlowski-Kordesch, E. & Kelts, K. (1994) Introduction. In *Global Geological Record of Lake Basins*, Vol. 1, Gierlowski-Kordesch, E. & Kelts, K. (Eds).Cambridge University Press, Cambridge.

Giles, N. (1992) *Wildlife after Gravel; Twenty Years of Practical Research by the Game Conservancy and ARC*. Game Conservancy Limited, Fordingbridge.

Gilbert, J.J. (1988) Suppression of rotifer populations by *Daphnia*: A review of the evidence, the mechanisms, and the effects on zooplankton community structure. *Limnology and Oceanography*, **33**, 1286–1303.

Giller, P.S. (2005) River restoration: seeking ecological standards. Editor's introduction. *Journal of Applied Ecology*, **42**, 201–207.

Giller, P.S. & Malmqvist, B. (1998) *The Biology of Streams and Rivers*. Oxford University Press.

Gislason, G.M., Olafsson, J.S. & Adalsteinsson, H. (1998) Animal communities in Icelandic rivers in relation to catchment characteristics and water chemistry. Preliminary results. *Nordic Hydrology*, **29**, 129–148.

Gliwicz, Z.M. (1986) Predation and the evolution of vertical migration behaviour in zooplankton. *Nature*, **320**, 746–748.

Godwin, H. (1978) *Fenland: its Ancient Past and Uncertain Future*. Cambridge University Press.

Goldman, C.R. & Horne, A.J. (1994) *Limnology*, 2nd edn. McGraw Hill, New York.

Goldman, J.C., McCarthy, J.J. & Peavey, D.G. (1979) Growth rate influence on the chemical composition of phytoplankton in oceanic waters. *Nature*, **179**, 210–215.

Goldschmidt, T. (1997) *Darwin's Dreampond. Drama in Lake Victoria*. MIT Press. Cambridge, Mass.

Goldschmidt, T. & Witte, F. (1992) Explosive speciation and adaptive radiation of haplochromine cichlids from Lake Victoria: an illustration of the scientific value of a lost species flock. *Mitteilungen internationale der Vereinigung theoretische und angewandte Limnologie*, **23**, 101–108.

Gorham, E. (1961) Factors influencing supply of major ions to inland waters with special reference to the atmosphere. *Geogical Society of America Bulletin*, **72**, 795–840.

Goudswaard, K.P.C., Witte, F. & Katunzi, E.F.B. (2008) The invasion of an introduced predator, Nile perch (*Lates niloticus* L.) in Lake Victoria (East Africa); chronology and causes. *Environmental Biology of Fish*, **81**, 127–139.

Goulding, M. (1980) *The Fishes and the Forest: Explorations in Amazonian Natural History*. University of California Press, Los Angeles.

Goulding, M. (1981) *Man and Fisheries on an Amazon Frontier*. Junk, The Hague.

Goulding, M., Smith, N.J.H. & Mahar, D.J. (1996) *Floods of Fortune. Ecology and Economy along the Amazon Frontier*. Columbia University Press, New York.

Gozlan, R.E. (2008) Introduction of non-native fish. Is it all bad? *Fish and Fisheries*, **9**, 106–115.

Graham, C.T. & Harrod, C. (2009) Implications of climate change for the fishes of the British Isles. *Journal of Fish Biology*, **74**, 1143–1205.

Gratton, C., Donaldson, J. & Vander Zanden, M.J. (2008) Ecosystem linkages between lakes and the surrounding terrestrial landscape in northeast Iceland. *Ecosystems*, **11**, 764–774.

Gray, L.J. (1981) Species composition and life histories of aquatic insects in a lowland Sonoran desert stream. *American Midland Naturalist*, **106**, 229–242.

Greathouse, E.A. & Pringle, C.M. (2006) Does the river continuum concept apply on a tropical island? Longitudinal variation in a Puerto Rican stream. *Canadian Journal of Fisheries and Aquatic Sciences*, **63**, 134–152.

Green, J. (1967) The distribution and variation of *Daphnia lumholtzi* (Crustacea: Cladocera) in relation to fish predation in Lake Albert, East Africa. *Journal of Zoology*, **151**, 181–97.

Green, W.J. & Lyons, W.B. (2009) The saline lakes of the McMurdo dry valleys, Antarctica. *Aquatic Geochemistry*, **15**, 321–348.

Gregory, K.J. & Walling, D.E. (1973) *Drainage Basin Form and Process*. Edward Arnold.

Grey, J., Thackeray, S.J., Jones, R.I. & Shine, A. (2002) Ferox trout (*Salmo trutta*) as 'Russian dolls': complementary gut content and stable isotope analyses of the Loch Ness food-web. *Freshwater Biology*, **47**, 1235–1243.

Gruber, N. & Galloway, J.N. (2008) An earth-system perspective of the global nitrogen cycle. *Nature*, **451**, 293–296.

Guinotte, J.M. & Fabry, V.J. (2008) Ocean acidification and its potential effects on marine ecosystems. *Annals of the New York Academy of Sciences*, **1134**, 320–342.

Gulati, R.D., Dionisio Pires, M. & Van Donk, E. (2008) Lake restoration studies: failures, bottlenecks and prospects of new ecotechnological measures. *Limnologica*, **38**, 233–247.

Guy, C.S. & Brown, M.L. (2007) *Analysis and Interpretation of Freshwater Fisheries Data*. American Fisheries Society, Bethesda, MD.

Gyllstrom, M., Hansson, L.-A., Jeppesen, E., et al. (2005) The role of climate in shaping zooplankton communities of shallow lakes. *Limnology and Oceanography*, **50**, 2008–2021.

Hahn, S., Bauer, S. & Klaassen, M. (2007) Estimating the contribution of carnivorous waterbirds to nutrient loading in freshwater habitats. *Freshwater Biology*, **52**, 2421–2433.

Hahn, S., Bauer, S. & Klaassen, M. (2008) Quantification of allochthonous nutrient input into freshwater bodies by herbivorous waterbirds. *Freshwater Biology*, **53**, 181–193.

Hairston, N.G. Jr & De Meester, L. (2008) *Daphnia* paleogenetics and environmental change: deconstructing the evolution of plasticity. *Internationale Revue der Hydrobiologie*, **93**, 578–592.

Hairston, N.G. Jr, Lampert, W., Cáceres, C.E., et al. (1999) Rapid evolution revealed by dormant eggs. *Nature*, **401**, 446.

Hakanson, L. (2004) Break-through in predictive modelling opens new possibilities for aquatic ecology and management – a review. *Hydrobiologia*, **518**, 135–157.

Hall, D.J. (1964) An experimental approach to the dynamics of a natural population of *Daphnia galeata* mendotae. *Ecology*, **45**, 94–111.

Hall, D.J., Threlkeld, S.T., Burns, C.W. & Crowley, P.H. (1976) The size and efficiency hypothesis and the size structure of zooplankton communities. *Annual Reviews of Ecology and Systematics*, **7**, 177–208.

Hameed, H.A., Kilinc, S., McGowan, S. & Moss, B. (1999) Physiological tests and bioassays – aids or superfluities to the diagnosis of phytoplankton nutrient limitation? A comparative study in the Broads and Meres of England. *European Phycological Journal*, **34**, 253–270.

Hanazato, T. & Ooi, T. (1992) Morphological responses of *Daphnia ambigua* to different concentrations of a chemical extract from *Chaoborus flavicans*. *Freshwater Biology*, **27**, 379–385.

Hansson, L.-A., Gustafsson, S., Rengefors, K. & Bomark, L. (2007) Cyanobacterial chemical warfare affects zooplankton community composition. *Freshwater Biology*, **52**, 1290–1301.

Harding, D. (1966) Lake Kariba, the hydrology and development of fisheries. In *Man-made Lakes*, Lowe-McConnell, R. (Ed.). Academic Press, London; 7–20.

Hargeby, A. (1990) Macrophyte associated invertebrates and the effect of habitat permanence. *Oikos*, **57**, 338–346.

Hargeby, A., Blindow, I. & Andersson, G. (2007) Long-term patterns of shifts between clear and turbid states in Lake Krankesjon and Lake Takern. *Ecosystems*, **10**, 28–35.

Harris, C.M., Calladine, J.R., Wernham, C.V. & Park, K.J. (2008) Impacts of piscivorous birds on salmonid populations and game fisheries in Scotland: a review. *Wildlife Biology*, **14**, 395–411.

Hart, R.C. (1986) Zooplankton abundance, community structure and dynamics in relation to inorganic turbidity, and their implications for a potential fishery in subtropical Lake Le Roux, South Africa. *Freshwater Biology*, **16**, 351–372.

Hartmann, J. (1977) Fischereiliche Veranderungen in kulturbedingt eutrophierenden Seen. *Schweizerische Zhurnal der Hydrologie*, **39**, 243–254.

Hauer, R. & Lamberti, G. (2006) *Methods in Stream Ecology*. Elsevier, New York.

Havel, J.E. (1987) Predator-induced defences: a review. In *Predation: Direct and Indirect Impacts on Aquatic Communities*, Kerfoot, W.C. & Sih, A. (Eds). University Press of New England, Hanover, NH; 263–278.

Haworth, E.Y. (1969) The diatoms of a sediment core from Blea Tarn, Langdale. *Journal of Ecology*, **57**, 429–39.

Haworth, E.Y. (1972) Diatom succession in a core from Pickerel Lake, Northeastern South Dakota. *Geological Society of America Bulletin*, **83**, 157–72.

Haworth, E.Y. (1980) Comparison of continuous phytoplankton records with the diatom stratigraphy in the recent sediments of Blelham Tarn. *Limnology and Oceanography*, **25**, 1093–1103.

Hayden, B. (1997) Observations on the prehistoric social and economic structure of the North American plateau. *World Archaeology*, **29**, 242–261.

Hayden, B. & Cannon, A. (1982). The corporate group as an archaeological unit. *Journal of Anthropological Archaeology*, **1**, 132–158.

Hayden, B. & Ryder, J.M. (1991) Prehistoric cultural collapse in the Lillooet area. *American Antiquity*, **56**, 50–65.

Heathwaite, A.L., Johnes, P.J. & Peters, N. (1996) Trends in nutrients. *Hydrological Processes*, **10**, 263–293.

Hecky, R.E. (1992) The eutrophication of Lake Victoria. *Verhandlungen internationale der Vereinigung theoretische und angewande Limnologie.* **25**, 39–48.

Hecky, R.E., Campbell, P. & Hendzel, L.L. (1993) The stoichiometry of carbon, nitrogen and phosphorus in particulate matter of lakes and oceans. *Limnology and Oceanography*, **38**, 709–724.

Heeg, J. & Breen, C.M. (1982) *Man and the Pongolo Floodplain.* South African National Scientific Programmes Report No. 56. Council for Scientific and Industrial Research, Pretoria, South Africa.

Heino, J. & Muotka, T. (2006) Landscape position, local environmental factors, and the structure of molluscan assemblages in lakes. Landscape *Ecology*, **21**, 499–507.

Heino, J., Virkkala, R. & Toivonen, H. (2009) Climate change and freshwater biodiversity: detected patterns, future trends and adaptations in northern regions. *Biological Reviews*, **84**, 39–54.

Helfield, J.M. & Naiman, R.J. (2006) Keystone interactions: salmon and bear in riparian forests of Alaska. *Ecosystems*, **9**, 167–180.

Hewlett, N.R., Snow, J. & Britton, J.R. (2009) The role of management practices in fish kills in recreational lake fisheries in England and Wales. *Fisheries Management and Ecology*, **16**, 248–254.

Hickley, P., Marsh, C. & North, R. (1995) Ecological management of angling. In *The Ecological Basis for River Management*, Harper, D.M. & Ferguson, A.J.D. (Eds) John Wiley & Sons, Chichester; 415–426.

Hickling, C.F. (1961) *Tropical Inland Fisheries.* Longman, London.

Hickling, R., Roy, D.B., Hill, J.K., Fox, R. & Thomas, C.D. (2006) The distributions of a wide range of taxonomic groups are expanding polewards. *Global Change Biology*, **12**, 450–455.

Hilt, S. & Grosse, E.M. (2008) Can allelopathically active submerged macrophytes stabilise clear-water states in shallow lakes? *Basic and Applied Ecology*, **9**, 422–432.

Hoback, W.W. & Stanley, D.W. (2001) Mini-review: insects in hypoxia. *Journal of Insect Physiology*, **47**, 533–542.

Hobbs, H.H., Jass, J.P. & Huner, J.V. (1989) A review of global crayfish introductions with particular emphasis on two North American species (Decapoda, Cambaridae). *Crustaceana*, **56**, 299–316.

Hobson, K.A. (1999) Tracing origins and migration of wildlife using stable isotopes: a review. *Oecologia*, **120**, 314–326.

Hodgson, D.A., Johnston, N.M., Caulketta, A.P. & Jones, V.J. (1998) Palaeolimnology of Antarctic fur seal *Arctocephalus gazella* populations and implications for Antarctic management. *Biological Conservation*, **83**, 145–154.

Hoffman, R.C. (2005) A brief history of aquatic resource use in mediaeval Europe. *Helgoland Marine Research*, **59**, 22–30.

Hohensinner, S., Habersack, H., Jungwirth, M. & Zauner, G. (2004) Reconstruction of the characteristics of a natural alluvial river-floodplain system and hydromorphological changes following human modifications: The Danube River (1812–1991). *River Research and Applications*, **20**, 25–41.

Holmes, N.T.H. (1998) Floodplain restoration. In *United Kingdom Floodplains*, Bailey, R.G., José, P.V. & Sherwood, B.R. (Eds). Westbury Academic and Scientific Publishing, Otley; 331–348.

Hooper, D.U., Chapin III, F.S., Ewel, J.J., et al. (2005) Effects of biodiversity on ecosystem functioning: A consensus of current knowledge. *Ecological Monographs*, **75**, 3–35.

Howard-Williams, C. (1977) Swamp ecosystems. *Malay Naturalists Journal*, **31**, 113–25.

Howell, P., Lock, M. & Cobb, S. (1988) *Jonglei Canal: Impact and Opportunity.* Cambridge University Press, Cambridge.

Hrbacek, J., Bvorakova, K., Korinek, V. & Prochazkova, L. (1961) Demonstration of the effect of the fish stock on the species composition of the zooplankton and the intensity of metabolism of the whole plankton association. *Verhandlungen internationale der Vereinigung theoretische und angewande Limnologie*, **14**, 192–195.

Hugueny, B. (1989) West African rivers as biogeography islands: species richness of fish communities. *Oecologia*, **79**, 236–243.

Huntingford, F.A. et al. (2006) Current issues in fish welfare. *Journal of Fish Biology*, **68**, 332–372.

Hurlbert, S.H., Zedler, J. & Fairbanks, D. (1971) Ecosystem alteration by mosquito fish (*Gambusia affinis*) predation. *Science*, **175**, 639–641.

Hurlbert, S.H., Loayza, W. & Moreno, T. (1986) Fish–flamingo–plankton interactions in the Peruvian Andes. *Limnology and Oceanography*, **31**, 457–468.

Hutchinson, G.E. (1957) *A Treatise on Limnology*, Vol. 1, *Geography, Physics, Chemistry.* John Wiley & Sons, New York.

Hutchinson, G.E. (1965) *The Ecological Theatre and the Evolutionary Play.* Yale University Press, New Haven, CT.

Hutchinson, G.E. (1967) *A Treatise on Limnology*, Vol. 2, *Introduction to Lake Ecology and the Limnoplankton.* John Wiley & Sons, New York.

Hutchinson, G.E. (1973) Eutrophication. *American Scientist*, **61**, 269–279.

Hutchinson, G.E. (1975) *A Treatise on Limnology*, Vol. 3, *Limnological Botany.* John Wiley & Sons, New York.

Hutchinson, G.E. (1993) *A Treatise on Limnology*, Vol. 4, *The Zoobenthos*, Edmondson, Y.H. (Ed.). John Wiley & Sons, New York.

Hutchinson, G.E. & Loffler, H. (1956) The thermal classification of lakes. *Proceedings of The National Academy of Sciences*, **42**, 84–86.

Hutchinson, G.E., Bonatti, E., Cowgill, U.M., et al. (1970) Ianula: an account of the history and development of the Lago di Monterosi, Latium, Italy. *Transactions of the American Philosophical Society*, **60**, 1–178.

Hynes, H.B.N. (1966) *The Biology of Polluted Waters.* Liverpool University Press.

Hynes, H.B.N. (1979) *The Ecology of Running Waters.* Liverpool University Press.

Ibelings, B.W., Portielje, R., Lammens, E.H.R.R., et al. (2007) Resilience of alternative stable states during the recovery of shallow lakes from eutrophication: Lake Veluwe as a case study. *Ecosystems*, **10**, 4–16.

Ilg, C., Dziock, F., Foeckler, F., et al. (2008) Long-term reactions of plants and macroinvertebrates to extreme floods in floodplain grasslands. *Ecology*, **89**, 2392–2398.

Imhof, G. (1973) Aspects of energy flow by different food chains in a reed bed-a review. *Polskii Archivum Hydrobiologii*, **20**, 165–8.

Infante, A. & Litt, A.H. (1985) Differences between two species of *Daphnia* in the use of 10 species of algae in Lake Washington. *Limnology and Oceanography*, **30**, 1053–1059.

IPCC (2007) *Climate Change 2007. Synthesis Report. Contribution of Working Groups I, II and III to the Fourth Assessment Report of the Intergovernmental Panel on Climate Change.* Core Writing Team, Pachauri, R.K. & Reisinger, A. (Eds). Intergovernmental Panel on Climate Change, Geneva.

Irfanullah, H.M. & Moss, B. (2005) A filamentous green-algae dominated temperate shallow lake: Variations on the theme of clear-water stable states. *Archiv fur Hydrobiologie*, **163**, 25–47.

Irvine, K., Moss, B. & Balls, H.R. (1989) The loss of submerged plants with eutrophication II. Relationships between fish and zooplankton in a set of experimental ponds, and conclusions. *Freshwater Biology*, **22**, 89–107.

Ishikawa, T., Narita, T. & Urabe, J. (2004) Long-term changes in the abundance of *Jesogammarus annandalei* (Tattersall). *Limnology and Oceanography*, **49**, 1840–1847.

Iversen, T.M., Kronvang, B., Madsen, B.L., Markmann, P. & Nielsen, M.B. (1993) Re-establishment of Danish streams: restoration and maintenance measures. *Aquatic Conservation: Marine and Freshwater Ecosystems*, **3**, 73–92.

Iwata, T., Nakano, S. & Inoue, M. (2003) Impacts of past riparian deforestation on stream communities in a tropical rain forest in Borneo. *Ecological Applications*, **13**, 461–473.

Jackson, M.B. & Colmer, T.D. (2005) Response and adaptation by plants to flooding stress. *Annals of Botany*, **96**, 501–505.

Jackson, M.B. & Ram, P.C. (2003) Physiological and molecular basis of susceptibility and tolerance of rice plants to complete submergence. *Annals of Botany*, **91**, 227–241.

Jackson, M.B., Ishizawa, K. & Ito, O. (2009) Evolution and mechanisms of plant tolerance to flooding stress. *Annals of Botany*, **103**, 137–142.

Jackson, R.B., Carpenter, S.R., Dahm, C.N., et al. (2001) Water in a changing world. *Ecological Applications*, **11**, 1027–1045.

Jacobs, S.M., Bechtold, J.S., Biggs, H.C., et al. (2007) Nutrient vectors and riparian processing: a review with special reference to African semiarid savanna ecosystems. *Ecosystems*, **10**, 1231–1249.

James, C., Fisher, J. & Moss, B. (2003) Nitrogen driven lakes: The Shropshire and Cheshire Meres? *Archiv fur Hydrobiologie*, **158**, 249–266.

James, C.S., Fisher, J., Russell, V., Collings, S. & Moss, B. (2005) Nitrate availability and hydrophyte species richness in shallow lakes. *Freshwater Biology*, **50**, 1049–1063.

James, R.T., Chimney, M.J., Sharfstein, B., et al. (2008) Hurricane effects on a shallow lake ecosystem, Lake Okeechobee, Florida, USA. *Fundamental and Applied Limnology*, **172**, 273–287.

Jauhiainen, J. et al. (2005) Carbon fluxes from a tropical peat swamp forest floor. *Global Change Biology*, **11**, 1788–1797.

Jeffrey, D.J. & Gilbert, J.J. (1997) Effects of metazoan predators on ciliates in freshwater plankton communities. *Journal of Eukaryotic Microbiology*, **44**, 194–199.

Jenkin, P.M. (1942) Seasonal changes in the temperature of Windermere (English Lake District). *Journal of Animal Ecology*, **11**, 248–69.

Jensen, J.P., Jeppesen, E., Olrik, K. & Kristensen, P. (1994) Impact of nutrients and physical factors on the shift from cyanobacterial to chlorophyte dominance in shallow Danish lakes. *Canadian Journal of Fisheries and Aquatic Sciences*, **51**, 1692–1699.

Jeppesen, E., Christoffersen, K., Landkildehus, F., et al. (2001) Fish and crustaceans in northeast Greenland lakes with special emphasis on interactions between Arctic charr (*Salvelinus alpinus*), *Lepidurus arcticus* and benthic chydorids. *Hydrobiologia*, **42**, 329–337.

Jeppesen, E., Christoffersen, K., Malmquist, H.J., Faafeng, B. & Hansson, L.-A. (2002) Food web interactions in five Faroese lakes tracked by stable isotopes. *Annales Societatis Scientiarum Faeroensis Supplementum*, **36**, 114–125.

Jeppesen, E., Søndergaard, M., Jensen, J.P., et al. (2005) Lake responses to reduced nutrient loading – an analysis of contemporary long-term data from 35 case studies. *Freshwater Biology*, **50**, 1747–1771.

Jhingran, V.G. (2002) *Fish and Fisheries of India*, 3rd edn. Hindustan Publishing Corporation, Delhi.

Johannes, R.E. (1965) Influence of marine protozoa on nutrient regeneration. *Limnology and Oceanography*, **10**, 434–442.

Johnes, P.J. (1996) Evaluation and management of the impact of land use change on the nitrogen and phosphorus load delivered to surface waters: the export coefficient modelling approach. *Journal of Hydrology*, **183**, 323–349.

Johnes, P., Moss, B. & Phillips, G. (1996) The determination of total nitrogen and total phosphorus concentrations in freshwaters from land use, stock headage and population data: testing of a model for use in conservation and water quality management. *Freshwater Biology*, **36**, 451–473.

Johnson, A.C., Acremana, M.C., Dunbar, M.J., et al. (2009) The British river of the future: How climate change and human activity might affect two contrasting river ecosystems in England. *Science of the Total Environment*, **407**, 4787–4798.

Johnson, M.G. & Brinkhurst, R.O. (1971a) Associations and species diversity in benthic macroinvertebrates of Bay of Quinte and Lake Ontario. *Journal of the Fisheries Research Board of Canada*, **28**, 1683–1697.

Johnson, M.G. & Brinkhurst, R.O. (1971b) Production of benthic macroinvertebrates of Bay of Quinte and Lake Ontario. *Journal of the Fisheries Research Board of Canada*, **28**, 1699–714.

Johnson, M.G. & Brinkhurst, R.O. (1971c) Benthic community metabolism in Bay of Quinte and Lake Ontario. *Journal of the Fisheries Research Board of Canada*, **28**, 1715–25.

Johnson, R.K. (1985) Feeding efficiencies of *Chironomus plumosus* (L.) and *C. anthracinus* Zett. (Diptera: Chironomidae) in mesotrophic Lake Erken. *Freshwater Biology*, **15**, 605–612.

Johnson, R.K., Boström, B., & van de Bund, W. (1989) Interactions between *Chironomus plumosus* (L.) and the microbial community in surficial sediments of a shallow, eutrophic lake. *Limnology and Oceanography*, **34**, 993–1003.

Johnson, W.C., Millett, B.V., Gilmanov, T., Voldseth, R.A., Guntenspergen, G.R. & Naugle, D.E. (2005) Vulnerability of northern prairie wetlands to climate change. *BioScience*, **55**, 863–872.

Jonasson, P.M. (1972) Ecology and production of the profundal benthos in relation to phytoplankton in Lake Esrom. *Oikos*, Suppl. **14**, 1–148.

Jonasson, P.M. (1977) Lake Esrom research, 1867–1977. *Folia Limnologica Scandinavica*, **17**, 67–90.

Jonasson, P.M. (1978) Zoobenthos of lakes. *Verhandlungen internationale der Vereinigung theoretische und angewande Limnologie*, **20**, 13–37.

Jonasson, P.M. (1996) Limits for life in the lake ecosystem. *Verhandlungen internationale der Vereinigung theoretische und angewande Limnologie*, **26**, 1–34.

Jones, J.B., et al. (1997) Organic matter dynamics in Sycamore Creek, a desert stream in Arizona, USA. *Journal of the North American Benthological Society*, **16**, 78–82.

Jones, J.D. (1964) Respiratory gas exchange in the aquatic pulmonate, Biomphalaria sudanica. *Comparative Biochemistry and Physiology*, **12**, 297–310.

Jones, J.I., Schade, J.D., Fisher, S.G. & Grimm, N.B. (1999) Do submerged aquatic plants influence their periphyton to enhance the growth and reproduction of invertebrate mutualists. *Oecologia*, **120**, 463–474.

Jones, J.I., Eaton, J.W. & Hardwick, K. (2000) The influence of periphyton on boundary layer conditions: a pH microelectrode investigation. *Aquatic Botany*, **67**, 191–206.

Jones, R.I. & Grey, J. (2004) Stable isotope analysis of chironomid larvae from some Finnish forest lakes indicates dietary contribution from biogenic methane. *Boreal Environment Research*, **9**, 17–23.

Jones, R.I., Grey, J., Sleep, D. & Quarmby, C. (1998) An assessment, using stable isotopes, of the importance of allochthonous organic carbon sources to the pelagic food web in Loch Ness. *Proceedings of The Royal Society of London Series B – Biological Sciences*, **265**, 105–111.

Jones, R.I., Carter, C.E., Kelly, A., Ward, S., Kelly, David, J. & Grey, J. (2008) Widespread contribution of methane-cycle bacteria to the diets of lake profundal chironomid larvae. *Ecology*, **89**, 857–864.

Jonsson, M., Malmqvist, B. & Hoffsten, P-O. (2001) Leaf litter breakdown rates in boreal streams: does shredder species richness matter? *Freshwater Biology*, **46**, 161–171.

Junk, W.J., Ohly, J.J., Piedade, M.T.F. & Soares, M.G.M. (Eds) (2000) *The Central Amazon Floodplain: Actual Use and Options for Sustainable Management*. Backhuys, Leiden.

Kalff, J. (2003) *Limnology*. Prentice Hall, New Jersey.

Kameda, K., et al. (2006) Pattern of natural $^{15}$N abundance in lakeside forest ecosystem affected by cormorant-derived nitrogen. *Hydrobiologia*, **567**, 69–86.

Karrow, P.F., Haas, J.N., Heiss, A.G., et al. (2009) The Fernbank interglacial site near Ithaca, New York, USA. *Quaternary Research*, **72**, 132–142.

Kernan, M., Battarbee, R.L. & Moss, B. (Eds) (2010) *Climate Change Impacts on Freshwater Ecosystems: Direct Effects and Interactions with Other Stresses*. Wiley-Blackwell, Oxford.

Kilham, P. & Kilham, S.S. (1990) Endless summer: internal loading processes dominate nutrient cycling in tropical lakes. *Freshwater Biology*, **23**, 379–389.

Kirk, J.T.O. (1994) *Light and Photosynthesis in Aquatic Ecosystems*, 2nd edn. Cambridge University Press.

Kiviranta, H., Vartiainen, T. & Tuomisto, J. (2002) Polychlorinated dibenzo-p-dioxins, dibenzofurans and biphenyls in fishermen in Finland. *Environmental Health Perspectives*, **110**, 355–361.

Klaassen, M. & Nolet, B.A. (2007) The role of herbivorous water birds in aquatic systems through interactions with aquatic macrophytes, with special reference to the Bewick's swan–fennel pondweed system. *Hydrobiologia*, **584**, 205–213.

Kling, G.W., Clark, M.A., Wagner, G.N., et al. (1987) The 1986 Lake Nyos gas disaster in Cameroun, West Africa. *Science*, **236**, 169–175.

Kling, G.W., Kipphut, G.W. & Miller, M.C. (1991) Arctic lakes and streams as gas conduits to the atmosphere: Implications for tundra carbon budgets. *Science*, **251**, 298–301.

Kolada, A., Soszka, H., Cydzik, D. & Golub, M. (2005) Abiotic typology of Polish lakes. *Limnologica*, **356**, 145–150.

Konishi, M., Nakano, S. & Iwata, T. (2001) Trophic cascading effects of predatory fish on leaf litter processing in a Japanese stream. *Ecological Research*, **16**, 415–422.

Kornijow, R. (1989) Macrofauna of elodeids of two lakes of different trophy. I Relationships between plants and structure of fauna colonizing them. *Ekologiska Polska*, **37**, 31–48.

Kortelainen, P., Mattsson, T., Rantakari, M. & Räike, A. (2004) Organic carbon concentrations in lakes and rivers. In *Inland and Coastal Waters of Finland*, Eloranta. P. (Ed.). Palmenia Publishing, Helsinki; 63–72.

Kudhongania, A.W. & Cordone, A.J. (1974) Batho-spatial distribution patterns and biomass estimates of the major demersal fishes in Lake Victoria. *African Journal of Tropical Hydrobiology and Fisheries*, **3**, 15–31.

Kufel, L. & Kufel, I. (2002) *Chara* beds acting as nutrient sinks in shallow lakes – a review. *Aquatic Botany*, **72**, 249–260.

Kuylenstierna, J.C.I., Hicks, W.K., Cinderby, S., Vallack, H.W. & Engardt, M. (2001) Variability in mapping acidification risk scenarios for terrestrial ecosystems in Asian countries. *Water, Air and Soil Pollution*, **130**, 1175–1180.

Kvet, J., Pokorny, J. & Cizkova, H. (2008) Carbon accumulation by macrophytes of aquatic and wetland habitats with standing water. *Proceedings of The National Academy of Sciences, India Section B Biological Sciences*, **78** (special issue S1), 91–98.

Kowalik, R.A., Cooper, D.M., Evans, C.D. & Ormerod, S.J. (2007) Acidic episodes retard the biological recovery of upland British streams from chronic acidification. *Global Change Biology*, **13**, 2439–2452.

Lake, P.S. (2003) Ecological effects of perturbation by drought in flowing waters. *Freshwater Biology*, **48**, 1161–1172.

Lamb, H., Roberts, N., Leng, M., Barker, P., Benkaddour, A. & van der Kaars, S. (1999) Lake evolution in a semi-arid montane environment: responses to catchment change and hydroclimatic variation. *Journal of Palaeolimnology*, **21**, 325–343.

Lampert, W. (2006) *Daphnia*: model herbivore, predator and prey. *Polish Journal of Ecology*, **54**, 607–620.

Lampert, W. & Sommer, U. (2007) *Limnoecology*, 2nd edn. Oxford University Press.

Last, W.M. & Smol, J.P. (2001) *Tracking Environmental Change Using Lake Sediments*, Vols 1–4. Kluwer, Dordrecht.

Laybourn-Parry, J. (1992) Protozoan Plankton Ecology. Chapman & Hall, London.

Laybourn-Parry, J. (1997) The microbial loop in Antarctic lakes. In *Ecosystem Processes in Antarctic Ice-free Landscapes*. Lyons, W.B., Howard-Williams, C. & Hawes, I. (Eds). Balkema, Rotterdam; 231–240.

Laybourn-Parry, J. (2009) No place too cold. *Science*, **324**, 1521–1522.

Lazzaro, X., Lacroix, G., Gauzens, B., Gignoux, J. & Legendre, S. (2009) Predator foraging behaviour drives food-web topological structure. *Journal of Animal Ecology*, **78**, 1307–1317.

Le Cren, E.D. (1972) Fish production in freshwaters. *Symposia of the Zoological Society of London*, **29**, 115–133.

Lean, D.R.S. (1973) Phosphorus dynamics in lake waters. *Science*, **179**, 678–80.

Lehman, J.T. & Caceres, C. (1993) Food-web responses to species invasion by a predatory invertebrate: *Bythotrephes* in Lake Michigan. *Limnology and Oceanography*, **38**, 879–891.

Lehman, J.T. & Scavia, D. (1982) Microscale patchiness of nutrients in plankton communities. *Science*, **216**, 729–730.

Lenton, T.M., Held, H., Kriegler, E., et al. (2007) Tipping elements in the Earth's climate system. *Proceedings of the National Academy of Sciences*, **105**, 1786–1793.

Leopold, L.B. (1994) *A View of the River*. Harvard University Press.

Leopold, L.B. (1997) *Water, Rivers and Creeks*. University Science Books.

Lesack, L.F.W., Marsh, P. & Hecky, R.E. (1998) Spatial and temporal dynamics of major solute chemistry among Mackenzie delta lakes. *Limnology and Oceanography*, **43**, 1530–1543.

Lester, R.E., & Boulton, A.J. (2008) Rehabilitating agricultural streams in Australia with wood: a review. *Environmental Management*, **42**, 210–326.

Leveque, C. & Mounolou, J.-C. (2003) *Biodiversity*. John Wiley & Sons, Chichester.

Lewis, W.M. & Wurtsbaugh, W.A. (2008) Control of lacustrine phytoplankton by nutrients: erosion of the phosphorus paradigm. *Internationale Revue der Hydrobiologie*, **93**, 446–465.

Likens, G.E., Bormann, F.H., Johnson, N.M., Fisher, D.W. & Pierce, R.S. (1970) Effects of forest cutting and herbicide treatment on nutrient budgets in the Hubbard Brook watershed-ecosystem. *Ecological Monographs*, **40**, 23–47.

Likens, G.E., Bormann, F.H., Pierce, R.S., Eaton, J.S. & Johnson, N.M. (1977) Biogeochemistry of a Forested Ecosystem. Springer-Verlag, New York.

Lindegaard, C. (1992) Zoobenthos ecology of Thingvallavatn: vertical distribution, abundance, population dynamics and production. *Oikos*, **64**, 257–304.

Lindegaard, C. & Jonasson, P.M. (1979) Abundance, population dynamics and production of zoobenthos in Lake Myvatn, Iceland. *Oikos*, **32**, 202–227.

Litchman, E. & Klausmeir, C.A. (2008) Trait-based community ecology of phytoplankton. *Annual Reviews of Ecology, Evolution and Systematics*, **39**, 615–639.

Lockaby, B.G. & Conner, W.H. (1999) N:P balance in wetland forests: productivity across a biogeochemical continuum. *The Botanical Review*, **65**, 171–185.

Lodge, D.M. (1985) Macrophyte-gastropod associations: observations and experiments on macrophyte choice by gastropods. *Freshwater Biology*, **15**, 695–708.

Lodge, D.M., Taylor, A., Holdich, D.M. & Skurdal, J. (2000) Nonindigenous crayfishes threaten North American freshwater biodiversity: Lessons from Europe. *Fisheries*, 7–20.

Logue, J.B., Burgmann, H. & Robinson, C.T. (2008) Progress in the ecological genetics and biodiversity of freshwater bacteria. *BioScience*, **58**, 103–113.

Logue, J.B. & Lindstrom, E. (2008) Biogeography of bacterioplankton in inland waters. *Freshwater Reviews*, **1**, 99–114.

Lovelock, J.E. (1965) A physical basis for life detection experiments. *Nature*, **207**, 568–570.

Lovelock, J. (1979) *Gaia: A New Look at Life on Earth*, Oxford University Press.

Lovelock, J.E. (1988) *The Ages of Gaia: a Biography of our Living Earth*. W.W. Norton, New York.

Lovelock, J.E. (2003) The living earth. *Nature*, **426**: 769–80.

Lovelock, J. (2006) *The Revenge of Gaia*. Penguin Books, London.

Lovelock, J. & Margulis, L. (1974) Atmospheric homeostasis: the Gaia hypothesis. *Tellus*, **26**, 2–10.

Lowe-McConnell, R.H. (Ed.) (1966) *Man-made Lakes. Symposia of the Institute of Biology, London, 15*. Academic Press, New York.

Lowe-McConnell, R.H. (1975) *Fish Communities in Tropical Freshwaters*. Longman, London.

Lowe-McConnell, R.H. (1987) *Ecological Studies in Tropical Fish Communities*. Cambridge University Press.

Lowe-McConnell, R.H. (1992) The changing ecosystem of Lake Victoria, East Africa. *Freshwater Forum*, **4**, 75–88.

Lund, J.W.G. (1949) Studies on *Asterionella*. 1. The origin and nature of the cells producing seasonal maxima. *Journal of Ecology*, **37**, 389–419.

Lund, J.W.G. (1950) Studies on *Asterionella formosa* Hass. II. Nutrient depletion and the spring maximum. *Journal of Ecology*, **38**, 1–14, 15–35.

Lund, J.W.G. (1954) The seasonal cycle of the plankton diatom Melosira italica (Ehr.) Kutz susp. subarctica O. Mull. *Journal of Ecology*, **42**, 151–179.

Lund, J.W.G. (1964) Primary productivity and periodicity of phytoplankton. *Verhandlungen internationale der Vereinigung theoretische und angewande Limnologie*, **15**, 37–56.

Lund, J.W.G. (1971) The seasonal periodicity of three planktonic desmids in Lake Windermere. *Mitteilungen internationale der Vereinigung theoretische und angewande Limnologie*, **19**, 3–25.

Lynn, D.E. & Waldren, S. (2003) Survival of *Ranunculus repens* L. (creeping buttercup) in an amphibious habitat. *Annals of Botany*, **91**, 75–84.

Maberley, S.C. & Spence, D.H.N. (1983) Photosynthetic inorganic carbon use by freshwater plants. *Journal of Ecology*, **71**, 705–724.

Macan, T.T. (1963) *Freshwater Ecology*. Longman, London.

Macan, T.T. (1970) *Biological Studies of the English Lakes*. American Elsevier, New York.

Macan, T.T. (1973) *Ponds and Lakes*. Allen and Unwin, London.

McCartney, M. (2009) Living with dams: managing the environmental impacts. *Water Policy*, **11** (Supplement 1), 121–139.

McDowall, R.M. (2006) Crying wolf, crying foul or crying shame: alien salmonids and a biodiversity crisis in the southern cool-temperate galaxioid fishes? *Reviews in Fish Biology and Fisheries*, **16**, 233–422.

McGinnity, P., Stone, J.B., Taggart, D., et al. (1997) Genetic impact of escaped farmed Atlantic salmon (*Slamo salar* L.) on native populations: use of DNA profiling to assess freshwater performance of wild, farmed, and hybrid progeny in a natural river environment. *ICES Journal of Marine Science*, **54**, 998–1008.

McGowan, S., Britton, G., Haworth, E. & Moss, B. (1999) Ancient blue-green blooms. *Limnology and Oceanography*, **44**, 436–439.

McIntosh, A.R. & Townsend, C.R. (1996) Interactions between fish, grazing invertebrates and algae in a New Zealand stream: a trophic cascade mediated by fish-induced changes to grazer behaviour? *Oecologia*, **108**, 174–181.

McLachlan, A.J. (1974) Development of some lake ecosystems in tropical Africa, with special reference to the invertebrates. *Biological Reviews*, **49**, 365–397.

McLachlan, A.J., Pearce, L.J. & Smith, J.A. (1979) Feeding interactions and cycling of peat in a bog lake. *Journal of Animal Ecology*, **48**, 851–861.

Mackereth, F.J.H. (1957) Chemical analysis in ecology illustrated from lake district tarns and lakes. 1. Chemical analysis. *Proceedings of the Linnean Society of London*, **67** (1954–1955), 159–164.

Mackereth, F.J.H. (1958) A portable core sampler for lake deposits. *Limnology and Oceanography*, **3**, 181–191.

Mackereth, F.J.H. (1965) Chemical investigations of lake sediments & their interpretation. *Proceedings of the Royal Society, Series B*, **161**, 293–375.

Mackereth, F.J.H. (1966) Some chemical observations on post-glacial lake sediments. *Philosophical Transactions of the Royal Society, Series B*, **250**, 165–213.

Madsen, B.L. (1995) *Danish Watercourses – Ten Years with the new Watercourse Act*. Ministry of Environment and Energy, Denmark, Danish Environment Protection Agency, Copenhagen.

Maitland, P.S. (1972) A key to the freshwater fishes of the British Isles. *Scientific Publications of the Freshwater Biological Association*, **27**, 1–137.

Maitland, P.S. (1995) Ecological impact of angling. In *The Ecological Basis for River Management*, Harper, D.M. & Ferguson, A.J.D. (Eds). John Wiley & Sons, Chichester; 443–452.

Makarewicz, J.C. & Likens, G.E. (1975) Niche analysis of a zooplankton community. *Science*, **190**, 1000–1002.

Malmqvist, B. (2002) Aquatic invertebrates in riverine landscapes. *Freshwater Biology*, 47, 679–694.

Malmqvist, B. & Rundle, S. (2002) Threats to running water ecosystems of the world. *Environmental Conservation*, **29**, 134–153.

March, J.G., Pringle, C.M., Townsend, M.J. & Wilson, A.I. (2002) Effects of freshwater shrimp assemblages on benthic communities along an altitudinal gradient of a tropical island stream. *Freshwater Biology*, **47**, 377–390.

March, J.G., Benstead, J.P., Pringle, C.M. & Scatena, F.N. (2003) Damming tropical island streams: problems, solutions, and alternatives. *BioScience*, **53**, 1069–1078.

Margulis, L. & Lovelock J.E. (1974) Biological modulation of the earth's atmosphere. *Icarus*, **21**: 1–19.

Margulis, L. & Sagan, D. (1987) *Microcosmos: Four Billion Years of Microbial Evolution*. Allen & Unwin, London.

Margulis, L. & Schwartz, K.V. (1998) *Five Kingdoms. An Illustrated Guide to the Phyla of Life on Earth*. W.H. Freeman, New York.

Mason, C.F. (2002) *Biology of Freshwater Pollution*, 4th edn. Pearson Educational, London.

Matsuishi, T., Muhoozi, L., Mkumbo, O., et al. (2006) Are the exploitation pressures on the Nile perch fisheries resources of Lake Victoria a cause for concern? *Fisheries Management and Ecology*, **13**, 53–71.

Matthews, C.P. & Westlake, D.F. (1969) Estimation of production by populations of higher plants subject to high mortality. *Oikos*, **20**, 156–60.

Matthews, G.V.T. (1993) *The Ramsar Convention on Wetlands: its History and Development*. Ramsar Convention Bureau, Gland.

Maxwell, G. (1957) *A Reed Shaken by the Wind*. Longmans, London. (1983; Penguin, Harmondsworth.)

Meerhoff, M., Fosalba, C., Bruzzone, C., Mazzeo, N., Noordoven, W. & Jeppesen, E. (2006) An experimental study of habitat choice by *Daphnia*: plants signal danger more than refuge in subtropical lakes. *Freshwater Biology*, **51**, 1320–1330.

Meerhoff, M., Iglesias, C., de Mello, F.T., et al. (2007a) Effects of habitat complexity on community structure and predator avoidance behaviour of littoral zooplankton in temperate versus subtropical shallow lakes. *Freshwater Biology*, **52**, 1009–1021.

Meerhoff, M., Clemente, J.M., de Mello, F.T., et al. (2007b) Can warm climate-related structure of littoral predator assemblies weaken the clear water state in shallow lakes? *Global Change Biology*, **13**, 888–1897.

Mehner, T., Arlinghaus, R., Berg, S., et al. (2004) How to link biomanipulation and sustainable fisheries management: a step-by-step guideline for lakes of the European temperate zone. *Fisheries Management and Ecology*, **11**, 261–275.

Meijer, M.-L. & Hosper, H. (1997) Effects of biomanipulation in the large and shallow lake Wolderwijd, The Netherlands. *Hydrobiologia*, **342/343**, 335–349.

Meijer, M.-L., De Boois, I., Scheffer, M., Portielje, R. & Hosper, H. (1999) Biomanipulation in shallow lakes in the Netherlands: an evaluation of 18 case studies. *Hydrobiologia*, **408/409**, 13–30.

Melack, J.M. (1979) Temporal variability of phytoplankton in tropical lakes. *Oecologia*, **44**, 1–7.

Michiels, I.C. & Traunspurger, W. (2005) Seasonal variation of biodiversity and assemblage structure in freshwater nematodes. *Archiv für Hydrobiologie*, **163**, 183–194.

Middelboe, M., Jacquet, S. & Weinbauer, M. (2008) Viruses in freshwater ecosystems: an introduction to the exploration of viruses in new aquatic habitats. *Freshwater Biology*, **53**, 1069–1075.

Miller, S.A. & Provenza, F.D. (2007) Mechanisms of resistance of freshwater macrophytes to herbivory by invasive juvenile common carp. *Freshwater Biology*, **52**, 39–49.

Milner, A.M., Brittain, J.E., Castella, E.l. & Petts, G.E. (2001) Trends of macroinvertebrate community structure in glacier-fed rivers in relation to environmental conditions: a synthesis. *Freshwater Biology*, **46**, 1833–1847.

Mitsch, W.J. & Gosselink, J.G. (2007) *Wetlands*, 4th edn. John Wiley & Sons, New York.

Mittelbach, G., Turner, A.M., Hall, D.J., Rettig, J.E. & Osenberg, C.W. (1995) Perturbation and resilience: a long-term, whole-lake study of predator extinction and reintroduction. *Ecology*, **76**, 2347–2360.

Moe, S.J., Dudley, B. & Ptacnik, R. (2008) REBECCA databases: experiences from compilation and analyses of monitoring data from 5000 lakes in 20 European countries. *Aquatic Ecology*, **42**, 183–201.

Monbiot, G. (2007) *Heat*. Penguin Books, London.

Monteith, D., Stoddard, J.L., Evans, C., et al. (2007) Dissolved organic carbon trends resulting from changes in atmospheric deposition chemistry. *Nature*, **450**, 537–541.

Mooij, W.M., Hülsmann, S., De Senerpont Domis, L.N., et al. (2005) The impact of climate change on lakes in the Netherlands: a review. *Aquatic Ecology*, **39**, 381–400.

Moore, J.W. (2006) Animal ecosystem engineers in streams. *BioScience*, **56**, 237–246.

Moore, N.W. (2002) Oaks, Dragonflies and People. Harley Books, Colchester.

Moore, P.D. (2002) The future of cool temperate bogs. *Environmental Conservation*, **29**, 2–20.

Moreau, M.A. & Coomes, O.T. (2007) Aquarium fish exploitation in western Amazonia: conservation issues in Peru. *Environmental Conservation*, 34, 12–22.

Moriarty, D.J.W., Darlington, J.P.E.C., Dunn, I.G., Moriarty, C.M. & Tevlin, M.P. (1973) Feeding and grazing in Lake George, Uganda. *Proceedings of the Royal Society of London, Series B*, **184**, 227–346.

Morrison, B.R.S. (1987) Uses and effects of piscicides. In *Angling and Wildlife in Fresh Waters ITE Symposium 19*, Maitland, P.S. & Turner, A.K. (Eds). Institute of Terrestrial Ecology, Wallingford; 47–52.

Mortimer, C.H. (1941–1942) The exchange of dissolved substances between mud and water in lakes. *Journal of Ecology*, **29**, 280–329; **30**, 147–201.

Moss, B. (1969) Limitation of algal growth in some Central African waters. *Limnology and Oceanography*, **14**, 591–601.

Moss, B. (1972) Studies on Gull Lake, Michigan. I. Seasonal and depth distribution of phytoplankton. *Freshwater Biology*, **2**, 289–307.

Moss, B. (1976) The effects of fertilization and fish on community structure and biomass of aquatic macrophytes and epiphytic algal populations: an ecosystem experiment. *Journal of Ecology*, **64**, 313–342.

Moss, B. (1977) Adaptations of epipelic and epipsammic freshwater algae. *Oecologia* (Berlin), **28**, 97–103.

Moss, B. (1990) Engineering and biological approaches to the restoration from eutrophication of shallow lakes in which aquatic plant communities are important components. *Hydrobiologia*, **200/201**, 367–377.

Moss, B. (1995) The microwaterscape – a four-dimensional view of interactions among water chemistry, phytoplankton, periphyton, macrophytes, animals and ourselves. *Water Science and Technology*, **32**, 105–16.

Moss, B. (2002) *The Broads: the People's Wetland*. Harper Collins New Naturalist, London.

Moss, B. (2005) Rapid shredding of leaves by crabs in a tropical African stream. *Verhandlungen internationale der Vereinigung theoretische und angewande Limnologie*, **29**, 147–150.

Moss, B. (2007) Lakes and society: Mirrors to our past, present and future. *Lake and Reservoir Management*, **23**, 457–465.

Moss, B. (2008a) The kingdom of the shore: achievement of good ecological potential in reservoirs. *Freshwater Reviews*, DOI: 10.1608/FRJ-1.1.2.

Moss, B. (2008b) The Water Framework Directive: Total environment or political compromise. *Science of the Total Environment*, **400**, 32–41.

Moss, B. (2010) Climate change, nutrient pollution and the bargain of Dr Faustus. *Freshwater Biology* (in press).

Moss, B. & Balls, H.R. (1989) Phytoplankton distribution in a floodplain lake and river system. II Seasonal changes in the phytoplankton communities and their control by hydrology and nutrient availability. *Journal of Plankton Research*, **11**, 839–867.

Moss, B., Stansfield, J. & Irvine, K. (1991) Development of daphnid communities in diatom- and cyanophyte-dominated lakes and their relevance to lake restoration by biomanipulation. *Journal of Applied Ecology*, **28**, 586–602.

Moss, B., McGowan, S. & Carvalho, L. (1994a) Determination of phytoplankton crops by top-down and bottom-up mechanisms in a group of English lakes, the West Midland meres. *Limnology and Oceanography*, **39**, 1020–1029.

Moss, B., Johnes, P. & Phillips, G. (1994b) August Thienemann and Loch Lomond – an approach to the design of a system for monitoring the state of north-temperate standing waters. *Hydrobiologia*, **290**, 1–12.

Moss B., Johnes, P.J. & Phillips, G. (1996a) The monitoring of ecological quality and the classification of standing waters in temperate regions: A review and proposal based on a worked scheme for British waters. *Biological Reviews*, **71**, 301–339.

Moss, B., Madgwick, J. & Phillips, G. (1996b) A Guide to the Restoration of Nutrient-Enriched Shallow Lakes. Environment Agency, Broads Authority and European Union, Norwich , UK.

Moss, B., Kornijow, R. & Measey, G.J. (1998) The effects of nymphaeid (*Nuphar lutea* L.) density and predation by perch (*Perca fluviatilis* L.) on the zooplankton communities in a shallow lake. *Freshwater Biology* **39**, 689–697.

Moss, B., Carvalho, L. & Plewes, J. (2002) The lake at Llandrindod Wells – a restoration comedy? *Aquatic Conservation: Marine and Freshwater Ecosystems*, **12**, 229–249.

Moss, B., Stephen, D., Balayla, D.M., et al. (2004) Continental-scale patterns of nutrient and fish effects on shallow lakes: synthesis of a pan-European mesocosm experiment. *Freshwater Biology*, **49**, 1633–1649.

Moss, B., Barker, T., Stephen, D., et al. (2005) Consequences of reduced nutrient loading on a lake system in a lowland catchment: deviations from the norm? *Freshwater Biology*, **50**, 1687–1705.

Moss, B., Hering, D., Green, A.J., et al. (2009). Climate change and the future of freshwater biodiversity in Europe: a primer for policy-makers. *Freshwater Reviews*, **2**, 103–130.

Mugidde, R. (1993) The increase in phytoplankton primary productivity and biomass in Lake Victoria (Uganda).

*Verhandlungen internationale der Vereinigung theoretische und angewande Limnologie*, **25**, 846–849.

Mulderij, G., Mau, B., van Donk, E. & Gross, E.M. (2007) Allelopathic activity of *Stratiotes aloides* on phytoplankton-towards identification of allelopathic substances. *Hydrobiologia*, **584**, 89–100.

Mulvihill, R.S., Newell, F.L. & Latta, S.C. (2008) Effects of acidification on the breeding ecology of a stream-dependent songbird, the Louisiana water thrush (*Seiurus motacilla*). *Freshwater Biology*, **53**, 2158–2169.

Naiman, R.J. & Rogers, K.H. (1997) Large animals and system-level characteristics in river corridors. *BioScience*, **47**, 521–529.

Naiman, R.J., Bilby, R.E., Schindler, D.E. & Helfield, J.M. (2002) Pacific salmon, nutrients and the dynamics of freshwater and riparian ecosystems. *Ecosystems*, **5**, 399–417.

Naiman, R.J., Bilby, R.E. & Kantor, S. (2009) *River Ecology and Management*. Springer-Verlag, New York.

NEGTAP (2001) *Transboundary Air Pollution: Acidification, Eutrophication and Ground level ozone in the UK*. National Expert Group on Transboundary Air Pollution, DEFRA, London.

Nelson, J.S. (2006) *Fishes of the World*, 4th edn. John Wiley & Sons, New York.

Netherlands Environmental Assessment Agency (2008) *The Netherlands in a Sustainable World*. MNP-Publication number 500084004, Bilthoven.

Newbould, C. (1998) The nature conservation importance of floodplains in England and Wales – with particular reference to their flora. In *United Kingdom Floodplains*, Bailey, R.G., José, P.V. & Sherwood, B.R. Westbury Academic and Scientific Publishing, Otley; 171–183.

Newbould, C., Purseglove, J. & Holmes, N. (1983) *Nature Conservation and River Engineering*. Nature Conservancy Council, Shrewsbury.

Newman, E.I. (1997) Phosphorus balance of contrasting farming systems, past and present. Can food production be sustainable? *Journal of Applied Ecology*, **34**, 1334–1347.

Nier, A.O. & Gulbransen, E.A. (1939) Variations in the relative abundance of the carbon isotopes. *Journal of the American Chemical Society*, **61**, 697–698.

Nishino, M. & Watanabe, N.C. (2000) Evolution and endemism in Lake Biwa, with special reference to its gastropod mollusc fauna. *Advances in Ecological Research*, **31**, 151–181.

Northcote, T.G. & Lobon-Cervia, J. (2008) Increasing experimental approaches in stream trout research – 1987–2006. *Ecology of Freshwater Fish*, **17**, 349–361.

Odada, E.O., Olago, D.O., Bugenyi, F., et al. (2003) Environmental assessment of the East African rift valley lakes. *Aquatic Sciences*, **65**, 254–271.

Odum, H.T. (1956) Primary production in flowing waters. *Limnology and Oceanography*, **1**, 102–17.

Ogutu-Ohwayo, R. (1992) The purpose, costs and benefits of fish introductions: with specific reference to the Great

Lakes of Africa. *Mitteilungen internationale der Vereinigung theoretische und angewandte Limnologie*, **23**, 37–44.

O'Keefe. J.H. & Davies, B.R. (1991) Conservation and management of the rivers of the Kruger National Park: suggested methods for calculating instream flow needs. *Aquatic Conservation: Marine and Freshwater Ecosystems*, **1**, 55–72.

Oliveira, A.C.B., Soares, M.G.M., Martinelli, L.A. & Moreira, M.Z. (2006) Carbon sources of fish in an Amazonian floodplain. *Aquatic Sciences*, **68**, 229–238.

O'Reilly, C.M., Alin, S.R., Plisnier, P-D., Cohen, A.S. & McKee, B.A. (2003) Climate change decreases aquatic ecosystem productivity of Lake Tanganyika, Africa. *Nature*, **424**, 766–768.

Ormerod, S.J. (1999) Three challenges for the science of river restoration. *Aquatic Conservation: Marine and Freshwater Ecosystems*, **9**, 551–558.

Ormerod, S.J. (2004) A golden age of river restoration science? *Aquatic Conservation: Marine and Freshwater Ecosystems*, **14**, 543–549.

Ormerod, S.J. & Durance, I. (2009) Restoration and recovery from acidification in upland Welsh streams over 25 years. *Journal of Applied Ecology*, **46**, 164–174.

Ormerod, S.J., O'Halloran, J.O., Gribbin, S.D. & Tyler, S.J. (1991) The ecology of dippers *Cinclus cinclus* in relation to stream acidity in upland Wales: breeding performance, calcium physiology and nestling growth. *Journal of Applied Ecology*, **28**, 419–433.

Ortiz-Zayas, J.R., Lewis, W.M., Saunders, J.F., McCutchan, J.H. & Scatena, F.N. (2005) Metabolism of a tropical rainforest stream. *Journal of the American Benthological Society*, **24**, 769–783.

Osborne, P.L. (1980) Prediction of phosphorus and nitrogen concentrations in lakes from both internal and external loading rates. *Hydrobiologia*, **69**, 229–33.

O'Sullivan, P.E. & Reynolds, C.S. (2004) *The Lakes Handbook*, Vol. 1, *Limnology and Limnetic Ecology*. Blackwell Science, Oxford.

O'Sullivan, P.E. & Reynolds, C.S. (2005) *The Lakes Handbook*, Vol. 2, *Restoration and Rehabilitation*. Blackwell Science, Oxford.

Page, S.E., Rieley, J.O., Shotyk, W. & Weiss, D. (1999) Interdependence of peat and vegetation in a tropical peat swamp forest. *Philosophical Transactions of the Royal Society, Series B*, **354**, 1885–1897.

Palacios-Fest, M.R., Alin, S.,Cohen, A.,Tanner, B. & Heuser, H. (2005) Paleolimnological investigations of anthropogenic environmental change in Lake Tanganyika: IV. Lacustrine paleoecology. *Journal of Paleolimnology*, **34**, 51–71.

Palmer, M.A., Reidy Liermann, C.A., Nilsson, C., et al. (2008) Climate change and the world's river basins: anticipating management options. *Frontiers in Ecology and the Environment*, **6**, doi:10.1890/060148.

Parejko, K. & Dodson, S. (1990) Progress towards characterization of a predator/prey kairomone: *Daphnia pulex* and *Chaoborus americanus*. *Hydrobiologia*, **198**, 51–59.

Parker, J.D., Burkepile, D.E., Collins, D.O., Kubanek, J. & Hay, M.E. (2007a) Stream mosses as chemically defended refugia for freshwater macroinvertebrates. *Oikos*, **116**, 302–312.

Parker, J.D., Caudill, C.C. & Hay, M.E. (2007b) Beaver herbivory on aquatic plants. *Oecologia*, **151**, 616–625.

Parker, P.L. (1964) The biogeochemistry of the stabe isotopes of carbon in a marine bay. *Geochemica et Cosmochemica Acta*, **28**, 1155–164.

Parker, S.M. & Huryn, A.D. (2006) Food web structure and function in two Arctic streams with contrasting disturbance regimes. *Freshwater Biology*, **51**, 1249–1263.

Parolin, P. (2009) Submerged in darkness: adaptations to prolonged submergence by woody species of the Amazonian floodplains. *Annals of Botany*, **103**, 359–376.

Parry, M.L., Canziani, O.F., Palutikof, J.P., van der Linden, P.J. & Hanson, C.E. (Eds) (2007) Cross-chapter case study. In: *Climate Change 2007: Impacts, Adaptation and Vulnerability*. Contribution of Working Group II to the Fourth Assessment Report of the Intergovernmental Panel on Climate Change. Cambridge University Press; 843–868.

Pauly, D., Christensen, V., Dalsgaard, J., Froese, R. & Torres, Jr., F. (1998) Fishing down marine food webs. *Science*, **279**, 860–863.

Pauly, D., Christensen, V., Guénette, S., et al. (2002) Towards sustainability in world fisheries. *Nature*, **418**, 689–695.

Pennak, R.W. (1985) The fresh-water invertebrate fauna: Problems and solutions for evolutionary success. *American Zoologist*, **25**, 671–687.

Peterson, B.J. (1999) Stable isotopes as tracers of organic matter input and transfer in benthic food webs: a review. *Acta Oecologica*, **20**, 479–487.

Phillips, G.L., Eminson, D.F. & Moss, B. (1978) A mechanism to account for macrophyte decline in progressively eutrophicated freshwaters. *Aquatic Botany*, **4**, 103–26.

Phillips, V.D. (1998) Peatswamp ecology and sustainable development in Borneo. *Biodiversity and Conservation*, **7**, 651–671.

Piao, S., Ciais, P., Friedlingstein, P., et al. (2007) Net carbon dioxide losses of northern ecosystems in response to autumn warming. *Nature*, **451**, 49–53.

Pimentel, D., McNair, S., Janecka, J., et al. (2002) Economic and environmental threats of alien plant, animal, and microbe invasions. In *Biological Invasions. Economic and Environmental Costs of Alien Plant, Animal, and Microbe Species*, Pimentel, D. (Ed.). CRC Press, Boca Raton, FL; 307–329.

Pickering, A.D. (2001) *Windermere: Restoring the Health of England's Largest Lake*. Freshwater Biological Association, Ambleside.

Pielou, E.C. (1998) *Fresh Water*. University of Chicago Press.

Pister, E.P. (1985) Desert pupfishes: reflections on reality, desirability and conscience. *Environmental Biology of Fishes*, **12**, 3–12.

Pitcher, T.J. & Hart, P.J.B. (1982) Fisheries Ecology. Croom Helm, London.

Pitcher, T.J. & Hart, P.J.B. (Eds) (2007) *The Impact of Species Changes in African Lakes.* Chapman & Hall, London.

Poff, N.L. (2002) Ecological response to and management of increased flooding caused by climate change. *Philosophical Transactions of the Royal Society of London, Series A,* **360**, 1497–1510.

Por, F.D. (1995) *The Pantanal of Mato Grosso (Brazil).* Kluwer, Dordrecht.

Porter, K.G. (1973) Selective grazing and differential digestion of algae by zooplankton. *Nature,* **244**, 179–80.

Porter, K.G. (1976) Enhancement of algal growth and productivity by grazing zooplankton. *Science,* **192**, 1332–1334.

Post, D.M. (2002) Using stable isotopes to estimate trophic position: Models, methods, and assumptions. *Ecology,* **83**, 703–718.

Poulson, T.L. & White, W.B. (1969) The cave environment. *Science,* **165**, 971–980.

Power, M.E., Matthews, W.J. & Stewart, A.J. (1985) Grazing minnows, piscivorous bass and stream algae: dynamics of a strong interaction. *Ecology,* **66**, 1448–1456.

Prentiss, A.M., Lyons, N., Harris, L., Burns, M.R.P. & Godin, T.M. (2007) The emergence of status inequality in intermediate scale societies: A demographic and socio-economic history of the Keatley Creek site, British Columbia. *Journal of Anthropological Archaeology,* **26**, 299–327.

Press, P., Siever, R., Grotzinger, J. & Jordan, T.H. (2003) *Understanding Earth,* 4th edn. W.H. Freeman & Co.

Pretty, J.L., Harrison, S.S.C., Shepherd, D.J., Smith, C., Hildrew, A.G. & Hey, R.D. (2003) River rehabilitation and fish populations: assessing the benefit of instream structures: Current issues with fish and fisheries. *Journal of Applied Ecology* **40**, 251–265.

Pretty, J.N., Mason, C.F., Nedwell, D.B., Hine, R.E., Leaf, S. & Dils, R. (2003) Environmental costs of freshwater eutrophication in England and Wales. *Environmental Science and Technology,* **37**, 201–208.

Pringle, C.M., Blake, G.A., Covich, A.P., Buzby, K.M. & Finley, A. (1993) Effects of omnivorous shrimp in a montane tropical stream: sediment removal, disturbance of sessile invertebrates and enhancement of understory algal biomass. *Oecologia,* **93**, 1–11.

Pringle, H. (1996) *In Search of Ancient North America.* John Wiley & Sons, New York.

Pringle, R.M. (2005a) The Nile Perch in lake Victoria: Local responses and adaptations. *Journal of the International African Institute,* 75, 510–538.

Pringle, R.M. (2005b) The origins of the Nile perch in Lake Victoria. *BioScience,* **55**, 780–787.

Prowse, T.D. & Beltaos, S. (2002) Climatic control of river–ice hydrology. *Hydrological Processes,* **16**, 805–822.

Prowse, T.D., Wrona, F.J., Reist, J.D., et al. (2006) Climate change effects on hydroecology of Arctic freshwater ecosystems. *Ambio,* **35**, 347–358.

Purseglove, J. (1988) *Taming the Flood.* Oxford University Press.

Randall, R.G., Kelso, J.R.M. & Minns, C.K. (1995) Fish production in freshwaters: are rivers more productive than lakes? *Canadian Journal of Fisheries and Aquatic Sciences,* **52**, 631–643.

Raven, J.A. (1970) Exogenous inorganic carbon sources in plant photosynthesis. *Biological Reviews,* **45**, 167–202.

Raven, P.J., Fox, P.J.A., Everard, M., Holmes, N.T.H. & Dawson, F.H. (1997) River Habitat Survey: a new system for classifying rivers according to their habitat quality. In *Freshwater Quality: Defining the Indefinable?,* Boon, P.J. & Howell, D.L. (Eds). The Stationery Office, Edinburgh; 215–234.

Reader, J. (1988) *Man on Earth.* Collins, London.

Renberg, I. & Hellberg, T. (1982) The pH history of lakes in south-western Sweden, as calculated from the subfossil diatom flora of the sediments. *Ambio,* **11**, 30–33.

Reynolds, C.S. (1996) The 1996 Founders' Lecture: Potamoplankters do it on the side. European. *Journal of Phycology,* **31**, 111–116.

Reynolds, C.S. (2008) A changing paradigm of pelagic food webs. *International Review of Hydrobiology,* **93**, 517–531.

Reynolds, C.S., Huszar, V., Kruk, C., Naselli-Flores, L. & Melo, S. (2002) Towards a functional classification of the freshwater phytoplankton. *Journal of Plankton Research,* **24**, 417–428.

Reynolds, C.S. & Walsby, A.E. (1975) Water-blooms. *Biological Reviews,* **50**, 437–481.

Reynoldson, T.B. (1966) The distribution and abundance of lake-dwelling triclads–towards a hypothesis. *Advances in Ecological Research,* **3**, 1–71.

Richardson, C.J. & Hussain, N.A. (2006) Restoring the Garden of Eden: An ecological assessment of the marshes of Iraq. *BioScience,* **56**, 477–489.

Richardson, J.L. & Richardson, A.E. (1972) History of an African rift lake and its climatic implications. *Ecological Monographs,* **42**, 499–534.

Ripple, W.J. & Beschta, R.I. (2004a) Wolves, elk, willows, and tropic cascades in the upper Gallantin Range of southwestern Montana, USA. *Forest Ecology and Management,* **200**, 161–181.

Ripple, W.J. & Beschta, R.I. (2004b) Wolves and the ecology of fear: can predation risk structure ecosystems? *BioScience,* **54**, 755–766.

Rodhe, H., Grennfelt, P., Wisniewski, J., et al. (1995) Acid reign '95? Conference summary statement. *Water, Air and Soil Pollution,* **85**, 1–14.

Rodhe, H., Dentener, F. & Schulz, M. (2002) The global distribution of acidifying wet deposition. *Environmental Science and Technology,* **36**, 4382–4388.

Rodhe, W. (1975) The SIL founders and our fundament. *Verhandlungen internationale der Vereinigung theeoretische und angewande Limnologie,* **19**, 16–25.

Rogers, K.H. 1980. The vegetation of Pongolo floodplain: distribution and utilization. In *Studies on the Ecology of Maputaland,* Bruton, M.N. & Cooper, K.H. (Eds). Rhodes

University, Grahamstown; and The Natal Branch of the Wildlife Society of Southern Africa; 69–77.

Rogers, K.H. & Breen, C.M. 1980. Growth and reproduction of *Potamogeton crispus* in a South African lake. *Journal of Ecology*, **68**, 561–571.

Rogers, K.H. & Breen, C.M. 1990a. Waterfowl of a sub-tropical African floodplain. 1. Seasonality of community composition and food resources. *Wetlands Ecology and Management*, **1**, 85–97.

Rogers, K.H. & Breen, C.M. 1990b. Waterfowl of a sub-tropical African floodplain. 2. Stability of the grazing system. *Wetlands Ecology and Management*, **1**, 99–109.

Romina-Schiaffino, M., Unrein, F., Gasol, J.M., et al. (2009) Comparative analysis of bacteripoplankton assemblages from maritime Antarctic lakes with contrasting trophic status. *Polar Biology*, **32**, 923–936.

Roni, P. & Beechie, T. (2008) Global review of the physical and biological effectiveness of stream habitat rehabilitation techniques. *North American Journal of Fisheries Management*, **28**, 856–890.

Rott, E., Cantonati, M., Fureder, L. & Pfifster, P. (2006) Benthic algae in high altitude streams of the Alps – a neglected component of the aquatic biota. *Hydrobiologia*, **562**, 195–216.

Round, F.E. (1961) The diatoms of a core from Esthwaite Water. *New Phytologist*, **60**, 43–59.

Rouquette, J.R., Posthumus, H., Gowing, D.J.G., et al. (2009) Valuing nature-conservation interests on agricultural floodplains. *Journal of Applied Ecology*, **46**, 289–296.

Rouse, W.R., Douglas, M.S.V., Hecky, R.E., et al. (1997) Effects of climate change on the freshwaters of Arctic and subarctic North America. *Hydrological Processes*, **11**, 873–902.

Rowland, S.J. (1989) Aspects of the history and fishery of the Murray cod, *Maccullochella peelii* (Mitchell) (Percichthyidae). *Proceedings of the Linnaean Society of New South Wales*, **111**, 201–213.

Rowlands, M. (2008) *The Philosopher and the Wolf*. Granta Publications, London.

Ruttner, F. (1953) *Fundamentals of Limnology*. Translated by D.G. Frey & F.E.J. Fry. University of Toronto Press, Toronto.

Ryder, J.M. & Church, M. (1986) The Lillooet terraces of Fraser River, a paleoenvironmental enquiry. *Canadian Journal of Earth Sciences*, **23**, 868–885.

Sahoo, G.B. & Schladow, S.G. (2008) Impacts of climate change on lakes and reservoirs dynamics and restoration policies. *Sustainability Science*, **3**, 189–199.

Salmi, P., Auvinen, H., Jurvelius, J. & Sipponen, M. (2000) Finnish lake fisheries and conservation of biodiversity: coexistence or conflict? *Fisheries Management and Ecology*, **7**, 127–138.

Salzburger, W. & Meyer, A. (2004) The species flocks of East African cichlid fishes: recent advances in molecular phylogenetics and population genetics. *Naturwissenschaften*, **91**, 277–290.

Sand Jensen, K., Pedersen, M.F. & Nielsen, S.L. (1992) Photosynthetic use of inorganic carbon among primary and secondary water plants in streams. *Freshwater Biology*, **27**, 283–293.

Sand-Jensen, K., Binzer, T. & Middelboe, A.L. (2007) Scaling of photosynthetic production of aquatic macrophytes: a review. *Oikos*, **116**, 280–294.

Sandlund, O.T., Gunnarsson, K., Jónasson, Pétur, M., et al. (1992) The arctic charr *Salvelinus alpinus* in Thingvallavatn. *Oikos*, **64**, 305–351.

Sarma, S.S.S., Nandini, S. & Gulati, R.D. (2005) Life history strategies of cladocerans: comparisons of tropical and temperate taxa. *Hydrobiologia*, **542**, 315–333.

Scavia, D., Laird, G.A. & Fahnenstiel, G.L. (1986) Production of planktonic bacteria in Lake Michigan. *Limnology and Oceanography*, **31**, 612–626.

Scheffer, M. v. (1993) Alternative equilibria in shallow lakes. *Trends in Ecology and Evolution*, **8**, 275–279.

Schilt, C.R. (2007) Developing fish passage and protection at hydropower dams. *Applied Animal Behaviour Science*, **104**, 295–325.

Schindler, D.E. & Scheuerell, M.D. (2002) Habitat coupling in lake ecosystems. *Oikos*, **98**, 177–189.

Schindler, D.W. (1974) Eutrophication and recovery in experimental lakes: implications for lake management. *Science*, **184**, 897–898.

Schindler, D.W. (1977) The evolution of phosphorus limitation in lakes. *Science*, **195**, 260–262.

Schindler, D.W. (1978) Factors regulating phytoplankton production and standing crop in the world's freshwaters. *Limnology and Oceanography*, **23**, 478–486.

Schindler, D.W., Welch, H.E., Kalff, J., Brunskdl, G.J. & Kritsch, N. (1974) Physical and chemical limnology of Char Lake, Cornwallis Island (75°N lat.) *Journal of the Fisheries Research Board of Canada*, **31**, 585–607.

Schlacher, T.A. & Cronin, G. (2007) A trophic cascade in a macrophyte based food web at the land–water ecotone. *Ecological Research*, **22**, 749–755.

Schmidt-Nielsen, K. (1997) *Animal Physiology: Adaptation and Environment*, 4th edn. Cambridge University Press.

Scudder, T. (2005) *The Future of Large Dams*. Earthscan, London.

Sculthorpe, C.D. (1967) *The Biology of Aquatic Vascular Plants*. Arnold, London.

Sear, D.A. (1994) River restoration and geomorphology. *Aquatic Conservation: Marine and Freshwater Ecosystems* **4**, 169–178.

Seeley, C.M. (1969) The diurnal curve in estimates of primary productivity. *Chesapeake Science*, **10**, 322–326.

Shapiro, J. (1980) The importance of trophic-level interactions to the abundance and species composition of algae in lakes. In *Hypertrophic Ecosystems*, Barica, J. & Mur, L. (Eds). Junk, The Hague.

Shapiro, J. (1990) Current beliefs regarding dominance by blue-greens: The case for the importance of $CO_2$ and pH.

*Verhandlungen internationale der Vereinigung theoretische und angewandte Limnologie*, **24**, 38–54.

Shapiro, J., Lamarra, V. & Lynch, M. (1975) Biomanipulation: an ecosystem approach to lake restoration. In *Water Quality Management through Biological Control*, Brezonik, P.L. & Fox, J.L. (Eds). Report ENV-07-75-1, University of Florida, Gainsville.

Shapiro, J. & Wright, D.I. (1984) Lake restoration by biomanipulation: Round Lake, Minnesota, the first two years. *Freshwater Biology*, **14**, 371–83.

Shearer, K.D. & Mulley, J.C. (1978) The introduction and distribution of carp, *Cyprinus carpio* Linnaeus, in Australia. *Australian Journal of Marine and Freshwater Research*, **29**, 551–563.

Sheehy Skeffington, M., Moran, J., Connor, A.O., et al. (2006) Turloughs: Ireland's unique wetland habitat. *Biological Conservation*, **133**, 265–290.

Sivonen, K., Halinen, K., Sihvonen, L.M., et al. (2007) Bacterial diversity and function in the Baltic Sea with an emphasis on Cyanobacteria. *Ambio*, **36**, 180–185.

Smid, P. (1975) Evaporation from a reed swamp. *Journal of Ecology*, **63**, 299–309.

Smith, R.A., Alexander, R.B. & Schwarz, G.E. (2003) Natural background concentrations of nutrients in streams and rivers of the conterminous United States. *Environmental Science and Technology*, **37**, 3039–47.

Smith, S.I. (1972) Factors of ecologic succession in oligotrophic fish communities of the Laurentian Great Lakes. *Journal of the Fisheries Research Board of Canada*, **29**, 717–30.

Smol, J.P. (2008) *Pollution of Lakes and Rivers: A Palaeoenvironmental Perspective*, 2nd edn. Blackwell Publishing.

Smolders, A.J.P., Lucassen, E.C.H.E.T. & Roelofs, J.G.M. (2002) The isoetid environment: biogeochemistry and threats. *Aquatic Botany*, **73**, 325–350.

Sobek, S., Algesten, G., Bergström, A-K., Jansson, M. & Tranvik, L.J. (2003) The catchment and climate regulation of $pCO_2$ in boreal lakes. *Global Change Biology*, **9**, 630–641.

Solomon, C., Carpenter, S.R., Cole, J.J. & Pace, M.L. (2008) Support of benthic invertebrates by detrital resources and current autochthonous primary production: results from a whole-lake $^{13}C$ addition. *Freshwater Biology*, **53**, 42–54.

Sommaruga-Wograth, S., Koinig, K.A., Schmidt, R., Sommaruga, R., Tessadri, R. & Psenner, R. (1997) Temperature effects on the acidity of remote alpine lakes. *Nature*, **387**, 64–67.

Sondergaard, M., Liboriussen, L., Pedersen, A.R. & Jeppesen, E. (2008) Lake restoration by fish removal: short- and long-term effects in 36 Danish lakes. *Ecosystems*, **11**, 1291–1305.

Speller, C.F., Yang, D.Y. & Hayden, B. (2005). Ancient DNA investigation of prehistoric salmon resource utilization at Keatley Creek, British Columbia, Canada. *Journal of Archaeological Science*, **32**, 1378–1389.

Spence, D.H.N. (1982) The zonation of plants in freshwater lakes. *Advances in Ecological Research*, **12**, 37–125.

Spence, D.H.N. & Chrystal, J. (1970a) Photosynthesis and zonation of freshwater macrophytes. I. Depth distribution and shade tolerance. *New Phytologistl*, **69**, 205–215.

Spence, D.H.N. & Chrystal, J. (1970b) Photosynthesis, zonation of freshwater macrophytes. II. Adaptability of species of deep and shallow waters. *New Phytologist*, **69**, 217–227.

Sraj-Krzic, N., Pongrac, P., Klemenc, M., Kladnik, A., Regvar, M. & Gaberščik, A. (2006) Mycorrhizal colonisation in plants from intermittent aquatic habitats. *Aquatic Botanist*, **85**, 331–336.

Steeman Nielsen, E. (1952) The use of radioactive carbon (C14) for measuring organic production in the sea. *Journal du Cinseil Internationale pour l'Exploration de la Mer*, **18**, 117–40.

Stoddard, J.L., Jeffries, D.S., Lükewille, A., et al. (1999) Regional trends in aquatic recovery from acidification in North America and Europe. *Nature*, **401**, 575–578.

Stoks, R. & McPeek, M.A. (2003) Predators and life histories shape *Lestes* damselfly assemblages along a freshwater habitat gradient. *Ecology*, **84**, 1576–1587.

Strayer, D.L. (1991) Projected distribution of the zebra mussel, *Dreissena polymorpha*, in North America. *Canadian Journal of Fisheries and Aquatic Sciences*, **48**, 1389–1395.

Strayer, D.L. (2009) Twenty years of zebra mussels: lessons from the mollusk that made headlines. *Frontiers in Ecology and the Environment*, **7**, 135–141.

Strayer, D.L., Eviner, V.T., Jeschke, J.M., & Pace, M.L. (2006) Understanding the long-term effects of species invasions. *Trends in Ecology and Evolution*, **21**, 645–651.

Sugina, Z.V. (2006) Endemic Bivalvia in ancient lakes. *Hydrobiologia*, **568** (S), 213–217.

Sullivan, T. (2000) *Aquatic Effects of Acid Deposition*. Lewis Publishers, CRC Press, New York.

Swaine, M.D., Adomako, J., Ameka, G., de Graft-Johnston, K.A.A. & Cheek, M. (2006) Forest river plants and water quality in Ghana. *Aquatic Botany*, **85**, 299–308.

Syvaranta, J., Hamalainen, H. & Jones, R.I. (2006) Within-lake variability in carbon and nitrogen stable isotope signatures. *Freshwater Biology*, **51**, 1090–1102.

Talling, J.F. (1966) The annual cycle of stratification and phytoplankton growth in Lake Victoria (E. Africa). *Internationale Revue der gesamten Hydrobiologie*, **51**, 545–621.

Talling, J.F. (1969) The incidence of vertical mixing, and some biological and chemical consequences, in tropical African lakes. *Verhandlungen internationale der Vereinigung theoretische und angewande Limnologie*, **17**, 998–1012.

Talling, J.F. (1971) The underwater light climate as a controlling factor in the production ecology of freshwater phytoplankton. *Mitteilungen internationale der Vereinigung theoretische und angewangte Limnologie*, **19**, 214–243.

Talling, J.F. (1976) The depletion of carbon dioxide from lake water by phytoplankton. *Journal of Ecology*, **64**, 79–121.

Talling, J.F. (1986) The seasonality of phytoplankton in African lakes. *Hydrobiologia*, **138**, 139–160.

Talling, J.F. (2008) The developmental history of inland-water science. *Freshwater Reviews*, **1**, 119–141.

Talling, J.F. & Lemoalle, J. (1999). *Ecological Dynamics of Tropical Inland Waters*. Cambridge University Press.

Talling, J.F. & Talling, l.B. (1965) The chemical composition of African lake water. *Internationale Revue der gesamten Hydrobiologie*, **50**, 421–463.

Taylor, B.E. (1988) Analyzing population dynamics of zooplankton. *Limnology and Oceanography*, **33**, 1266–1273.

Ter Braak, C.J.F. & van Dam, H. (1989) Inferring pH from diatoms: A comparison of old and new calibration methods. *Hydrobiologia*, **178**, 209–223.

Templeton, R. (Ed.) (1995) *Freshwater Fisheries Management*, 2nd edn. Fishing News Books, Blackwell Scientific, Oxford.

Texeira-de-Mello, F. et al. (2009) Substantial differences in littoral fish community structure and dynamics in subtropical and temperate lakes. *Freshwater Biology*, **54**, 1202–1215.

Theel, H.J., Dibble, E.D. & Madsen, J.D. (2008) Differential influence of a monotypic and diverse native aquatic plant bed on a macroinvertebrate assemblage: an experimental implication of exotic plant induced habitat. *Hydrobiologia*, **600**, 77–87.

Thesiger, W. (1964) The Marsh Arabs. Longmans, London.

Thirtle, C., Beyers, L., Ismael, Y. & Piesse, J. (2003) Can GM-technologies help the poor? the impact of Bt cotton in Makhathini Flats, KwaZulu-Natal. *World Development*, **31**, 717–732.

Threlkeld, S. (1979) Estimating cladoceran birth rates: the importance of egg mortality and the egg age distribution. *Limnology and Oceanography*, **24**, 601–612.

Tibby, J. & Haberle, S.G. (2007) A late-glacial to present diatom record from Lake Euramoo, wet tropics of Queensland, Australia. *Palaeography, Palaeoclimatology, Palaeoecology*, **251**, 46–56.

Tilman, D. (1977) Resource competition between planktonic algae: an experimental and theoretical approach. *Ecology*, **58**, 338–348.

Timms, R.M. & Moss, B. (1984) Prevention of growth of potentially dense phytoplankton populations by zooplankton grazing in the presence of zooplanktivorous fish, in a shallow wetland ecosystem. *Limnology and Oceanography*, **29**, 472–486.

Titman, D. (1976) Ecological competition between algae: experimental confirmation of resource-based competition theory. *Science*, **192**, 463–465.

Tockner, K. & Stanford, J.A. (2002) Riverine flood plains: present state and future trends. *Environmental Conservation*, **29**, 308–330.

Tockner, K., Ward, J.V., Arscott, D.B., et al. (2003) The Tagliamento river: a model system of European importance. *Aquatic Sciences*, **65**, 239–253.

Tomanova, S., Goitia, E. & Helesic, J. (2006) Trophic levels and functional feeding groups of macroinvertebrates in neotropical streams. *Hydrobiologia*, **556**, 251–264.

Thompson, K., Shewry, P.R. & Woolhouse, H.W. (1979) Papyrus swamp development in the Upemba Basin, Zaire: studies of population structure in *Cyperus papyrus* stands. *Botanical Journal of the Linnean Society*, **78**, 299–316.

Traunsperger, W. (1996) Distribution of benthic nematodes in the littoriprofundal and profundal of an oligotrophic lake (Konigssee, National Park Berchtesgaden, FRG). *Archiv für Hydrobiologie*, **135**, 557–575.

Trosper, R.L. (2003) Resilience in Pre-contact Pacific Northwest Social ecological systems. Conservation Ecology, 7, 6–17.

Turner, R.C. & Scaife, R.G. (Eds) (1995) *Bog Bodies: New Discoveries and New Perspectives*. British Museum Press, London.

Turunen, A.W., Verkasalo, P.K., Kiviranta, H., et al. (2008) Mortality in a cohort with high fish consumption. *International Journal of Epidemiology*, **37**, 1008–1017.

Uhlmann, D. (1980) Stability and multiple steady states of hypereutrophic ecosystems. In *Hypertrophic Ecosystems*, Barica, J. & Mur, L. (Eds). Developments in Hydrobiology, Vol. 2. Junk, The Hague; 235–248.

Vallentyne, J.R. (1969) Sedimentary organic matter and palaeolimnology. *Mitteilungen internationale der Verein theoretische und angewande Limnology*, **17**, 104–110.

Van der Gucht, K., Cottenie, K., Muylaert, K., et al. (2007) The power of species sorting: local factors drive bacterial community composition over a wide range of scales. *Proceedings of The National Academy of Sciences*, **104**, 20404–20409.

Van der Valk, A.G. (2006) *The Biology of Freshwater Wetlands*. Oxford University Press.

Van Donk, E. (2005) Planktonic interactions: developments and perspectives. *Verhandlungen intyernationale der Vereinigung theretische und angewande Limnologie*, **29**, 61–72.

Van Donk, E. (2007) Chemical information transfer in freshwater plankton. *Ecological Informatics*, **2**, 112–120.

Van Doorslaer, W., Stoks, R., Jeppesen, E. & de Meester, L. (2007) Adaptive micro-evolutionary responses to simulated global warming in *Simocephalus vetulus*: a mesocosm study. *Global Change Biology*, **13**, 878–886.

Van Geest, G.J., Hessen, D.O., Spierenburg, P., et al. (2007) Goose-mediated nutrient enrichment and planktonic grazer control in arctic freshwater ponds. *Oecologia*, **153**, 653–662.

Van Noordwijk, M. (1984) *Ecology Textbook for the Sudan*. Khartoum University Press.

Van Wyk, E., Breen, C.M., Roux, D.J., Rogers, K.H., Sherwill, T. & van Wilger, B.W. (2000) The ecological reserve: towards a common understanding for river management in South Africa. *Water SA*, **32**, 403–410.

Vander Zanden, M.J. & Vadeboncoeur, Y. (2002) Fishes as integrators of benthic and pelagic food webs in lakes. *Ecology*, **83**, 2152–2161.

Vannote, R.L. et al. (l980) The river continuum concept. *Canadian Journal of Fisheries and Aquatic Sciences*, **37**, 120–37.

Vitousek, P.M., Minshall, G.W., Cummings, K.W., Sedell, J.R. & Cushing, C.E. (1997) Human domination of Earth's ecosystems. *Science*, **277**, 494–499.

Vollenweider, R.A. (1975) Input output models with special reference to the phosphorus loading concept in limnology. *Schweizerische Zhurnal fur Hydrologie*, **37**, 53–84.

Vollenweider, R.A. & Kerekes, J.J. (1981) Appendix I: Background and summary results of the OECD cooperative programme on eutrophication. In *The OECD Cooperative Programme on Eutrophication Canadian Contribution*, Janus, L.L. & Vollenweider, R.A. (compilers). Scientific Series 131, Environment Canada.

Wagner, C. & Adrian, R. (2009) Exploring lake ecosystems: hierarchy responses to long-term change? *Global Change Biology*, **15**, 1104–1115.

Ward, P. (2009) *The Medea Hypothesis*. Princeton University Press, Princeton, NJ.

Ward, R.C. & Robinson, M. (1990) *Principles of Hydrology*, 3rd edn. McGraw Hill, New York.

Warfe, D.M. & Barmuta, L.A. (2006) Habitat structural complexity mediates food web dynamics in a freshwater macrophyte community. *Oecologia*, **150**, 141–154.

Wassen, M.J. & Olde Venterink, H. (2006) Comparison of nitrogen and phosphorus fluxes in some European fens and floodplains. *Applied Vegetation Science*, **9**, 213–222.

Wassen, M.J., Barendregt, A., Palczybski, A., De Smidt, J.T. & de Mars, H. (1990) The relationship between fen vegetation gradients, groundwater flow and flooding in an undrained valley mire at Biebrza, Poland. *Journal of Ecology*, **78**, 1106–1122.

Wassen, M.J., Peeters, W.H.M. & Olde Venterink, H. (2002) Patterns in vegetetaion, hydrology and nutrient availability in an undisturbed river floodplain in Poland. *Plant Ecology*, **165**, 27–43.

Weatherly, N.S. (1988). Liming to mitigate acidification in freshwater ecosystems: a review of the biological consequences. *Water, Air and Soil Pollution*, **39**, 421–437.

Weber, C.A. (1907) Aufbau und Vegetation der Moore Norddeutschlands. *Beiblatt zu den Botanischen Jahrbuchern*, **90**, 19–34.

Weisse, T. (2006) Biodiversity of freshwater microorganisms – achievements problems and perspectives. *Polish Journal of Ecology*, **54**, 633–652.

Welcomme, R.L. (1979) *Fisheries Ecology of Floodplain Rivers*. Longman, London.

Welcomme, R.L. (2002) An evaluation of tropical brush and vegetation park fisheries. *Fisheries Management and Ecology*, **9**, 175–188.

Westlake, D.F. (1967) Some effects of low velocity currents on the metabolism of aquatic macrophytes. *Journal of Experimental Botany*, **18**, 187–205.

Westlake, D.F. (1982) The primary productivity of water plants. In *Studies on Aquatic Vascular Plants*, Symoens, J.J., Hooper, S.S. & Compere, P. (Eds) Royal Botanical Society of Belgium, Brussels; 165–180.

Wetzel, R.G. (1990) Land-water interfaces: Metabolic and limnological regulators. *Verhandlungen internationale der Vereinigung theoretische und angewande Limnologie*, **24**, 6–24.

Wetzel, R.G. (2001) *Limnology. Lake and River Systems*. Elsevier, New York.

Whitehead, P.G., Wilby, R.L., Butterfield, D. & Wade, A.J. (2006) Impacts of climate change on in-stream nitrogen in a lowland chalk stream: an appraisal of adaptation strategies. *Science of the Total Environment*, **365**, 260–273.

Wiegand, C. & Pflugmacher, S. (2005) Ecotoxicological effects of selected cyanobacterial secondary metabolites a short review. *Toxicology and Applied Pharmacology*, **203**, 201–218.

Wilcox, H.R., Hildrew, A.G. & Nichols, R.A. (2001). Genetic differentiation of a European caddisfly: past and present gene flow among fragmented larval habitats. *Molecular Ecology*, **10**, 182–184.

Wilhelm, S.W. & Matteson, A.R. (2008) Freshwater and marine virioplankton: a brief overview of commonalities and differences. *Freshwater Biology*, **53**, 1076–1089.

Williams, D.D. (2006) *The Biology of Temporary Waters*. Oxford University Press.

Williams, P., Whitfield, M. & Biggs, J. (2008) How can we make new ponds biodiverse? A case study monitored over 7 years. *Hydrobiologia*, **597**, 137–148.

Williams, P., Biggs, J., Whitfield, M., et al. (1999) *The Pond Book: a Guide to the Management and Creation of Ponds*. The Ponds Conservation Trust, Oxford.

Williams, W.D. (2002) Environmental threats to salt lakes and the likely status of inland saline ecosystems in 2025. *Environmental Conservation*, **29**, 154–167.

Williams, W.D. & Aladin, N.V. (1991) The Aral Sea: recent limnological changes and their conservation significance. *Aquatic Conservation: Marine and Freshwater Ecosystems*, **1**, 3–24.

Winder, M. & Schindler, D.E. (2004) Climate change uncouples trophic interactions in an aquatic ecosystem. *Ecology*, **85**, 2100–2106.

Winfield, I.J. (1990) Predation pressure from above: observations on the activities of piscivorous birds at a shallow eutrophic lake. *Hydrobiologia*, **191**, 223–231.

Winfield, I.J., Fletcher, J.M. & James, J.B. (2008a) The Arctic charr (*Salvelinus alpinus*) populations of Windermere, UK: population trends associated with eutrophication, climate changes and increased abundance of roach (*Rutilus rutilus*). *Environmental Biology of Fishes*, **83**, 25–35.

Winfield, I.J., James, J.B. & Fletcher, J.M. (2008b) Northern pike (*Esox lucius*) in a warming lake: changes in population size and individual condition in relation to prey abundance. *Hydrobiologia*, **601**, 29–40.

Winter, H.V., Lapinska, M. & De leeuw, J.J. (2009) The River Vecht fish community after rehabilitation measures: a comparison to the historical situation by using the River Biebrza as a geographical reference. *River Research and Applications*, **25**, 16–28.

Witte, F., Goldschmidt, T., Wanink, J., et al. (1992) The destruction of an endemic species flock: quantitative data on the decline of the haplochromine cichlids of lake Victoria. *Environmental Biology of Fishes*, **34**, 1–28.

Wium-Andersen, S. (1971) Photosynthetic uptake of free $CO_2$ by roots of Lobelia dortmanna. *Physiologia Plantarum*, **25**, 245–248.

Wium-Andersen, S. & Andersen, J.M. (1972) The influence of vegetation on the redox profile of the sediment of Grane Langsø, a Danish Lobelia lake. *Limnology and Oceanography*, **17**, 948–952.

Wooton, R.J. (1998) *Ecology of Teleost Fishes*, 2nd edn. Kluwer, Dordrecht.

World Commission on Dams (2000) *Dams and Development. A New Framework for Decision Making*. Earthscan Publications, London.

Worthington, S. & Worthington, E.B. (1933) *Inland Waters of Africa*. Macmillan, London.

Wright, J.F. (1995) Development and use of a system for predicting the macroinvertebrate fauna in flowing waters. Australian. *Journal of Ecology*, **20**, 181–197.

Wright, M.S. & Covich, A.P. (2005) The effect of macro-invertebrate exclusion on leaf breakdown rates in a tropical headwater stream. *Biotropica*, **37**, 403–408.

Wurtsbaugh, W. (1992) Food-web modification by an invertebrate predator in the Great Salt lake (USA) *Oecologia*, **89**, 168–175.

Yong-De, C., Xue-Qin, L., & Wang, H.Z. (2008) Macro-zoobenthic community of Fuxian Lake, the deepest lake of southwest China. *Limnologica*, **38**, 116–125.

Young, G. & Wheeler, N. (1977) *Return to the Marshes*. Collins, London.

Yule, C.M. (1996) Trophic relationships and food webs of the benthic invertebrate fauna of two aseasonal tropical streams on Bougainville Island, Papua New Guinea. *Journal of Tropical Ecology*, **12**, 517–534.

Zambrano, L., Perrow, M.R., Sayer, C.D., Tomlinson, M.L. & Davidson, T.A. (2006) Relationships between fish feeding guild and trophic structure in English lowland shallow lakes subject to anthropogenic influence: implications for lake restoration. *Aquatic Ecology*, **40**, 391–405.

Zaret, T.M. (1969) Predation-balanced polymorphism of *Ceriodaphnia cornuta* Sars. *Limnology and Oceanography*, **14**, 301–303.

Zaret, T.M. & Paine, R.T. (1973) Species introduction in a tropical lake. *Science*, **218**, 444–445.

Zong, Y., Chen, Z., Chen, C., Wang, Z. & Wang, H. (2007) Fire and flood management of coastal swamp enabled first rice paddy cultivation in east China. *Nature*, **449**, 459–463.

Zonneveld, C. 1998. Light-limited microalgal growth: a comparison of modelling approaches. *Ecological Modelling*, **113**, 41–54.

# INDEX

Page numbers in *italics* represent figures, those in **bold** represent tables.